W9-BMH-426

A DICTIONARY OF FOREIGN WORDS AND PHRASES

A DICTIONARY OF

FOREIGN WORDS AND PHRASES

IN CURRENT ENGLISH

A. J. BLISS

LONDON

ROUTLEDGE AND KEGAN PAUL

First published in 1966
by Routledge & Kegan Paul Ltd
Broadway House, 68–74 Carter Lane
London, E.C.4

Printed in Great Britain
by C. Tinling & Co. Ltd
Liverpool, London and Prescot

For J.A.P.

'How charmingly and effectively these foreign tags assist one in the great task of calling a spade by some other name!'

Aldous Huxley, *Antic Hay*

PREFACE AND ACKNOWLEDGMENTS

As Henry Sweet wrote in the Preface to his *Anglo-Saxon Dictionary*, 'a dictionary which is good from a practical point of view—that is, which is finished within a reasonable time, and is kept within reasonable limits of space—must necessarily fall far short of ideal requirements'. Although I hope that my own dictionary may be found serviceable from a practical point of view, I am acutely conscious of its deficiencies, and well aware that several more years' work would have made it a much better book. I can only plead in extenuation that nothing of quite the same kind has been attempted before, so that the plan of the dictionary had to be worked out from first principles, and the material collected afresh; moreover, the need for such a work is so pressing that longer delay seemed ill-advised.

This dictionary would have fallen even further short of ideal requirements if it had not been for the generous help I have received from many sources, and it is both a duty and a pleasure to acknowledge my indebtedness. My thanks are due first to all those correspondents, many of them personally unknown to me, who wrote to suggest words and phrases for inclusion in the dictionary; the plan of the work did not allow me to accept all the suggestions made, but the fact that so many persons of varying tastes and interests co-operated in this way has moderated if not quite eliminated the bias which a purely personal choice must have introduced. Next I must thank the numerous friends and colleagues who have patiently answered my questions about the most diverse subjects; if, as I hope, there is no actual error of fact in the dictionary, the credit is largely due to them. My thanks are also due to my publishers for their forbearance in the matter of last-minute alterations and additions, and to the printers for the skill with which they have accomplished an exceedingly difficult task.

My chief indebtedness, however, is to Mr. J. A. Porter, who for several years has devoted much of his scanty leisure to assisting me in the preparation of the dictionary. He has not only suggested a large number of words and phrases for inclusion, but he has been indefatigable in hunting out quotations to illustrate the use of the expressions included, and information throwing light on their meaning, origin, and history. He has discussed the plan of the work with me, and has read the whole of it several times both in manuscript and in proof; I am ashamed to remember the number of errors and omissions that his vigilance has enabled me to avoid.

PREFACE]

The obligation under which I have been placed by so many people would be poorly discharged if I did not point out that the responsibility for the dictionary, both in general and in detail, remains mine alone. I have frequently found myself unable to accept advice which might have made the work better than it is; if my judgment has been at fault, no one is to blame but myself.

A.J.B.

LIST OF CONTENTS

INTRODUCTION

I. The Contents of the Dictionary

Preliminary

The number of foreign words and phrases used in current English, both written and spoken, is very large. To the ordinary cultivated man many of these will already be familiar, but there will be others of whose precise meaning he is ignorant or uncertain; and in these cases it is not always easy for him to discover the meaning unless he has access to a well-stocked reference library. The smaller English dictionaries, with their limited vocabulary, naturally tend to include relatively few foreign words, and list only those which have entered the language of everyday intercourse and occur with great frequency; most of these will already be known to the inquirer. The larger dictionaries, like the *New English Dictionary*[1] and the American *Webster*, aim at completeness, and include a great many terms used only by specialists in some art or science, who already know their meaning; not only are the foreign words as a whole lost among the much more numerous native words, but the more widely current foreign words are lost among a mass of highly technical terms rarely encountered in general reading. The *New English Dictionary* has the additional disadvantage (from this special point of view) that it is a historical dictionary, and therefore of set purpose includes a very large number of words which have long been obsolete. Moreover, these dictionaries include very few phrases. Naturally enough, an English dictionary will not list many English phrases, since the meaning of the vast majority of these can be deduced from the meanings of the words of which they consist, all of which will be entered separately. But foreign phrases used in English have a different status: they are indivisible units, corresponding in this respect to English words rather than to English phrases; the words of which they are composed are not normally used except in the one set context, and will not therefore be individually entered in any English dictionary.

Dictionaries of foreign languages are likely to be more helpful, if they are available in sufficient number—words and phrases from more than fifty different languages are in use in English—but even these may not always serve the purpose unless they are unusually comprehensive. It so happens that many of the foreign expressions

[1] For further details of this important work see p. 61.

used in English are, though not limited in their use to specialists, more or less technical in their connotation, and many of the smaller foreign dictionaries are deficient in technical terms. (For these more technical expressions there are, of course, special technical dictionaries—Dictionaries of Law, Dictionaries of Music, Dictionaries of Geography and so on; but each of these deals with only a small proportion of the foreign words and phrases used in English). Foreign phrases are often highly idiomatic—this may well be one of the reasons for their adoption into English—so that their meaning cannot be readily deduced from the meanings of the words of which they are composed; and the smaller foreign dictionaries do not contain many such idiomatic phrases. But the strongest objection to the use of foreign dictionaries depends on the fact that the meaning, or at least the connotation, of many of the foreign expressions used in English differs substantially from the meaning or connotation they have in the language from which they come; in such cases the use of a foreign dictionary will be actively misleading. Some of the more extreme examples of such changes of meaning are discussed below, p. 13, but there are numerous other examples in which the change of meaning or connotation, though less striking, is none the less significant.

There are indeed dictionaries of foreign expressions used in English, but none of these is wholly satisfactory. Much the best is *The Stanford Dictionary of Anglicised Words and Phrases*[1], but even this has many disadvantages. It is now antiquated—it was published in 1892—and contains none of the very numerous expressions first introduced into English in the twentieth century; as the title implies, it includes a very large number of words which have been fully anglicized, and which are therefore not now 'foreign' in any ordinary sense of the term; and (like the *New English Dictionary*) it is historical in plan, so that its pages are overloaded with words and phrases which have long been obsolete. Other more recent dictionaries of foreign expressions are even less useful: all swell their bulk by the inclusion of numerous words and phrases which have either long been obsolete, or have only a very limited currency; some appear to aim at providing a kind of compact polyglot dictionary for those travelling abroad, since they include expressions which could not conceivably have any currency in an English context.

In this dictionary I have tried to supply the needs of the general reader in search of a single work of reference which will explain at least the majority of the foreign words and phrases likely to be

[1] For further details of this work see p. 61.

encountered in current English, both written and spoken. I have tried to restrict the volume to a manageable size by excluding expressions which are either obsolete or have only a limited technical currency. For this reason I have found it necessary to compile the list of words and phrases to be included without reference to earlier dictionaries—though I have, of course, consulted dictionaries and other works of reference in search of information about the expressions included in the list. With very few exceptions all the words and phrases in this dictionary have been culled from recent books and journals; the exceptions are expressions which I would use myself or have heard in conversation, but which I have not happened to find in print. No doubt this method must result in the omission of words and phrases which I have accidentally overlooked, though I hope the omissions will not be found to be very numerous; but the ransacking of dictionaries for additional entries could only have made this volume more bulky, more expensive, and less convenient to use.

The remainder of the first part of this Introduction is devoted to a discussion and appraisal from different points of view of the words and phrases actually listed in the dictionary. The second part deals with various difficulties arising in connection with the use of foreign expressions in English. The third part explains the arrangement of the dictionary.

The historical background

A visitor to Britain during the first half of the fifth century would have found two languages in common use: in the rural districts British (the language which eventually developed into Welsh, Cornish and Breton), in the Romanized cities Latin. About the middle of the century a new language, the language which ultimately developed into modern English, was brought to the country by invaders from across the Channel. According to the Venerable Bede the invading force was composed of Angles, Saxons, and Jutes; but archæological investigation has thrown some doubt on the validity of Bede's distinctions. The original homes of the invaders were in the districts which now constitute northern Germany and the Danish peninsula, but it is very probable that they had migrated first to the lowlands of Frisia and western Holland, and that the original tribal differences had been largely eliminated in the course of their residence there. At all events it is now generally agreed that the invaders spoke a single, more or less homogeneous language, and that the dialectal divergences observable at a later date developed in Britain, not on the Continent. The language spoken by the invaders is sometimes known as Anglo-Saxon, but it is better called Old English, since this latter name emphasizes the essential continuity of the English language from the fifth century to the present day.

Old English was a Germanic language, and contained few words alien to the original native stock. Like the other Germanic languages of this period, it contained a few words of Latin origin picked up on the Continent, long before the invaders came to Britain, through trade with the Romans; examples, in their modern English form, are *cheese* < *caseus*, *kitchen* < *coquina*, and *street* < *strata* (*via*). However, the Anglo-Saxons did not very readily accept foreign words into their speech, and there are very few words in English which can be attributed to borrowing from the British-speaking and Latin-speaking inhabitants whom the invaders found in possession of the country: *brock* 'badger', *combe* 'valley' and the adjective *dun* 'dark-coloured' are examples of words borrowed from British; *chest*<*cista*, *fork*<*furca*, and *pail*<*pagella* are examples of borrowings from Latin during this early period. The advent of Christianity about the year 600 introduced into the language a number of Latin ecclesiastical terms, such as *bishop*<*episcopus*, *devil*<*diabolus*, and *priest*<*presbyter*; all three Latin words are in turn derived from Greek. But even in this sphere the Anglo-Saxons preferred either to apply new Christian meanings to native words like *Easter*, *heaven*, *hell* and *sin*, or to form new compound words from native stems to express the new Christian concepts; thus, for the mystery which we now call by the Latin name *Trinity*, the Anglo-Saxons used the native compound *Threeness*. During the later Anglo-Saxon period, from the latter part of the ninth century onwards, the north-eastern part of England was occupied by Danish invaders, and a large number of Scandinavian words found their way into the local dialects of this area, many of which still survive in the modern dialects. Relatively few Scandinavian words, however, found their way into the English spoken in the Southern part of the country; examples are *fellow*, *outlaw*, *wrong*, and the verb *call*.

It is difficult to overestimate the importance of the influence of the Norman Conquest on the English language. Before the Conquest the vocabulary of English was almost entirely native; by the end of the fourteenth century, when Chaucer was writing his *Canterbury Tales*, about half[1] the words used in English were of foreign origin, though the basic structure of the language remained (and still remains)

[1] Half the words as listed in a dictionary or glossary, that is; in a passage of continuous writing not more than one fifth of the words would be of foreign origin, because the foreign words were used relatively much less frequently than the surviving native words.

Germanic. Within a short time after the Conquest all the important positions in the country, both secular and ecclesiastical, had been filled by Normans; for nearly two hundred years the 'upper crust' of English society spoke French amongst themselves. From the beginning there must have been influences at work against the use of French: many of the Norman nobles married English wives, and Norman mothers had their children suckled by English nurses, so that all the Norman children in England must have spoken some English, at least as a nursery-language; and every Norman landowner or cleric must have needed to speak some elementary English to his English subordinates and servants. Yet as long as the Norman nobility owned estates in Normandy as well as in England, and spent some part of the year on the other side of the Channel, French must have been the more convenient language for their general use. With the loss of Normandy by King John in 1204, circumstances changed; those nobles who chose to remain in England now spent the whole of their time there; residence in France no longer served to counteract the natural encroachment of English. Linguistic nationalism seems hardly to have existed in the Middle Ages, yet the fact that France became and remained the traditional enemy of England for many hundreds of years can hardly have failed to exert some influence against French in favour of English as the language of the upper classes in England.

From the thirteenth century onwards the upper classes in England made increasing use of English; but, because at first English came less naturally to them than French, they tended to interlard their speech with French words—partly because the native English vocabulary was somewhat defective in certain fields (notably in those concerned with abstract concepts and with the luxuries of life), partly from ignorance of the appropriate native term. The numerous French words adopted in this way were fully absorbed into the English language, so much so that many of them cannot easily be recognized as French except by professional students of language. The following words, for instance, would scarcely strike the ordinary user of English as being 'foreign': *assets, bargain, broker, chair, coat, dance, faith, fruit, fur, ink, joy, pen, pray, roast*. This extensive acceptance of French words into the vocabulary of English made it easier for words from other foreign languages to be accepted too, and from this time onwards foreign words entered English in abundance; words were taken not only from French, but from the Classical languages, from other European languages, and in due course, as more and more of the world became accessible to travellers, from remoter languages as well.

The anglicization of foreign words

The French words absorbed into English during the Middle Ages were fully anglicized both in pronunciation and in form. There was less difference between the pronunciations of the two languages in the Middle Ages than there is today, but there were already a number of sounds in French that had no counterpart in English; these were all replaced by English sounds. There was also a marked difference in stress between the two languages, in so far as the stress in French tended (and tends) to fall towards the end of a word, and the stress in English tended (and tends) to fall towards the beginning of a word; the French stress was nearly always rejected in favour of the English stress. The substitution of the English for the French stress can be observed in such words as *beauty*, *memory*, *palace*, and *service*; and it will be noticed that these words contain no sounds which are not fully English. In a similar way French words were provided with English inflections. Nouns offered little difficulty, since the addition of a final *-s* was the most common way of forming the plural in both languages. Verbs, on the other hand, lost their French inflections and were conjugated according to the English pattern—usually one of the simpler English patterns; but such French verbs as *catch/caught* and *strive/strove/striven* show that even the more irregular of the English patterns could be brought into play.

In the same way words adopted at a later period, not only from modern languages but from the Classical languages, tended to be anglicized. Until recent times Greek and Latin were pronounced in each individual country with the sounds of the vernacular language of that country[1], so that the question of modifying the pronunciation of borrowed words did not arise. In form, however, these words underwent substantial changes: the original inflectional endings were dropped, and were replaced either by the appropriate English endings or by special endings, not fully English, but felt to be less alien from English than those of Greek or Latin. An example of the first process is to be found in the numerous verbs formed from the past participles of Latin verbs: such forms as *select*, *situate*, and *convict*, all three from Latin past participles, were originally borrowed in an adjectival function; the first is still often used as an adjective, the second only in the jargon of the law, the third never (though with a variant stress it is used as a noun); but all three are now in use as verbs, and are conjugated with the ordinary English verbal inflections. An example of the second process is to be found in the numerous adjectives of Latin

[1] The pronunciation of Latin and Greek in England is discussed at length below, pp. 37-40 and 42-44.

origin which in English end in -ous, such as *obvious*, *tremendous*, *various*; in these the original ending *-us* of the Latin nominative singular masculine has been replaced by the French ending *-ous*[1] found in such words as *famous* and *generous*, an ending which historically corresponds not to Latin *-us* but to Latin *-osus*.

The anglicization of words adopted since about 1600 has been less systematic. French words adopted during the seventeenth century tend to show a curious combination of French stress with English sounds: such words as *campaign*, *festoon*, *gazette* and *grimace*, for instance, are pronounced with the stress on the last syllable as in French, though the sounds have been fully anglicized. More recent borrowings vary considerably in the treatment they receive; both the extent of the anglicization they undergo and the rapidity with which it takes place tend to depend on frequency of usage; in general the more frequently a word is used the more completely and the more rapidly it is anglicised. The word *picnic*, for instance, was first used in the eighteenth century (usually in the form *pique-nique*) to describe a function considered essentially foreign, to be encountered only abroad; not until after 1800 was it first applied to an *al fresco* meal in England. On the other hand the word *garage* was first used in English as recently as 1902, and for several years thereafter was still always printed either in italics or within quotation marks; yet owing to the rapid development of the internal combustion engine the word has become so familiar that, although more conservative speakers still prefer a quasi-French pronunciation of the final syllable, a fully anglicized pronunciation is now probably more common, and will certainly eventually prevail.

However, anglicization is not entirely a question of long standing in the language, or of frequency of usage; there are some words of foreign origin which have been used, even frequently used, for many hundreds of years and have still not been anglicized. More remarkable still, it sometimes happens that a foreign word becomes fully anglicized, and yet at a later date reappears in a 'foreign' form. The French word *bévue*, for instance, was introduced and anglicized in the eighteenth century as *bevew*; but this anglicized form is now obsolete, and the only form in current use is the original *bévue*, so spelt, and pronounced approximately as in French. Some of the reasons for the failure of anglicization, or for the re-appearance of a 'foreign' form, are discussed below, pp. 21–25. This dictionary is concerned only with those words which have not been anglicized, or which have re-appeared in a 'foreign' form; and, amongst these, only with those

[1] The ending *-ous* is a Norman dialect form corresponding to the *-eux* of standard French: *fameux*, *généreux*.

which can be said to belong to current English.[1] Unfortunately, it is exceedingly difficult to define precisely what it is that characterizes a word as 'foreign', and nearly as difficult to define what is meant by 'current' English. These two concepts will therefore have to be discussed at some length.

THE MEANING OF 'FOREIGN'

There is no difficulty in distinguishing a 'foreign' phrase from an English phrase: one is composed of foreign words, the other of English words. However, to draw an equally sharp distinction in the case of single words is to oversimplify. In point of fact, words of foreign origin form a spectrum graduating imperceptibly from words like *faith* at one end, the foreign origin of which would be obvious only to the professional student of language, to words like *éclat*, which no one would consider anything but 'foreign', at the other; it would be possible to prepare a sequence of words, each slightly but perceptibly more 'foreign' than the preceding one, covering the whole range between these two extremes. Unfortunately, for the purpose of such a dictionary as this it is necessary to draw a hard-and-fast line somewhere across this spectrum, and to call all words on one side of it 'foreign', all words on the other side 'not foreign'; and the right point at which to draw the line is not easy to determine.

It would be very satisfactory if it were possible to draw up a list of objective criteria by means of which 'foreign' words can be distinguished from those which are 'not foreign', and up to a point it is indeed possible; at least the attempt is worth making. These criteria may be either positive or negative; that is to say, they may prescribe characteristics the presence of which implies that a word *is* 'foreign', or characteristics the presence of which implies that a word is *not* 'foreign'. As will appear, most of the possible criteria are open to obvious objections, and none is wholly free from difficulty; yet, taken together, they are of considerable help in distinguishing 'foreign' words.

SOME POSITIVE CRITERIA

The following is a list of some positive criteria, with the objections that might be urged against each.

(1) *The use of italics in printing*. At first sight this seems to be an admirable criterion, since one of the accepted uses of italic type is for

[1] The dictionary also, of course, deals with foreign phrases; but these are normally anglicized (if at all) by translation, and therefore present fewer problems; see below, pp. 22-23.

distinguishing words in foreign languages; and it is true that a word which is invariably printed in italics can safely be regarded as 'foreign'. But authors and compositors are as much afflicted by the difficulty of drawing a line across the spectrum as the compiler of a dictionary; there is a large class of words for which the presence or absence of italics varies from printer to printer and from publisher to publisher; and there is no obvious reason for accepting as final the usage of one printer or publisher in preference to that of another.

(2) *The use of accent-marks or other diacritic signs.* Again the criterion would seem to be useful, since no accent-marks or diacritic signs are used in native English words; but again the usage of writers and compositors is far from standardized. The lack of standardization can by no means be attributed to the absence of suitable diacritic signs from the type-face being used: it is not uncommon to see the same word printed with and without diacritics in the same paragraph[1]. Moreover, there is an additional disadvantage here not applicable to the preceding criterion: this one can obviously be of no help at all in judging the very numerous 'foreign' words which are not written with any accent-marks or other diacritics in their language of origin.

(3) *The presence in the accepted pronunciation of sounds never heard in native English words*[2]. The presence in the accepted pronunciation of a word of such foreign sounds as the French nasal vowels, or the German 'front rounded' vowels *ö* and *ü*, is conclusive proof that it is 'foreign'. But although usage in pronunciation is rather more stable than usage in spelling, variations do occur; for instance, although the normal pronunciation of the noun *envelope* is fully anglicized, there are still many speakers who use an approximation to a French nasal vowel in the first syllable. Again, this criterion can be of no service when the pronunciation of a word in its language of origin contains no sound substantially different from the sounds of English.

(4) *A different correspondence of sound and symbol from the normal correspondence in native English words.* The word *rouge*, for example, as normally pronounced in English, contains no sound not heard in

[1] Current usage as it affects accent-marks and other diacritics is discussed at greater length below, pp. 46–48.

[2] Under this heading might be included the occurrence of a stress which would not seem natural in a native English word. But usage is too variable for this consideration to be of much value: such words as *bureau* and *garage* can be heard stressed on either syllable.

native or fully anglicized English words; but the use of *ou* to represent the sound usually spelt *oo*, and the use of *g* to represent the sound normally heard only in such words as *pleasure* and *invasion*, mark the word out as 'foreign'. But even in this respect usage varies. The majority of speakers pronounce the word *trait* like the word *tray*, and thus mark the word out as 'foreign' by their failure to pronounce the final *-t*; but a substantial number of speakers now pronounce the final *-t*, and the number is likely to increase. Moreover, the strict application of this criterion would class the word *machine* as 'foreign', a conclusion repugnant to common sense.

(5) *The use in English of foreign feminine or plural forms.* English has no distinctive feminine form for the adjective, and the few distinctively feminine nouns (like *actress*) are easy to recognize; thus the existence of a special feminine form like *contadina* beside *contadino*, or *danseuse* beside *danseur*, is conclusive proof that the words concerned are 'foreign'. But only adjectives and nouns referring to persons can have a feminine form, and these represent only a small minority of the total. Moreover, there are some curious anomalies in the use of feminine forms in English: the feminine *naïve* has largely displaced the masculine *naïf* (perhaps because of the influence of the derived abstract noun *naïveté*), and the feminine *blonde* is often applied to men; on the other hand, such words as *protégé* often retain their masculine forms in English even when applied to women (doubtless because in such cases the addition of a final *-e* does not affect the pronunciation). Foreign plurals also present some difficulties. Since the normal formation of the plural in both French and Spanish consists of the addition of a final *-s*, exactly as in English, this criterion fails us for the majority of the very numerous nouns and adjectives adopted from these two languages[1]. Some words may take either a foreign plural or an English plural according to the circumstances. In some cases it is reasonable to conclude that the word is 'foreign' when it takes a foreign plural, but English when it takes an English plural; thus, *medium* with plural *media* is clearly

[1] The plural *s* is normally not pronounced in French, so that failure to pronounce it might be considered an indication that the word concerned is 'foreign'; unfortunately the plural *s* is often pronounced in English even when added to unmistakably 'foreign' nouns like *trait;* the normal pronunciation of the plural *traits* is like *trays*, a pronunciation which is neither fully English nor fully French. The word *corps* has the same spelling in both singular and plural, in English as in French; the final *-s* is always silent in French, but in English it is pronounced in the plural, though not in the singular.

'foreign', but *medium* with plural *mediums* is fully anglicized. Unfortunately other instances are not so clear-cut[1].

SOME NEGATIVE CRITERIA

The following is a list of some negative criteria, with the objections that might be urged against each.

(1) *The existence of derivatives formed in accordance with English rules.* It is true that the majority of 'foreign' words do not form derivatives (verbs from nouns, nouns from adjectives, and so on) in accordance with English rules. There are many pairs of 'foreign' words in English, one of which is formed from the other in accordance with foreign rules of derivation: *gêné* from *gêne*, *bourgeoisie* from *bourgeois*, and numerous others. Yet there are not a few words which, although clearly 'foreign' by the criteria of the preceding section, none the less have derivatives formed in accordance with English rules. The pronunciation of *qu* as *k* shows that *coquette* is 'foreign', yet the derived adjective is *coquettish*. An even more striking example is *subpœna*, which when used as a verb has a past participle *subpœnaed* or *subpœna'd*; yet the use of the symbol *œ* shows that the word is 'foreign', and in fact few of those who use it can be unaware that it comes from the Latin phrase *sub pœna*.

(2) *The use of a different spelling from that in the language of origin.* Anglicization often involves a change of spelling as well as of pronunciation, and words which remain 'foreign' usually retain their spelling unchanged; so that any change of spelling in English suggests that the word is no longer 'foreign'. This criterion is not, of course, applicable to words adopted from languages written in special characters, since in such cases some kind of transliteration is unavoidable; and even when it is applicable it needs to be used with the greatest of caution. Many apparent discrepancies of spelling are to be explained by the fact that English has preserved a spelling formerly in use but now obsolete in the language of origin: thus, English *connoisseur*, *ditto*, *duenna*, *inamorato*, *maelstrom* and *Thalweg* preserve obsolete but perfectly genuine forms of contemporary *connaisseur*, *detto*, *dueña*, *innamorato*, *maalstroom* and *Talweg*. Certain discrepancies in spelling which cannot be explained in this way nevertheless follow a consistent pattern and serve a clear purpose. Many foreign words, for instance, are stressed on the final syllable, contrary

[1] Current usage in respect of foreign feminines and plurals is discussed at greater length below, pp. 51–55.

to normal English usage; and in a number of words a final *-e*, not present in the language of origin, has been added to indicate this stress on the final syllable, especially when there already exists an English word identical in spelling with the foreign word concerned, but differently stressed. Thus, the existence of English *choral*, *local* and *moral* (stressed on the first syllable) justifies the spellings *chorale*, *locale* and *morale* for German *Choral(gesang)* and French *local*, *moral*[1]. Another systematic tendency, though one which serves no very obvious purpose, is the simplification of double consonants in foreign languages: English *lazaretto* and *seraglio* correspond to Italian *lazzaretto* and *serraglio*, English *macaroni* to obsolete Italian *maccaroni* (modern *maccheroni*). The form *guerilla* for Spanish *guerrilla*, though scarcely standard English, has been very common ever since the word was first introduced at the time of the Peninsular War. The opposite tendency seems to affect some Spanish words: English *peccadillo* and *incommunicado* correspond to Spanish *pecadillo* and *incomunicado*; in the latter case the spelling has doubtless been assimilated to that of English *communicate*. Yet another systematic tendency is the preference for final *-ée* in words of French origin: English *couchée* and *levée* correspond to French *coucher* and *lever*, and *toupée* is very commonly written for French *toupet*. Occasionally a change of spelling seems to be designed to make a word look more 'foreign': Portuguese *aia*, *ama* and *varanda*, all three associated in English usage primarily with the Orient, are written *ayah*, *amah* and *verandah*, with an Oriental-looking final *-h*. A complicated example of change of spelling is to be found in *confidante* for French *confidente*. Probably the change of spelling originally served to differentiate the masculine *confidant* from the English adjective *confident;* but the masculine form has now been anglicized, and the feminine form is sufficiently differentiated by its final *-e*, so that the reason for the change of spelling no longer applies; yet the traditional spelling persists.

(3) *The existence of a different meaning from that in the language of origin*. This criterion is even more hazardous. 'Foreign' words are less likely to undergo a change of meaning than native words, since their meaning in the language from which they come (which may be known to many of those who use them) will normally act as a restraining influence. However, the precise correspondence of meaning may be modified in a number of ways. The meaning of an expression may

[1] For some further possible examples of this tendency see below, p. 48. The final *-e* of the word *forte* (French *fort*) may be intended to distinguish it from the military term *fort*, though here no question of stress arises.

undergo change in its language or origin—in extreme cases an expression may become wholly obsolete in its language of origin, though it remains current in English: an example is *à pur et à plein*, which is to all intents and purposes obsolete in French. If an expression becomes obsolete in this way, the language of origin can exercise no restraining influence. Sometimes the only current meaning of an expression in English is one which, though it exists in the language of origin, is subsidiary and relatively unimportant. Thus, the basic French meanings of *allure*, *passe-partout* and *trousseau* are 'gait', 'master-key', and 'bunch (of keys)' respectively. Sometimes English has specialized the meaning of an expression in a way not countenanced by the language of origin: in French *chauffeur* means merely 'driver', and can be applied to an owner-driver, but in English it means only 'paid driver'; in Spanish *copita* can be applied to any kind of wine-glass, but in English it means only 'tulip-shaped sherry-glass'. Sometimes the English meaning of an expression is quite unknown in the language of origin: in French *bonne bouche* means only 'pleasant taste', *rôtisserie* only 'cook-shop'. A very curious instance is to be found in the phrase *papier mâché*, which seems to have been formed in English from two French words; in French it has only its literal meaning 'chewed paper'. It is only a step from a spurious phrase like this to such 'pseudo-foreign' words as *agapemone*, *glissando* and *imponderabilia*, which look like Greek, Italian and Latin respectively, but are not. These words look 'foreign', and can hardly be omitted from a dictionary such as this, since the user of the dictionary cannot be expected to know that they are not genuinely 'foreign' until he has looked them up.

Practical conclusions

The application of these criteria is difficult, particularly since the results derived from the negative criteria often seem to conflict with those derived from the positive criteria; each word must be carefully weighed in the balance. However, used with discretion they can be very useful, and with their help it is possible to mark off a large number of expressions as clearly 'foreign', and a large number of others as fully anglicized. Nevertheless, there will remain a substantial proportion of words to which none of the criteria is applicable, or for which usage varies in a way which leaves the result in doubt. For such words there is no alternative but to apply a wholly subjective criterion: a word is 'foreign' if it 'feels' foreign to the speaker or writer who uses it. The objections to such a subjective criterion are obvious: no two speakers or writers will agree at all points in the application of the criterion. The apprehension of a word as 'foreign' will vary according to the education, environment, and even the profession of the person who uses it. This does not mean that there will not be substantial agreement between educated speakers about a very large number of words to which the objective criteria listed above are not applicable, but there will be an extensive fringe-area in which there is room for disagreement.

From the practical point of view this fringe-area might be treated in various ways in the compilation of a dictionary such as this. All doubtful words might be admitted: this procedure would swell the bulk of the dictionary very substantially, and a large number of the words added would be so familiar to the majority of speakers of English that their usage could never be in doubt; the presence of so many unwanted words would make the genuinely 'foreign' ones more difficult to find. Alternatively, all doubtful words might be excluded: but this procedure would mean the exclusion of numerous words which might seem 'foreign' and therefore difficult to a large number of potential users of the dictionary. In fact I have adopted neither of these procedures: where objective criteria fail I have accepted as decisive my own subjective judgment of the status of each word, in the hope that, although my choice of words will certainly not be identical with that of any user or critic of the dictionary, it is not so eccentric as to imperil the usefulness of the dictionary as much as the wholesale admission or exclusion of doubtful words would certainly do.

'CURRENT' WORDS

The adjective 'current' combines in its meaning two distinct ideas, 'belonging to the present time' and 'in general circulation'. If a 'foreign' word is properly to be considered 'current' it must conform to both these conditions; it must belong to the present time, and it must be in general circulation.

It is obvious that the first condition excludes words which have long been obsolete, but it is less obvious how far back the 'present time' can be considered to extend. As far as the spoken language is concerned, only words still in use at this very moment can be considered 'current' in the temporal sense; but the written language is more permanent, and the reading of the man of today is not limited to what was written yesterday. A reader of the older literature normally adopts (perhaps unconsciously) a historical approach, and is prepared to encounter obsolete words which must be looked out in a historical dictionary; historical novels, too, may contain obsolete words which are recognized at once for what they are; but the reader who picks up a straight novel written thirty or forty years ago tends to look on it as a 'modern' work, and to feel that any word found in it is in a sense 'current'; the writer in a reminiscent vein, writing of a period now passed away but within his own memory, may well use words which would no longer seem natural to him in his everyday speech. As a rough rule of thumb it seems fair to say that any word which has been extensively used at any time during the present century, even if it is now obsolescent or obsolete, is in this general sense 'current'.

The second condition excludes words which are not in general circulation; that is, words which are incomprehensible to the majority of those who use English. There are, indeed, innumerable terms in use at the present day which are very limited in their usage—technical terms which, though well understood and used with unthinking freedom by those professionally connected with the particular field concerned, are unintelligible to the uninitiated. As it happens, rather a large number of the 'foreign' words used in English are technical terms, especially in the field of the arts. It is clear that words never used except by those professionally occupied with a given discipline must be excluded from the list of 'current' words; but there is a large fringe-area of words which, though in a sense technical terms, are nevertheless known to and extensively used by amateurs in the fields concerned. The cultivated man often has a wide range of amateur interests in the arts, and to a lesser extent in certain of the less abstruse sciences.

Words which are used not only by professionals but by amateurs of the arts and sciences, even though their currency is limited, must be considered 'current' in a sense. It is perhaps fair to say that any technical term known to and used by persons other than those who are professionally occupied with the discipline concerned must be considered to be 'current'. A useful practical criterion of 'currency' in this sense is the appearance of a word in the pages of the weekly non-technical journals which expressly cater for the interests of the educated amateur: 'foreign' words to be classified in this category are frequent enough in articles on literary criticism, music, the plastic arts, architecture, foreign travel, and so on. A further justification of the inclusion of such quasi-technical words is to be found in the fact that their technical status is far from stable. Terms which were originally limited in their application to some specific art or science are now in much more general usage, either in connection with other arts or sciences, or in familiar colloquial contexts. Such culinary terms as *macédoine* and *roux*, such musical terms as *crescendo* and *staccato*, for instance, are now very frequently used in figurative senses in general non-technical contexts.

There are certain fields in which the 'currency' of a word is particularly difficult to determine, notably the fields of culinary and medical terms. The technical language of cooking includes a very large number of 'foreign' words, mainly from French; similarly the technical language of medicine includes a large number of Greek and Latin words; but by no means all the technical words in either field are likely to be encountered by the non-specialist. It is obviously not a function of this dictionary to define all the terms which might be found in a menu, since if the menu is written in French these words are not current *in English*. On the other hand, many cookery books and culinary articles in newspapers and journals include a good many 'foreign' words, usually referring either to general categories of dishes or to processes involved in the preparation of food; and an attempt has been made to include all the most common of these. Similarly, words never found outside the pages of a medical textbook or journal are not included, but an attempt has been made to include those likely to be found in writings of more general interest in non-technical journals. Other fields are even more remote from the purpose of the dictionary. For instance, none of the Latin names of plants and shrubs is included in the dictionary, though many are known to people who are not professional botanists; but those who use the terms are normally keen gardeners and have a special if not a professional interest in such matters; and the terms are so numerous that to include them would overload the dictionary.

'Current' phrases

So far we have been mainly concerned with single words rather than with phrases, since there is rarely any doubt whether a phrase is 'foreign' or not; but the question of 'currency' affects phrases just as much as single words. All the considerations discussed in the preceding section apply with equal strength to phrases; but there is one special difficulty which applies to phrases only, not to single words. This difficulty is both theoretical and practical, and arises from the fact that many 'foreign' phrases used in English are quotations from foreign authors. The number of possible foreign quotations is very large indeed, since a speaker or writer well versed in foreign literatures and endowed with a good memory has a vast stock of phrases to draw on; and the listener or reader, provided he is familiar with the language in question, will understand what is meant, even if he does not recognize the origin of the quotation. But the majority of such quotations are not in any sense 'current', since they are not in general circulation; a quotation may well be used once and never used again. From the theoretical point of view, therefore, the majority of quotations have no place in such a dictionary as this; there are many good Dictionaries of Quotations in which their meanings may be looked out. From the practical point of view also it would be impossible to include a very large number of quotations, since they would add enormously to the bulk of the volume without adding appreciably to its usefulness.

A simple solution would be to exclude all quotations from the pages of the dictionary; that is, to exclude any phrase which is to be found in the works of a well-known foreign author. However, to do this would be to introduce a number of anomalies, and to exclude a great many phrases which are unquestionably 'current' in the sense defined in the preceding section. Many 'foreign' expressions in common use are in fact quotations, even though those who use them may be unaware of the fact; how many of those who use the phrase *cherchez la femme* know that it is a quotation from *Les Mohicans de Paris* by Alexandre Dumas the younger? Again, many 'foreign' expressions in common use are not exact quotations but adaptations of phrases used by well-known writers: thus, *cacoethes scribendi* is an adaptation of Juvenal's *scribendi cacoethes*, and *cacoethes loquendi* is a further adaptation of *cacoethes scribendi*. Are these phrases to be considered as quotations or not?[1] Then there are phrases of the type which may be called 'verbal quotations'—phrases supposed on more or less trustworthy authority to have been spoken by well-known persons; many of these, like *après nous le déluge* (Mme de Pompadour), *eppur si muove* (Galileo) or *ils n'ont rien appris ni rien oublié* (Talleyrand) are commonly used with some kind of awareness of the attribution. Many other phrases, though not attributed to any author, and not to be found in dictionaries of quotations, have all the appearance of quotations: such, for instance, are *cucullus non facit monachum*, *palmam qui meruit ferat*, and *spes ultima gentis*.

Another kind of difficulty is raised by phrases which appear in the works of more than one author, or more than once in the works of the same author. Such phrases are not uncommon, and the following represent only a selection: *ab ovo* (Horace, *Satires* and *Ars Poetica*); *æquo animo* (Cicero, Vulgate); *hinc illæ lacrymæ* (Terence, Horace); *rara avis* (Horace, Juvenal); *siccum lumen* (Tibullus, Lucan). In some cases one writer may be quoting from another: Horace's use of *hinc*

[1] The adaptation of quotations is discussed at greater length below, pp. 30–32.

illæ lacrymæ is almost certainly a conscious quotation from Terence, and Juvenal's use of *rara avis* a conscious quotation from Horace. In other cases it seems more probable that the phrase was already proverbial and formed part of the common stock of the language; so, no doubt, with *æquo animo* and *siccum lumen.* But it can only be an accident if such proverbial phrases have survived in the work of more than one writer, so that many phrases used by one writer only may have been equally proverbial, even if they cannot be identified with any confidence. Yet a further difficulty is raised by phrases which are now quoted, not in the language in which they were originally written, but in some other language into which they have been translated. Euclid's ὅτι ἔδει δεῖξαι is familiar in its Latin form *quod erat demonstrandum*; Quintilian's *cædes videtur significare sanguinem et ferrum* is known only in Bismarck's German translation *Blut und Eisen.*

These considerations leave no doubt that the exclusion of a phrase from the dictionary merely because it appears in a known source, or closely resembles a phrase in a known source, would result in many arbitrary inconsistencies. Many common phrases would have to be omitted even though no one but a specialist could recognize them as quotations or adaptations; amongst these would be a number which were proverbial or even hackneyed phrases long before they were used in any extant writing. On the other hand, many other phrases would be included which are almost certainly quotations from sources not yet identified, merely because their origin is not known; and at any time the discovery of their origin might render them inadmissible for inclusion. It would seem, then, that quotations need not be excluded as such; but only those quotations qualify for inclusion which are really in general circulation; that is, those which have become more or less proverbial, so that their origin in the work of an earlier writer is not consciously present in the mind of the user.

Inevitably the choice of such phrases must be mainly subjective; different persons will differ widely in their awareness of the origins of such phrases—the Classical scholar, for instance, can hardly fail to be conscious of the origins of Greek and Latin phrases, and will use them less unselfconsciously than the man in the street. I have tried to err rather on the side of inclusion than of exclusion: thus, the fact that *sunt lacrymæ rerum* is to be found somewhere in Virgil is probably known to most of those who use the phrase, but I have included it none the less. Although this is not a dictionary of quotations, I have tried to ascertain the origin of all phrases which obviously are, or which seem to be, quotations; in a number of cases I have failed in the attempt; dictionaries of quotations are not always reliable, and the references they give are sometimes misleading and occasionally quite inexplicable.

THE CLASSIFICATION OF 'FOREIGN' EXPRESSIONS

As soon as the list of words and phrases for inclusion in the dictionary has been completed it becomes obvious that they fall naturally into a number of more or less well defined categories, which are nearly if not quite mutually exclusive.

(1) *Expressions for which no tolerable English equivalent happens to exist*. The absence of a suitable English equivalent is presumably due to some historical accident, but it is rarely possible even to conjecture a plausible reason for the lack. Thus, although *chic* may reasonably be considered a quality characteristically French, or at least not English, *esprit de corps* is often quoted as a virtue in which the English excel[1]; and *flair* is a gift peculiar to individuals rather than to nations. Expressions of this type usually denote abstract qualities, but they may occasionally refer to concrete things. It is difficult to understand why there should be no English equivalent of the useful term *guichet*; 'ticket-window' is perhaps the nearest approach, but would not cover many common uses of *guichet*; 'grill through which business is transacted' is intolerably cumbersome.

(2) *Expressions which display a markedly felicitous turn of phrase*. All expressions in this category are naturally phrases; they could be translated into English, but any translation would lack some of the succinctness and force of the original. Most quotations and pseudo-quotations belong in this category. It would not be difficult to find a passable translation for, say, *esprit d'escalier*, *ich kann nicht anders*, *monumentum ære perennius*, or *oderint dum metuant*, but no translation could match the lapidary quality of the original.

(3) *Expressions picked up by British servicemen in foreign countries*. These expressions, first incorporated into service slang, often later find their way into the general slang of the people at large. Examples from the First World War are *ça ne fait rien*, *dekko*, *imshi*, *Kamerad*; from the Second World War, *bambino*, *kaputt*, *shufti*.

(4) *Expressions couched in a foreign language for reasons of decorum*. Gibbon's 'decent obscurity of a learned language' still prevails in such terms as *genitalia* or *pudendum;* but now the obscurity of any foreign language seems to be considered decent, with a strong preference for

[1] The alternative term for this quality is German: *Gemeinschaftsgefühl*.

French—perhaps because of the persistent English superstition that the French are remarkably licentious. Nearly all the less reputable aspects of sexual behaviour are conveniently designated by French expressions: *allumeuse*, *cabinet particulier*, *fricatrice*, *maison de rendezvous*, *maîtresse en titre*, *quartier toléré*, and many others. German contributes only *Stundenhotel*, Italian only *bordello*. Such expressions are becoming less common now that the climate of opinion allows of increasing frankness in the discussion of sexual matters, and they will doubtless eventually become obsolete.

(5) *Expressions which, though not connected with any specific art or science, are in a sense 'technical'*. The expression *au pair* is used because it is related to the employment of foreigners; certainly there is no equivalent, even approximate, in English. The term *ombudsman* retains its Scandinavian form because the office is a Scandinavian invention which until recently had no counterpart in English-speaking countries.

(6) *Expressions which are strictly technical and belong to the professional vocabulary of some art or science*. It is characteristic of such expressions that they have acquired in their language of origin special connotations lacking from their English equivalents. Thus, such technical terms of music as *allegro* 'cheerful', *largo* 'spacious', *scherzo* 'joke' have specific meanings not conveyed by the corresponding English words; Italian *staccato* and French *détaché*, both meaning 'detached', have quite distinct meanings as technical terms. Similarly such technical terms of the plastic arts as *fresco* 'fresh' have special meanings which could not easily be deduced from a literal translation.

(7) *Quasi-technical expressions only recently introduced into the language*. The 'foreign' status of such expressions seems likely to be only temporary; in due course they will doubtless be either anglicized or translated. Examples in the transitional stage are *comédie noire*, *nouvelle vague* and *roman-fleuve*, now often translated as 'black comedy', 'new wave' and 'river novel' respectively.

(8) *Expressions which acquire a temporary vogue and rapidly become obsolete*. An excellent example is *discothèque*. In the course of a few years this word has passed through the following stages of meaning: a record library; a record shop; a record shop providing refreshments for its customers; a club providing recorded music and refreshments; a night-club providing recorded music and dancing. It is safe to predict that this word will either become obsolete or undergo some kind of translation within a very short time. A very

similar example is *boutique*. Expressions referring to women's fashions are particularly unstable: as fashions change, so do the current terms; and since Paris is still the cradle of fashion, the terms are very often French. It sometimes happens that with the change of fashions the same foreign expression may be introduced more than once into the language in different senses, to the confusion of lexicographers: the word *pèlerine*, for instance has been in vogue at least six times, in 1740–50, 1764, 1825–35, 1855–68, 1884–1904, and again in recent years. Though the currency of expressions of this type, whether connected with fashion or not, may be evanescent, they may eke out a prolonged existence in reminiscences of the fairly recent past; thus, *Backfisch* has exactly the same status as the English *flapper*, and a photograph album may stimulate reference to *bandeaux* and *chignons*.

(9) *Expressions referring to foreign institutions or things*. In many cases the only alternative to the use of a 'foreign' expression is a more or less elaborate description. A French *château*, for instance, is not at all the same thing as an English castle, nor is there any precise counterpart in England; the Russian *dacha* has political connotations not easily rendered into English without periphrasis; the avoidance of *præsidium* would involve a description of the Soviet bureaucratic organization.

(10) *Expressions used rather to convey local colour than because there is no English equivalent*. These expressions, like those in the previous category, refer to foreign institutions and things, but the obvious English equivalent is avoided for the sake of local colour. In a book about France the word *gendarme* conveys nothing that would not be conveyed by the English word *policeman* except a vaguely foreign atmosphere—a suggestion of unfamiliar uniforms and broken English. In a book about Germany the word *Rathaus* may be preferable to the English *town hall* because of a vague suggestion of stepped gables or Gothic pinnacles.

(11) *Expressions used for purposes of stylistic decoration*. Some writers and speakers prefer to use a 'foreign' expression merely because it is not English; it makes a pleasant change, and impresses the reader or listener with the superior culture and erudition of the user. The desirability of the use of 'foreign' words and phrases for such purposes is discussed at length below, pp. 35–36.

Why some expressions remain 'foreign'

This classification of 'foreign' words and phrases throws considerable light on the problem raised on p. 7 above and left in abeyance: why it is that certain 'foreign' expressions remain 'foreign' instead of being anglicized. If an expression is adopted because it has been picked up by servicemen in foreign countries (3); or for reasons of decorum (4); or because it is a technical term carrying a special connotation (5), (6); or because it refers to a foreign institution or thing, or conveys local colour (9), (10); or because it gives an impression of the culture and erudition of the user (11)—in all these cases the reason for the original adoption from a foreign language will suffice to explain the failure of anglicization. Doubtless the desire to display erudition plays its part also in maintaining the 'foreign' status of expressions in these and the other categories; but for expressions in the remaining categories some special influences can be observed.

As we have already seen (p. 7), mere duration of time and frequency of usage are important. Anglicization is never immediate, and an expression must remain in the language for a certain time and acquire a certain frequency of usage before it stands any chance of anglicization. The quasi-technical expressions of category (7) have only recently been introduced into the language, and are in fact undergoing a process of anglicization (in most cases by translation), as the examples show. Expressions in category (8) by the very definition of the category do not remain in the language long enough to undergo anglicization; once they become obsolete and are used only in reminiscent mood, their form is fossilized and anglicization is out of the question. Many of the expressions in categories (1) and (2) are recent introductions; others, though of some standing in the language, are seldom enough used for anglicization to be unlikely. For instance, the word *guichet*, quoted as an example of category (1), was introduced as long ago as 1848; but although it is a useful term it is not in everday use, and is likely to remain 'foreign'[1]. However, many of the expressions in categories (1) and (2) have been in frequent use for a considerable period, and for the enduring 'foreign' status of these some other explanation must be found.

Many of the expressions in category (1) and all the expressions in category (2) are not words but phrases; and the anglicization of phrases is less straightforward than that of single words. A phrase may be anglicized in one or other of two ways: the sounds and stresses may be accommodated to those of English, as in the case of

[1] In fact the word exists in the language in an anglicized form: English *wicket*, anglicized in the thirteenth century, represents a Norman dialect form of French *guichet*. In the sense 'small door in a large door' it retains the sense 'opening'; in the sense 'set of stumps and bails in cricket' it retains the sense 'grill'.

single words, or the phrase may be translated into English. The accommodation of sounds and stresses to the English pattern is comparatively rare, for obvious reasons: the result would be a collocation of unfamiliar words, the syntactic relationship between which could only be a matter of conjecture. Accommodation of this kind seems only to happen when all the words of which the phrase is composed already exist in English in an anglicized form. Thus the anglicization of *court martial* depends on the prior existence of *court* and *martial* as anglicized words; despite the unEnglish word-order—noun followed by adjective—the syntactic relationship between the two words is obvious. Yet the unusual word order is so far objectionable that the phrase is now tending to be replaced by a compound noun *court-martial*, with plural *court-martials* instead of the traditional *courts martial*. Another interesting example is the legal phrase *malice prepense*, which has the same unEnglish word-order; here the great rarity of the adjective *prepense*, which scarcely occurs outside this phrase, has encouraged the development of the partially translated form *malice aforethought*, in which the unEnglish word-order accords ill with the conspicuously Saxon adjective *aforethought*[1]. The translation of a 'foreign' phrase is also comparatively rare. French *ça va sans dire* has entered English in translation as 'that goes without saying', which despite the objections of purists no longer has a 'foreign' ring. On the other hand, the translation of *ça saute aux yeux* as 'it jumps to the eyes' sounds awkward, and is rarely used. It should be noted that, by the very definition of the category, the translation of phrases in category (2) is out of the question.

The anglicization of a substantial number of words is put out of court by the fact that the normal accommodation of sounds and stress to the English pattern would result in a word identical in form with an existing word of quite different meaning. Thus, the French word *emplacement* would, if anglicized, become identical with the English military term 'emplacement'; French *enfilade* with the military term 'enfilade'; French *facile* with English 'facile', which has quite a different connotation; French *franchise* with English 'franchise'; and so on. Of course the 'English' word with which confusion is

[1] A special form of anglicization, in which a foreign phrase is anglicized as a single word, is illustrated by the word *paramour*, from the French phrase *par amour* 'by way of love'. French *débonnaire*, though it has now been re-adopted as a 'foreign' word, was fully anglicized as early as the thirteenth century; but this is not really an example of the anglicization of a phrase, since *de bonne aire* had already become a single word in French before it was introduced into English.

likely is in every case an anglicization of earlier date; the point is that if a foreign word already anglicized in one sense is adopted again in a slightly different sense it must remain forever 'foreign', since otherwise its distinctive meaning would not be discernible. Similarly, if French *conservatoire* were to be anglicized it could only become 'conservatory'; and there already exists in English a word of this form with quite a different meaning—'a glass-house opening out of a drawing-room'. It is noteworthy that in the United States, where the meaning 'glass-house' is not in use, the French word has in fact been anglicized as *conservatory*.

In a slightly different class are such technical or quasi-technical terms as *gravitas* and *scientia*, which could only be anglicized as 'gravity' and 'science'; but each of these two words has undergone a special development of sense in English which is inappropriate to the technical use. Although *gravity* still retains the meaning 'weightiness (of demeanour)', there is a likelihood of confusion with the scientific sense 'the force attracting two bodies one to another'; and *science* now means only 'the study of natural physical phenomena', not 'systematic knowledge (of any subject)'. Still more complicated are the cases in which two or more similar or closely related words have been borrowed from different languages, each with its own special connotation. One example has been given above (p. 20): *staccato* and *détaché* both mean 'detached', but each has a distinct technical connotation lacking from the English word. Similarly *maniéré* and *manieroso* both correspond to English 'mannered', yet neither means quite the same as the English word. Perhaps the most complicated example of all is provided by the three words *nouvelle* (French), *novella* (Italian), and *Novelle* (German); each of these is a term of literary criticism, and each has a distinct connotation; if any of them were to be anglicized it could only be as 'novel', identical in form with an English term of literary criticism which means something quite different again.

But over and above these special considerations there is a general consideration of compelling force. Just as the technical terms in categories (5) and (6) have special connotations in their various languages of origin, so every word in every language has special connotations not all of which will be associated with the equivalent word in some other language. If a word refers to some concrete object or to some commonplace idea it is unlikely that the connotations will be of any great importance, and the anglicization of a foreign word of this type will occasion no noticeable loss. But if a word refers to some vague abstract concept difficult to define, it is likely that the field of connotation (ultimately derived from numerous literary and spoken usages more or less familiar to those who use the word) will be of the first importance; and anglicization is likely to destroy this field of connotation. Thus, to take only one instance out of a large number, such a word as *frisson* could very easily be anglicized in pronunciation, so that it would rhyme with the English word *listen*; but the word so anglicized would fail to call to mind the various occurrences of the word in French literature and in French spoken idiom which are ultimately responsible for the characteristic and practically untranslatable meaning of the word in its French form. Words of this kind are very frequent among the 'foreign' expressions used in English, and no duration of time or frequency of usage is likely to result in their anglicization.

The dating of 'foreign' expressions

It is interesting and in some respects enlightening to classify the 'foreign' expressions in English according to the language from which they come and the approximate date at which they were introduced into English. Unfortunately the accurate dating of these expressions is somewhat difficult. The only authorities are the *New English Dictionary* and *The Stanford Dictionary of Anglicised Words and Phrases*[1], and neither is wholly satisfactory from this point of view. The earlier volumes of the *New English Dictionary* are markedly deficient in 'foreign' terms, and although many of the deficiencies are supplied in the *Supplement* of 1933, the work as a whole includes only a relatively small number of phrases. *Stanford* includes a much larger selection of phrases than the *New English Dictionary*, but its dating is much less trustworthy; if a word or phrase appears in both works the earliest quotation in the *New English Dictionary* is very often earlier, sometimes much earlier, than the earliest in *Stanford*. For a number of phrases I have been able to supply from my own reading an earlier date than that given in *Stanford*; but much work still remains to be done in hunting out early quotations illustrating the use of 'foreign' phrases. However, even allowing for possible error in the dating of the phrases, the study of the dates at which 'foreign' expressions were introduced into English reveals many points of interest. Full details are given in the Appendix, pp. 369–89, but the Tables in the following section give the information in summary form.

Some tables of statistics

Table I shows the actual number of words and phrases adopted from each language or group of languages, subdivided according to the

[1] For further details of these works see p. 61.

century in which they were introduced. Words and phrases are listed under the language from which they were actually adopted; in many cases the ultimate origin of the expression is to be found in a different language; *odalisque*, for instance, is listed as French, though its ultimate origin is to be found in Turkish. Greek and Latin are listed together as 'Classical', for reasons which will become apparent below, pp. 40–42. The first fact which emerges from these figures is

	Mediæval	16c.	17c.	18c.	19c.	20c.
French	19	42	166	316	736	1103
Classical	89	237	371	173	328	250
Italian		26	48	100	90	153
German		2	2	4	58	240
Spanish		13	14	14	47	32
Other European	4	10	13	22	49	53
Non-European	2	12	56	35	97	55
Total	114	342	670	664	1405	1886

TABLE I

the general increase in the total for each century. This increase is in part to be accounted for by the fact that the table includes only words and phrases still current in English: the longer ago an expression was introduced from a foreign language, the more chance it has had of being anglicized, or of becoming obsolete. Nevertheless, it seems likely that the number of foreign words and phrases adopted into the language has in fact increased, even though this conjecture cannot be proved from the figures. The second fact is that the total number of words and phrases attributable to the eighteenth century is actually less than the number attributable to the seventeenth century; in other words, there is a setback in the general rate of increase at this point. Since there is no likelihood that expressions adopted in the eighteenth century were more readily anglicized or more rapidly became obsolete than those adopted in the seventeenth century, it would seem certain that the number adopted in the eighteenth century really was smaller. This phenomenon is probably to be explained by the linguistic purism of the eighteenth century, as exemplified by the abortive attempts early in the century to found an English Academy on the lines of the Académie Française, and by the great prestige attained by Johnson's *Dictionary* (1755) as an arbiter of permissible usage. Much more surprising is the third fact, that the number of Classical words and phrases introduced during the eighteenth century is only about half the number adopted in either the preceding or the following century; the popular belief that eighteenth-century gentlemen heavily interlarded their conversation with Classical tags would seem to be unjustified.

The same figures can also be expressed as percentages, and some further facts are more clearly revealed by this form of presentation. Table II shows the proportion of words and phrases from a given

	Mediæval	16c.	17c.	18c.	19c.	20c.
French	16·7	12·2	24·8	47·7	52·3	58·6
Classical	78·0	69·4	55·3	25·9	23·4	13·2
Italian		7·6	7·2	15·1	6·4	8·1
German		0·6	0·3	0·6	4·1	12·7
Spanish		3·8	2·1	2·1	3·4	1·7
Other European	3·5	2·9	1·9	3·3	3·5	2·8
Non-European	1·8	3·5	8·4	5·3	6·9	2·9

TABLE II

language, expressed as a percentage of the total of words and phrases adopted from all foreign languages during a given century. Since there is no serious likelihood of selective anglicization or selective obsolescence, these percentages will hardly be affected by the fact that the table includes only those words and phrases still in current use; they can be accepted as representative of the actual proportion of expressions adopted from each language during a given century. The most striking feature of this table is the steady decline in the proportion of Classical words and phrases, from 78 per cent in the Middle Ages down to 13 per cent in the twentieth century. This decline is counterbalanced by an almost equally steady rise in the proportion of French words and phrases; there is a small drop in the sixteenth century, but apart from this the proportion rises steadily from a mere 16 per cent in the Middle Ages to over 50 per cent in the nineteenth and twentieth centuries. Italian words and phrases show a steady proportion of 6 to 8 per cent from the sixteenth to the twentieth century, except for a sudden peak of 15 per cent in the eighteenth century; this peak is certainly to be attributed to the large number of technical terms of art and music adopted during that period. Borrowings from German represent less than 1 per cent of the total from the sixteenth to the eighteenth century, but rise to 4 per cent in the nineteenth and to nearly 13 per cent in the twentieth century; this latter high proportion is attributable to the effect of two successive world wars.

The figures of Table I can also be expressed as cumulative totals, which show the total number of words and phrases from a given language still in use at a given period—still with the proviso that words and phrases not in current use are excluded. Table III gives

	Mediæval	16c.	17c.	18c.	19c.	20c.
French	19	61	227	543	1279	2382
Classical	89	326	697	870	1198	1448
Italian		26	74	174	264	417
German		2	4	8	66	306
Spanish		13	27	41	88	120
Other European	4	14	27	49	98	151
Non-European	2	14	70	105	202	257
Total	114	456	1126	1790	3195	5081

TABLE III

such cumulative totals. The effect of the limitation to words and phrases still in current use can again be eliminated by the use of percentages, and Table IV gives the cumulative totals of Table III

	Mediæval	16c.	17c.	18c.	19c.	20c.
French	16·7	13·4	20·2	30·4	40·0	46·9
Classical	78·0	71·5	61·9	48·6	37·5	28·5
Italian		5·7	6·6	9·7	8·3	8·2
German		0·4	0·3	0·4	2·1	6·0
Spanish		2·8	2·4	2·3	2·7	2·4
Other European	3·5	3·1	2·4	2·7	3·1	3·0
Non-European	1·8	3·1	6·2	5·9	6·3	5·0

TABLE IV

expressed as percentages of the whole in any given century. The Classical languages show the same steady decline, and French shows the same steady increase (apart from the slight drop in the sixteenth century); but these percentages enable us to see that it was not until about 1800 that the proportion of French words and phrases in use actually exceeded the proportion from the Classical languages. At the present day very nearly half the 'foreign' words and phrases in current use are from French; but more than a quarter are from the Classical languages; all the other languages put together only account for a little less than a quarter of the total.

THE HISTORICAL SIGNIFICANCE OF 'FOREIGN' EXPRESSIONS

Interesting though these figures are, the study of the actual lists of words and phrases in the Appendix is even more rewarding; there is much enlightenment here for the student of social history. The gradual extension of the number of languages drawn upon illustrates the expansion of the known world between the Middle Ages and the present day. During the Middle Ages only six languages contributed words and phrases to English: French, which until the end of the period was still much used in polite conversation; the learned languages Latin, Greek and Arabic; and two Celtic languages spoken in the British Isles—Gaelic and Irish. Nine more were added in the sixteenth century: the more important European languages, Italian and Spanish (strongly represented), German, Dutch and Portuguese (only sparsely represented); two languages extending beyond the borders of Europe, Russian and Turkish; and two Oriental languages, Hindustani and Malay. The seventeenth century saw the advent of some of the less important European languages, Danish, Norwegian and Welsh; two more learned languages, Hebrew and Sanskrit; and a larger number of Oriental languages—Persian, Chinese and Japanese, Tamil and Tibetan. The eighteenth century saw the introduction of only two new languages, Australian and Eskimo. In the nineteenth century were added one more European language, Magyar, and a number of languages from distant continents—Afrikaans, Swahili, Javanese, Hawaiian and Maori. So far the twentieth century has seen the addition of only one language hitherto unrepresented, Swedish; and it is doubtless a historical accident that no Swedish words have entered the language at an earlier date. In addition to the languages listed above there are about a score of languages which have contributed to English only one word each, at various dates from the seventeenth century onwards.

A study of the individual words and phrases contributed by the various languages yields only uneven results: sometimes a clear pattern emerges, sometimes not—French, for instance, has contributed so much more liberally than any other language that expressions of every possible type are to be found among the borrowings of each century. Expressions from Latin and Greek are, as might be expected, nearly all of a 'learned' type—technical expressions from the more sedate arts and sciences, and quotations from literary texts. A conspicuous feature of the Latin borrowings is the high proportion of phrases introduced from the earliest period; among the borrowings from other languages phrases tend to be rather rare until comparatively recent times. Latin expressions introduced during the

Middle Ages include, as is natural, a large proportion of terms connected with religion; but Latin religious terms disappear almost completely between the Reformation in the early sixteenth century and the restoration of the Roman hierarchy in 1850, after which they again become plentiful. During the intervening period 'foreign' religious terms are nearly all from Italian: *biretta*, *nuncio*, *padre* (sixteenth century); *baldacchino*, *monsignore* (seventeenth century); *beato*, *campo santo*, *zucchetto* (nineteenth century); the complete absence of Italian religious terms in the eighteenth century is perhaps counterbalanced by the occurrence of *abbé* and *prie-dieu* from French.

The vast majority of words and phrases from Italian are connected either with music or with the plastic arts. Expressions connected with architecture and painting have entered English in a steady flow since the sixteenth century; in the eighteenth century there was a sudden cataract of expressions connected with music; since that time musical terms have continued to be introduced, but recently there has been a renewed rise in the number of terms connected with architecture and painting. Expressions from German are negligibly few until the nineteenth century, and nineteenth-century borrowings are mostly of the kind brought back by English tourists: *Alpenstock*, *Edelweiss*, *Gasthof*, *Kursaal*, *Pretzel*, *Schloss*, and so on. More recent introductions from German reflect only too clearly the most conspicuous features of German history during the twentieth century, totalitarian rule and the two successive wars resulting from it. Various aspects and consequences of dictatorship are illustrated by *Führerprinzip*, *Gleichschaltung*, *Judenhetze*, *Lebensraum*, *Machtübernahme*, *Putsch*, *Realpolitik*, *Totschläger*, *Vernichtungslager*, and many others; the two wars have contributed *Blitzkrieg*, *Ersatz*, *Feldgrau*, *Festung Europa*, *Flammenwerfer*, *Kriegsgefangene(r)*, *Minenwerfer*, *Panzer*, *Schnorchel*, *Schrecklichkeit*, and others. A study of the expressions introduced from other languages can be equally rewarding—the borrowings from Hindustani, for instance, illustrate the rise and fall of the East India Company and the eventual withdrawal of the British from India—but space does not permit a full analysis; however, the materials for such a study are given in full in the Appendix to the dictionary.

The origins of quotations

Many of the 'foreign' phrases used in English are quotations, and it is of some interest to examine the sources from which they are drawn. The first striking point is the high proportion of quotations which have been adapted or altered in some way. Only rarely does the alteration seem to be stylistic: *nihil tetigit quod non ornavit* seems a clear improvement on the original *nullum quod tetigit non ornavit* (Dr Johnson); *c'est pire qu'un crime, c'est une faute* is more forceful than the original *c'est plus qu'un crime* . . . (Fouché). Nearly all the altered quotations are from Latin, and there is a special reason for this. The majority of Latin quotations are from sources in verse, and Latin poetic style often results in the wide separation of closely related words; if the words to be quoted are thus separated, the intervening words have to be left out. Thus, Horace's

> *Æquam* memento rebus in arduis
> *Servare mentem*

is quoted as *æquam servare mentem*, and Juvenal's

> *Da* spatium vitæ, *multos* da, Jupiter, *annos*

as *da multos annos*. Sometimes the order of the words is altered too: thus, Horace's

> Ille *terrarum* mihi præter omnis
> *Angulus* ridet

is quoted as *angulus terrarum*, and Virgil's

> *fugit* irreparabile *tempus*

as *tempus fugit*. Moreover, the requirements of Latin syntax sometimes lead to the appearance of a quotable phrase in an inappropriate case. Thus, Horace's

> *Auream* quisquis *mediocritatem*
> Diligit . . .

is quoted as *aurea mediocritas* in the nominative, and Sallust's

> Appius ait, *fabrum* esse *suæ* quemque *fortunæ*

as *faber fortunæ suæ*. This latter example is particularly interesting, since although the original is in prose the quoted form has been altered in three ways: intervening words have been omitted, the order of the words has been transposed, and the case has been changed. (There are a few instances in which an inappropriate case is retained in English usage: Juvenal's *panem et circenses* is always quoted in the accusative, irrespective of the English syntax; the verb required to govern the accusative in *ex ungue leonem* and its congener *ex pede Herculem* is never expressed, though it is present in the Greek phrase from which the former is translated.) Sometimes the alteration of case may result in a different meaning from that of the original: Horace's *disjecti membra poetæ* 'the limbs of a dismembered poet' is always quoted in the form *disjecta membra* 'dismembered limbs', and applied to fragmentary literary remains.

Latin quotations heavily outnumber those from foreign languages. Among the quotations included in this dictionary 161 are from Latin, compared with forty-eight from French, eight from German, and four from Italian. The majority of the Latin quotations are drawn from a few favourite authors. At the head of the list is Horace, with thirty-two quotations in all, eighteen from the *Odes*, five from the *Satires*, five from the *Ars Poetica*, and four from the *Epistles*. Rather surprisingly, the next in order of frequency is the Vulgate version of the Bible, from which no less than twenty-nine quotations are drawn; the substantial contribution made by the Vulgate to the stock of phrases used in English is usually overlooked. Next comes Virgil, with twenty-one quotations in all, sixteen from the *Æneid*, three from the *Georgics*, and two from the *Eclogues*; then Cicero with fourteen quotations, Juvenal with nine, Suetonius with seven, Ovid with six, and Tacitus with four. No other writer contributes more than three quotations, but few writers of the Golden or Silver Age are not represented by at least one quotation.

The quotations from French follow quite a different pattern. The forty-eight French quotations are drawn from thirty-seven different writers, and only six writers are represented by more than one quotation: Molière with five, Voltaire with four, Balzac, Diderot, Dumas and Proust with two each. Many of the writers represented are relatively unknown: no one but a student of French literature is likely to have heard of Émile Augier (*nostalgie de la boue*), Edmond Harancourt (*partir, c'est mourir un peu*), Jouvenot and Micard (*fin de siècle*), or Alphonse Karr (*plus ça change, plus c'est la même chose*). Another oddity of the French quotations is the fact that a high proportion of them are taken, not from the text of a work, but from its title. The following represent no more than a selection of such quotations: *demi-monde* (Dumas), *demi-vierge* (Prévost), *démon de midi* (Bourget), *embarras des richesses* (d'Allainval), *femme de trente ans* (Balzac), *femme savante* (Molière), *poète maudit* (Verlaine), *princesse lointaine* (Rostand), *saison en enfer* (Rimbaud), *trahison des clercs* (Benda), *vie de Bohème* (Murger). Among the eight German quotations there is only one duplication of origin: both *Blut und Eisen* and *Eisen und Blut* were used by Bismark, on different occasions. Of the four Italian quotations three, as one might expect, are from Dante; the fourth, *se non è vero è molto ben trovato*, was used by Giordano Bruno but may already have been proverbial.

II. The Use and Abuse of 'Foreign' Words and Phrases

'Description' and 'prescription'

The functions of the lexicographer, as of the grammarian, are traditionally two-fold—to describe and to prescribe; that is, he must record all the variations of usage which in fact exist, and at the same time point out which usages are more and which less desirable. It is the fashion at present to decry prescription in grammar and lexicography, and to insist that both should be purely descriptive. Since any language—so runs the argument—is no more than the sum total of the usage of those who speak and write it, the only possible criterion of 'correctness' is usage; hence the only legitimate function of the grammarian and lexicographer is to record and systematize the facts of current usage. The argument is not wholly without substance, and it is certainly difficult to defend the procedure of certain grammarians in the past who were so much misled by their pre-occupation with Latin grammar that the rules they laid down prescribed usages which not only were not, but never had been, current English. Nevertheless, the argument in its extreme form overlooks two important facts.

In the first place, usage is never uniform; different classes of speakers and writers will differ substantially in their modes of expressing ideas, and even within the usage of a single speaker or writer there is often room for variation according to the occasion of the utterance, or even according to mood or whim. In the second place, the primary function of language is communication, so that clarity and intelligibility are qualities without which language cannot fulfil its purpose. If for the expression of any idea there is only one current turn of phrase, and this is lacking in clarity and intelligibility, obviously nothing can be done about it—the deficiency must be regretfully accepted. But if, as is more commonly the case, there is more than one turn of phrase available, equally obviously the one which is superior in clarity and intelligibility must be preferred to the others; and it is not only the right but the duty of the grammarian and lexicographer to point out which of a number of concurrent usages is to be preferred on such grounds. It is not possible to evade this issue. If, for instance, we choose to prefer the usage of one set of speakers to that of another, the evasion is only apparent, not real, since the set of speakers chosen as the standard will inevitably be those whose usage is preferable on grounds of clarity and intelligibility.

The compiler of a dictionary of 'foreign' words and phrases must, of course, record all the words and phrases which are in fact in current use, together with all the important variations in spelling and pronunciation which in fact occur; but he cannot well avoid the task of discussing 'correctness' in the use of such words and phrases. He must first of all consider the question whether there are any expressions amongst those which he lists which ought either not to be used at all in English, or to be used only in certain well-defined circumstances; in discussing this question he must be guided by the principles governing the use of language in general. Secondly, granted that certain 'foreign' words and phrases may be used (at least on certain occasions), he must consider the question of 'correctness' in the spelling and pronunciation of these expressions, and in the use of foreign feminine and plural forms. In this second task he must take into account not only general principles, but also the usage in the various languages from which the 'foreign' expressions have come. This is not to say, of course, that where English usage is in question the usage of a foreign language can ever be decisive; we have already seen (pp. 11–13) that the spelling of a foreign word may be altered in English (often for very good reasons), and that the meaning, too, may undergo change. Nevertheless, usage in the language of origin cannot be entirely neglected; such aberrations, for instance, as the spurious plural *apparati* are due merely to ignorance; and every departure from the usage of the language of origin must be carefully considered on its merits.

The use of 'foreign' expressions

Any objection to the use of 'foreign' words and phrases as such, or to any class of them in particular, must be based on the principle that the primary function of language is communication. The use of any expression or turn of phrase, whether English or 'foreign', ought to be limited by two considerations: that the expression used is the most apt to express the meaning intended; and that it should be immediately intelligible to the reader or listener envisaged. It might be thought that if all speakers and writers were conscientious there would be no need for a dictionary such as this. However, even the most conscientious writer can only consider the needs of one class of readers, the class he considers most likely to be interested in his work; and he is not to be blamed if his work falls into the hands of another class of readers who do not find his modes of expression so readily intelligible. Thus, the writer on technical or quasi-technical subjects is fully entitled to make use of technical words and expressions not easily intelligible to the uninitiated; so that the cultivated reader who takes a general interest in subjects in which he has no *expertise*—the reader who, though not a lawyer, enjoys the law reports, or the reader who, though not a musician, follows the accounts of recent concerts, and so on—is likely to encounter technical words and expressions, used in all good faith by the writer, which he does not understand. The speaker is in rather a different position from the writer. Unlike the writer, the speaker can normally see the people who are listening to him and can moderate his modes of expression accordingly. However, even the speaker may in certain circumstances be unable to judge with any accuracy the range of understanding of those who are listening. The lecturer addressing an unfamiliar audience, even the casual speaker talking in a group not all the members of which are known to him—these may in all good faith use expressions which are not readily intelligible. Hence, even if all writers and speakers were conscientious there would still be a need for a dictionary of 'foreign' expressions; and moreover there are many writers and speakers who use 'foreign' expressions for quite illegitimate purposes.

The use of 'foreign' expressions is justified only if there is no English equivalent (or no adequate English equivalent), and if the expression in question is likely to be understood without difficulty by all probable readers or listeners. It follows that the legitimacy of the use of these expressions will depend almost wholly on the occasion of the utterance. A speaker conversing on general matters in mixed company, a writer discussing a general topic in a book or article likely to be read by all and sundry—these should be careful to use only those non-technical 'foreign' expressions which have achieved wide currency because there is no true equivalent in English. The writer or lecturer on technical subjects, addressing an audience of like-minded enthusiasts, is naturally free to make extensive use of the accepted technical terms of his subject, even if they are 'foreign'; even so, he should first make sure that there is no acceptable English equivalent. Similarly, the writer or speaker who has to deal with the institutions and customs of foreign countries is entitled to make use of 'foreign' expressions to describe them, provided that by so doing he can save time without loss of clarity. The validity of the use of 'foreign' expressions merely to provide local colour is more questionable; it is difficult not to feel that a really competent speaker or writer ought to be able to achieve the effect he requires by suitably manipulating the extensive resources of his proper medium, the English language.

But the use of 'foreign' expressions for their own sake is altogether a different matter. To use an expression merely because it is 'foreign', not because it expresses the required meaning better than any available English equivalent; to use a 'foreign' expression not in the confidence that it will be perfectly intelligible to the reader or listener, but in the hope that it will not: this is to display a peculiarly unpleasant type of intellectual arrogance and snobbery[1]. It is not too difficult to forgive a writer who is genuinely so well versed in a foreign language that an expression from that language springs to his mind as readily as an English one; it is a very human failing to use such a 'foreign' expression for decorative purposes without pausing to consider whether it will be readily intelligible to one's readers. If, on the other hand, a writer racks his brains to think up a 'foreign' equivalent for the English expression which springs naturally to his mind; if (still worse) he hunts through a dictionary such as this to find a 'foreign' expression that can somehow be dragged in to what he is writing, in order to convey to his readers that his command of foreign languages is better than it really is, or to pretend to a profound knowledge of foreign languages which does not really exist—this is not only deceitful, it is prostituting the function of language to unworthy purposes.

It follows from all this that a dictionary of 'foreign' words and phrases differs from all other dictionaries in so far as it should be, as it were, a 'one-way' dictionary: it is for the use of readers, not of writers; of listeners, not of speakers. If a writer or a speaker has occasion to consult such a dictionary, even to check some minor point of spelling or pronunciation, or some shade of meaning, the word or phrase he is looking up cannot have sprung so naturally to his mind that he is justified in using it; the mere fact that he has looked an expression up in the dictionary should debar him from using it. One result of this peculiarity is that the definitions in such a dictionary can often be simplified or compressed: they are intended to throw light on an expression already standing in a context, not to delimit the kind of context into which an expression may be placed. This point is illustrated more fully below, p. 59.

THE PRONUNCIATION AND SPELLING OF 'FOREIGN' EXPRESSIONS

Granted that in certain circumstances it is permissible to use 'foreign' words and phrases in an English context, certain problems arise in connection with their spelling and pronunciation. The problems vary from language to language, and it will be convenient to divide foreign languages into three main groups: the Classical languages, Latin and Greek; languages written in scripts or alphabets other than the Roman alphabet; and European languages written in the Roman

[1] For a scathing denunciation of this kind of vulgarity see H. W. Fowler *A Dictionary of Modern English Usage* (1926) s.v. FRENCH WORDS.

alphabet. European languages can be further divided into two sub-groups: those (like French, German and Italian) of which a large number of cultivated people have some knowledge, and those (like, for instance, the Scandinavian languages) which are known to comparatively few. The most difficult problems are presented by the Classical languages, Latin and Greek, and these must be discussed first.

The pronunciation and spelling of Latin

There are no less than three different pronunciations of Latin current in England at the present day, each with its own appropriate peculiarities of spelling.

(1) *The traditional or 'English' pronunciation.* This system, in which both vowels and consonants are pronounced as in English, is the historical descendant of the pronunciation used in England during the Middle Ages. In the Middle Ages the association of sound with alphabetic symbol differed little from language to language, so that although each nation pronounced Latin with the sounds of its own language, Latin could be used as a medium of communication from one end of Europe to the other. But whereas the vowels of most other European languages have not altered much since the Middle Ages, the English vowels during the period 1400–1700 underwent an extensive series of changes collectively known as the 'Great Vowel Shift', as a result of which the vowel-symbols acquired their present values, very different from those represented by the same symbols in other languages[1]; and, as the vowels of English changed, so the vowels of Latin (as spoken in England) changed with them. This 'English' pronunciation is no longer used when Latin is read aloud, except for certain formal purposes in the older universities; but it is the only acceptable pronunciation for the numerous Latin terms and phrases used by lawyers, and remains the normal pronunciation for the great majority of other Latin words and phrases used in English. Certain peculiarities of spelling are appropriate to this pronunciation: 'consonant *i*' and 'consonant *u*' are written *j* and *v* respectively (as they must be, since they are pronounced like English *j* and *v*), and the original diphthongs *ae* and *oe* are written *æ* and *œ* respectively (both are pronounced like English *ee*). There has been some confusion between *æ* and *e*, so that *et cetera* is much commoner than *et cætera*,

[1] The vowels of German and Dutch underwent a similar series of changes; but in these languages the spelling was altered to correspond with the new pronunciation, so that the value of each vowel-symbol remained unaltered.

and *ceteris paribus* is at least as common as *cæteris paribus;* the two distinct words *cæstus* and *cestus* are regularly confused in spelling. Confusion between *œ* and *e* is much less frequent, but the spelling *fœtus* has completely ousted the historical *fetus.* Until comparatively recently certain accent-marks were used in writing and printing Latin tags pronounced in the 'English' way, the grave accent to indicate that final *-e* is syllabic, not (as usually in English words) silent, and the circumflex to distinguish the ablative singular of the first declension from the nominative singular; both usages are illustrated in the phrases *bonâ fidè* and *vicè versâ.* It is to be regretted that this useful custom has now been given up.

(2) *The ecclesiastical or 'Italian' pronunciation.* This system, in which both vowels and consonants are pronounced approximately as in Italian, was introduced into England at the time of the restoration of the Roman hierarchy in 1850, and has since been adopted by many Anglican clergy of High Church inclinations[1]. This pronunciation is appropriate to the fairly numerous words and phrases of ecclesiastical connotation. The spelling appropriate to this system is the same as that appropriate to the 'English' system, though *j* is pronounced like English *y*, and *æ* and *œ* are pronounced like Italian *e*.

(3) *The reformed or 'Classical' pronunciation.* This system—a reconstruction of the pronunciation used in Rome during the Golden Age of Latin literature—was introduced into English schools about 1900, and is now (with some modifications) used almost universally for pædagogic purposes. In this system the vowels are pronounced as in Italian; the diphthongs *æ* and *œ* (always so written) are pronounced with the diphthongs of English *by* and *boy*; 'consonant *i*' (written *i*) and 'consonant *u*' (written *u*) are pronounced like English *y* and *w* respectively; *c* is always pronounced like English *k*, *g* always like English *g* in *got*, even before a following *e* or *i*[2]. There is little doubt that this 'Classical' pronunciation reproduces with consider-

[1] Before 1850 the Roman clergy in England had used a compromise pronunciation, the origin of which is disputable, combining 'Italian' vowels with 'English' consonants; for some time after 1850 the pronunciation of Latin in the 'Italian' style was one of numerous bones of contention between the pre-Emancipation clergy and the new ultramontane hierarchy. The Society of Jesus in England still makes use of a pronunication resembling the old compromise pronunciation.

[2] Before *e* and *i* Latin *c* and *g* are pronounced like English *s* and *j* in the 'English' system, like English *ch* and *j* in the 'Italian' system.

able accuracy that current in Rome at the beginning of the Christian era; whether it is the ideal pronunciation to use in the teaching of Latin is another question, which it is fortunately unnecessary to discuss here. Suffice it to say that the 'Classical' pronunciation in its pure form is never used for Latin words and phrases in an English context—he would be a bold man who would write *ueni, uidi, uici* and pronounce it with the appropriate *w*- and *k*-sounds; but some of its features have influenced the pronunciation of the longer and less frequently used phrases.

The majority of Latin words and phrases are currently pronounced according to the 'English' system of pronunciation[1]. Words and phrases of ecclesiastical connotation are usually pronounced according to the 'Italian' pronunciation, though there are some curious anomalies here. In such expressions as *Agnus Dei* and *Magnificat* the combination *gn* should, in the 'Italian' pronunciation, be pronounced as in Italian (that is, approximately like *ni* in English *onion*); in the 'Classical' pronunciation like English *ng* followed by *n*; in the 'English' pronunciation like English *g* followed by *n*. In fact the 'English' pronunciation of the combination *gn* is always used in these expressions, so that in *Agnus Dei* the first word is pronounced with the 'English' pronunciation and the second with the 'Italian'. However, the real difficulty arises with the longer Latin phrases, particularly those which can be recognized as quotations from well-known writers. Until about 1900 these were certainly pronounced according to the 'English' pronunciation, since this pronunciation was used in the study of Latin literature; now the conflict of pronunciations has led to uncertainty. The speaker who will refer without hesitation to a 'decree *nisi*', making *nisi* rhyme with English *I sigh*, will hesitate to use the same pronunciation in the phrase *de mortuis nil nisi bonum*; and the most convinced exponent of the 'Classical' pronunciation, when quoting the phrase *aut Cæsar aut nullus*, will hesitate to pronounce the familiar *Cæsar* like German *Kaiser*. This doubt about the appropriate pronunciation leads to an avoidance of the longer phrases and quotations, and to a lack of uniformity of pronunciation when they are used. Doubtless the 'English' pronunciation is the most appropriate for any Latin phrase or quotation used in an English context; but, though the pronunciation of most of the more frequent words and tags is familiar through constant use, the 'English' version of the longer phrases may be unknown, or accessible only after some thought; and the fear of

[1] In Ireland such common words and phrases as *a priori, data, status,* etc. are often pronounced with 'Italian' vowels even by educated people, doubtless because of their familiarity with ecclesiastical Latin.

seeming eccentric may also hinder its use. In so far as it is possible to generalize for these difficult cases, there seems to be a tendency to combine 'Classical' vowels with 'English' consonants.

THE SPELLING OF GREEK

The transliteration of the Greek alphabet by the Romans differs in some respects from the transliteration now considered to represent the Greek sounds best. The following are the symbols and combinations of symbols for which the transliterations differ:

υ	u	y
ει	ei	ī
ου	ou	ū
αι	ai	æ
οι	oi	œ
κ	k	c
χ	kh	ch

The first column shows the Greek symbols, the second the accepted modern transliteration, the third the Roman transliteration[1]. In addition, the Romans adapted the endings of many of the Greek declensions to conform with their own Latin declensions: in particular, the masculine ending -ος (*-os*) becomes *-us*[2], the neuter ending -ον (*-on*) becomes *-um*, and the feminine ending -η (*-ē*) becomes *-a*.

It would seem to be a simple matter to decide whether a given word entered English through Latin or direct from Greek by observing its form: words which show the Roman transliteration and the Latin endings must have come through Latin, those which show the modern transliteration and the Greek endings must have come direct from Greek. Unfortunately the problem is not nearly so simple as it looks. In the first place, later Latin did not always substitute its own inflectional endings for those of Greek; in particular, the neuter ending *-on* often survives[3]. In the second place, the Roman method of

[1] The Roman transliteration is not always always wholly self-consistent. The rendering of Greek καρύκειον as *caduceus*, for instance, is eccentric in a number of ways.

[2] Not every Latin *-us* in a word of Greek origin is from -ος. Latin *periplus* is from Greek περίπλους. Latin *polypus*, from Greek πολύπους, exceptionally has a plural *polypi* as if the *-us* were indeed from -ος. The *-os* in *tripos* is a spurious Greek form based on the Latin *tripus* from Greek τρίπους.

[3] The ending *-on* in Latin words of Greek origin is sometimes from Greek -ων, as in *cacodæmon, colophon, dæmon;* this *-on* is naturally never at any period replaced by *-um*.

transliteration became so familiar (because of the numerous Greek words that have entered English through Latin) that until very recently it was often used in preference to the modern system, even in rendering Greek words which have never been adopted into Latin. The Roman system was used almost without exception until the nineteenth century, though the Greek inflectional endings were often preserved, as in *cosmos*. Apparent exceptions like *boustrophedon*, *hoi polloi*, and *nous* (all introduced during the seventeenth century) were until recently always written or printed in Greek characters, even in an English context, so that their transliteration is quite modern; another apparent exception is *peripeteia*, which has recently replaced an earlier *peripetia* transliterated according to the Roman system. Even when the Roman system began to be abandoned, the modern system was not adopted in its entirety to replace it; there are many instances of compromise, due to dislike of the appearance of certain combinations in English. Thus, though the representation of the Greek diphthongs by *ei*, *ou*, *ai* and *oi* has been normal since the last century[1] in such forms as *eidolon*, *parousia*, *korai* and *koine*, the use of *u* instead of *y* is rare (*hubris* and *kudos* are the only examples); *k* instead of *c* is often avoided (as in the twentieth-century borrowing *catharsis*)[2], and there is no example in English of *kh*—such forms as *kat' exochen* (formerly written or printed in Greek characters and only recently transliterated), *encheiridion*, and the nineteenth century *chiton* all use *ch*, though the first has the modern *k* and the second the modern *ei*. The history of the word now written *ankylosis* is enlightening. This word was first introduced in the eighteenth century in the Roman transliteration *ancylosis*; then, since such a spelling might lead the unwary to pronounce the *c* as *s*, it was soon replaced by *anchylosis* with a *ch* that has no warrant in the Greek; it is only recently that *anchylosis* has in turn given place to *ankylosis*, with modern *k* but Roman *y*. Other curious forms are the nineteenth-century *ikon* and *kerygma*, which also combine a modern consonant with a Roman vowel. Quite inexplicable is *eureka*, which according to either system of transliteration ought to begin with an *h*; the form *heureca* was in use about 1600, but since 1650 *eureka* has been the standard form, though *heureka* occurs as an occasional pedantry.

In the light of such inconsistencies it is impossible to determine from the form alone whether a given word came into English through

[1] Already in the eighteenth century the form *homoousion* had been used by Gibbon, a man of exceptional learning. *Noumenon* is not a relevant example, since the Greek form has *οου*.

[2] A very early example of the use of *k* is *kyrie eleïson* (fourteenth century).

Latin or directly from Greek; and there are, of course, a number of Greek words which would have the same form in either of the systems of transliteration, and which have inflectional endings (such as -*ις*, Latin -*is*) which would not be altered in Latin. As a practical solution to the problem I have adopted the following principles: (1) if a word is transliterated according to the Roman system, and a corresponding form exists in Latin (even in modern Latin) I have assumed that it entered English through Latin; if there is no corresponding form in Latin I have assumed that it came direct from Greek; (2) if a word shows any single feature of the modern transliteration, even in combination with other features drawn from the Roman system, I have assumed that it came direct from Greek; (3) if a word would have the same form in either system of transliteration, I have arbitrarily assumed that it came direct from Greek, even if a corresponding form exists in Latin. These principles are sufficient to classify all but a few of the words of Greek origin; but one or two problems remain. The most puzzling is the word *amœba* from Greek *ἀμοιβή*; here the diphthong *οι* appears as *œ* according to the Roman system, and the ending -*η* has been replaced by -*a*; yet the word appears never to have been used in Latin, even in modern Latin. Since the inflectional endings are not normally altered in direct borrowings from the Greek, even when the Roman transliteration is used, I have felt bound to assume that the word has been used in modern Latin, but has escaped the notice of the lexicographers. Special difficulties are presented by pseudo-Greek words—that is, words which are based on Greek stems, but which have never actually existed in Greek. One such word is *telæsthesia*, which despite its origin at the end of the nineteenth century uses the Roman transliteration *æ* for *αι*; another is *anonyma*, which not only used the Roman *y* for *υ*, but has the Latin ending -*a*. In view of these doubts and difficulties it has seemed preferable to class Greek and Latin words together in the statistical tables on pp. 26–28.

The pronunciation of Greek

The pronunciation of words of Greek origin presents as many difficulties as the pronunciation of Latin words, since once again three different systems are in use.

(1) *The traditional pronunciation*. This system has the same history as the traditional or 'English' pronunciation of Latin: it is the descendant of the pronunciation in use before the completion of the sound-changes which transformed the English vowels. It corresponds

closely to the traditional pronunciation of Latin, and in the numerous cases where a Greek word appears in English in a Latin form the 'English' pronunciation is appropriate. Even some of the Greek words which appear in a modern transliteration follow the traditional pronunciation: thus, *nous* rhymes with English *house*, and *hubris* and *kudos* are pronounced with English *u* as in *due*.

(2) *The reformed pronunciation.* This system purports to reproduce the pronunciation of ancient Greek, and is used for the teaching of Greek in schools[1]. It reproduces the ancient pronunciation much less accurately than the 'Classical' pronunciation of Latin: for instance, although there can be little doubt that in ancient Greek the characters θ (*th*), φ (*ph*), and χ (*kh*) were pronounced as aspirated stops (i.e. as in *pothook*, *taphouse* and *Lockheed* respectively), no attempt is ever made to reproduce these difficult sounds. There is a special difficulty in finding the position of the stress in Greek words. The accent-marks now customarily used in writing and printing Greek were the invention of post-Classical grammarians in Alexandria; there is no reason to doubt the accuracy of the tradition they recorded, since in modern Greek the stress always falls on the syllable which bears the accent-mark[2]. Yet in the reformed pronunciation the position of the accent-mark is wholly ignored, and the stress is placed according to the rules of stress in Latin, which require a knowledge of the length of vowels. In the case of two of the Greek vowels there is no difficulty, since η (*ē*) and ω (*ō*) are always long, and ϵ (*e*) and ο (*o*) are always short; but the length of α (*a*), ι (*i*) and υ (*u*) can only be determined on etymological grounds, so that those who are ignorant of Greek are necessarily at a loss. Fortunately this reformed pronunciation is used only for the very few words which are transliterated wholly according to the modern system.

(3) *The pronunciation of Modern Greek.* Since Greek, unlike Latin, is not a dead language, the pronunciation of Modern Greek (which differs extensively from that of ancient Greek) must also be taken into account. Since there are only three words in this dictionary which are derived from Modern Greek—*moussaka*, *ouzo*, and *retsina*—

[1] This pronunciation has had a chequered history. As early as the sixteenth century attempts to reform the pronunciation of Greek led to high feelings and ecclesiastical censure.

[2] It is possible, even probable, that the accent-marks were intended to record a 'pitch-accent' rather than a 'stress-accent' in ancient Greek; i.e. that the accent consisted rather of a change of pitch than of an increase in intensity as in modern English. If so, the pitch-accent of ancient Greek has been replaced by stress-accent in Modern Greek.

there is no need to discuss the modern pronunciation in detail; it is sufficient to remark that *a*, *e*, *i* and *o* are pronounced as in Italian, and *ou* as in French.

Languages written in non-Roman scripts

With the exception of Russian all the languages written in scripts or alphabets other than the Roman alphabet are Oriental languages; and with them must be included Turkish which, though it is now written with the Roman alphabet, was written in the Arabic script when the vast majority of English borrowings from it were introduced into the language. Here too it is convenient to include languages like Eskimo and Hawaiian, which have no native script and until recent times were never written down. Most of the languages included in this group offer few difficulties of pronunciation, since the accepted English form is usually one which will convey, in terms of English spelling conventions, an approximation to the correct pronunciation. Thus, such words as *anorak*, *charpoy*, *howdah*, *kilim*, *mahout*, *sampan*, *sarong*, *sepoy*, *tarboosh* can hardly be mispronounced if the combinations of letters are given their ordinary English values.

The problem here, if problem there is, is rather one of spelling: the few who have some knowledge of a little-known language may tend to become impatient with what seems to them an unscientific system of transliteration, and to substitute one which seems to them preferable. For this reason it is not uncommon to find such words as *krees*, *ranee*, *sheikh*, *suttee*, *syce* and *taboo* written *kris*, *rani*, *shaikh*, *sati*, *sais* and *tabu* respectively. In some cases the supposedly more scientific form seems to have ousted the traditional form completely: *babu*, *guru*, *hammam*, *sari* and *umiak* must now be considered the standard forms in place of the earlier and preferable *baboo*, *gooroo*, *hummum*, *saree* and *oomiak* (though *igloo* still retains its *oo*). Of course in a systematic treatise on a foreign language a 'scientific' system of transliteration is eminently desirable; but those who alter, or attempt to alter, the traditional spelling overlook the fact that for 'foreign' words in current speech the most important factor is that the approximate pronunciation should be immediately obvious. The interpretation of the traditional spellings requires no special knowledge, but a 'scientific' transliteration is meaningless unless the principles of the system are properly understood, and the value to be attributed to each symbol has been memorized. The spelling *syce*, for instance, is obviously based on English spelling conventions, and there can be no doubt at all what pronunciation is intended. The spelling *sais*, on the other hand, is ambiguous: if the word had entered

English through French it would suggest one pronunciation, if through Italian another; in itself the spelling does not supply enough information for the pronunciation to be determined with confidence.

There are in fact a number of words from languages in this group which have entered English by way of other European languages, especially French; in these cases the combinations of letters must be pronounced according to the spelling conventions of the language concerned. In *couscous* and *souk* the combination *ou* must be pronounced as in French (that is, like English *oo*); in *comitadji* and *djibbah* the *dj* is to be pronounced like English *j*; and so on. Occasionally the standard form combines elements from a French and an English transliteration: in *djinnee*, for instance, the *dj* is French and the *ee* is English. In none of these cases is any doubt or difficulty likely to arise in practice.

Words from Russian present a few special problems. The more recent adoptions normally appear in a sensible transliteration which is more or less self-explanatory: consonants and consonant groups are pronounced as in English, vowels as in Italian. In such a word as *dacha*, for instance, the two *a*'s have their 'Continental' value, but *ch* is to be pronounced as in English, not as in French or as in German. Some difficulty arises with the Russian character properly transliterated *shch*, since this awkward collocation of consonants tends to be avoided in English. Russian *borshch* normally appears as *bortsch* in English, Russian *yamshchik* as *yamschik* or *yamstchik*[1]. The accepted English spelling of some of the earlier borrowings from Russian retains vestiges of the spelling-systems of other European languages through which they have passed: in *moujik*, for instance, the *ou* and the *j* have to be pronounced as in French; a more modern transliteration would be *muzhik*. The most irrational spelling of all is to be found in the word *czar*, from Russian *tsarĭ*, and efforts have been made (without conspicuous success) to substitute the spelling *tsar*, which certainly represents the Russian pronunciation much more accurately. One obstacle in the way of this reform is the existence of the form *czarina* as the accepted English name for the wife of a *czar*. This word has a curious history: it is formed from *czar* (itself an obsolete German transliteration of the Russian word) by the addition, first of the German feminine ending *-in*, then of the Italian feminine ending *-a*. Purists are obliged to insist on the substitution of the true Russian feminine form *tsaritsa*; and since the public is naturally unwilling to accept an innovation which involves

[1] However, English *s(t)ch* does not always correspond to the Russian *shch;* English *izvoschik* is from Russian *izvozchik*.

a radical change of pronunciation, *czarina* still holds the field and has tended to reinforce the tenacity of the spelling *czar*.

The spelling of European languages

In general the spelling of words and phrases introduced into English from European languages is the spelling current in the language of origin. However, there are a number of exceptions to this rule; some are justified either by long usage or by common sense, others are due either to ignorance or to carelessness, and ought to be discouraged. Many of the traditional divergences from contemporary foreign usage have been discussed above, pp. 11–12. The preservation of obsolete foreign spellings in English is justified partly by reverence for tradition, partly by considerations of expediency. English *duenna*, for example, preserves the older spelling of Spanish *dueña*; the older spelling must obviously be retained, since *dueña* would conflict with the English pronunciation of the word. English *foible* preserves the older spelling of French *faible*; any interference with the traditional spelling *foible* would not only conflict with the English pronunciation but would lead to confusion between two distinct words, since the Modern French *faible* has been introduced into English in a different sense. In other cases, too, the adoption of a current foreign spelling is ruled out by the English pronunciation. French *avant-coureur*, for instance, appears in English as *avant-courier*, in which the second element (but not the first) has been anglicized[1]; restoration of the French spelling would conflict with the accepted pronunciation. The English form *pistachio* appears to be a compromise between the Spanish *pistacho* and the Italian *pistacchio*; the accepted pronunciation is based on that of the Spanish form but is not identical with it, so that any change of spelling would be inappropriate[2].

The use of accent-marks and other diacritics in words and phrases of foreign origin presents a special problem. The difficulty here is in part merely typographical: many of the founts used in printing

[1] In fact a different word has been substituted for the second element: French *courrier* (from Italian *corriere*) is distinct from French *coureur*, but some of the meanings of *coureur* have been taken over by the anglicized *courier*.

[2] English usage in the writing and printing of German nouns is far from stable. In German all nouns normally take a capital letter, and this custom is often followed when German nouns are used in English; but the capital is sometimes omitted in accordance with normal English usage. In this dictionary all German nouns are printed with a capital letter.

popular newspapers are deficient in the special characters required,[1] so that the printers have no choice but to omit the accent-marks; and the appearance of a word without an accent-mark may become so familiar that the accent-mark is omitted even when a special character is available. The lack of a suitable special character may account for the rarity of the Scandinavian symbol *ø* in such words as Danish *smørrebrød*; the fact that Swedish uses *ö* where Norwegian uses *ø* encourages the use of the more familiar and more easily obtainable *ö*, so that the spelling *smörrebröd* is not uncommon. In this particular instance the largely accidental resemblance to Norwegian *smørgåsbord*, Swedish *smörgåsbord*, may have something to do with the substitution. In the same way *skijöring* has become the accepted English spelling of Norwegian *skikjøring* (the omission of the *k* is doubtless due to the fact that Norwegian *k* is very lightly pronounced in such a position).

However, peculiarities in the use of accent-marks are not wholly to be accounted for by a lack of suitable special characters. Certain accent-marks seem to be highly acceptable to English taste, and are rarely omitted; some may even be inserted where they are not called for. German words which call for the use of the diæresis ¨ are rarely printed without it, though *Fräulein* occasionally appears as *Fraulein*, probably through confusion with *Frau*; the diæresis is never omitted from French *naïf*, though curiously enough it is often omitted from the feminine *naïve*. The French circumflex accent ˆ is also relatively stable. It would be mere pedantry to insist on *châssis* and *hôtel* (though *hôtelier* is still very common); *bâton* in some of its more common senses normally drops the circumflex; *rêverie*, too, is very frequently written without the circumflex. However, such common word as *dépôt*, *entrepôt* and *rôle* still very generally retain it; perhaps the commonest spelling of *dépôt* is *depôt*, without the acute but with the circumflex accent. What is rather surprising is the fact that in a large number of words the circumflex accent is either substituted for another accent-mark or introduced without any justification in French. The circumflex is sometimes substituted for the acute accent (*crêpon* for *crépon*) or for the grave accent (*crêche*, *crême de la crême* for *crèche*, *crème de la crème*); in a great many cases it is introduced

[1] In writing by hand or with a typewriter an accent-mark can be added without difficulty to the ordinary symbol; but, in printing, each combination of symbol and accent-mark has to be individually cast, and these special types have to be separately stored. Where mechanical setting by Linotype is used the number of types available is limited by the structure of the Linotype machine, and it is not possible (as it is with mechanical setting by Monotype) to insert special characters later by hand.

without any justification at all (*châlet*, *chênet*, *compôte*, *côterie*, *rôturier* for *chalet*, *chenet*, *compote*, *coterie*, *roturier*)[1].

The least stable of the accent-marks is the acute accent in words of French origin. Here the stability depends to a large extent on the position of the *é* in the word. The omission of the accent-mark from *é* at the end of a word could easily lead to mispronunciation, and there are in English use many pairs of French words distinguished only by the presence or absence of the acute accent: *comble* and *comblé*, *gêne* and *gêné*, *manque* and *manqué*, and others. The omission of the acute accent from a word like *communiqué* would lead to confusion with words like *critique*[2]. So important is this final *-é*, in fact, that it is sometimes reinforced by an additional, unetymological, *e*, as in *rechauffée*, *soufflée* for *rechauffé*, *soufflé*; we have already seen (p. 12) that final *-ée* is sometimes preferred to other French endings in *couchée*, *levée* and *toupée*. At the beginning of a word *é* is relatively stable when it is followed by only one consonant, since there are few English words beginning with *e* and a single consonant: such words as *élan*, *élite*, *épergne*, *étape*, *étude* rarely lose the acute accent. But when *e* at the beginning of a word is followed by two consonants, as in *éclair*, *éclat*, *écru*, *épris*, *étrier* and other words, omission is much more common. Most vulnerable of all is *é* preceded by a single consonant, as in *débris*, *début*, *décor*, *dépôt*, *réclame*, *régime*, *répertoire*, *résumé*; in such words the acute accent is perhaps more often omitted than not. Occasionally an overanxiety for correctness in words of this type may lead to the addition of an acute accent where none is called for, as in *récherché* for *recherché*.

It must not be overlooked that frequency of usage has something to do with the use and disuse of accent-marks. The words in which accent-marks are most commonly omitted are those which are most commonly used; the spelling of less frequent words, especially of technical or quasi-technical words, tends to conform fully to that of the language from which they come.

The pronunciation of European languages

The question of the pronunciation of words and phrases from modern European languages is a very thorny one. The basis of the difficulty

[1] Some of these errors may be due to erroneous associations with other words: *chalet* with *château*, *chenet* with *chêne*, *coterie* with *côte*, *roturier* with *rôtir*.

[2] The omission of the acute accent at the end of a word is much more common in the United States, where words like *canapé* and *coupé* are often written *canape* and *coupe*; the omission is sometimes accompanied by a corresponding change in the pronunciation.

is the fact that the sounds of what is often called 'Received Standard English' differ very substantially from those of most European languages. In particular, Standard English makes extensive use of diphthongs and contains relatively few pure vowels, so that the pronunciation of the pure vowels so common in most European languages does not come easily to the speaker of Standard English. From this point of view the speaker of dialectal English, or of one of the Regional Standards, is at an advantage over the speaker of Standard English, since the dialects use many pure vowels never heard in Standard English. There is a further difficulty which affects all speakers of English more or less equally: many European languages make use of sounds unknown either in Standard English or in the dialects. The French nasal vowels, for instance, are never used in any form of English; the 'front rounded' vowels *ö* and *ü* are not used in Standard English, and are rare in the dialects[1].

It follows that the pronunciation of a 'foreign' word or phrase in an English sentence exactly as it is pronounced in its language of origin will require the use of a number of sounds not used in the rest of the discourse. The achievement of such a pronunciation is exceedingly difficult, even for a speaker who knows the language in question really well; it is undesirable, since it interrupts the natural flow of discourse—the listener will be temporarily more occupied in admiring a feat of lingual agility than in following the meaning of the sentence; and it is above all unnecessary—it can serve no useful purpose to pronounce a 'foreign' expression in an English sentence with a perfect native accent. (Speakers who attempt such feats are commonly those who will use 'foreign' expressions merely for the sake of conveying an impression of their superior culture and erudition.) On the other hand, complete anglicization of pronunciation is equally undesirable. We have already seen (pp. 21–25) that there are many excellent reasons why certain words and phrases have remained 'foreign' instead of being anglicized, and it is important that such expressions should be recognizable as 'foreign' in speech as well as in writing[2]. What is required, therefore, is a pronunciation which will not be so far removed from that of English as to stand out abruptly from its context, yet which will be sufficiently distinctive to ensure that the expression concerned can be readily recognized as 'foreign'.

[1] There are minor differences between English and other languages in the articulation of nearly all sounds, consonants as well as vowels. These need not be listed here, but reinforce the argument of the next paragraph.

[2] In printing, of course, a 'foreign' expression can easily be distinguished as such by the use of italics.

There are certain characteristics shared by many foreign languages but not by English which can be called into play to achieve the desired effect. The most important of these is the general tendency in languages other than English to pronounce unstressed vowels distinctly, instead of slurring them and obscuring their quality as in English; by pronouncing unstressed vowels in 'foreign' expressions distinctly, the speaker of English can mark these expressions out as 'foreign' without making use of any sound which does not occur in English. Another characteristic, most noticeable in French but discernible in some other languages, is a tendency to place the stress in a position different from that which would seem most natural in English. The reproduction of these two characteristics will be sufficient to distinguish as 'foreign' a great many words and phrases—though obviously neither is applicable to monosyllabic words of foreign origin. Such words as *étagère* and *jalousie*, for instance, can be marked out as 'foreign' without the use of any foreign sounds by placing the stress on the last syllable and pronouncing the unstressed vowels clearly and distinctly. In precisely the same way the technical term *caractère* can be distinguished from English 'character' without the use of any foreign sounds; to attempt to reproduce the French '*r grasseyé*' twice over would make the word unnecessarily conspicuous in its context.

For the rest, the pronunciation of individual vowels and consonants depends to a certain extent on the nature of the expression concerned and on the context in which it is used. The more technical an expression, the stronger the tendency to reproduce with some accuracy its pronunciation in the language from which it comes; less technical expressions, especially those in frequent use, should be pronounced with as few foreign sounds as possible. When pronouncing expressions of this latter kind the prudent speaker will avoid pedantry or eccentricity and aim at a simple, natural effect. Whenever an English sound provides a reasonable approximation to a foreign sound he will substitute it for the foreign sound; whenever there is no reasonable English equivalent to a foreign sound he will imitate the foreign sound as closely as is consistent with the general pattern of English sounds. He will, for instance, in general substitute an English vowel-sound (impure or diphthongal though it may be) for a foreign vowel-sound, and ignore minor differences in the pronunciation of the consonants; but he will produce an unostentatious approximation to, say, the nasal vowels of French, the 'front rounded' vowels *ö* and *ü*, or the *ch*-sounds of German. In some cases linguistic discretion will suggest an even more extensive substitution of English sounds: the phrase *hors d'œuvre*, for instance, is pronounced without any foreign sounds at all—no 'front rounded' vowel is normally attempted in the second word.

The use of foreign feminine forms in English

A great many foreign languages preserve a more extensive system of genders than English does: whereas with few exceptions English preserves a distinction of gender only in the pronouns of the third person singular, in many languages the distinction extends throughout the inflection of nouns and adjectives. No attempt is ever made in English to imitate the grammatical gender of a foreign language when a 'foreign' adjective is used—that is, the form of the adjective is never adjusted to suit the grammatical gender (in the language from which the adjective comes) of the noun which it qualifies—but it is normal to adjust the form of 'foreign' nouns and adjectives to suit the feeling for natural gender in English. Special feminine forms are therefore used only with 'foreign' nouns referring to persons, or with 'foreign' adjectives which in their English context happen to refer to persons.

By far the most numerous special feminine forms are to be found amongst words of French origin, and these are in general used correctly. A great many French adjectives used in English are formed from past participles: *accablé*, *borné*, *déclassé*, *déséquilibré*, *distingué*, *empressé*, *froissé*, *maquillé*, *passé*, *soigné* and numerous others. The feminine of these is formed by adding an *e* which does not affect the pronunciation, and it is perhaps because the pronunciation is not affected that the omission of the final *-e*, though not common, is more frequent than with most other types of French adjective. When an adjective of this type is used as a noun the omission of the feminine *-e* is much more common: *habitué* and *protégé* are as often as not left uninflected when they refer to women. When the pronunciation of the feminine differs from that of the masculine the neglect of the special feminine form is very rare. Various regular types can be distinguished. (1) Adjectives formed from present participles in *-ant*, feminine *-ante* (*clairvoyant*, *exigeant*, *intransigeant*, *piquant*); with these may be included *méchant*, though it is no longer felt as a present participle in French. (2) Nouns (and a few adjectives) formed with the agent-suffix *-eur*, feminine *-euse* (*charmeur*, *chauffeur*, *coiffeur*, *danseur*, *enjôleur*, *entrepreneur*, *farceur*, *poseur*, *siffleur*, *souffleur*); with these may be classed adjectives in *-eux*, feminine *-euse* (*précieux*, *sérieux*). (3) Other French nouns and adjectives in which the feminine differs in pronunciation from the masculine: *bourgeois* (*bourgeoise*), *épris* (*éprise*), *gamin* (*gamine*), *mesquin* (*mesquine*), *métis* (*métisse*), *mignon* (*mignonne*), *naïf* (*naïve*), *roturier* (*roturière*), *sournois* (*sournoise*); the oddity here is *naïf*, since the feminine *naïve* is often used in preference to the masculine even when it refers to a male person. Italian and Spanish nouns and adjectives ending in *-o* form their feminine by changing *-o* into *-a*, and this adjustment is usually carried out in English with such words as *aficionado*, *beato*, *contadino*, *majo*, *mestizo*, *simpatico*. There are two exceptions: though feminine forms are sometimes used in English, *incognito* and *incommunicado* are often left unchanged in such sentences as 'she was travelling *incognito*' and 'she was held *incommunicado* by the police', doubtless because the words are felt to be adverbial rather than adjectival in such sentences. Another exception, this time in French, is to be found in the phrase *nouveau riche*: the feminine *nouvelle riche* is exceedingly rare, doubtless because the phrase is felt to mean 'newly rich', with *nouveau* in an adverbial function. Phrases sometimes offer a little difficulty, since more than one word may need to be put into the feminine form: *croyant et pratiquant* (*croyante et pratiquante*), *faux dévot* (*fausse dévote*), *petit bourgeois* (*petite bourgeoise*), *premier danseur* (*première danseuse*). Another kind of difficulty is offered by *enfant chéri*, feminine *enfant chérie*—the first word remains unchanged.

The use of foreign plurals in English

The question of foreign plurals is much more complicated. There are in general no English feminines to compete with the foreign feminines, so that the only question which arises is whether the foreign feminine is used or not; but any 'foreign' word can with a little difficulty be fitted with an English plural, so that either an English or a foreign plural may be used; certain words sometimes take an English plural, sometimes a foreign one. Words from little-known languages nearly always take an English plural—no doubt because the correct foreign plural is unknown to most of those who use the words. A few such words, however, mostly technical, generally take a foreign plural: Welsh *cynghanedd* (*cynganeddion*) and *eisteddfod* (*eisteddfodau*), Arabic *fellah* (*fellahin*) and *hadith* (*hadithat*), Hebrew *kibbutz* (*kibbutzim*), Russian *izvoschik* (*izvoschiki*), *stilyaga* (*stilyagi*) and *zastruga* (*zastrugi*). In the case of Classical words and words from the more familiar modern languages the correct plural is widely known, or can easily be ascertained, and the difficulty is to know whether it should be used or not.

The majority of Latin masculines in *-us* form their plural in *-i*, and this rule is very generally observed in English, probably because of the awkwardness of an ending *-uses*: *bacillus, caduceus, modulus, papyrus, stylus*, and a great many others. However, there are some traps for the unwary. Certain fourth-declension nouns in *-us* remain unchanged in the plural: *apparatus, excursus, fœtus, ictus, tractatus*—though the use of *apparati* is not unknown amongst scientists. Other nouns in *-us* were originally verbs in the first person plural, and with these there is no alternative to the awkward *-uses: ignoramus, inspeximus, mandamus, vidimus*. A trap of a different kind is to be found in the word *polypus*, which has plural *polypi* although something like *polypodes* might have been expected. The few Greek nouns which retain the singular *-os* form their plural in *-oi* instead of the rather awkward *-oses*, which would in any case be liable to confusion with the plural of nouns in *-osis*: *kouros, pithos, stichos*. Latin neuters in *-um* regularly form their plural in *-a* in English, because of the awkwardness of an ending *-ums*: *addendum, bacterium, consortium, curriculum, datum, desideratum, memorandum, quinquennium, stratum, ultimatum*. A few nouns like *fulcrum* do have a plural in *-ums*, and *medium* has two plurals *media* and *mediums*, differentiated according to the meaning. Greek neuters in *-on* more often than not form their plural in *-a*: *acroterion, criterion, ganglion, megaron, noumenon, phenomenon, prolegomenon*. However, the ending *-ons* is much less objectionable than *-ums* because it is familiar in the very numerous, fully anglicized words ending in *-ation, -ition*, etc., so that although *phenomenons* and *prolegomenons* are unthinkable, *criterions* and *ganglions* are sometimes preferred to *criteria* and *ganglia*. The use of the Latin plural of feminines in *-a* is much less frequent, and with many such nouns a plural in *-as* is much more frequent than the Latin plural in *-æ*: *abscissa, amphora, cicada, lamina, nebula*—only in a highly technical context is a plural in *-æ* to be expected. On the other hand such words as *differentiæ* and *sequelæ* are so much better known in the plural than in the singular that the use of any other plural is unlikely.

The less common Greek and Latin plurals tend to be avoided. The plurals *lemmata, œdemata, traumata* and the like are giving place to *lemmas, œdemas, traumas*. Though *ambo* still has a plural *ambones, cento* prefers *centos* to *centones*. So also *calx* and *vortex* tend to prefer *calxes* and *vortexes* to *calces* and *vortices*; *ikon* and *strophe* tend to prefer *ikons* and *strophes* to *ikones* and *strophai*. Words like *proboscis* are particularly difficult: the Greek plural *proboscides* seems strange, the English plural *proboscises* seems awkward; a common way out (but one which cannot be recommended) is to write *probosces*, without any justification either in Greek or in English. Some of the more technical Greek and Latin words still retain their irregular plurals: *cognomen* (*cognomina*), *genus* (*genera*), *kore* (*korai*), *stoa* (*stoai*). Expressions involving Latin verbs, which are fortunately rare, may have two different kinds of plural according to the meaning. The distinction is well illustrated by the word *exit* '(a stage-direction that) he goes out'; if the required meaning in the plural is '(stage-directions that) he goes out' the appropriate form is *exits*, but if the required meaning is '(a stage-direction that) they go out' the appropriate form is *exeunt*. The majority of such expressions take either one form or the other. Examples of the first type are *affidavit* (*affidavits*), *caret* (*carets*), *cognovit* (*cognovits*) and *tenet* (*tenets*)[1]. Examples of the second type are *ipse dixit* (*ipsi dixerunt*), *peccavi* (*peccavimus*), *proxime accessit* (*proxime accesserunt*).

In one or two instances the identity of form between the Latin neuter plural in *-a* and the Latin feminine singular in *-a* has led to confusion in English: *effluvia*, the plural of *effluvium*, has sometimes been misapprehended as a feminine singular and given a spurious plural *effluviæ*; conversely, the feminine singular *scoria* has sometimes been misapprehended as a neuter plural and given a spurious singular *scorium*. An even more flagrant (though rare) example of this latter error is *propaganda* (feminine singular, ablative case), which has occasionally been treated as a plural and supplied with a singular *propagandum*. Even when no spurious forms have been invented the misapprehension of a Latin form may be revealed by the structure of the sentence in which it is used; such plural forms as *agenda* and *data* are sometimes erroneously used with singular verbs.

Words from modern languages present fewer difficulties. Words from French are particularly simple, since the normal method of forming the plural in French is by adding an *s*, exactly as in English. Works ending in *-eau*, however, a large number of which have entered English, form their plural in *-eaux*: *bureau*, *château*, *flambeau*, *gâteau*, *morceau*, *plateau*, *portmanteau*, *rouleau*, *trousseau*. In English these words are often given a plural in *-s*, but in the more technical contexts a plural in *-x* is still frequent; however, although the plural *-x* is silent in French, it is often sounded as a *z* in English. Spanish also forms its plural by adding an *s* when the singular ends in a vowel, but a little care is needed with Spanish words ending in a consonant: *conquistador*, for instance, has plural *conquistadores*. German words are usually given German plurals—no other plural for *Lied* than *Lieder* is thinkable; but *Poltergeists* is much commoner than *Polter-*

[1] The plural *tenent* was formerly in use but is now obsolete.

geister. Italian words present to a lesser degree the same kind of difficulties as bedevil Latin words. Many Italian masculines in *-o* regularly take the Italian plural in *-i*: *amoretto*, *bozzetto*, *contadino*, *graffito*, *illuminato*, *palazzo*, *pentimento*, *putto*, *spolvero*, and many others. Many words of the same type, however, vary between *-i* and *-os*: *concerto*, *contralto*, *impresario*, *solo*, *soprano*, *tempo*, *torso*, *virtuoso;* in these cases *-i* is preferred in the more technical contexts, *-os* in the more general contexts[1]. The rare Italian masculines in *-e* (like *dilettante*) vary between *-i* and *-es*. Masculines in *-a* (like *quadratista* and *vedutista*) always take *-i* in the plural. Some Italian feminines in *-a* regularly form a plural in *-e*: *carrozza*, *fioritura*. Others vary between *-e* and *-as* according to the context: *loggia*, *piazza*. An enlightening example is the word *regatta*. This word originally meant, and can still mean, a local contest on the Venetian lagoon, and in this sense the plural is regularly *regatte*; but it is more commonly applied to almost any type of aquatic sporting event, and in this sense the plural is *regattas*.

Phrases from foreign languages may be divided into two general categories according to the way the plural is formed. In the first category only one word, usually the first, is altered in the formation of the plural: *amicus curiæ* (*amici curiæ*), *chargé d'affaires* (*chargés d'affaires*), *desco da parto* (*deschi da parto*), *felo de se* (*felones de se*), *jeu de mots* (*jeux de mots*), *objet d'art* (*objets d'art*). In the second category, consisting entirely of two-word phrases, both words have to be adjusted in the plural: *bel esprit* (*beaux esprits*), *corpus vile* (*corpora vilia*), *editio princeps* (*editiones principes*), *fons vivus* (*fontes vivi*), *novus homo* (*novi homines*), *tableau vivant* (*tableaux vivants*), *varia lectio* (*variæ lectiones*). A few phrases like *hors d'œuvre* remain unchanged in the plural in their language of origin; these generally add an *s* in English.

It is possible to summarize the detailed information given in this section without much loss of accuracy. In general it can be said that 'foreign' words and phrases form their plurals in English as they do in their languages of origin. However, Latin feminines in *-a*, most Italian nouns, and French nouns ending in *-eau* may take either a foreign or an English plural. In these cases a foreign plural is more common in a technical context, an English plural in a non-technical context; but the correct usage in any given passage is a question which must be left to the linguistic discretion of the writer or speaker.

[1] The ending *-oes* is appropriate only when a word is fully anglicized, and forms like *soloes* are better avoided.

III. The Arrangement of the Dictionary

The alphabetic arrangement

The order of the entries in this dictionary is strictly alphabetic. In most dictionaries a strictly alphabetic arrangement of this kind is very properly avoided: groups of related and derived words can most conveniently be discussed under a single heading; idiomatic phrases may need to be discussed under one or more of the most conspicuous words contained in them. Since, however, each 'foreign' expression used in English is, as it were, a self-contained entity only very indirectly related to any other, neither of these considerations applies to the present work. A strictly alphabetic sequence is the simplest to consult; moreover, any departure from it would involve ambiguities in the case of expressions like *ex tempore* or *ex post facto*, sometimes written as a single word and sometimes as two or three, or those like *laissez-faire* which are sometimes hyphenated and sometimes not. The characters *æ* and *œ* are alphabetized as *ae* and *oe* respectively. Accent-marks and diacritics of all kinds are ignored in alphabetization, unless two words are distinguished only by the presence or absence of a diacritic; in this case the form without the diacritic comes before the form with the diacritic. Thus, *comble* comes before *comblé*, *manque* before *manqué*, and so on.

Phrases are alphabetized as if they consisted of a continuous string of letters, no account being taken of the spaces between words. Their alphabetic position is always dictated by the first word, unless this is the definite or indefinite article in the language in question; any such article is enclosed in round brackets and ignored in alphabetization, so that (*le*) *style, c'est l'homme*, for instance, will be found under *S*. This arrangement is rendered necessary by the fact that a number of phrases are used sometimes with and sometimes without a foreign article: *le Grand Siècle* and *la belle époque* may sometimes appear as 'the *Grand Siècle*' and 'the *belle époque*', *die neue Sachlichkeit* as 'the *neue Sachlichkeit*'. Since, however, the French definite article *l'* (used only before a vowel or silent *h*) is too closely connected with the following word ever to be omitted in this way, an exception is made in this case: *l'homme même*, for instance, will be found under *L*, not *H*.

The information given in each entry in the dictionary is arranged in a standard sequence, which is described in the following paragraphs; not all the items described, however, will be found in every entry, since some of them are not always applicable or relevant.

The head-word

The head-word (or head-phrase) is given in **bold type**. Alternative forms of the head-word are divided by an oblique stroke, the preferable form being given first. Alternative forms which are very rare, or which are clearly erroneous, are mentioned later in the entry. Cross-references to alternative forms are given in the appropriate alphabetic place if this is not immediately adjacent to the main entry, and a brief definition is given there to avoid unnecessary hunting to and fro; if more precise or extensive information is needed it must, of course, be sought under the head-word indicated. There are numerous phrases of which a part is sometimes omitted and sometimes included; in this case the part which is sometimes omitted is enclosed in round brackets. Thus, *se non è vero, è* (*molto*) *ben trovato* implies that the phrase is sometimes found in the form *se non è vero, è ben trovato*. Where omissions are very substantial the shortened form is given a separate entry; thus, there is a separate entry for *ben trovato*, with a cross-reference to the full form of the phrase. Parts of words omitted when a word or phrase is abbreviated are also enclosed in round brackets, the addition of full stops being taken for granted; thus, *op*(*ere*) *cit*(*ato*) implies an abbreviation *op. cit.*; the abbreviation is given a cross-reference in the appropriate alphabetic place if this is not immediately adjacent to the main entry. Sometimes it is more convenient to give the abbreviation separately later in the entry; thus, the abbreviation of *varia lectio* to *v.l.* with plural *vv.ll.* could not easily be indicated by the use of brackets. Immediately after the head-word, and still in **bold type,** come special foreign feminine and plural forms, given in full to avoid any possibility of ambiguity. The mention of a foreign plural at this point does not imply that it is the only, or even the most frequent, plural in use—merely that, if a foreign plural is to be used, this is the correct form[1]. If no foreign plural is given the implication is either that no plural is in use, or that the plural is formed according to normal English rules.

The etymology

The etymology immediately follows the head-word, and is enclosed in square brackets. A full etymology is divided into three parts, but not all of these are always necessary.

(1) *An indication of the language of origin.* I have not attempted full academic accuracy in this indication; I have not attempted, for

[1] The use of foreign plurals has been discussed above, pp. 52–55.

instance, to distinguish between Hindi and Urdu, but have included both under the better known name Hindustani. For the abbreviations used, see p. 62. In the majority of entries this indication is all that is called for by way of etymology.

(2) *The spelling in the language of origin.* If the spelling of a word or phrase in English differs substantially from the spelling in its language of origin, the latter is given in *italics*. If the language of origin is not written in the Roman alphabet, some standard transliteration is used, except in the case of Greek, which is reproduced in Greek type; this exception is very necessary, since Greek words and phrases are still sometimes printed in English contexts without transliteration. If the language of origin is written in the Roman alphabet the current spelling is used, so that further information can easily be found in a modern dictionary of the language in question. Many English dictionaries still use obsolete spelling-systems when quoting foreign words, so that consultation of a specialist dictionary is made unnecessarily difficult. Turkish, for instance, has officially used the Roman alphabet since as long ago as 1928; yet many English dictionaries still quote Turkish words in an obsolete transliteration of the Arabic script used before 1928. Similarly the spelling of Irish was officially simplified in 1948, and this simplified spelling has been adopted in the present work when Irish words are quoted.

(3) *The meaning in the language of origin.* If the literal meaning of the word or phrase differs substantially from the meaning given in the definition and is of some intrinsic interest, it is added at this point, enclosed in inverted commas. The insertion of the literal meaning does not necessarily imply that the figurative meaning current in English is not also current in the language of origin.

Specialized and technical usage

If a word or phrase is a technical term, an indication is given (in *italics*) of the special field of interest to which the expression belongs; for the abbreviations used, see p. 62. These indications are designedly very general: for instance *Ling.* 'Linguistics' includes not only the technical terms of Linguistics proper but those used in the more technical type of literary criticism and in the study of metre. It is often not possible to define very exactly the boundaries of the fields of study in which a term may be used; but it is important to indicate that it is a specialized term and therefore not in general use, since this fact may influence the extent to which it remains 'foreign', and hence its spelling, pronunciation and inflection.

The definition

The definitions are intended to be as self-contained as possible, and are designed for the enlightenment of those who have little specialized knowledge of the subject concerned; technical accuracy has therefore sometimes been sacrificed to clarity of exposition. Definitions of slightly different senses of the same expression are divided from each other by semicolons; if there are markedly different senses, these are numbered and dealt with separately. Grammatical categories are not defined; if necessary the usage of a word is indicated by the addition of an appropriate context, enclosed in round brackets. Round brackets are also used in another way. Many 'foreign' words and phrases are used in English in senses which, though closely related, are not identical with each other, and it is often possible to save space by enclosing part of a definition in round brackets. For instance, the definition of the word *trek* runs as follows: '(one stage of) a journey by ox-wagon; to make a journey by ox-wagon; (to make) any kind of arduous journey across country.' Fully expanded, this definition would read as follows: 'a journey by ox-wagon; one stage of a journey by ox-wagon; to make a journey by ox-wagon; any kind of arduous journey across country; to make any kind of arduous journey across country.' If the dictionary were intended as an arbiter of usage there might be some ambiguity between the two ways of using round brackets; but, as has been explained above (p. 36), this is a 'one-way' dictionary, designed only to elucidate the meaning of an expression in a given context; no 'foreign' expression should be used by a writer or speaker who is in doubt about the limits of permissible usage. Many words used in the definitions which are also head-words in the dictionary are printed in SMALL CAPITALS, so that the use of small capitals is equivalent to the addition of *q.v.* after the word; this device is used only when the consultation of the entry thus referred to will throw further light on the definition.

The date of introduction

After the definition comes a note of the date at which the word or phrase was introduced into English. Some expressions may have a long history of use in England in contexts other than English contexts (legal terms in Latin or Law-French, for instance); but it is the date of their first appearance in an English context which is given here. The difficulty of establishing the date of first introduction has already been discussed above, p. 25. The dates are indicated by centuries: *16c.* stands for 'sixteenth century', and so on. Sometimes different senses of the same word or phrase have entered English at different periods; whenever such a difference is interesting or significant the appropriate date is given under each section of the definition.

Notes on points of interest

Notes are often added on points of interest arising in connection with the head-words. If the precise connotation of a word or phrase cannot easily be brought out in a concise definition it is elaborated here. Rare or erroneous alternative forms and peculiarities of pronunciation, spelling and usage are discussed, especially in cases which cannot be brought under the general rules given in Section II of this introduction. The notes are also intended to obviate as far as possible the necessity of consulting any other work of reference. Quotations are traced to their origins, though no attempt is made to elucidate dubious attributions. A certain amount of encyclopædic information is provided where it seems likely that the reader's general knowledge may be at fault; but it is obviously impossible to cater for all classes of users of the dictionary, and there are doubtless many cases where some readers will feel that the explanatory notes labour the obvious, and many cases where other readers will feel that more information would have been welcome.

Cross-references

After the notes will be found cross-references, given in SMALL CAPITALS, to other words or phrases related by etymology or meaning to the head-word; distinct cross-references are divided from each other by semicolons. It is hoped that these cross-references will be both useful, since they call attention to groups of words and phrases which are nearly but not quite synonymous, and interesting, since they call attention to groups of words having the same ultimate origin but quite different meanings—for instance, *bodega*, *bottega* and *boutique*, etymologically identical, have wholly different connotations in English.

Illustrative quotations

The plan of the dictionary does not allow for the inclusion of quotations illustrating 'foreign' words and phrases in English; such quotations would have increased the bulk and the cost of the work enormously. However, each entry ends with an indication (enclosed in square brackets) of the places where illustrative quotations may be found. References are to *A New English Dictionary on Historical Principles* (1884–1928; Supplement 1933)[1] and to *The Stanford Dictionary of Anglicised Words and Phrases* (1892; Supplement of the same date). The abbreviations used are the following:

N	New English Dictionary
N*	New English Dictionary (Supplement)
N(*)	New English Dictionary and Supplement
S	Stanford
S*	Stanford (Supplement)
S(*)	Stanford and Supplement

This dictionary thus serves as an index to those 'foreign' words and phrases in the *New English Dictionary* and in *Stanford* which are still current.

[1] This work was re-issued by the Clarendon Press in 1933 as *The Oxford English Dictionary*. The majority of writers on language continue to use the original name, partly to ensure conformity with the universal practice before 1933, partly to avoid confusion with the other Oxford dictionaries—*The Shorter Oxford English Dictionary*, *The Concise Oxford Dictionary*, and others.

LIST OF ABBREVIATIONS

Afrik.	Afrikaans
A.-I.	Anglo-Indian
Arab.	Arabic
Arch.	Architecture
Austr.	Australian
c.	century
Chin.	Chinese
Cing.	Cingalese
Cul.	Culinary
Dan.	Danish
Dip.	Diplomacy
Du.	Dutch
Eccles.	Ecclesiastical
Equ.	Equitation
Esk.	Eskimo
esp.	especially
f.	feminine
facet.	facetious(ly)
Finn.	Finnish
Fr.	French
Gael.	Gaelic
Geog.	Geography
Ger.	German
Gk.	Greek
Haw.	Hawaiian
Heb.	Hebrew
Hind.	Hindustani
Hist.	Historical
Ir.	Irish
It.	Italian
Jap.	Japanese
Jav.	Javanese
Lat.	Latin
Ling.	Linguistics
Mal.	Malay
Math.	Mathematics
Med.	Medical
Mil.	Military
Mus.	Music
Myth.	Mythology
N,N*,N(*)	*see* p. 61
Norw.	Norwegian
Obs.	Obsolete
occ.	occasionally
orig.	originally
Pers.	Persian
pl.	plural
Pol.	Polish
Port.	Portuguese
Prov.	Provençal
Psych.	Psychology
Rel.	Religion
Russ.	Russian
S,S*,S(*)	*see* p. 61
Sansk.	Sanskrit
Sp.	Spanish
Swed.	Swedish
Theol.	Theology
Tib.	Tibetan
Turk.	Turkish
U.S.	United States (usage)
usu.	usually
Yidd.	Yiddish
<	derived from

A

a=ANTE, before.

abandon [Fr.] freedom from constraint, freedom from self-consciousness. 19c. Distinguished in pronunciation from the English verb *abandon*. [N,S(*)]

à bas [Fr.] down with . . .!; always followed by the name of the person execrated. 19c. Less drastic in its implications than À LA LANTERNE or AU POTEAU. [S]

abat-jour [Fr.] (1) a skylight; (2) a device for reflecting daylight into a dark room; (3) a shutter or awning to exclude daylight. 19c. In French the word also has the meaning 'lamp-shade'. [S]

abattoir [Fr.] a public slaughter-house. 19c. Introduced by Napoleon in 1810. [N,S]

abattu, *f.* **abattue** [Fr.] dejected, despondent. 18c. [S]

abat-voix [Fr.] a sounding-board, a wooden canopy (*esp.* over a pulpit) to reduce the dispersion of sound. 19c. [S]

abbé [Fr.] a cleric; one who, although in (minor) orders and wearing clerical dress, fulfills no ecclesiastical function. 18c. [N,S]

abbé de cour [Fr.] an ABBÉ who has obtained a lucrative and influential appointment at court; *usu.* with the implication that he is more worldly than a cleric should be. 19c.

Aberglaube [Ger.] superstition, reverence for the unknown. 19c. Used by Goethe and introduced into English by Matthew Arnold *Literature and Dogma* (1873); the connotation is less pejorative than that of English *superstition*. [N*]

ab extra [Lat.] *Theol.* from outside; not emanating from the mind. 17c. Opposed to *ab intra* 'from within', which however is much less used. [S]

à bientôt [Fr.] see you again soon! 20c. A common form of farewell in French, adopted in English because no English equivalent conveys the implication of a proximate meeting. Cf. HASTA LUEGO.

ab initio [Lat.] *Law* from the beginning; *esp.* of contracts, etc., which are null and void from the beginning, as distinct from those which are voided or voidable. 16c. Distinct in meaning from AB ORIGINE. [S]

Ablaut [Ger.] *Ling.* gradation, systematic variation of the root-vowel of a word in derivation. 19c. Sometimes known as *apophony*, as UMLAUT is sometimes known as *metaphony*. The vowels of such groups of English forms as *sing*, *sang*, *sung* are related by *Ablaut*. [N,S]

abondance [Fr.] an undertaking to win nine tricks at solo whist. 19c. Now often anglicized as *abundance*.

abondance déclarée [Fr.] an undertaking to win all thirteen tricks at solo whist. 19c. Now often anglicized as *abundance declared*.

abonnement [Fr.] subscription (to a journal, society, etc.) 20c.

ab origine [Lat.] from the beginning, from the creation of the world. 16c. Distinct in meaning from AB INITIO. [S]

aborigines *pl.* [Lat.] the original inhabitants of a country, *esp.* the natives found in possession of a country by European settlers. 16c. The Latin word is plural only; the correct English singular is *aboriginal*, and the form *aborigine* is etymologically indefensible. [N,S]

ab ovo [Lat. 'from the egg'] from the beginning. 16c. Horace *Ars Poetica* 147; *Satires* I iii 6. [S(*)]

à bras ouverts [Fr.] with open arms, with a cordial welcome. 19c. [S]

abscissa, *pl.* **abscissæ** [Lat. (*linea*) *abscissa* '(line) cut off'] *Math.* the portion of a line between a given point in it and an ordinate drawn from a given point outside it. 17c. [N,S]

Abseil [Ger.] a method of descending a cliff or rock-face on a double rope secured in such a way that the last man down can recover it; to descend a rock-face in this way. 20c. Cf. RAPPEL.

absinthe [Fr. 'wormwood'] a potent alcoholic liquor distilled from wine and wormwood. 19c. The manufacture and consumption of *absinthe* became illegal in France on 16th March, 1915; but the name is often applied to the less potent liquor known as *Pernod*. [N,S]

absit omen! [Lat. 'may the omen be absent!'] touch wood!, God forbid! 16c. Used to avert the misfortune possibly invoked by the inadvertent mention of an undesirable circumstance. [S(*)]

Abteilung, *pl.* **Abteilungen** [Ger.] a section, a division (of a book, etc.) 20c.

ab uno disce omnes [Lat.] judge them all from a single one; one is very like another. 17c. Virgil *Æneid* ii 65-6: *Accipe nunc Danaum insidias, et crimine ab uno Disce omnes* 'now take the tricks of the Greeks, and learn them all from a single crime'. The variant *ex uno disce omnes*, once common, seems now to be obsolete. [S]

a buon fresco [It.] *Art* (painting) on plaster while it is still wet; opposed to A SECCO (painting on dry plaster). 20c. Finishing touches may be added IN SECCO after the plaster is dry. Cf. BUON FRESCO.

ab urbe condita [Lat.] from the foundation of the city (of Rome). 18c. The foundation of Rome in 753 B.C. was the epoch from which the Romans calculated their dates; commonly abbreviated to *A.U.C.* [S]

abusus non tollit usum [Lat.] *Law* the abuse (of a right, etc.) does not invalidate its use. 19c.

académicien [Fr.] a member of an academy, *esp.* of the Académie Française (founded in 1635). 20c.

acanthus [Lat.] *Arch.* a conventional representation of the leaf of the plant Bear's Breech, used in the capital of the Corinthian column. 18c. As the name of the plant the word has been in use since 16c. [N,S(*)]

a cappella [It.] *Mus.* (1) (choral music) in ecclesiastical style, *usu.* unaccompanied but *occ.* with organ or orchestral accompaniment in unison with the singers; (2) = ALLA BREVE. 20c. The form *a capella* is incorrect; the earlier form *alla cappella* (19c.) is also incorrect.[N*]

accablé, *f.* **accablée** [Fr.] crushed, overwhelmed. 19c. [S]

accapareur de femmes [Fr.] a lady-killer, a 'wolf'. 20c.

accelerando [It.] *Mus.* with increasing speed. 19c. [S]

accidia/acedia [Lat. < Gk. ἀκηδία] *Theol.* (Spiritual) apathy and indifference; sloth tending towards despair. 17c. The anglicized form *accidie* was current 13c.–16c., and is still the most current form amongst non-theologians. [S]

accouchement [Fr.] child-bed, confinement. 19c. [N,S]

accoucheur, *f.* **accoucheuse** [Fr.] a man-midwife, an obstetrician; a midwife. 18c. The feminine form is of much later introduction (19c.); previously the masculine form was used for both sexes. [N,S]

acedia=ACCIDIA, (spiritual) apathy.

à chacun son goût = CHACUN À SON GOÛT, every man to his taste.

acharné, *f.* **acharnée** [Fr.] eager, relentless, ruthless. 20c.

acharnement [Fr.] ferocity, desperation. 18c. *Orig.* a military term, 'bloodthirsty fury'. [N,S]

à cheval [Fr. 'on horseback'] (1) *Mil.* (a line of troops) extending on both sides of a road or river; (2) *Roulette* (a stake placed) on the line dividing two adjacent numbers. 19c. [S(*)]

acme [Gk. ἀκμή] culmination, point of perfection. 16c. Cf. COMBLE. [NS]

à contrecœur [Fr.] reluctantly, in defiance of one's true feelings. 19c. [S]

acqua forte=AQUA FORTIS, nitric acid.

acroterion, *pl.* **acroteria** [Gk. ἀκρωτήριον] *Arch.* a pedestal for a statue at the corner of a pediment. 17c. The Latinized form *acroterium* is also in use. [N,S]

acte gratuit [Fr.] a motiveless or inconsequent act, performed on impulse. 20c. The term is borrowed from the writings of André Gide, in whose individualist morality the *acte gratuit* is a preliminary to self-control.

actualité [Fr.] topical interest, contemporary realism. 20c. Fr. *actualités* is the term for 'newsreel'.

acumen [Lat.] shrewdness, penetration. 16c. [N,S(*)]

acushla [Ir. *a chuisle* (*mo chroí*) 'O pulse (of my heart)'] darling; a common and conventional term of endearment. 19c. The full phrase *acushla mochree* is also found. The form *macushla* (Ir. *mo chuisle* 'my pulse') is *occ.* found in English, but would not be used in Irish as a form of address. Cf. ALANNA; ASTHORE; MAVOURNEEN; MOCHREE. [S]

A.D.=ANNO DOMINI, in the year of the Lord.

adagio [It. 'at leisure'] *Mus.* in slow time (slower than LARGO); a movement in slow time. 18c. First used in an English musical score by Purcell in 1683. [N,S(*)]

A.D.C.=AIDE DE CAMP, a confidential attendant.

ad captandum (vulgus) [Lat.] (an argument) intended to appeal to popular prejudice. 17c. [S]

ad clerum [Lat.] *Eccles.* (a sermon or pastoral letter) addressed to the clergy. 16c. [S(*)]

ad crumenam [Lat.] (an argument) addressed to the purse, intended to appeal to the listener's financial sense. 18c. Often *argumentum ad crumenam.* [S]

addendum, *pl.* **addenda** [Lat.] something to be added; an appendix. 17c. [N,S]

adelantado [Sp.] the governor of a (Spanish) province. 16c. [N,S]

ad eundem (gradum) [Lat. 'to the same (degree)'] (the admission of a graduate of one University) to the same degree of another without examination. 18c. [S]

à deux [Fr.] (a meeting, meal, etc.) for two persons; (two persons) in private together, without the presence of a third person; TÊTE-À-TÊTE. 19c. Cf. À TROIS. [S]

ad finem [Lat.] towards the end (of a page, chapter, etc.) 17c. Used to make a reference more precise. [S]

ad hoc [Lat.] for this special purpose or occasion. 17c. Used of a body, committee, etc., or of an argument; often with the disparaging implication of hasty improvisation. [N*,S(*)]

ad hominem [Lat. 'to the man'] (an argument) designed to appeal to the personal sentiments or prejudices of the listener. 16c. Often *argumentum ad hominem.* [S(*)]

adieu, *pl.* **adieux** [Fr. 'to God'] farewell! 14c. *Orig.* a distinction was made between *farewell!* said to the person leaving and *adieu!* said to the person remaining. The pronunciation is fully anglicized, but the word is felt to be foreign. Cf. ADIOS. [N,S]

ad infinitum [Lat.] endlessly, to infinity; forming an infinite series. 17c. [N,S]

ad inquirendum [Lat.] *Law* (a writ) ordering inquiry to be made into some matter of public interest. 17c. [S]

ad interim [Lat. 'for the meantime'] temporary, provisional(ly). 18c. [N,S]

adios [Sp.] farewell! 20c. Cf. ADIEU.

ad lib(itum) [Lat.] (1) at pleasure, as much as desired; (2) *Mus.* optional, to be played or omitted at will; the opposite of OBBLIGATO. 17c. [N,S(*)]

ad litem [Lat.] *Law* (a guardian appointed to represent an infant) in a suit or action. 18c. [S]

ad majorem Dei gloriam [Lat.] to the greater glory of God. 17c. The motto of the Society of Jesus; commonly abbreviated to *A.M.D.G.* [S]

ad misericordiam [Lat.] (a plea) for mercy; (an argument) appealing to the compassion of the listener. 19c. [S]

ad nauseam [Lat.] to the pitch of causing disgust. 17c. [N*,S(*)]

adobe [Sp.] an unbaked brick dried in the sun. 19c. Pronounced either as in Spanish or as in French. [N(*),S(*)]

ad personam [Lat.] (an argument) designed to appeal to the personal sentiments or prejudices of the listener. 20c. A variant of AD HOMINEM, used in the erroneous belief that the latter cannot be applied to a woman.

ad rem [Lat.] relevant to the subject under discussion. 17c. Cf. NIHIL AD REM. [N*,S(*)]

adscriptus glebæ, *pl.* **adscripti glebæ** [Lat.] *Hist.* bound to the land, in feudal servitude. 19c. A variant is *adstrictus glebæ*. [S(*)]

adsum [Lat.] 'I am present', *esp.* at school in responding to a roll-call. 16c. The first recorded use (Shakespeare *II Henry VI* I iv 26) is by a spirit in response to an invocation. [S]

ad usum Delphini=IN USUM DELPHINI, bowdlerized.

ad usum filioli [Lat.] for the use of a child, expurgated, bowdlerized. 19c. Cf. IN USUM DELPHINI.

ad valorem [Lat.] (a tax) proportional to the value (of the goods taxed). 17c. [N,S]

ad vitam aut culpam [Lat. 'for life or until default'] *Law* during good behaviour. 19c. [S]

ad vivum [Lat.] (painted) from the living model, life-like. 17c. Cf. AU VIF; SUR LE VIF. [S]

advocatus diaboli [Lat.] *Eccles.* the 'devil's advocate', the person appointed by the Papal CURIA to oppose a process of canonization; *hence*, a fault-finder. 19c. [S]

adytum, *pl.* **adyta** [Lat. < Gk. ἄδυτον] *Hist.* the SANCTUM or holy of holies of a pagan temple. 17c. [N,S(*)]

ægis [Lat. < Gk. αἰγίσ] shield; protection, patronage. 18c. [N,S]

ægrotat [Lat. 'he is ill'] a certificate that an undergraduate is too ill to attend University examinations; *hence*, a degree awarded without examination in case of illness. 18c. An *ægrotat* is unclassed and therefore inferior to an Honours Degree. [S]

æquam servare mentem [Lat.] to keep one's mind undisturbed. 19c.

Horace *Odes* II iii 1–2: *Æquam memento rebus in arduis Servare mentem* 'remember in troubled times to keep your mind undisturbed'.

æquo animo [Lat.] with an unruffled mind. 19c. Cicero *Ad Atticum* vi 8, Vulgate *III Kings* xxi 7, etc.; probably already a CLICHÉ.

æs alienum [Lat. 'other people's money'] debt. 19c. Cicero *Ad Familiares* v 6, but doubtless already a legal tag. [S]

æs triplex [Lat. 'triple brass'] an impenetrable defence. 19c. Horace *Odes* I iii 9.

ætat(is suæ) [Lat.] aged . . .; always followed by a number. 17c. Cf. ANNO ÆTATIS SUÆ. [S]

affairé, *f.* **affairée** [Fr.] busy, preoccupied. 20c. Often with the implication that the preoccupation is to some extent assumed.

affaire (de cœur) [Fr.] a love affair. 19c. The French phrase may imply a more sentimental attachment than its English equivalent. [S(*)]

affaire d'honneur [Fr.] a matter of honour, *esp.* a duel. 19c. [S]

Affektenlehre [Ger.] *Psych.* the theory of the emotions. 20c. Applied *esp.* to the theory developed by Philipp Lersch (b.1898).

affiche [Fr.] a notice or advertisement fastened or pasted to a wall, etc. 18c. [N*,S]

affiché, *f.* **affichée** [Fr.] conspicuous, notorious (in one's relationship to another person). 20c.

affidavit [Lat. 'he (she) has affirmed'] *Law* a deposition made under oath before a magistrate or commissioner for oaths. 16c. The phrase 'to swear (*or* make) an *affidavit*' is sometimes incorrectly replaced by 'to take an *affidavit*'. [N,S]

afflatus [Lat. 'breathing on'] poetic or prophetic inspiration. 17c. [N,S(*)]

afición [Sp. 'affection'] an eager and informed interest in bull-fighting. 20c. Popularized by Ernest Hemingway's *Fiesta* (1926).

aficionado, *f.* **aficionada** [Sp.] having AFICIÓN, devoted to bull-fighting; *hence*, taking an eager and informed interest in any pursuit; a 'fan'. 20c. Cf. PASSIONNÉ.

à fleur d'eau [Fr.] just at water-level. 19c.

à fond (perdu) [Fr.] to the bottom, thoroughly. 19c.

a fortiori [Lat.] *Logic* all the more; *usu.* in the form 'if A is true, then *all the more* must B be true'. 16c. [N,S]

agape, *pl.* **agapæ** [Gk. ἀγάπη] *Eccles.* a 'love-feast', a charitable repast which in the early Church accompanied the Eucharist. 16c. [N,S]

agapemone [Gk. ἀγάπη + μονή] 'abode of love', the name given to the settlement in Somerset founded by H. J. Prince in 1845 for the practice of free love. See W. H. Dixon *Spiritual Wives* (1868). [N*,S]

agar-agar [Mal.] an East-Indian seaweed from which is extracted a gelatinous substance used for dressing silk and in the preparation of cultures of BACTERIA. 19c. [N*,S]

agenda *pl.* [Lat.] things to be done; items of business to be transacted at a meeting. 17c. The singular *agendum* seems not to be in use. [N(*),S(*)]

agent provocateur [Fr.] a person who incites another to commit a crime so as to secure evidence sufficient for conviction. 19c. [N*]

aggiornamento [It.] bringing up to date, modernization. 20c. The term employed to describe the policy of church reform adopted by the Second Vatican Council.

agitato [It.] *Mus.* in an agitated manner, expressing emotion and perturbation. 19c. [N,S]

Agnus Dei [Lat.] a part of the Mass consisting of three versicles beginning with the words *Agnus Dei* 'Lamb of God'; *hence*, a musical setting of these versicles. 14c. Vulgate *St John* i 29. [N,S(*)]

à gogo [Fr.] galore, in plenty. 20c. The phrase became familiar in England through the French title *Whisky à Gogo* of Sir Compton Mackenzie's *Whisky Galore*.

agon, *pl.* **agones** [Gk. ἀγών] *Hist.* a public celebration of games in ancient Greece; *hence*, a contest, a struggle. 17c. [N,S]

agonistes [Gk. ἀγωνιστής] an athlete, a wrestler; *hence*, a person at grips with some powerful and inimical force. 17c. Familiar from Milton's *Samson Agonistes* (1671).

agora [Gk. ἀγορά] *Hist.* a market-place, a place of assembly. 16c. Cf. FORUM. [N,S(*)]

agoraphobia [Gk. ἀγορά + φοβία] *Psych.* a morbid fear of open places. 19c. [N]

à grands frais [Fr.] at great expense. 19c.

agraphon, *pl.* **agrapha** [Gk. ἄγραφον] *Rel.* an uncanonical saying of Christ; an item of traditional information about Christ. 19c. First used in 1776 by J. G. Körner; brought into general usage by Alfred Resch in 1889.

agrégé, *f.* **agrégée** [Fr.] successful at the *concours d'agrégation*, a competitive examination for teaching posts. 20c. The nearest English equivalent is *M.A.*, but the competitive element is absent from English degrees.

agréments *pl.* [Fr.] (1) the refinements of social life, courtesies; (2) *Mus.* ornaments in harpsichord music. 18c. The earlier spelling was *agrémens*. [S]

agrogorod [Russ.] a Soviet agricultural 'new town'. 20c.

aguardiente [Sp.] a fiery liquor distilled from grain or potatoes. 19c. [N*,S]

ahimsa [Sansk. *ahiṃsā*] *Rel.* harmlessness, the Hindu doctrine of the sacredness of life. 20c. A leading tenet of the Jain sect.

à huis clos [Fr.] behind closed doors, in secret. 19c. Cf. IN CAMERA; JANUIS CLAUSIS. [S]

aide (de camp), *pl.* **aides (de camp)** [Fr.] *Mil.* an officer in attendance on a general; a confidential attendant. 17c. *Usu.* abbreviated to *A.D.C.* [N,S(*)]

aide-mémoire [Fr.] a help to the memory, a note of headings (for a speech, etc.); a mnemonic; a detailed diplomatic note sent to a foreign government. 19c. [N*,S]

aigre-doux [Fr.] bitter-sweet. 19c. [N,S]

aigrette [Fr. 'egret'] a bunch of feathers, cluster of jewels, etc., worn on the head as an ornament. 17c. [N,S]

aigreur [Fr.] tartness, bitterness (of tone, speech, manner, etc.) 19c. [S]

aiguille [Fr. 'needle'] a sharply-pointed mountain-peak. 19c. [N,S]

aiguillette [Fr.] (1) *Mil.* a tagged braid on a full-dress uniform; (2) *Cul.* a small strip of cooked meat or fish. 19c. [N,S(*)]

aîné [Fr.] (the) elder; always preceded by a name, and opposed to CADET '(the) younger'. 19c. Cf. FILS; PÈRE. [S]

akvavit [Dan.] an ardent spirit flavoured with caraway seed. 20c. From the Latin AQUA VITÆ.

à la [Fr.] after the manner of; as prepared for, or by; always followed by a name. 17c. The phrase is short for *à la mode de*; hence the feminine article *la* is appropriate even when followed by a masculine name. [N,S]

à la bonne heure [Fr. 'at the right time'] well done!; capital! 18c. [S]

à la carte [Fr.] according to the (itemized) menu, each dish charged for separately in the account. 19c. Opposed to TABLE D'HÔTE; PRIX FIXE. [N*,S]

à la guerre comme à la guerre [Fr. 'in war as in war'] one must take the rough with the smooth. 20c. Cf. C'EST LA GUERRE.

à la lanterne [Fr. 'to the lamp'] (let him be hanged) from the lamp-chain! 19c. Many of the victims of the French Revolution were hanged from the chains supporting the street-lamps; the phrase occurs in the refrain of the revolutionary song ÇA IRA. Cf. AU POTEAU. [S]

alambiqué [Fr. 'distilled'] over-refined, over-subtle. 18c. [S]

à la mode [Fr.] in the fashion, fashionable. 17c. [N,S]

alanna [Ir. *a leinbh* 'O baby'] darling; a common and conventional term of endearment. 19c. The English form is perhaps rather from *a lenbh*, grammatically incorrect in Irish. Cf. ACUSHLA; ASTHORE; MOCHREE.

à la page [Fr.] up to date, in the know, familiar with the latest fashions. 20c.

à la recherche du temps perdu [Fr.] in quest of the past. 20c. From the general title of the sequence of novels by Marcel Proust, translated by C. K. Scott Moncrieff as 'Remembrance of Things Past'. The phrase is often used with reference to Proust's view that trivial sensations may produce 'involuntary memory' and vividly re-create past experiences.

à la rigueur [Fr.] if absolutely necessary. 20c.

a latere [Lat. 'from the side (of the Pope)'] *Eccles.* (a Cardinal legate) having plenipotentiary powers. 16c. Cf. LEGATUS A LATERE. [S(*)]

alberello, *pl.* **alberelli** [It.] a jar of glass or earthenware designed for holding medicinal substances. 20c.

albino [Port.] (an animal or human being) lacking pigment in skin, hair and eyes. 18c. [N,S]

album [Lat. 'white'] a blank book into which are inserted autographs, verses, photographs, postage-stamps, etc. 17c. *Orig.* a tablet on which public notices, etc., were inscribed. [N,S(*)]

al dente [It.] *Cul.* cooked so as to be firm to the tooth, not too soft. 20c.

alea jacta est=JACTA EST ALEA, the die is cast.

à l'étroit [Fr.] in straitened circumstances. 20c.

al fresco [It.] in the open air; open-air. 18c. Sometimes written as one word *alfresco.* Cf. EN PLEIN AIR. [N,S(*)]

algæ *pl.* [Lat.] sea-weed or fresh-water weeds. 16c. The singular *alga* seems not now to be in use. [N,S]

alias [Lat. 'otherwise'] otherwise known as . . .; an assumed name. 16c. Often with the implication that the assumption of an alternative name is for criminal purposes. The plural is *aliases.* [N,S]

alibi [Lat. 'elsewhere'] *Law* the plea of having been elsewhere at the time a crime was committed. 18c. The use of the word in the general sense 'excuse' is increasingly common, but is to be reprehended. [N,S]

à l'impériale [Fr.] in the imperial manner, as it was done in the (British) Empire. 20c.

à l'improviste [Fr.] unexpectedly; on the spur of the moment. 20c.

aliquot [Lat. 'so many'] in the phrase '*aliquot* part', contained in a greater quantity an integral number of times. 16c. [N,S]

alla breve [It.] *Mus.* a TEMPO of two minims to the bar; quick common time. 18c. *Orig.* a *tempo* of four minims or one breve to the bar; the breve, in spite of its name, being the longest note now in use. [N,S]

alla marcia [It.] *Mus.* in the style of a march. 19c.

alla prima [It.] *Art* (a technique of painting in which the picture is completed) in one session, so that all under-painting, etc. is obliterated. 20c. The technique was not used for finished painting until the nineteenth century. Cf. AU PREMIER COUP.

allée [Fr.] an avenue; a path between trees and shrubs. 18c. [S]

allegretto [It.] *Mus.* in moderately fast time (slower than ALLEGRO); a movement in moderately fast time. 18c. [S]

allegro [It. 'cheerful'] *Mus.* in quick time, lively; a movement in quick time. 18c. First used in an English musical score by Purcell in 1683. [S]

allocutus [Lat.] *Law* advice to a criminal convicted of felony that he is entitled to make a plea in bar or mitigation of sentence. 20c.

allonge [Fr.] a slip of paper pasted to the end of a bill of exchange or promissory note to make room for further endorsements. 19c. [N,S]

allumeuse [Fr.] a pathological flirt, a woman who excites men's passions with no intention of satisfying them. 20c.

allure [Fr.] behaviour; the sum of physical features and mannerisms which reveal the personality. 19c. The primary meaning in French is 'gait'; the full extension of meaning is peculiar to English. [N,S]

alluvium, *pl.* **alluvia** [Lat.] *Geog.* a deposit of earth or sand formed in a river valley or delta. 17c. [N,S]

alma mater [Lat. 'bounteous mother'] a title given to Universities, Colleges and Schools, looked on as the foster-mothers of their ALUMNI. 18c. Now hardly used except with a flavour of irony. [N,S]

aloha [Haw. 'love'] greetings! farewell! 20c. A common form of salutation in Hawaii.

à l'outrance [Fr. *à outrance*] to the bitter end. 19c. The form *à l'outrance* is so well established in English that to insist on *à outrance* is pedantry. [S(*)]

Alpenhorn [Ger.] *Mus.* a primitive Swiss wind-instrument playing only the notes of the natural scale. 19c. Cf. RANZ-DES-VACHES. [N*]

Alpenstock [Ger.] a stick fitted with an iron point used in mountain-climbing. 19c. An earlier name was *bâton ferré.* Cf. STOCK. [N,S]

alta moda [It.] fashionable dress-designing, dress-designing considered as a fine art. 20c. Now replacing HAUTE COUTURE because of the growing influence of Italian designers.

alter ego [Lat. 'other self'] an intimate and trusted friend. 16c. Used by Cicero, but a translation of Greek *ἄλλος ἐγώ, ἕτερος ἐγώ. Occ.* misused in the sense 'secondary personality'. [N*,S(*)]

alternatim [Lat.] *Mus.* alternately (of two choirs, orchestras, etc.) 20c.

altiplano [Sp.] an elevated tract of level land, a PLATEAU, *esp.* in South America. 20c.

alto, *pl.* **alti** [It. 'high'] *Mus.* the highest male voice, the counter-tenor; a singer having such a voice; (an instrument) having a compass similar to that of the highest male voice. 18c. The use of *alto* for CONTRALTO is confusing and should be avoided. [N,S]

alto rilievo [It.] *Art* high relief, sculpture in which the figures project more than half their true proportion from the surface. 17c. Formerly often written *alto relievo.* Cf. BASSO RILIEVO; CAVO RILIEVO; MEZZO RILIEVO; SCHIACCIATO RILIEVO. [N,S]

alumnus, *pl.* **alumni** [Lat. 'foster-child'] a student of a University; a pupil of a school. 17c. The feminine *alumna,* pl. *alumnæ,* is *U.S.* only. Cf. ALMA MATER. [N(*),S]

a.m.=ANTE MERIDIEM, before noon.

amah [Port. *ama* 'nurse'] *A.-I.* a native wet-nurse. 19c. Distinct from AYAH 'nurse-maid, lady's maid'; but the distinction is not always clearly maintained. [N,S]

amant attitré [Fr.] an official lover, one who defrays the expenses of a lady of easy virtue. 20c. Cf. MAÎTRESSE EN TITRE.

amant de cœur [Fr.] a chosen lover; a lover taken in addition to, and *usu.* without the knowledge of, the AMANT ATTITRÉ. 20c.

amanuensis, *pl.* **amanuenses** [Lat.] one who writes from dictation or makes a fair copy of a draft. 17c. [N,S]

amateur [Fr. 'lover'] one who follows any pursuit as a pastime; one who is not a professional; *hence*, one who is careless or inefficient. 18c. The etymological sense (e.g. 'an *amateur* of painting') is now hardly in use except in the combination GRAND AMATEUR. Cf. DILETTANTE. [N,S(*)]

amazone [Fr.] *Equ.* a riding-habit. 19c. [S]

ambiance [Fr.] atmosphere (in the metaphorical sense). 20c. The connotation of *ambiance* is more extensive and general than that of *atmosphere*. Cf. AMBIENTE. [N*]

ambiente [It.] atmosphere (in the metaphorical sense); the circumstances and surroundings which affect one's life. 20c. Not identical in connotation with AMBIANCE.

ambo, *pl.* **ambones** [Lat. < Gk. ἄμβων] *Hist.* the reading-desk in an early Christian church. 17c. [N,S]

ambrosia [Gk. ἀμβροσία] *Myth.* the food of the Gods (in Classical mythology); *hence*, any delicious comestible. 16c. Cf. NECTAR. [N,S]

A.M.D.G.=AD MAJOREM DEI GLORIAM, to the greater glory of God.

âme damnée [Fr. 'damned soul'] one who is entirely and unscrupulously devoted to the interests of another. 19c. [S]

âme d'élite [Fr.] a soul specially marked out (for spiritual favours). 20c. Cf. ÉLITE.

âme incomprise [Fr.] one whose spiritual or intellectual aspirations are misunderstood or denigrated by his associates. 20c.

amende honorable [Fr.] a public apology for an insult or offence, with or without reparation. 17c. [N,S]

a mensa et thoro [Lat. 'from board and bed'] *Law* (a dispensation to man and wife) from the obligation to cohabit. 17c. Used of a judicial separation as distinct from a divorce. The spelling *toro* is also in use; but the (less correct) *thoro* is sanctioned by usage. [S]

à merveille [Fr.] wonderfully well. 18c. [S]

amicus curiæ, *pl.* **amici curiæ** [Lat.] *Law* a friend of the Court, one who advises the Court in an action in which he has no interest. 17c. [S]

amie [Fr.] a mistress. 18c. Cf. PETITE AMIE. [S]

amitié amoureuse [Fr.] a friendship (between man and woman) with a sentimental or erotic element. 20c.

amnesia [Gk. ἀμνησία] (1) forgetfulness; (2) *Med.* loss of memory. 17c. [N,S]

amœba, *pl.* **amœbæ** [Lat. < Gk. ἀμοιβή 'change'] a single-cell animalcule of inconstant shape. 19c. [N]

amontillado [Sp.] a dry, nutty sherry from the hill-districts of Montilla in Spain; *hence*, dry (in manner, style, etc.) 19c. [N*,S]

amoretto, *pl.* **amoretti** [It.] a Cupid (in decoration, sculpture, etc.) 17c. The form *amorello* is also found, but is not Italian. Cf. AMORINO; PUTTO. [N,S]

amorino, *pl.* **amorini** [It.] a Cupid (in decoration, sculpture, etc.) 19c. Cf. AMORETTO; PUTTO. [N,S]

amor patriæ [Lat.] love of the fatherland, patriotism. 18c. [S]

amour [Fr. 'love'] an illicit love-affair, an intrigue. 17c. Naturalized in 14c. in its etymological sense, without implications of immorality; re-introduced in the pejorative sense. [N,S]

amour courtois [Fr.] 'courtly love', the mediæval social and literary convention in which love assumes a quasi-feudal aspect. 20c. Cf. FRAUENDIENST.

amour de voyage [Fr.] a temporary infatuation such as is frequently experienced in the course of a sea-voyage. 20c.

amourette [Fr.] a trivial love-affair. 19c. [N,S]

amour propre [Fr.] self-love, self-esteem; desire for admiration. 19c. [N,S]

amphora, *pl.* **amphoræ** [Lat.] *Hist.* a two-handled vessel used in Classical antiquity for holding wine, oil, etc. 15c. [N,S]

ampoule [Fr.] (1) *Eccles.* a vessel for holding consecrated oil. 17c. (2) *Med.* a glass bulb containing a drug. 20c. [N,S]

anabasis [Gk. ἀνάβασις 'going up'] a military advance. 19c. From the title of Xenophon's description of the advance of Cyrus into Asia (401 B.C.) Cf. KATABASIS. [N,S]

anacoluthon, *pl.* **anacolutha** [Lat. < Gk. ἀνακόλουθον] *Ling.* want of grammatical sequence; the juxtaposition of two incomplete constructions. 18c. [N,S]

anacrusis, *pl.* **anacruses** [Lat. < Gk. ἀνάκρουσις] (1) *Ling.* one or more extra-metrical syllables at the beginning of a line of verse; (2) *Mus.* the part of a piece of music before the first strong beat. 19c. Cf. AUFTAKT. [N,S]

anæsthesia [Lat. < Gk. ἀναισθησία] (1) absence of feeling, insensibility; (2) *Med.* the artificial production of insensibility to pain. 19c. [N,S]

ananke [Gk. ἀνάγκη] absolute necessity, the force of destiny to which even the Gods are subject. 19c. *Usu.* written in Greek characters. [S]

anathema [Gk. ἀνάθεμα] *Eccles.* the curse of God; ecclesiastical excommunication; *hence*, any imprecation; something to be hated; detestable. 16c. [N,S]

anathema sit [Gk. + Lat.] *Eccles.* 'let him be accursed!', the formula of ecclesiastical excommunication. 16c. Vulgate *I Corinthians* xvi 22.

anchylosis, *see* ANKYLOSIS, the stiffening of a joint.

ancien régime [Fr.] the old RÉGIME, the state of affairs in France before the French Revolution; *hence*, the state of affairs in existence before any significant date. 18c. [S]

andante [It. 'going'] *Mus.* in moderately slow time (slower than ALLEGRETTO); a movement in moderately slow time. 18c. [N,S]

andantino [It.] *Mus.* in moderately slow time (slower than ANDANTE); a movement in *andantino* time. 19c. Confusingly, *andantino* is sometimes intended to mean 'rather faster than *andante*'. [N,S]

angelus [Lat.] *Eccles.* the sequence of prayers beginning *angelus Domini nuntiavit Mariæ*, recited at 6 a.m., noon and 6 p.m. at the sound of a bell; *hence*, the bell rung as a signal for these prayers. 17c. [N,S]

angina (pectoris) [Lat. 'strangling (of the breast)'] *Med.* a dangerous heart-disease characterized by acute pain near the heart. 18c. The accepted English pronunciation *angīna* is due to an erroneous belief that the second vowel was long in Latin. [N,S]

Anglice [Lat.] in English; properly introducing the translation of a foreign phrase, but often ironically in explanation of a solecism. 17c. [S]

Angst [Ger.] anguish, fear, anxiety, disquiet. *usu.* without obvious cause; a feeling of estrangement from a hostile world. 20c. Popularized by Cyril Connolly's *The Unquiet Grave* (1944) and by post-war interest in Existentialism.

anguis in herba [Lat.] a snake in the grass. 16c. The full phrase is LATET ANGUIS IN HERBA. [S]

angulus terrarum [Lat.] a (favourite or familiar) corner of the earth, the place in which one feels most at home. 20c. Horace *Odes* II vi 13–14: *Ille terrarum mihi præter omnis Angulus ridet* 'that corner of the earth smiles for me more than all others'.

anima [Lat.] (1) the animal soul, the soul shared by mankind with the animal kingdom; (2) *Psych.* the true inner self, the inward personality. 20c. In the first sense contrasted with ANIMUS, in the second with PERSONA. Cf. PSYCHE.

anima naturaliter Christiana [Lat.] a soul naturally Christian, one who practises the Christian virtues without the help of the Christian revelation. 20c. Tertullian *Apologia* xvii.

animateur [Fr.] a writer or dramatist capable of presenting abstruse and complicated philosophical ideas in clear, vivid and attractive form. 20c. Cf. HAUTE VULGARISATION; VULGARISATEUR.

animus [Lat. 'mind'] (1) animosity, hostility, malice. 19c. (2) Creative breadth of vision. 20c. (3) the rational soul. 20c. In the third sense contrasted with ANIMA. Cf. PNEUMA. [N,S]

animus furandi [Lat.] *Law* the intention of stealing, the state of mind which converts mere removal into theft. 19c. [S]

animus revertendi [Lat.] *Law* the intention to return home, the habit in domesticated animals of seeking shelter where they were reared. 17c. [S]

animus revocandi [Lat.] *Law* the intention of revoking (a will, codicil, etc.) 19c.

ankylosis [Gk. *ἀγκύλωσις*] *Med.* the stiffening of a joint, the growing together of two bones not normally united. 18c. The earlier (less correct) spelling *anchylosis* has now very generally been given up. [N,S]

anna [Hind. *ānā*] *A.-I.* a coin worth one sixteenth of a RUPEE. 18c. [N,S]

anno ætatis suæ [Lat.] in the year of his (her) age . . ., aged . . .; always followed by a number. 17c. Cf. ÆTATIS SUÆ.

anno Domini [Lat.] (1) in the year of our Lord . . ., in the year of the Christian era . . .; always followed by a date. 16c. (2) *facet.* the approach of old age. 19c. In the first sense normally abbreviated to *A.D.* [N(*),S(*)]

anno regni [Lat.] in the year of the reign . . .; always followed by a number. 19c.

annulus, *pl.* **annuli** [Lat.] a ring or ring-shaped formation (in various technical applications). 16c. The Latin word is a mediæval error for Classical *anulus*, but the form is well established in English. [N,S]

annus mirabilis, *pl.* **anni mirabiles** [Lat.] a wonderful or remarkable year, *esp.* the year 1666. 17c. First used in Evelyn's *Diary* 1659–60; the title of a poem by Dryden (1667). [N,S]

anonyma [Pseudo-Gk.] a fashionable woman of ill fame; an amateur prostitute. 19c. [S]

anonymus, *pl.* **anonymi** [Lat. < Gk. *ἀνώνυμος*] one whose name is unknown or concealed; *esp.* a painter or sculptor whose work can be recognized but whose name is unknown. 16c. [S]

anorak [Esk. *ánorâq*] a light waterproof jacket with a hood, for use out of doors in bleak weather. 20c. The Eskimo *anorak* was originally made of skins. The spelling *anarak* is erroneous. Cf. PARKA.

Anschluss [Ger.] the union of Austria with Germany, *esp.* that achieved under the National Socialist RÉGIME in 1938. 19c.

an sich [Ger.] in itself, in its true nature. 20c. Cf. DING AN SICH.

ante [Lat.] (1) before . . . (giving a TERMINUS AD QUEM); always followed by a date; (2) above, previously mentioned. 19c. [S]

ante meridiem [Lat.] before noon. 16c. *Usu.* abbreviated to *a.m.* Cf. POST MERIDIEM. [S(*)]

antenna, *pl.* **antennæ** [Lat. 'yardarm'] a projecting sensory organ found in various living beings; *hence*, a sensitive mechanical device of similar form, a wireless aerial. 17c. [N(*),S]

anti [Gk. ἀντι-] against, opposed to. 20c. The prefix *anti-* is of great antiquity in English; in 19c. it came to be used as an independent noun meaning 'one who is opposed to something'; the common adjectival use is of recent origin. [N*]

antipasto, *pl.* **antipasti** [It.] *Cul.* an appetizing dish eaten at the beginning of a meal; HORS D'ŒUVRE. 16c. [S]

antipodes *pl.* [Gk. ἀντίποδες] parts of the terrestrial sphere directly opposite our own. 16c. An earlier meaning in English, now obsolete, was 'people living on the opposite side of the earth'. [N,S(*)]

antistrophe [Gk. ἀντιστροφή] *Ling.* part of a metrical composition corresponding in rhythm to the STROPHE. 17c. [N,S]

antithesis, *pl.* **antitheses** [Gk. ἀντίθεσις] *Logic* a contrast of ideas; two propositions juxtaposed so as to reveal their dissimilarity. 16c. [N,S(*)]

anus [Lat.] the posterior opening in animals through which excrement is ejected. 16c. [N,S]

aorta [Lat. < Gk. ἀορτή] *Med.* the great artery leading from the left ventricle of the heart.

à outrance, *see* À L'OUTRANCE, to the bitter end.

apache [Fr.] a ruffian, *esp.* one haunting Paris or other cities; a person who treats women with violence; (a dance) in which the male simulates cruelty towards the female partner. 20c. *Orig.* the name of a warlike tribe of American Indians. [N*]

apartheid [Afrik. 'separation'] the system of rigorous segregation between Europeans and others practised by the Government of South Africa. 20c.

aperçu [Fr.] an intuitive understanding; an inspired appreciation; a general survey. 19c. [N,S]

apéritif [Fr.] an alcoholic drink taken before a meal to stimulate the appetite. 19c. Commonly a fortified wine flavoured with (bitter) herbs. [N*]

à perte de vue [Fr.] as far as the eye can see. 18c. [S*]

Apfelstrudel [Ger.] *Cul.* a sweetmeat made of cooked apple and flaky pastry. 20c. *Strudel* in German means 'whirlpool', but in South German dialects 'flaky pastry'.

aphasia [Gk. ἀφασία] *Med.* loss of the faculty of speech, dumbness. 19c. [N,S]

aplomb [Fr.] self-assurance, self-possession. 19c. [N,S]

apocrypha *pl.* [Lat. < Gk. ἀπόκρυφα] writings of doubtful authorship or authenticity; *esp.* those books of Holy Scripture excluded from the canon by the Reformers. 16c. The singular *apocryphon* is now obsolete; *apocrypha* is normally construed with a plural verb, but sometimes with a singular, in which case a plural *apocryphas* may be used. [N,S(*)]

apodyterium [Lat. < Gk. ἀποδυτήριον] *Hist.* the dressing-room for those about to make use of the Greek or Roman baths or PALÆSTRA. 17c. [N,S]

apologia [Gk. ἀπολογία] a written defence of the opinions or conduct, *usu.* of the writer, but *occ.* of another. 19c. Popularized in English by the success of Cardinal Newman's *Apologia pro Vita Sua* (1864). [N*,S]

aposiopesis, *pl.* **aposiopeses** [Gk. ἀποσιώπησις] *Ling.* breaking off in the middle of a sentence. 16c. [N,S]

a posteriori [Lat.] *Logic* (argument or reasoning) from effects to causes; inductively. 16c. Cf. A PRIORI. [N,S(*)]

apotheosis, *pl.* **apotheoses** [Gk. ἀποθέωσις] deification; the supreme exaltation of a principle or person. 16c. Often misused as if it meant 'an outstanding example'. [N,S]

apparat [Russ.] the Soviet bureaucracy. 20c.

apparatchik [Russ.] a member of the Soviet bureaucracy. 20c.

apparatus, *pl.* **apparatus** [Lat.] (1) materials and instruments required for a specific purpose, *esp.* the requisites for a scientific experiment; (2)= APPARATUS CRITICUS. 17c. [N,S]

apparatus criticus, *pl.* **apparatus critici** [Lat.] materials for the critical study of a document, *esp.* palæographical and critical notes designed to assist the study of a text printed from manuscript. 18c. [N(*),S]

appartement [Fr.] a suite of rooms occupied by an individual or family. 19c. An *appartement* is more select and luxurious than a flat, and is *usu.* located abroad. [S]

appartement de parade [Fr.] a suite of elegant reception rooms. 20c. Cf. BEL ÉTAGE; PIANO NOBILE.

appartement meublé [Fr.] a furnished flat, *esp.* one provided by a wealthy lover for his mistress. 20c. Cf. PETITE MAISON.

appliqué [Fr.] a pattern produced by stitching designs cut from one material on to another. 18c. [N,S(*)]

appoggiatura, *pl.* **appoggiature** [It.] *Mus.* a grace-note which takes the accent and part of the time-value from the following note. 18c. [N,S]

après coup [Fr.] as an afterthought, late in the day. 19c. [S]

après nous le déluge [Fr.] after us the deluge, when we are dead let the heavens fall. 19c. Attributed to Mme de Pompadour (1721–64) by Mme de Hausset *Mémoires* (1824) 19; often misquoted as *après moi le déluge*. [S]

après-ski [Fr. + Norw.] recreation after skiing, *usu.* comprising dancing and drinking; (clothes, etc.) designed for such recreation; to take part in such recreation. 20c.

a priori [Lat.] *Logic* (argument or reasoning) from causes to effects; deductively; presumptively, in accordance with general probability. 17c. Cf. A POSTERIORI. [N,S]

à propos [Fr.] pertinent(ly), opportune(ly); in the nick of time. 17c. *Occ.* written as a single word *apropos*. The usage '*à propos* of . . .' seems to be obsolete. Cf. MAL À PROPOS. [N,S(*)]

à propos de bottes [Fr. 'talking of boots'] by the way, to change the subject (where the sequence of ideas has no logical connection). 18c. The phrase is found in J.-F. Reynard's play *Le Distrait* (1697). [S]

à propos de rien [Fr.] *à propos* of nothing, while I think of it. 20c. Less facetious than À PROPOS DE BOTTES.

à pur et à plein [Fr.] pure and simple; completely, without any doubt. 20c. The phrase is obsolete in current French.

aqua fortis [Lat. 'strong water'] nitric acid; a powerful solvent or corrosive. 16c. The Italian form *acqua forte* is also occasionally used. Cf. EAU FORTE. [N,S]

aqua regia [Lat. 'royal water'] a mixture of nitric acid and hydrochloric acid which will dissolve gold and platinum. 17c. [N,S]

aquarelle [Fr. 'water-colour'] *Art* a method of painting in which a drawing in waterproof ink is tinted with transparent water-colour. 19c. [N,S]

aquarium, *pl.* **aquaria** [Lat.] a glass tank for the preservation and observation of water-creatures. 19c. Introduced about 1854 to replace the earlier 'marine VIVARIUM' or 'aquatic VIVARIUM'; an alternative form, soon displaced, was *aquavivarium.* [N,S]

a quattr' occhi [It. 'between four eyes'] (two people) face to face, in private conversation. 19c. Cf. TÊTE-À-TÊTE. [S]

aqua vitæ [Lat. 'water of life'] ardent spirits, *esp.* brandy, but also whisky. 15c. *Orig.* an alchemical term for unrectified alcohol. Cf. AKVAVIT. [N,S]

aquila [Lat. 'eagle'] a lectern in a church. 20c. So called because such lecterns are often designed in the form of an eagle with wings outspread.

à quoi bon? [Fr.] what's the use? 20c.

arabesque [Fr.] (1) *Art* a form of surface decoration consisting of intricate and fanciful tracery. 17c. (2) *Ballet* a pose in which one leg and both arms are fully extended so as to give the longest possible line from finger-tip to toe. 20c. [N(*),S(*)]

arabesque fondue [Fr.] *Ballet* an ARABESQUE performed with the leg on which the body is supported bent instead of straight. 20c.

arabesque penchée [Fr.] *Ballet* an ARABESQUE performed with the body bent forwards instead of vertical. 20c.

arak [Arab. *'araq* 'juice'] an Oriental ardent spirit distilled from the sap of the palm-tree or from rice and sugar. 17c. Formerly spelt *arrack*. Cf. RAKI. [N,S]

arbiter [Lat.] a judge, *usu.* of a question of taste. 16c. Some former senses have now been taken over by *arbitrator*. [N,S]

arbiter elegantiarum [Lat.] a judge of good taste, one whose opinion is deferred to in matters of æsthetics. 19c. Tacitus *Annals* xvi 18: ELEGANTIÆ ARBITER. [S]

arbitrium [Lat.] power to decide or act, absolute authority. 18c. [S]

arboretum, *pl.* **arboreta** [Lat.] a garden devoted to the cultivation and display of rare trees. 19c. [N,S]

Arcades ambo [Lat. 'both Arcadians'] (two people) having tastes in common, *esp.* æsthetic or literary tastes. 19c. Virgil *Eclogues* vii 4. [N*,S]

arcanum, *pl.* **arcana** [Lat.] a secret, a mystery. 16c. More often in the plural than in the singular. [N,S]

arcanum imperii, *pl.* **arcana imperii** [Lat.] a secret of state. 17c. Now nearly always in the plural. [S]

arcus senilis [Lat.] *Med.* a narrow yellowish band gradually encircling the CORNEA with advancing age. 20c.

à rebours [Fr.] against the grain, perversely. 20c. Often with implicit reference to the novel by J.-K. Huysmans (1884) of which this is the title.

arête [Fr.] *Geog.* a knife-edge mountain ridge. 19c. The word was *orig.* peculiar to French Switzerland, but has been disseminated by climbers. [N,S]

argot [Fr.] a form of jargon or slang peculiar to some class of people, *orig.* and *esp.* thieves. 19c. A class dialect as distinct from a PATOIS or local dialect. [N,S]

argumentum, *see* AD CRUMENAM; AD HOMINEM.

argumentum a silentio [Lat.] an argument based on the failure of some authority to refer to the point at issue. 20c. Cf. EX SILENTIO.

aria, *pl.* **arie** [It.] *Mus.* a song, *esp.* (in opera) a solo song contrasted with the recitative which precedes it. 18c. [S]

arietta, *pl.* **ariette** [It.] *Mus.* a short ARIA. 18c. [S]

arioso [It.] *Mus.* a style of singing between ARIA and recitative; (instrumental music) in a vocal style. 18c. Cf. SPRECHGESANG. [N,S]

a rivederci [It. 'until we meet again'] farewell! 17c. Also written *arrivederci.* A common form of farewell in many languages: cf. AUF WIEDERSEHEN; AU REVOIR; HASTA LA VISTA. [S]

armoire [Fr.] a free-standing cupboard. 16c. The only word in English use which distinguishes a free-standing from a built-in cupboard. [N,S]

aroma [Gk. ἄρωμα] fragrance; an elusive charm. 18c. [N,S]

arpeggio, *pl.* **arpeggi** [It.] *Mus.* playing the notes of a chord in succession instead of together; a broken chord. 18c. [N,S]

arricciato/arricciatura/arriccio [It.] *Art* the layer of rough plaster beneath the INTONACO on which the FRESCO is painted. 20c. Strictly *arricciato* refers to the wall when the application of the *arricciatura* is completed, but the words are not clearly distinguished in English. Cf. GESSO GROSSO; RINZAFFATO.

arriéré [Fr.] backward, behind the times, old-fashioned. 20c.

arrière-goût [Fr.] an after-taste, *esp.* an unpleasant after-taste. 20c.

arrière-pensée [Fr.] a mental reservation, an ulterior motive. 19c. [N*,S]

arrière-plan [Fr.] *Art* background. 20c.

arrivé, *f.* **arrivée** [Fr.] successful, having made one's way, having established a position in the world. 20c.

arrivederci=A RIVEDERCI, farewell!

arriviste [Fr.] determined to succeed, on the make; a careerist. 20c. [N*]

arrondissement [Fr.] an administrative subdivision of the departments of France, *esp.* one of the subdivisions of Paris corresponding roughly to 'postal districts'. 19c. [N,S]

arroyo [Sp.] *U.S.* a gully, the dried-up bed of a stream. 19c. [N(*),S]

ars est celare artem [Lat.] (true) art is to conceal art; the finest art seems the most natural and inevitable. 17c. Also formerly *artis est celare artem;* the origin of the phrase is unknown. [S]

ars gratia artis [Lat.] art for art's sake. 19c. Cf. L'ART POUR L'ART.

arsis, *pl.* **arses** [Gk. ἄρσις] (1) *Ling.* a stressed syllable in metre; (2) *Mus.* the first note of the bar, the beat; always in contrast to THESIS. 14c. By some writers the meanings of *arsis* and *thesis* are interchanged, and they are therefore best avoided. Cf. ICTUS. [N,S]

ars longa, vita brevis [Lat.] art is long, life is short. 16c. Translated into English by Chaucer as 'the lyf so short, the craft so long to lerne'. Seneca *De Brevitate Vitæ* 1: *vita brevis est, longa ars.* A translation of Hippocrates *Aphorisms* i 1: ὁ βίος βραχύσ, ἡ δὲ τέχνη μακρή. [S]

ars nova [Lat. 'new art'] *Mus.* the polyphonic music of the later Middle Ages, as contrasted with the ORGANUM it displaced. 20c.

art autre [Fr. 'other art'] *Art* a new movement in painting developed after the Second World War. 20c. An example of *art autre* is TACHISME.

art brut [Fr.] primitive or pseudo-primitive art. 20c. The phrase was coined by Jean Dubuffet about 1945.

artel [Russ.] a Russian co-operative organization of workers. 19c.

art engagé [Fr.] artistic activities or works of art undertaken with a political or sociological purpose. 20c. Cf. ENGAGÉ; THÉÂTRE ENGAGÉ.

artiste [Fr.] a public performer (*usu.* professional) in music, dancing, etc.; one who makes a fine art of his employment. 18c. The word is more and more frequently replaced by *artist*, for which it was substituted when the latter came to mean primarily 'painter'. [N,S]

art moderne [Fr.] modern art. 20c. A vague term embracing the products of all the AVANT-GARDE movements from Impressionism onwards.

art nouveau [Fr. 'new art'] (in) a style of drawing and domestic decoration characterized by flowing lines and Japanese influence. 19c. Developed in 1893–4 by Victor Horta (1861–1947) and Alphonse Mucha (1860–1939) and introduced into England shortly before 1900; at first a minority fad, *art nouveau* ultimately had considerable influence on the development of taste. Cf. JAPONAISERIE; JUGENDSTIL.

ascesis [Gk. ἄσκησις] the practice of self-discipline, *esp.* within a religious or monastic framework. 19c. [N*,S]

Aschenbrödel [Ger.] Cinderella, a despised underling who ultimately achieves wealth and happiness. 20c.

a secco [It.] *Art* (painting) on dry plaster; opposed to A BUON FRESCO. 20c. Cf. FRESCO SECCO; IN SECCO; SECCO.

asphyxia [Lat. < Gk. ἀσφυξία 'stoppage of the pulse'] *Med.* suffocation. 18c. [N,S]

assegai [Port. *azagaia* < Arab. *az-zaghāyah*] a light spear or lance of hard wood tipped with iron; properly Berber or Moorish, but extended to similar weapons used by all African tribes. 17c. Normally spelt *assagai* until the end of 19c. [N,S]

assemblage [Fr.] *Art* a technique by which a sculpture is built up by fastening together fragmentary objects; a sculpture produced in this way. 20c. *Assemblage* is the equivalent in sculpture of MONTAGE in painting.

assemblé [Fr.] *Ballet* a leap in which the dancer brings his feet together before alighting. 20c.

assoluta=PRIMA BALLERINA ASSOLUTA, leading ballet-dancer.

asthore [Ir. *a stóir* 'O treasure'] darling; a common and conventional term of endearment. 19c. Cf. ACUSHLA; ALANNA; MOCHREE.

asyndeton [Lat. < Gk. ἀσύνδετον] *Ling.* a rhetorical figure in which the (copulative) conjunction is omitted. 16c. Cf. POLYSYNDETON. [N,S]

ataman [Russ. < Ger. *Hauptmann* 'captain'] a Cossack leader. 19c. [N*]

atap [Jav.] thatch made of palm-fronds. 19c. The spelling *attap*, formerly more common, is now disused. [N*,S]

à tâtons [Fr.] groping, feeling one's way, tentatively. 20c.

atelier [Fr.] (1) *Art* the studio of a painter or sculptor; a studio at which pupils are admitted and a model is provided, but no instruction is given. 19c. (2) a leading fashion-house. 20c. Cf. GRAND ATELIER. [N,S]

a tempo [It.] *Mus.* in (exact) time; reverting to the previous time. 18c. Cf. TEMPO. [S]

atoll [Maldive *atoll(on)*] *Geog.* a ring-shaped coral reef enclosing a lagoon. 19c. The word is probably ultimately from Mal. *aḍal* 'closing'. The form *atollon* is recorded once in English in 17c. [N,S]

atrium, *pl.* **atria** [Lat.] *Hist.* the central hall or court of a Roman house. 16c. [N,S(*)]

à trois [Fr.] (a meeting, meal, etc.) for three persons; (three persons) without other company. 20c. Cf. À DEUX; MÉNAGE À TROIS.

attaché [Fr.] *Dip.* a member of the suite of an ambassador. 19c. An '*attaché* case' is so called because it is suitable for carrying diplomatic papers. [N,S]

attentat [Fr.] an attempted assassination. 19c. [S]

attentat aux mœurs [Fr.] an indecent assault. 20c.

attitude [Fr.] *Ballet* a position in which the dancer extends one leg backwards, holding the corresponding arm above the head and the other extended backwards or sideways. 20c. Cf. PROMENADE EN ATTITUDE.

attrapé [Fr.] well-caught (likeness), successful (imitation). 20c.

aubade [Fr.] a song or serenade at dawn. 17c. [N,S]

auberge [Fr.] an inn. 16c. [N,S(*)]

aubergine [Fr.] the fruit of the plant *Solanum esculentum*, used as a vegetable; *hence*, a greenish colour used in FAMILLE VERTE porcelain. 18c. The translation 'egg-plant' commonly given in dictionaries is not used; those who use the vegetable call it by its French name. [N,S]

A.U.C.=AB URBE CONDITA, from the foundation of the city.

au contraire [Fr.] on the contrary. 18c. [S]

au courant [Fr.] in the swim, well-informed, conversant with current affairs. 19c. Formerly construed with *of* or *with;* the construction with *with* is still possible, but *au courant* is now *usu.* absolute, though 'AU FAIT with' is normal. [N*,S]

auctoritate [Lat.] on the authority of . . .; always followed by a name. 20c. Used in justifying a statement which might be considered dubious.

auctoritate suo [Lat.] on his (her) own authority; with no authority from anyone else. 20c. Implying that an action or statement was unjustified.

au désespoir [Fr.] in despair. 18c. [S]

audi alteram partem [Lat.] *Law* hear the other side; one must hear both sides of a case before reaching a decision. 15c. St Augustine *De Duabus Animabus* xiv 2. [S]

auditorium, *pl.* **auditoria** [Lat.] a hall used for listening to lectures or recitals; the part of a theatre, etc., occupied by the audience. 17c. [N,S(*)]

au fait [Fr.] thoroughly conversant (with), well-informed. 18c. Formerly construed with *of, at, in* or *to;* now commonly construed with *with*, less common used absolutely. Cf. AU COURANT. [N,S]

Aufklärung [Ger.] the (German) Age of Reason, the Age of Enlightenment. 20c. The term means 'clearing up', and is derived from the frontispiece of Baron C. F. von Wolff's *Vernünfftige Gedancken* (1725), which depicts the dawn breaking through the clouds.

Auflage, *pl.* **Auflagen** [Ger.] an edition or impression (of a book). 19c. Cf. AUSGABE.

au fond [Fr.] fundamentally. 19c. Often with the implication 'in spite of appearances'. [S]

Auftakt [Ger.] (1) *Ling.* one or more extra-metrical syllables at the beginning of a line; (2) *Mus.* the part of a piece of music before the first strong beat. 19c. Cf. ANACRUSIS.

auf Wiedersehen [Ger. 'until we meet again'] farewell! 19c. A common form of farewell in many languages: cf. A RIVEDERCI; AU REVOIR; HASTA LA VISTA. [S]

au grand galop [Fr.] at full gallop, full tilt. 20c.

au grand sérieux [Fr.] in all seriousness, perfectly seriously. 19c. The implication is that the matter is not one which would normally, or by normal people, be taken seriously. Cf. AU SÉRIEUX. [S]

au gratin [Fr.] *Cul.* dressed with bread-crumbs or grated cheese and baked in the oven or grilled. 19c. [S]

au naturel [Fr.] (1) in the natural state; (2) *Cul.* uncooked; plainly and simply cooked. 19c. [N*,S]

au pair [Fr.] (an arrangement) whereby services are exchanged without cash payment, *esp.* (an arrangement) whereby light domestic service is rendered in exchange for board and lodging; one who renders service in exchange for board and lodging. 20c. [N*]

au pied de la lettre [Fr.] absolutely literally. 18c. [S]

au poteau [Fr. 'to the post'] (let him be hanged) from the lamp-post! 20c. Many of the victims of the French Revolution were hanged from the street-lamps. Cf. À LA LANTERNE.

au premier abord [Fr.] at first acquaintance. 20c.

au premier coup [Fr.] *Art* (a technique of painting in which the picture is completed) in one session. 20c. Cf. ALLA PRIMA.

aura [Gk. *αὔρα* 'breeze'] a subtle emanation from any substance; *esp.* a visible emanation supposed (by theosophists, etc.) to surround the human body. 18c. [N(*),S]

aurea mediocritas [Lat.] the golden mean, the happy medium. 19c. Horace *Odes* II x 5: *Auream quisquis mediocritatem Diligit* 'whoever loves the golden mean . . .' Cf. JUSTE MILIEU; VIA MEDIA. [S]

au revoir [Fr. 'until we meet again'] farewell! 17c. A common form of farewell in many languages: cf. A RIVEDERCI; AUF WIEDERSEHEN; HASTA LA VISTA. [N*,S]

aurora australis [Lat.] a celestial phenomenon similar to the AURORA BOREALIS but observable in the southern hemisphere. 18c. [N,S]

aurora borealis [Lat. 'northern dawn'] the Northern Lights; electrical disturbances visible in the northern sky, particularly in Arctic regions. 18c. [N,S(*)]

aurum fulminans [Lat.] an explosive precipitate formed by adding ammonia to chloride of gold. 17c. [N,S]

aurum mosaicum [Lat.] bisulphide of tin, used in the preparation of paints and stains. 16c. The meaning of the second word is uncertain; the forms *musicum* and *musivum* were also formerly in use. [N,S]

aurum potabile [Lat.] a cordial containing fine particles of gold suspended in some volatile oil. 15c. [N,S]

au sérieux [Fr.] seriously, in earnest. 19c. Cf. AU GRAND SÉRIEUX. [S]

Ausgabe, *pl.* **Ausgaben** [Ger.] an edition (of a work). 19c. Distinct from AUFLAGE: a new edition of a book, even with corrections and additions, is an *Auflage; Ausgabe* implies that a work has been completely re-edited.

Ausgleich [Ger.] a settlement, an agreement; *esp.* the agreement between Austria and Hungary concluded in 1867. 19c.

Ausländer, *pl.* **Ausländer** [Ger.] a foreigner. 20c. *Usu.* with the implication of 'outlandishness' or lack of civilization. Cf. UITLANDER.

Aussprache [Ger.] (good) pronunciation, elocution. 20c.

aut Cæsar aut nullus/aut Cæsar aut nihil [Lat.] a king or nothing; either complete success or utter failure. 17c. Perhaps based on a saying of the Emperor Caligula (Suetonius *Caligula* xxxvii): *aut frugi hominem esse oportere dictitans, aut Cæsarem* 'he was always saying that one must either be thrifty, or Cæsar'; but the implications of this saying are entirely different. [S]

Autobahn, *pl.* **Autobahnen** [Ger.] a motor-way, a road specially designed for high-speed traffic. 20c. Cf. AUTOSTRADA.

autocritique [Fr.] self-criticism, *esp.* as a disciplinary exercise undertaken by a devout Communist. 20c.

auto-da-fé, *pl.* **autos-da-fé** [Port. 'act of faith'] the execution of a sentence of the Inquisition, *esp.* the public burning of a heretic. 18c. Cf. SANBENITO. [N,S]

autogenesis [Gk. *αὐτο* + *γένεσις*] spontaneous generation. 19c. Cf. PARTHENOGENESIS. [N*]

automaton, *pl.* **automata** [Gk. *αὐτόματον*] a piece of mechanism designed to simulate a living being; a human being whose actions are (or appear to be) entirely mechanical. 17c. Cf. ZOMBIE. [N,S]

autostrada [It.] a motor-way, a road specially designed for high-speed traffic. 20c. Imitated from the German AUTOBAHN.

autrefois acquit [Obs. Fr.] *Law* the plea of 'previously acquitted' of the charge now being preferred. 18c. [S]

autrefois convict [Obs. Fr.] *Law* the plea of 'previously convicted' of the charge now being preferred. 19c. In law a previous conviction is as much a bar to further proceedings as a previous acquittal.

autres temps, autres mœurs [Fr.] other days, other ways; manners change with the times; modern customs or feelings must not be imputed to earlier periods. 20c.

au vif [Fr.] (painted) from the living model. 20c. Cf. AD VIVUM; SUR LE VIF.

avalanche [Fr.] a mass of snow and earth, loosened from a mountain-side, plunging into the valley below. 18c. *Orig.* a Swiss French dialect form, now adopted into most languages. [N,S(*)]

avant-courier [Fr. *avant-coureur*] one who rides ahead, a scout or skirmisher; a precursor. 17c. The second element is fully anglicized, as in *courier*, but the first element is often pronounced as in French. [N,S]

avant-garde [Fr.] the vanguard, the leading part of an army; *hence*, (characteristic of) an advanced æsthetic (*esp.* literary) movement. 15c. The figurative use, dating only from the end of the 19c., has almost displaced the older meaning. [S]

avant-goût [Fr.] a foretaste, something to whet the appetite. 19c. [S]

avanti [It.] forward!, carry on! 20c. Cf. EN AVANT.

avatar [Sansk. *avatāra*] the incarnation of a deity; the manifestation (of a principle, etc.) in concrete form. 18c. [N,S]

ave atque vale [Lat.] hail and farewell! 19c. Catullus *Carmina* ci 10: *atque in perpetuum, frâter, ave atque vale*! 'and for eternity, brother, hail and farewell!' Catullus' lament at his brother's grave is now often applied facetiously to a brief or passing visit.

avec empressement [Fr.] eagerly, enthusiastically. 20c.

ave Maria [Lat.] *Eccles.* hail, Mary! (the angelic salutation); the hour at which the prayer beginning with these words is commonly recited; the bell summoning the faithful to this prayer. 13c. [N,S]

avete [Lat.] greetings! 20c. Common in school magazines, etc. as a heading to a list of new members. A better and more frequent form is SALVETE. Cf. VALETE.

avizandum [Lat.] *Law* consideration (by a judge in private). 19c. The term is peculiar to Scottish law. [N,S]

avoirdupois [Obs. Fr. *avoir de pois* 'goods of weight'] the name of the standard system of weights used in the British Isles; *hence facet.*, excess bodyweight. 15c. The current form with *du* is merely erroneous; a pseudo-French pronunciation is out of place. [N,S]

ayah [Port. *aia* 'governess'] *A.-I.* a native nursemaid or lady's maid. 18c. Distinct from AMAH 'wet-nurse'; but the distinction is not always clearly maintained. [N,S]

azione (sacra) [It.] *Mus.* a sacred drama with music, an acted ORATORIO. 20c.

B

baas [Du.] master, employer; *usu.* as a form of address by an African slave or servant. 17c. This word is the origin of the American *boss*, the latter spelling reflecting the American pronunciation of short *o*. [N*,S]

babu [Hind. *bābu*] *A.-I.* a native clerk who writes English; *hence*, applied to a stilted and unidiomatic yet florid English supposed to be characteristic of native clerks. 18c. *Orig.* a title of respect accompanying a name; formerly spelt *baboo*. [N,S]

baccalauréat [Fr.] the French school-leaving examination corresponding roughly to matriculation. 20c. Etymologically *baccalauréat* means 'bachelor's degree', but in France it is a pre-University examination. Cf. BACHOT.

baccara(t) [Fr. *baccara*] a card-game played for money, somewhat resembling VINGT-ET-UN, in which one of the players holds the bank. 19c. Cf. CHEMIN DE FER. [N,S]

Bacchanalia *pl.* [Lat.] *Hist.* the triennial feast held by the Romans in honour of Bacchus, the god of wine; *hence*, an orgy, an occasion of drunken revelry. 16c. [N,S]

Bacchantes *pl.* [Lat.] *Hist.* priestesses of Bacchus; *hence*, drunken women. 16c. A singular *Bacchante* is in common use: this is partly an erroneous derivation from the plural, and partly an adoption of Fr. *Bacchante;* in the first case the word is pronounced as a trisyllable, in the second case as in French. [N,S]

bachot [Fr.] the colloquial French name for the BACCALAURÉAT, the French school-leaving examination. 20c. Another colloquial French form is *bac*.

bacillus, *pl.* **bacilli** [Lat. 'little rod'] *Med.* a rod-shaped vegetable organism of microscopic size, found in diseased tissues. 19c. Etymologically identical with BACTERIUM, but distinct in meaning. [N,S]

Backfisch [Ger. 'small fry'] a girl in her teens, a bobby-soxer. 19c. Now obsolescent or obsolete.

bacterium, *pl.* **bacteria** [Lat. < Gk. βακτήριον 'little rod'] *Med.* a rod-shaped vegetable organism of microscopic size, found in decomposing organic matter. 19c. Etymologically identical with BACILLUS, but distinct in meaning. [N,S]

badinage [Fr.] chaff, banter, raillery, light-hearted fooling. 17c. Cf. PERSIFLAGE. [N,S]

badinerie [Fr.] *Mus.* a piece of music of light and playful character. 20c. Cf. SCHERZO.

bafoué, *f.* **bafouée** [Fr.] mocked at, derided; (a person) whose destiny it is never to be taken seriously. 20c.

bagarre [Fr.] a rumpus, a racket, a scuffle. 20c.

bagatelle [Fr.] (1) a trifle, something of no importance; (2) *Mus.* a piece of music not intended seriously by its composer; (3) a form of billiards in which the balls are cued from one end of the table into numbered sockets at the other. 17c. [N,S]

bagnio [It. *bagno* 'bath'] (1) a brothel; (2) an Oriental prison, *esp.* a slave-prison. 16c. The semantic development from 'Turkish bath' to 'brothel' is straightforward; it is said that the slave-prison in Constantinople occupied the site of a former public bath. [N,S]

baguette [Fr.] an ornament in the form of a half-cylinder; a small jewel cut into a thin rectangular shape. 20c. Cf. BÂTON.

baignoire [Fr. 'bath-tub'] a stage-box, a box at the theatre on the same level as the stalls. 19c. [N,S]

bain-marie [Fr.] a flat vessel of boiling water into which saucepans, etc., are placed to simmer or to keep hot. 19c. Latin *balneum Mariæ*, in the same sense, was in use in English as early as 15c.; the association with the Blessed Virgin is obscure. [N,S]

baksheesh [Pers. *bakhshīsh*] a gratuity, a tip. 17c. Spelt in a wide variety of ways by travellers, and anglicized as *buckshee* 'free'. [N,S]

balalaika [Russ.] a Slavonic musical instrument resembling a guitar, but with a triangular body. 18c. [N*,S]

baldacchino, *pl.* **baldacchini** [It.] a canopy of brocade (or of wood or metal in a similar form) over an altar, throne, or doorway. 17c. *Orig.* with reference to brocade from Baghdad, It. *Baldacco.* [N,S]

ballade [Fr.] *Ling.* a poem consisting of three stanzas of eight lines each and one (the 'Envoy') of four lines, all four stanzas ending in the same line. 14c. Formerly seven-line stanzas were also permissible. [N]

balle à la main [Fr.] *Tennis* a ball moving in such a way as to offer an opportunity for a decisive stroke. 19c.

ballerina, *pl.* **ballerine** [It.] a female dancer who sustains the chief rôles in BALLETS. 18c. Cf. PRIMA BALLERINA (ASSOLUTA). [N,S]

ballet [Fr.] an entertainment consisting of group and solo dancing with a musical accompaniment. 17c. [N,S]

ballet blanc [Fr.] a BALLET in which the DANSEUSES wear white dresses based on Taglioni's costume in *La Sylphide* (1832). 20c.

ballet chanté [Fr.] a BALLET in which the performers accompany their actions with song. 20c.

ballet d'action [Fr.] a BALLET in which the whole of the movement is designed to tell a story rather than to provide a graceful spectacle. 18c. Cf. PAS D'ACTION. [S]

ballista, *pl.* **ballistæ** [Lat.] *Hist.* an ancient siege-engine which discharged missiles by the release of a spring. 16c. [N,S]

ballon [Fr. 'balloon'] (1) *Ballet* elasticity (of a dancer's action); (2) a large globe-shaped brandy-glass designed to facilitate the savouring of the BOUQUET. 20c.

ballon d'essai [Fr. 'trial balloon'] a project undertaken to test public feeling. 19c. [N*,S]

ballonné [Fr.] *Ballet* a leaping movement in which the dancer extends one leg and lands on the other foot. 20c.

ballotté [Fr.] *Ballet* an upward leap on one leg accompanied by a DÉVELOPPÉ. 20c.

bal masqué [Fr.] a ball at which the dancers wear masks. 18c. [S*]

bal musette [Fr.] a cheap dance-hall with an accordion band. 20c. Properly *musette* is a bag-pipe.

bambino, *pl.* **bambini** [It.] a baby in swaddling-clothes, *esp.* a representation of the infant Jesus; *facet.* a child of one of the Mediterranean races. 18c. [N,S(*)]

banal [Fr.] commonplace, trite. 19c. Anglicized in the 19c., but now commonly pronounced as in French. [N,S]

banc [Fr.] *Law* the judges' bench; *hence,* a plenary session of a bench of judges. 20c.

banco [Fr. < It.] an offer by a player (in CHEMIN DE FER and similar games) to put down a stake equal to that put down by the bank. 20c.

Band, *pl.* **Bände** [Ger.] a volume (of a book or journal). 19c.

bandeau, *pl.* **bandeaux** [Fr.] (1) a ribbon or narrow strip of cloth used to bind the hair; (2) *Tennis* the strip of wall immediately below a penthouse. 18c. [N,S]

banderilla [Sp.] a dart decorated with a small streamer thrust into the neck or shoulder of a bull at a bull-fight. 18c. [N,S]

banderillero [Sp.] a bull-fighter whose function it is to use the BANDERILLA. 18c. [N,S]

banlieue [Fr.] suburbs. 20c. Singular in French although the English equivalent is plural. Cf. FAUBOURG.

banquette [Fr.] (1) *Mil.* a platform behind a rampart or in a trench. 17c. (2) a long cushioned seat with a cushioned back (*usu.* against a wall), *esp.* as used in restaurants, etc., as a substitute for individual seats. 20c. [N]

banshee [Ir. *bean sí* 'woman of the fairies'] a supernatural being which wails under the windows of a house where death is imminent. 18c. [N,S]

banzai [Jap. '10,000 years'] a cry used by the Japanese in battle or to greet the emperor. 20c. [N*]

barbeau [Fr.] a pattern of cornflowers, *esp.* on porcelain. 20c.

barbette [Fr.] a gun-turret. 18c. *Orig.* of military guns, but subsequently mainly of naval guns fired from a turret instead of through a port. [N,S]

barbotine [Fr.] 'slip', a creamy mixture of kaolin and water used to ornament pottery; pottery ornamented in this way. 19c. Cf. PÂTE-SUR-PÂTE. [N(*)]

barcarolle [Fr.] *Mus.* a piece of music resembling the songs sung by Venetian gondoliers (It. *barcaruoli*). 18c. [N,S]

baroque [Fr. < Port. *barroco* 'imperfect pearl'] *Arch.* a style of architecture characterized by florid and eccentric ornamentation. 19c. The *baroque* style first appeared towards the end of 16c., flourished in the 17c., and spread throughout Europe during the 18c. Cf. ROCOCO. [N(*),S]

baroquerie [Fr.] the prevalence of the BAROQUE style; a collection of objects ornamented in the BAROQUE style. 20c.

barouche [Ger. *Barutsche*] a four-wheeled four-seater carriage with a hood. 19c. Despite the pseudo-French form of the English word, the word has never been used in French. [N,S]

barrage [Fr.] a concentration of continuous artillery or machine-gun fire; *hence*, any continuous attack. 20c. Introduced during the First World War. [N*]

barre [Fr.] *Ballet* the bar which runs at waist height round the mirror-lined walls of a ballet-school. 20c. The *barre* is used for supporting the body while practising leg-movements.

baryton-Martin [Fr.] *Mus.* a baritone voice which can pass smoothly from the bass to the tenor register. 20c. Named from the French singer Jean-Blaise Martin (1769–1837).

bas bleu [Fr.] a blue-stocking, a learned woman, a woman who makes a parade of cultural interests. 18c. The French term is a translation of the English, which is derived from Benjamin Stillingfleet's habit of wearing informal worsted stockings at the assemblies at Montagu House. Cf. FEMME SAVANTE. [N,S(*)]

bascule [Fr.] *Equ.* the rocking movement made by a horse when jumping high obstacles correctly. 20c.

basenji [Basuto] a small brown African hunting-dog. 20c.

basilica [Lat. < Gk. βασιλική (οἰκία) 'royal (dwelling)'] (1) *Hist.* a large hall used as a court of justice or place of assembly; (2) *Eccles.* a building resembling the Roman *basilica* used as a place of Christian worship. 16c. [N,S]

basque [Fr.] the part of a (woman's) tailored jacket below the waist-line. 19c. [N,S]

bas-relief [Fr.] *Art* low relief, sculpture in which the figures project less than half their true proportion from the surface. 17c. The first element is commonly pronounced as in French, the second as in English. Cf. BASSO RILIEVO. [N,S*]

basse-taille [Fr. 'low-cut'] *Art* EN PLEIN (enamel work), (enamel work) in which the ground (*usu.* of gold or silver) is carved in INTAGLIO, the hollows being filled with translucent enamel through which the modelling can still be seen. 20c. Cf. SUR FOND RÉSERVÉ.

basso al ottava [It.] *Mus.* a bass part to be played an octave lower than it is written. 20c.

basso continuo [It.] *Mus.* thorough-bass, figured bass; the bass part of a piece of music accompanied by figures indicating the harmonies to be extemporized at the keyboard. 18c. Cf. CONTINUO. [N,S]

basso ostinato [It.] *Mus.* ground-bass, a bass figure repeated over and over again though the melody it accompanies may vary. 20c. Cf. OSTINATO.

basso profondo [It.] *Mus.* (a singer having) a deep bass voice. 19c. The form *basso profundo* is common, but is not Italian. [N*,S]

basso rilievo [It.] *Art* low relief, sculpture in which the figures project less than half their true proportion from the surface. 17c. Formerly often written *basso relievo.* Cf. ALTO RILIEVO; CAVO RILIEVO; MEZZO RILIEVO; SCHIACCIATO RILIEVO. [N,S]

bateau-mouche, *pl.* **bateaux-mouches** [Fr. 'fly-boat'] a passenger-steamer on the river Seine. 20c.

bathos [Gk. *βάθος*] anticlimax, descent from the sublime to the ridiculous. 18c. Introduced by Alexander Pope in his essay *Bathos, the art of sinking in Poetry* (1727–8). [N,S]

batik [Jav. *'mbatik* 'drawing'] *Art* a method of dyeing fabric in patterns by coating the part not to be dyed in wax; a fabric dyed in this way. 19c. After dyeing the wax is removed; the process may be repeated several times to produce a pattern in different colours. [N*]

batiste [Fr.] cambric, fine linen or cotton. 17c. Perhaps so called from its use for wiping babies' heads after baptism. [N,S(*)]

bâton [Fr.] (1) a stick, *esp.* a kind of truncheon or cudgel. 16c. Long obsolete but recently revived. (2) *Mus.* the light stick used by a conductor for directing an orchestra. 19c. The *bâton* was first used in England about 1820. (3) a jewel cut into a long rectangular shape. 20c. A small jewel cut into a thin rectangular shape is known as a BAGUETTE. (4) one of a series of thin rectangular marks used as a substitute for numerals on some modern watches and clocks. 20c. Cf. SANS HEURES. The spelling *baton* is increasingly prevalent, *esp.* in the second sense. [N,S]

battement [Fr.] *Ballet* one of a variety of movements in which the leg is agitated in the air or struck against some part of the supporting leg. 20c.

battement dégagé [Fr.] *Ballet* a movement in which the free leg is moved backwards and forwards without touching the ground. 20c.

battement tendu [Fr.] *Ballet* a movement in which the leg is extended to the front, side, or back, the toe resting lightly on the ground and then returning across the other leg. 20c.

batterie de campagne [Fr.] a picnic-outfit, supplies and equipment sufficient for the preparation of simple meals in the open air. 20c.

batterie de cuisine [Fr.] *Cul.* a complete set of cooking utensils. 18c. No English equivalent is so all-embracing. [S]

battue [Fr.] a method of shooting in which the game are driven from cover by beaters to a point where the guns are waiting. 19c. [N,S]

Bauhaus [Ger.] *Arch.* the name of a school of modern design aiming to reconcile art with technology; (architecture) influenced by this school. The *Bauhaus* was founded at Weimar in 1919 by Walter Gropius, transferred to Dessau in 1925, and closed down in 1933.

bayadère [Fr.] a Hindu dancing-girl. 19c. [N,S]

bayou [Fr. *boyau* 'gut'] *U.S.* a sluggish offshoot of a river or lake. 19c. [N,S]

bazaar [Pers. *bāzār*] an Oriental market; *hence,* a sale of work for charitable purposes. 17c. Cf. SOUK. [N,S]

béarnaise [Fr.] *Cul.* a sauce made of butter, egg-yolks and vinegar, flavoured with tarragon. 20c. Named from the ancient French province of Béarn, in the western Pyrenees.

beatæ memoriæ [Lat.] of blessed memory; properly with reference to a near-saint, but often ironical. 19c. [S]

beata simplicitas [Lat.] holy simplicity, the NAÏVETÉ of the saintly. 19c. Thomas à Kempis *The Imitation of Christ* iv 18. Cf. SANCTA SIMPLICITAS.

beato, *f.* **beata,** *pl.* **beati,** *f. pl.* **beate** [It.] a holy man; one who, though not canonized, is venerated by the Church. 19c.

beau, *pl.* **beaux** [Fr.] one who attracts attention by fine clothes and manners; one who pays marked attentions to a woman. 17c. Cf. BELLE. [N,S]

beau geste [Fr.] a magnanimous gesture. 20c. Cf. GESTE. [N*]

beau idéal [Fr. 'ideal Beautiful'] (1) the abstract idea of beauty; (2) the ideal type or model of anything. 19c. The second meaning comes from a mistaken interpretation of *beau* as adjective and *idéal* as noun; when this meaning is intended the second word is commonly written and pronounced as in English. [N,S]

beau monde [Fr.] 'Society', the world of fashion. 17c. Cf. HAUT MONDE. [N,S]

beau-pot [Fr. 'beautiful pot'] a large ornamental vase for cut flowers. 18c. [N]

beaux arts *pl.* [Fr.] the Fine Arts. 20c.

beaux yeux *pl.* [Fr. 'beautiful eyes'] good looks, *esp.* as a motive for benefiting someone. 19c. [S]

Bebung [Ger.] *Mus.* a device of clavichord technique in which a fluctuation of pitch is produced by varying the pressure of the finger on the key. 20c.

bêche-de-mer [Fr. 'sea-spade' < Port. *bicho do mar* 'sea-worm'] the sea-slug, eaten as a delicacy by the Chinese. 18c. [N(*),S]

bedouin [Fr. < Arab. *badāwīn* pl.] (an Arab) of the desert. 14c. [N,S]

béguin [Fr.] infatuation. 20c.

béguinage [Fr.] an establishment of BÉGUINES. 19c. [N]

béguine [Fr.] a member of a religious sisterhood, not bound by strict vows but free to leave the order and marry. 15c. These sisterhoods were founded in the Low Countries in the 12th century by Lambert le Bègue, from whom the name is derived. [N,S]

bel canto [It.] *Mus.* a type of singing characterized by a full rich tone. 20c. [N*]

bel esprit, *pl.* **beaux esprits** [Fr.] a brilliant wit. 17c. Often used with a tinge of irony. [N,S]

bel étage [Fr.] the most splendid storey of a house, *usu.* the first floor. 19c. Cf. APPARTEMENT DE PARADE; PIANO NOBILE. [S]

belle [Fr.] a beautiful woman, *esp.* the reigning beauty of a place or circle. 17c. The feminine of BEAU, but lacking the disparaging implications of the masculine. [N,S]

(la) belle époque [Fr. 'the fine period'] the period from about 1890 to 1914, the culmination of the way of life destroyed by the First World War. 20c.

belle indifférence [Fr.] *Psych.* serene indifference, an abnormal condition of abstraction from the realities of life. 20c.

belle laide [Fr.] (a woman) whose plainness or ugliness of feature is itself attractive or charming. 20c. Cf. JOLIE-LAIDE.

belle peinture [Fr.] 'straight' painting, naturalistic painting, as distinct from Impressionism, etc. 20c.

belles lettres *pl.* [Fr.] the study of literature from an æsthetic standpoint; works of literary criticism or philosophical reflection. 17c. A useful term denoting serious literature which is neither poetry nor fiction. [N,S]

belvedere [It. *bel vedere* 'fine view'] *Arch.* a turret or summerhouse (*usu.* open on three sides) designed to command a fine prospect. 16c. Now often pronounced as if English. [N,S]

bene decessit [Lat. 'he has left well'] a testimonial given to a person leaving an establishment or employment, certifying that his departure was not due to misconduct. 19c. [S]

benedicite [Lat. 'bless!'] the invocation of a blessing, *esp.* at table. 13c. [N,S]

Benedictus [Lat.] the part of the Mass immediately following the SANCTUS; a musical setting of this part of the Mass. 19c. From the opening words: *Benedictus qui venit in nomine Domini* 'blessed is he who comes in the name of the Lord'. [N,S]

bene esse [Lat.] prosperity, well-being, comfort, luxury; opposed to ESSE, mere existence. 17c. [S]

bénéficiaire [Fr.] one who benefits or profits by something. 19c. [S]

ben trovato, *pl.* **ben trovati** [It.] ingeniously invented; a happy invention. 19c. Cf. BIEN TROUVÉ; SE NON È VERO, È (MOLTO) BEN TROVATO. [S]

berceau [Fr.] a covered walk, *esp.* one formed from plants trained over a framework. 17c. Cf. PERGOLA. [S]

berceuse [Fr.] *Mus.* a cradle-song, a lullaby. 20c. Cf. WIEGENLIED.

béret [Fr.] a cap without a peak, like that worn by Basque peasants. 19c. [N(*)]

bergère [Fr. 'shepherdess'] a deep easy chair. 19c. [S]

bergerie [Fr.] *Art* sophisticated imitation of the rustic and primitive; a work of art in this style. 20c.

Bergfall [Ger.] the fall of a mountain crag; the visible results of such a fall. 19c. [N]

Bergschrund [Ger.] *Geog.* a large CREVASSE formed at the head of a glacier as the ice moves down. 19c. [N(*)]

beri-beri [Cing. 'great weakness'] *Med.* an Oriental disease resulting in dropsy and paralysis. 19c. The disease is due to lack of vitamin B. [N,S]

bersagliere, *pl.* **bersaglieri** [It.] a rifleman, an Italian infantry private. 19c. [S]

betel [Port. < Mal. *vettila*] the leaf of an evergreen plant commonly chewed by natives of India and neighbouring countries. 16c. The chewing is followed by the expectoration of scarlet juice. [N,S]

bête noire [Fr. 'black beast'] an object of special aversion. 19c. [N*,S]

bêtise [Fr.] an act of stupidity, lack of tact. 19c. Often 'to make a *bêtise*' after Fr. *faire une bêtise.* To be distinguished from FAUX PAS and GAFFE, which imply social ignorance or lack of sensibility rather than inadvertence. [S]

bévue [Fr.] an inadvertent error. 19c. Naturalized in 18c. as *bevew,* but re-adopted in 19c. [N,S]

bey [Turk.] the governor of a Turkish district; a title of rank following a proper name. 16c. [N,S]

bhang [Hind. *bhāng*] a preparation of Indian hemp, the leaves and seeds of which are narcotic and intoxicating. 16c. Cf. HASHISH; MARIJUANA. [N,S]

bianco-sopra-bianco [It.] *Art* decoration in white enamel on a white ground, characteristic of English Delft ware. 20c.

bibelot [Fr.] a small curio or article of VIRTÙ. 19c. Cf. BIJOUTERIE. [N*,S]

bidet [Fr. 'nag'] a small low rectangular bath for intimate personal hygiene. 19c. Common in France but rare in England. In English *occ.* written *bidette.* [N]

bidonville [Fr.] a shanty-town, a settlement of houses built of petrol-cans hammered flat. 20c.

bien élevé, *f.* **bien élevée** [Fr.] nicely brought up, well educated in conventional morality. 20c. Cf. JEUNE FILLE BIEN ÉLEVÉE.

bien entendu [Fr.] of course, naturally. 19c. [S]

biennale [It.] (a fair, exhibition, etc.) held every two years. 20c. Cf. TRIENNALE.

bien pensant [Fr.] right-thinking, holding all the right opinions. 20c.

bien rangé, *f.* **bien rangée** [Fr.] steady, methodical, given to regular habits, leading a serious life. 20c.

bienséance [Fr.] decorum, propriety, good breeding. 17c. Often in the plural *bienséances* 'the demands of good breeding, the proprieties'. [N,S]

bien trouvé [Fr.] ingeniously invented, a happy invention. 20c. Based on the It. BEN TROVATO.

bien vu [Fr.] well thought-of, highly esteemed. 20c.

bifolium, *pl.* **bifolia** [Lat.] a pair of conjugate leaves in a manuscript or printed book. 20c.

bijou, *pl.* **bijoux** [Fr.] a jewel, a trinket; a 'gem' of architecture, etc.; any small work of art of outstanding excellence. 17c. Now vulgarly in adjectival use: 'a *bijou* residence', etc. [N,S]

bijouterie [Fr.] jewellery, small articles of VIRTÙ. 19c. Cf. BIBELOT. [N,S]

Bildungsroman [Ger.] a novel concerned with the education, *usu.* the emotional education, of its hero. 20c. The classic example is Flaubert's *L'Éducation Sentimentale* (1869). Cf. ERZIEHUNGSROMAN.

billabong [Austr. *billa bung* 'dead river'] a stagnant backwater. 19c. [N*]

billet doux, *pl.* **billets doux** [Fr. 'sweet note'] a love-letter. 17c. Not now in serious usage. Cf. POULET. [N,S]

biltong [Afrik.] strips of lean meat dried in the sun. 19c. [N,S]

bimbashi [Turk. *bin başı* 'head of a thousand'] a Turkish colonel. 19c. [N*,S]

bint [Arab.] a woman, *esp.* a woman of easy virtue. 20c.

biretta [It.] *Eccles.* a square clerical cap of black, red or purple. 16c. [N,S]

bis dat qui cito dat [Lat.] he gives twice who gives quickly. 19c. Publilius Syrus *Aphorisms* 245: *inopi beneficium bis dat, qui dat celeriter* 'he who gives alms to a poor man quickly gives it twice'. [S]

bise [Fr.] a cold dry north wind prevalent in Switzerland and neighbouring districts. 13c. Cf. MAESTRALE; MISTRAL; TRAMONTANA. [N,S]

bisque [Fr.] (1) *Cul.* crayfish soup; (2) *Tennis* a form of odds whereby one player is allowed to score a point at his own choice once in a set; *hence,* odds in any game. 17c. The term *bisque* applied to pottery fired once without a glaze is not French, but an English abbreviation of *biscuit* in the same sense. [N,S]

bistre [Fr.] *Art* a brown pigment prepared from soot, often used for monochrome water-colour painting. 18c. [N]

bistro [Fr.] a wine-shop, a public house. 20c.

bivouac [Fr. < Swiss Ger. *Beiwacht*] an open-air encampment; to set up such an encampment. 19c. In military use since 18c. [N,S]

bizarre [Fr.] eccentric, extravagant, odd; grotesque, appealing by oddity rather than by beauty. 17c. [N,S]

bizarrerie [Fr.] oddity, eccentricity, grotesqueness. 18c. [N,S]

blague [Fr.] pretentious falsehood, humbug, 19c. [N,S]

blagueur, *f.* **blagueuse** [Fr.] a practical joker. 19c. [S]

blanc de blancs [Fr.] a light delicate champagne made wholly out of the juice of white grapes. 20c.

blanc-de-Chine [Fr.] *Art* a white porcelain with a milky glaze, manufactured under the Ming dynasty at Tê-hua in the province of Fukien. 20c.

blancmange [Obs. Fr. *blanc manger* 'white food'] a pudding made of cornflour, milk and flavouring. 15c. Formerly also a dish of white meat or fish (from 14c.) The current pseudo-French pronunciation is fairly recent. [N,S]

blanquette [Fr.] (1) a kind of pear; (2) *Cul.* a white FRICASSÉE or stew, made with a rich white sauce. 19c. [S]

blasé, *f.* **blasée** [Fr.] surfeited with pleasure; unexcited by any novelty. 19c. [N,S]

(der) Blaue Reiter [Ger. 'the blue horseman'] the name chosen by a group of German artists who came together in Munich in 1911. 20c. The aim of the group (founded by Kandinsky and Marc) was to break with the past and create a new spiritual tradition; the name is that of a picture by Kandinsky.

bleu-jaune [Fr.] an amethystine spar showing STRATA of blue and yellow, used for making ornaments, vases, etc. 20c. Often corrupted to *Blue John.*

(ein) Blick ins Chaos [Ger.] a glimpse of the abyss, a revelation of the proximate dissolution of contemporary social order. 20c.

Blitzkrieg [Ger.] lightning war; a surprise attack carried through to victory. 20c. *Orig.* of German tactics during the Second World War; now *usu.* metaphorically.

bloc [Fr.] a combination of groups, parties or nations formed to promote a certain purpose. 20c. [N*]

blond, *f.* **blonde** [Fr.] fair-haired, *usu.* with the implication that the skin is fair also. 17c. The feminine *blonde* is now sometimes used for the masculine. [N,S]

blonde Bestie [Ger.] a 'blond beast', a member of the 'Aryan' HERRENVOLK. 20c. Used by Nietzsche (in his *Zur Genealogie der Moral*) in comparing the cruelty of the master-race to the innocent cruelty of the beast of prey. Cf. ÜBERMENSCH.

blouson [Fr.] (a jacket or similar garment) with a tight waistband and considerable fullness above it. 20c.

blouson doré, *pl.* **blousons dorés** [Fr.] a juvenile delinquent from the upper or wealthy classes. 20c. An ingenious combination of BLOUSON NOIR and JEUNESSE DORÉE.

blouson noir, *pl.* **blousons noirs** [Fr.] a (French) teddy-boy. 20c. So called from the black leather windjammers popular amongst them. Cf. HALBSTARKE(R); JEUNE VOYOU; STILYAGA; VITELLONE.

Blut und Boden [Ger.] 'blood and earth'. 20c. A phrase popularized by the propagandists of the German National Socialist Party. The precise connotation seems to be uncertain: the general intention is to assimilate a modern nation to a primitive tribal community, but whether *Blut* refers to blood-relationship or to the shedding of blood in defence of tribal territory is doubtful.

Blut und Ehre [Ger.] 'blood and honour'. 20c. A slogan of the German National Socialist Party; often inscribed on daggers worn by members of the Hitler Youth Movement.

Blut und Eisen [Ger.] 'blood and iron', military power used to achieve a specific purpose. 20c. Used by Bismarck in the Prussian House of Deputies, 28th January 1886; but he had already used the phrase in the form EISEN UND BLUT as early as 1862. Bismarck was quoting from Quintilian *Declamationes* 350: *cædes videtur significare sanguinem et ferrum* 'warfare obviously means blood and iron'.

Blutwurst [Ger.] black pudding. 20c.

bocage [Fr.] (1) thicket, woodland. 17c. Revived during the Normandy campaign of 1944 in the special meaning 'fields and meadows interspersed with hedges and trees forming cover for tanks'. (2) a background of foliage and flowers supporting the figures in a pottery set-piece. 20c. [N]

bodega [Sp.] a wine-cellar, a vault for storing and maturing wine; a wine-shop. 19c. Cf. BOTTEGA; BOUTIQUE.

Boer [Afrik.] a (South African Dutch) farmer, *esp.* one living in the Transvaal. 19c. [N(*),S]

bohereen [Ir. *bóthairín*] a minor road, a country lane, a cart-track. 19c. Also in the form *boreen.* [N(*),S]

bois clair [Fr.] unstained and unvarnished wood. 20c.

bois de rose [Fr.] rosewood. 20c.

boiserie [Fr.] domestic woodwork, *esp.* panelling. 20c.

boîte [Fr. 'box'] a disreputable club or dance-hall; a 'low dive'. 20c.

boîte de nuit [Fr.] a night-club. 20c.

bolas *pl.* [Sp. 'balls'] a device consisting of two or more heavy balls connected by cords, used for capturing animals by flinging it at them in such a way that their legs become entangled. 19c. Now often used as a singular with plural *bolases.* [N,S(*)]

bolero [Sp.] (1) *Mus.* a lively Spanish dance; (2) a short jacket reaching barely to the waist. 19c. [N(*),S]

bolshevik [Russ. 'bigger'] a member of the extreme wing of the Russian Socialist Party, later the Communist Party. 20c. Often interpreted as the 'majority' party at the Second Congress of the Russian Social-Democratic Party, 1903. Cf. MENSHEVIK. [N*]

bolus, *pl.* **boli** [Lat. < Gk. βῶλος] *Med.* a large pill. 16c. [N,S]

bombe [Fr.] *Cul.* a conical confection, *usu.* of ice-cream. 19c. [N*]

bombé [Fr.] convex, bulging. 20c. In common use applied to furniture in which surfaces normally plane are convex.

bombe surprise [Fr.] *Cul.* a conical confection of unspecified ingredients; *hence,* a 'surprise packet', something the consequences of which cannot be foreseen. 20c.

bonæ memoriæ [Lat.] of gracious memory, (a person) whom it is pleasant to call to mind. 20c.

bona fide [Lat.] in good faith, with sincerity; honest, sincere. 16c. Now often with reference to licensing laws, which in some countries offer special privileges to '*bona fide* travellers'. Cf. MALA FIDE. [N,S]

bona fides [Lat.] good faith, honest intention, absence of intent to defraud. 18c. Cf. MALA FIDES. [N,S]

bonanza [Sp. 'prosperity'] *U.S.* (yielding) rich ore; *hence,* sudden unexpected wealth. 19c. [N(*),S]

bona vacantia [Lat.] *Law* unclaimed goods, goods the legal ownership of which cannot be determined. 19c. [S]

bonbon [Fr.] a sweetmeat, a sugarplum, a comfit. 19c. [N,S]

bonbonnière [Fr.] a small fancy box to hold sweets. 19c. [N,S]

bon copain [Fr.] an agreeable companion; a loyal friend; aggressively good-natured, selfconsciously friendly (manners, behaviour, etc.) 20c. Replacing the earlier *bon camarade* (19c.). The feminine *bonne copine* seems not to be in use.

Bond [Afrik.] the *Afrikaander Bond,* a political league formed in South Africa in 1882 to promote the unification and independence of the South African colonies. 19c. [N(*)]

bondieuserie [Fr. < *bon Dieu* 'good God'] cloying piety, *esp.* as manifested in 'repository art'. 20c. The term was invented by Jules Vallès (1832–1885). Cf. OBJET DE PIÉTÉ.

bon enfant, *pl.* **bons enfants** [Fr. 'good child'] an agreeable companion, one who is always good company. 19c. [N*,S]

bon goût [Fr.] good taste. 18c. [S(*)]

bonheur-du-jour [Fr. 'joy of the day'] a lady's small writing-table with drawers below and small drawers and cupboards at the back; an ESCRITOIRE. 20c. It has been conjectured that the name refers to the sudden popularity achieved by the design about 1770.

bonhomie [Fr.] good nature, easy good-humour, 'clubbability'. 18c. [N,S]

boni et legales (homines) *pl.* [Lat.] decent, law-abiding (people). 20c.

bon marché [Fr.] cheap. 19c. The name of a well-known cut-price shop in Paris. [S]

bon mot, *pl.* **bons mots** [Fr.] a clever remark, an epigram, a witticism. 18c. Cf. MOT. [N,S]

bonne [Fr.] a (French) maidservant or nursemaid. 18c. [N,S]

bonne amie [Fr.] a woman who is a good friend (to someone); often with the implication that she is more than a friend. 20c.

bonne à tout faire [Fr.] a maid of all work, a 'general'. 20c.

bonne bouche, *pl.* **bonnes bouches** [Fr.] a tasty morsel (literally or figuratively). 18c. The English sense is not known in French, where the meaning is 'pleasant taste'. [N,S]

bonnes fortunes *pl.* [Fr.] love-affairs; success with the ladies. 18c. [S]

bonsai [Jap. 'tray-cultivation'] the (Japanese) art of constructing minature gardens from trees and shrubs dwarfed by repeated root-pruning. 20c.

bonsens [Fr.] good sense, common sense. 20c. *Occ.* (from 18c.) anglicized as *bonsense* and rhymed with *nonsense*.

bon ton [Fr.] good breeding; 'Society'; the world of fashion. 18c. Obsolete by about 1850, but revived with ironical overtones. Cf. HAUT TON. [N,S]

bon vivant, *pl.* **bons vivants** [Fr.] one who enjoys life, one fond of good living, *esp.* of the pleasures of the table. 18c. Cf. GOURMAND. [N,S]

bon viveur, *pl.* **bons viveurs** [Pseudo-Fr.] a BON VIVANT. 19c. The phrase is not used in French; VIVEUR means 'loose liver'. The reason for the substitution is not clear. [N*,S]

bon voyage [Fr.] a prosperous journey; good wishes for a prosperous journey! 15c. [N,S]

boomerang [Austr. *wo-mur-rāng*] a curved wooden missile so designed that it can be made to return to the thrower. 18c. [N,S]

bordello [It.] a brothel, a house of prostitution. 16c. There is no etymological connection with *brothel*, which *orig.* meant a person, not a place. [N,S]

bordereau [Fr.] a memorandum, a 'scrap of paper'. 20c. *Usu.* with reference to the treasonable memorandum which led to the imprisonment of Alfred Dreyfus (1859–1935) from 1894 to 1906.

boreen=BOHEREEN, a minor road.

borné, *f.* **bornée** [Fr.] limited in breadth of outlook, narrow-minded. 19c. [N,S]

bortsch [Russ. *borshch*] *Cul.* a Russian soup coloured with beetroot juice. 19c. Numerous different spellings have been current, including *borsch* and *borscht;* none represents the Russian accurately. [N*]

borzoi [Russ. 'swift'] the Siberian wolfhound. 19c. There is no justification for the pseudo-French pronunciation sometimes heard. [N*]

bossa nova [Port. 'new bump'] a South American dance somewhat resembling the tango. 20c.

bottega [It.] a CAFÉ, a wine-shop. 19c. Cf. BODEGA; BOUTIQUE. [S]

boucharde [Fr.] *Art* a sculptor's hammer, one face of which is cut into small pyramidal points. 20c.

bouché, *f.* **bouchée** [Fr. 'corked'] (1) blocked, stopped up; (2) (wine or cider) corked while still fermenting, so that it remains fizzy. 20c. Not the same as English *corked* 'tasting of the cork'.

bouche bée, *pl.* **bouches bées** [Fr.] *Mus.* (singing) with the mouth open, but without articulating words. 20c. Cf. BOUCHE FERMÉE.

bouchée [Fr.] *Cul.* a small patty or pastry. 19c. [N]

bouche fermée, *pl.* **bouches fermées** [Fr.] *Mus.* (singing) with the mouth shut, humming. 20c. Cf. BOUCHE BÉE.

bouclé [Fr.] (kind of knitting wool) consisting of numerous small loops; fabric knitted from such wool. 20c.

boudoir [Fr. 'sulking-place'] a small room where a lady can be alone or receive her intimate friends. 18c. Scarcely now used without irony. Cf. VIE DE BOUDOIR. [N,S]

bouffant [Fr.] puffed out; now *esp.* of the style of hair-dressing known as COIFFURE BOUFFANTE. 19c. [N,S]

bougie [Fr.] *Med.* a thin flexible instrument for probing or dilating passages in the body. 18c. In French the word also has the meanings 'wax taper' and 'sparking plug'. [N,S]

bouillabaisse [Fr.] *Cul.* a Provençal dish of fish stewed in water or wine. 19c. [N*]

bouilli [Fr.] *Cul.* boiled or stewed meat, *usu.* beef. 17c. [N,S]

bouillon [Fr.] (1) *Cul.* broth, *usu.* of beef or chicken. 17c. (2) *Med,* a broth used for the culture of BACTERIA. 20c. [N(*),S]

boule [Fr.] a game resembling ROULETTE, in which a rubber ball is rolled round a wooden bowl pierced with numbered holes. 20c. [N*]

boulevard [Fr.] a broad street or walk planted with trees, *esp.* considered as a place for lounging and gossiping. 18c. The word is ultimately cognate with *bulwark.* [N(*),S]

boulevardier [Fr.] one who frequents the BOULEVARDS, a lounger. 19c. Cf. FLÂNEUR. [N,S]

bouleversé, *f.* **bouleversée** [Fr.] upset, turned upside down; overwhelmed, overcome (with emotion). 19c. [S]

bouleversement [Fr.] turning upside down, complete oversetting. 18c. [N,S]

bouquet [Fr.] (1) a bunch of flowers, a nosegay; (2) the AROMA exhaled from wine. 18c. [N,S]

bouquet garni [Fr.] *Cul.* a bunch of herbs (*usu.* parsley, thyme and bay) used for flavouring. 20c. Cf. GARNI.

bouquiniste [Fr.] a second-hand bookseller. 20c. Rather the vendor of miscellaneous bargains than the proprietor of a properly organized bookshop.

bourgeois, *f.* **bourgeoise** [Fr.] a member of the middle classes; related to or typical of the middle classes; *hence*, philistine in æsthetic matters; indifferent to socialist principles. 17c. The secondary meanings have developed fairly recently. Cf. BÜRGERLICH; PETIT BOURGEOIS. [N,S]

bourgeoisie [Fr.] the middle classes, *esp.* considered as philistine in æsthetic matters or indifferent to socialist principles. 17c. Cf. HAUTE BOURGEOISIE; PETITE BOURGEOISIE. [N,S]

bourrée [Fr.] (1) *Mus.* a lively dance of French or Spanish origin. 18c. (2) *Ballet* a series of rapid PAS DE BOURRÉE; a series of small rapid steps on the POINTES. 20c. [N*]

Bourse [Fr. 'purse'] the French Stock Exchange. 19c. [N,S]

boustrophedon [Gk. βουστροφηδόν 'ox-turning'] (written) alternately from right to left and left to right. 17c. The term is drawn from an analogy with ploughing. [N,S]

boutade [Fr.] a sudden fit of temper, a sudden unpredictable action. 17c. [N(*),S]

boutique [Fr.] a small expensive shop in a fashionable district, a small shop catering for expensive and exotic tastes. 20c. Etymologically related to BODEGA, BOTTEGA, though the sense development is very different.

boutonné, *f.* **boutonnée** [Fr. 'buttoned up'] reticent, unforthcoming, laconic. 20c. Cf. CONTENU; DÉBOUTONNÉ.

boutonnière [Fr.] a spray of flowers worn in the buttonhole. 19c. Cf. CORSAGE. [N*,S]

bouts rimés [Fr. 'rhymed ends'] (the composition of) verse, the rhymes for which are provided by another hand; a game in which each player completes the couplet started by the preceding player, and begins another for the next player. 18c. The second meaning (not recorded by the dictionaries) is now much the more common. [N,S]

boyar [Russ. *boyarin*, pl. *boyare*] a grandee in the old Russian aristocracy; a Russian landed proprietor. 16c. [N,S]

bozzetto, *pl.* **bozzetti** [It.] a small-scale model for a large piece of statuary, a sculptural sketch. 20c. Cf. MAQUETTE.

bras de lumière, *pl.* **bras de lumière** [Fr.] a lamp-bracket affixed to a wall, a wall-light. 20c.

brassard [Fr.] a badge worn on the arm, a distinctive armlet. 19c. [N]

brasserie [Fr. 'brewery'] an establishment in which food and beer are sold. 19c. [N*,S]

brassière [Fr. 'bodice'] an underbodice designed to support the breasts. 20c. A euphemism; the corresponding word in French is *soutien-gorge*, another euphemism. [N*]

bravura [It.] display of daring or brilliance, *esp. Mus.* (a piece of music) requiring great skill and spirit in the performer. 18c. [N,S(*)]

breccia [It.] *Geog.* a composite rock formed of angular fragments held together by a natural cement; a composite mass of gravel and ice. 18c. [N,S]

Breitschwanz [Ger. 'broad-tail'] artificial sable fur. 20c. [N*]

breviora *pl.* [Lat.] the shorter works (of some writer). 20c. Cf. PARERGON.

bric-à-brac [Fr.] antiquarian odds and ends, miscellaneous curios. 19c. [N,S]

bricole [Fr.] *Tennis* the rebound of a ball from the wall of the court; *hence*, any oblique or indirect action. 16c. [N,S]

brio [It.] liveliness, vivacity. 19c. Cf. CON BRIO. [N,S]

brioche [Fr.] a small light cake made with yeast. 19c. The 'cake' of Marie Antoinette's 'Let them eat cake!' [N,S]

briolette [Fr.] a pear-shaped diamond with triangular facets cut in all directions. 19c. The French word is perhaps from *briller* 'to sparkle'. [N,S]

brisé [Fr. 'broken'] *Ballet* a leap during which the feet are lightly beaten in the air. 20c.

brise-bise [Fr. 'break-wind'] a net curtain over the lower part of a window. 20c. [N*]

brise-soleil [Pseudo-Fr. 'break-sun'] *Arch.* a louvred screen designed to protect the walls and windows of buildings from tropical sunshine. 20c. Introduced by Le Corbusier as an ornamental feature in non-tropical climates.

brisé volé [Fr.] *Ballet* a BRISÉ in which the dancer alights on one foot with the other extended. 20c.

brocatelle [Fr.] a kind of brocade, a heavy figured fabric with an embossed pattern. 17c. [N,S]

broch/brogh [Dan. *borg* 'stronghold'] *Hist.* a prehistoric stone fort found in north-eastern Scotland, Orkney and Shetland, consisting of a small circular enclosure for cattle, with rooms for habitation in the thickness of the wall. 17c. The word is a Scottish variation on the Scandinavian equivalent of English *borough*. [N]

broché [Fr.] (sheets of paper) stitched together, not bound. 20c.

brochure [Fr.] a pamphlet stitched or stapled together, not bound. 18c. [N,S]

broderie anglaise [Fr. 'English embroidery'] open embroidery on white cambric. 19c. Often written *broderie Anglaise*, though French usage does not require the capital. [N*]

brogh=BROCH, a prehistoric stone fort.

bronchi *pl.* [Lat. < Gk. *βρόγχοι*] *Med.* the two main branches of the TRACHEA or wind-pipe. 18c. The singular *bronchus* is very rare. [N]

bronco [Sp. 'rough'] *U.S.* an untamed or half-tamed horse. 19c. [N,S]

brouhaha [Fr.] fuss and bother, hubbub, uproar. 20c.

brouillon [Fr.] a rough draft (of a letter or document). 19c. [N*,S(*)]

(die) Brücke [Ger. 'the bridge'] the name chosen by a group of artists who came together in Dresden in 1905. 20c. The work of the group was characterized by dramatic subject-matter treated in harsh colour. Cf. (LES) FAUVES.

bruit [Fr.] rumour. 20c. Anglicized in 15c., but recently re-adopted with a French pronunciation.

brûlé, *f.* **brûlée** [Fr. 'burnt'] (1) compromised, having lost one's reputation; (2) *Cul.* made or flavoured with burnt sugar. 20c.

brûle-parfums, *pl.* **brûle-parfums** [Fr.] a small ornamental brazier for the burning of aromatic substances. 20c. Cf. CASSOLETTE.

brunette [Fr.] (a woman) of dark complexion, *usu.* with brown or black hair. 18c. No masculine equivalent is in use, though BLOND is used of men. [N,S]

brusque [Fr.] rough or abrupt in manner. 17c. [N,S(*)]

brusquerie [Fr.] roughness or abruptness of behaviour; an instance of such behaviour. 18c. [N,S]

brut [Fr.] (of wines) unsweetened, raw, rough. 19c. Cf. SEC. [N*]

brutum fulmen, *pl.* **bruta fulmina** [Lat.] a harmless thunderbolt, an empty threat. 17c. Pliny *Natural History* ii 43. [S]

bruyant, *f.* **bruyante** [Fr.] noisy, rackety. 20c.

buffet [Fr.] a refreshment bar; light refreshments (*usu.* cold) set out on a side-table at an informal social function. 19c. The earlier meaning 'sideboard' is now obsolete. [N,S]

buffo [It.] comic, burlesque; a comic actor or singer. 18c. Cf. OPÉRA BOUFFE; OPERA BUFFA. [N,S(*)]

bulbul [Arab.] a species of thrush admired in the East for its song. 17c. [N,S]

Bundeswehr [Ger.] the Federal German Armed Forces established by the Treaty of Paris (1954–5) under Supreme Allied Command. 20c.

buon fresco [It.] *Art* wet plaster ready for painting; painting executed on wet plaster. 20c. Cf. A BUON FRESCO.

bureau, *pl.* **bureaux** [Fr. 'baize'] (1) a writing-desk; (2) an office for the transaction of official business. 17c. The *bureau* is properly a desk with small drawers, pigeon-holes and cupboards above, enclosed by a sloping front which can be let down to form a writing-surface, as distinct from the SECRÉTAIRE in which the writing-surface is vertical when closed; but the word is often used, like ESCRITOIRE, to denote any form of writing-desk, even a BUREAU PLAT. [N(*),S]

bureau à cylindre, *pl.* **bureaux à cylindre** [Fr.] a writing-desk with a lid consisting of a rigid quarter-cylinder of wood which slides round behind the drawers at the back when open. 20c. In French the word is also applied to a roll-top desk.

bureau de change, *pl.* **bureaux de change** [Fr.] a money-changer's office. 20c.

bureau plat, *pl.* **bureaux plats** [Fr.] a flat-topped writing-table with drawers on each side of the knee-hole, a library table. 20c.

bürgerlich [Ger.] BOURGEOIS, characteristic of the middle classes, philistine in æsthetic matters. 20c.

burla [It.] (1) a joke, *esp.* a joke at the expense of another person; (2) *Mus.* a playful composition, a musical joke. 20c. Cf. SCHERZO.

burnous [Fr. < Arab. *burnus*] a hooded cloak extensively worn by Moors and Arabs. 17c. [N,S]

burra [Hind. *barā*] *A.-I.* large, *usu.* in the phrase *burra peg* 'large drink'. 19c. The word *peg* in this sense, though confined to *A.-I.*, is English. Cf. CHOTA (peg).

burra sahib [Hind. *barā çāḥib* 'great master'] *A.-I.* an important person, *esp.* the head of a department, etc. 19c. Cf. SAHIB. [N*]

burro [Sp.] a donkey. 19c. [N(*)]

Burschenschaft, *pl.* **Burschenschaften** [Ger.] a (German) students' association, *usu.* of a political character. 19c. [S]

bushido [Jap.] the ethical code of the SAMURAI, the Japanese military caste. 19c. [N*]

but du promenade [Fr.] the aim of the excursion, the object of the exercise. 20c.

butte [Fr.] *U.S.* an isolated hill rising abruptly from a plain. 19c. [N]

buvette [Fr.] a roadside inn; a refreshment bar. 18c. [N(*),S]

bwana [Swahili] master; *usu.* as a term of address by a Swahili servant. 19c. [N*]

byssus [Lat. < Gk. *βύσσος*] *Hist.* a fine linen fabric prized by the ancients. 14c. [N]

C

c.=CIRCA, about . . . .

cabaret [Fr. 'tavern'] a light entertainment provided in a restaurant, etc., as an accompaniment to refreshments. 20c. [N*]

cabinet particulier, *pl.* **cabinets particuliers** [Fr.] a private room, *esp.* one provided for the temporary accommodation of a man and his mistress. 20c. Cf. MAISON DE RENDEZVOUS.

cabochon [Fr.] (a precious stone) smoothed and polished but not cut into facets; (a moulding) with a smooth convex surface surrounded by ornamentation. 16c. Cf. EN CABOCHON. [N,S]

cabriole [Fr.] (1) *Ballet* a leap in which one leg is extended before the dancer leaves the ground. 20c. (2) a form of curved leg frequently used in 18th-century furniture. 18c. The curved leg is so called because it resembles the fore-leg of an animal leaping. Cf. CAPRIOLE. [N(*),S]

cabriolet [Fr.] (1) a light two-wheeled one-horse vehicle with a large hood and an apron. 18c. (2) a motor-car constructed with a sliding glass partition between the driver and the occupants of the back seats. [N,S]

cache [Fr.] a hiding-place, *esp.* for stores of provisions; a store of provisions hidden by an explorer, etc., for future use. 16c. [N(*),S]

cache-misère [Fr. 'hide-shabbiness'] any close concealing garment, *esp.* a hat or turban which conceals the hair. 20c.

cache-sexe [Fr. 'hide-sex'] the minimum garment consistent with decency, a G-string. 20c.

cachet [Fr. 'seal'] (1) an unmistakable mark, a 'certain something'; (2) *Med.* a nauseous medicine enclosed in a soluble casing; (3) a special impression made by a rubber-stamp on a first-flight envelope in addition to the normal postal markings. 19c. Cf. DRAGÉE. [N(*),S]

cache-torchons [Fr.] a receptacle for keeping cleaning-rags, etc., out of sight. 20c.

cachou [Fr.] a fragrant tablet used by smokers and others to sweeten the breath. 19c. [N(*),S]

cacodæmon [Gk. *κακοδαίμων*] an evil spirit, an evil genius. 16c. [N,S]

cacoethes loquendi [Lat.] an itch for speaking, an irresistible urge to talk. 19c. Based on CACOETHES SCRIBENDI. [S]

cacoethes scribendi [Lat.] an itch for writing, an irresistible urge to write. 19c. Juvenal *Satires* III vii 51–2: *insanabile . . . scribendi cacoethes* 'the incurable itch for writing'. The more correct *scribendi cacoethes* was in use from 17c., but is now obsolete. Lat. *cacoethes* is from Gk. κακοήθης 'bad habit'. [S]

cadenza [It.] *Mus.* an elaborate, florid passage for voice or solo instrument, *usu.* at the end of a song or instrumental movement. 18c. [N,S]

cadet [Fr.] (the) younger; always preceded by a name, and opposed to AÎNÉ '(the) elder'. 19c. [S]

cadit quæstio [Lat.] the question lapses, there is nothing left to discuss. 19c. [S]

cadre [Fr. 'frame'] a minimum establishment of key men, which can be expanded as or when necessary. 19c. *Orig. Mil.*, but now in more general use. [N,S]

caduceus, *pl.* **caducei** [Lat. < Gk. καρύκειον] *Hist.* the staff of office of a Greek or Roman herald, *esp.* that carried by Hermes (Mercury) the messenger of the gods. 16c. Gk. καρύκειον is Doric; the Attic form is κηρύκειον. [N,S]

cæcum, *pl.* **cæca** [Lat.] *Med.* the blind-gut, a closed tube forming part of the large intestine in man and many animals. 18c. [N,S]

cæl(avit) [Lat.] (he) engraved (it); always accompanied by a name and appended to an engraving. 20c. Cf. DEL(INEAVIT); FEC(IT); PINX(IT); SCULPS(IT).

cæstus [Lat.] *Hist.* a Roman boxing-glove, *usu.* loaded with iron or lead. 18c. Often written *cestus*, and confused with the distinct word CESTUS. [N,S]

cæsura [Lat.] *Ling.* the interruption of a rhythm, a pause for breath which divides a line of verse. 16c. There is commonly only one *cæsura* in each line of verse, but there may on occasion be more than one. [N,S]

cætera desunt/cetera desunt [Lat.] the rest is lacking. 19c. Used to indicate that the remainder of a manuscript, etc., is not extant. Cf. DESUNT CÆTERA. [S]

cæteris paribus/ceteris paribus [Lat.] other things being equal. 17c. [N*,S]

cafard [Fr.] depression, often accompanied by nostalgia. 20c.

café [Fr.] (1) coffee; (2) a coffee-house; *hence*, an establishment where light meals are served. 19c. The monosyllabic pronunciations sometimes heard are gross vulgarisms. [N,S]

café au lait [Fr.] coffee with (hot) milk, as opposed to CAFÉ NOIR; *hence*, a light brown colour. 18c. Cf. CAPPUCCINO. [N*,S]

café chantant, *pl.* **cafés chantants** [Fr.] a CAFÉ in which vocal and musical entertainment is provided. 19c. [N*,S(*)]

café-concert [Fr.] a music-hall. 20c.

café filtre [Fr.] a cup or glass of coffee made by allowing hot water to filter down through a detachable vessel containing ground coffee. 20c. Cf. FILTRE.

café littéraire [Fr.] a CAFÉ patronized by men of letters. 20c.

café noir [Fr.] black coffee, coffee without milk. 19c. Cf. CAFÉ AU LAIT; CAPPUCCINO. [N*,S]

caftan [Turk. *kaftan*] an Oriental garment consisting of a long tunic with a girdle at the waist. 16c. [N,S]

cagnotte [Fr.] (in many games of chance) the percentage gain accruing to the bank as a result of the deliberate adjustment of the odds; (in BACCARA(T) and CHEMIN DE FER) the percentage of the stakes reserved to the proprietor of the gaming-rooms. 20c.

cagoule [Fr.] (a head-covering resembling) a cowl or hood. 20c.

cahier [Fr.] a notebook; now *usu.* the technical notebook of a writer or artist. 19c. [N(*),S]

cailleach [Ir.] an old hag; a term of abuse or abusive reference. 19c. [N,S]

caïque [Fr. < Turk. *kayık*] a light rowing-boat; a Levantine sailing-vessel. 16c. [N,S]

ça ira [Fr.] all will go well. 19c. From the refrain of a popular song composed in 1789 by a street-singer named Ladré: *Ah, ça ira, ça ira, ça ira! Les aristocrates* À LA LANTERNE! [S]

calando [It.] *Mus.* growing softer and slower. 19c. [N]

calculus, *pl.* **calculi** [Lat.] (1) *Med.* a stone, any hard accretion inside the body. 18c. (2) a system or method of calculation, *esp.* that involving differentiation. 17c. The second meaning derives from the primitive use of pebbles to facilitate counting. [N,S]

caldarium [Lat.] *Hist.* the hottest room of a Roman bath. 18c. Cf. FRIGIDARIUM, TEPIDARIUM. [N,S]

callus [Lat.] *Med.* hardened skin; bony substance formed during the healing of a fracture. 16c. [N,S]

calque [Fr.] an exact copy, a slavish imitation. 20c.

calvaire [Fr.] an open-air representation of the Crucifixion, a wayside cross. 19c. [S]

calx, *pl.* **calces** [Lat.] the powdery residue resulting from the calcining of a metal. 15c. [N,]

camaraderie [Fr.] good fellowship, jovial intimacy, loyalty among intimates. 19c. [N,S]

camarilla [Sp. 'little room'] a group of secret intriguers. 19c. [N,S]

cameo [It.] *Art* a carving in low relief on a substance having two layers of different colours (e.g. onyx, sardonyx, or certain kinds of shell) so that the figure is in one colour and the ground in another; a small ornament carved in this way; *hence*, a representation in miniature, perfect of its kind. 16c. Cf. VIGNETTE. [N(*),S(*)]

camera lucida [Lat. 'light room'] a device for projecting a coloured image through a prism on to a sheet of paper on which the outline of the image can be traced. 17c. Invented by Dr Robert Hooke (1635–1703) in 1668; the *camera lucida* differs from the earlier CAMERA OBSCURA in that the lightness of the room allows copying. [N,S]

camera obscura [Lat. 'dark room'] a device whereby a coloured image is projected through a small hole or a lens on to a suitable surface in a dark room. 17c. Invented by G. B. Porta (1542–97). Cf. CAMERA LUCIDA. [N,S]

camino reál [Sp.] the 'royal road', the best or most successful means of achieving an end. 20c.

camouflage [Fr.] *Mil.* disguising the appearance of an object used in war; *hence*, disguising the appearance of any object or the purpose of any action; to disguise (the appearance of anything). 20c. *Orig.* used of disguise by means of a smoke-screen; cf. CAMOUFLET. [N*]

camouflet [Fr. 'puff of smoke'] Mil. a small explosive charge intended to destroy enemy troops engaged in mining. 19c. [N,S]

campanile, *pl.* **campanili** [It.] a bell-tower (*usu.* detached). 17c. [N,S]

campo santo [It. 'holy field'] a burial ground. 19c. [S]

campus [Lat. 'field'] the grounds of a college or university. 18c. First used at Princeton, and until recently *U.S.* only; now increasingly current in newly-founded English universities and educational establishments to denote the concentration of residences for staff and students in the same area as the university or educational buildings proper. No plural is in use. [N*]

canaille [Fr. 'pack of dogs'] the populace, the rabble, the crowd, the mob. 17c. Cf. HOI POLLOI. [N,S]

canapé [Fr. 'sofa'] (1) a high-backed sofa large enough to seat several people. 20c. (2) *Cul.* a piece of fried or toasted bread on which a savoury titbit is served. 19c. (3) *Bridge* a convention by which a short suit is bid before a long suit. 20c. [N*]

canard [Fr. 'duck'] an absurd story, a false report, a hoax. 19c. The development of the meaning from 'duck' remains mysterious, though numerous conjectures have been put forward. [N,S]

cancan [Fr.] an indecorous dance popular in Paris dancing-halls in the nineteenth century; a less offensive modern version of this dance. 19c. Cf. CHAHUT. [N,S]

cancellandum [Lat.] (part of) a leaf of a book for which another is to be substituted. 20c. The substituted (part of a) leaf is called a *cancel.* [N*]

ça ne fait rien [Fr.] it doesn't matter, it's of no importance. 20c. Also *cela ne fait rien.* Popularized during and after the First World War.

canelloni, *see* CANNELLONI, a kind of PASTA.

canephorus [Lat. < Gk. κανεφόρος] *Arch.* the figure of a youth bearing a basket on his head. 19c. The feminine is *canephora*, but *canephorus* is commonly used to denote a figure of either sex. [N,S]

cannelloni *pl.* [It.] *Cul.* a kind of PASTA resembling large-sized MACARONI, stuffed with cheese or meat and served with a sauce after baking. 20c. Often mis-spelt *canelloni, canneloni*. Cf. SPAGHETTI; VERMICELLI.

cannula [Lat. 'small pipe'] *Med.* a tubular instrument introduced into a cavity of the body to allow the escape of a fluid. 17c. [N,S]

cañon [Sp.] *U.S.* a deep precipitous gorge through which a river flows. 19c. Now often spelt *canyon* to avoid the use of the TILDE. [N(*),S]

cantabile [It.] *Mus.* in a smooth, flowing vocal style; a piece of music in such a style. 18c. Cf. SOSTENUTO. [N,S]

cantata [It.] *Mus.* a choral work resembling an ORATORIO but shorter. 18c. Formerly contrasted with SONATA in the obsolete sense 'instrumental composition'. [N,S]

cantatrice [It.] *Mus.* a female professional singer. 19c. [N,S]

cantharus [Lat. < Gk. κάνθαρος] *Hist.* a large two-handled drinking-vessel; a fountain in the courtyard of a church. 19c. [N*]

cantilena [It.] *Mus.* the air or melody of a piece of music. 18c. [N,S]

canto [It. 'song'] a division of a long poem. 16c. [N,S]

canto fermo, *pl.* **canti fermi** [It.] *Mus.* a simple melody to which contrapuntal parts are added; *esp.* a plainsong melody so treated. 18c. The Latin equivalent *cantus firmus*, once common, is now scarcely used. [N,S]

canton [Fr.] a subdivision of a country, *esp.* one of the small sovereign states which form the Swiss confederation. 16c. [N,S]

cantoris [Lat. 'of the singer'] *Mus.* (the side of the church) belonging to the precentor; the north side of the church; opposed to DECANI. 18c. [N*,S]

canyon=CAÑON, a deep precipitous gorge.

capable de tout [Fr.] likely to do anything, entirely unpredictable in one's activities. 20c.

cap-a-pié [Obs.Fr.] from head to foot, *usu.* with reference to full armour. 16c. The modern French form is *de pied en cap*. [N,S]

capax imperii nisi imperasset, *see* (OMNIUM CONSENSU,) CAPAX IMPERII NISI IMPERASSET, (everyone thought him) capable of exercizing authority until he tried it.

capias [Lat. 'you may seize'] *Law* one of a number of types of writ authorizing the sheriff to arrest (a person) or seize (goods). 15c. [N,S]

capo d'opera [It.] a masterpiece. 19c. Cf. CHEF D'ŒUVRE. [S]

caporal [Fr. 'corporal'] a kind of light shag tobacco; a cigarette made from such tobacco. 19c. [N,S]

cappa magna [Lat.] *Eccles.* the long ceremonial cloak with train and hood worn by cardinals and some other ecclesiastical dignitaries. 20c. The *cappa magna* is red for cardinals, violet for bishops. The Italian form *cappamagna* is sometimes used in English.

cappuccino [It.] black coffee topped with frothed hot milk or cream. 20c. In Italian usage, 'black coffee with a little hot milk'; so named from the dark brown habit of the Capuchin friar. Sometimes miswritten *cappucino*, *capuccino*.

capriccio [It.] *Mus.* a lively composition in free form; *hence*, a light-hearted exercise in any artistic technique, a JEU D'ESPRIT. 17c. [N,S]

caprice [Fr.] a sudden whim, a decision formed without adequate motive; a temperament addicted to such decisions. 17c. [N,S]

capriole [Obs.Fr.] *Equ.* a vertical leap at the top of which the horse jerks its hind legs out together. 16c. The modern French form is CABRIOLE. [N,S]

caput lupinum [Lat. 'wolf's head'] an outlaw. 18c. An outlaw could be killed as freely as a wolf. [N*,S]

caput mortuum [Lat. 'dead head'] the residue left after prolonged distillation; worthless residue; red oxide of lead used as a pigment. 17c. [N,S]

caqueteuse/caquetoire [Fr. 'gossip-seat'] a chair with a triangular seat, narrow back, and widespread arms. 20c.

carabiniere, *pl.* **carabinieri** [It.] an Italian policeman armed with a rifle. 20c.

caracole [Fr.] *Equ.* a half-turn to the right or left. 17c. [N,S]

caractère [Fr.] *Ballet* (a dance) based on a national or traditional dance, or on the movements of a trade or manner of living. 20c. Cf. DEMI-CARACTÈRE.

carafe [Fr. < Arab. *gharrāf* 'full of water'] an ornamental glass bottle for holding water; a similar bottle for wine, a decanter. 18c. [N,S]

caravanserai [Fr. *caravansérail* < Pers. *kārwān-sarāī*] an Oriental inn with a courtyard where caravans can put up. 16c. [N,S]

carcinoma, *pl.* **carcinomata** [Lat. < Gk. καρκίνωμα 'crab'] *Med.* cancer. 18c. *Orig.* applied only to the early stages of cancer, but now rapidly becoming the accepted name for the disease when referring to a specific organ. [N,S]

caret [Lat. 'it is wanting'] a mark in a line of writing used to show that something is omitted at that point. 17c. The missing words are written above the line or in the margin. [N,S]

carillon [Fr.] *Mus.* a set of bells so arranged that a tune can be played on them by hand or by machinery. 18c. [N,S]

caritas [Lat.] *Theol.* Christian charity, the love of God and one's neighbour. 20c. Used in English because of the different connotation of the word *charity*.

carmagnole [Fr.] a lively song and dance popular among the French revolutionaries in 1793. 18c. [N,S]

carnet [Fr.] a small booklet, *usu.* of official documents. 20c.

carnet vert [Fr. 'green CARNET'] the international insurance certificate required for touring the Continent by car. 20c.

carnivora *pl.* [Lat.] flesh-eating animals. 19c. [N]

carpe diem [Lat.] make the most of the present; eat, drink, for tomorrow we die! 19c. Horace *Odes* I xi 8. Cf. DUM VIVIMUS, VIVAMUS. [S]

carrousel [Fr.] *U.S.* a roundabout, a merry-go-round; *hence*, a rotating stand for the display of merchandise in a shop. 20c. Formerly in the sense 'a festive tournament'. [N,S]

carrozza, *pl.* **carrozze** [It.] a coach; a cab. 20c.

carte blanche [Fr. 'blank paper'] full discretionary power, absolute freedom of action. 18c. [N,S]

carte de visite [Fr.] a size of photograph, 3½ by 2¼ inches. 19c. Introduced in 1858, these photographs were intended for use as visiting cards. [N,S(*)]

carte d'identité [Fr.] an identity card, an official document to prove identity. 20c.

cartel [Fr.] (1) *Mil.* (a written agreement concerning) the exchange of prisoners in time of war. 17c. (2) an agreement between a number of firms to regulate prices, etc.; a syndicate. 20c. [N(*),S(*)]

cartellino, *pl.* **cartellini** [It.] *Art* a painted representation of a small paper scroll bearing an inscription. 20c.

cartonnier [Fr.] an ornamental cabinet containing large flat drawers for the storage of prints, drawings, etc. 20c.

carton-pierre [Fr.] a kind of PAPIER MÂCHÉ made to imitate stone. 19c. [N*]

cartouche [Fr.] a framework for an inscription simulating a sheet of paper with the ends rolled; an oval or rectangular outline enclosing a proper name in Egyptian hieroglyphics. 17c. [N,S]

casa [It.] a house, a villa (in Italy). 19c. Sp. *casa* is used in *U.S.* in a similar sense. [N*,S]

ça saute aux yeux [Fr. 'it jumps to the eyes'] it is quite obvious, it cannot be overlooked. 20c. Also in the form *cela saute aux yeux*.

cascara (sagrada) [Sp. '(sacred) bark'] *Med.* the bark of the Californian buckthorn, used as a laxative. 19c. [N*]

cas de conscience [Fr.] a case of conscience, a question of morality. 20c. Cf. CRISE DE CONSCIENCE.

caserne [Fr.] *Mil.* a (French) barracks, *esp.* temporary barracks. 19c. [N,S]

casino [It. 'little house'] a club-house, *esp.* one where gambling provides the chief entertainment. 18c. Until recently music and dancing were the chief attractions of a *casino*, but the word is not now used unless games of chance are played. [N,S]

cassant [Fr.] abrupt, curt, peremptory. 20c.

casse-croûte [Fr.] a snack, a light meal. 20c.

casserole [Fr.] *Cul.* a covered stew-pan, *usu.* of thick earthenware. 18c. Cf. EN CASSEROLE. [N(*),S]

cassette [Fr.] a small box, *esp.* one designed for containing photographic plates or film. 19c. Now normally with reference to a small cylindrical box designed to feed film direct into a camera without the risk of exposure to light. [N]

cassis [Fr.] a syrup or liqueur flavoured with black-currant. 20c.

cassolette [Fr.] a vessel for burning incense or perfumes in; a box with a perforated lid to allow the perfume of the contents to diffuse. 19c. Cf. BRÛLE-PARFUMS. [N,S]

cassone, *pl.* **cassoni** [It.] *Art* a large (Italian) dower-chest, *usu.* elaborately decorated and incorporating painted panels. 19c. [N*,S]

caste [Fr. < Sp. Port. *casta* 'pure'] one of the numerous immutable hereditary groups into which Indian society is divided; *hence*, any socially exclusive class of people. 17c. [N,S]

castrato, *pl.* **castrati** [It.] *Mus.* a male singer castrated in boyhood so as to preserve his SOPRANO voice. 18c. [N,S]

casus belli [Lat.] an occasion of war, an act justifying war; grounds for a quarrel. 19c. [N*,S]

casus fœderis [Lat.] an act or circumstance bringing into effect the provisions of a treaty. 18c. [N*,S]

casus omissus [Lat.] a circumstance not envisaged by a law or treaty. 18c. [S]

catachresis [Lat. < Gk. *κατάχρησις*] *Ling.* the use of a term in a sense which it does not properly possess; misuse of words. 16c. [N,S]

catafalque [Fr.] an elaborate bier for the display of a coffin during a lying-in-state or a funeral, or as a permanent memorial. 17c. [N,S]

catalogue raisonné, *pl.* **catalogues raisonnés** [Fr.] a systematic descriptive catalogue; *hence*, a systematic list of any kind. 18c. Cf. RAISONNÉ. [N*,S(*)]

catalysis [Gk. *κατάλυσις*] the process whereby a substance can facilitate a chemical reaction while itself remaining unchanged. 19c. [N,S]

catamaran [Tamil *kaṭṭa-maram* 'tied wood'] a boat the stability of which is assured by means of a float (or floats) secured to the ends of transverse members. 17c. [N,S]

catena, *pl.* **catenæ** [Lat. 'chain'] a connected series, *esp.* of writings testifying to belief in some doctrine. 17c. Common only since 19c. [N,S]

catharsis [Lat. < Gk. *κάθαρσις* 'purging'] the purification of the emotions through vicarious experience, *esp.* through the tragic drama. 20c. Aristotle *Poetics* vi. [N*]

catholicon [Gk. *καθολικόν* 'universal'] (1) a universal remedy; (2) a comprehensive treatise. 17c. Cf. PANACEA. [N]

cauchemar [Fr.] a nightmare; a bugbear, a nagging worry. 20c.

caudillo [Sp.] the leader of a group, a captain. 20c. The title *El Caudillo* given to Generalissimo Franco is exactly equivalent to *Il* DUCE and (DER) FÜHRER; but unlike the last it has not acquired a more general connotation.

causa causans [Lat.] the cause which is actually operating in given circumstances to produce an effect. 19c. Contrasted with CAUSA SINE QUA NON. [S]

causa movens [Lat.] the reason for undertaking an action. 20c.

causa sine qua non [Lat.] a cause which is a necessary precondition of a result but plays no active part in its production. 17c. Contrasted with CAUSA CAUSANS. Cf. SINE QUA NON. [S]

cause célèbre [Fr.] a celebrated law-suit, a legal action which gives rise to great public interest. 19c. [N*,S]

causerie [Fr.] an informal discussion, *esp.* a light-hearted article on a literary topic. 19c. [N*,S]

causeuse [Fr.] a small sofa on which two people can sit and talk. 19c. [N,S]

cavaletti *pl.* [It. 'trestles'] *Equ.* low barriers with crossed end-pieces, used in schooling horses. 20c.

cavaliere servente, *pl.* **cavalieri serventi** [It.] the recognized lover of a married woman; one who attends to all the needs of a woman not his wife. 18c. Cf. CICISBEO. [S]

ça va sans dire [Fr.] that goes without saying, that is too obvious to mention. 19c. Also *cela va sans dire*. Until recently the English translation 'that goes without saying' was reprehended as unEnglish, but it now passes unnoticed. [S(*)]

cavatina [It.] *Mus.* a short simple song with no second section or recapitulation. 19c. [N,S]

cave [Lat.] beware! (of the approach of an enemy). 19c. Mainly as school slang, but widely understood. [N*,S]

caveat [Lat. 'let him beware'] *Law* a notice to refrain from some action pending the decision of the court; *hence,* a warning that action will be taken in certain circumstances. 18c. [N,S]

caveat emptor [Lat.] *Law* let the buyer beware; (the principle that) the buyer must ascertain the good quality of the goods he purchases. 16c. [N*,S]

cavo rilievo [It.] *Art* hollow relief; sculpture in which only the outlines of the figures are incised, so that their highest parts are on a level with the ground. 19c. Not the same as INTAGLIO, in which the figures themselves are hollowed out as in a seal. Cf. ALTO RILIEVO; BASSO RILIEVO; MEZZO RILIEVO; SCHIACCIATO RILIEVO. [N,S]

C.D.=CORPS DIPLOMATIQUE, embassy staff.

céad míle fáilte [Ir.] a hundred thousand welcomes; the conventional form of welcome in Irish. 19c. Cf. FÁILTE. [S]

cedant arma togæ [Lat.] let martial rule give place to civil authority. 17c. The first half of a hexameter verse *Cedant arma togæ, concedat laurea laudi* (or *linguæ*) 'let arms give place to the toga, laurels to praise'; the verse is twice quoted by Cicero, *De Officiis* I xxii 82, *In Pisonem* xxx 73. [S]

cedilla [Sp.] a mark like a comma written beneath a *c* to indicate that it has a 'soft' not a 'hard' sound: *ç*. 16c. *Orig.* the mark was a small *z*, and this is the meaning of the name. [N,S]

céilidhe [Ir. *céilí*] (1) an informal social gathering, *usu.* in the evening, at which conversation is the main form of entertainment; (2) an organized social gathering with music and (Irish) dancing. 20c. The English spelling is the older Irish spelling.

cela . . ., *see* ÇA . . .

cendré [Fr.] ash-blond; having ash-blond hair. 20c.

ce n'est pas une révolte, c'est une révolution [Fr.] it isn't a rebellion, it's a revolution. 19c. Said by the Duc de Liancourt to Louis XVI, 14th July 1789; cf. Carlyle *The French Revolution* I v 7.

ce n'est que le premier pas qui coûte = IL N'Y A QUE LE PREMIER PAS QUI COÛTE, it is only the first step that counts.

censor morum [Lat.] a regulator of morals, one whose business it is to punish moral delinquency. 18c. [S]

census [Lat.] an enumeration of individuals, *esp.* of the population of a country for official purposes. 18c. [N(*),S]

cento, *pl.* **centones** [Lat. 'patchwork'] a work composed by piecing together scraps from earlier writers. 17c. The anglicized plural *centos* is now more common. [N,S]

cercle privé [Fr.] a party of gamblers playing in a private room (in a CASINO, etc.) 20c. Cf. SALLE PRIVÉE.

cerebellum [Lat.] *Med.* the smaller hind-portion of the brain, the seat of the higher faculties. 16c. [N,S]

certiorari [Lat. 'to be certified'] *Law* a writ issued by a superior court directing an inferior court to submit the records of an action in which it appears that justice has not been or cannot be done. 15c. [N,S]

certum est quia impossible est [Lat.] it is certain because it is impossible. 20c. Tertullian *De Carne Christi* ii 5. Very commonly misquoted (from 18c.) as *credo quia impossible est* 'I believe (it) because it is impossible'. The paradox is to be resolved in the sense that the apparently impossible would not have been proposed for belief unless it were true. [S]

c'est à dire [Fr.] that is to say . . . 19c. [S]

c'est la guerre [Fr.] that's war, that's the way things happen in wartime. 19c. Cf. À LA GUERRE COMME À LA GUERRE. [S]

c'est la vie [Fr.] that's life, that's the way things happen. 20c.

c'est magnifique, mais ce n'est pas la guerre [Fr.] it's magnificent, but it's not war. 20c. Said of the Charge of the Light Brigade by Maréchal Bosquet (1810–61); hence applied to any heroic waste of effort.

c'est pire qu'un crime, c'est une faute [Fr.] it's worse than a crime, it's a blunder. 20c. *Mémoires de Joseph Fouché* (1824) i 310: *C'est plus qu'un crime, c'est une faute.* The attribution to Fouché (1759–1820) has been questioned, but seems reliable.

cestui que trust [Obs.Fr.] *Law* the person for whose benefit anything is held in trust by another. 18c. Sometimes misused as if it meant 'trustee'; sometimes mis-spelt *cestui qui trust.* [N,S]

cestus [Lat. < Gk. *κεστός* 'stitched'] a girdle or belt, *esp.* that of Venus, the source of her irresistible fascination. 16c. Often written *cæstus*, and confused with the distinct word CÆSTUS. [N,S]

c'est Vénus tout entière à sa proie attachée [Fr.] it is Venus herself fastened on her prey. 20c. Racine *Phèdre* I iii. Used of a woman in pursuit of a man to whom she is irresistibly attracted.

cetera desunt=CÆTERA DESUNT, the rest is lacking.

ceteris paribus = CÆTERIS PARIBUS, other things being equal.

cf. = CONFER, compare.

chaconne [Fr. < Sp. < Basque *chucun* 'pretty'] *Mus.* a slow Spanish dance in 3/4 time. 17c. Cf. PASSACAGLIA. [N,S]

chacun à son goût [Fr.] every man to his taste. 19c. Also in the form, more usual in French, *à chacun son goût.* [S]

chacun à son métier [Fr.] every man to his trade, let the cobbler stick to his last. 20c.

chagrin [Fr. < Turk. *sağrı* 'rump'] acute vexation, mortification. 17c. *Orig.* 'rough leather' (English *shagreen*); *hence*, something that abrades the mind. [N,S]

chagrin d'amour [Fr.] the distress resulting from an unhappy love-affair. 20c. The phrase occurs repeatedly in *Plaisir d'Amour* by Jean Pierre Claris de Florian (1755–94), familiar in the musical setting by Martini.

chahut [Fr.] a noisy dance resembling the CANCAN. 20c.

chaise [Fr. 'chair'] a light four-wheeled carriage. 18c. [N,S]

chaise-longue [Fr.] a kind of sofa with a back but one end; a day-bed. 19c. Cf. DUCHESSE. [N,S(*)]

chalet [Fr.] the small wooden house of a Swiss peasant; any house built in a similar style. 18c. The spelling *châlet* is erroneous. [N,S]

chalumeau [Fr.] *Mus.* a simple rustic reed-instrument, a shepherd's pipe; the lower register of a clarinet. 18c. [N,S*]

chamade [Fr.] *Mil.* the sounding of a drum to ask for a parley. 17c. [N,S(*)]

chambré [Fr.] (wine) brought to room-temperature. 20c. It is customary to serve red wines *chambré* and white wines chilled.

chamois [Fr.] the European antelope or mountain goat; the skin of this animal used as a wash-leather. 16c. The skin is commonly called *shammy-leather*, and this spelling is sometimes used in writing. [N,S]

champlevé [Fr. *champ levé* 'raised field'] *Art* (a kind of enamel work) in which the metal ground is engraved or hollowed out, the hollows being filled with opaque enamel. 19c. A strip of metal is left between each of the hollowed-out sections. Cf. CLOISONNÉ; (EN) TAILLE D'ÉPARGNE. [N*,S]

chandelier [Fr.] a branched candle-holder, *usu.* suspended from the ceiling and often ornamented with cut-glass lustres. 18c. The word is fully anglicized, except that the initial *ch* is still pronounced as in French. [N,S]

chanson de geste, *pl.* **chansons de geste** [Fr.] one of a group of French historical verse romances, often connected with Charlemagne, current from the 11th to the 13th century, 19c. [S]

chanson de toile, *pl.* **chansons de toile** [Fr.] a short sentimental narrative poem sung by women working at the loom. 20c. Also in the form *chanson à toile.*

chansonnier [Fr.] (1) a (mediæval French) collection of songs or lyrics; (2) a writer of satirical songs or lampoons. 20c.

chantage [Fr.] blackmail, extorting money by the threat of scandalous revelations. 19c. [N,S*]

chaparejos *pl.* [Sp.] *U.S.* stout leather trousers worn by cowboys as a protection against thorns. 19c. Now often abbreviated to *chaps.* [N*]

chaparral [Sp.] *U.S.* a dense undergrowth of thorns, brambles, and briars, of a kind commonly found on poor soil in Mexico and Texas. 19c. [N(*),S]

chapati [Hind. *chapāti*] *A.-I.* a small flat cake of unleavened bread. 19c. The staple food of Upper India. Often spelt *chapatti*, and formerly *chupatty.* [N(*),S(*)]

chapeau-bras [Fr.] a flat three-cornered hat which can be carried under the arm. 18c. Also *chapeau de bras.* [N,S]

chapelle ardente [Fr. 'burning chapel'] a chapel illuminated for the lying-in-state of a distinguished person. 19c. [S]

chaperon [Fr. 'little hood'] a woman (*usu.* married or elderly) who accompanies a young unmarried woman for the sake of propriety. 18c. Sometimes erroneously written *chaperone* as appearing more feminine; but the current meaning derives from the abstract idea of 'protection'. Cf. DUENNA; GOUVERNANTE. [N,S]

char-à-banc [Fr.] a vehicle for a large number of passengers with seats facing forwards. 19c. *Orig.* horse-drawn, later mechanically propelled; the word has been replaced in contemporary usage by '(motor-)coach'. [N,S]

charade [Fr.] a riddle in which each syllable of a word, and finally the word itself, forms part of a brief dramatic scene; *hence*, mummery. 18c. Formerly used also of a written puzzle of similar type. [N,S]

charcuterie [Fr.] (1) a pork-butcher's shop; (2) *Cul.* small pieces of pork cooked in various ways. 19c. [N*]

chargé d'affaires, *pl.* **chargés d'affaires** [Fr.] *Dip.* a diplomatic representative of lower rank than an ambassador; the official in charge of an embassy during the absence of the ambassador. 18c. [N,S]

charisma, *pl.* **charismata** [Gk. χάρισμα] *Theol.* a special grace, a spiritual gift. 17c. [N(*),S]

charivari [Fr.] cacophonous music made in derision of some unpopular person; any disagreeable noise. 17c. [N,S]

charmeur, *f.* **charmeuse** [Fr.] fascinating; (a person) who makes use of charm to achieve success. 20c.

charmeuse [Fr.] a soft smooth fabric (*usu.* of silk) with a satin-like surface. 20c. [N*]

charpoy [Hind. *chārpāī*] *A.-I.* a light Indian bed, a camp-bed. 19c. [N,S(*)]

chasse [Fr.] a liqueur or spirit taken after coffee. 19c. Short for *chasse-café*, formerly also used in full in English; the current French form is POUSSE-CAFÉ. [N,S]

chassé [Fr.] *Ballet* a gliding step in which one foot is moved forwards on the ground. 19c. A similar step was used in country-dancing. [N,S]

chasse-cousin(s) [Fr.] an inferior dinner with bad wine, designed to discourage the visits of unwanted guests. 20c. So called because in rural France most visitors are related, however remotely, to their host.

chassé-croisé [Fr.] a dance-movement in which partners repeatedly change places; *hence*, any circumstance in which people or things repeatedly change places. 19c. [N*,S]

chasseur [Fr.] a tout, *usu.* for a night-club or similar establishment. 20c.

chasseur alpin, *pl.* **chasseurs alpins** [Fr.] a member of a French light infantry regiment composed of skilled mountaineers. 20c. Cf. JÄGER.

chassis [Fr. *châssis*] (1) the framework (and mechanism) of a mechanically propelled vehicle, as opposed to the coachwork; (2) *Art* the frame on which an artist's canvas is stretched. 20c. [N*]

château, *pl.* **châteaux** [Fr.] a large (French) mansion or country house. 18c. Frequently with reference to the bottling of wines on a French estate. [N,S]

château en Espagne [Fr.] a castle in Spain, a day-dream of fantastic good fortune. 19c. [N*,S]

châtelaine [Fr.] (1) the mistress of a household; (2) a bunch of keys, scissors, trinkets, etc. worn suspended from the waist. 19c. [N(*),S]

chatoyance [Fr.] iridescence, variable colour or lustre. 20c.

chatoyant [Fr.] iridescent, changeable in colour or lustre. 19c. Applied to materials like shot silk and to certain jewels and minerals. [N,S]

chaud-froid [Fr. 'hot-cold'] *Cul.* a dish composed of cooked chicken served cold in jelly or sauce. 19c. [N*]

chauffeur, *f.* **chauffeuse** [Fr.] a servant paid to drive a car. 20c. Formerly applied also to an owner-driver, as it still is in French. [N*]

chef [Fr.] a head cook; any male cook. 19c. Short for *chef de cuisine*, but the full form is not in use. [N,S]

chef d'école [Fr.] the founder of a 'school' of art, one who is enthusiastically imitated. 19c. Cf. ÉCOLE; FAIRE ÉCOLE. [S]

chef d'œuvre, *pl.* **chefs d'œuvre** [Fr.] a masterpiece. 17c. The *f* is not pronounced. Cf. CAPO D'OPERA. [N,S]

chef d'orchestre [Fr.] the conductor or leader of an orchestra. 20c.

chef-lieu [Fr.] the chief town of a district, *esp.* of a French *département*. 19c. [S]

chemin de fer [Fr. 'railway'] a card-game resembling BACCARA(T). 20c. [N*]

chemise [Fr.] a woman's linen undergarment, a long bodice; *hence*, any garment resembling an undervest or long bodice. 18c. [N,S]

chemise de bain [Fr.] a linen gown worn in the bath for the sake of modesty. 20c. Customary in some Continental convents.

chemise de nuit [Fr.] a (woman's) nightgown. 20c.

chemisette [Fr.] an ornamental 'front' of lace or muslin which fills the open neck of a woman's dress. 19c. Cf. PLASTRON. [N,S]

chenet [Fr.] a fire-dog, an andiron. 20c. Sometimes mis-spelt *chênet*, as if intended to support logs of oak (*chêne*); the word is a diminutive of *chien* 'dog'.

chenille [Fr. 'hairy caterpillar'] a thread consisting of a core surrounded by a fine silk nap; cloth woven from such threads. 18c. [N,S]

cheong-sam [Chin.] a long red dress worn by women in China on ceremonial occasions such as weddings; a tight-fitting quasi-Oriental dress with a split at each side seam. 20c.

cherchez la femme [Fr.] look for the woman; there's bound to be a woman at the bottom of it. 20c. A. Dumas *Les Mohicans de Paris* (1864) III x and elsewhere; dramatized version III vii.

chère amie [Fr. 'dear friend'] a mistress. 18c. A polite and inoffensive euphemism. [S(*)]

chéri, *f.* **chérie** [Fr.] darling; *usu.* as a form of address. 19c. [S]

cher maître [Fr.] dear master; *usu.* as a form of address. 20c. Often ironically addressed to someone from whom one has learnt much but whom one now excels.

chernozem [Russ.] *Geog.* the fertile black earth of Southern Russia. 20c. Similar soil is found also in a belt extending from Canada through the United States.

che sarà, sarà [It.] what will be, will be. 16c. [S]

chétif, *f.* **chétive** [Fr.] frail, under-developed, sickly-looking. 20c. [N*]

cheval de bataille [Fr. 'battle-horse'] a favourite subject, a favourite argument, a 'King Charles's head'. 19c. The implication is always that the subject or argument is grievously overworked. [S]

chevalier d'industrie [Fr.] an adventurer, a swindler, one who lives by his wits. 18c. [S]

chevaux de frise *pl.* [Fr. 'Frisian horses'] a rotating bar bristling with spikes set on the top of a wall to discourage entry; a line of fixed spikes, fragments of broken glass, etc. on top of a wall. 19c. In use from 17c. in military contexts; the singular *cheval de frise* was also used. The plural is now sometimes misconstrued as a singular. [N,S]

chevet [Fr.] *Arch.* the apse of a church, *usu.* with an ambulatory and radiating chapels. 19c. [N]

chevron [Fr.] a pattern like an inverted V, used in decorative art; a similar shape used as a badge on the sleeve of a uniform. 17c. [N,S]

chez [Fr.] at the house of . . ., at . . .'s house. 20c. A useful expression for which there is no kind of equivalent in English.

chez nous [Fr.] at our house, at home. 19c. The similar forms *chez vous, chez lui* 'at your (his) house' were in use in 18c., but seem now to be obsolete. [S(*)]

chiaroscuro [It. *chiar'* 'bright' *oscuro* 'dark'] *Art* the effect of light and shade in paintings, drawings, etc., *esp.* when the contrast is considerable. 17c. [N,S]

chiasmus [Lat. < Gk. *χιασμός*] *Ling.* a figure of speech in which the sequence of ideas in one of two parallel clauses is inverted in the other. 19c. From the shape of the Greek letter X 'chi'. [N,S]

chic [Fr.] elegance, style, unmistakable but indefinable superiority; possessing such elegance or style. 19c. Probably abbreviated from CHICANE. [N,S]

chicane [Fr.] (1) a trick, a subterfuge, a quibble; trickery, cunning, scheming. 17c. (2) *Bridge* a void, the absence of cards in any suit. 20c. (3) a barrier used in motor-racing, etc. 20c. Probably from mediæval Greek *τζυκανίζειν* 'to play golf', from Pers. *chaugān* 'polo stick'. The origin of the second and third meanings is not clear. [N(*),S]

chichi [Fr.] affected, pretentious, 'precious'. 20c. Of unknown origin: the original meaning seems to have been 'a single curl of false hair'. Distinguished by its quasi-French pronunciation from CHI-CHI; but there may have been some contamination of meaning.

chi-chi [Hind *chhī-chhī* 'dirt'] *A.-I.* the mincing English spoken by Eurasians in India; (characteristic of) a Eurasian who speaks such English. 18c. Formerly also written *chee-chee.* [N]

chiffon [Fr. 'rag'] a diaphanous silk muslin; *pl.* **chiffons**, ornamental accessories of feminine dress. 19c. [N(*),S]

chiffonnier/chiffonnière [Fr.] a low set of shelves with a mirror back and a marble top. 18c. [N,S]

chignon [Fr.] a large coil of hair wound round a pad, worn at the back of the head. 18c. [N,S]

chimæra [Lat. < Gk. *χίμαιρα*] a grotesque monster formed of parts of different animals; a figment of the imagination, an impossible dream, an extravagant fancy. 16c. [N,S]

chinoiserie [Fr.] a taste for the Chinese style, a scheme of decoration or collection of objects in the Chinese style. 19c. Cf. JAPONAISERIE. [N]

chiton [Gk. *χιτών*] (1) *Hist.* the tunic worn by the ancient Greeks; (2) *Ballet* a similar costume worn by a dancer. 19c. In ballet contexts the word is pronounced as in French. [N,S]

chlamys [Gk. *χλαμύς*] *Hist.* a short cloak worn by men in ancient Greece. 17c. [N,S]

chorale [Ger. *Choral(gesang)*] *Mus.* a choral hymn, a sacred song sung in unison by a choir or congregation; the tune of such a hymn. 19c. The *chorale* is particularly associated with the names of Luther and J. S. Bach. A trisyllabic pronunciation is *occ.* heard, as if the word were from Italian. [N,S]

chose jugée [Fr.] a question already decided, which it is therefore idle to discuss. 19c. Cf. RES JUDICATA. [N*]

chota [Hind. *chhoṭa*] *A.-I.* small, *usu.* in the phrase *chota peg* 'small drink'. 19c. The word *peg* in this sense, though confined to *A.-I.*, is English. Cf. BURRA (peg). [N*]

chota hazri [Hind. *chhoṭa hāẓ(i)ri*] *A.-I.* a light early breakfast. 19c. [N*]

chou(x) [Fr. 'cabbage(s)'] *Cul.* the name given to a special paste or cake-mixture used for making ÉCLAIRS, etc. 19c. *Orig.* the name of a globular custard-tart. [N*]

chronique scandaleuse, *pl.* **chroniques scandaleuses** [Fr.] a chronicle of scandal, memoirs relating the gossip of the day. 19c. The phrase is taken from the title of a reprint (1611) of a life of Louis XI of France attributed to Jean de Troyes. [S]

chypre [Fr. 'Cyprus'] an exotic kind of perfume made in Cyprus. 19c. [N*]

ciao [It.] greetings! a familiar form of salutation on meeting or parting. 20c. A corruption of *schiavo* (*suo*) 'your slave', a Venetian variant of *servo suo* 'your servant'. Now a vogue-word in international student circles.

ciborium, *pl.* **ciboria** [Lat.] *Eccles.* a vessel for reserving the Eucharist, *usu.* in the form of a chalice with a lid. 17c. [N,S]

cicada, *pl.* **cicadæ** [Lat.] the tree-cricket, *esp.* the male tree-cricket which emits a continuous shrill chirping sound. 15c. The *cicada* is found only in tropical and sub-tropical climates, and is unrelated to the cricket and grasshopper. [N,S]

cicerone [It.] a guide who explains the antiquities of a place to visitors. 18c. From the name of Cicero the orator, with reference to the learning and eloquence of the guides. [N,S]

cicisbeo, *pl.* **cicisbei** [It.] the recognized lover of a married woman. 18c. Cf. CAVALIERE SERVENTE. [N,S]

ci-devant [Fr.] former, that was formerly, that used to be. 18c. After the French Revolution used as a noun meaning 'former aristocrat'. Cf. QUONDAM. [N,S]

ci-gît [Fr.] here lies . . .; an epitaph. 20c.

cilia *pl.* [Lat.] hairs forming a fringe resembling eye-lashes; hair-like organs, *usu.* in constant motion, found in animal and vegetable tissues. 18c. [N(*),S]

ciment fondu [Fr. 'cast cement'] *Arch.* a cement of exceptional strength, used in building to support great weights; also used for the casting of statues, reliefs, etc., *esp.* for architectural decoration. 20c.

cinéaste [Fr.] a film-producer; a technical collaborator in the production of a film. 20c.

cinéma-vérité [Fr. 'cinema-truth'] realism in film-making, achieved by the use of inconspicuous equipment and news-reel technique. 20c. Cf. VÉRITÉ.

cinq-à-sept [Fr. 'five until seven'] a visit to one's mistress or to a brothel. 20c.

cinquecento [It. '500'] the fifteen hundreds, the sixteenth century, *esp.* the art and architecture of that century; characteristic of that century. 18c. Cf. QUATTROCENTO; SEICENTO; SETTECENTO; TRECENTO. [N,S]

cipollata [It.] *Cul.* any food strongly flavoured with onion, *esp.* a small Italian sausage strongly flavoured with onion. 20c. Now very commonly anglicized as *chipolata.*

cipollino [It. 'little onion'] an Italian marble veined with alternate streaks of white and pale green. 19c. [N,S]

cippus, *pl.* **cippi** [Lat.] a low monumental column bearing an inscription. 18c. [N,S]

circa [Lat.] about . . .; always followed by a date. 19c. Normally abbreviated to *c.* [N,S]

circus [Lat.] *Hist.* an oblong or oval arena surrounded by tiers of seats, for the celebration of games or the exhibition of spectacles; *esp.* the Circus Maximus of ancient Rome. 16c. The meanings 'acrobatic display' and 'circular space at the intersection of a number of streets' are no older than 19c. [N,S]

ciré [Fr. 'waxed'] (silk or other fabric) with a smooth shiny surface. 20c. Cf. GLACÉ. [N*]

cire perdue [Fr. 'lost wax'] *Art* a method of casting in bronze by making a clay model with a wax surface, enclosing it in a mould, melting out the wax and replacing it by molten bronze. 19c. [N*]

cirque [Fr.] *Geog.* a deep rounded hollow with steep sides, a natural amphitheatre. 19c. Cf. CWM. [N]

ciselé [Fr. 'chiselled'] finely and laboriously worked (of literary style, etc.) 20c.

clachan [Gael.] a hamlet or small village in the Western Highlands of Scotland. 15c. [N]

clair de lune [Fr. 'moonlight'] a kind of bluish glass with an opalescent lustre. 20c.

cláirseach [Ir.] the ancient Celtic harp strung with wire. 15c. Pronounced and *occ.* written *clarshach.* [N]

clairvoyance [Fr.] the faculty of perceiving something concealed from sight or beyond the range of sight; second sight; *hence*, clearness of insight or mental perception. 19c. [N,S]

clairvoyant, *f.* **clairvoyante** [Fr.] one gifted with the faculty of perceiving something concealed from sight or beyond the range of sight. 19c. Cf. VOYANT. [N,S]

claque [Fr.] a group of people paid to clap in a theatre; *hence*, a group of toadies always ready to applaud their leader. 19c. [N,S]

claqueur [Fr.] someone paid to applaud, a member of a CLAQUE. 19c. [N,S]

clausula, *pl.* **clausulæ** [Lat.] *Ling.* a short clause forming the conclusion of a period in Latin prose. 20c. Cf. CURSUS.

clausura [It.] *Eccles.* the part of a monastery or convent from which visitors (*esp.* those of the opposite sex) are excluded. 20c.

claveciniste [Fr.] a player on the harpsichord. 19c. The English *harpsichordist* is clumsy, and is avoided. [N]

clef de voûte [Fr.] a keystone; a person or thing whose presence is indispensable to an organization. 20c.

clepsydra, *pl.* **clepsydræ** [Lat. < Gk. κλεψύδρα 'steal-water'] a water-clock, in which the leaking of water from a small hole marks the passage of time. 17c. [N,S]

clerici vagantes *pl.* [Lat.] wandering scholars; mediæval students who left their Universities to take to the roads. 20c. These *clerici vagantes* were responsible for much of the best mediæval Latin poetry. Cf. GYROVAGI; VAGANTES.

cliché [Fr.] a commonplace phrase, a stereotyped expression. 19c. *Orig.* the French name for a stereotype block in printing; the meaning is now 'photographic negative'. Cf. PHRASE TOUTE FAITE. [N*]

clientèle [Fr.] the whole body of those who consult a professional man or patronize a commercial establishment; regular customers. 19c. [N,S]

clique [Fr.] a small and exclusive group of people banded together for unworthy motives. 18c. Probably *orig.* identical with CLAQUE. A more offensive term than COTERIE: a *clique* is felt to be actively exclusive and to cultivate a sense of superiority to others. [N(*),S]

cloaca, *pl.* **cloacæ** [Lat. 'sewer'] the common excretory canal found in birds, reptiles, and some fishes and mammals. 19c. [N,S]

clochard [Fr.] a tramp, a lie-about. 20c.

cloche [Fr. 'bell'] (1) a glass cover, *orig.* bell-shaped, for the protection of seedlings and delicate plants. 19c. (2) a close-fitting bell-shaped woman's hat. 20c. [N(*)]

cloisonné [Fr. 'partitioned'] *Art* a kind of enamel work in which the cavities containing the enamel are formed by soldering thin strips of metal to the metal ground; *hence*, (any work of art) having the brilliance and clear-cut outlines of such enamel-work. 19c. Cf. CHAMPLEVÉ. [N,S]

cloqué [Fr.] (silk fabric, etc.) embossed with a raised pattern, regular or random. 20c.

clou [Fr. 'nail'] the central idea (of a work of art, etc.); the chief point of interest (in an exhibition, etc.). 19c. [N*]

cocotte [Fr.] a prostitute; a woman of the DEMI-MONDE. 19c. Cf. GRANDE COCOTTE. [N*]

coda [It. 'tail'] *Mus.* a concluding passage introduced after the completion of the essential parts of a movement. 18c. [N(*),S]

codex, *pl.* **codices** [Lat.] an ancient manuscript written in book form, not in the form of a roll. 19c. In use from 16c. in the obsolete sense 'code of laws'. [N,S]

(le) cœur a ses raisons que la raison ne connaît point [Fr.] the heart has its reasons that the reason knows nothing of; i.e., intuitive convictions may have greater force than rational arguments. 20c. Pascal *Pensées* iv 277.

cogito, ergo sum [Lat.] I think, therefore I am. 17c. Descartes *Discours de la Méthode* (1637). [S]

cognomen, *pl.* **cognomina** [Lat.] a nickname; a surname. 19c. *Orig.* the third name (the family name) of a Roman citizen. [N,S]

cognoscenti *pl.* [It.] those who have expert knowledge (*usu.* of the fine arts). 18c. The singular, hardly now in use, is *cognoscente*. The word implies a more professional knowledge than CONNOISSEUR, but is now often used with a flavour of irony. [N,S]

cognovit [Lat. 'he knows'] *Law* an acknowledgment by the defendant that the plaintiff's case is good, made to escape the costs of a trial. 18c. [N,S]

cohue [Fr.] an unruly crowd, a noisy mob. 19c. [N,S]

coiffeur, *f.* **coiffeuse** [Fr.] a hair-dresser. 19c. Used by hair-dressers (or their clients) who wish to imply French CHIC. [N(*),S]

coiffeur de dames [Fr.] a women's hair-dresser. 20c.

coiffure [Fr.] a style of dressing the hair. 17c. Formerly also in the sense 'head-dress'. [N,S]

coiffure bouffante [Fr.] a style of hair-dressing in which the hair is made to stand away from the head and is often swept round in a bee-hive shape. 20c. Cf. BOUFFANT.

coitus [Lat.] copulation. 18c. [N]

col [Fr. 'neck'] *Geog.* (1) a high pass across a range of mountains; (2) a region of level pressure between two depressions and two anticyclones diagonally disposed. 19c. [N(*),S]

coleslaw [Du. *koolsla*] *Cul.* a salad of sliced cabbage dressed with vinegar, salt and pepper. 19c. Sometimes corrupted to *cold slaw*. [N]

collage [Fr. 'sticking'] *Art* a technique in which materials and objects are glued to a canvas or panel as part of a picture; a picture produced in this way. 20c. Distinct from MONTAGE in which the whole picture is composed of materials pasted to a surface. Cf. PAPIERS COLLÉS.

collectanea *pl.* [Lat.] notes and quotations collected from various sources. 18c. [N,S]

colleen [Ir. *cailín*] a young (Irish) girl. 19c. [N,S]

colleen bawn [Ir. *cailín bán* 'white girl'] darling girl, sweetheart. 19c. [N]

col legno [It.] *Mus.* (a note on a violin or similar instrument) produced by striking the string with the wood of the bow. 20c.

colloquium, *pl.* **colloquia** [Lat.] a discussion; a discourse or address. 17c. Now *usu.* as an academic pedantry. [N,S]

colon [Fr.] a colonist, a settler in a (French) colonial territory. 19c. [S]

colophon [Lat. < Gk. *κολοφῶν* 'finishing touch'] an inscription or device at the end of a manuscript or printed book, corresponding in the information it gives to the modern title-page. 18c. [N,S]

coloratura [It. 'colouring'] *Mus.* runs, trills and florid passages in vocal music, which add brilliance and display the skill of the singer; (a voice) suitable for such singing. 18c. [N(*)]

colossus [Lat. < Gk. *κολοσσός*] a gigantic statue; anything which impresses by its mere size. 14c. The original *colossus* was the bronze statue of Apollo which stood astride the entrance to the harbour of Rhodes. [N,S]

colostrum [Lat.] beestings, the first milk secreted by a mammal after parturition. 16c. [N]

colporteur [Fr. 'neck-bearer'] a travelling bookseller, one who sells books and pamphlets (*esp.* bibles and religious tracts) from door to door. 18c. [N,S(*)]

columbarium, *pl.* **columbaria** [Lat. 'dove-cot'] a building the walls of which are formed of niches or recesses for cinerary urns. 18c. Until recently only *Hist.*, with reference to Roman sepulchres; now common with reference to similar arrangements in a CREMATORIUM. [N,S]

comble [Fr.] the culmination (of something), the point of perfection. 19c. Cf. ACME, which however can only be used with a dependent genitive. The most common French use 'culmination of misfortune' seems not to be current in English. [N*,S]

comblé, *f.* **comblée** [Fr.] brought to a state of perfection, superbly finished. 20c.

(la) comédie humaine [Fr.] the comedy of human life, the panorama of society. 19c. From the title of Balzac's sequence of novels.

comédie larmoyante [Fr.] sentimental comedy, the comedy of domestic sentiment from which the element of farce is wholly absent. 20c. An eighteenth-century GENRE originated by Marivaux; but the phrase is used with a wider application.

comédienne [Fr.] an actress specializing in comedy. 19c. Cf. TRAGÉDIENNE. [N]

comédie noire [Fr. 'black comedy'] a dramatic work which, though without a tragic ending, has a tragic tone. 20c. *Occ.* translated as *black comedy*. Cf. PIÈCE NOIRE.

comédie rose [Fr. 'pink comedy'] a dramatic work wholly optimistic in tone. 20c. Cf. PIÈCE ROSE.

comédie rosse [Fr.] a bitter, ironical comedy. 20c.

comitadji [Turk. *komitacı* 'committee-man'] a member of a revolutionary secret society, *esp.* in the Balkans at the turn of the century. 20c. Other spellings formerly in use seem to have become obsolete. [N*]

commando [Port.] (1) an expedition by European settlers against (South African) natives; a unit of the BOER militia. 19c. (2) a soldier specially trained for hand-to-hand fighting. 20c. The second meaning has practically displaced the first. [N(*),S]

commedia dell'arte [It.] improvised drama performed by professional actors, *esp.* in sixteenth-century Italy. 20c.

commedietta [It.] a short or trifling comedy. 20c. The older Italian and English form *comedietta* seems to have become obsolete. [N,S]

comme il faut [Fr.] in accordance with etiquette; correct in behaviour, presentable in society. 18c. [N*,S]

comme il se doit [Fr.] as is right and proper, as is fitting. 20c.

(le) commencement de la fin [Fr.] the beginning of the end. 20c. The phrase is attributed to Talleyrand, who is reputed to have used it during the Hundred Days' War.

commerçant [Fr.] a merchant, a dealer, a trader (on a large scale). 20c. More impressive than any of the English equivalents.

commère [Fr.] a female COMPÈRE. 20c.

commis [Fr.] a (French) clerk; a waiter. 17c. [N,S]

commissar [Russ. *kommissar*] the head of a government department in Soviet Russia. 20c. [N*]

commissionnaire [Fr.] one entrusted with a message; a hotel messenger or porter. 18c. The *Corps of Commissionnaires*, an association of army pensioners, was founded in 1859. [N,S]

commis voyageur [Fr.] a (French) commercial traveller. 20c.

commode [Fr. 'convenient'] (1) a low chest of drawers; (2) a chair enclosing a chamber-pot, a night-stool. 18c. [N,S]

communard [Fr.] a supporter of the Paris COMMUNE in 1871; *hence*, a communalist, a believer in the widest possible extension of the autonomy of local authorities. 19c. [N,S]

commune [Fr.] the smallest administrative division in France, governed by a mayor and council; applied also to similar divisions in other countries. 17c. Used *esp.* of the Parisian insurrection of 18th March – 29th May 1871. [N,S]

communiqué [Fr.] an official announcement or report by a government, etc. 19c. Often with the implication that the full truth has not been told. [N*,S]

compagnon de voyage [Fr.] a travelling companion. 18c. [N*,S]

compendium, *pl.* **compendia** [Lat.] (1) an abridgment, an EPITOME; an embodiment in miniature, a personification. 16c. (2) a compact outfit comprising all the necessary equipment for some occupation. 20c. [N,S]

compère [Fr. 'gossip'] one who introduces and comments upon the items of an entertainment, show, or contest; to introduce and comment in this way. 20c. The reference may be to either sex: the feminine COMMÈRE, once fairly common, is now very rare. [N*]

compos mentis [Lat.] of sound mind, competent to transact legal business. 17c. Tacitus *Annals* xv 76: *compote mentis pectore* 'with a spirit sound of intellect'. Less common than NON COMPOS MENTIS. [S(*)]

compote [Fr.] *Cul.* fruit stewed in syrup, *esp.* fruit salad in syrup. 17c. The common spelling *compôte* is not French. [N(*),S]

compte rendu [Fr.] an official report of work done, progress made, etc. 19c. [S]

con=CONTRA, against.

con amore [It.] (performed) with fire and enthusiasm due to love of the subject; as a labour of love. 18c. [N,S]

con brio [It.] *Mus.* with spirit and force. 19c. Cf. BRIO; CON FUOCO; CON SPIRITO. [N]

concertante [It.] *Mus.* (a style of musical composition) which provides an opportunity for virtuosity by the instrumentalists; (instrumental parts) written in such a style. 18c. Cf. SINFONIA CONCERTANTE. [N,S]

concerto, *pl.* **concerti** [It.] *Mus.* a composition for one or more solo instruments accompanied by an orchestra. 18c. Formerly, and still historically, applied to a CONCERTO GROSSO. [N,S(*)]

concerto de chasse [It. + Fr.] *Mus.* a CONCERTO for hunting-horns. 20c.

concerto grosso, *pl.* **concerti grossi** [It.] *Mus.* a composition in which all the instruments of the orchestra play together. 18c. Sometimes confusingly abbreviated to CONCERTO. [S]

concessionnaire [Fr.] one who has been granted exclusive rights by a government or public authority. 19c. The spelling *concessionaire*, not found in French, is common in English. [N,S]

concierge [Fr.] the man or woman in charge of a block of flats (in France), a porter, a door-keeper. 17c. [N,S]

concordat [Fr.] an agreement between Church and State about ecclesiastical privileges. 17c. [N]

concours [Fr.] a contest or competition, *esp.* a motor-race. 20c.

concours d'élégance [Fr.] a contest, *usu.* held at the end of a motor-car rally, in which the beauty and finish of a car (but not its speed) are considered. 20c.

condominium [Lat.] joint rule or sovereignty, *usu.* by a number of States. 18c. [N(*),S]

condottiere, *pl.* **condottieri** [It.] the leader of a troop of mercenaries. 18c. [N,S]

confer [Lat.] compare . . .; introducing a cross-reference. 19c. Normally abbreviated to *cf.*

conférencier [Fr.] a lecturer, one who delivers an address. 19c. The implication is of less dogmatism than is suggested by *lecturer*. [S]

confessio fidei [Lat.] a confession of faith, a public avowal of allegiance to a cause. 20c.

confetti *pl.* [It.] small disks of coloured paper thrown during a carnival or at a wedding. 19c. *Orig.* applied to small sweetmeats thrown on similar occasions. [N*,S]

confidante [Fr. *confidente*] (1) a woman entrusted with confidences, an intimate woman friend. 17c. (2) an upholstered settee with a triangular seat beyond the arm at each end. 18c. The English spelling has not been adequately explained. [N(*),S]

confiserie [Fr.] a shop at which pastries and sweetmeats are sold. 20c.

confiseur [Fr.] a maker of pastries and sweetmeats, a confectioner. 19c. [S]

confit [Fr.] *Cul.* a piece of meat preserved in its own fat. 20c.

confiteor [Lat.] *Eccles.* the form of confession used at the beginning of the Mass; *hence*, any confession or avowal. 13c. From the first words of the prayer, *Confiteor Deo omnipotenti* . . . 'I confess to almighty God . . . [N,S]

confort moderne [Fr.] every modern convenience. 20c. *Usu.* ironically.

confrère [Fr.] a fellow-member of a learned profession or academic society. 18c. There is no exact equivalent in English: *colleague* implies a closer bond of union. [N,S]

confrérie [Fr.] a brotherhood, a group of associates. 19c. *Usu.* with a somewhat contemptuous connotation absent from the simple CONFRÈRE.

con fuoco [It.] *Mus.* with fire and spirit. 19c. Cf. CON BRIO; CON SPIRITO. [N]

congé [Fr.] permission to depart; dismissal (from service). 15c. The meaning 'bow (*orig.* on taking leave)' is now obsolete except *Hist.* Cf. POUR PRENDRE CONGÉ. [N,S]

congé définitif [Fr.] final leavetaking, final dismissal. 20c. Often with reference to death.

congé d'élire [Fr.] permission given to a Dean and Chapter to elect a bishop or archbishop nominated by the Crown: *hence*, any formal permission to elect a nominated candidate. 16c. During the Middle Ages the election of bishops was real; the right of nomination was assumed by Henry VIII. [N,S]

congeries [Lat.] a collection of things heaped together in disorder. 17c. The word has sometimes been taken as plural, so that a false singular *congerie*, *congery* has been formed from it. The plural, identical with the singular, seems not to be in use. [N,S]

con moto [It.] *Mus.* with spirited movement. 19c. [N]

connaissance [Fr.] acquaintanceship. 20c.

connoisseur [Obs. Fr.] a critical judge in matters of taste, *esp.* in the fine arts. The word implies a less professional knowledge than COGNOSCENTI. [N,S]

conquistador, *pl.* **conquistadores** [Sp.] one who took part in the Spanish conquest of Mexico and Peru in the sixteenth century. 19c. [N,S]

consecutio temporum [Lat.] *Ling.* the 'sequence of tenses', the grammatical rule whereby the use of a given tense in the principle clause requires the use of one of a prescribed group of tenses in the subordinate clause. 20c.

conseil d'état [Fr. 'council of state'] a French judicial body which examines administrative regulations and acts as a court of appeal against them. 20c.

consensus [Lat.] agreement (of opinion); a majority verdict. 19c. Often mis-spelt *concensus*, as if related to CENSUS. [N,S]

conservatoire [Fr.] a school or academy of music (and sometimes of elocution). 19c. Used to render Ger. *Konservatorium* and It. *conservatorio*, and also applied to establishments in England. The normal *U.S.* form is *conservatory*, which has a different connotation in English. [N,S]

console [Fr.] (1) a table or wide shelf supported by a bracket fixed to a wall; a side-table with legs at the front only. 19c. (2) *Mus.* the keyboard(s) and stop-mechanism of an organ, *esp.* when separated from the body of the instrument. 19c. (3) a free-standing cabinet containing electronic equipment. 20c. [N,S]

consommation [Fr.] light refreshments, *esp.* a drink bought in a CAFÉ. 20c.

consommé [Fr.] *Cul.* a strong clear soup produced by the prolonged boiling of meat; a cold jelly made in a similar way. 19c. Often *facet.* in the phrase 'in the *consommé*' for 'in the soup, in trouble'. [N(*),S]

con sordino [It.] *Mus.* muted, (an instrument played) with a mute. 20c. Cf. EN SOURDINE.

consortium, *pl.* **consortia** [Lat.] (1) partnership, association; action in concert, *esp.* of states and large organizations; a group of states or organizations acting in concert; (2) *Law* company and cohabitation (of spouses). 19c. [N,S]

conspectus [Lat.] a general survey or comprehensive view; a SYNOPSIS or summary. 19c. [N,S]

con spirito [It.] *Mus.* with spirit. 19c. Cf. CON BRIO; CON FUOCO. [N]

constatation [Fr.] verification, the establishing of something as a fact. 20c.

contadino, *f.* **contadina,** *pl.* **contadini,** *f. pl.* **contadine** [It.] an Italian countryman or peasant. 17c. [N,S]

conte [Fr.] a short story (as a literary GENRE). 19c. [N*]

contenu, *f.* **contenue** [Fr.] self-contained, reserved, sober in manner. 20c. Cf. BOUTONNÉ.

conte philosphique [Fr.] a short story designed to illustrate a philosophical or moral theme or thesis. 20c.

continuo [It.] *Mus.* BASSO CONTINUO, a figured bass; often applied to the instrument (harpsichord or organ) on which the figured bass is to be performed. 19c. [N*]

continuum, *pl.* **continua** [Lat.] a field of continuous extension. 20c. Used in a variety of technical contexts: the phrase 'space-time *continuum*' is currently used to denote the extension of physical objects in three dimensions of space and a fourth dimension of time.

contour [Fr.] (1) an outline; (2) *Art* the line separating the different sections of a design; (3) *Geog.* a line on a map marking points of equal elevation. 17c. [N,S]

con(tra) [Lat.] against (a proposition), *usu.* in the phrase '*pro* and *con*(*tra*)', for and against (or in the plural '*pros* and *cons*', arguments for and against). 15c. Even when used alone, as in 'Mr X argued *contra*', the opposition with *pro* is implied. [N,S]

contra bonos mores [Lat.] contrary to the accepted canons of decent behaviour. 18c. [S]

contralto, *pl.* **contralti** [It.] *Mus.* the lowest female voice, corresponding to the male ALTO or counter-tenor; a singer having such a voice. 18c. Formerly used also for *alto;* the use of *alto* for *contralto* is confusing and should be avoided. [N,S]

contra mundum [Lat.] against the world; in complete isolation. 18c. [S]

contrapposto [It.] *Art* a pose in which hips and shoulders are in different planes; the opposition or contrast of masses. 20c. Most commonly used of the work of Michelangelo. [N*]

contrarier [Fr.] to thwart, to vex, to upset. 20c.

contrat de majorité [Fr.] a political system whereby the members of parliament who vote a government into power undertake to support all its measures for a prescribed period. 20c.

(le) contrat social [Fr.] the social contract whereby the individual voluntarily surrenders his freedom to the community and undertakes to abide by the common will. 20c. Jean-Jacques Rousseau *Du Contrat Social* (1762), in which the doctrine of the social contract is used to prove the sovereignty of the people.

contre-coup [Fr.] (1) repercussion; (2) *Med.* an injury produced exactly opposite the position of a blow. 18c. [N,S]

contrepartie [Fr.] (in inlay work) the ground which is cut away in places to receive the inlaid veneers.

contretemps [Fr.] an inopportune event, a tiresome or mortifying mischance. 18c. *Orig.* a term of fencing, in use from 17c., meaning 'an ill-timed thrust'. [N,S]

convenable [Fr.] in conformity with the customs and proprieties of polite society. 19c. Cf. INCONVENABLE. [S]

(les) convenances *pl.* [Fr.] the customs and proprieties of polite society. 19c. [N,S]

conversazione, *pl.* **conversazioni** [It.] a social assembly for the purposes of conversation, an 'at home'; an assembly organized by a learned body, partly to exhibit the work of the body, partly to provide an occasion for the meeting of those interested. 18c. Cf. SOIRÉE. [N,S]

copaiba/copaiva [Sp. *copaiba*] *Art* a resinous substance obtained from various South American shrubs, used as a MEDIUM in painting. 18c. [N,S]

copita [Sp.] a tulip-shaped sherry-glass. 20c. The specialized connotation is English: in Spanish the word denotes any kind of wine-glass.

copula, *pl.* **copulæ** [Lat.] *Ling.* the present tense of the verb *to be,* when used merely to link the subject of a sentence to the predicate. 17c. [N,S]

coquette [Fr.] a woman who sets out to attract the admiration of men without any intention of responding to the feelings aroused in them; a woman who habitually trifles with the affections of men. 17c. [N,S]

coquillage [Fr.] a carved or inlaid ornament in the form of a shell. 20c. Common in the decoration of eighteenth-century furniture.

coram episcopo [Lat.] *Eccles.* (a liturgical ceremony) performed in the presence of a bishop. 20c.

coram populo [Lat.] in public, in full view. 19c. [N]

cor anglais, *pl.* **cors anglais** [Fr. 'English horn'] *Mus.* the tenor oboe; an organ stop resembling the tone of this instrument. 19c. [N]

cordée [Fr.] a group of climbers roped together on a single rope. 20c.

cordon bleu [Fr.] the blue ribbon worn by the Knights Grand Cross of the French Order of the Holy Ghost; *hence,* any first-class distinction; a person entitled to any first-class distinction, *esp.* a first-class cook or CHEF. 18c. The application to cooks dates only from 19c. Cf. CORDON ROUGE. [N,S]

cordon militaire [Fr.] *Mil.* a chain of military posts, a line of troops set to guard an area. 20c. The simple *cordon* has been in use in this sense since 18c.

cordon rouge [Fr.] (1) the red sash worn by members of the LÉGION D'HONNEUR; (2) a distinction second only to the CORDON BLEU; a person entitled to any second-class distinction, *esp.* a second-class cook or CHEF. 20c.

cordon sanitaire [Fr.] a line of guards posted round an infected district to prevent the spread of disease; *hence,* the political or military encirclement of a foreign power whose intentions are distrusted. 19c. [S]

corgi [Welsh 'dwarf-dog'] a small short-legged Welsh breed of dog. 20c. [N*]

cornea [Lat. 'horny'] *Med.* the transparent part of the outer covering of the eye, the lens of the eye. 14c. [N,S]

cornet à piston(s) [Fr.] *Mus.* a concert trumpet fitted with valves so as to produce notes additional to the natural harmonics. 19c. [N,S]

corniche [Fr. 'cornice'] a coastal road running along a ledge cut into the side of a cliff or steep hillside, *esp.* along the Mediterranean seaboard of France or Italy. 20c.

cornucopia [Lat. < *cornu copiæ* 'horn of plenty'] *Art* a goat's horn overflowing with flowers, fruit and corn, used as a symbol of plenty. 16c. [N,S]

corona, *pl.* **coronæ** [Lat. 'crown'] a luminous halo surrounding a celestial body, *esp.* that surrounding the sun, visible only during a total eclipse. 17c. [N,S]

coronach [Ir. *coranach*] a funeral lament or dirge used in Ireland and the Highlands of Scotland. 16c. [N,S]

corps, *pl.* **corps** [Fr. 'body'] *Mil.* the largest division of an army, forming a tactical unit; *hence,* any quasi-military organization. 18c. An abbreviation of *corps d'armée* 'army *corps*'. Though the written form of the word is invariable in the plural, a distinction is made in speech by adding the customary *z*-sound to the plural. [N,S]

corps de ballet [Fr.] *Ballet* the dancers in a ballet, *esp.* those not classed as soloists, who dance together in a body. 19c. [N,S]

corps de bataille [Fr.] *Mil.* the central part of an army drawn up for battle. 18c. [N,S]

corps d'élite [Fr.] a body of picked men; a society of the elect. 19c. Cf. ÉLITE. [S]

corps diplomatique [Fr.] *Dip.* the foreign representatives at the court of any country; members of the staff of an embassy. 18c. Often abbreviated to C.D. and inscribed on a plate attached to motor-vehicles as a symbol of diplomatic immunity. [N,S(*)]

corpus [Lat. 'body'] a complete collection of writings of a certain type, or by a certain person or group of persons, or about a certain subject. 18c. The plural *corpora* seems not to be in use. [N,S]

Corpus Christi [Lat. 'body of Christ'] *Eccles.* the feast of the Blessed Sacrament, observed on the Thursday after Trinity Sunday; *hence,* (the type of mediæval play) formerly performed on that feast. 14c. The feast was first officially celebrated in 1311. [N]

corpus delicti [Lat.] *Law* the sum of the various ingredients which make an act a breach of the law. 19c. Often misused in the sense of a material object in connection with which a crime is alleged; or more particularly in the sense of the body in a case of murder. [N,S]

corpus juris [Lat.] *Law* a complete code of law. 19c. [N,S]

corpus vile, *pl.* **corpora vilia** [Lat. 'vile body'] a worthless object, *usu.* one used in an experiment unlikely to be successful. 19c. Cf. FIAT EXPERIMENTUM IN CORPORE VILI. [S]

corral [Sp.] *U.S.* a stockade or enclosure for horses or cattle; a circle of wagons formed for defensive purposes. 19c. Cf. KRAAL. [N(*),S]

corrida (de toros) [Sp. 'running (of bulls)'] a bull-fight; bull-fighting. 19c. [N*]

corrigendum, *pl.* **corrigenda** [Lat.] something to be corrected; *esp. pl.* a list of corrections to be made in a printed book. 19c. Cf. ERRATUM. [N,S]

corroboree [Austr.] an Australian aboriginal dance, either festive or warlike; *hence,* any noisy and ill-organized assembly. 18c. Numerous different spellings have been in use; the current one is probably influenced by *corroborate.* [N,S]

corruptio optimi pessima [Lat.] when the best is corrupted it becomes the worst. 17c. Often used with reference to people: notable talents misapplied lead to extreme wickedness. [S]

corsage [Fr.] a spray of flowers worn on the bodice of a dress. 20c. In earlier use (19c.) with reference to the bodice itself, Cf. BOUTONNIÈRE. [N*]

corsetière [Fr.] a fitter of women's corsets, who takes measurements and orders the corsets from the manufacturers. 19c. The masculine *corsetier* appears to have been in use, but the occupation is naturally mainly one for women. [N*,S]

cortège [Fr.] a retinue, a procession of people, *esp.* a funeral procession. 17c. Until about 1900 spelt *cortége* in French and in English. [N,S]

cortes *pl.* [Sp. 'courts'] the two chambers of the legislative assembly of Spain or Portugal. 17c. [N,S]

cortex, *pl.* **cortices** [Lat.] bark, husk, *esp. Med.* the outer grey matter of the brain. 17c. [N,S]

cortile, *pl.* **cortili** [It.] *Arch.* a courtyard, *usu.* surrounded by buildings. 18c. [N,S]

corvée [Fr.] forced labour, unpaid labour owed by a vassal to his feudal lord; *hence*, drudgery, any laborious task. 18c. [N,S]

coryphée [Fr.] *Ballet* the leading (male) dancer in a BALLET. 19c. Despite its appearance the word is masculine. [N,S]

coryza [Lat. < Gk. κόρυζα] *Med.* the running at the nose which accompanies a cold in the head. 17c. Used loosely for 'a cold in the head'. [N]

cosmos [Gk. κόσμος] the universe considered as an ordered system. 17c. Sometimes contrasted with *chaos*, the universe in a state of disorder. [N,S]

costumier [Fr.] a maker or vendor of costumes, *esp.* theatrical costumes. 19c. [N,S]

coteau, *pl.* **coteaux** [Fr.] a sloping hillside, the lower slope of a mountain; *hence U.S.* a flat-topped hill, a small PLATEAU. 19c. [N*]

coterie [Fr.] a select or exclusive set of people. 18c. The exclusiveness may be social or intellectual. The term is less offensive than CLIQUE, which implies a sense of superiority and a nefarious aim. *Occ.* miswritten *côterie.* [N,S]

cotillon [Fr.] a favour or SOUVENIR given away at a ball or dance. 20c. Formerly the name of a popular dance.

cotta [Lat.] *Eccles.* a short surplice worn with a cassock. 19c. [N]

cottage orné [Fr.] a villa or small country house built with an affectation of rusticity. 19c. *Occ.* miswritten *cottage ornée.* [S]

couchée [Fr. *coucher*] a reception held during the King's evening toilet; *hence*, any evening reception. 17c. Cf. LEVÉE. [N,S]

couchette [Fr.] a sleeping-berth, *usu.* on a train. 20c.

coulant [Fr.] accommodating, easy to get on with. 20c.

coulé [Fr.] *Mus.* a grace-note used to fill the gaps in a series of descending thirds. 20c.

couleur de rose [Fr.] pink; rose-coloured, optimistic; deliberately optimistic. 18c. [N,S]

couleur du temps [Fr. 'the colour of the weather'] 'the way the wind blows', the general tendency of circumstances at a given moment. 20c.

coulisse [Fr.] a piece of scenery at the side of a stage designed to mask the wings; the wings of a stage; *hence Art* part of a picture serving a purpose similar to that of the side-scenery on a stage. 19c. [N,S]

coup [Fr. 'blow'] a stroke or hit in any game; a (successful) stroke of policy; an unexpected success. 18c. [N,S]

coup de foudre [Fr. 'thunder-stroke'] love at first sight, an instantaneous and overwhelming passion. 20c.

coup de grâce [Fr.] the final stroke, the stroke that puts a victim out of his misery. 18c. [N,S]

coup de main [Fr.] *Mil.* a sudden, vigorous and resolute attack. 18c. [N,S]

coup de maître [Fr.] a master-stroke, an action worthy of a master. 18c. [N,S]

coup de piston [Fr.] a helping hand, the exercise of influence in favour of a candidate, 'string-pulling'. 20c. Cf. PISTON.

coup-de-poing [Fr. 'blow with the fist'] a primitive hand-axe, a flint with one side flaked to a cutting-edge and the other shaped to fit the hand. 20c.

coup de savate [Fr.] a kick with the flat of the foot. 20c. Cf. ZAPATEADO.

coup d'essai [Fr.] an experimental work, a first attempt. 18c. [N,S]

coup d'état [Fr.] a violent political action, *esp.* one in which the government is changed by force of arms, or in which opposition is illegally suppressed by the government. 17c. Cf. MACHTÜBERNAHME; PUTSCH. [N,S]

coup de temps [Fr.] *Tennis* a stroke made when the ball is very near the angle between the back wall and the ground. 19c.

coup de théâtre [Fr.] a sudden sensational action, an action designed to achieve dramatic effect. 18c. [N,S]

coup d'œil [Fr.] a glimpse giving a general view; the effect of a scene at first glance. 18c. [N,S]

coupe [Fr.] *Cul.* a pudding served in a goblet-shaped glass. 20c.

coupé [Fr. 'cut'] (1) a compartment at the end of a railway-carriage, with seats on one side only. 19c. (2) a motor-car (*usu.* a sports-car) with only two doors and tilt-up front seats. 20c. (3) *Ballet* a step in which the weight is transferred from one foot to the other, the free foot being rested against the lower part of the other leg. 20c. [N(*),S]

coupé de ville [Fr.] an open COUPÉ with a hood which can be raised so as to cover either the back seats only or the front seats as well. 20c.

coup en passant [Fr.] *Bridge* an end-play in which the defender is given the choice of allowing declarer either a useful discard or a trump trick which could not otherwise have been made. 20c. Cf. EN PASSANT, the term applied to a move in chess to which this play is supposed to bear some resemblance.

courbette [Fr.] *Equ.* a leap made by a horse in which the fore-legs are raised together and the hind-legs raised before the fore-feet have reached the ground. 17c. [N,S]

coureur [Fr.] a man who runs after women, a man whose affections are rapidly transferred from one woman to another. 20c.

coureur de bois [Fr.] *Hist.* a wandering hunter in the early French settlements in Canada. 18c. [N*]

couscous [Arab. *kuskus*] an African dish made by steaming flour over a bowl of boiling broth. 17c. [N,S]

coûte que coûte [Fr.] no matter what it may cost, whatever the penalty may be. 18c. [N*,S]

couture [Fr.] dress-making; fashion in women's clothing. 20c. Cf. HAUTE COUTURE.

couturier, *f.* **couturière** [Fr.] a dressmaker, *esp.* a fashionable dress-designer. 19c. Cf. MODISTE. [N*,S]

couvade [Fr. 'hatching'] a custom observed in certain primitive tribes whereby after the birth of a child the father simulates a physical condition appropriate to the mother. 19c. [N,S]

couvert [Fr.] a 'place' at table, a set of the cutlery and napery used in consuming a meal. 20c. There has never been an English term for this useful concept.

crampon [Fr.] a small iron plate set with spikes, which can be fastened to the foot for walking over ice. 18c. Cf. ÉTRIER. [N]

cranium, *pl.* **crania** [Lat. < Gk. *κρανίον*] *Med.* the bones which enclose the brain, the upper part of the skull. 16c. [N,S]

crannog [Ir.] *Hist.* an ancient Celtic lake-dwelling. 19c. [N,S]

craquelure [Fr.] *Art* (1) the fine cracks in the surface of an ancient painting; (2) controlled crazing in the glaze of pottery, introduced for artistic effect. 20c.

craquelure anglaise [Fr.] *Art* excessive cracking in the surface of English paintings of the eighteenth century, due to the use of bitumen as a medium. 20c.

crèche [Fr.] a public nursery, a place where small children can be left while their mothers are at work. 19c. Sometimes miswritten *crêche*. [N,S]

credenza [It.] a low cupboard, *usu.* of walnut, with panelled doors and drawers above; a sideboard, *esp.* one resting on the floor without legs. 20c.

credo [Lat. 'I believe'] a formula of belief, a statement of principles. 19c. in use from 12c. as a name for the Apostles' Creed or the Nicene Creed; the more general meaning is new. [N,S]

credo quia impossibile (est) [Lat.] I believe it because it is impossible. 18c. The standard misquotation of Tertullian's CERTUM EST QUIA IMPOSSIBILE EST. [S]

crematorium, *pl.* **crematoria** [Lat.] a building designed for the incineration of corpses. 19c. The awkward plural *crematoria* is avoided when possible. [N,S]

crème brûlée [Fr. 'burnt cream'] *Cul.* caramel custard, custard flavoured with burnt sugar. 20c. Cf. BRÛLÉ.

crème de la crème [Fr. 'cream of the cream'] the pick of society, the best people, the ÉLITE. 19c. Often miswritten *crême de la crême*. [N*,S]

crêpe [Fr.] a gauze-like silk fabric embossed with minute wrinkles; (paper, rubber, etc.) so manufactured as to have many small wrinkles. 19c. Anglicized as *crape* in the special sense of black *crêpe* used as mourning wear. [N(*),S]

crêpe de Chine [Fr.] a kind of CRÊPE (*usu.* light in colour) *orig.* made of raw silk. 19c. [N]

crêpe lisse [Fr.] a smooth gauze-like silk fabric. 19c. Cf. LISSE. [N,S]

crépon [Fr.] a thick firm heavy CRÊPE fabric. 19c. Now often miswritten *crêpon*. [N]

crépuscule [Fr.] twilight, *esp.* as a time of day favourable to romantic feelings. 20c.

crescendo [It. 'growing'] *Mus.* (a passage) gradually increasing in loudness; *hence*, a gradual increase in the loudness of any sound, a gradual increase in strength. 18c. Cf. DIMINUENDO. [N,S]

crevasse [Fr.] *Geog.* a deep fissure in the ice of a glacier. 19c. [N,S]

crève-cœur [Fr.] heartbreak, bitter disappointment. 20c.

criant/criard [Fr.] garish, full of discordant colour. 19c. [N*,S]

cri de cœur [Fr.] a heart-felt utterance of anguish or passion. 20c. The French form is *cri du cœur*, also *occ.* used in English. [N*]

crime passionnel [Fr.] a crime dictated by the passions, *usu.* a murder prompted by the infidelity of a wife or mistress. 20c. The second word is often miswritten *passionel* or *passion(n)elle*.

crise d'adolescence [Fr.] the critical period of adolescence, emotional growing-pains. 20c.

crise de cœur [Fr.] an emotional crisis, a love-affair of exceptional poignancy. 20c.

crise de combat [Fr.] *Mil.* a turning-point in warfare, a vital passage of arms. 20c.

crise de conscience [Fr.] an overwhelming moral doubt, a severe attack of scruples or remorse. 20c.

crise (de nerfs) [Fr.] a nervous breakdown, *usu.* of short duration; an attack of hysteria. 20c.

crisis, *pl.* **crises** [Lat. < Gk. κρίσις] a turning-point, a decisive moment (in a plan, career, etc.); a time of insecurity and suspense. 17c. [N,S(*)]

criterion, *pl.* **criteria** [Gk. κριτήριον] a distinctive mark, standard or rule by which something is judged. 17c. [N,S(*)]

critique [Fr.] a critical essay, a well-considered assessment of a work of art or literature. 17c. Whereas a review is normally of a new book, a *critique* need not be so, and is *usu.* a more substantial and important work. [N,S(*)]

crochet [Fr. 'little hook'] a kind of knitting done with a single small hook instead of a pair of needles. 19c. [N,S]

croissant [Fr.] a rich crescent-shaped roll made by rolling flakes of butter into the dough. 20c.

croix de guerre [Fr.] a French military decoration, first awarded in 1915. 20c.

cromlech [Welsh 'crooked stone'] *Hist.* a prehistoric Celtic structure consisting of a large flat stone supported on three or more upright stones. 17c. The Welsh plural *cromlechau* is rare: the normal plural is *cromlechs*. Cf. DOLMEN. [N,S]

croquet [Fr. 'shepherd's crook'] a game in which wooden balls are driven with wooden mallets through a series of hoops. 19c. The game was introduced into Ireland from France before 1850 and from Ireland into England in 1852. [N,S]

croquette [Fr.] *Cul.* a ball of potato or rice, or of minced meat or fish, seasoned and fried brown. 18c. [N,S]

croquis [Fr.] *Art* a rough sketch. 19c. Cf. ÉBAUCHE; ESQUISSE. [N,S]

croupier [Fr.] an official in a gambling saloon who superintends the game and rakes in the stakes. 18c. [N,S]

croûte [Fr. 'crust'] *Cul.* a piece of fried bread used as a foundation or to garnish certain dishes. 20c. [N*]

croûton [Fr.] *Cul.* a sippet of bread or toast, cut into a cube and fried, served with soups or as a garnish to certain dishes. 19c. [N*,S]

croyant, *f.* **croyante** [Fr.] (a Christian) who accepts the creed of his faith, *usu.* with the implication that he neglects religious observance. 20c.

croyant et pratiquant, *f.* **croyante et pratiquante** [Fr.] (a Christian) who both accepts the creed of his faith and is scrupulous about religious observance; a practising Christian. 20c.

cru [Fr.] growth (of a vine); a vineyard or group of vineyards. 19c. Cf. GRAND CRU; PREMIER CRU. [S]

cruauté [Fr.] ruthlessness, absence of sentimentality. 20c.

crudités *pl.* [Fr.] *Cul.* raw vegetables, *usu.* in a sauce, eaten as an appetizer at the beginning of a meal. 20c.

crustacea *pl.* [Lat.] the class of aquatic creatures with hard shells and jointed limbs, including crabs, lobsters, crayfish, prawns and shrimps. 19c. The term was introduced by Lamarck in 1801. [N,S]

crux, *pl.* **cruces** [Lat. 'cross'] (1) a point of particular difficulty, and obscurity very hard to explain. 19c. Very common in the phrase 'a textual *crux*', a reading in a manuscript which editors find very hard to explain. (2) the central point of a problem, the crucial difficulty; *hence*, the most important part (of an argument). 20c. [N,S]

crux ansata [Lat. 'cross with a handle'] the form of cross, known in ancient Egypt by the name *ankh*, in which the upright above the cross-piece is replaced by a circle. 20c.

cucullus non facit monachum [Lat.] 'a cowl doesn't make a monk', i.e. you cannot acquire an interior quality merely by adopting the appropriate external appearance. 17c. [S]

cuesta [Sp.] *Geog.* a plain sloping gently up to the crest of a cliff or steep escarpment. 20c.

cui bono? [Lat.] for whose benefit? who profits by it? 17c. Used by Cicero (*Pro Milone* xii 32, etc.), but probably already a familiar tag. Now often misused in the sense 'for what purpose?'. [N,S]

cuirasse musclée [Fr.] a breast-plate modelled on the nude male torso, adopted by the Romans from the Greeks. 20c.

cuir bouilli [Fr.] leather boiled until soft, moulded into the form required, then allowed to dry and harden. 19c. Anglicized in 14c., but re-adopted from French. [N]

cuir ciselé [Fr.] leather tooled in pictorial designs, used as a material for binding books. 20c.

cuisine [Fr. 'kitchen'] style of cooking; culinary resources (of a person or establishment). 18c. Cf. HAUTE CUISINE. [N,S]

cujus regio, ejus religio [Lat.] *Eccles.* the principle that the inhabitants of a region should accept the religion of its ruler. 20c. This principle was adopted at the Diet of Augsburg (1555).

cul-de-lampe, *pl.* **culs-de-lampe** [Fr. 'lamp-bottom'] (1) *Arch.* a bracket or pendant of an inverted conical shape; (2) an ornament used to fill up a page in a printed book, a tail-piece. 18c. [N,S]

cul-de-sac, *pl.* **culs-de-sac** [Fr. 'bottom of a bag'] (1) *Med.* a vessel or tube open at one end only, like the CÆCUM or blind gut; (2) a blind alley, a lane or passage closed at the end. 18c. Not generally used in the latter sense in French: the French equivalent is usually *impasse*. [N,S]

culotte [Fr.] a pair of women's wide flared trousers (long or short) so designed as to resemble a skirt when the wearer is standing still; a divided skirt. 20c.

culte du moi [Fr.] the religion of self, the systematic placing of one's own interests before those of others. 20c. Cf. JE-M'EN-FOUTISME.

cultus [Lat.] *Eccles.* an organized system of religious ceremonial, *esp.* the formal veneration of saints. 19c. [N,S]

cum [Lat.] with, together with. 19c. Used in a variety of ways: (1) in the names of combined parishes, e.g. 'Chorlton-cum-Hardy'; (2) in certain fixed phrases, e.g. '*cum* dividend'; (3) *facet.*, e.g. 'chauffeur *cum* valet *cum* gardener'. [N,S]

cum grano salis [Lat.] with a grain of salt, with some caution or mistrust. 17c. Cf. Pliny *Natural History* xxiii 8: *addito salis grano* 'with a grain of salt added'. [N,S]

cum laude [Lat.] with praise, with distinction; always of the result of an examination. Cf. MAXIMA CUM LAUDE; SUMMA CUM LAUDE.

cummerbund [Pers. *kamar-band* 'loin-cloth'] *A.-I.* a sash worn round the waist. 17c. [N,S]

cum notis variorum [Lat.] with the notes of various commentators; (an edition of a text) in which the conjectures of all previous editors are recorded. 19c. Cf. VARIORUM.

cum privilegio (ad imprimendum solum) [Lat.] with privilege (of exclusive printing rights). 16c. [N,S]

cupola [It.] a domed roof, *esp.* a glazed dome or lantern. 16c. [N,S]

curé [Fr.] a (French) parish priest. 17c. Not 'curate', for which the French term is *vicaire*. [N,S]

curettage [Fr.] *Med.* the removal of a growth by scraping with a CURETTE. 20c. The reference is almost invariably to abortion. The current French spelling is *curetage*, but English seems to prefer the older French form *curettage*. [N*]

curette [Fr.] *Med.* a small spoon-shaped surgical instrument used for scraping; to scrape with such an instrument. 18c. [N]

curia [Lat.] *Eccles.* the group of ecclesiastical officials forming the ENTOURAGE of the Pope, or of any bishop. 19c. [N,S]

curiosa *pl.* [Lat.] remarkable objects, rarities. 19c. Often with the implication of erotic or pornographic interest. [S]

curiosa felicitas [Lat.] careful felicity (of phrase), beauty of style which is the result of thought and care. 18c. Petronius *Satyricon* cxviii 5: *Horatii curiosa felicitas* 'the careful felicity of Horace'. [S]

curragh [Ir. *curach*] a coracle, a boat made of wickerwork covered with hide. 15c. Cf. UMIAK. [N,S]

currente calamo [Lat. 'with running pen'] (written) straight off, without pausing to think. 18c. [S]

curriculum, *pl.* **curricula** [Lat.] a regular course of training or study, *esp.* at a school or university; a description of such a course of study. 19c. [N,S]

curriculum vitæ [Lat. 'course of life'] a brief autobiographical account attached to an application for a post. 20c.

cursus [Lat.] (1) *Hist.* a prehistoric earthwork consisting of two long parallel banks joined by a semicircle at each end; (2) *Ling.* a type of rhythmical cadence used at the end of a sentence in Greek and Latin prose. 19c. Cf. CLAUSULA. [N(*)]

cursus honorum [Lat.] *Hist.* the sequence of offices (quæstor, ædile, prætor) held by a Roman official before attaining the consulate; *hence*, any sequence of junior posts leading to a position of high authority. 20c.

cursus litterarum [Lat. 'course of letters'] the process by which the true readings of a text are corrupted in copying. 20c. The older and better form is DUCTUS LITTERARUM.

cuvée [Fr. 'vatful'] a quantity of wine, *usu.* of superior quality, reserved for special customers of a wine-merchant. 19c. [S]

cwm [Welsh] *Geog.* a deep rounded hollow with steep sides, a natural amphitheatre. 20c. Cf. CIRQUE.

Cymru am byth [Welsh] Wales forever! 20c.

cynghanedd, *pl.* **cynganeddion** [Welsh] an elaborate form of alliterative metre used in Welsh poetry; one of the varieties of this alliterative metre. 20c.

cy-près [Obs. Fr. 'as near (as possible)'] *Law* the procedure by which, when the literal execution of a testator's wishes is impossible, their general intention is carried out in some other way. 19c. [N,S]

czar [Russ. *tsarĭ*] the emperor of Russia. 16c. The title is derived ultimately from the Roman *Cæsar*. The spelling *czar* is without historic or linguistic justification: Slavonic languages written in the Roman alphabet use the spelling *car*, and the pronunciation is more accurately represented by the spelling *tsar*. The latter spelling, though strongly supported by purists, has failed to make headway. [N,S]

czardas [Magyar *csárdás*] the Hungarian national dance, a dance involving numerous leaps and much use of turned-in feet. 19c. The spelling *csardas*, though more correct and once common, is now pedantic. [N*]

czarevitch [Russ. *tsarevich*] the son of a CZAR. 18c. In Russia the stress is on the second syllable. The eldest son of the *czar* had the differentiated title *tsesarevich*, but the two forms are not normally distinguished in English. The Newmarket long-distance handicap known as the 'Cesarewitch', instituted in 1839, was named in honour of the prince who acceded to the throne as Alexander II. [N,S]

czarina [It. < Obs. Ger. *Czarin*] the wife of a CZAR, the Empress of Russia. 18c. Formed from *czar* by the addition of the German feminine suffix *-in* and the Italian feminine ending *-a;* the Russian feminine is represented by CZARITZA. [N,S(*)]

czaritza [Russ. *tsaritsa*] the wife of a CZAR, the Empress of Russia. 17c. More correct but less common than CZARINA. [N]

D

d.=DENARIUS, a penny.

δ=DELE, delete.

da capo [It.] *Mus*, (to be repeated) from the beginning. 18c. Cf. DAL SEGNO. [N,S]

dacha [Russ.] a country house or villa in Russia, *esp.* as a symbol of bureaucratic status. 20c.

Dachshund [Ger. 'badger-dog'] a German breed of short-legged long-bodied dogs, formerly used for hunting badgers. 19c. German *chs* is pronounced as English *x*. [N,S]

dacoit [Hind. *ḍakait*] *A.-I.* a member of a band of armed robbers (in India or Burma). 19c. [N,S]

dacoity [Hind. *ḍakaitī*] *A.-I.* an act of robbery with violence committed by an armed band (in India or Burma). 19c. [N,S]

dada [Fr. 'hobby-horse'] an anarchic movement, primarily in poetry but extended to the other arts, in which meaning and coherence are deliberately rejected. 20c. The movement, the name of which is taken from that of a review, was founded by Tristan Tzara at Zürich in 1916. Cf. FORMES LIBRES. [N*]

dæmon [Lat. < Gk. *δαίμων*] a demi-god or deified hero; a tuletary spirit or GENIUS. 16c. Identical in origin with *demon*, from which the Latin spelling serves to distinguish it. [N,S]

dahabiyeh [Arab. *ðahabīyah*] a large sailing boat used to carry passengers up the Nile. 19c. Current in a wide variety of spellings; *dahabiyeh* corresponds approximately to the pronunciation of modern Egyptian Arabic. [N,S]

Dáil [Ir. 'assembly'] the Parliament of the Republic of Ireland. 20c. The full form *Dáil Eireann* 'assembly of Ireland' is rarely used. Cf. TEACHTA DÁLA. [N*]

daimio [Jap. *dai myo* 'great name'] a Japanese prince or nobleman, a feudal vassal of the MIKADO. 18c. Cf. SAMURAI. [N,S]

dak [Hind. *ḍāk*] *A.-I.* travel by a system of relays of horses or bearers; the carriage of mail by relays of bearers. 18c. [N(*),S(*)]

dalle de verre, *pl.* **dalles de verre** [Fr.] *Arch.* a slab of (coloured) glass used as a building material. 20c.

dal segno [It.] *Mus.* (to be repeated) from the sign. 19c. The 'sign' resembles a highly ornamental *S*. Cf. DA CAPO. [S]

dame de compagnie [Fr.] a paid (female) companion. 18c. [N*,S]

dame d'honneur, *pl.* **dames d'honneur** [Fr.] a lady-in-waiting (to a royal personage). 19c. [S]

damnosa hæreditas [Lat.] a ruinous inheritance, a legacy which involves loss or imposes hardship on the legatee. 19c. Gaius *Institutes* ii 163. [S]

damnum sine injuria [Lat.] *Law* a loss for which there is no remedy by process of law. 19c. Also *damnum absque injuria*. [S]

da multos annos [Lat.] 'grant many years', a wish for the long life of a person, *esp.* on the occasion of a birthday, etc. 20c. Juvenal *Satires* IV x 188: *Da spatium vitæ, multos da, Jupiter, annos* 'grant a stretch of life, Jupiter, grant many years'.

danse d'école [Fr.] *Ballet* the Classical style of ballet-dancing as taught in the classroom. 20c.

danse de vertige [Fr.] a whirling dance calculated to induce dizziness in the performer and hence in the spectators. 20c.

danse du ventre [Fr.] a style of Oriental dancing characterized by visible flexion of the abdominal muscles. 20c.

danse macabre [Fr.] the Dance of Death, an allegorical representation of Death leading all conditions of men in a dance to the grave. 19c. Fr. *macabre* is an error for earlier *macabré*, of unknown origin; the earlier English phrase (from 15c.) was *dance of Machabree*. Cf. MACABRE; TOTENTANZ. [N,S]

danseur, *f.* **danseuse** [Fr.] *Ballet* a ballet-dancer. 19c. The feminine form is both earlier and more common; the masculine seems not to have been used before 20c. [N,S]

danseur noble [Fr.] *Ballet* a dancer with a noble Classical style. 20c.

datum, *pl.* **data** [Lat.] something known or assumed as fact and made the basis of a hypothesis or calculation. 17c. The plural is much more common than the singular, which is *usu.* attributive, as in '*datum*-line', etc. Cf. DONNÉE. [N,S(*)]

Dauphin [Fr. 'dolphin'] the title of the eldest son of the King of France from 1349 to 1830. 15c. The title was conferred on the occasion of the cession of the province of Dauphiné to Philip of Valois. Cf. IN USUM DELPHINI. [N,S]

débâcle [Fr.] a sudden complete downfall or ruin, a stampede. 19c. The original meaning is 'the breaking up of ice in a river'. [N,S]

de bene esse [Lat. 'as being good'] *Law* without prejudice, subject to further examination. 17c. [N,S]

débonnaire [Fr.] gentle, gracious, kindly, affable. 18c. Fully anglicized in 13c., but borrowed again with French spelling and pronunciation. [N,S]

déboutonné, *f.* **déboutonnée** [Fr.] unbuttoned, wearing careless or informal dress; lacking in reserve, fond of making intimate confidences. 19c. Cf. BOUTONNÉ. [S]

débris [Fr.] the broken fragments of anything ruined or destroyed. 18c. Now often written *debris*. [N,S]

débrouillard, *f.* **débrouillarde** [Fr.] full of resource, able to shift for one's self. 20c. Cf. SYSTÈME D.

début [Fr.] a first entry into society; a first public appearance as an actor, etc. 18c. [N,S]

débutante [Fr.] a young woman making her first entry into society, *usu.* by presentation at Court. 19c. The presentation of *débutantes* at Court was discontinued in 1958, and the connotation of the word is now less precise. [N,S]

decani [Lat. 'of the dean'] *Mus.* (the side of the church) on which the Dean sits; the south side of the church; opposed to CANTORIS. 18c. [N,S]

decessit sine prole [Lat.] (he, she) died without issue. 20c. Frequent in genealogical works and in family trees; normally abbreviated to *d.s.p.* Cf. OBIIT SINE PROLE; SINE PROLE.

déchéance [Fr.] decline; failure. 20c.

déclassé, *f.* **déclassée** [Fr.] displaced or degraded from one's proper station in society, having lost CASTE. 19c. [N*]

décolletage [Fr.] exposure of the neck and shoulders by the wearing of a low-cut dress; the low-cut neck of a dress. 19c. [N*]

décolletée [Fr.] (a woman) wearing a low-cut dress which exposes the neck and shoulders. 19c. [N,S]

décor [Fr.] (1) the scenery and furnishing of the stage of a theatre; (2) the interior decoration and fittings of a public building or of a luxurious private residence; (3) *Art* the decorative background of a work of art. 20c. [N*]

décor simultané [Fr.] a stage-setting in which several different locations are visible at the same time. 20c. Common in the Middle Ages when realism was not attempted, and revived in recent times for special effects.

découpage [Fr.] continuity, cutting (of a film script); the division of a film SCENARIO into scenes, with technical directions. 20c.

décousu [Fr. 'unsewn'] desultory, disconnected, lacking in cohesion. 19c. [S]

dedans [Fr. 'inside'] *Tennis* the open gallery at the service end of a tennis-court. 18c. [N,S]

de die in diem [Lat.] daily, every day without intermission. 17c. [S]

deësis [Gk. δέησις 'prayer'] *Art* a group representing Christ enthroned, the Virgin on one side and St John on the other. 20c.

de facto [Lat.] in fact, in reality, as a matter of fact; opposed to DE JURE.

17c. Commonly used of circumstances which have to be recognized as existing though they have no justification in law or morality. [N,S]

défaillance [Fr.] faintness, flagging, exhaustion. 20c.

(les) défauts de ses qualités [Fr.] the weaknesses that go with his (her) virtues. 20c.

de fide [Lat.] *Rel.* (a matter) of faith, (a doctrine) to be held as an essential article of religious belief. 17c. [N,S]

déformation professionnelle [Fr.] a physical deformity peculiar to a certain trade; *hence*, a psychological peculiarity or weakness characteristic of a certain occupation or profession, an 'occupational disease'. 20c.

dégagé, *f.* **dégagée** [Fr.] (1) unconstrained or informal in manner or appearance. 17c. (2) not ENGAGÉ, not committed to any particular party or social philosophy. 20c. (3) *Ballet* the freeing of a foot in preparation for a step. 20c. [N,S]

dégringolade [Fr.] a rapid deterioration, a sudden fall. 19c. [N*,S]

de gustibus (non est disputandum) [Lat.] there is no arguing about matters of taste, there's no accounting for tastes. 17c. Cf. QUOT HOMINES, TOT SENTENTIÆ. [S(*)]

déhanchement [Fr.] *Art* a stance characteristic of mediæval statues in which one hip is raised and the other lowered. 20c.

de haut en bas [Fr. 'from high to low'] with an air of conscious superiority. 17c. [N(*),S]

Dei gratia [Lat.] by the grace of God. 17c. [S]

déjà vu [Fr. 'already seen'] (1) *Art* unoriginal (work), a repetition of hackneyed formulæ; (2) *Psych.* the feeling that one has had previous experience of a place visited or an event witnessed for the first time. 20c.

déjeuner à la fourchette [Fr.] a fork luncheon, a substantial but informal meal taken in the middle of the day. 19c. [N,S]

de jure [Lat.] according to law, by rights; opposed to DE FACTO. 17c. [N,S]

dekko [Hind. *dekho* 'look!'] a look (at something). 19c. *Orig.* army slang, but now in wider usage. Cf. SHUFTI. [N*]

délassement [Fr.] relaxation, recreation. 19c. [N*,S]

del credere [It. 'of trust'] (an arrangement) whereby a broker or agent guarantees the solvency of the purchasers of his employer's goods; (a broker or agent) acting on such terms. 18c. [N,S]

dele [Lat.] delete; an instruction to the printer (written on the proof of a printed work) that a letter, word, etc. is to be deleted. 18c. *Usu.* abbreviated to δ. [N,S]

Delikatessen [Ger.] (a shop selling) exotic foods, *usu.* expensive and of foreign origin, purchased to supplement a meal or to accompany cocktails. 20c. Ultimately from Fr. *délicatesse*, and sometimes written *delicatessen* in English. [N*]

del(ineavit) [Lat.] (he) drew (it); always accompanied by a name and appended to a drawing. 18c. Cf. CÆL(AVIT); FEC(IT); PINX(IT); SCULPS(IT).

delirium, *pl.* **deliria** [Lat.] *Med.* temporary mental derangement, accompanied by hallucination, *usu.* caused by high fever; *hence*, frenzied excitement. 16c. [N,S]

delirium tremens [Lat. 'trembling DELIRIUM'] *Med.* a form of DELIRIUM, characterized by optical delusions and terror, induced by excessive consumption of alcohol. 19c. The term was invented by Dr T. Sutton in 1813. Abbreviated to *d.t.* and spoken of in the plural (*d.t.'s*) as if *tremens* were a plural noun. [N,S]

de longue haleine [Fr.] long and exacting (labour). 20c. Cf. D'UNE LONGUE HALEINE.

de luxe [Fr.] luxurious, superior, sumptuous. 19c. In English usage normally placed before a common noun but after a brand-name. [N*,S]

démarche [Fr.] proceeding, method of action. 17c. In contemporary usage the implication is *usu.* of the beginning of a new course of action. [N,S(*)]

déménagement [Fr.] moving house, moving one's goods and chattels to another place. 20c.

démenti [Fr.] a contradiction, *esp.* an official contradiction of a published statement. 17c. [N(*),S]

dementia [Lat.] *Med.* a form of insanity characterized by loss of mental powers. 19c. [N,S]

dementia præcox [Lat. 'early insanity'] *Med.* split personality, SCHIZOPHRENIA. 20c. So called because the symptoms frequently appear early in life.

démeublé [Fr.] stripped of furniture. 20c.

demi-caractère [Fr.] *Ballet* (a dance) based on a national or traditional dance, but executed with steps based on the classical technique. 20c. Cf. CARACTÈRE.

demi-castor [Fr.] an upper-class prostitute. 20c.

demi-mondaine [Fr.] a woman belonging to the DEMI-MONDE, a woman of doubtful reputation. 19c. Cf. COCOTTE. [N*]

demi-monde [Fr.] the class of women of doubtful reputation and standing, on the fringes of society. 19c. From the title of a comedy by Alexandre Dumas the younger, *Le Demi-Monde* (1855). [N,S]

de minimis non curat lex [Lat.] *Law* the law takes no account of trifles. 17c. [S]

demi-pension [Fr.] half-board, an arrangement by which some meals but not all are regularly eaten at an establishment at which the person concerned is lodging. 20c. Cf. EN PENSION; PENSION.

demi-pointe [Fr.] *Ballet* a position of the foot in which the heel is raised until the line of the foot is at about 45° to the horizontal. 20c. Cf. POINTE.

demi-saison [Fr.] spring or autumn (fashions); a light (spring or autumn) overcoat. 20c.

demi-tasse [Fr. 'half-cup'] a small after-dinner coffee-cup. 20c.

demi-toilette [Fr.] (a woman's) evening dress, elaborate but less formal than GRANDE TOILETTE. 20c.

demi-vierge [Fr. 'half-virgin'] a woman who, though still technically a virgin, has been morally depraved by frequent sexual experiences. 20c. From the title of a novel by Marcel Prévost, *Les Demi-Vierges* (1894).

démodé [Fr.] out of fashion, not up-to-date. 19c. Cf. VIEUX JEU. [N*]

(le) démon de midi [Fr.] the resurgence of sexual inclination in middle age. 20c. The title of a novel (1914) by Paul Bourget. Cf. Vulgate *Psalm* xc (xci) 6: *ab incursu et dæmonio meridiano;* in the Great Bible 'the sickness that destroyeth in the noon-day', in the Authorized Version 'the destruction that wasteth at noon-day'. In the French phrase the 'demon' is taken to refer to sexual temptation, and 'noon-day' to the meridian of life.

de mortuis (nil nisi bonum) [Lat.] (say) nothing but good of the dead; the failings of the dead should not be mentioned. 18c. [S]

denarius, *pl.* **denarii** [Lat.] (1) *Hist.* an ancient Roman gold or silver coin; (2) a penny. 16c. In the latter sense *usu.* abbreviated to *d.*, and used both in the combinations *L.S.D.*, *L.s.d.*, *£.s.d.* (LIBRÆ, SOLIDI, *denarii*) and in such forms as 2*d.*, etc.; 2*d.* is normally read as 'twopence', but *facet.* sometimes as 'two dee'. [N,S]

denier [Fr.] a unit of weight employed for measuring silk or nylon yarn. 19c. The lower the number of *deniers* the finer the yarn. Now *usu.* stressed on the first syllable but with a quasi-French vowel. [N*]

de nos jours [Fr.] of our times; always preceded by a proper name, e.g. 'the Robespierre *de nos jours*'. 20c.

dénouement [Fr.] the final unravelling of the plot of a novel or play; the final solution of a mystery. 18c. The alternative French spelling *dénoûment*, less common than *dénouement*, seems never to be used in English. An exactly parallel form is ENGOUEMENT. [N,S]

de novo [Lat.] anew, afresh, again. 17c. [N,S]

dentelle [Fr.] an ornamental pattern or border resembling lace, *esp.* in bookbinding. 19c. [N(*)]

dentellière [Fr.] a (female) lace-maker. 20c.

deoch-an-doruis [Gael. 'drink of the door'] a stirrup-cup, a parting drink. 20c.

Deo Optimo Maximo [Lat.] for God the best and greatest. 20c. The motto of the Benedictine order. Often abbreviated to *D.O.M.*, and in this form used on the corks and labels of Benedictine bottles.

Deo volente [Lat.] God willing; unless unforeseen circumstances prevent it. 18c. *Usu.* abbreviated to *D.V.* [S(*)]

dépaysé, *f.* **dépaysée** [Fr.] far from home, homesick, out of one's element, at a loss. 20c. Cf. DÉRACINÉ.

déplacé [Fr.] out of place, uncalled-for, ill-timed. 18c. [S]

déplacement [Fr.] (a sense of) being away from home, being out of place. 20c.

dépôt [Fr.] (1) *Mil.* the headquarters of a regiment, the place where recruits are assembled and drilled. 18c. (2) a warehouse, a place where goods are stored. 19c. (3) *U.S.* a railway station. 19c. (4) a garage for public service vehicles. 20c. Now often written *depot*, but still pronounced approximately as in French; in *U.S.* usage fully anglicized in pronunciation, and sometimes applied also to bus-stations and air-terminals. [N, S]

de profundis [Lat.] (a cry) from the depths of despair. (a cry) of bitter misery. 15c. Vulgate *Psalm* cxxix (cxxx)1: *De profundis clamavi ad te* 'Out of the depths I have cried unto thee'. [N,S]

de propaganda fide [Lat. 'concerning the propagation of the faith'] *Eccles.* a congregation of cardinals instituted in 1622 to superintend foreign missions. 17c. Cf. PROPAGANDA. [S]

dépucellage [Fr.] the deflowering (*usu.* by violence) of a virgin; loss of virginity. 20c.

député [Fr.] a member of the lower house of representatives in France. 19c. [S]

déraciné, *f.* **déracinée** [Fr.] uprooted from one's natural environment, out of one's element. 20c. Cf. DÉPAYSÉ.

de règle [Fr.] required by rule or convention. 19c. Whereas DE RIGUEUR invokes the pressure of public opinion, *de règle* invokes an explicit rule or convention. Not to be confused with EN RÈGLE.

de rigueur [Fr. 'in strictness'] indispensable, absolutely required by etiquette. 19c. Cf. DE RÈGLE. [N,S]

(le) dernier cri [Fr. 'the latest cry'] the very latest fashion. 19c. [N*]

dernier ressort [Fr.] a final court from which there is no appeal; *hence*, a last resource. 17c. [N,S]

dervish [Turk. *derviş* < Pers. *darvīsh* 'religious mendicant'] a Moslem friar or religious mendicant. 16c. Some of the orders practise fantastic rites involving dancing, whirling, or howling. Cf. FAKIR. [N,S]

desco da parto, *pl.* **deschi da parto** [It.] *Art* an elaborately painted tray used for carrying gifts to a woman in childbed. 20c.

déséquilibré, *f.* **déséquilibrée** [Fr.] mentally unbalanced. 20c. *Usu.* with reference to a slight and temporary mental derangement.

déshabillé [Fr.] a state of undress, carelessness or informality of costume; a garment worn in undress. 17c. Found in a variety of partially anglicized spellings, of which the most common is *déshabille*. Cf. EN DÉSHABILLÉ. [N,S]

desideratum, *pl.* **desiderata** [Lat.] something desired or needed; something the want of which is widely felt. 17c. [N,S]

designatum, *pl.* **designata** [Lat.] *Ling.* something designated by a word, *esp.* the noun antecedent of a pronoun. 20c.

désinvolture [Fr.] unselfconsciousness, lack of deference, flippancy of manner. 20c. Cf. SANS-GÊNE.

desipere in loco [Lat.] to be frivolous on occasion. 18c. Horace *Odes* IV xii 28: *dulce est desipere in loco* 'it is pleasant to be frivolous on occasion'. [S]

désœuvré, *f.* **désœuvrée** [Fr.] unoccupied, having nothing to do, at a loose end. 18c. [N,S]

désœuvrement [Fr.] lack of occupation, idleness. 19c. [N,S]

désordonné [Fr.] ill-planned, badly arranged, chaotic. 20c.

désorienté, *f.* **désorientée** [Fr.] having lost one's bearings, bewildered, at a loss. 20c.

desperado [Obs. Sp.] a desperate man, a man ready for violence. 17c. [N,S]

dessus de table [Fr.] an ornamental centre-piece for a dinner-table, an ÉPERGNE. 20c.

desunt cætera/desunt cetera [Lat.] the rest is lacking. 17c. Used to indicate that the remainder of a manuscript, etc., is not extant. Cf. CÆTERA DESUNT. [S]

desunt nonnulla [Lat.] not a little is lacking. 19c. Used to indicate that there is a substantial LACUNA in a manuscript, etc.

détaché [Fr.] *Mus.* (a passage played) with each successive note distinctly separated but not STACCATO; *esp.* (a violin passage) with each note played alternately with up- and down-bow. 20c.

de te fabula (narratur) [Lat.] it is of you that the tale is told, the circumstances apply to you exactly. 19c. Horace *Satires* I i 69–70: *mutato nomine de te Fabula narratur* 'with the name changed the tale is told of you'.

détente [Fr.] a relaxation of tension, *esp.* in political and international affairs. 20c. [N*]

détour [Fr.] a deviation from the straight road, a circuitous way round. 18c. Now often written *detour*. [N,S]

détournement de jeunesse/détournement de mineurs [Fr.] the abduction (and *usu.* the seduction) of young people. 20c.

détraqué, *f.* **détraquée** [Fr.] mildly unbalanced, harmlessly insane. 20c.

detritus [Lat.] *Geog.* fragments of rock detached by erosion. 18c. [N,S]

de trop [Fr.] one too many, in the way, 'playing gooseberry'. 18c. [N,S]

Deus absconditus [Lat.] *Theol.* the hidden God, God considered as inaccessible to human cognition. 20c. Vulgate *Isaias* xlv 15: *Vere, tu es Deus absconditus* 'Truly thou art a hidden God'.

deus ex machina, *f.* **dea ex machina** [Lat. 'a god from a machine'] a superior being who resolves problems insoluble by ordinary means. 19c.

The reference is to stage machinery used in the Greek drama to present a divinity in an elevated position. [S]

deux-chevaux [Fr.] a two-horse-power car, *esp.* a baby Citroën. 20c.

Deuxième Bureau [Fr. 'second BUREAU'] the French department of Military Intelligence, corresponding to the English M.I.5. 20c. The nature of the *Premier Bureau*, if it exists, appears to be secret.

deux-temps [Fr.] a dance consisting of two steps, a GLISSADE and a CHASSÉ. 19c. From *valse à deux temps* 'waltz in two-time'. Cf. TROIS-TEMPS. [N]

dévalisé, *f.* **dévalisée** [Fr.] robbed, burgled. 20c.

développé [Fr.] *Ballet* a movement in which one leg is raised until the toe is opposite the knee of the other leg and then fully extended, while the arms open first to the front and then to the side. 20c.

devoir [Fr.] an act of civility or respect. 16c. *Usu.* in the plural, 'to pay one's *devoirs*'. [N,S]

devoirs d'état *pl.* [Fr.] *Theol.* the duties of society, the obligation of each man to do the best for himself according to the customs of society as it is. 20c.

dévot, *f.* **dévote** [Fr.] religious, pious; a pious or religious person. 18c. Cf. FAUX DÉVOT. [N,S]

dghajsa [Maltese] a small Maltese sailing-boat used for ferrying passengers to and from liners in Grand Harbour. 20c.

dhobi [Hind. *dhōbī*] *A.-I.* a native (Indian) washer-man. 19c. [N,S]

dhoti [Hind. *dhōtī*] *A.-I.* the loin-cloth worn by Hindus. 17c. [N,S]

dhow [Unknown] an Arab sailing vessel, *esp.* a vessel used in the slave trade. 19c. [N,S]

diablerie [Fr.] (1) *Art* a portrayal of the powers of Hell; (2) devilment, mischief, fascination. 18c. [N,S]

diabolus in musica [Lat. 'the devil in music'] *Mus.* the interval of the diminished fifth (B to F in the scale of C). 20c. So called because of the unpleasant effect its misuse can cause.

diæresis, *pl.* **diæreses** [Lat. < Gk. διαίρεσις] *Ling.* the pronunciation of two consecutive vowels separately, not as a diphthong; the diacritic sign ¨ commonly used to mark such a pronunciation. 17c. The diacritic sign is sometimes also called UMLAUT, but this practice is to be deprecated. [N,S]

diagnosis, *pl.* **diagnoses** [Gk. διάγνωσις] *Med.* the identification of a disease by a study of its symptoms; *hence*, the determination of the cause of some trouble or difficulty. 17c. Cf. PROGNOSIS. [N,S]

diagonale [Fr.] *Ballet* a series of steps made diagonally across the stage. 20c. Cf. EN DIAGONALE.

dialogue des sourds [Fr.] a conversation between the deaf. 20c. Applied to discussions or negotiations in which each party is totally indifferent to the interests of the other.

diamanté [Fr.] cloth to which a sparkling effect is given by the application of crystal or paste brilliants. 20c. Sometimes miswritten *diamantée.* [N*]

diaspora [Gk. *διασπορά*] the Dispersion, the body of Jews living amongst the Gentiles. 19c. From the Septuagint version of *Deuteronomy* xxviii 25: 'thou shalt be a *diaspora* into all the kingdoms of the earth'. [N]

Dichtung und Wahrheit [Ger.] poetry and truth, a mixture of poetic fiction and fact which gives a more accurate impression of reality than truth undiluted could do. 20c. *Dichtung und Wahrheit* is the subtitle of Goethe's autobiography *Aus Meinem Leben* (1811–14, 1833).

dictum, *pl.* **dicta** [Lat.] a formal pronouncement, an authoritative statement; a current saying. 18c. Cf. OBITER DICTUM. [N,S]

dies iræ [Lat.] the Day of Wrath, the Day of the Last Judgment. 19c. From the first words of the Latin hymn ascribed to Thomas of Celano, about 1250. [N,S]

dies non (juridicus) [Lat.] a day on which no legal business is transacted; a legal day of rest. 17c. [N,S]

Diesseitigkeit [Ger. 'this-sided-ness'] the doctrine of materialism, a concern only with what appertains to this world. 20c.

Dieu et mon droit [Fr.] 'God and my rights', the motto of the sovereigns of England since Henry VI. 17c. [S]

differentia, *pl.* **differentiæ** [Lat.] a distinguishing mark or characteristic, *esp.* one which distinguishes one species from another within the same GENUS. 19c. [N,S]

difficile [Fr.] hard to please, given to making difficulties, troublesome to deal with. 19c. [N]

difficilior lectio potior [Lat.] 'the more difficult reading is preferable', the canon of textual criticism that an unusual reading is more likely to be original than a commonplace one. 19c.

Diktat [Ger.] a treaty or settlement imposed on a vanquished enemy by the victor. 20c. Often used of the Treaty of Versailles (1919).

dilemma [Gk. *δίλημμα*] *Logic* an argument which involves an opponent in the choice of two alternatives equally unfavourable to him; *hence*, a choice between two equally unpleasant alternatives, a state of perplexity. 16c. The two unfavourable alternatives are known as the 'horns of the *dilemma*'. Strictly speaking a *dilemma* cannot involve more than two possible choices; if there are more than two possible choices the appropriate terms are *trilemma*, etc., but these are little used. [N,S]

dilettante, *pl.* **dilettanti** [It. 'lover'] one who cultivates the fine arts as a pastime, not as a profession; *hence*, one whose interest in art or science is neither serious nor systematic. 18c. Cf. AMATEUR. [N,S]

diligente [It.] *Art* (the work) of industry, not of inspiration or genius. 20c. Contrasted with MANIEROSO.

diminuendo [It.] *Mus.* (a passage) gradually decreasing in loudness; *hence*, a gradual decrease in the loudness of any sound. 18c. Cf. CRESCENDO. [N,S]

Ding an sich [Ger.] a thing in itself, the reality underlying the appearance of an object, the NOUMENON. 20c. Introduced by Immanuel Kant (1724–1804) in his *Kritik der reinen Vernunft* (1781). Cf. AN SICH.

diplomate de carrière [Fr.] a professional diplomat, a diplomat who has followed the normal CURSUS HONORUM. 20c.

directeur de conscience [Fr.] a spiritual director. 20c.

Directoire [Fr.] (characteristic of) the styles and fashions current under the French Directory, 1795–9. 19c. The *Directoire* style is one of extravagant imitation of Greek and Roman models, and anticipates the English Regency style. [N*]

dirigisme [Fr.] planned economy, the system of state planning of the national economy. 20c.

dirigiste [Fr.] (characteristic of) an advocate of state planning. 20c.

Dirndl [Ger.] the Bavarian and Austrian woman's traditional costume, consisting of a blouse with short puffed sleeves and a skirt gathered tightly at the waist and very full below. 20c. In English usage applied *esp.* to a skirt of this type. The word is a South German diminutive of *Dirne* 'girl'.

dis aliter visum [Lat.] the gods decided otherwise, it was not fated to happen. 20c. Virgil *Æneid* ii 428.

discordia concors [Lat.] harmonious discord, the artistic device whereby harmony is achieved through the juxtaposition of apparently incompatible elements. 20c. Adapted from Horace *Epistles* I xii 19: *concordia discors*. The reason for the adaptation is not clear, since the meaning is scarcely altered.

discothèque [Fr.] a record-library or record-shop, *esp.* as the resort of teen-age enthusiasts; *hence*, a night-club at which recorded music is played; (clothing, etc.) favoured by those frequenting such an establishment. 20c. The French word is formed from *disque* 'record' on the analogy of *bibliothèque* 'library'; in both French and English the word is post-1960.

diseuse [Fr.] a woman entertainer who specializes in dramatic monologue. 19c. [N*]

disjecta membra [Lat.] scattered remains, fragments of literary work not put into any coherent order. 18c. Altered from Horace *Satires* I iv 62: *disjecti membra poetæ* 'the limbs of a dismembered poet'. [N,S]

distingué, *f.* **distinguée** [Fr.] having an air of distinction. 19c. [N,S]

distinguo [Lat.] I make a distinction. 20c. Used in argument when one's adversary seems to be confusing two distinct things or issues. [N*]

distrait, *f.* **distraite** [Fr.] pre-occupied, thinking of something else. 18c. [N,S]

ditto [Obs. It. 'said'] aforesaid, the same. 17c. *Orig.* only used of months, but now of general application. [N,S]

diva [It. 'goddess'] a distinguished female opera singer, a PRIMA DONNA. 19c. [N]

divertimento, *pl.* **divertimenti** [It.] *Mus.* a light and simple piece of instrumental music; a piece of instrumental music in a number of movements. 19c. [N,S]

divertissement [Fr.] *Ballet* a short self-contained dance, often performed as an ENTR'ACTE between longer pieces. 19c. [N,S]

divide et impera [Lat.] divide and conquer, impose order by fomenting the dissensions of subject peoples. 17c. The maxim is attributed to Louis XI of France by Prosper Mérimée in his *Chronique du Règne de Charles IX* (1829). [S]

divorcée [Fr.] a divorced woman. 19c. The masculine *divorcé* was formerly in use but seems now to be obsolete; the anglicized *divorcee* is used of both sexes. [N,S]

dix-huitième [Fr.] (characteristic of) the eighteenth century. 20c. Cf. SETTECENTO. [N*]

djellaba/djellâba [Fr. < Arab. *jilyāb*] a cloak with a hood and wide sleeves, worn in Algeria and Morocco. 20c.

djibbah [Arab. *jubbah*] a long straight cloth coat, open in front, with long sleeves, worn by Moslems; a similar garment worn as an affectation by European women. 19c. The English spelling reflects the pronunciation of Egyptian Arabic. [N(*)]

djinnee, *f.* **djinneeyeh,** *pl.* **djinn** [Arab. *jinnī*] *Myth.* a supernatural being of a lower order than the angels, able to appear in human form and to benefit or injure men. 17c. The plural *djinn* is often used as a singular. The singular *djinnee* is sometimes written *genie,* and the unrelated *genii* (plural of GENIUS) is used as its plural. [N,S]

doctrinaire [Fr.] (a theorist) who tries to apply an arbitrary doctrine without regard to practical considerations. 19c. *Orig.* applied about 1815 to a French political party which advocated constitutional monarchy and parliamentary government. [N,S]

dogma, *pl.* **dogmata** [Gk. δόγμα] an article of belief propounded by some authority, *usu.* a religious authority; the whole body of systematized belief. 17c. [N,S]

dolce far niente [It.] pleasant idleness, total relaxation. 19c. [N,S]

dolce stil nuovo [It. 'musical new style'] the school of love-poetry developed in Italy in the thirteenth century, in which the beloved woman is spiritualized and etherealized. 20c. The phrase was invented by Dante, *Purgatorio* xxiv 57.

dolce vita [It.] a life of luxury combining opulence with sensuality. 20c. Popularized by the Italian film *La Dolce Vita,* directed by Federico Fellini.

dolman [Obs. Turk. *dolaman*] the uniform jacket of a Hussar, worn with the sleeves hanging loose; *hence,* a woman's garment with loose cape-like sleeves; *hence*, (a sleeve) very wide at the shoulder and tapering to the wrist, not inserted but continuous with the front and back of the bodice. 19c. The current Turkish form is *dolama*. [N,S]

dolmen [Fr. < Cornish *tolmen* 'hole of stone'] a CROMLECH, a prehistoric Celtic structure consisting of a large flat stone supported on three or more upright stones. 19c. [N,S]

D.O.M.=DEO OPTIMO MAXIMO, for God the best and greatest.

domino [Fr.] a loose cloak worn at masquerades with a half-mask; *hence*, the half-mask itself. 17c. The word is found in French, Italian and Spanish, but the ultimate origin is uncertain; it seems to have entered English from French. The plural is *dominoes*, as in the familiar game. [N,S]

Dominus illuminatio mea [Lat.] the Lord is my light. 19c. The motto of the University of Oxford; Vulgate *Psalm* xxvi (xxvii) 1.

dompteur [Fr.] a tamer of wild animals. 20c.

donnée [Fr.] the subject or theme of a story, the material on which a writer founds his work. 19c. Cf. DATUM. [N*]

Doppelgänger [Ger.] the apparition of a living person, a supernatural manifestation identical in appearance with a living person. 19c. [N*,S]

dossier [Fr.] a file of papers or documents referring to the same subject, *usu.* the life and activities of some person. 19c. [N,S]

dot [Fr.] a marriage-portion, a dowry. 19c. The *t* is pronounced in French and in English. [N,S]

douane [Fr.] a custom-house, *esp.* in France or the Mediterranean countries. 17c. Cf. OCTROI. [N,S]

douanier [Fr.] a customs officer. 18c. [N,S]

double entendre [Fr.] a double meaning; a phrase having two meanings, one innocent and the other indelicate or indecent. 17c. The current French phrase is *double entente*, occasionally used in English by pedants; but *double entendre* is well established and unlikely to be displaced. [N,S]

doublure [Fr.] an ornamental lining on the inside of the cover of a book. 19c. [N]

douceur [Fr.] a gratuity, a bribe. 18c. The basic meaning is that of payment for favours received or expected; the word is more gracious than 'tip' or 'bribe'. Cf. POURBOIRE; TRINKGELD. [N,S]

douceur de vivre [Fr.] the pleasure of civilized living, the enjoyment of the good things of life. 20c. Adapted from Talleyrand's phrase *plaisir de vivre*, used with reference to the years before 1789; Guizot *Mémoires pour Servir à l'Histoire de mon Temps* (1858–67) I 6.

douche [Fr.] a jet of water applied to some part of the body, *usu.* for medicinal purposes; a shower-bath. 18c. [N,S]

doukhobors *pl.* [Russ. *dukhobortsy* 'spirit-wrestlers'] members of a Russian fanatical sect refusing military service, many of whom emigrated to Canada shortly before 1900. 19c. A spurious singular *doukhobor* has been formed from the plural; the Russian singular is *dukhoborets*. [N*]

douleia=DULIA, the veneration of saints.

doyen, *f.* **doyenne** [Fr.] the senior member of a body, institute, etc. 17c. [N,S]

doyenné [Fr.] the state of being the senior member of a body, institute, etc. 20c.

Dozent [Ger.] a university lecturer, *usu.* a foreigner employed to teach his own language. 19c. Formerly often written *Docent*. Cf. PRIVATDOZENT. [S]

dragée [Fr.] a nauseous medicine enclosed in a sugary casing, a sugary pill; a chocolate drop; a small silvered ball for decorating iced cakes. 19c. Cf. CACHET. [N,S]

dragoman [Fr. < Obs. Arab. *targumān*] a guide and interpreter, *esp.* in a country where Arabic, Turkish or Persian is spoken. 14c. The plural is *dragomans;* but *dragomen*, formed as if the termination *-man* were the English word *man*, is of long standing in English. [N,S]

dramatis personæ [Lat.] (a list of) the characters in a play or story. 18c. [N,S]

drame à thèse [Fr.] a play with a purpose, a play that is designed primarily to illustrate some doctrine or theory. 20c. Cf. ROMAN À THÈSE.

drame bourgeois [Fr.] a play about everyday life, as distinct from Classical drama and melodrama. 20c.

dramma per (la) musica [It.] *Mus.* a serious opera, *esp.* one the LIBRETTO of which has been specially written for setting to music. 20c. Cf. OPERA SERIA.

Drang nach Osten [Ger.] the thrust to the East, the traditional urge of German politicians to annex territories in the East. 20c.

draperie mouillée [Fr. 'wet drapery'] *Art* clinging drapery, as portrayed in painting and sculpture. 20c. The name is due to the device adopted by certain artists of wetting the model's clothing to secure the required effect.

Dreigroschenoper [Ger. 'threepenny opera'] *Mus.* an opera expressing social satire in modern popular idiom. 20c. From the title of the adaptation of Gay's *Beggar's Opera* made in 1928 by Bert Brecht and Kurt Weill.

dressage [Fr.] *Equ.* the breaking-in and training of a horse; a demonstration of the skill and obedience of a trained horse. 20c.

droit administratif [Fr.] the (French) system of rules concerning the organization of the public services. 20c.

droit de cité [Fr.] the freedom of a city, free admission into some circle or organization. 20c.

droit de seigneur [Fr.] *Hist.* the supposed right of a feudal overlord to deflower the bride of any of his tenants on the first night of her marriage. 20c. Cf. JUS PRIMÆ NOCTIS.

droit naturel [Fr.] the natural right of man to a decent livelihood, *esp.* as the basis of a political philosophy. 20c.

drôle [Fr.] comic, amusing; queer, odd. 20c. Fully anglicized from 17c. as *droll*, but re-introduced from French. [N]

d.s.p.=DECESSIT SINE PROLE, died without issue.

d.t.=DELIRIUM TREMENS, alcoholic hallucination.

duce [It.] the leader of a group, *esp.* as the title adopted by Benito Mussolini. 20c. Cf. CAUDILLO; (DER) FÜHRER.

duchesse [Fr.] (1) lustrous and smooth (satin fabric, etc.); (2) a CHAISE-LONGUE with a concave head and foot curving round along the open side; a CHAISE-LONGUE consisting of two arm-chairs joined by a matching upholstered stool which can be removed; (3) (a set of covers) for a dressing-table, *usu.* consisting of one large and two small mats. 19c. Cf. PÉCHÉ MORTEL. [N*]

ductus litterarum [Lat. 'course of letters'] the process by which the true readings of a text are corrupted in copying. 19c. The study of this process may enable an editor to restore a true reading to a corrupt text. Cf. CURSUS LITTERARUM. [S]

du dernier bateau [Fr. 'from the latest boat'] in the height of fashion, in the very latest fashion. 20c.

duenna [Obs. Sp.] a woman (*usu.* married or elderly) who accompanies a young unmarried woman for the sake of propriety, a CHAPERON. 17c. The current Spanish form is *dueña*, in which the TILDE represents the second *n* written over the first. Cf. GOUVERNANTE. [N,S]

dulce domum [Lat.] home, sweet home. 19c. The refrain of a Latin song popular at Winchester College. [S]

dulce et decorum est pro patria mori [Lat.] it is pleasant and proper to die for one's country. 18c. Horace *Odes* III ii 13. [S]

dulia [Lat. < Gk. δουλεία 'slavery'] *Theol.* the inferior kind of veneration due to angels and saints. 17c. Also *occ.* in the Greek form *douleia.* [N,S]

duma [Russ.] the Russian elective legislative council established in 1905 and abolished in 1917. 20c. [N*]

du meilleur rang [Fr.] belonging to the highest rank in society, aristocratic. 20c.

dum sola (et casta) [Lat.] *Law* so long as she shall live alone (and chaste). 20c. Used to ensure that a legacy or allowance shall be conditional on the chastity of the beneficiary. [N*]

dum spiro, spero [Lat.] while I breathe, I hope; while there's life there's hope. 17c. [S]

dum vivimus, vivamus [Lat.] while we are alive, let us live to the full; eat, drink, for tomorrow we die! 20c. Cf. CARPE DIEM.

d'un certain âge [Fr. 'of a certain age'] middle-aged (*usu.* of a woman).

20c. The phrase implies chivalrous reluctance to be too specific. Cf. ENTRE DEUX ÂGES.

d'une longue haleine [Fr. 'of a long breath'] long-term, which cannot be accomplished quickly. 20c. Cf. DE LONGUE HALEINE.

duo [It.] *Mus.* a duet, a piece for two voices or instruments. 16c. Cf. TRIO. [N,S]

duomo [It.] a cathedral church (*usu.* in Italy). 16c. [N,S]

durbar [Pers. *darbār*] *A.-I.* a public audience held by a native Indian ruler, or by a British governor or viceroy in India; the hall or place in which such an audience is held. 17c. [N,S]

Durchlaucht [Ger.] 'Serene Highness', the title given to German princes. 20c.

durum [Lat.] (a kind of wheat) producing hard grains rich in protein, used in the preparation of PASTA. 20c. From the botanical name of the wheat, *Triticum durum*.

du tout [Fr.] *Tennis* the score of a player who requires one stroke to win the set. 19c.

duvet [Fr.] an eiderdown quilt. 20c.

D.V.=DEO VOLENTE, God willing.

E

eau de Cologne [Fr.] a perfume made of alcohol and the essential oils of various flowers, *esp.* lemon-flowers. 19c. [N,S]

eau de Nil [Fr.] a pale green colour supposed to resemble that of the waters of the Nile. 19c. [N*]

eau de vie [Fr. 'water of life'] brandy, *esp.* that of inferior quality. 19c. Cf. AQUA VITÆ. [N,S]

eau forte, *pl.* **eaux fortes** [Fr. 'strong water'] nitric acid; *hence,* an etching. 19c. An etching is made by dissolving away with nitric acid those parts of the copper plate from which a protective film of wax has been scraped. Cf. AQUA FORTIS. [N,S]

eau sucrée [Fr.] a summer drink made by dissolving sugar in water. 19c. [N*,S]

ébauche [Fr.] (1) a sketch, a rapid drawing; (2) the component parts of the movement of a watch. 18c. Cf. CROQUIS; ESQUISSE [S]

ébéniste [Fr.] a skilled cabinet-maker. 20c. *Orig.* 'worker in ebony', but in current usage contrasted with MENUISIER 'skilled joiner'.

ébénisterie [Fr.] skilled cabinet-making; the work of a skilled cabinet-maker. 20c.

écarté [Fr.] a card-game for two players, in which a player may discard certain cards and replace them with others from the pack. 19c. [N,S]

ecce Homo [Lat.] *Art* a representation of Christ crowned with thorns and wearing a purple robe. 17c. Vulgate *St John* xix 5: *ecce Homo* 'behold the Man!' [N,S]

ecce signum [Lat. 'behold the sign!'] here is the proof of it. 15c. Used when producing evidence in support of a statement just made. [N,S]

ecclesiola, *pl.* **ecclesiolæ** [Lat.] *Rel.* a little church, a church within a church, *esp.* a group of enthusiasts who believe that they alone preserve the true doctrine. 20c.

échange de vues [Fr.] an exchange of opinions, a statement of principles as a preliminary to negotiations. 20c.

échappé [Fr.] *Ballet* a step in which the dancer leaps into the air and alights on the toes or the POINTES, *usu.* with the feet apart. 20c.

échelon [Fr.] (1) *Mil.* a formation of troops in parallel divisions, each having its front clear of the next in advance; a staggered formation of troops. 18c. (2) a group of persons of equal status in some hierarchical organization. 20c. Cf. EN ÉCHELON. [N,S]

échoppe [Fr.] *Art* a scorper, a flat or semi-circular gouge. 20c.

echt [Ger.] genuine, pure, unadulterated. 20c.

éclair [Fr. 'lightning'] a small pastry made of CHOU(x) paste, filled with whipped cream and coated with chocolate icing. 19c. The origin of the name is unknown. [N*]

éclaircissement [Fr.] a revelation; an explanation, *esp.* the resolution of a misunderstanding between two parties. 17c. [N,S]

éclat [Fr.] brilliance, dazzling effect; conspicuous success; universal acclamation. 17c. [N,S]

école [Fr.] a 'school', a group of disciples imitating the style and manner of an artist or writer. 20c. Cf. CHEF D'ÉCOLE; FAIRE ÉCOLE.

écorché [Fr. 'flayed'] *Art* a representation of a human or animal figure displaying the muscular system. 19c. [N*,S]

écrasez l'infâme [Fr.] 'crush the beast!' i.e. fight unceasingly against intolerance and fanaticism. 20c. The variant form *écrasons l'infâme* was Voltaire's regular war-cry, but the current form actually occurs in a letter to d'Alembert, 28th November 1762.

écrin [Fr.] a jewel-box. 19c. [N*,S]

écritoire [Fr.] a writing-desk, a BUREAU or SECRÉTAIRE. 20c. The modern French form of the long-established ESCRITOIRE.

écriture artiste [Fr.] an 'impressionist' prose style which attempts to achieve life and vigour by the use of unusual vocabulary and syntax. 20c.

écru [Fr.] the colour of unbleached linen. 19c. [N,S]

écuelle [Fr.] a two-handled porringer. 19c. [N*]

écurie [Fr. 'stable'] a fleet of cars entered for a motor-race by some manufacturer or combine, a 'works' team'. 20c.

edax rerum [Lat.] (Time) the devourer of all things. 17c. Ovid *Metamorphoses* xv 234. Cf. TEMPUS EDAX RERUM.

Edda [Icelandic] a collection of Old Norse poetry on mythical and traditional subjects, made about 1200. 18c. The same name is also given to a collection of miscellaneous prose works made by Snorri Sturluson about 1230: the two are sometimes distinguished as the 'Elder' or 'Poetic' *Edda* and the 'Younger' or 'Prose' *Edda*. The original meaning of the word was perhaps 'grandmother'. [N,S]

Edelweiss [Ger. 'noble-white'] a white alpine plant growing in nearly inaccessible places, prized because of the difficulty of obtaining it. 19c. [N,S]

édition de luxe [Fr.] an edition of a printed book prepared regardless of expense. 19c. [N,S]

editio princeps, *pl.* **editiones principes** [Lat.] the first printed edition of a work, *usu.* of a Classical text. 19c. [N*,S]

effendi [Turk. *efendi*] a gentleman, a (Turkish) government official; a title of respect added after a name. 17c. [N,S]

effleurage [Fr.] a stimulating light MASSAGE administered with fur gloves. 20c.

effluvium, *pl.* **effluvia** [Lat.] an exhalation, an emanation, *usu.* one producing a disagreeable smell. 17c. The plural *effluvia* has sometimes been taken for a singular and supplied with a fictitious plural *effluviæ.* [N,S]

e.g.=EXEMPLI GRATIA, for example.

égalité [Fr.] a draw, an equal score in any game, *esp.* one in which money is staked. 20c.

égaré [Fr.] misguided, astray from the truth. 20c. *Usu.* of an idea, an argument, etc.

ego [Lat. 'I'] *Psych.* the conscious thinking subject, as opposed to the object of contemplation; the subjective personality. 19c. The term *ego,* though popularized by the works of Sigmund Freud, was in use long before his time. Cf. ID; NON-EGO. [N,S]

ego et rex meus [Lat.] 'I and my king', a phrase quoted as the extreme example of the vice of putting oneself first. 17c. Attributed to Cardinal Wolsey (cf. Shakespeare *Henry VIII* III ii 314); but the word-order is correct in Latin, and no egotism is implied. [S]

Ehepaar [Ger.] a married couple, *esp.* a couple considered as a happy example of the marital state. 20c.

eheu fugaces [Lat.] alas, (the years are) fleeting. 20c. Horace *Odes* II xiv 1: *Eheu, fugaces, Postume, Postume, Labuntur anni* 'Alas, Postumus, Postumus, the fleeting years are slipping by'.

eidolon, *pl.* **eidola** [Gk. εἴδωλον] an unsubstantial image, a phantasm. 19c. [N,S]

eirenicon [Gk. εἰρηνικόν] an attempt to reconcile differences, an overture of peace. 19c. In earlier use (17c.) with a strictly religious connotation. [N,S]

Eisen und Blut [Ger.] 'iron and blood', military power used to achieve a specific purpose. 20c. Used by Bismarck in the Prussian House of Deputies, 30th September 1862; in 1886 he repeated the phrase in the alternative form BLUT UND EISEN.

eisteddfod, *pl.* **eisteddfodau** [Welsh 'session'] a congress of Welsh bards and minstrels; a competition in poetry, singing, music, etc. 19c. Cf. FEIS. [N,S]

ejusdem generis [Lat.] *Law* of the same kind. 17c. [S]

élan [Fr.] ardour, impetuousness. 19c. [N,S(*)]

élan vital [Fr.] life force. 20c. A phrase introduced by the philosopher Henri Bergson to denote the force of creative evolution underlying all activity in the universe.

eldorado [Sp. *el dorado* 'the gilded'] a fictitious country rich in gold, believed by the Spaniards of the sixteenth century to exist on the Upper Amazon; *hence,* any region or prospect of enormous wealth. 16c. [N,S]

elegantiæ arbiter [Lat.] a judge of good taste, one whose opinion is deferred to in matters of æsthetics. 20c. Tacitus *Annals* xvi 18, referring to Petronius. More commonly used in the adapted form ARBITER ELEGANTIARUM.

elenchus, *pl.* **elenchi** [Lat. < Gk. ἔλεγχος] *Logic* the refutation of a proposition in logic; a sophistical argument, a fallacy. 17c. Cf. PETITIO ELENCHI. [N,S]

élévation [Fr.] *Ballet* the totality of movements in which the dancer leaps into the air; agility in aerial movements. 20c.

élite [Fr.] the choice part, the flower (of society or of any group of people). 18c. Often with the implication that the people concerned are aware of their superiority to the herd. Cf. CRÈME DE LA CRÈME. [N,S]

elixir [Lat. < Arab. *al-iksir*] a substance supposed to have the power of transmuting base metals into gold; a drug supposed to have the power of indefinitely prolonging life; a sovereign remedy, a PANACEA. 14c. [N,S]

éloge [Fr.] a funeral oration, a panegyric; an ENCOMIUM. 16c. [N,S]

émaillerie à jour [Fr.] Art a kind of CLOISONNÉ-work in which the ground is removed when the application of transparent enamels is complete, so that the result resembles stained glass in miniature. 20c. The method was popular in the fourteenth century. Cf. PLIQUÉ À JOUR.

embargo [Sp. 'arrest'] an order forbidding the passage of ships to and from a country; a suspension of commerce; any prohibition or restraint. 17c. [N,S]

embarras de choix [Fr.] difficulty in making a choice, *usu.* because of the large number of possibilities available. 19c. The French phrase is *embarras du choix*, also sometimes used in English; but the less correct alternative seems better established. [S]

embarras de(s) richesse(s) [Fr.] an abundance which gives rise to difficulties, *esp.* an abundance of fine details which spoils the general effect of a work of art. 18c. The phrase comes from the title of a comedy by the Abbé d'Allainval (1700–53), *L'Embarras des Richesses* (1726), and this is the most authentic form of the phrase; but *embarras de richesses* is the normal form in French, and *embarras de richesse* is common in English. [N,S]

embarras du choix=EMBARRAS DE CHOIX, difficulty in making a choice.

embonpoint [Fr.] plumpness, a well-nourished appearance. 17c. Often, but not always, in a complimentary sense. [N,S]

embouchure [Fr.] *Mus.* the mouthpiece of a wind instrument; the manner of using the mouth to produce a musical tone from a wind instrument. 18c. [N,S]

embourgeoisement [Fr.] the gradual admission of primitive peoples to citizenship of a civilized state. 20c.

embusqué [Fr. 'in ambush'] one who avoids military service by entering a reserved occupation, a shirker. 20c. [N*]

emeritus, *pl.* **emeriti** [Lat.] (a professor) who has retired from his Chair. 19c. In the singular *emeritus* may precede or follow the noun 'professor'; in the plural *emeriti* always follows the noun. [N,S]

émeute [Fr.] a riot, a popular rising. 19c. [N,S]

émigré, *f.* **émigrée** [Fr.] one who has left his country, *usu.* for political reasons; *esp.* one who left France during the Revolution. 18c. [N,S]

éminence grise [Fr. 'grey eminence'] a power behind the throne, one who exercises great power while remaining in obscurity. 20c. The title given to Father Joseph, the Capuchin friar who exercised great influence over Cardinal Richelieu.

émotionné, *f.* **émotionnée** [Fr.] moved, thrilled (by some experience). 20c.

empennage [Fr. 'feathering (of an arrow)'] the tail-unit of an aircraft, including the tail-plane and the fin. 20c. [N*]

emphyteusis [Lat. < Gk. ἐμφύτευσις] *Law* perpetual leasehold, perpetual tenancy of property subject to the payment of ground-rent. 17c. [N,S]

emplacement [Fr.] the site, situation, and location of a building, etc., considered as a suitable background for it. 19c. Distinguished in its pronunciation, and by the use of italics, from the military term of identical form. [S]

emporium, *pl.* **emporia** [Lat. < Gk. ἐμπόριον] a principal centre of commerce; a market-place, a BAZAAR. 16c. Often pompously applied to a large shop. [N,S]

empressé, *f.* **empressée** [Fr.] anxiously cordial, eager to display good will and civility. 19c. [N*,S]

empressement [Fr.] an eager display of cordiality and civility. 18c. [N,S]

en avant [Fr.] forward, ahead, *esp.* as a cry of encouragement. 19c. Cf. AVANTI. [N*,S]

en axe [Fr.] *Arch.* in alignment; (two objects) in alignment one with another. 20c. [N*]

en bloc [Fr.] as a whole, wholesale, in a lump. 19c. [N*]

en brochette [Fr.] *Cul.* (pieces of food served) on a skewer. 20c.

en brosse [Fr. 'like a brush'] (hair cut) very short, following the contours of the head; crew-cut. 20c.

en cabochon [Fr.] (a precious stone) smoothed and polished but not cut into facets. 20c. Cf. CABOCHON.

encænia [Lat. < Gk. (τὰ) ἐγκαίνια] an annual commemoration of the dedication of a building; *esp.* the annual Commemoration of the founders and benefactors of the University of Oxford. 14c. [N,S]

en camaïeu [Fr.] *Art* (an underpainting) in monochrome. 20c. Cf. GRISAILLE.

en casserole [Fr.] *Cul.* (cooked) in a CASSEROLE or covered stew-pan of thick earthenware. 20c.

enceinte [Fr.] (1) pregnant, great with child. 17c. (2) *Mil.* a space enclosed by fortifications; the fortifications surrounding an enclosure. 18c. [N,S]

enchaînement [Fr.] *Ballet* a sequence of a number of steps forming a single movement. 20c.

encheiridion/enchiridion [Gk. ἐγχειρίδιον] a handbook, a manual, a short treatise serving as a book of reference. 18c. The spelling *encheiridion*, closer to the Greek, seems now to be the commoner. Cf. VADE MECUM. [N,S]

en clair [Fr.] in plain language, not in code or cypher. 19c. [N*]

enclave [Fr.] a district belonging to one country, but entirely surrounded by the territory of another; *hence*, anything wholly surrounded by something alien to it. 19c. [N]

encoignure [Fr.] a corner-cupboard with short legs, designed to stand on the floor. 20c.

encomium, *pl.* **encomia** [Lat. < Gk. ἐγκώμιον] a formal expression of praise, a laudatory composition, a panegyric. 16c. [N,S]

encore [Fr. 'again'] the repetition of an item in a public performance, or the performance of an additional item; a call for such an addition to the programme. 18c. The word is used by the audience to call for a repetition; the origin of the usage is obscure, since the French equivalent is *bis!* [N,S]

en dedans [Fr.] *Ballet* (a movement) in which the free leg or the body itself is rotated or turned towards the supporting leg. 20c.

en dehors [Fr.] *Ballet* (a movement) in which the free leg or the body itself is rotated or turned away from the supporting leg. 20c.

en déshabillé [Fr.] in a state of undress, informally dressed. 17c. For variant spellings cf. DÉSHABILLÉ. [N,S]

en détail [Fr.] in detail. 20c.

en diagonale [Fr.] *Ballet* diagonally across the stage. 20c. Cf. DIAGONALE.

endimanché, *f.* **endimanchée** [Fr.] dressed up in one's Sunday best; *hence*, a style, etc., which has been deliberately made ornate. 20c.

en échelon [Fr.] *Mil.* in staggered formation, in parallel divisions each having its front clear of the next in advance. 19c. Cf. ÉCHELON. [N,S]

en évidence [Fr.] much in evidence, in the forefront, conspicuous. 19c. [N*,S]

en face [Pseudo-Fr.] *Art* from the front, full-face. 20c. The French for 'full-face' is *de face*.

en famille [Fr.] (treated) like one of the family, without formality; (dining, etc.) with one's family alone, without guests. 18c. [N*,S]

enfant chéri, *f.* **enfant chérie,** *pl.* **enfants chéris** [Fr.] a much-loved child, a pampered child. 20c.

enfant de miracle [Fr. 'child of a miracle'] a child whose birth is welcome but wholly unexpected, *usu.* one born late in its parents' life. 20c.

enfant de son siècle [Fr.] a child of his century, one whose character and actions seem to reflect the spirit of the period in which he lived. 20c.

enfant gâté, *pl.* **enfants gâtés** [Fr.] a spoilt child, one who is showered with unmerited favours. 19c. The feminine form is properly *enfant gâtée*, but the masculine form seems to be used freely of both sexes. [S(*)]

enfantillage [Fr.] a childish action, a foolish prank. 20c. [N*]

enfant perdu, *pl.* **enfants perdus** [Fr.] a member of a 'forlorn hope', one who is held to be expendable. 16c. Nearly always in the plural. [S]

enfant terrible, *pl.* **enfants terribles** [Fr. 'terrible child'] a child whose precocious chatter or unruly behaviour embarrasses his elders; *hence*, any person who embarrasses his associates by indiscreet or ill-considered words or actions. 19c. *Les Enfants Terribles* was the title of a series of prints by the French engraver Sulpice-Guillaume Gavarni (1804–1866). [N*,S]

en fête [Fr.] in festival array, keeping high holiday. 19c. [N*,S]

enfilade [Fr.] an open VISTA; a suite of rooms in a straight line offering an open VISTA from one end to the other. 20c. Distinguished by its French pronunciation from the military term anglicized in 18c.

en flèche [Fr. 'like an arrow-head'] at the head (of a literary or artistic movement, etc.) 20c.

engagé [Fr.] committed to the support of a political party or social philosophy; dedicated to the promulgation of the doctrines of such a party or philosophy. 20c. Cf. ART ENGAGÉ; DÉGAGÉ; THÉÂTRE ENGAGÉ.

engagement [Fr.] the condition of being ENGAGÉ, of being committed to the support of a political party or social philosophy. 20c.

en garçon [Fr.] as a bachelor, living as a bachelor. 19c. Cf. GARÇONNIÈRE. [N*,S]

en garde [Fr.] on guard, on the alert. 20c. Used in fencing to warn one's opponent of an impending attack.

englyn, *pl.* **englynion** [Welsh] *Ling.* a four-line stanza of prescribed form, written in the CYNGHANEDD metre. 17c. [N]

engobe [Fr.] a white coating of pipe-clay on an earthenware or pottery vessel, *usu.* covered with a transparent glaze. 19c. [N]

engouement [Fr. 'obstruction in the throat'] infatuation, unreasoning admiration. 19c. The alternative French spelling *engoûment*, less common than *engouement*, is only very rarely used in English. An exactly parallel form is DÉNOUEMENT. [N,S]

en grande tenue [Fr.] in full dress, *esp.* military or naval full dress; in evening dress; in court dress. 19c. Cf. GRANDE TENUE. [N*,S]

enjambement [Fr.] *Ling.* running on the sense from one metrical unit to another, *esp.* from one couplet to another; *hence*, maintaining continuity across a normal division of anything. 19c. Still commonly printed in italics, but found also in the anglicized form *enjambment*. Cf. HAKENSTIL. [N,S]

enjôleur, *f.* **enjôleuse** [Fr.] (a person) who secures advantages by coaxing or wheedling. 20c.

en l'air [Fr.] (1) in the air, quite vague, a matter for discussion; (2) *Mil.* (troops) too far away to give or receive support. 19c. [N*,S]

en masse [Fr.] in a body, as a whole; bodily, all together. 18c. [N,S]

en ménage [Fr.] (living together) as husband and wife. 20c. *Usu.* with the implication that the couple concerned are not in fact husband and wife.

ennui [Fr.] boredom, mental dissatisfaction due to lack of occupation. 18c. [N,S]

ennuyeux [Fr.] tiresome, vexatious. 20c. Not necessarily 'causing ENNUI'.

enosis [Gk. ἕνωσις] re-union; now *esp.* the movement for the re-union of Cyprus with Greece. 20c.

en pantoufles [Fr.] in slippers, in the unconstrained atmosphere of familiar intercourse. 20c. [N*]

en passant [Fr.] (1) in passing, by the way, while attending to something else. 17c. (2) *Chess* (a pawn taken) as if on the square through which it passes when making its initial move of two squares. 19c. A pawn can only be taken *en passant* by another pawn, not by another piece, and only immediately after its initial move. Cf. COUP EN PASSANT. [N]

en pension [Fr.] living as a boarder, paying a fixed sum for board and lodging. 19c. Cf. DEMI-PENSION; PENSION. [N]

en plein [Fr.] (1) *Roulette* (a stake placed) on a single number, not on a sequence or combination of numbers; (2) *Art* (enamel work) in which the ground (*usu.* of gold or silver) is carved in INTAGLIO, the hollows being filled with translucent enamel through which the modelling can still be seen. 20c. Cf. BASSE-TAILLE; SUR FOND RÉSERVÉ.

en plein air [Fr.] in the open air. Cf. AL FRESCO. [N*]

en poste [Fr.] *Dip.* having a diplomatic appointment (at a certain place). 20c.

en prince [Fr.] like a prince, in a princely style. 17c. [N,S]

en principe [Fr.] in principle. 20c. Implying that while the principle is accepted details still remain to be settled.

en prise [Fr.] *Chess* (a piece) in such a position that it can be taken at the next move. 19c. [N*,S]

en rapport [Fr.] in harmony, in sympathy. 19c. Used *esp.* of a sympathetic and intuitive understanding between two people. Cf. RAPPORT. [N*,S]

en règle [Fr.] in order, in due form. 19c. Not to be confused with DE RÈGLE. [N*,S]

en retraite [Fr.] in retirement, on the retired list, superannuated, living on a pension. 19c. [N*,S]

en revanche [Fr.] in return, as a retaliation. 19c. [N*,S]

en route [Fr.] on the road, on the way. 18c. Construed with *for*, not *to:* '*en route* for' = 'on the way to'. [N,S]

en secondes noces [Fr.] in a second marriage, as a second spouse. 20c.

ensemble [Fr. 'together'] (1) all the details of something considered together as contributing to the general effect; (2) *Mus.* the joint performance of all those taking part in a concerted piece of music; a group of performers accustomed to play together. 18c. Cf. TABLEAU D'ENSEMBLE; TOUT ENSEMBLE. [N(*),S]

en sourdine [Fr.] (1) *Mus.* muted; (2) secretly, stealthily, on the sly. 20c. Cf. CON SORDINO; SOURDINE.

en suite [Fr.] in agreement (with), of the same kind; (a set of rooms) opening one into another. 18c. [N,S]

en taille d'épargne [Fr.] *Art* CHAMPLEVÉ (enamel work), (enamel work) in which the metal ground is engraved or hollowed out, the hollows being filled with opaque enamel. 20c. Cf. CLOISONNÉ; ÉPERGNE; TAILLE D'ÉPARGNE.

entasis [Gk. *ἔντασις* 'stretching'] *Arch.* a slight swelling in the outline of a shaft or column, designed to produce the illusion that the column is straight. 17c. The device is intended to frustrate the optical illusion whereby a column of equal thickness appears to have a slightly concave outline. [N,S]

entente [Fr.] an understanding, *esp.* between states or political powers; a group of states linked by such an understanding. 19c. Later than ENTENTE CORDIALE, and probably an abbreviation of it. [N*,S]

entente cordiale [Fr.] a friendly understanding, *esp.* between states or political powers. 19c. Often used with reference to the understanding between England, France and Russia, 1904–08. [N*,S]

entêté, *f.* **entêtée** [Fr.] obstinate, stubborn, strong-willed, headstrong. 19c. [S]

entia non (sunt) multiplicanda præter necessitatem [Lat.] suppositions must not be unnecessarily multiplied, i.e. the best explanation (of a phenomenon, etc.) is that which requires the fewest suppositions. 20c. The principle, attributed to the fourteenth-century nominalist philosopher William of Occam or Ockham, is known as 'Ockham's razor', or 'the law of parsimony'. Cf. HYPOTHESES NON FINGO.

Entmythologisierung [Ger.] the historical process by which a story or fable, originally mythical, comes to be presented as one of actual fact. 20c.

entourage [Fr.] surroundings, environment; *hence*, a retinue, the SUITE of friends and advisers of a person of consequence; the supporters and disciples of an artist, writer, etc. 19c. [N,S]

entourloupette [Fr.] an underhand means of obtaining a commercial advantage. 20c.

en tout cas [Fr. 'in any emergency'] an umbrella which is designed to serve also as a sunshade. 19c. [N*,S]

entr'acte [Fr.] the interval between the acts of a play or opera; a musical interlude or other performance designed to occupy the interval. 19c. Cf. DIVERTISSEMENT. [N,S]

entrain [Fr.] liveliness, spirit, animation. 19c. [S]

en train [Fr.] into the way (of doing something), in the mood (for doing something); in high spirits. 18c. [S]

en transi, *pl.* **en transis** [Fr.] *Art* (a sculptured figure on a tomb) in a recumbent position as if asleep. 20c.

en travesti [Fr.] *Ballet* (a woman dancer) dressed as a man. 20c.

entrechat [Fr.] *Ballet* a leap during which the dancer rapidly crosses and uncrosses his legs. 18c. The number of times the legs are crossed and uncrossed is often indicated by a (French) number after the word, the starting and finishing positions being counted together as one. Nijinski is reputed to have performed the *entrechat dix.* [N,S]

entrecôte [Fr.] *Cul.* rib-steak. 19c. [S]

entredeux [Fr. 'between two'] an insertion, *usu.* of lace but sometimes of embroidered linen, etc., in a woman's dress. 19c. [N*,S]

entre deux âges [Fr.] middle-aged, neither young nor old. 20c. *Usu.* applied to a woman. Cf. D'UN CERTAIN ÂGE.

entre deux guerres [Fr.] (the period) between the two wars of 1914–18 and 1939–45. 20c.

entrée [Fr.] (1) the right or privilege of admission (to a house, company of distinguished people, etc.); (2) *Ballet* the entry of a dancer or group of dancers; *hence*, a dance performed by a single dancer or small group of dancers, forming part of a larger work; (3) *Cul.* a dish served between the fish course and the meat course. 18c. Cf. GRANDE ENTRÉE; PETITE ENTRÉE. [N,S]

entremets [Fr.] *Cul.* a side-dish; any dainty served between two main courses; a sweet dish. 17c. The word is often used in the plural, which is identical with the singular; hence a false singular *entremet* is sometimes found. [N,S]

entre nous [Fr.] between ourselves, in strict confidence. 18c. [N,S]

entrepôt [Fr.] a warehouse where goods may be temporarily deposited; a commercial centre to which goods are brought for distribution. 18c. [N,S]

entrepreneur, *f.* **entrepreneuse** [Fr.] (1) a contractor acting as an intermediary between capital and labour; (2) the organizer of an entertainment or musical performance, the manager of an establishment used for purposes of entertainment. 19c. [N,S]

entresol [Fr.] a mezzanine floor, a series of rooms contrived in the upper part of a section of a high ground floor. 18c. [N,S]

enuresis [Lat.] *Med.* incontinence of urine, bed-wetting. 19c. The modern Latin word is irregularly formed from a Greek stem. [N*]

en ventre sa mère [Obs. Fr.] *Law* in his mother's womb, as yet unborn. 19c. Used in connection with the legal rights of an unborn child. Cf. IN UTERO. [N*]

en villégiature [Fr.] staying in the country, on holiday in the country. 20c. Cf. VILLEGGIATURA.

en voyage [Fr.] travelling, on a journey. 20c.

épanchement [Fr.] an outpouring of emotion; effusiveness. 20c.

épaule en dedans [Fr. 'shoulder in'] *Equ.* a forward DRESSAGE movement in which the horse is flexed over his whole length away from the direction in which he is moving. 20c.

épaulement [Fr.] *Ballet* the proper placing of a dancer's shoulders. 20c.

épée [Fr.] the foil, with the point protected by a button, used in fencing; a similar, sharp-pointed, weapon used in duelling. 19c. [N*]

épergne [Fr. *épargne* 'economy'] an ornamental centre-piece for a dinner-table. 18c. The *épergne* is commonly a support for a number of silver dishes, *orig.* used to hold pickles, but now more usually filled with flowers or fruit. The relationship between French *épargne* and English *épergne* is obscure, but there is perhaps some connection through EN TAILLE D'ÉPARGNE. Cf. DESSUS DE TABLE. [N,S]

ephebus, *pl.* **ephebi** [Lat. < Gk. ἔφηβος] a young man. 17c. *Orig.* a Greek citizen between the ages of eighteen and twenty. *Occ.* in the Greek form *ephebos*, pl. *epheboi*. [N,S]

ephemeris, *pl.* **ephemerides** [Gk. ἐφημερίς] an astronomical almanac in which the positions of the heavenly bodies are forecast for each day of the year. 16c. [N,S]

ephemeron, *pl.* **ephemera** [Gk. ἐφήμερον] an insect that lives only for a day; *hence*, any person or thing that has only a transitory existence. 17c. Since 18c. the plural *ephemera* has often been taken as if a Latin feminine singular, with plural *ephemeræ* or *ephemeras*. [N,S]

epicedium, *pl.* **epicedia** [Lat. < Gk. ἐπικήδειον] a funeral song or ode, a dirge. 16c. [N,S]

epidermis [Gk. ἐπιδερμίς] the outer layer of the skin of an animal. 17c. [N,S]

epiphenomenon [Lat. < Gk. ἐπι- + φαινόμενον] a secondary development, a secondary symptom. 18c. [N]

episcopus vagans, *pl.* **episcopi vagantes** [Lat.] *Eccles.* a wandering bishop, a cleric in bishop's orders (*usu.* of one of the Eastern churches) who has no see and considers himself free to administer priest's orders in any part of the world. 20c.

epithalamium, *pl.* **epithalamia** [Lat. < Gk. ἐπιθαλάμιον] a nuptial song, an ode in praise of bride and bridegroom. 16c. Found also in the form *epithalamion*, direct from the Greek. Cf. PROTHALAMION. [N,S]

epitome [Gk. *ἐπιτομή*] an abridgment, an abstract, a COMPENDIUM; anything which represents some thing or idea on a reduced scale. 16c. Cf. RÉSUMÉ. [N,S]

épopée [Fr.] an epic poem; epic poetry in general. 17c. [N,S]

epos [Gk. *ἔπος*] a sequence of unwritten narrative poems such as were later put together into epic poems; a series of heroic events fit to be recorded in an epic; an epic poem. 19c. [N,S]

eppur si muove [It.] and yet it does move. 20c. Also in the form *e pur si muove*. Attributed to Galileo after he had recanted his theory that the earth moves round the sun, but almost certainly apocryphal; used as an example of heroism (or obstinacy) in adhering to a belief in the face of hostile pressure.

épris, *f.* **éprise** [Fr.] captivated, on the point of falling in love. 19c. [S]

épuisé, *f.* **épuisée** [Fr.] exhausted, worn out. 18c. Apparently not in use during 19c. but revived in 20c. [S]

équestrienne [Pseudo-Fr.] a female horse-rider, *esp.* a female circus rider. 19c. The word does not exist in standard French. [N,S]

equilibrium [Lat. *æquilibrium*] a state of even balance; neutrality or indifference in judgment. 17c. The word was spelt as in Latin until the middle of 18c. [N,S]

équipe [Fr.] a team of competitors taking part in a sporting event. 20c.

Erdgeist [Ger.] the Earth Spirit, the active spiritual force of the world. 20c. The *Erdgeist* is summoned by Faust in Part I of Goethe's *Faust* (1808).

ergastulum, *pl.* **ergastula** [Lat.] *Hist.* a private prison or place of punishment for slaves. 19c. [N*]

ergo [Lat.] therefore. 14c. Used to introduce the conclusion of a syllogism. [N,S]

Erin go bragh [Pseudo-Ir.] Ireland forever! 20c. The Irish form is *Éire go brách*; in Old Irish *Érinn* is the accusative or dative of *Ériu* 'Ireland', modern *Éire*; the phrase as a whole is an English invention.

erotica, *pl.* [Gk. *ἐρωτικά*] books, etc., concerned with sexual love; pornographic writings. 19c. [N*]

erratum, *pl.* **errata** [Lat.] an error, *esp.* in a printed book; in *pl.*, a list of corrected errors appended to a printed book. 16c. Cf. CORRIGENDUM. [N,S]

Ersatz [Ger.] a substitute, an inferior article used to replace another which is not readily obtainable; not genuine, inferior. 20c. Introduced during the First World War, but mainly current during the Second World War and the period of 'austerity' which immediately followed it; most common as an adjective, and *usu.* written without a capital letter. [N*]

Erziehungsroman [Ger.] a novel concerned with the education, *usu.* the emotional education, of its hero. 20c. The classical example of the

Erziehungsroman is Flaubert's *L'Éducation Sentimentale* (1869). Cf. BILDUNGSROMAN.

escargot [Fr.] *Cul.* an edible snail. 19c. [N*]

esclandre [Fr.] a public scandal, a disturbance causing notoriety, a 'scene'. 19c. [N,S]

escritoire [Obs. Fr.] a writing-desk, a BUREAU or SECRÉTAIRE. 17c. Until 19c. often mysteriously written *escrutoire*, *escrutore;* now *occ.* replaced by the modern French ÉCRITOIRE. [N,S(*)]

espadrille [Fr.] a shoe with a sole of twisted rope and uppers of canvas. 19c. [N*]

espiègle [Fr.] roguish, sprightly, mischievous. 19c. [N,S]

espièglerie [Fr.] roguishness, playfulness. 19c. [N,S]

espresso [It. 'squeezed out'] (coffee) made by using the pressure of steam to force water at near boiling-point through a pierced vessel containing the coffee-grains. 20c. Now often partially anglicized as *expresso.*

esprit [Fr.] vivacious wit, liveliness of temperament. 16c. [N,S]

esprit de corps [Fr.] the loyalty of the members of some body, association, etc., to their common traditions and interests. 18c. Cf. GEMEINSCHAFTSGEFÜHL. [N,S]

esprit de notaire [Fr.] the soul of a lawyer, a pettifogging mind, a tendency to be overmuch concerned with trivial detail. 20c.

esprit d'escalier [Fr. 'staircase wit'] a witty remark or telling retort which comes to mind only after the occasion for its use has passed. 20c. The 'staircase' is the one leading down from the SALON to the front door. The French phrase is *esprit de l'escalier*, coined by Denis Diderot (1713–84) *Paradoxe sur le Comédien.*

esprit fort, *pl.* **esprits forts** [Fr.] one who professes superiority to current prejudices, a free-thinker. 18c. [N,S]

esprit gaulois [Fr.] a spirit of mocking criticism, supposedly characteristic of the French. 20c.

esprit laïc [Fr.] an attitude of mind hostile to clerical or doctrinal influence, *esp.* in educational institutions. 20c.

esprit libre [Fr.] an untrammelled spirit, one who is not hampered by conventional prejudices or reticences; freedom from care. 20c.

esquisse [Fr.] *Art* a sketch, the first rough drawing for a picture, or the first rough model for a statue. 18c. Cf. CROQUIS; ÉBAUCHE. [N,S]

esse [Lat.] essential nature; mere existence; opposed to BENE ESSE, prosperity, well-being. 17c. Cf. IN ESSE. [N(*),S]

estaminet [Fr.] a small public-house. 19c. Formerly also a CAFÉ where smoking was allowed. [N,S]

estancia [Sp.] a cattle-farm in Spanish America. 18c. [N,S]

esthéticien, *f.* **esthéticienne** [Fr.] a specialist in beauty treatment. 20c. Cf. VISAGISTE.

esto [Lat. 'let it be'] *Law* admitting that it is so. 20c. Used to claim that one's own contention is valid even if one's opponents' statements are correct.

esto perpetua [Lat.] may it last forever! 18c. Since the Latin phrase is feminine it can properly be applied only to things which can be considered as feminine; but this limitation is not always observed. [S]

étagère [Fr.] a set of open shelves, either on legs or attached to the wall like a hanging bookshelf; a what-not. 19c. [N,S]

étalage [Fr.] display, *esp.* of goods in the window of a shop. 20c. [N*]

et alia/et alii [Lat.] and other things (*alia*), and other people (*alii*). 15c. Both forms are normally abbreviated to *et al.*, in which case it is not possible to distinguish whether things or people are referred to except from the context. [S]

étape [Fr.] a stage in a journey; a stopping-place between the stages of a journey (now *esp.* the stages of a cycle-race, etc.) 20c. [S]

étatisme [Fr.] state management, state control; the extension of the power of the state over the individual citizen. 20c. [N*]

et cætera/et cetera [Lat.] and the rest, and so forth; *hence* as a noun (*usu.* in the plural *etceteras*), extras, appurtenances, 'sundries'. 15c. Normally abbreviated to *etc.* in writing, but always pronounced in full. [N,S]

e tenebris lux [Lat.] light out of darkness, illumination in a dark place. 20c.

et hoc genus omne [Lat.] and all that kind of thing, and all that kind of people. 19c. Cf. HOC GENUS OMNE. [S]

ethos [Gk. ἦθος] the characteristic spirit of a people or community. 19c [N,S]

et in Arcadia ego [Lat.] I too have lived in Arcadia, I too have known the delights of the earthly paradise. 20c. *Orig.* an inscription on a tomb. The current interpretation is probably wrong: the true meaning may be 'even in Arcadia, there am I (i.e. Death)'.

étoile [Fr.] a design in the shape of a star; the intersection of streets radiating from a point. 18c. Cf. ROND-POINT. [N,S]

étourderie [Fr.] thoughtlessness, heedlessness; a thoughtless act, a blunder 18c. [S]

étourdi, *f.* **étourdie** [Fr.] thoughtless, scatter-brained. 17c. [S]

étrenne [Fr.] a New Year's gift. 19c. Rare in the singular, much more common in the plural *étrennes* in both French and English. [N*,S]

étrier [Fr. 'stirrup'] a climbing-iron, an iron device strapped to a climbing-boot to provide a foothold on a difficult surface. 20c. Cf. CRAMPON.

et sequentes/et sequentia [Lat.] and the following (pages, chapters, etc.) 19c. The first form is masculine or feminine, the second neuter; they are distinguished according to the Latin gender of the following noun. Fortunately both are normally abbreviated to *et seq.*, so that this difficulty is avoided.

et tu, Brute! [Lat.] you too, Brutus! 16c. A reproach spoken to a friend who has joined with others to do one an injury. Attributed to Julius Cæsar when he recognized Brutus (his friend, and perhaps his son) amongst his assassins: Suetonius *Divus Julius* lxxxii. [S]

étude [Fr.] *Mus.* a study, a composition designed to exercise or display the virtuosity of the performer. 19c. [S]

étui [Fr.] a small pocket-case for holding needles and similar small objects. 17c. [N,S]

etymon, *pl.* **etyma** [Lat. < Gk. ἔτυμον] *Ling.* the primitive form of a word, the original from which a word is derived. 16c. [N,S]

euphoria [Gk. εὐφορία] a feeling of well-being and good health, *esp.* in a person whose health is not normally good. 20c.

eureka [Gk. εὕρηκα] I have found it, I have found the answer to the problem. 16c. The ejaculation of Archimedes when he discovered the principle of specific gravity: Vitruvius *De Architectura* ix 215. The correct transliteration *heureka* is rarely used. [N,S]

euthanasia [Gk. εὐθανασία] a gentle and pleasant death, *esp.* such a death medically induced in those suffering from incurable and painful diseases. 17c. [N,S]

Ewigkeit [Ger. 'eternity'] in the phrase 'into the *Ewigkeit*', into thin air. 19c. [N*,S]

(das) Ewig-Weibliche [Ger.] the eternal feminine, the unchanging power of woman to inspire and spiritualize mankind. 20c. From the conclusion of Goethe's *Faust* Part II (1832): *Das Ewig-Weibliche Zieht uns hinan* 'the eternal feminine draws us on'.

ex [Lat. 'out of'] (1) directly from (as in '*ex* warehouse'). 19c. (2) without (as in '*ex* dividend'). 19c. (3) prefixed to English words with a hyphen, former, sometime (as in '*ex*-king'). 14c. [N(*),S]

ex abundanti cautela [Lat.] from excessive caution, to be well on the safe side. 19c. A variant is *ex abundantiori cautela* 'to be even more on the safe side'. Cf. OB MAJOREM CAUTELAM. [S]

exalté, *f.* **exaltée** [Fr.] in a state of mind elevated above the normal by excitement, enthusiasm, etc. 20c.

ex animo [Lat.] from the heart, sincerely, without reservation. 17c. Used by Cicero, but probably already a current phrase. [N,S]

ex cathedra [Lat. 'from the throne'] authoritative(ly), (spoken) by virtue of judicial office. 17c. Used *esp.* of pronouncements made by the Pope in Consistory. [N,S]

exceptio probat regulam [Lat.] the exception proves the rule. 20c. A legal maxim of which the complete text is: *exceptio probat* [or *(con)firmat*] *regulam in casibus non exceptis* 'the fact that certain exceptions are made (in a legal document) confirms that the rule is valid in all other cases'. The meaning is often misunderstood, and the phrase is correspondingly misapplied.

exceptis excipiendis [Lat.] when the appropriate exceptions have been made. 19c. Used when applying a principle or rule not all the provisions of which are applicable to the case in question. Cf. MUTATIS MUTANDIS. [S]

exclusivité [Fr.] exclusiveness. 20c.

excreta *pl.* [Lat.] excreted matter, the waste products of the animal or human body, *esp.* the FÆCES. 19c. [N,S]

excursus, *pl.* **excursus** [Lat.] a digression in which some point of detail is discussed at length; an appendix devoted to the discussion of some marginal question. 19c. [N,S]

ex debito justitiæ [Lat.] as a debt of justice, as a legal obligation. 17c. Opposed to EX GRATIA. [S]

ex delicto [Lat.] *Law* as a result of a crime, arising out of a crime. 19c. [S]

ex dono [Lat.] as a gift (from); an inscription, *usu.* on a book, recording that it is a gift from the person specified. 17c. [S]

exeat [Lat. 'let him go out'] leave of absence from a school or college. 18c. [N,S]

exécutant, *f.* **exécutante** [Fr.] *Mus.* a performer, *usu.* a VIRTUOSO performer, on some instrument. 20c.

exegesis [Gk. ἐξήγησις] explanation, interpretation, *esp.* the interpretation of Holy Scripture. 17c. [N,S]

(exegi) monumentum ære perennius [Lat.] (I have wrought) a monument more lasting than bronze. 17c. Horace *Odes* III xxx 1. [S]

exempli gratia [Lat.] for example. 17c. Commonly abbreviated to *e.g.* [S(*)]

exemplum, *pl.* **exempla** [Lat.] an anecdote or brief story used in a mediæval sermon to illustrate a moral point. 20c.

exercice au milieu [Fr.] *Ballet* an exercise performed in the middle of the practice-room, not against the BARRE. 20c.

exercice de style [Fr.] a literary work, painting, etc., performed as a technical exercise and not intended as a serious work of art. 20c.

exergue [Fr.] the space on the reverse of a coin or medal, marked off from the main design by a horizontal line, which contains the date. 17c. [N,S]

exeunt [Lat.] they go out; (a stage-direction indicating that) certain specified characters, or the characters who have just spoken, leave the stage. 15c. Cf. EXIT. [N,S]

exeunt omnes [Lat.] they all go out; (a stage-direction indicating that) all the characters leave the stage. 16c. [N,S]

ex gratia [Lat.] (a payment made) as a favour, not EX DEBITO JUSTITIÆ. 20c. [N*]

ex hypothesi [Lat.] as a result of the assumptions made; *hence*, as a matter of course. 17c. The second meaning 'as a matter of course' is an unwarrantable extension of the first, but appears to be firmly established. [N*,S]

exigeant, *f.* **exigeante** [Fr.] hard to please, asking a lot, insisting on one's rights. 18c. [N,S]

exit [Lat.] he (she) goes out; (a stage-direction indicating that) a specified character, or the character who has just spoken, leaves the stage. 16c. Cf. EXEUNT. [N,S]

ex libris [Lat.] from the library (of the person whose name follows); an inscription or label recording the ownership of a book. 19c. As a noun, often written *ex-libris*; the plural is unchanged. [N,S]

ex necessitate [Lat.] from necessity, having no alternative. 20c.

ex nihilo nihil fit [Lat.] nothing can be made out of nothing. 16c. Based on Persius *Satires* iii 84: *de nihilo nihil*. Persius himself was adapting Lucretius *De Rerum Natura* i 155–6: *nil posse creari De nilo* 'nothing can be created out of nothing'. [S]

exodus [Lat. < Gk. ἔξοδος] a mass departure from some place, *esp.* a mass emigration from one country to another. 17c. [N,S]

ex officio [Lat.] by virtue of one's office. 16c. *Usu.* with reference to the automatic appointment of a person to a committee without election. [N,S]

ex opere operato [Lat.] *Theol.* by virtue of the thing done, irrespective of the merit of the person doing it. 16c. Used primarily of the sacraments, which are not invalidated by the defects of the minister. Cf. OPUS OPERATUM. [S]

exordium, *pl.* **exordia** [Lat.] the opening or introductory part of a speech or composition. 16c. Cf. PROLEGOMENON; PROŒMIUM. [N,S]

ex parte [Lat.] *Law* (evidence) given by one party only or in the interest of one party only; (an interim injunction) granted to the plaintiff for a short time in the absence of the defendant. 17c. [N,S]

ex pede Herculem [Lat.] (you can judge) the size of Hercules from his foot, you can judge the whole by a part. 17c. The Latin *Herculem* in the accusative presupposes a verb which is never supplied. Cf. EX UNGUE LEONEM. [S]

expéditeur [Fr.] an agent who arranges the despatch of goods on behalf of another person. 20c.

experientia docet [Lat.] experience teaches (us), we learn from experience. 19. Macrobius *Saturnalia* vii 5: *experientia docebit* 'experience will teach (us)' [S]

experimentum crucis [Lat.] a crucial experiment, an experiment the result of which will decide the course of future investigation. 18c. [S]

expertise [Fr.] expert knowledge, skill and experience in a particular activity or branch of study. 19c. [N*]

experto crede [Lat.] believe me, I know. 16c. Virgil *Æneid* xi 283: *experto credite*. There seems to have been a mediæval proverb *experto crede Roberto* 'believe Robert who has tried it', which may be the origin of the current phrase. [S]

explication de texte [Fr.] the detailed, formal stylistic analysis of a literary passage. 20c. This process forms the basis of the study of literature in France; its value is still a matter for argument in England.

explicit, *pl.* **expliciunt** [Lat.] (here) ends (the book, etc.); *hence*, the last few words of a manuscript treatise, recorded for purposes of identification. In the Middle Ages *explicit* was used like FINIS to mark the end of a book. Cf. INCIPIT. [N,S]

exposé [Fr.] (1) a reasoned statement or explanation of some thing or idea; (2) a revelation of something discreditable. 19c. [N,S]

ex post facto/expostfacto [Lat.] retrospective, *esp.* (a law) which changes the legal status of an act committed before its enactment. 17c. Cf. POSTFACTO. [N,S]

ex professo [Lat.] professedly, according to one's own claim or avowal. 20c.

ex silentio [Lat.] (an argument) from silence, i.e. based on the fact that no mention is made (in a text, etc.) of something which might be expected on certain hypotheses to be mentioned. 20c. Cf. ARGUMENTUM A SILENTIO.

ex tempore/extempore [Lat. 'out of the moment'] (a speech, musical performance, etc. performed) without preparation, on the spur of the moment. 16c. Cicero *De Oratore* iii 50, but probably already a current phrase. Cf. IMPROMPTU. [N,S]

extra metrum [Lat.] *Ling.* outside the metre, (a syllable or syllables) not to be counted in scansion. 20c.

ex ungue leonem [Lat.] (you can identify) a lion from its claw, you can judge the whole by a part. 19c. The phrase *ex ungue leonem* (*pingere*) is a translation of the Greek phrase ἐξ ὄνυχος τὸν λέοντα γράφειν attributed by Plutarch to Alcæus and by Lucian to Phidias. Cf. EX PEDE HERCULEM. [S]

exuviæ *pl.* [Lat.] cast-off skins, shells, etc. of living creatures. 17c. [N,S]

ex voto [Lat.] (an offering) made in pursuance of a vow, *esp.* an offering made in recognition of an answer to prayer. 18c. [N(*),S]

F

faber fortunæ suæ [Lat.] the builder of his own fortune, the architect of his own destiny. 17c. Sallust *Ad Cæsarem* I i 2: *Appius ait, fabrum esse suæ quemque fortunæ* 'Appius [i.e. Appius Claudius the blind] says that each man is the maker of his own fate'. [S(*)]

fabliau, *pl.* **fabliaux** [Obs. Fr.] a short verse narrative in Old French, *usu.* satirical or obscene. 19c. The form *fabliau* belongs to the Picard dialect; the more regular form is *fableau.* [N,S]

façade [Fr.] the front of a building; the visible part of anything, often with the implication that what is visible is inferior; *hence*, an appearance of respectability which conceals unworthy motives. 17c. [N,S]

façade d'honneur [Fr.] the principal front of a large building. 20c.

face-à-main [Fr.] an eye-glass with a folding handle, a LORGNETTE. 20c. A recent pedantry introduced because Fr. *lorgnette* properly means 'field-glass'.

facetiæ *pl.* [Lat.] jokes, witticisms, short humorous paragraphs. 17c. [N,S]

facia/fascia [Lat. *fascia*] a board running round the top of a wall under the eaves of a house; the board over a shop-front bearing the owner's name and business; the control or instrument panel of any mechanical or electronic device, *esp.* the dashboard of a car. 16c. The less correct spelling *facia* is now much more common than *fascia*, though the latter is still in use. [N,S]

facile [Fr.] compliant, easily influenced; easily led into immorality. 20c. Distinct in pronunciation and meaning from English *facile.*

facile princeps [Lat.] easily first, the acknowledged leader. 19c. [N*,S]

facilis descensus Averno [Lat.] the way down to Hell is easy, it is easy to slip into bad habits. 17c. Virgil *Æneid* vi 126; some manuscripts read *Averni* for *Averno*, and the phrase is often quoted in this form, with the same meaning. [S]

façon de parler [Fr.] a manner of speaking; something said without sincerity for effect. 19c. [S]

façonné [Fr.] (a fabric) woven with a small regular figured design. 20c.

facsimile [Lat. *fac simile* 'make alike!'] an exact copy or representation. 17c. Until about 1800 written as two words, or with a hyphen. Cf. REPLICA. [N,S]

factotum [Lat. *fac totum* 'do everything!'] a Jack-of-all-trades; a general servant who can turn his hand to anything. 16c. Until about 1800 written as two words, or with a hyphen. [N,S]

fæces *pl.* [Lat.] excrement discharged from the bowels. 17c. Formerly used in the sense 'lees, sediment', and for EXCRETA in general. [N,S]

faible [Fr.] a weakness, a partiality (for some thing or person). 20c. Distinct in meaning from FOIBLE, the older French form.

faïence [Fr.] any kind of glazed earthenware or porcelain, *esp.* MAJOLICA, earthenware glazed with tin enamel. 18c. From the name of the town Faenza in northern Italy, a home of the ceramic industry; formerly often spelt *fayence*. [N,S]

faille [Fr.] a kind of heavy ribbed silk fabric. 20c.

fáilte [Ir.] welcome. 20c. Cf. CÉAD MÍLE FÁILTE.

fainéant [Fr. 'do-nothing'] idle, indolent, indifferent; an idler, one who takes no action. 17c. Cf. ROI FAINÉANT. [N,S]

fainéantise [Fr.] indolence, indifference, apathy. 17c. The rare French alternative form *fainéance* is *occ.* used in English. [N,S]

faire école [Fr.] to found a 'school', to attract a group of disciples who imitate one's style or manner. 20c. Cf. CHEF D'ÉCOLE; ÉCOLE.

faisandé [Fr.] highly-flavoured, highly seasoned; 'spicy', mildly indecent, in doubtful taste. 20c. The proper meaning is 'high' (of game, etc.).

faiseur de mots [Fr.] a word-spinner, one who can talk or write indefinitely while saying very little. 20c.

fait accompli [Fr.] an accomplished fact, something done which cannot easily be reversed. 19c. [N,S]

faites vos jeux [Fr.] place your stakes! 20c. The warning by the CROUPIER that play is about to begin. Cf. RIEN NE VA PLUS.

faits divers *pl.* [Fr.] news in brief, short passages retailing interesting though unimportant items of news. 20c.

fakir [Arab. *faqīr* 'poor (man)'] a Moslem friar or religious mendicant, a DERVISH; *hence*, a poor or naked ascetic of any Oriental sect. 17c. [N,S]

falsetto [It.] *Mus.* a voice pitched above the natural register of the singer, a head-voice. 18c. [N,S]

famille jaune; famille noire; famille rose; famille verte [Fr.] types of Chinese porcelain of the Ch'ing dynasty (1644–1912), in which the colours are predominantly yellow, black, pink and green respectively. 19c. The earliest of these 'families' is *famille verte*, introduced from the reign of K'ang Hsi (1662–1722); next comes *famille rose* from the reign of Yung Chêng (1723–36). [N*]

fandango [Sp.] a lively Spanish dance originating in the West Indies; the music accompanying this dance. 18c. The word is probably of negro origin. [N,S]

fanfaronnade [Fr.] arrogant, boastful or ostentatious speech or behaviour. 17c. [N,S]

fantaisie [Fr.] imagination run riot; wilful fancy, eccentric desire. 20c.

fantaisiste [Fr.] one who indulges in extravagant fancies or eccentric whims. 20c.

fantasia [It.] *Mus.* a composition free in form and giving full rein to the imagination, a composition which appears to be improvised. 18c. A *fantasia* often consists of variations on several themes. Cf. RICERCARE. [N,S]

farandole [Fr.] a lively dance or jig popular in Provence. 19c. [N,S]

(la) farce est jouée [Fr.] the comedy is over. 20c. Attributed to Rabelais on his deathbed. Cf. FINITA LA COMMEDIA.

farceur, *f.* **farceuse** [Fr.] a buffoon, a practical joker, one who tries to be funny; one who is not to be taken seriously. 19c. [N,S]

farci [Fr.] *Cul.* stuffed. 20c.

farouche [Fr.] sullen, ill at ease, unused to company, savage. 18c. [N,S(*)]

farrago [Lat. 'mixed fodder'] an incongruous mixture, a confused jumble. 17c. [N,S]

fas [Lat.] right and proper. 18c. The implication is *usu.* of social or conventional rather than of moral rightness. Cf. NEFAS. [S]

Fasching [Ger.] a (German) carnival. 20c.

fascia=FACIA, a board; the dashboard of a car.

fasciculus, *pl.* **fasciculi** [Lat.] a single number of a volume issued in parts. 19c. The anglicized form *fascicle* appears earlier (17c.). Cf. HEFT; LIEFERUNG; LIVRAISON. [N,S]

fascine [Fr.] *Mil.* a bundle of brushwood used for facing earthworks, filling ditches, etc. 17c. [N,S]

fas est et ab hoste doceri [Lat.] it is right to learn even from the enemy. 17c. Ovid *Metamorphoses* iv 428. [S]

fata morgana [It. '(the) fairy Morgan'] a kind of mirage seen in the Straits of Messina; *hence*, any mirage or illusory appearance. 19c. The phenomenon was supposed to be the work of the notorious enchantress Morgan la Fée, the step-sister of King Arthur in Arthurian romance. [N,S]

faubourg [Fr.] part of a town lying outside the walls, an inner suburb. 15c. The obsolete French spelling *fauxbourg* is sometimes still used in English. Cf. BANLIEUE. [N,S]

fauna, *pl.* **faunæ** [Lat.] the whole range of animal life proper to any particular district or period. 18c. Often associated with FLORA. [N,S]

faunesque [Fr.] faun-like, shy but sensual. 20c.

fausse dévote, *see* FAUX DÉVOT, a pious hypocrite.

fausse maigre [Fr.] a woman who has achieved a slender figure by dieting, massage, etc. 20c.

faute de mieux [Fr.] for want of better. 18c. Cf. PIS ALLER. [N,S]

fauteuil [Fr.] an armchair; a seat with arms in a theatre, etc.; the seat of a Member of the Académie Française. 18c. [N(*),S(*)]

fauve [Fr.] tawny; savage, like a wild beast. 20c.

(Les) Fauves [Fr.] 'wild beasts', a term of opprobrium applied to Matisse and his school after the Paris Autumn Salon, 1905. 20c. Cf. (DIE) BRÜCKE.

fauvisme [Fr.] the style and technique of LES FAUVES (Matisse and his school). 20c.

faux amis [Fr. 'false friends'] pairs of words which have the same or a similar form in two languages but wholly different meanings, e.g. English *deception*, French *déception* 'disappointment'. 20c. From the title of a well-known collection of such pairs by Koessler and Derocquigny (1928).

faux bonhomme [Fr.] one whose apparent good nature is merely assumed, a hypocritical good fellow. 20c. In French the implication of hypocrisy is stronger than in English.

faux bourdon [Fr.] *Mus.* a mediæval system of harmonization in thirds and sixths. 20c. Anglicized in 15c. as *faburden*, recently re-introduced in the French form.

faux dévot, *f.* **fausse dévote** [Fr.] one who pretends to piety, a pious hypocrite. 20c. Cf. DÉVOT.

faux ménage [Fr.] an ill-assorted married couple; a marriage of incompatibles. 20c. Cf. MÉNAGE.

faux naïf [Fr.] one whose apparent simplicity is merely assumed. 20c. Cf. NAÏF.

faux pas [Fr.] a mistake, an act for which one feels regret or shame, a social solecism. 17c. Formerly much stronger in meaning, and often applied to a woman's fall from virtue. Cf. GAFFE. [N,S]

favete linguis [Lat. 'be gracious with (your) tongues'] listen in silence! 20c. Horace *Odes* III i 2.

fay ce que vouldras [Obs. Fr.] 'do what you will', the sole rule of the Abbey of Thélème. 20c. Rabelais *Gargantua* I lvii.

fec(it) [Lat.] (he) made (it); always accompanied by a name and inscribed on a work of art. 19c. Cf. CÆL(AVIT); DEL(INEAVIT); PINX(IT); SCULPS(IT). [S]

féerie [Fr.] a theatrical representation of fairyland; a landscape, etc., suggesting fairyland. 19c. [N,S]

féerique [Fr.] fairylike, magical, bewitching. 20c.

feis, *pl.* **feiseanna** [Ir.] an (Irish) competition in singing, dancing, music, etc. 19c. Cf. EISTEDDFOD. [N*]

Feldgrau [Ger. 'field-grey'] a dark bluish-grey, the traditional colour of the uniform of the German army. 20c.

feldsher [Russ.] a (Russian) medical auxiliary or half-trained doctor. 19c. The Russian word is from German *Feldscher* 'army surgeon'. [N*]

fellah, *pl.* **fellahin** [Arab. *fellāḥ*] an Egyptian peasant. 18c. [N,S]

felo de se, *pl.* **felones de se** [Lat. 'felon of himself'] *Law* one who kills himself, either deliberately, or accidentally while committing a felony; *hence*, the crime of suicide. 17c. The use of *felo de se* to mean 'suicide' is improper, but has been well established since 18c. [N,S]

felucca [It. < Arab. *falūkah*] a small Mediterranean ship propelled by sails or oars or both. 17c. [N,S]

feme covert [Obs. Fr.] *Law* a woman under the protection of her husband. 17c. The modern French form *femme couverte* has *occ.* been substituted, but legal usage prefers the older form. [N,S]

feme sole [Obs. Fr.] *Law* a woman not under the protection of a husband. 17c. The phrase may be applied to a spinster, a widow, or a married woman whose husband has no control over her property. [N,S]

femme de chambre [Fr.] a lady's maid; a (French) chambermaid. 18c. [N,S]

femme de trente ans [Fr.] a 'woman of thirty', who may be expected to suffer much from unsatisfactory love-affairs. 20c. From the title of a novel (1831–4) by Balzac.

femme du monde [Fr.] a woman well acquainted with the ways of the world, a woman not easily shocked. 20c. In French the meaning is rather 'society woman'. Cf. GENS DU MONDE; HOMME DU MONDE.

femme du peuple [Fr.] a working-class woman; a woman whose manners betray her humble origins. 20c. Cf. HOMME DU PEUPLE.

femme fatale [Fr.] a woman who brings disaster on all who love her. 20c. Cf. JEUNE FILLE FATALE.

femme incomprise [Fr.] a misunderstood woman, a woman whose good qualities are not appreciated. 19c. [S]

femme savante, *pl.* **femmes savantes** [Fr.] a learned woman, a bluestocking. 19c. *Usu.* with implied reference to Molière's *Les Femmes Savantes* (1672). Cf. BAS BLEU. [S]

femme sérieuse [Fr.] an earnest woman, a woman who is not frivolous. 20c. Cf. HOMME SÉRIEUX; JEUNE FEMME SÉRIEUSE; SÉRIEUX.

feræ naturæ [Lat.] (animals) of savage disposition; undomesticated. 17c. Cf. MANSUETÆ NATURÆ. [S]

ferraiuolo [It.] *Eccles.* a garment worn by priests, consisting of a width of cloth hanging from the shoulders nearly to the ground and fastened round the neck. 20c. The more usual spelling in Italian is *ferraiolo*.

ferula [Lat. 'fennel-stalk'] a cane, any instrument used for punishment in schools; *hence*, school discipline. 16c. [N,S]

festa [It.] a holiday or carnival in honour of the feast-day of a saint. 19c. Cf. FÊTE; FIESTA. [N,S]

festa teatrale [It.] *Mus.* a spectacular operatic production designed to celebrate some public festivity, e.g. a victory, a royal marriage, etc. 20c.

festina lente [Lat. 'hasten slowly!'] more haste, less speed. 17c. The Latin form of the Greek tag σπεῦδε βραδέως attributed to the Emperor Augustus by Suetonius *Divus Augustus* xxv. [S]

Festschrift [Ger.] a volume of papers by pupils and colleagues published in honour of the birthday of a distinguished scholar. 20c.

Festung Europa [Ger.] the 'fortification of Europe' planned and achieved by Hitler during the Second World War; *hence*, any plan for the defence of Europe against aggression. 20c.

fête [Fr.] a festival, an entertainment on a large scale; to provide a sumptuous entertainment for (someone). 18c. Cf. EN FÊTE; FESTA; FIESTA. [N,S]

fête champêtre [Fr.] an outdoor entertainment, a sumptuous garden-party. 18c. [N,S]

fête galante [Fr.] *Art* (a picture of) dancing, music and love-making in a rural setting. 20c. The great master of the *fête galante* was Watteau (1684–1721).

feu de joie [Fr.] a salute fired by rifles on an occasion of rejoicing. 18c. A *feu de joie* should consist of rapid shots in succession up and down the rows of riflemen, so as to produce a continuous rattle of sound. The same phrase was in earlier use with the meaning 'bonfire'. [N,S]

feuilleton [Fr.] a literary or scientific article published in a newspaper, *esp.* an episode in a serial story; *hence*, a novel considered fit only for publication in serial instalments, a novelette. 19c. [N,S]

fiacre [Fr.] a small four-wheeled hackney-carriage, a cab. 17c. [N,S]

fiançailles *pl.* [Fr.] a betrothal ceremony. 17c. [N,S]

fiancé, *f.* **fiancée** [Fr.] the person to whom one is betrothed. 19c. [N,S]

fianchetto [It.] *Chess* the moving of the Bishop to the Knight's second square in order to control the long diagonal. 20c.

fiasco [It. 'bottle'] an ignominious failure, a total breakdown in performance. 19c. The process by which the word for 'bottle' acquired this meaning is wholly unknown, though various stories have been invented to explain it. [N,S]

fiat [Lat. 'let it be'] an authoritative sanction, an authorization; a command that something should be done. 17c. [N,S(*)]

fiat experimentum in corpore vili [Lat.] let the experiment be carried out on something worthless. 19c. Cf. CORPUS VILE. [S]

fiat justitia, ruat cœlum [Lat.] let justice be done, though the heavens fall. 19c. The variant *ruat mundum* 'though the world come to ruin', was in use from 16c., but seems now to be obsolete. Cf. RUAT CŒLUM. [S]

fiat lux [Lat.] let there be light. 17c. Vulgate *Genesis* i 3. [S]

fibula, *pl.* **fibulæ** [Lat.] *Hist.* an ancient clasp or brooch. 17c. [N,S]

fiche [Fr.] a slip of paper, *esp.* an official registration form. 20c.

fichu [Fr.] (1) a shawl of muslin or lawn, *usu.* triangular, worn round the shoulders or head. 19c. (2) done for, finished. 20c. In the latter sense *fichu* is a euphemism for the less polite FOUTU. [N,S]

fidus Achates [Lat.] an intimate friend, a trusted companion. 16c. Virgil *Æneid* vi 158 and elsewhere. [S]

fieri facias [Lat. 'cause to be done'] *Law* a writ authorizing the sheriff to recover the amount of a judgment by distraint on goods. 15c. [N,S]

fiesta [Sp.] a holiday or carnival in honour of the feast-day of a saint; a carnival associated with a bull-fight. 19c. Cf. FESTA; FÊTE. [N*,S]

figurant, *f.* **figurante** [Fr.] a character in a play who has a 'walking-on' part, a supernumerary actor; (*f. only*) a chorus-girl, a show-girl. 18c. Cf. PERSONA MUTA. [N,S]

figurine [Fr.] *Art* a small carved figure. 19c. [N]

fil d'Ariane [Fr.] Ariadne's thread, the key to a labyrinth. 20c. A reference to the story of Theseus, who escaped from the labyrinth at Minos by using a thread given him by Ariadne.

filet [Fr.] (1) *Cul.* the undercut of a sirloin or rump of beef; (2) a kind of lace net with a square mesh. 19c. [N*,S]

filet mignon [Fr.] *Cul.* tenderloin, the undercut of sirloin. 20c.

filioque [Lat.] 'and from the Son', the clause of the Nicene creed which asserts the 'double procession' of the Holy Ghost, not accepted by the Eastern churches. 19c. [N,S]

filius nullius [Lat. 'son of nobody'] an illegitimate child of unacknowledged paternity. 20c.

fille de joie, *pl.* **filles de joie** [Fr. 'daughter of joy'] a prostitute. 18c. [S]

fille du régiment [Fr.] a female camp-follower, an army prostitute. 20c.

fils [Fr.] (the) son; always preceded by a name, and opposed to PÈRE '(the) father'. 19c. Cf. AÎNÉ; CADET. [S]

filtre [Fr.] (coffee) made by allowing hot water to filter down through a detachable vessel containing ground coffee. 20c. Cf. CAFÉ FILTRE.

finale [It.] the conclusion of anything, *esp.* the last movement of a symphony or the last chorus of an act of an opera; the final catastrophe. 18c. [N,S]

fin de guerre [Fr.] (characteristic of) the end of a war. 20c.

fin de non-recevoir [Fr.] *Law* a plea in bar, a demurrer; a plea that the opponents' point, even if valid, is not relevant to the issue. 20c.

fin de race [Fr.] (characteristic of) the decline of the human race. 20c.

fin de siècle [Fr.] (characteristic of) the end of a century, *esp.* of the nineteenth century; *hence*, decadent, devoted to æstheticism. 20c. From the title of a novel by F. de Jouvenot and H. Micard (1888).

fine à l'eau [Fr.] brandy and water, brandy and soda. 20c.

fine (Champagne) [Fr.] fine brandy of Champagne (Angumois and Saintonge), old liqueur brandy. 19c. [N*]

fine (de la) maison [Fr.] old brandy 'of the house', i.e. a speciality of the hotel or restaurant. 20c. Cf. MAISON. [N*]

fines herbes *pl.* [Fr.] *Cul.* a mixture in equal parts of chopped parsley, chervil, chives and tarragon, used as a seasoning. 20c.

finesse [Fr.] (1) delicacy, refinement; delicate skill. 16c. (2) *Bridge* an attempt to win a trick by playing a card not the highest out, in the hope or expectation that the opponent who has still to play holds no higher card. 19c. [N,S]

Fingerfertigkeit [Ger.] *Mus.* digital dexterity. 20c.

fin gourmet [Fr.] a CONNOISSEUR of the pleasures of the table. 20c. Now often used in preference to GOURMET to avoid the risk of confusion with GOURMAND.

finis [Lat.] the end, the conclusion, *esp.* of life. 17c. Formerly (from 15c.) often written at the end of a book; since about 1850 *The End* has been more common. Cf. EXPLICIT. [N,S]

finis coronat opus [Lat. 'the end crowns the work'] the finishing touches are the making of a work of art; a man's last acts reveal the purpose of his life. 17c. [S]

finita la commedia [It.] the comedy is over, the pretence has come to an end. 20c. Cf. (LA) FARCE EST JOUÉE.

fino [Sp.] a delicate pale dry sherry. 20c.

fin sourire [Fr.] a knowing smile. 20c.

fioritura, *pl.* **fioriture** [It.] *Mus.* a florid ornament or embellishment of a musical theme. 19c. [N,S]

firman [Pers. *fermān*] a licence, authorization or permit issued by an Oriental sovereign, *esp.* the Sultan of Turkey. 17c. [N,S]

Firn [Ger. 'last year's (snow)'] *Geog.* the granulated snow on the upper part of a glacier, which has not yet been compressed into ice. 19c. Cf. NÉVÉ. [N]

fjord [Norw.] *Geog.* a long narrow arm of the sea running between high cliffs. 17c. Formerly commonly spelt *fiord.* [N,S]

flagrante delicto [Lat.] *Law* during or immediately after the commission of a crime. 17c. Cf. IN FLAGRANTE DELICTO. [N,S]

flair [Fr. 'sense of smell'] intuition, instinctive discernment. 19c. [N,S]

flambé [Fr.] (1) *Cul.* (any dish) which while still hot is soaked in brandy which is ignited as the dish is served; (2) (a piece of Chinese porcelain) iridescent as a result of the application of a streaky glaze, or as the result of uneven firing. 19c. Cf. ROUGE FLAMBÉ. [N*]

flambeau, *pl.* **flambeaux** [Fr.] a lighted torch, a firebrand. 17c. [N,S]

flamenco [Sp. 'flamingo'] a kind of Spanish dance; the music appropriate to such a dance. 19c. So called because of the garish costume of the dancers. The Spanish word also means 'Flemish', but there is no etymological connection. [N*]

Flammenwerfer, *pl.* **Flammenwerfer** [Ger.] a flame-thrower, a tank equipped with apparatus for projecting an intensely hot flame. 20c.

flâneur [Fr.] a lounger, an idle man-about-town. 19c. Cf. BOULEVARDIER. [N,S]

flauto d'echo [It.] *Mus.* an organ stop the sound of which resembles that of a distant flute. 20c.

flèche [Fr.] *Arch.* a slender spire, *esp.* one at the intersection of the nave and transepts of a church. 19c. [N,S]

fleur-de-lis/fleur-de-lys [Fr.] the heraldic lily, *esp.* as part of the royal arms of France. 15c. [N,S]

flic [Fr.] a (French) policeman. 20c. A common French slang term.

flora, *pl.* **floræ** [Lat.] the whole range of vegetable life proper to any particular district or period; a catalogue of plant life. 18c. Often associated with FAUNA. [N,S]

floreat [Lat.] may . . . flourish!; always followed by the name of a school, institution, etc. 20c.

florilegium, *pl.* **florilegia** [Lat.] a collection of the flowers of literature, an anthology. 17c. The word is the exact Latin equivalent of the Greek *anthology*. [N,S]

fl(oruit) [Lat.] he flourished, he was working; followed by a date or dates. 19c. Used to indicate the period of activity of an artist the dates of whose birth and death are unknown. Also used as a noun to denote 'the period during which he was working'. [N]

flou [Fr.] hazy, blurred, woolly, imprecise; haziness, lack of precision. 20c.

fœderatus, *pl.* **fœderati** [Lat.] *Hist.* an ally (of the Romans). 20c. Used with reference to the Roman principle of invoking the aid of each tribe conquered in reducing the next tribe to be attacked.

fœtus, *pl.* **fœtus** [Lat.] *Med.* the young of an animal while still in the womb or the egg, a full-grown embryo. 17c. The spelling *fetus* is etymologically more correct, but is never in practice used. [N,S]

Föhn [Ger.] *Geog.* the warm dry wind which blows down the valleys of the leeward side of a mountain range, *esp.* on the north side of the Alps. 19c. [N,S]

foible [Obs. Fr.] a failing, a weakness, an idiosyncrasy. 17c. The modern French FAIBLE is used in quite a different sense. [N]

foie gras [Fr.] the liver of a fattened goose. 19c. Also used as an abbreviation for PÂTÉ DE FOIE GRAS 'Strasburg pie'. [N*,S]

folâtre [Fr.] playful, frolicsome. 19c. [S]

folie [Fr.] *Psych.* a condition in which a normal but suggestible person is infected with the delusions of a forceful psychotic. 20c.

folie de doute [Fr.] *Psych.* a morbid compulsion to reassure onself repeatedly that certain everyday actions have in fact been done. 20c.

folie de grandeur [Fr.] MEGALOMANIA, an illusion of greatness, the mistaken belief that one is a most important person; a mania for surrounding oneself with magnificent objects and objects of large size. 20c.

folklorique [Fr.] (an event) likely to be long remembered and embroidered by the common people. 20c. From the English word *folk-lore*.

fonctionnaire [Fr.] a minor civil servant, a petty official. 20c. Cf. ROND-DE-CUIR.

fondant [Fr. 'melting'] *Cul.* a flavoured sugary paste; a sweetmeat made from this paste. 19c. [N]

fond de teint [Fr.] foundation colour (in make-up). 20c.

fondo d'oro [It.] *Art* the gilded background used to set off figures in mediæval illumination and Primitive painting. 20c.

fond(s) [Fr.] groundwork, foundation; basis, fundamental nature; capital as a security for some venture. 17c. Modern French distinguishes *fond* 'foundation' and *fonds* 'funds', but the distinction is recent and is not observed in English; both forms are used indiscriminately, though *fonds* seems to be preferred in current usage. [N,S]

fondue [Fr.] *Cul.* a traditional Swiss Alpine dish, of which the main ingredients are melted cheese and wine, sometimes with the addition of eggs, liqueurs, etc. 19c. [N]

fons et origo (mali) [Lat.] the source and origin (of the evil). 19c. [N*,S]

fons vivus, *pl.* **fontes vivi** [Lat.] the living spring, the perennial source (of some influence, etc.) 20c.

force de frappe [Fr.] *Mil.* a striking force. 20c. Now used *esp.* of a nuclear striking force.

force majeure [Fr.] irresistible force, overwhelming power. 19c. [N*,S]

format [Fr.] the shape and size of a book; *hence*, the arrangement or pattern of any organization, entertainment, etc. 19c. [N,S]

formes libres *pl.* [Fr.] *Art* free forms, incoherent forms derived from fantasy and the unconscious, characteristic of the DADA movement. 20c.

formicarium, *pl.* **formicaria** [Lat.] an ant-hill, *esp.* an artificial ant-hill designed for the observation of ant life. 19c. [N]

forte [Fr. *fort* 'strong'] the thing in which a person (or group of persons) excels. 17c. [N,S]

forum, *pl.* **fora** [Lat.] *Hist.* the market-place or place of assembly in a Roman town, *esp.* in its function as a court of justice; *hence*, an assembly for the open discussion of some serious topic. 17c. Cf. AGORA. [N,S]

fouetté [Fr. 'whipped'] *Ballet* a step executed on the POINTE, in which the free foot is rapidly rotated in a horizontal circle at knee-level. 20c.

fougasse [Fr.] *Mil.* a small land-mine. 19c. Replacing the earlier *fougade* (17c.). [N(*),S]

foulard [Fr.] a head-scarf or neckerchief of silk or of silk and cotton. 19c. [N,S]

fourchette [Fr. 'fork'] *Bridge* a holding consisting of the cards immediately above and below a card held by the preceding player. 19c. [N*]

fourgon [Fr.] the luggage van of a train; a baggage-wagon. 19c. [N,S]

fou rire [Fr.] hysterical laughter, uncontrollable giggling. 20c.

foutu [Fr.] done for, finished. 20c. The literal meaning is indecent, and the word is often replaced in French and in English by the euphemism FICHU.

foyer [Fr. 'hearth'] the public entrance-hall or promenade of a theatre, etc. 19c. [N,S]

fracas [Fr.] disturbance, uproar; a noisy quarrel. 18c. [N,S]

Fraktur [Ger.] a black-letter typeface, a German typeface. 20c.

franchise [Fr.] frankness, candour. 20c. Distinguished by the French pronunciation from the English *franchise*.

franc-tireur [Fr.] a sharp-shooter, a member of an irregular army corps of snipers. 19c. [N,S]

Franglais [Fr.] French heavily interlarded with English words and expressions. 20c. The word is a PORTMANTEAU formation from *français* and *anglais*.

Frankfurter [Ger.] a highly-seasoned German sausage. 20c. [N*]

frappé [Fr.] iced, chilled; an iced drink; *hence*, thick, viscous. 19c. [N(*),S]

Frau [Ger.] a (German) housewife; a woman with the characteristics of a German housewife. 19c. Cf. HAUSFRAU. [N,S]

fraude pieuse [Fr.] a pious deceit, something dishonest done in the interest of religion or morality. 20c. Cf. PIA FRAUS.

Frauendienst [Ger. 'service of women'] the mediæval code of courtly love, according to which the lover is a vassal of his lady. 20c. Cf. AMOUR COURTOIS.

Fräulein [Ger.] a young unmarried (German) woman, *esp.* a German governess in an English household. 17c. Cf. MADEMOISELLE. [N,S]

fredaine [Fr.] an escapade, indiscreet behaviour. 19c. [S]

Fremdwort, *pl.* **Fremdwörter** [Ger.] a foreign word, a word introduced from another language, *usu.* with the nationalistic implication that such borrowings are undesirable. 20c.

fresco [It. 'fresh'] *Art* a method of painting on plaster while it is still wet; a painting so executed. 16c. Cf. A BUON FRESCO; BUON FRESCO. [N,S]

fresco secco [It.] *Art* painting on plaster which has been allowed to dry. 20c. Painting on dry plaster is not strictly a form of *fresco* at all, and the phrase is a contradiction in terms. Cf. A SECCO; IN SECCO; SECCO.

fricandeau [Fr.] *Cul.* stewed veal served with a savoury sauce. 18c. [N,S]

fricassée [Fr.] *Cul.* a dish consisting of small pieces of flesh cut up, fried or stewed, and served in sauce. 16c. [N,S]

fricatrice [Fr.] a female homosexual, a Lesbian. 20c.

frigidarium [Lat.] *Hist.* the cold room of a Roman bath. 18c. Cf. CALDARIUM; TEPIDARIUM. [N,S]

frisson [Fr.] a shiver, a shudder, a thrill. 20c.

fritto misto [It.] *Cul.* a mixed dish of fried sea-food. 20c.

froissé, *f.* **froissée** [Fr.] vexed, offended, ruffled, hurt. 20c.

fronde [Fr. 'sling'] a party of malcontents, a violent political opposition. 19c. From *La Fronde*, the name given to the party which attacked Mazarin and the French Court during the minority of Louis XIV. [N,S]

frondeur [Fr.] a (political) malcontent, a rebellious critic, an irreconcilable. 19c. [N,S]

frottage [Fr.] *Art* a method of producing patterns by rubbing graphite over paper laid on some rough texture. 20c. Patterns produced in this way are sometimes used in COLLAGE-work.

frou-frou [Fr.] the rustle of a woman's dress, *esp.* a silk dress; *hence*, 'frills', superfluous and ostentatious ornamentation. 19c. The figurative meaning is perhaps connected with the French phrase *faire du frou-frou* 'to show off'. [N,S]

fruit de mer, *pl.* **fruits de mer** [Fr.] sea-food, any edible crustacean. 20c.

frustum, *pl.* **frusta** [Lat.] the portion of a solid figure which remains when the apex has been sliced off. 17c. [N,S]

fuchigashira [Jap.] the pommel of a (Japanese) sword. 20c. Cf. TSUBA.

fugue [Fr.] *Psych.* a flight from sanity; the flight of a neurotic from intolerable circumstances, *usu.* accompanied by loss of memory. 20c. [N*]

(der) Führer [Ger.] the leader of a group, *esp.* as the title adopted by Adolf Hitler; *hence*, any dictatorial and oppressive functionary. 20c. Cf. CAUDILLO; DUCE.

Führerprinzip [Ger.] the theory or doctrine that dictatorship is efficient and desirable. 20c.

fulcrum, *pl.* **fulcra** [Lat.] the point of resistance about which a lever works. 17c. Cf. POINT D'APPUI. [N,S]

fumage [Fr.] *Art* a COLLAGE made with smoked paper. 20c.

fumaruola, *pl.* **fumaruole** [It.] a smoke-hole, a hole through which smoke issues from a volcano. 19c. Often in the anglicized form *fumarole*. Cf. SOLFATARA. [S]

fumiste [Fr.] (1) a hoaxer, a practical joker; (2) *Art* an artist who practises FUMAGE. 20c.

functus officio [Lat.] having completed one's term of office, having ceased to hold some public appointment. 20c.

furore [It.] enthusiastic popular acclamation, wild excitement. 19c. [N,S]

fuselage [Fr.] the body of an aeroplane. 20c.

fustanella [It. < Gk. *φούστανι*] the stiff full petticoat of white cotton or linen worn by men in modern Greece, *esp.* by Greek soldiers. 20c. The modern Greek word is perhaps connected with English *fustian.* [N,S]

G

gaffe [Fr.] a blunder, clumsy tactlessness, saying the wrong thing. 20c. Cf. FAUX PAS. [N*]

gala [Fr., It.] a festive occasion, an occasion suitable for fine clothes, etc.; (clothes, etc.) suitable for a festive occasion; (a theatrical performance, etc.) conducted with special pomp and ceremony. 18c. Formerly pronounced as if English, now always as in French or Italian. [N,S]

galant [Fr.] *Mus.* light-hearted, elegant, and technically accomplished (music). 20c.

galanterie [Fr.] flattering attention to women, mild flirtation. 20c.

Galanteriekunst [Ger.] *Art* a style (of painting, etc.) which aims chiefly at elegance and technical accomplishment. 20c.

galantine [Fr.] *Cul.* boned white meat (*usu.* veal or chicken) boiled and served cold in its own jelly. 18c. [N,S]

galantuomo [It.] a decent, respectable man. 20c. Cf. HONNÊTE HOMME.

galbe [Fr.] *Art* curve, contour, outline, sweep; line, style, elegance. 20c.

galère [Fr. 'galley'] set-up, set of people, circle. 18c. In allusion to Molière's QUE DIABLE ALLAIT-IL FAIRE DANS CETTE GALÈRE? [S]

Galgenhumor [Ger. 'gallows-humour'] morbid humour, 'sick' humour. 20c. Cf. HUMOUR NOIR.

galop [Fr.] a lively dance in 2/4 time, forming part of a set of QUADRILLES. 19c. In Ballet a *galop* often forms the conclusion of a DIVERTISSEMENT. [N]

gamin, *f.* **gamine** [Fr.] a street-urchin; (a man or woman) having an attractive impertinence supposedly characteristic of street-urchins. 19c. [N(*),S]

gaminerie [Fr.] an attractive impertinence like that of a street-urchin. 20c. [N*]

ganglion, *pl.* **ganglia** [Gk. γάγγλιον] *Med.* a knot on a nerve from which nerve-fibres radiate; *hence*, a centre of activity. 18c. [N,S]

garçon [Fr. 'boy'] a (French) waiter. 19c. [N,S]

garçon gratuit [Fr.] an unwanted boy, a boy who feels himself or is felt to be alien to his family. 20c.

garçonne [Fr.] a bachelor girl, an ostentatiously independent woman. 20c.

garçonnière [Fr.] a bachelor flat. 20c. Cf. EN GARÇON.

garde champêtre [Fr.] a game-keeper; a rural constable. 19c. [S]

garde mobile [Fr.] a corps of militia, *esp.* in France in 1848 and 1868–71. 19c. [S]

garderobe [Fr. 'wardrobe'] a mediæval privy. 19c. [N]

garni [Fr.] *Cul.* (a dish) accompanied by the appropriate vegetables, etc. 20c. Cf. BOUQUET GARNI.

Gasthaus [Ger.] a (German) inn or small hotel. 19c. A *Gasthaus* is a more modest establishment than a GASTHOF. [N*,S]

Gasthof [Ger.] a (German) hotel. 19c. [N*,S]

gastronome [Fr.] an expert on the pleasures of the table. 19c. Cf. FIN GOURMET; GOURMET. [N,S]

gâteau, *pl.* **gâteaux** [Fr.] *Cul.* any dish of which the basis is a cake; any dish served in the form of a cake or pudding. 19c. [N]

gauche [Fr. 'left (hand)'] awkward, lacking in tact or social grace. 18c. [N,S]

gaucherie [Fr.] tactlessness, lack of good manners or social grace. 18c. [N,S]

gaucho [Sp.] a half-breed mounted herdsman in South America. 19c. The word is probably *orig.* from some native American language. [N]

gaudeamus igitur [Lat.] let us therefore rejoice! 20c. From the German students' drinking song, *gaudeamus igitur juvenes dum sumus* 'let us therefore rejoice while we are young!'

gaudium certaminis, *pl.* **gaudia certaminis** [Lat.] the pleasure of the contest, the enjoyment of a good argument. 19c. [S]

gaufrette [Fr.] a wafer-biscuit, a sugar wafer. 20c.

Gauleiter [Ger.] 'district leader', a rank in the National Socialist hierarchy in Germany; *hence*, a petty dictator, a local FÜHRER. 20c.

gauloise [Fr. 'Gaulish'] a cheap and popular brand of French cigarettes. 20c.

gavotte [Fr.] a lively dance resembling a minuet; the music accompanying such a dance. 17c. The *gavotte* is in common time, and the melody always begins on the third beat of the bar. [N,S]

gazpacho [Sp.] *Cul.* a highly-seasoned cold vegetable soup popular in Andalusia. 19c. [N*,S]

Gebrauchsmusik [Ger.] *Mus.* music written for a special purpose or occasion. 20c. A common example of *Gebrauchsmusik* is film music.

geisha [Jap.] a Japanese dancing-girl versed in the arts of entertainment. 19c. [N]

Geistesgeschichte [Ger.] the history of the spiritual development (of a writer, artist, etc.) 20c.

Gemeinde [Ger.] a (German) municipality. 20c.

Gemeindehaus [Ger.] a (German) town-nall. 20c. Cf. RATHAUS.

Gemeinschaft [Ger.] a community, an association. 20c.

Gemeinschaftsgefühl [Ger.] community spirit, the feeling of belonging to some association or of possessing some common heritage; social interest. 20c. Cf. ESPRIT DE CORPS.

gemütlich [Ger.] kindly, amiable, easy to get on with; homely, congenial, comfortable. 20c.

Gemütlichkeit [Ger.] kindliness, friendliness; comfort, homeliness. 20c. The qualities denoted by *Gemütlichkeit* are supposed to be characteristic of the German family and the German home.

gendarme [Fr.] (1) an armed policeman, a soldier used on police duties. 18c. (2) a pinnacle or tower of rock on a mountain ridge. 19c. It has been conjectured that the mountain pinnacle is so called because it frequently halts travellers. [N,S(*)]

gendarmerie [Fr.] a body of armed police, a troop of soldiers used on police duties. 18c. [N,S]

gêne [Fr.] constraint, embarrassment, social discomfort. 19c. Cf. SANS GÊNE. [S]

gêné, *f.* **gênée** [Fr.] constrained, embarrassed, ill at ease. 19c. [S]

générale=RÉPÉTITION GÉNÉRALE, dress rehearsal.

generalia *pl.* [Lat.] general principles, first principles. 19c. [N,S]

generalissimo [It.] the supreme commander of a combined force, *esp.* of military or naval forces, or of the armies of several nations. 17c. Cf. SUPREMO. [N,S]

genesis [Gk. γένεσις] origin, manner of formation or production, *esp.* of intellectual concepts or works of art. 17c. [N,S]

genitalia *pl.* [Lat.] the external reproductive organs, *esp.* of the male. 19c. Cf. PUDENDUM. [N]

genius, *pl.* **genii** [Lat.] (1) a tutelary spirit guarding a person or place; (2) a good or evil spirit influencing the character or actions of a person; (3) intellectual power or creative imagination of an exalted and exceptional kind; (4) a person endowed with exceptional intellectual power or creative imagination. 16c. Sense (3)—and hence sense (4)—depends on the supposition that exceptional gifts result from the intervention of supernatural beings. Senses (1) and (2) have been influenced by the fact that the plural *genii* has come to be used as the plural of *genie*, a variant spelling of the wholly unrelated DJINNEE. Cf. DÆMON. [N,S]

genius domus [Lat.] the tutelary spirit of a house; the influence of a house on the minds of its inhabitants. 20c. Adapted from GENIUS LOCI.

genius loci [Lat.] the tutelary spirit of a place; the influence of a place on those who visit it. 18c. Virgil *Æneid* vii 136. [N,S]

genizah, *pl.* **genizoth** [Heb.] a repository for damaged or discarded manuscripts. 20c. [N*]

genre [Fr.] (1) kind, sort, style, *esp.* some particular category of work of art; (2) *Art* (naturalistic painting) of objects from everyday life, still-life (painting). 19c. [N(*),S]

genre pittoresque [Fr.] a style of writing or composition aiming primarily at evocative description. 20c. Cf. (LE) PITTORESQUE.

gens de bien [Fr.] respectable people. 19c. [S]

gens de couleur [Fr.] coloured people, half-castes. 20c.

gens du monde [Fr.] society people. 19c. Cf. FEMME DU MONDE; HOMME DU MONDE. [S]

gentilhommière [Fr.] a small country estate suitable for a gentleman in modest circumstances. 20c.

genus, *pl.* **genera** [Lat.] a class of things which includes a number of subordinate kinds (known as 'species') which share certain common attributes. 16c. [N,S]

Gesamtkunstwerk [Ger. 'total work of art'] *Art* a work of art in the achievement of which all the different art forms (music, poetry, dancing, painting, etc.) have their part to play. 20c. The idea is Wagner's, and he attempted to realize it at Bayreuth.

Gesellschaft [Ger.] a society formed for some special purpose; a commercial company. 20c.

gesso [It.] *Art* a mixture of plaster of Paris and size, used as a ground for painting. 16c. [N,S]

gesso grosso [It.] *Art* a layer of coarse granular plaster forming the basis of the surface prepared for FRESCO painting. 20c.

gesso sottile [It.] *Art* a layer of fine plaster over the underlying GESSO GROSSO. 20c. Cf. INTONACO.

Gestalt [Ger. 'form'] *Psych.* an object of perception forming a unity incapable of being expressed in terms of its parts; *hence*, a work of art considered as a unity. 20c. The term was introduced in 1890 by Christian von Ehrenfels. [N*]

Gestaltpsychologie [Ger.] a system of psychology based on the assumption that objects of perception are perceived as unities. 20c.

geste [Fr.] a (magnanimous) gesture. 20c. Cf. BEAU GESTE.

Gesundheit! [Ger.] (your) health! 20c. Used as a toast when drinking in company; also as an equivalent to 'bless you!', said when a person sneezes. Cf. PROSIT; SKÅL; SLÁINTE.

get [Aramaic] a Jewish formal bill of divorcement. 19c. [N*]

gharry [Hind. *gāṛī*] *A.-I.* an Indian carriage. 19c. Cf. TONGA. [N,S]

ghat [Hind. *ghāṭ*] *A.-I.* a mountain pass; a flight of steps leading to the water's edge. 17c. Formerly more commonly spelt *ghaut*. [N,S]

ghetto, *pl.* **ghetti** [It.] a Jewish quarter, a Jewry (*orig.* in Italy, but now used of a Jewish quarter in any country); *hence*, any district inhabited exclusively by persons of a (supposedly inferior) race, colour, or religion; *hence*, (the mentality or state of mind) induced by living in such a district. 17c. The Italian plural *ghetti* is now very rare. [N,S]

giallo antico [It. 'antique yellow'] a rich yellow marble found among Roman ruins in Italy. 18c. Cf. ROSSO ANTICO; VERDE ANTICO. [N,S]

gigolo [Fr.] a professional (male) dancing partner; *hence*, a young man who accepts payment for escorting women (*usu.* elderly); a male prostitute. 20c. [N*]

gigot [Fr.] *Cul.* a leg of mutton prepared for the table. 18c. [N,S]

gilet [Fr.] *Ballet* a bodice shaped like a man's waistcoat. 19c. [N,S]

gillie [Gael. *gille*] a servant of a Highland chief; *hence*, a servant accompanying a sportsman in the Scottish Highlands. 18c. [N,S]

girandole [Fr.] a branched support for candles, or other lights, *usu.* in the form of a wall-bracket, but *occ.* free-standing. 18c. The word has also been used to denote a kind of Catherine-wheel, a revolving jet of water, and a pendant consisting of a large stone surrounded by smaller stones; but these meanings seem to be obsolete. [N,S]

glacé [Fr.] (1) (leather or fabric) with a highly polished or lustrous surface; (2) *Cul.* (fruit, etc.) coated with sugar. 19c. Cf. CIRÉ. [N,S]

glacis [Fr.] *Mil.* a gradual slope, *esp.* one leading from a rampart to ground level, so designed as to expose an attacking enemy to continuous fire from the rampart. 17c. Cf. TALUS. [N,S]

Gleichberechtigung [Ger.] equality of status, *esp.* in connection with armaments. 20c.

Gleichgültigkeit [Ger.] indifference, a feeling of 'don't care'. 20c. Cf. JE-M'EN-FOUTISME.

Gleichschaltung [Ger.] the elimination of political opposition by coercing or liquidating one's opponents. 20c.

glissade [Fr.] (1) the action of sliding down a slope of snow or ice; (2) *Ballet* a sliding step in which the position of the feet is changed in succession without lifting them from the ground. 19c. [N,S]

glissando, *pl.* **glissandi** [Pseudo-It.] *Mus.* (1) the action of playing successive notes on a keyboard instrument by running the finger over the keys; (2) the production of a smoothly gliding tone on a bowed string instrument or a trombone. 19c. No such word exists in Italian: the form used in English is adapted from Fr. *glissant*. Cf. PORTAMENTO. [N*]

Glockenspiel [Ger.] *Mus.* a musical instrument consisting of a series of small bells struck with a hammer. 19c. The instrument is now sometimes equipped with a keyboard, and the bells may be replaced by resonant bars. [N*]

gloire [Fr.] glory, honour, fame. 20c. Always with the implication that the French conception of glory is quite different from the English.

gloria (in excelsis) [Lat.] 'glory be (to God) on high', the beginning of the prayer which follows the Introit of the Mass; a musical setting of this prayer. 14c. [N,S]

Glühwein [Ger.] mulled wine. 20c.

gnome, *pl.* **gnomæ** [Gk. *γνώμη*] a maxim, an aphorism, a proverb. 16c. *Usu.* pronounced as a disyllable. [N,S]

gnomon [Gk. *γνώμων* 'carpenter's square'] the rod or plate which casts a shadow on a sun-dial. 16c. [N,S]

gnosis [Gk. *γνῶσις*] *Rel.* a special knowledge or understanding of spiritual mysteries. 16c. [N,S]

gnothi seauton [Gk. *γνῶθι σεαυτόν*] know yourself! 17c. Quoted by Juvenal *Satires* xi 27, but already proverbial. Cf. NOSCE TEIPSUM. [S]

godet [Fr.] a gore, a triangular piece of cloth inserted in a skirt or other garment to make it flare. 19c. [N*]

godille [Fr. 'stern-oar'] *Ski* a rapid descent of a snow-slope in which the skier follows a wavy course by means of a regular oscillating movement of his skis. 20c. Cf. WEDELN.

gombeen [Ir. *gaimbín*] usury. 19c. The 'gombeen-man' in an Irish village is a petty money-lender. [N,S]

gondola [It.] a light Venetian boat rising sharply to a point at each end, *usu.* propelled by a single oar at the stern. 16c. [N,S]

gorsedd [Welsh 'throne'] a meeting of Welsh bards and druids, *esp.* as a preliminary to an EISTEDDFOD. 18c. [N*]

gossoon [Ir. *garsún* < Fr. *garçon*] a boy, a hobbledehoy, a young countryman. 19c. [N,S]

Götterdämmerung [Ger.] the twilight of the Gods, the end of the world in Scandinavian mythology. 20c. A translation of Icelandic *ragna røkkr*, a variant of *ragna rök* 'the doom of the Gods'. Often used with explicit or implicit reference to the last episode of Wagner's *Ring*.

gouache [Fr.] *Art* (a method of painting in) opaque water-colour; a painting executed in opaque water-colour. 19c. Cf. PEINTURE À LA COLLE. [N,S]

goulash [Magyar *gulyás* 'herdsman'] (1) *Cul.* a highly-seasoned stew of steak and vegetables; (2) *Bridge* a re-deal without shuffling, sometimes made when all four players pass, or when the bidding fails to pass the level of one. 20c. The *goulash* deal, popular in the early days of Contract Bridge, has been recently revived. [N*]

gourmand, *f.* **gourmande** [Fr.] (one who is) over-fond of the pleasures of the table. 18c. Anglicized from 16c. as *gormand*, etc., but re-adopted as a French word in 18c. Cf. BON VIVANT. [N,S]

gourmandise [Fr.] gluttony, self-indulgence at table. 19c. Anglicized from 16c. as *gormandize*, etc., but re-adopted as a French word in 19c. [N,S]

gourmet [Fr.] one who makes a study of the pleasures of the table, an epicure. 19c. Cf. FIN GOURMET; GASTRONOME. [N,S]

gouvernante [Fr.] a woman (*usu.* married or elderly) who accompanies a young unmarried woman for the sake of propriety; a CHAPERON. 18c. Cf. DUENNA. [N,S]

goy, *pl.* **goyim** [Heb. 'nation'] a gentile, a Christian. 20c. Cf. SHIKSA.

gradatim [Lat.] gradually, step by step. 16c. [N,S]

gradus (ad Parnassum) [Lat.] a dictionary of poetical words and phrases designed to facilitate the composition of Latin verse; *hence,* a similar manual facilitating verse composition in other languages. 18c. [N,S]

graffito, *pl.* **graffiti** [It.] (1) a drawing or writing (often indecent) scribbled or scratched on a wall, *esp.* the wall of an ancient building; (2) *Art* a method of architectural decoration produced by scratching through a thin layer of plaster to a layer of a different colour. 19c. Cf. SGRAFFITO. [N,S]

grand amateur, *pl.* **grands amateurs** [Fr.] an ardent lover of beautiful things, a collector of OBJETS D'ART on a grand scale. 20c. This phrase preserves the original meaning, now obsolete, of AMATEUR.

grand atelier, *pl.* **grands ateliers** [Fr.] a leading fashion-house. 20c.

grand coup [Fr.] (1) a bold and successful stroke (of policy, etc.); (2) *Bridge* disposing of a superfluous trump (*usu.* by ruffing a winner) to avoid a disadvantageous lead. 19c. The *grand coup* was already familiar in the days of whist. [N*,S]

grand cru [Fr.] (a wine from) a well-known vineyard or group of vineyards. 20c. Cf. CRU; PREMIER CRU.

grande amoureuse [Fr.] a woman who loves on a grand scale, a woman who devotes all her time and energy to her love-affairs. 20c.

(la) Grande Armée [Fr. '(the) great army'] the army assembled by Napoleon for his invasion of Russia in 1812. 19c. [S]

grand écart [Fr.] 'the splits', the gymnastic feat in which the legs are separated until they are at right angles to the body, which rests upright on the floor. 20c.

grande cocotte, *pl.* **grandes cocottes** [Fr.] a high-class prostitute, a woman whose lover maintains her in great luxury. 20c. Cf. POULE DE LUXE.

grande dame [Fr.] a great lady, a woman of dignified and aristocratic bearing. 19c. Now mainly ironical, with an implication of offensive condescension for which there is no justification. Cf. GRAND SEIGNEUR. [N*,S]

grande école, *pl.* **grandes écoles** [Fr.] a French quasi-military technical college. 20c. The best known of the *grandes écoles* are the École Polytechnique and the École Normale Supérieure.

grande entrée [Fr.] the privilege of admission (to Court, etc.) on state occasions only, not for private functions. 19c. Cf. ENTRÉE; PETITE ENTRÉE. [S]

grande épreuve, *pl.* **grandes épreuves** [Fr.] an important motor-race. 20c.

grande marque, *pl.* **grandes marques** [Fr.] a famous make (of motor-car, etc.) 20c. Cf. MARQUE.

grande passion [Fr.] an overpowering love, the love of one's life. 19c. [N*,S]

grandes machines *pl.* [Fr.] *Art* 'heavy stuff', large-scale works of art. 20c.

grande sonnerie [Fr.] a system of striking in clocks and watches whereby the quarter and the hour is struck at every quarter. 20c. Cf. MONTRE GRANDE SONNERIE.

grande tenue [Fr.] full dress, *esp.* military or naval full dress; evening dress; court dress. 19c. Cf. EN GRANDE TENUE. [N*,S]

grande toilette [Fr.] (a woman's) full evening dress. 20c. Cf. DEMI-TOILETTE.

grande vedette [Fr.] a major star (of stage or screen). 20c. Cf. VEDETTE.

Grand Guignol [Fr.] (characteristic of) an entertainment consisting of a number of horrific short plays. 20c. From the name of a theatre in Paris where such plays used to be performed. [N*]

grand luxe [Fr.] the highest degree of luxury. 20c. Cf. LUXE.

grand mal [Fr.] *Med.* the more violent form of epilepsy characterized by convulsive spasms. 19c. Cf. PETIT MAL.

(le) Grand Monarque [Fr.] the French king Louis XIV; *hence*, any absolute ruler. 18c. [N*,S]

Grand Prix [Fr. 'great prize'] a major international race, now *usu.* for motor-cars. 19c. First used of the *Grand Prix de Paris*, a race for three-year-olds run annually at Longchamps since 1863. [N*]

grand seigneur [Fr.] a great nobleman, a gentleman of dignified and aristocratic bearing. 17c. Now mainly ironical, with an implication of offensive condescension for which there is no justification. Cf. GRANDE DAME; SEIGNEUR. [S]

(le) Grand Siècle [Fr. '(the) great century'] the reign of Louis XIV, the Classical age of French literature. 20c. [N*]

(il) gran rifiuto [It.] the great refusal, the refusal of a high honour or reward. 20c. Dante *Inferno* iii 60; the reference is not explicit, but the passage is commonly taken to refer to Pietro di Morone, Pope Celestine V, who in 1294 resigned the Papacy to return to a hermit's cell.

gran turismo [It.] a high-performance car with ample luggage-space and comfortable seats for two persons. 20c.

grappa [It.] an ardent spirit distilled from wine, a kind of strong brandy. 20c.

grasseyé [Fr.] *Ling.* (an *r*-sound) produced by vibration of the uvula. 20c. In French used mainly of an exaggeratedly harsh and unpleasant sound.

gratin [Fr.] the 'upper crust' (of society), the most exclusive people. 20c.

gratis [Lat.] free of charge; unjustifiably, gratuitously. 15c. [N,S]

gravamen, *pl.* **gravamina** [Lat.] a grievance; the weightiest part of a charge or accusation. 17c. [N,S]

gravitas [Lat.] seriousmindedness, dignity and solemnity of bearing, *esp.* as cultivated by the ancient Romans. 20c.

greffier [Fr.] a notary, *esp.* the clerk to a JUGE D'INSTRUCTION. 16c. [N,S]

Grenzgänger, *pl.* **Grenzgänger** [Ger.] one who crosses a political boundary, *esp.* from East Germany or one of the other Iron Curtain countries. 20c.

grille [Fr.] (1) *Tennis* a square opening near the corner of the end wall on the hazard side. 18c. (2) a grating, *esp.* the grating through which enclosed nuns communicate with visitors. 19c. [N,S(*)]

grimoire [Fr.] a manual of black magic. 19c. Derived from Lat. *grammatica*, *grimoire* is a doublet of English *grammar*. [N*]

gringo [Sp.] any stranger in Mexico, *esp.* a North American. 19c. [N(*)]

grippe [Fr.] influenza. 18c. [N,S]

grisaille [Fr.] *Art* (a design, painting, etc.) executed in various shades of grey. 19c. Stained-glass windows may also be executed in *grisaille*. Cf. EN CAMAÏEU. [N,S]

grisette [Fr.] a young Frenchwoman of the working class, *esp.* a shop-assistant. 18c. So called from a cheap grey cloth formerly much worn by such persons. [N,S]

gros de Naples [Fr.] a heavy silk fabric formerly manufactured at Naples. 19c. [N]

grosgrain [Fr.] a strong corded silk fabric, *esp.* as used for ribbons and hat-bands. 19c. [N*]

gros point [Fr.] (embroidery executed in) cross-stitch. 20c. Cf. PETIT POINT.

grotesquerie [Pseudo-Fr.] fantastic absurdity, picturesque extravagance. 17c. The form does not exist in French. [N]

grottesca, *pl.* **grottesche** [It.] *Art* a style of decoration in which human and animal figures are fantastically interwoven with foliage and flowers; a work of art in this style. 16c. So named from the mural paintings found in *grottoes*, the excavated chambers of ancient houses. [N,S]

Gründerzeit [Ger.] the period of reckless financial speculation which followed the Franco-Prussian war. 20c.

Grundgedanke, *pl.* **Grundgedanken** [Ger.] basic conception, fundamental idea. 20c.

guano [Sp.] a natural manure formed from the excrement of generations of sea-birds. 17c. [N,S]

guéridon [Fr.] a small round pedestal-table. 20c.

guerilla=GUERRILLA, warfare by irregular troops.

guerre à outrance [Fr.] total war, war to the death. 19c. [S]

guerrilla [Sp.] (warfare) carried on by small bodies of irregular troops, *usu.* behind the enemy's lines; *hence*, (a combatant) engaged in such irregular warfare; a GUERRILLERO. 19c. Introduced into English at the time of the Peninsular War; from the date of its first introduction the erroneous spelling *guerilla* has been very common. [N,S]

guerrillero, *f.* **guerrillera** [Sp.] a member of an irregular troop waging war behind the enemy's lines. 19c. [N,S]

guichet [Fr.] a grating through which business is transacted, a ticket-window. 19c. It is curious that no English word should exist to express so useful a concept. [N*,S]

guilloche [Fr.] *Art* a pattern formed by the interlacing of two bands twisted one over the other. 19c. [N,S]

guillotine [Fr.] (1) a heavy knife falling by its own weight between grooved posts, used for executing criminals; *hence*, any similar machine used for other purposes (e.g. for cutting paper). 18c. Named after Joseph-Ignace Guillotin, professor of anatomy, who in 1789 recommended its use as the most humane method of execution. (2) a parliamentary device whereby the government imposes an arbitrary limit on the time for the discussion of a controversial measure. 20c. [N,S]

guindé [Fr.] stilted, stiff, formal. 20c.

guipure [Fr.] a kind of lace in which the MOTIFS are loosely linked together without a ground. 19c. [N,S]

guru [Hind.] a Hindu spiritual teacher or head of a religious sect. 17c. Formerly often spelt *gooroo*. Cf. SWAMI. [N,S]

gusto [It. 'taste'] zest, relish, keen enjoyment. 17c. [N,S]

gutta percha [Mal. *getah percha*] a durable, resistant, waterproof, and easily moulded substance made from the hardened gum of various Oriental trees. 19c. [N,S]

gymnasium, *pl.* **gymnasia** [Lat. < Gk. *γυμνάσιον*] (1) a place or building designed for the practice of athletic exercises; (2) a German high-school. 16c. In the second meaning the German plural *Gymnasien* may be used. [N,S]

gyrovagi *pl.* [Lat.] wandering monks, mediæval clerics who wandered from monastery to monastery. 20c. Sometimes anglicized as *gyrovagues*. Cf. CLERICI VAGANTES; VAGANTES.

H

habeas corpus [Lat. 'you shall have the body'] *Law* a writ requiring the custodian of a prisoner to produce him in court so that the lawfulness of his detention may be determined. 15c. The granting and enforcing of the writ was much facilitated by the Habeas Corpus Act of 1679. [N,S]

habitat [Lat. 'it lives'] the native region of a plant or animal; *hence*, a dwelling-place or place of resort. 18c. [N,S]

habitué, *f.* **habituée** [Fr.] a habitual visitor, one who frequents a place. 19c. [N,S]

habitué de la maison [Fr.] a regular visitor to a house; a regular customer of a CAFÉ, RESTAURANT, etc. 20c.

hacienda [Sp.] a country estate, a plantation. 18c. [N,S]

hadith, *pl.* **hadithat** [Arab. *ḥadīþ*] *Rel.* the body of tradition about Mahomet, which forms an appendix to the Koran called the SUNNA. 19c. [N*]

hæc olim meminisse juvabit [Lat.] one day it will be pleasant to remember these things. 18c. A consolation for present unhappiness: Virgil *Æneid* i 203. [S(*)]

Haff [Ger.] *Geog.* a salt-water lake formed by a long spit of sand extending nearly across the entrance of a bay. 20c. Cf. NEHRUNG.

haiku [Jap.] the shortest form of Japanese poem, consisting of three lines of 5, 7 and 5 syllables respectively. 20c. Also sometimes spelt *hokku.*

hajji [Arab. *ḥājī*] a Moslem who has made a pilgrimage to Mecca. 17c.

haka [Maori] a New Zealand aboriginal dance. 19c. [N*]

Hakenstil [Ger.] *Ling.* a poetic style in which the sense is run on from line to line; opposed to ZEILENSTIL. 20c. Cf. ENJAMBEMENT.

hakim [Arab. *ḥakīm*] a Moslem physician. 17c. Distinct from *hakim* (Arab. *ḥākim*), a Moslem judge or ruler. [N,S]

Halbgelehrte(r) [Ger.] a half-educated person; one with a mere smattering of a subject. 20c. For the form cf. HALBSTARKE(R).

Halbstarke(r), *pl.* **Halbstarke(n)** [Ger. 'half-strong'] a young hooligan, a juvenile delinquent. 20c. In German the word is an adjectival noun, and its form depends on the presence or absence of the definite article: *ein Halbstarker*, pl. *Halbstarke;* with the definite article, *der Halbstarke*, pl. *die Halbstarken.* In English the forms seem to be used indiscriminately. Cf. BLOUSON NOIR; JEUNE VOYOU; STILYAGA; VITELLONE.

halitus [Lat.] vapour, exhalation. 17c. [N,S]

hamartia [Gk. ἁμαρτία] a tragic error or flaw, a mistake or defect of character involving tragic consequences or precipitating tragedy. 20c. The term is taken from Aristotle's *Poetics*.

hammam [Arab. *ḥammām*] a Turkish bath. 17c. Formerly often written *hummum*. [N,S]

hapax legomenon, *pl.* **hapax legomena** [Gk. ἅπαξ λεγόμενον] a word or expression found only once in the surviving records of a language. 17c. Often still written in Greek characters. [N*,S]

hara-kiri [Jap. 'belly-cut'] ceremonial suicide by disembowelling, formerly practised by Japanese gentlemen when faced with disgrace. 19c. Often wrongly written *hari-kari*. [N,S]

harem [Arab. *ḥaram* 'unlawful'] the part of a Moslem house where the women live in seclusion; Moslem women living in seclusion; *hence*, any collection of concubines. 17c. The form *harim*, *hareem*, also *occ.* used, is from the synonymous Arab. *ḥarīm*. Cf. SERAGLIO, ZENANA. [N,S]

harmattan [Fanti *haramata*] a dry land wind which blows on the coast of West Africa between December and February, filling the air with reddish dust. 17c. [N,S]

hashish [Arab. *ḥashīsh*] a preparation of Indian hemp, the leaves and seeds of which are narcotic and intoxicating. 16c. The preparation may be smoked, or drunk as an infusion. Cf. BHANG; MARIJUANA. [N,S]

hasta la vista [Sp. 'until we meet again'] farewell! 20c. A common form of farewell in many languages: cf. A RIVEDERCI; AUF WIEDERSEHEN; AU REVOIR.

hasta luego [Sp. 'until then'] goodbye! 20c. Implying, in contrast to *hasta la vista*, that a further meeting has been arranged or is to be expected the same day. Cf. À BIENTOT.

Hauptfeind [Ger.] the main enemy, the chief enemy. 20c.

Hausfrau [Ger.] a German housewife; *hence*, a woman displaying all the domestic virtues but little sexual attraction. 19c. Cf. FRAU. [N*,S]

Hausmalerei [Ger.] *Art* the painting of porcelain as a cottage industry; (porcelain) produced in this manner. 20c. *Hausmalerei* porcelain is generally Meissen of the 18th century.

haute bourgeoisie [Fr.] the upper middle classes, the professional classes. 19c. Cf. BOURGEOISIE. [S]

haute couture [Fr.] fashionable dress-designing, dress-designing considered as a fine art. 20c. Cf. ALTA MODA; COUTURE.

haute cuisine [Fr.] cookery considered as a fine art. 20c. Cf. CUISINE.

haute école [Fr.] *Equ.* the more difficult feats of professional horsemanship. 19c. [N*,S]

haute époque [Fr.] (the architecture and furniture of) the reigns of Louis XIV, XV and XVI of France (1643–1793). 20c.

haute-lice [Fr.] high-warp (loom), in which the warp threads are vertical; (a textile fabric, *esp.* tapestry) produced on such a loom. 20c.

haute politique [Fr.] high politics, negotiations conducted by persons of high standing; intrigue beyond the understanding of the ordinary man. 20c.

hauteur [Fr.] haughtiness; a contemptuous manner. 18c. [N,S]

haute vulgarisation [Fr.] scholarly popularization, skilled presentation of a technical subject for non-specialists. 20c. Cf. ANIMATEUR; VULGARISATEUR.

haut monde [Fr.] 'Society', the world of fashion. 20c. Cf. BEAU MONDE. [N*]

haut ton [Fr.] the highest social distinction; people of the world of fashion. 19c. The phrase is perhaps now obsolete. Cf. BON TON. [N,S]

havildar [Hind. *ḥavildār* < Pers. *ḥawāl-dār*] *A.-I.* a SEPOY holding a non-commissioned rank corresponding to that of sergeant. 17c. [N,S]

Heft [Ger.] a single number of a volume issued in parts, a fascicle. 20c. Cf. FASCICULUS; LIEFERUNG; LIVRAISON.

hegira/hejira [Lat. *hegira* < Arab. *hijrah*] Mahomet's flight from Mecca to Medina in 622; *hence*, any flight or sudden departure. 16c. [N,S]

Heimweh [Ger.] home-sickness. 18c. [N*,S]

Heldentenor [Ger.] *Mus.* a tenor voice suited to the singing of the hero's RÔLE in opera; a singer having such a voice. 20c. Cf. ROBUSTO.

helix, *pl.* **helices** [Lat. < Gk. ἕλιξ] anything having the shape of the thread of a screw. 16c. Distinct in meaning from *spiral*, which refers to an outline on a plane surface: a 'spiral' staircase is properly a 'helical' staircase. [N,S]

hendiadys [Lat. < Gk. ἓν διὰ δυοῖν 'one by means of two'] *Ling.* a figure of speech in which a concept normally expressed by adjective and noun is expressed by two nouns joined by *and*. 16c. [N,S]

herbarium, *pl.* **herbaria** [Lat.] a collection of dried plants systematically arranged, a HORTUS SICCUS. 18c. [N,S(*)]

Herrenvolk [Ger.] the master-race, a race predestined to rule the world. 20c. Used under the influence of National Socialism by the Germans of themselves. Cf. BLONDE BESTIE.

hetæra, *pl.* **hetæræ** [Lat. < Gk. ἑταίρα] a mistress; a prostitute. 19c. Sometimes used in a form nearer to the Greek: *hetaira*, pl. *hetairai*. The Greek *hetaira* was often a highly-educated woman. [N,S]

Heurige(r), *pl.* **Heurige(n)** [Ger.] wine of less than one year's vintage; *hence*, a place where new wine is sold as soon as it is fit to drink. 20c. For the form cf. HALBSTARKE(R); in English *Heuriger* is the normal form.

Hexentanz [Ger.] a witches' sabbath, *esp.* as represented in art or music. 20c.

hiatus, *pl.* **hiatus** [Lat.] (1) a gap in some logical or continuous sequence, a LACUNA; (2) *Ling.* the juxtaposition of two vowels (not forming a dipthong) with no intervening consonant. 17c. [N,S]

hic et ubique [Lat.] here, there and everywhere; a person who is always gadding about. 17c. [S]

hic jacet [Lat.] 'here lies'; a sepulchral inscription, an epitaph. 17c. [S]

hidalgo [Sp.] a gentleman by birth. 16c. From *hijo de algo* 'a son of something'. [N,S]

hinc illæ lacrymæ [Lat. 'hence those tears'] that is the cause of all the trouble. 16c. Terence *Andria* I i 99; quoted by Horace *Epistles* I xix 41. [S]

Hinterland [Ger.] the 'back country', the district lying behind a coastal district, *esp.* a savage or recently subjugated district in such a position; *hence,* a sphere of activity on the fringes of law-abiding society. 19c. [N(*),S]

historien de salon [Fr.] an amateur historian; a popularizer of history. 20c.

hoc genus omne [Lat.] all that kind of thing, all that kind of people. 18c. Horace *Satires* I ii 2; also in the form ET HOC GENUS OMNE. [S]

Hochkonjunktur [Ger.] a period of exceptional commercial prosperity, a boom; *esp.* the peak holiday period in the tourist industry. 20c.

hoc opus, hic labor (est) [Lat.] this is the work, this is the toil; this is the task that has to be undertaken. 16c. Virgil *Æneid* vi 129. [S]

hoi polloi [Gk. *οἱ πολλοί*] the masses, the common throng. 17c. Although the first word is the Greek definite article, the English definite article is commonly prefixed: 'the *hoi polloi*'. Cf. CANAILLE. [N*,S]

hokku=HAIKU, a type of Japanese poem.

homme de bien [Fr.] a man of good disposition, a respectable man. 18c. [S]

homme de cœur [Fr.] a man of feeling, a sensitive man. 20c. Cf. HOMME SENSIBLE.

homme de lettres [Fr.] a man of letters, a professional literary man. 19c. [S]

homme d'esprit [Fr.] a wit, a man of sparkling repartee. 18c. [S]

homme du monde [Fr.] a man of the world; a man who moves in good society; a man who takes for granted the frailties of human nature. 20c. In English usage *homme du monde* combines the connotations of FEMME DU MONDE and GENS DU MONDE.

homme du peuple [Fr.] a working-class man, a man who betrays his humble origins. 20c. Cf. FEMME DU PEUPLE.

homme moyen sensuel [Fr.] the average unintellectual man, the man in the street. 20c.

homme-orchestre [Fr.] a one-man band; *hence,* a man who performs several skills simultaneously. 20c.

homme sensible [Fr.] a man of feeling, a sensitive man. 20c. Cf. HOMME DE CŒUR.

homme sérieux [Fr.] an earnest man, a man who is not frivolous. 20c. Cf. FEMME SÉRIEUSE; JEUNE FEMME SÉRIEUSE; SÉRIEUX.

homœoteleuton, *pl.* **homœoteleuta** [Lat. < Gk. ὁμοιοτέλευτον] the occurrence of two words or phrases with the same ending, as a cause of an omission in copying; an instance of this error in copying. 19c. Cf. SAUT DU MÊME AU MÊME. [N]

homoiousion [Gk. ὁμοιούσιον] *Theol.* the (heretical) doctrine of the Trinity which holds that the Father and the Son are of like substance. 19c. Opposed to HOMOOUSION. [N*]

homo ludens [Lat.] the sportive man, the aspect of the human personality which leads to irresponsible joking. 20c.

homoousion [Gk. ὁμοούσιον] *Theol.* the (orthodox) doctrine of the Trinity which holds that the Father and the Son are of the same substance. 18c. This doctrine, opposed to HOMOIOUSION, was formulated by the Council of Nicæa in 325. [N*]

homo sapiens [Lat.] rational man, (a member of) the human species, the species of Man represented by the races of the world today. 19c. [N*]

homo trium litterarum [Lat. 'three-letter man'] a thief. 19c. The three letters are *f*, *u*, *r*, spelling the Latin word for 'thief': Plautus *Aulularia* II iv 46. [S]

homo unius libri [Lat.] a man of one book, a man exceedingly well versed in a single favourite work. 17c. The implication is often that the *homo unius libri* is ignorant of everything but his one favourite book. Attributed to St Thomas Aquinas by Southey *The Doctor* (1834–47) i 164. [S]

homunculus, *pl.* **homunculi** [Lat.] a tiny man, a pigmy; a miniature man made by artificial means. 17c. [N,S]

honi soit qui mal y pense [Obs. Fr.] 'shame on him who thinks evil of it!', the motto of the Order of the Garter. 16c. [S]

honnête homme [Fr.] a decent, respectable man. 17c. Cf. GALANTUOMO. [S]

honorarium, *pl.* **honoraria** [Lat.] a fee for professional services. 17c. [N,S]

honoris causa [Lat.] (a University degree) conferred in recognition of public distinction, without the customary examination. 19c. The early, more general meaning 'out of respect (for a person)' seems now to be obsolete. Cf. JURE DIGNITATIS. [N,S]

hookah [Arab. *ḥuqqah*] an Oriental pipe in which the smoke bubbles through scented water before being inhaled through a long flexible tube. 18c. Cf. NARGHILE. [N,S]

horæ subsecivæ *pl.* [Lat.] moments of leisure, periods away from one's normal occupations. 19c. [S]

horizontale [Fr.] a high-class prostitute. 20c.

horresco referens [Lat.] I shudder to say it. 17c. *Usu.* as an interpolation or parenthesis. Virgil *Æneid* ii 204. [S]

horribile dictu [Lat.] horrible to relate. 20c. *Usu.* as an interpolation or parenthesis. Formed on the basis of MIRABILE DICTU 'wonderful to relate'.

hors catalogue [Fr.] not mentioned in the catalogue (of an exhibition, or of the complete work of an artist). 20c.

hors concours [Fr. 'outside the competition'] without a rival, unequalled. 19c. [N*,S]

hors de combat [Fr.] disabled from fighting, out of action. 18c. [N,S]

hors d'œuvre, *pl.* **hors d'œuvre** [Fr. 'outside the work'] *Cul.* a savoury dish to whet the appetite at the beginning of a meal. 18c. Though the plural is unchanged in French, an *s* is often added in English; the pronunciation, however, remains unchanged in the plural. Cf. ANTIPASTO. [N,S]

hors du jeu [Fr. 'out of the game'] not practical politics. 20c. [N*]

hors série [Fr.] not included in the series, added as an afterthought. 20c.

hors texte [Fr.] (an illustration) on a separate leaf tipped or folded into a book, not printed with the text. 20c.

hortus conclusus [Lat.] *Art* a picture portraying the Madonna seated in an enclosed garden. 20c.

hortus inclusus [Lat.] an enclosed garden, an area to which access is strictly controlled or limited. 20c.

hortus siccus [Lat. 'dry garden'] a collection of dried plants systematically arranged, a HERBARIUM. 17c. [N,S]

hôtel de ville [Fr.] a (French) town-hall. 18c. [S]

hôtelier [Fr.] the proprietor or manager of a hotel. 20c. [N*]

houille blanche [Fr. 'white coal'] hydro-electric power. 20c.

houri [Pers. *ḥūri*] one of the virgins of the Moslem paradise; *hence*, a seductively beautiful woman. 18c. The Persian word is from Arabic, and the basic meaning is 'with gazelle-like eyes'. [N,S]

howdah [Pers. *haudah*] a seat with a rail and a canopy, placed on the back of an elephant. 18c. [N,S]

hubris [Gk. ὕβρις] wanton arrogance deserving a rebuke from the gods. 19c. [N*]

hula/hula-hula [Haw.] a lascivious dance performed by Hawaiian women; (a grass skirt) worn while performing the dance; (a hoop of cane or wire) rotated round the waist by contortions resembling this dance. 19c. [N*]

humanitas [Lat.] the study of the liberal arts; *hence*, the attitude towards human problems and the moral standards inculcated by such a study. 20c.

humour noir [Fr.] morbid humour, 'sick' humour. 20c. Cf. GALGENHUMOR.

hwyl [Welsh] (1) a sing-song intonation adopted by Welsh preachers in moments of exaltation; (2) the emotional fervour characteristic of gatherings of Welsh people. 19c. [N*]

hydra [Lat. < Gk. ὕδρα] *Myth.* a fabulous many-headed water-monster, whose heads grew again as fast as they were cut off; *hence*, any mischief or menace which renews itself in spite of efforts to eliminate it, *esp.* the populace considered as the enemy of some purpose or organization. 16c. In use from 14c. in the form *ydre, ydra.* [N,S]

hydrophobia [Lat. < Gk. ὑδροφοβία] *Med.* the fear of water characteristic of the disease of rabies; *hence*, the disease itself. 17c. [N,S]

hyperæsthesia [Lat. < Gk. ὑπερ- + -αισθησία] morbid sensitiveness, *esp.* of the nerves; a preternatural sensitivity, a 'sixth sense'. 19c. [N,S]

hyperbole [Lat. < Gk. ὑπερβολή] exaggeration, an extravagant statement not intended to be taken literally. 16c. [N,S]

hypochondria [Lat. < Gk. ὑποχόνδρια 'internal organs'] a morbid state of depression, *esp.* a morbid anxiety about one's own health. 17c. The stomach and adjacent organs were formerly supposed to be the seat of melancholy; the current sense of the word was developed in English. [N,S]

hypogeum, *pl.* **hypogea** [Lat. < Gk. ὑπόγειον] an underground room or vault. 18c. [N]

hypotheses non fingo [Lat.] 'I do not invent suppositions', i.e. the best explanation (of a phenomenon, etc.) is that which requires the fewest suppositions. 20c. Attributed to Sir Isaac Newton. Cf. ENTIA NON (SUNT) MULTIPLICANDA PRÆTER NECESSITATEM.

hysteron proteron [Lat. < Gk. ὕστερον πρότερον] *Ling.* an inversion of a natural sequence of ideas, putting the cart before the horse. 16c. [S]

I

ibid(em) [Lat. 'in the same place'] in the same book. 17c. Used to avoid the repetition of a reference. Cf. LOC(O) CIT(ATO); OP(ERE) CIT(ATO). [N,S]

ich dien [Obs. Ger.] 'I serve', the motto of the Prince of Wales. 16c. Adopted with the crest of ostrich feathers after the battle of Crécy in 1346. [S]

ich grolle nicht [Ger] I bear no grudge, I don't complain. 20c. The first words of a poem in Heine's *Buch der Lieder* (1827); familiar in Schumann's setting.

ich kann nicht anders [Ger.] I can do no other, I have no alternative. 20c. Martin Luther in a speech to the Diet of Worms, 18th April 1521: *Hier stehe ich; ich kann nicht anders* 'Here I stand; I can do no other'. Used of a man standing by his principles against all opposition.

iconostasis [Lat. < Gk. *εἰκονόστασις*] *Eccles.* a screen dividing the sanctuary from the nave of an Orthodox church, on which sacred pictures (IKONES) are displayed. 19c. [N]

ictus, *pl.* **ictus** [Lat.] *Ling.* metrical stress; a stressed syllable in metre. 18c. Cf. ARSIS. [N,S]

id [Lat. 'it'] *Psych.* the inherited instinctive impulses of the individual. 20c. A translation of the German *es*, the Latin form being chosen to avoid the ambiguity of English 'it'. Cf. EGO. [N*]

idée fixe, *pl.* **idées fixes** [Fr.] a fixed idea, an obsession, a monomania. 19c. [N*,S]

idées reçues *pl.* [Fr.] accepted ideas, conventional outlooks or doctrines. 20c.

id(em) [Lat.] the same, *esp.* the same author. 15c. Used to avoid repetition, *esp.* of the name of an author referred to. [N,S]

idem sonans [Lat. 'sounding the same'] *Law* identity of pronunciation; the miswriting of one word or name for another having the same sound. 19c. [N*]

id est [Lat.] that is, that is to say. 16c. *Usu.* abbreviated to *i.e.* [N,S]

i.e.=ID EST, that is (to say).

Iesus Hominum Salvator [Lat.] Jesus, Saviour of mankind. 19c. A phrase invented in the Early Church to explain the initials IHS, the first three letters of Greek *ΙΗΣΟΥΣ* 'Jesus', in which *H* is the Greek long *Ē*.

igloo [Esk. *igdlo* 'house'] a small dome-shaped hut built of compressed snow. 19c. The word is a misnomer, since the Eskimo form is used only of a permanent house; the snow-hut is called *igdluvigaq* in Eskimo. [N]

ignis fatuus, *pl.* **ignes fatui** [Lat. 'foolish fire'] a phosphorescent light seen flitting over marshy ground; *hence*, any delusive idea or purpose. 16c. The *ignis fatuus* is supposedly due to the spontaneous combustion of marsh-gas. [N,S]

ignoramus [Lat. 'we do not know'] an ignorant person. 17c. *Orig.* the endorsement with which a grand jury rejected a bill of indictment; *hence*, a nickname given to an ignorant lawyer (from 16c.); *hence*, by extension, any ignorant person. The plural of the word is not, of course, *ignorami*. [N,S]

ignorantia legis neminem excusat [Lat.] *Law* ignorance of the law excuses no man. 20c.

ignoratio elenchi [Lat. 'ignoring the argument'] *Logic* the fallacy of refuting a proposition different from that set forth by one's opponent; *hence*, any irrelevant argument. 16c. Cf. ELENCHUS; PETITIO PRINCIPII. [N,S]

ignotum per ignotius [Lat.] an attempt to explain something about which little is known by reference to something about which still less is known. 15c. Cf. OBSCURUM PER OBSCURIUS. [N,S]

ignotus [Lat.] a person unknown. 20c. Used in catalogues of works of art where the authorship of a work is unknown. Cf. INCONNU.

ikon, *pl.* **ikones** [Gk. εἰκών] *Eccles.* a sacred picture venerated in the Orthodox Church. 19c. The unsatisfactory spelling *ikon* seems to have prevailed against the Greek *eikon* and the Latin *icon*, both formerly in use. [N,S]

il faut cultiver notre jardin [Fr. 'we must cultivate our garden'] we must attend to our own affairs. 20c. The last words of Voltaire's *Candide* (1758); the atheist's practical remedy for the evils of the world.

il faut souffrir pour être belle [Fr.] one must suffer in order to be beautiful. 20c. Applicable only to women, *usu.* with references to painful cosmetic processes voluntarily undergone.

illuminato, *pl.* **illuminati** [It.] a person claiming to possess special enlightenment or knowledge. 19c. Applied (*usu.* in the plural) *esp.* to a sect of Spanish heretics of the 16c., and to the members of a German secret society, akin to Freemasonry, founded in 1776. [N,S]

il n'y a que le premier pas qui coûte [Fr.] it's only the first step that counts. 20c. Used by Mme du Deffand in a letter (7th July 1763) in reference to the legend that St Denis walked two leagues carrying his head in his hands; now often misused in the sense 'the first step is the most difficult'. Also current in the variant form *ce n'est que le premier pas qui coûte*.

ils ne passeront pas [Fr.] they shall not get past. 20c. From the Order of the Day issued by Marshal Pétain at Verdun, February 1916.

ils n'ont rien appris ni rien oublié [Fr.] they have learned nothing and forgotten nothing. 20c. The reference is to the Court of Louis XVIII. Attributed to Marshal Dumouriez (1739–1823) in the form *les courtisans qui l'entourent n'ont rien oublié et n'ont rien appris;* but also attributed to Talleyrand.

imago [Lat.] (1) a perfect or typical example (of some concept); (2) *Psych.* a subconscious image of an ideal type of person, which influences behaviour and emotions. 20c. [N*]

imam [Arab. *imām*] a Moslem priest; a title given to the Caliph and certain other Moslem leaders. 17c. [N,S]

imbroglio [It.] a state of great confusion, a difficult situation, a complicated misunderstanding. 19c. [N,S]

immobiliste [Fr.] (a person) who opposes all kinds of progress and reform; an obscurantist. 20c.

immortelle [Fr.] a flower of papery texture which retains its colour and shape when dried. 19c. [N,S]

(les) Immortels [Fr. 'the immortals'] the members of the Académie Française. 20c.

impair [Fr.] *Roulette* any one of the odd numbers. 19c. Cf. PAIR. [N*]

impasse [Fr.] a situation from which there is no escape, an insoluble difficulty. 19c. [N,S]

impasto [It.] *Art* the application of thick layers of opaque pigment. 18c. [N,S]

impayable [Fr.] 'priceless', impossible to equal. 19c. [N]

impedimenta *pl.* [Lat.] encumbrances, *esp.* baggage, parcels, etc. 17c. [N,S]

imperium [Lat.] supreme power, sovereignty. 17c. [N,S]

imperium in imperio [Lat.] an independent authority claimed or exercised within the jurisdiction of another authority. 18c. [N,S]

impetus [Lat.] the force with which a body moves; *hence*, motive power, moving force; a STIMULUS, an incentive. 17c. Cf. MOMENTUM. [N,S]

impluvium [Lat.] the square water-cistern in the centre of the ATRIUM of a Roman house. 19c. [N,S]

imponderabilia *pl.* [Pseudo-Lat.] factors the influence of which on some project it is not easy to evaluate in concrete terms. 20c.

impresario, *pl.* **impresarii** [It.] an organizer of public entertainments, *esp.* the manager of an operatic company. 18c. [N,S]

imprimatur [Lat. 'let it be printed'] the formula licensing the publication of a book, an official licence to publish; *hence*, sanction, authoritative approval. 17c. Now used mainly of a licence granted by a bishop for the publication of a religious work: cf. NIHIL OBSTAT. [N,S]

imprimatura [It.] *Art* a coloured wash laid over a panel or canvas, either before or after the preliminary drawing is made. 20c.

imprimé [Fr.] a printed dress-fabric, *usu.* of linen or cotton. 20c.

imprimis [Lat. < *in primis* 'amongst the first'] in the first place, *esp.* introducing the first of a sequence of items. 15c. [N,S]

impromptu [Lat. *in promptu* 'in readiness'] (a speech, musical performance, etc. performed) without preparation, on the spur of the moment; *hence*, *Mus.* a composition resembling an improvisation. 17c. Cf. EX TEMPORE. [N,S]

imshi [Arab. 'walk!'] go away!, be off! 20c. [N*]

in absentia [Lat.] in the absence (of the person concerned). 20c. *Usu.* of the conferment of an academic distinction or of trial for a criminal offence.

in æternum [Lat.] for ever and ever. 20c. Cf. IN PERPETUUM.

inamorato, *f.* **inamorata** [Obs. It.] a lover, a sweetheart, one who is in love. 16c. The current Italian spelling is *innamorato.* [N,S]

in articulo mortis [Lat.] at the point of death, at death's door. 16c. Cf. IN EXTREMIS. [N(*),S]

in bona parte/in bonam partem [Lat.] (to be interpreted) on the favourable side, in a favourable manner. 17c. Cf. IN MALA PARTE. [S]

in camera [Lat.] (legal proceedings) conducted in secret, not in open court. 19c. Formerly such cases were heard in the judge's chambers. Cf. À HUIS CLOS; JANUIS CLAUSIS. [N,S]

in capite [Lat.] *Hist.* (a tenant) in chief, (holding land) directly from the Crown. 16c. Cf. MESNE. [N,S]

incipit [Lat. '(here) begins (the book, etc.)'] the first few words of a manuscript treatise, recorded for purposes of identification. 19c. Cf. EXPLICIT. [N]

incognito, *f.* **incognita,** *pl.* **incogniti** [It. 'unknown'] (a person) living or travelling in disguise, or under an assumed name, to avoid recognition. 17c. [N,S]

in commendam [Lat. 'in trust'] *Eccles.* (the holding of a benefice or see) pending the appointment of the proper incumbent. 17c. [N,S]

incommunicado, *f.* **incommunicada** [Sp. *incomunicado*] detained or imprisoned without communication with the outside world. 20c. Introduced at the time of the Spanish Civil War. The spelling *incommunicado,* though not justified by the Spanish form, seems well established in English.

inconnu, *f.* **inconnue** [Fr.] a person whose identity is unknown. 19c. Cf. IGNOTUS. [S]

inconséquence [Fr.] behaviour lacking in logical coherence or sequence; the habit of such behaviour. 20c.

in consimile casu [Lat.] *Law* in a (legally) similar or identical position. 20c.

in contumaciam [Lat.] *Law* in contempt (of court). 19c. [N*,S]

inconvenable [Fr.] not in accordance with propriety or decency. 20c. Cf. CONVENABLE.

incubus, *pl.* **incubi** [Lat.] an evil spirit which cohabits with a woman during her sleep; *hence*, a nightmare; *hence*, a person or thing exercising an oppressive influence. 13c. Cf. SUCCUBUS. [N,S]

incunabula *pl.* [Lat. 'swaddling-clothes'] books produced during the infancy of printing, *usu.* specifically before 1500. 19c. The singular (rarely needed) is either *incunabulum* (not in use in Latin) or the anglicized *incunable*. Cf. WIEGENDRUCK. [N,S]

indaba [Zulu] a conference with or between South African natives. 19c. [N]

index expurgatorius [Lat.] *Eccles.* a list of passages to be deleted or altered in works otherwise permitted for the reading of the faithful. 17c. The first *index expurgatorius* was authorized by the Council of Trent and published in 1571; in English usage the phrase is often confused with INDEX LIBRORUM PROHIBITORUM. [N,S]

index librorum prohibitorum [Lat.] *Eccles.* an authorative list of the books which the faithful are not permitted to read without express permission. 17c. The first *index librorum prohibitorum* was authorized by the Council of Trent and published in 1564; the current edition incorporates an INDEX EXPURGATORIUS. [N]

index locorum [Lat.] an index of places (mentioned in a book). 19c. [N]

index nominum [Lat.] an index of names (mentioned in a book). 19c. Cf. ONOMASTICON. [N,S]

index rerum [Lat.] an index of subjects (discussed in a book). 19c. [N,S]

index verborum [Lat.] an index of words (discussed in a book). 19c. [N,S]

indicium, *pl.* **indicia** [Lat.] an indication, a symptom, an item of evidence. 17c. [N,S]

inertia [Lat.] the tendency of matter to remain at rest (or to continue to move in a straight line) unless influenced by external forces; *hence*, a tendency to remain at rest, sloth. 18c. Formerly called VIS INERTIÆ. [N,S]

in esse [Lat.] actually, in real fact; contrasted with IN POSSE 'potentially'. 16c. Cf. ESSE. [N,S]

in excelsis [Lat.] in the highest degree. 19c. Vulgate *St Mark* xi 10. [N,S]

in extenso [Lat.] at full length, in its entirety. 19c. [N,S]

in extremis [Lat.] in the last agonies, at the point of death. 16c. Vulgate *St Mark* v 23. Cf. IN ARTICULO MORTIS. [N,S]

infanta [Sp., Port.] a royal princess of Spain or Portugal. 17c. [N,S]

inferno, *pl.* **inferni** [It. 'hell'] a place of torment or misery; a conflagration. 19c. [N,S]

in flagrante delicto [Lat.] in the very act, red-handed. 18c. The technical legal sense is normally denoted by FLAGRANTE DELICTO. [N,S]

in forma pauperis [Lat.] *Law* in the guise of a poor person, without liability for costs. 16c. [N,S]

infra [Lat.] below, further on (referring to a later passage in a book, etc.) 19c. Cf. SUPRA; UT INFRA. [N,S]

infra dig(nitatem) [Lat.] beneath one's dignity, not consonant with one's position. 19c. The abbreviated form is now only *facet.* [N,S]

infusion [Fr.] a draught of medicinal herbs steeped in hot or boiling water. 20c. A favourite remedy of the French housewife. Cf. TISANE.

ingénue [Fr.] a young woman of artless simplicity; such a character represented upon the stage; an actress who plays such parts. 19c. Cf. JEUNE INGÉNUE. [N*,S]

in globo [Lat.] in its entirety, as a whole, taking a general view. 20c. Cf. IN TOTO.

in jure uxoris [Lat.] *Law* by the right of his wife. 20c. Of a title, privilege, etc., inherited by the wife but held or exercised by the husband.

in limine [Lat. 'on the threshold'] at the very outset. 19c. [N,S]

(in) loco parentis [Lat.] in the place of a parent, having parental responsibility and authority. 18c. [N,S]

in mala parte/in malam partem [Lat.] (to be interpreted) on the bad side, in an unfavourable manner. 17c. Cf. IN BONA PARTE. [S]

in medias res [Lat.] into the middle of the affair or narrative. 18c. Horace *Ars Poetica* 148: *Semper ad eventum festinat, et in medias res . . . auditorem rapit* 'he always hurries to the outcome, and drags the listener into the middle of things'. Sometimes misused in the sense '*in* the middle . . .' instead of '*into* the middle . . .' [N,S]

in memoriam [Lat.] in memory of (a dead person); *hence*, a commemorative writing. 19c. The currency of the phrase dates from the publication of Tennyson's *In Memoriam* (1850). [N,S]

Innigkeit [Ger.] intimacy, sincerity and warmth of feeling, *esp.* in a work of art. 20c.

innuendo [Lat. 'by intimating'] an indirect suggestion, an allusive remark, *esp.* one of uncomplimentary implication. 17c. *Orig.* a legal term referring to a parenthetic interpretation of terms allegedly slanderous or libellous. [N,S]

in pari materia [Lat.] (a test or experiment, etc., made) on comparable material; (words, etc.) referring to comparable ideas. 20c.

in partibus (infidelium) [Lat. 'in the regions (of unbelievers)'] *Eccles.* (a bishop or see) merely titular, without real authority. 17c. It is customary to appoint suffragan bishops to such nominal sees, which are *usu.* in countries once Christian but now pagan. [N,S]

in perpetuum [Lat.] in perpetuity, for ever. 17c. Cf. IN ÆTERNUM. [N,S]

in petto [It. 'in the breast'] secretly, without disclosure. 18c. Often, by confusion with English *petty*, misused as if it meant 'in little'. [S]

in pontificalibus [Lat.] *Eccles.* in the proper vestments of a pope, cardinal, or bishop; in the vestments of a priest. 14c. Cf. PONTIFICALIA. [N,S]

in posse [Lat.] potentially; having the possibility of existing; contrasted with IN ESSE 'actually'. 17c. [N,S]

in propria persona [Lat.] in his (her) own person, personally, undisguised. 17c. [N,S(*)]

in puris naturalibus [Lat.] in a state of nature, stark naked. 17c. [N,S]

in re [Lat.] in the matter of, concerning. 19c. Properly a legal expression, 'in the case of'; formerly (17c.) used in the sense of 'in fact, in reality'. [N(*),S]

in rebus [Lat.] *Law* in the affairs of (some person). 20c. The plural of IN RE, but retaining its legal connotation.

in rem [Lat.] *Law* into the matter of (some person). 20c. Related to IN RE (accusative instead of ablative), but retaining its legal connotation.

in sæcula sæculorum [Lat.] for ever and ever, world without end. 16c. Vulgate *Galatians* i 5 and elsewhere. [N,S]

in secco [It.] Art (the touching-up of a FRESCO) when the plaster is dry. 20c. Distinct from A SECCO, which refers to painting on dry plaster, not to FRESCO proper. Cf. FRESCO SECCO; SECCO.

ins Gesamt/insgesamt [Ger.] altogether, taken as a whole. 20c.

insiemi [It.] *Mus.* together. 20c.

insignia *pl.* [Lat.] badges of office, symbols or emblems of a nation, order, institution, etc.; distinguishing marks. 17c. The Latin singular *insigne* has *occ.* been used; and the plural *insignia* has been taken as a singular, with plural *insignias*. [N,S]

in situ [Lat.] in its original place, undisturbed; (a test, experiment, etc.) carried out on the spot, without the removal of the object tested to a laboratory. 19c. [N,S]

insolite [Fr.] unusual, out of the ordinary. 20c.

insomnia [Lat.] *Med.* (morbid) inability to sleep. 18c. The word has sometimes been taken as a plural with singular *insomnium*. [N,S]

insouciance [Fr.] unconcern, a devil-may-care attitude. 18c. [N,S]

insouciant, *f.* **insouciante** [Fr.] unconcerned, heedless. 19c. [N,S(*)]

inspeximus [Lat. 'we have inspected'] *Hist.* a charter confirming and quoting an earlier charter which the grantor has examined. 17c. Cf. VIDIMUS. [N,S]

instantané [Fr.] instantaneous. 20c. In French the word also has the meaning 'snapshot'.

instanter [Lat.] immediately, at once, without delay. 17c. *Orig*. a legal term. [N,S]

in statu pupillari [Lat.] as a pupil or ward; under scholastic or academic discipline. 19c. [N*,S]

in statu quo (ante) [Lat.] in the same position or condition (as before). 17c. Cf. STATUS QUO ANTE. [N,S]

intaglio [It.] a method of carving or engraving in which the design is hollowed out in reverse, as in a seal; a design or work of art produced in this way. 17c. To be distinguished from CAVO RILIEVO 'hollow relief', in which the outlines of the figures are incised, but the figures themselves are not hollowed out. [N,S]

intarsiatore, *pl.* **intarsiatori** [It.] a worker in INTARSIATURA. 19c. [N*,S]

intarsiatura, *pl.* **intarsiature** [It.] inlaid work in wood, bone, ivory and mother-of-pearl. 19c. [N*,S]

intarsio [It.] INTARSIATURA, inlaid work in wood, bone, ivory and mother-of-pearl. 19c. *Occ*. written *intarsia*, by confusion with TARSIA or *intarsiatura*. Cf. LAVORO DI COMMESSO. [N*,S]

intelligentsia/intelligentzia [Russ.] a class of society characterized by superior intelligence and advanced political views. 20c. Now nearly always in an ironical or pejorative connotation. [N*]

inter alia [Lat.] amongst other things. 17c. Sometimes misused with reference to persons. [N,S]

intéressante [Fr.] 'in an interesting condition', pregnant. 20c.

interim [Lat. 'meanwhile'] an interval of time, *usu*. in the phrase 'in the *interim*', in the meantime; temporary, provisional. 16c. [N,S]

intermezzo, *pl.* **intermezzi** [It.] (1) a short entertainment inserted between the acts of a play or opera; (2) *Mus*. a short movement linking the main divisions of a larger work; an independent composition of similar character. 19c. [N,S]

interregnum [Lat.] the interval between the reigns of successive rulers, during which the state is ruled by some provisional authority; a suspension of authority; a breach of continuity. 16c. [N,S]

inter vivos [Lat.] *Law* (a deed of gift, etc., executed) between living persons. 20c.

intime [Fr.] cosy, homely, confidential. 20c.

intimiste [Fr.] *Art* (a late form of Impressionist painting) devoted wholly to domestic interiors. 20c. The most important practitioners of *intimiste* painting were Pierre Bonnard (1867–1947) and Édouard Vuillard (1868–1940).

intonaco, *pl.* **intonachi** [It.] *Art* a final layer of wet plaster on which the FRESCO artist works. 19c. Cf. ARRICCIATO; GESSO GROSSO; GESSO SOTTILE; RINZAFFATO. [N,S]

in toto [Lat.] as a whole, completely, without exception. 18c. Cf. IN GLOBO. [N,S]

intra muros [Lat.] within the walls (of a city or institution); concerned with the internal politics (of an institution, etc.) 20c.

intransigeant, *f.* **intransigeante** [Fr.] uncompromising, unaccommodating. 19c. The French form holds its own against the anglicized *intransigent.* [N,S]

intra vires [Lat.] within the legal power or authority (of a person, institution, etc.); opposed to ULTRA VIRES. 19c. [N*,S]

in usum Delphini [Lat. 'for the use of the DAUPHIN'] bowdlerized, expurgated. 17c. From the title of an edition of the Latin Classics prepared by the order of Louis XIV for the use of his son; also current in the variant form *ad usum Delphini.* [S]

in utero [Lat.] in the womb, unborn. 18c. In legal and medical usage. Cf. EN VENTRE SA MÈRE. [N*,S]

in vacuo [Lat.] (an experiment conducted) in a vacuum; *hence,* (an argument, etc.) in the abstract, not applied to any concrete circumstances. 17c. The latter, metaphorical, meaning is very recent. [N,S]

inv(enit) [Lat.] (he) discovered (it), (he) invented (it); always accompanied by a name and inscribed on a model, etc. 19c.

in vino veritas [Lat.] there is truth in wine, the drunken man always tells the truth. 17c. [S]

invité, *f.* **invitée** [Fr.] a guest. 20c.

in vivo [Lat.] *Med.* (reactions, etc.) occurring only in the living body, not under laboratory conditions. 20c. [N*]

ipecacuanha [Port.] an emetic and expectorant drug derived from the root of a South American shrub. 17c. The Portuguese word is derived from a South American Indian name. [N,S(*)]

ipse dixit, *pl.* **ipsi dixerunt** [Lat.] a dogmatic assertion made on the unsupported authority of the speaker. 16c. A translation of the Greek *αὐτὸς ἔφα,* used by the Pythagoreans. Cf. Cicero *De Natura Deorum* I v 10: '*Ipse dixit.*' '*Ipse*' *autem erat Pythagoras* ' "He himself said it", and the "he himself" was Pythagoras.' [N,S(*)]

ipsissima verba *pl.* [Lat.] the exact words, the precise words. 19c. [N*,S]

ipso facto [Lat.] by that very fact, as an immediate and necessary consequence. 16c.

ipso jure [Lat.] *Law* by the operation of the law itself. 20c. [N*]

Islam [Arab. *islām* 'resignation'] the religious system founded by Mahomet. 19c. The word *Moslem* 'follower of Mahomet' is from Arab. *muslim,* a participle formed from the same root *s-l-m,* which is also found in SALAAM. [N,S]

istoriato [It.] (a porcelain vase) whose surface is wholly covered with representative decoration. 20c.

Italia irredenta [It.] the parts of Italy still under foreign domination after the war of 1866. 20c.

item [Lat.] also, likewise; used to introduce each article in an enumeration or catalogue. 14c. From this is derived the fully anglicized noun *item.* [N,S]

izba [Russ.] a Russian log-house or wooden hut. 18c. [N*]

izvoschik, *pl.* **izvoschiki** [Russ. *izvozchik*] a Russian cab-driver. 20c. Cf. YAMSCHIK.

J

jabot [Fr.] a frill, often of lace, worn at the throat of a woman's costume. 19c. Formerly the term was applied also to a kind of neck-ruffle worn by men. [N,S]

j'accuse [Fr.] 'I accuse . . .'; a pamphlet, etc., accusing some authority of injustice or intolerance. 20c. From the title of Emile Zola's letter to *L'Aurore* (January 1898) in which he demanded a re-examination of the Dreyfus case.

jacquerie [Fr.] an insurrection of the peasantry, a peasants' revolt. 16c. *Orig.* of the peasants' rising in northern France in 1357–8; from the name *Jacques*, a nickname for a French peasant. [N,S]

jacta est alea [Lat.] the die is cast, there is no going back. 16c. Suetonius *Divus Julius* xxxii: *jacta alea est*—Cæsar's words at the crossing of the Rubicon. Suetonius' word-order seems never to be used in English: the current forms are *jacta est alea* and *alea jacta est.* [S]

j'adoube [Obs. Fr.] *Chess* 'I adjust', the formula used by a player to intimate that he is touching a piece merely to adjust its position. 19c.

Jäger [Ger.] a huntsman; a servant in huntsman's costume; a rifleman of certain German and Austrian regiments, *orig.* recruited from foresters. 18c. Cf. CHASSEUR ALPIN. [N,S]

jalousie [Fr.] a blind or shutter made of sloping slats so as to exclude sun and rain while admitting air and diffused light. 19c. Cf. PERSIENNES. [N,S]

januis clausis [Lat.] behind closed doors, in secret, IN CAMERA. 20c. Vulgate *St John* xx 26. Cf. À HUIS CLOS.

jardinière [Fr.] (1) an ornamental flower-pot, a stand for the display of cut flowers or flowers in pots; (2) *Cul.* a vegetable soup or garnish. 19c. [N(*),S]

jaspé [Fr.] mottled, marbled so as to resemble jasper. 19c. [N*]

jehad [Arab. *jihād*] a holy war by Moslems against unbelievers; *hence*, a crusade, a war or campaign inspired by some doctrine or principle. 19c. [N,S]

je m'en fiche [Fr.] I don't care. 20c. A euphemism for the less decent *je m'en fous*. 20c.

je-m'en-foutisme [Fr.] the philosophy of 'don't care', 'I'm all right'. 20c. From the phrase *je m'en fous*=JE M'EN FICHE. Cf. CULTE DU MOI; GLEICHGÜLTIGKEIT.

je-ne-sais-quoi [Fr. 'I don't know what'] an inexpressible or indescribable something. 17c. [N,S]

jet d'eau, *pl.* **jets d'eau** [Fr.] a jet of water issuing from a pipe in an ornamental fountain. 17c. [N,S]

jeté [Fr. 'thrown'] *Ballet* a leap from one foot to the other, during which the free leg may be extended in any direction. 20c. [N*]

jeté battu [Fr.] *Ballet* a JETÉ accompanied by a BATTEMENT. 20c.

jeu de mots, *pl.* **jeux de mots** [Fr.] a play upon words, a pun. 18c. [N,S(*)]

jeu d'esprit, *pl.* **jeux d'esprit** [Fr.] a witticism, a witty trifle, an exercise of wit; a light-hearted exercise in any artistic technique. 18c. Cf. CAPRICCIO. [N,S]

jeune amour, *pl.* **jeunes amours** [Fr.] young love, adolescent love. 20c. The French phrase lacks the pejorative connotation of *calf love*, and is sentimental in tone.

jeune femme sérieuse [Fr.] an earnest young woman, a young woman who is not frivolous. 20c. Cf. FEMME SÉRIEUSE; HOMME SÉRIEUX; SÉRIEUX.

jeune fille [Fr.] a young girl; (clothes, etc.) suitable for a young girl. 20c.

jeune fille bien élevée [Fr.] a nicely brought-up girl. 20c. *Usu.* with a slightly contemptuous connotation.

jeune fille fatale [Fr.] a young woman who brings disaster on all who love her. 20c. Adapted from the more usual FEMME FATALE.

jeune ingénue [Fr.] a young woman of artless simplicity. 20c. Identical in sense with INGÉNUE, but lacking the theatrical connotations of the latter.

jeune premier [Fr.] an actor who plays the part of the young hero or the young lover, a male juvenile lead. 19c. [N*,S]

jeune première [Fr.] an actress who plays the part of the young heroine, a female juvenile lead. 19c. [N*]

jeune refusé [Fr.] an 'angry young man'. 20c. Cf. RÉVOLTÉ.

jeunesse dorée [Fr. 'gilded youth'] young people of wealth and fashion. 19c. The invention of the term is attributed to Louis-Marie-Stanislas Fréron (1754–1802), who applied it to the fashionable counter-revolutionary group formed after the fall of Robespierre in 1794. [N*,S]

jeune voyou, *pl.* **jeunes voyous** [Fr.] a young hooligan, a teddy-boy. 20c. Cf. BLOUSON NOIR; HALBSTARKE(R); STILYAGA; VITELLONE.

(les) jeux sont faits [Fr.] *Roulette* 'the stakes are laid'; called by the CROUPIER and immediately followed by RIEN NE VA PLUS. 20c.

jinrickshaw [Jap. *jin-riki-sha* 'man-strength-vehicle'] a light hooded two-wheeled carriage, drawn by one or two men. 19c. First used in Japan about 1870, subsequently introduced into other Oriental countries. [N,S]

jiu-jitsu [Jap. *jūjutsu* 'yielding science'] a Japanese system of wrestling in which the opponent's own strength is made use of to throw him. 19c. Cf. JUDO. [N*]

joie de vivre [Fr.] a feeling of happiness and physical well-being, high spirits. 20c. [N*]

jolie-laide [Fr.] (a woman) whose plainness or ugliness of feature is itself attractive or charming. 20c. Cf. BELLE LAIDE.

jongleur [Fr.] *Hist.* a wandering minstrel. 18c. [N,S(*)]

joue [Fr. 'cheek'] *Tennis* the inner vertical wall of one of the winning openings. 19c. A ball which has touched a *joue* and rebounded is not held to have entered the opening.

jour [Fr.] an 'at home' day, a specified day of the week on which visits are expected without invitation. 20c.

jour de fête [Fr.] a feast-day, *esp.* the feast-day of a patron saint. 20c.

journal intime [Fr.] a confidential diary, *esp.* one which although intended for publication records intimate details of the life of the writer and his associates. 20c.

jubé [Fr.] *Eccles.* a rood-screen and gallery dividing the chancel of a church from the nave. 20c. In current usage the spelling with an acute accent shows that the word is felt to be from French; but from 18c. the Latin form *jube* without an accent was in use in the same sense. The ultimate origin is the Latin phrase *Jube, domine, benedicere,* spoken by the deacon from the rood-loft before the reading of the Gospel. [N]

Judenhetze [Ger.] anti-Semitism, persecution of the Jews. 20c.

judo [Jap. *jūdō* 'soft way'] a more developed form of JIU-JITSU, the Japanese system of wrestling. 19c. In practice *judo* and *jiu-jitsu* are commonly used without distinction. [N*]

juge d'instruction [Fr.] an 'examining magistrate', a French magistrate who examines the evidence against a person accused of a crime, to decide whether there is a case for trial. 19c. [S]

Jugendstil [Ger. 'youth-style'] ART NOUVEAU, a style of drawing and domestic decoration introduced between 1890 and 1900. 20c. The name is taken from *Jugend,* the title of a journal devoted to the new movement and published in Munich from 1896.

juju [W. African] an object (often incongruous) made the object of religious or superstitious veneration by the native tribes of West Africa. 19c. Ultimately from the French *joujou* 'toy'. [N]

Junggrammatiker, *pl.* **Junggrammatiker** [Ger. 'young grammarian'] a neo-grammarian, one of a group of German philologists who in the period after 1870 laid the foundations of modern linguistic science. 20c. The most outstanding of the *Junggrammatiker* was Karl Brugmann (1849–1919) of Leipzig.

Junker [Ger. < *jung Herr* 'young nobleman'] an arrogant, overbearing member of the Prussian aristocracy, *esp.* a member of the aristocratic party at the time of Bismarck. 16c. [N,S]

junta [Sp.] an administrative council, *esp.* one of those formed in districts of Spain during the Napoleonic wars; *hence,* a secret and self-elected committee exercising undue influence on the affairs of some organization. 17c. In the more general sense the mis-spelling *junto* was formerly very common, but it seems now to be obsolete. The pronunciation is fully anglicized. [N,S]

jure dignitatis [Lat.] (a degree awarded) by right of distinction, to one who has achieved a distinguished position in public life. 20c. Cf. HONORIS CAUSA.

jure divino [Lat.] by divine right, by right depending on the law of God. 16c. [N,S]

jus accrescendi [Lat.] *Law* the right of survivorship peculiar to joint ownership, joint rights, or joint liabilities, whereby the surviving party accedes without formality to the ownership, rights, or liabilities of the deceased party. 20c.

jus gentium [Lat.] the law of nations, the principles of equity common to all civilized peoples. 16c. [N*,S]

jus primæ noctis [Lat. 'law of the first night'] *Hist.* the supposed right of a feudal overlord to deflower the bride of any of his tenants on the first night of marriage. 20c. Cf. DROIT DE SEIGNEUR.

juste milieu [Fr.] the happy mean, judicious moderation, *esp.* in political principles. 19c. Denis Diderot *Salon de 1767: garder en tout un juste milieu, voilà la règle du bonheur* 'to observe a judicious moderation in everything, that is the key to happiness'. The phrase was taken up in a political context by Louis-Philippe of France. Cf. AUREA MEDIOCRITAS; VIA MEDIA. [S]

justification du tirage [Fr.] an enumeration of the copies of a work printed, with details of the paper, binding, etc. used, often appended to fine books printed in France. 20c.

juvenilia *pl.* [Lat.] works of art or literature produced during youth. 17c. Often used as the title of a collection of such works. [N*]

j'y suis, j'y reste [Fr.] here I am and here I stay. 20c. Used by General MacMahon (1808–93) at the taking of Sebastopol during the Crimean War.

K

kabuki [Jap.] the Japanese realistic popular drama. 20c. Contrasted with Noh, the formal quasi-religious drama.

Kaffeeklatsch [Ger.] gossip over a cup of coffee; a coffee- or tea-party devoted to the exchange of gossip, *esp.* of literary and artistic tittle-tattle. 20c.

kaimakam [Turk. < Arab. *qā'im maqām* 'lieutenant'] a deputy governor in the Turkish administrative system. 17c. [N,S]

Kaiser [Ger.] the emperor of Germany or Austria. 19c. The word, ultimately from Lat. *Cæsar*, has been in use in English in a more general sense since 12c.; the current use dates from about 1800, and the more general sense has become obsolete. [N,S(*)]

kakemono [Jap. 'hang-thing'] *Art* a Japanese scroll-picture, mounted on rollers so that it can be rolled up for storage. 19c. Cf. MAKIMONO. [N]

Kamerad [Ger.] 'comrade!', the term used by German soldiers when surrendering to the enemy; *hence*, an appeal for clemency. 20c. [N*]

kamikaze [Jap. 'divine wind'] a (Japanese) suicide plane, the pilot of which faces certain death in the destruction of an enemy vessel. 20c. The reference is to the providential TYPHOON which frustrated the Mongol invasion of 1281.

kanaka [Haw.] a native of the South Sea Islands, *esp.* one in the service of a European employer; *hence*, any native employee. 19c. [N]

Kapellmeister [Ger.] *Mus.* the conductor of an orchestra (with or without a choir) such as used to be maintained in the German courts. 19c. Cf. MAESTRO DI CAPPELLA. [N]

kaputt [Ger.] done for, no good, useless. 20c.

Karabiner [Ger.] a steel ring with a spring clip on one side, used in mountaineering to attach a climber securely to a rope. 20c.

karate [Jap. 'open hand'] a system of inflicting injury by striking vital nerve-centres in the body with the edge of the open hand. 20c.

karma [Sansk.] the sum total of a Buddhist's actions in one incarnation, which determines his fate in the next; *hence*, fate, destiny. 19c. [N]

karroo [Hottentot] *Geog.* an arid clayey plateau in South Africa. 18c. [N,S]

kasbah [Arab. *qaṣ(a)bah*] the palace-citadel of an Arab chieftain in North

Africa; the district surrounding such a citadel; *hence*, the native quarter in a North African town. 20c.

katabasis [Gk. κατάβασις 'going down'] a military retreat. 19c. With reference to the retreat of Xenophon, as related by him in his *Anabasis*. Cf. ANABASIS. [N]

kat' exochen [Gk. κατ' ἐξοχήν] pre-eminently, PAR EXCELLENCE. 16c. Nearly always written in Greek characters. [S]

Katzenjammer [Ger. 'caterwauling'] the spiritual or physical discomfort following sensual excess, *esp*. the headache and nausea resulting from the excessive consumption of alcohol. 20c.

kayak [Esk. *qajaq*] an Eskimo canoe consisting of a light framework covered with sealskin, the aperture in which is laced round the waist of the user. 18c. The *kayak* is designed for fishing and is used only by men. Cf. UMIAK. [N,S]

kebab [Turk. < Arab. *kabāb*] *Cul*. one of a variety of Oriental dishes consisting of meat cut into small pieces, seasoned, and roasted. 17c. The Turkish spelling is now the current one; but formerly various spellings reflecting the Arabic form were in use, such as *cabob*, *kabob*. Now often used as an abbreviation for SHISH KEBAB. Cf. SHASHLIK. [N,S]

keef=KIF, Indian hemp.

kelim=KILIM, a carpet without a pile.

kendo [Jap. *kendō*] the Japanese science of swordsmanship. 20c.

képi [Fr.] a French military cap with a flat top and a peak. 19c. [N,S]

Kerbschnitt [Ger.] *Art* chip-carving, a form of wood-carving in which slivers of wood are gouged out from a flat surface. 20c.

kermesse [Fr. < Obs. Du. *kerkmisse* 'church-mass'] an annual fair or carnival in the Low Countries. 16c. [N,S]

kerygma [Gk. κήρυγμα] *Rel*. systematic preaching, proclamation of religious truth. 19c. [N]

khaki [Hind. *khākī* 'dusty'] a cloth of a characteristic dull greenish-brown colour, used for military uniforms. 19c. Introduced in India about 1850, and extended to the British Army in general from the time of the Boer War. [N,S]

khamsin [Arab. *khamsīn* 'fifty'] an oppressively hot south-east wind which blows in Egypt and neighbouring countries for about fifty days during March, April and May. 17c. Cf. SIROCCO. [N]

khan [Arab. *khān*] an unfurnished building for the accommodation of travellers in the East. 14c. [N,S]

khitmutgar [Hind. *khidmat-gār* 'servant'] *A.-I.* a male servant who waits at table. 18c. [N,S]

kibbutz, *pl.* **kibbutzim** [Heb.] an Israeli collective farm. 20c.

kibitka [Russ.] a Tartar tent of lattice and felt; a Russian covered cart or sledge. 18c. [N,S]

kibitzer [Ger. *Kiebitz* 'lapwing'] *Bridge* a bystander who comments (*usu.* ignorantly) on the play of the cards. 20c. From the title of an American play (February 1929) in which Edward G. Robinson played the part of such a bystander; the German *Kiebitz* in this sense is much older, and is supposed to derive from the alleged inquisitiveness of the lapwing.

kif/keef [Arab. *kaif*] a state of dreamy intoxication induced by a narcotic; *hence*, Indian hemp. 19c. [N]

kilim [Turk.] a woven carpet without a pile. 20c. Sometimes mis-spelt *kelim*.

kimono [Jap. 'silk-thing'] a long Japanese robe with loose sleeves. 19c. [N]

Kindergarten [Ger. 'children's garden'] a nursery school conducted on the principles devised by Friedrich Fröbel (1782–1852). 19c. The Fröbel system aims at developing the intelligence of children by means of games which will retain their interest. [N,S]

Kinder, Kirche, Küche [Ger.] 'children, church, cooking', an enumeration of the occupations fit for a woman. 20c. The words are sometimes arranged in other orders, of which *Küche, Kirche, Kinder* is perhaps the most common.

kismet [Turk. < Arab. *qisma*(*t*)] fate, destiny. 19c. The spelling *kismat*, formerly common, reflects the Arabic form. [N,S]

Kitsch [Ger.] worthless rubbish, *esp.* as a derogatory term for forms or works of art which are felt to be shoddy or gaudy. 20c.

Klaviertiger [Ger. 'keyboard-tiger'] a virtuoso pianist whose attack upon his instrument appears ferocious. 20c.

Kletterschuh, *pl.* **Kletterschuhe** [Ger.] a climbing-boot. 20c.

kohl [Arab. *koḥ'l*] powdered antimony, used in the East for darkening the eyelids. 18c. The same Arabic word, with the Arabic definite article, forms the word *alcohol*, the common idea being 'sublimation'. [N,S]

koine [Gk. *κοινή*] the common literary language of the ancient Greeks; *hence*, any standard literary language accepted over a wide area. 20c. [N*]

kolkhoz [Russ.] a Russian collective farm. 20c. Contrasted with SOVKHOZ, a state-owned farm.

kolossal [Ger.] splendid, excellent. 20c. Properly 'colossal, huge', but common as a colloquial term of approbation. Cf. WUNDERBAR.

Konzertstück [Ger.] *Mus.* a piece of music designed to display the virtuosity of the performer(s) at a concert. 20c.

kopje [Du. 'little head'] a small rounded hill in South Africa. 19c. [N]

kore, *pl.* **korai** [Gk. *κόρη*] *Art* a statue of a young girl. 20c. Gk. *κόρη* is the feminine of *κόρος*, introduced into English in its Ionic form *κοῦρος* KOUROS.

kosher [Heb. *kāshēr* 'right'] (food) prepared in accordance with Jewish law; (a shop) supplying such food. 19c. [N,S]

kouros, *pl.* **kouroi** [Gk. κοῦρος] *Art* a statue of a boy or young man. 20c. κοῦρος is Ionic (Homeric) Greek; the Attic form is κόρος. Cf. KORE.

kowtow [Chin. *k'o-t'ou* 'knock the head'] the Chinese custom of knocking the forehead on the ground in token of submission to a superior; *hence*, a display of obsequiousness; to make an act of complete submission, to defer obsequiously to the wishes of a superior. 19c. The form *kotow*, which represents the Chinese form more accurately, seems to have been entirely displaced by *kowtow*, in which the first vowel has been assimilated to the second. [N(*),S]

kozuka [Jap.] a knife carried in the scabbard of a sword. 20c.

kraal [Du.] a native village consisting of a collection of huts surrounded by a stockade, with a space for cattle in the middle. 18c. The South African Dutch word is from Sp. CORRAL. [N,S]

Kraft durch Freude [Ger.] 'Strength through Joy', the name of an organization sponsored by the National Socialist Party in Germany, which provided regimented leisure for the masses under government control. 20c.

kraken [Norw.] a mythical sea-monster of enormous size, supposed to have been seen off the coast of Norway. 18c. The final *-n* is the Norwegian definite article, but the English definite article is commonly prefixed: 'the *kraken*'. [N,S]

Krankheit [Ger.] physical sickness and mental disturbance resulting from excessive executive responsibility. 20c. Cf. MANAGERKRANKHEIT.

Krankheitsgewinn [Ger.] *Psych.* the benefits (avoidance of responsibility, etc.) resulting from mental illness, considered as the cause of that illness. 20c.

kranz/krantz [Afrik. 'chaplet'] *Geog.* a wall of rock round the summit of a mountain; an overhanging cliff enclosing a valley. 19c. [N]

krees/kris [Mal. *kris*] a Malayan dagger. 16c. Numerous different spellings have also been in use. [N,S]

Kriegsgefangene(r), *pl.* **Kriegsgefangene(n)** [Ger.] a prisoner of war. 20c. For the form cf. HALBSTARKE(R); in English usage *Kriegsgefangener* seems to be much the more common form.

Kriegsspiel [Ger.] a game, designed to develop skill in strategy and tactics, in which blocks representing military or naval forces are moved about on a map or chart. 19c. The game was apparently invented in Switzerland about 1811. [N,S]

Kriminalroman [Ger.] a novel about crime. 20c. The term is more general than the English 'detective story' or 'thriller'. Cf. ROMAN POLICIER.

kris=KREES, a Malayan dagger.

Küche, Kirche, Kinder=KINDER, KIRCHE, KÜCHE, 'children, church, cooking'.

kudos [Gk. κῦδος] credit, fame, reputation. 19c. [N,S]

kukri [Hind. *kukṛī*] a curved knife, broader near the point than at the haft, with the cutting edge inside the curve, used by the Gurkhas. 19c. The vocalic *ṛ* has given rise to numerous different spellings: *kukeri*, *kookaree*, etc. [N,S]

kulak, *pl.* **kulaki** [Russ. 'fist'] a prosperous Russian peasant, a peasant-proprietor. 19c. So called because the prosperous peasant is notoriously tight-fisted. [N,S]

Kultur [Ger.] 'culture' as conceived by the Germans; racial arrogance, a desire to impose one's own values on all the world. 20c. [N*]

Kulturbolschewismus [Ger.] intellectual and artistic anarchy or nihilism; decadence in modern (non-representational) art. 20c. The term originated in National Socialist Germany.

Kulturgeschichte [Ger.] the history of civilization and of art. 20c. Cf. KUNSTGESCHICHTE.

kulturgeschichtlich [Ger.] related to the history of civilization and of art. 20c.

Kulturkampf [Ger.] a struggle for the control of the system of education in a country, *esp.* that between Bismarck and the Pope between 1872 and 1887; an attempt by one nation to achieve cultural supremacy over others. 19c. [N*,S]

Kulturkreis, *pl.* **Kulturkreise** [Ger.] one of a series of successive overlapping waves of civilization spreading out from a centre, postulated to explain the diffusion of cultures in various parts of the world. 20c.

kulturny [Russ.] cultural, *esp.* conducive to the propagation of Marxist culture. 20c.

Kunstgeschichte [Ger.] the history of art. 20c. Cf. KULTURGESCHICHTE.

Kunsthistoriker [Ger.] a student of or expert in the history of art. 20c.

Kunstprosa [Ger.] literary prose, prose designed to serve an artistic rather than a utilitarian end. 20c.

Kuomintang [Chin. 'people's national party'] the radical nationalist party formed in China by Sun Yat-sen in 1912 after the fall of the emperor. 20c. [N*]

kurgan [Russ.] a prehistoric sepulchral TUMULUS in Southern Russia. 19c. The word is ultimately of Tartar origin. [N]

Kurhaus [Ger.] the building at a health-resort where the medicinal water is obtained, the pump-room at a spa. 19c. [S]

Kursaal [Ger.] a set of public rooms for the entertainment of visitors at a health-resort. 19c. [S]

kvas [Russ.] rye beer. 16c. [N]

kyrie eleïson [Gk. *κύριε ἐλέησον*] *Eccles.* the petition 'Lord, have mercy' spoken at the beginning of the Mass; a musical setting of this petition, *esp.* as the first movement of a choral Mass. 14c. The words occur in the Greek text of *Psalm* cxxii (cxxiii) 3, *St Matthew* xv 22 and elsewhere. [N,S]

L

£=LIBRA, LIBRÆ, pound(s) sterling.

la . . . [Fr.] the (famous, notorious) . . .; always followed by the name of a woman. 20c. The connotation is always vaguely proprietorial, sometimes conveying admiration but sometimes slightly contemptuous.

laager [Afrik. *lager*] an encampment, a temporary halting-place defended by a circle of wagons; *esp.* an encampment of BOER migrants; to form such a defensive encampment. 19c. [N(*),S]

labarum [Lat. < Gk. λαβαρόν] *Hist.* the imperial standard of the emperor Constantine, consisting of the Roman standard with the addition of the Christian XP symbol; *hence*, any symbolic banner; *hence*, any moral ideal or incentive. 17c. [N,S]

laborare est orare [Lat.] 'to work is to pray', God is best served by conscientious attention to duty. 19c. [S]

lacrymæ rerum [Lat. 'tears of things'] the innate sadness of human life, the tragedy of human destiny. 20c. Also in the fuller form SUNT LACRYMÆ RERUM. Virgil *Æneid* i 462: *Sunt lacrymæ rerum, et mentem mortalia tangunt* 'there are tears in life, and human sufferings distress the mind'. Virgil's well-known line is nearly untranslatable.

lacuna, *pl.* **lacunæ** [Lat.] a gap, a blank, a HIATUS, *esp.* in a manuscript or in the text of an author. 17c. [N,S]

lahar [Jav.] *Geog.* an avalanche of mud formed from volcanic ash impregnated with rain. 20c.

laissez-aller/laisser-aller [Fr.] absence of constraint, excessive ease of manner. 19c. The current French form *laisser-aller* is formed from the infinitive, the more common English form *laissez-aller* from the imperative. Cf. SANS-GÊNE.

laissez-faire/laisser-faire [Fr.] the principle or policy that the government should not interfere in the affairs of the individual. 19c. For the form cf. LAISSEZ-ALLER.

laissez-passer [Fr.] a pass, a permit, *esp.* a diplomatic passport. 20c.

lakh [Hind. *lākh*] *A.-I.* one hundred thousand. 17c. A *lakh* of RUPEES is worth nearly £10,000. [N,S]

lama [Tib. *blama*] a Buddhist priest or monk in Tibet. 17c. The chief *lama* is known as the *Dalai Lama.* [N,S]

lambris d'appui [Fr.] waist-high panelling. 20c.

lambris de hauteur [Fr.] panelling from floor to cornice. 20c.

lamé [Fr.] (a fabric) made of interwoven threads of silk and silver or gold. 20c.

lamina, *pl.* **laminæ** [Lat.] a thin plate, *usu.* of metal. 17c. [N,S]

Ländler [Ger.] *Mus.* a slow waltz of Tyrolean origin. 20c.

landsmål [Norw.] a variety of written Norwegian based on forms drawn from various spoken dialects, used by certain writers in preference to the official RIKSMÅL which differs little from Danish. 19c. The *landsmål* was developed after Norway became independent of Denmark in 1814 by the philologist Ivar Aasen, who based it mainly on his own dialect of Søndmøre.

Langlauf [Ger.] long-distance skiing, skiing across country. 20c. Opposed to PISTE-skiing.

langouste [Fr.] a rock-lobster, a spiny lobster. 20c.

langue-de-chat, *pl.* **langues-de-chat** [Fr. 'cat's tongue'] a piece of chocolate shaped into a long flat strip with rounded ends. 20c.

lapis lazuli [Lat.] a silicious mineral of a vivid blue colour, used as a pigment and for decorative purposes. 14c. The second word is from Pers. *lāzhward.* [N,S]

lapsus calami [Lat.] a slip of the pen, an accidental error in writing. 19c. [N,S]

lapsus linguæ [Lat.] a slip of the tongue, an accidental error in speech. 17c. [N,S]

lapsus memoriæ [Lat.] a slip of the memory, a defective or inaccurate remembrance. 20c.

lares et penates *pl.* [Lat.] household gods; *hence*, the familiar comforting things of home. 18c. Apparently *lares* were the individual tutelary deities of each family, *penates* gods chosen from amongst the common Pantheon; *lares* alone occurs much earlier in English (17c.), but the two seem always to be used in conjunction in current English. [N,S]

larghetto [It.] *Mus.* in slow time, slower than ANDANTE but not so slow as LARGO; a movement in slow time. 18c. [S]

largo [It.] *Mus.* in slow time (slower than LARGHETTO but not so slow as ADAGIO) and in a broad dignified manner; a movement so performed. 17c. [N,S]

larmes dans la voix [Fr.] tears in the voice, a tone of voice suggesting that the speaker is on the verge of tears. 20c.

larnax [Gk. λάρναξ] *Hist.* a cinerary urn. 20c.

larva, *pl.* **larvæ** [Lat. 'ghost'] a winged insect in the grub state, before its transformation into a pupa. 18c. [N,S]

l'art pour l'art [Fr.] art for art's sake, the doctrine that art should be untrammelled by social or moral restrictions. 20c. First used in 1804 in Benjamin Constant's *Journal Intime*, and again in 1818 in Victor Cousin's

Sorbonne lectures on Art. The doctrine was repeatedly formulated by Théophile Gautier, but not in these words. Cf. ARS GRATIA ARTIS.

lasagna, *pl.* **lasagne** [It.] a flat strip of PASTA used mainly in preparing MINESTRONE. 20c. Rare in the singular.

lasciate ogni speranza, voi ch'entrate [It.] all hope abandon, ye who enter here. 20c. The inscription over the gates of Hell in Dante's *Inferno* iii 9.

latet anguis in herba [Lat.] there is a snake hidden in the grass, there is a concealed drawback in the affair. 16c. Virgil *Eclogues* iii 93. [S]

latifundia *pl.* [Lat.] large estates, *esp.* in Spain and in Spanish South America. 19c. [N]

latticinio [It. 'milk-product'] a method of making ornamental stems for wine-glasses by stretching a glass cylinder in which rods of coloured glass have been embedded. 20c. So called because of the milky appearance of the resulting stem. Cf. MILLEFIORI.

laudator temporis acti, *pl.* **laudatores temporis acti** [Lat.] one who praises former periods at the expense of the present. 18c. Horace *Ars Poetica* 173: *laudator temporis acti Se puero* 'a praiser of time past when he was a boy'. [S]

laus Deo semper [Lat.] praise be to God for ever! 19c. Often used in conjunction with AD MAJOREM DEI GLORIAM; commonly abbreviated to *L.D.S.*

lava [It. 'stream'] the flow of molten or semi-liquid rock from a volcano; *hence*, this molten rock after it has cooled and hardened. 18c. [N,S]

lavabo [Lat. 'I shall wash'] *Eccles.* the washing of the priest's hands after the offertory of the Mass; *hence Arch.* a mediæval wash-basin. 19c. From the words used during the ritual washing, Vulgate *Psalm* xxv (xxvi) 6: *Lavabo inter innocentes manus meas* 'I will wash my hands among the innocent'. [N]

lavoro di commesso [It.] inlay or mosaic of bone, ivory, mother-of-pearl or semi-precious stones. 20c. Cf. INTARSIO; PIETRA COMMESSA; PIETRA DURA.

layette [Fr.] a complete set of clothes, bedding and other requisites for a new-born child. 19c. [N]

lazaretto [It. *lazzaretto*] (1) a building for the reception of persons detained in quarantine; (2) a store-compartment in the fore part of a ship. 17c. [N,S]

lazzarone, *pl.* **lazzaroni** [It.] a beggar or casual worker in Naples. 18c. [N,S(*)]

lb.=LIBRA, LIBRÆ, pound(s) weight.

L.D.S.=LAUS DEO SEMPER, praise be to God for ever!

Lebensmut [Ger.] zest for life, indomitable spirit, pluck, 20c.

Lebensphilosophie [Ger.] philosophy of life. 20c.

Lebensraum [Ger.] room for living, space for an expanding population. 20c. A slogan of the Nationalist Socialist party in Germany.

Leberwurst [Ger.] liver-sausage. 20c.

Lederhosen *pl.* [Ger.] short trousers of soft leather, *usu.* with leather braces, as worn in Germany, Austria and Switzerland. 20c.

legato [It. 'tied'] *Mus.* smoothly, with no break between successive notes. 19c. [N,S]

legatus a latere, *pl.* **legati a latere** [Lat. 'a legate from the side (of the Pope)'] *Eccles.* a Cardinal legate having plenipotentiary powers. 16c. Cf. A LATERE. [S]

légèreté [Fr.] frivolity, irresponsibility. 18c. [S]

Légion d'Honneur [Fr.] an order founded by Napoleon in 1802, membership of which is conferred as a reward for civil or military distinction. 20c. Cf. CORDON ROUGE.

Légion Étrangère [Fr.] the French Foreign Legion, a corps of foreign volunteers serving in the French colonies. 20c.

légionnaire [Fr.] a member of a legion, *esp.* of the French Foreign Legion, or of one of the associations of ex-service men so designated. 20c. [N*]

lei [Haw.] a thickly-woven garland of flowers, the gift of which is a token of esteem in Hawaii. 20c.

Leitmotiv [Ger.] (1) *Mus.* a musical theme associated throughout an opera with a particular person or situation; *hence* (2) a recurrent or characteristic theme in any work of art. 19c. The term was introduced by Wagner; in English it is often mis-spelt *Leitmotif* by association with MOTIF. [N]

lemma, *pl.* **lemmata** [Gk. λῆμμα] the heading or title of a literary work; the head-word of an entry in a glossary or dictionary. 17c. [N,S]

leprechaun [Ir. *leipreachán*] a diminutive supernatural creature who makes himself useful to those who display good will towards him. 19c. The word is an alteration of Old Irish *lugchorpán* 'small body'; it had some currency in English in 17c. in the form *lubrican.* [N,S]

léproserie [Fr.] a settlement for the care of lepers. 20c. The anglicized form *leprosery* has been in use since 19c.

les . . . [Fr.] 'the . . .', often prefixed to the name of a group of entertainers, as if to suggest a Continental daring in their performance. 20c.

lèse-majesté [Fr.] an offence against the majesty of a sovereign or nation, high treason; *hence,* an attack on any person who assumes quasi-regal dignity. 16c. The French phrase is from Lat. *læsa majestas* 'injured majesty', used by the 4th-century historian Ammianus. [N,S]

l'état, c'est moi [Fr.] I am the State, all power is in my hands. 20c. Used by Louis XIV to the Parlement de Paris, 13th April 1655.

lettre de cachet, *pl.* **lettres de cachet** [Fr.] a sealed letter from the King of France ordering the governor of the Bastille to imprison the person named; *hence,* any arbitary warrant for arrest. 18c. [S]

lettre de marque, *pl.* **lettres de marque** [Fr.] a royal warrant authorizing a subject to carry out reprisals on the subjects of a hostile state, a licence authorizing piracy. 20c. In use in anglicized forms since 15c. The practice was officially abolished by the Congress of Paris in 1856. Cf. MARQUE. [N]

lettriste [Fr.] *Art* (an art form) in which alphabetic symbols are used for decorative purposes, or in which sounds are arranged without reference to sense. 20c.

levade [Fr.] *Equ.* a DRESSAGE movement in which the horse rises with its forefeet in the air and remains in this position for a few seconds without moving. 20c.

levée [Fr. *lever*] a reception held during the King's morning toilet; *hence*, a reception held by a King or his representative at which only men are present. 17c. Court usage does not permit a French pronunciation of this word, which is stressed on the first syllable. Cf. COUCHÉE. [N,S]

levée en masse [Fr.] general mobilization, the mobilization of all persons capable of bearing arms. 19c. [S]

lever de rideau [Fr.] a 'curtain-raiser', a short play performed before the main theatrical performance of the evening. 19c. [S]

lex domicilii [Lat.] *Law* the law in force in the place of domicile, *esp.* in cases concerning marriage, divorce, and annulment. 20c.

lex fori [Lat.] *Law* the law of the court in which proceedings are being conducted. 20c.

lex loci celebrationis [Lat.] *Law* the law in force in the place of celebration (of a marriage). 20c. Cf. LOCUS CELEBRATIONIS.

lex non scripta [Lat.] *Law* unwritten law, the customary law of a county or district as distinct from statute law. 19c. [S]

lex talionis [Lat.] the law of retaliation, 'an eye for an eye and a tooth for a tooth'. 16c. [S]

l'homme même [Fr. 'the man himself'] the personality of a writer as reflected in his style. 20c. Buffon *Discours sur le Style* (1753): *le style est l'homme même*, often misquoted as (LE) STYLE, C'EST L'HOMME.

liaison [Fr.] (1) an illicit intimacy between a man and a woman; (2) *Ling.* the pronunciation of a final consonant (which would otherwise be silent) when the following word begins with a vowel or mute *h;* (3) *Mil.* exchange of information between two units, (an officer) deputed to convey and receive information. 19c. In the third sense a verb 'to liaise' has been formed. [N,S]

liane/liana [Fr. *liane*] one of a group of climbing and twining plants common in tropical jungles. 18c. The form *liana*, not in use in any foreign language, seems to be due to the mistaken belief that the word is of Latin or Spanish origin. [N,S]

libertin [Fr.] a free-thinker, one who holds unorthodox views on religious questions. 20c. The French form has been recently revived as a substitute for the anglicized *libertine*, now limited to the meaning 'rake, profligate'.

libido [Lat.] *Psych.* the energy of the instinctive desires, *esp.* those connected with sexual activities. 20c. First used by Jung, and adopted by Freud. [N*]

libra, *pl.* **libræ** [Lat.] a pound weight; a pound sterling (*orig.* a pound weight of silver). 14c. Commonly abbreviated in the first sense to *lb.* and in the second to £ or *L.* (in the combination *L.S.D., L.s.d.*) [N,S]

libretto, *pl.* **libretti** [It.] *Mus.* the 'book of words' of an opera, the text to which a musical composition is set. 18c. [N,S]

Liebeserklärung [Ger.] a declaration of love. 20c.

Lied, *pl.* **Lieder** [Ger.] *Mus.* a (German) song. 19c. Cf. VOLKSLIED; WIEGENLIED. [S]

Lieferung, *pl.* **Lieferungen** [Ger. 'delivery'] a single number of a volume issued in parts. 20c. Cf. FASCICULUS; HEFT; LIVRAISON.

lignum vitæ [Lat. 'wood of life'] the exceptionally hard wood of the West Indian tree *Guaiacum officinale*; a resin derived from this tree. 16c. [N,S]

limæ labor [Lat. 'work of the file'] careful correction and revision (of a literary work). 18c. Horace *Ars Poetica* 291. [S]

limbo [Lat. (*e*) *limbo* '(out of) the edge (of hell)'] *Rel.* a region on the borders of Hell, the abode of those who have not received grace but have not merited damnation; *hence*, any region to which useless or neglected persons or things are consigned. 14c. [N,S]

limes, *pl.* **limites** [Lat.] *Hist.* a Roman frontier, consisting of a string of forts normally joined by a military road. 20c.

linctus [Lat.] *Med.* a thick syrupy medicine prescribed to relieve irritation of the throat. 17c. [N,S]

lingerie [Fr.] women's underwear, now *esp.* underwear of fine quality or ornamental design. 19c. [N(*)]

lingua franca [It. 'Frankish tongue'] a mixed language, resembling a much simplified Italian, used in the Levant; *hence*, any language used for communication between people of different nationalities. 17c. [N,S]

liqueur [Fr.] a beverage made of ardent spirits, sugar and flavouring (*usu.* a herbal flavouring). 18c. Current usage discountenances a fully French pronunciation. [N,S]

lira organizzata [It.] *Mus.* a hurdy-gurdy, a stringed instrument in which the sound is evoked by the friction of a rosined wheel. 20c.

lisse [Fr.] CRÊPE LISSE, a smooth gauze-like silk fabric, sometimes used for repairing torn pages in valuable books. 19c. [N]

lit-bateau [Fr.] a bed with head and foot curved up so as to resemble the prow and stern of a boat. 20c.

lit de justice [Fr. 'bed of justice'] *Hist.* the king's throne in the French parliament; *hence*, a royal state visit to parliament for the purpose of registering an edict. 18c. [S]

lite pendente [Lat.] *Law* while the case is pending. 17c. [S]

literati *pl.* [It.] men of letters, men of learning, the learned classes. 17c.

The singular *literato* is rare; the alternative singular *literatus*, as if the plural represented Lat. *lit(t)erati*, seems to be obsolete. [N,S]

literatim=LITTERATIM, literally.

litotes [Gk. λιτότης 'meagre'] *Ling.* a figure of speech by which an affirmative is expressed by the negative of the contrary. 17c. The figure is one form of MEIOSIS, a more general kind of understatement. [N,S]

litteræ humaniores *pl.* [Lat.] the humanities, the study of the Greek and Roman classics, *esp.* as the subject of an Honours Course in the University of Oxford. 18c. [S]

littera scripta manet [Lat.] the written word remains, it is safer to put it in writing. 16c. The first words of a proverbial punning hexameter: *littera scripta manet, sed manant lubrica verba* 'the written letter remains, but slippery words flow away'. [S]

littérateur, *f.* **littératrice** [Fr.] a (professional) man of letters, *esp.* a writer of critical works. 19c. [N,S]

litteratim/literatim [Lat.] letter by letter, literally. 17c. The more Classically correct spelling *litteratim* seems recently to have prevailed over the earlier *literatim.* [N,S]

littoral [Fr.] a coastal region, a district bordered by the sea. 19c. [N]

livraison [Fr. 'delivery'] a single number of a volume published in parts. 19c. Cf. FASCICULUS; HEFT; LIEFERUNG. [N,S]

livre de chevet [Fr.] a bedside book, a favourite book which one wishes to have always within easy reach. 20c.

locale [Fr. *local*] the place or locality where some event happens or is envisaged as happening. 18c. The mis-spelling *locale* has been current since the early 19c., and is securely established. Cf. MISE EN SCÈNE; MORALE. [N,S]

locataire [Fr.] a tenant or lodger, one who rents a house or room. 19c. [S]

loc. cit.=LOCO CITATO, in the passage quoted.

loch [Gael.] a lake; a partially landlocked arm of the sea. 14c. In Ireland the same word is written in the anglicized form *lough.* [N,S]

loc(o) cit(ato) [Lat.] in the passage quoted. 19c. Used to avoid the repetition of a reference. Cf. IBID(EM); OP(ERE) CIT(ATO). [S]

loco parentis, *see* (IN) LOCO PARENTIS, in the place of a parent.

locum tenens [Lat.] a deputy, one who holds office in place of another, or temporarily performs the professional duties of another. 17c. Now used *esp.* of a doctor who provides medical services during the absence of the regular practitioner; in this special sense *usu.* abbreviated to *locum.* [N,S]

locus, *pl.* **loci** [Lat.] (1) the place in which a thing is or an event happens; (2) *Math.* the path followed by a point the position of which is defined by some equation or fixed relationship. 18c. [N,S]

locus celebrationis [Lat.] *Law* the place of celebration (of a marriage). 20c. Cf. LEX LOCI CELEBRATIONIS.

locus classicus, *pl.* **loci classici** [Lat.] a standard passage (*usu.* in an ancient author) which is specially important for the understanding of some word or subject. 19c. [N,S]

locus communis, *pl.* **loci communes** [Lat.] a commonplace, a passage always quoted in some particular context. 16c. [N]

locus desperatus, *pl.* **loci desperati** [Lat.] a passage in a text transmitted by manuscript whose meaning is so corrupt as to be almost beyond conjecture. 20c.

locus pœnitentiæ, *pl.* **loci pœnitentiæ** [Lat.] (1) a place of repentance; (2) *Law* an opportunity of withdrawing from an engagement, provided some definitive step has not been taken. 18c. Vulgate *Hebrews* xii 17: *non enim invenit pœnitentiæ locum, quamquam cum lacrymis inquisisset eam* 'for he found no place of repentance, though he sought it carefully with tears.' [N,S]

locus standi [Lat.] (1) a recognized position (in connection with some activity); (2) *Law* the right of appearing in court. 19c.

Loden [Ger.] a thick woollen cloth used for making cloaks. 20c.

l'œil du maître [Fr.] the eye of the master, the vision of the artist. 20c.

loess [Ger. *Löss*] *Geog.* a loamy deposit of silt or dust, often of a yellowish colour, believed to have been transported by the wind. 19c. [N]

loge [Fr.] a box in a theatre or at the opera; a theatrical dressing-room. 18c. [N,S]

loggia, *pl.* **loggie** [It.] a gallery or arcade, open to the air on one side at least. 18c. [N,S]

logos [Gk. *λόγος*] *Rel.* the Word, the divine Mind or Reason envisaged by Greek philosophers; the Second Person of the Blessed Trinity. 16c. The Christian use of the term is taken from the first words of the Gospel of St John. [N,S]

Lokal [Ger.] a CAFÉ or tavern, *esp.* one used by its patrons as a clubhouse. 20c. Compare the similar use of 'the local' in English. Cf. NACHTLOKAL.

longueur [Fr.] a tedious passage in a work of literature, speech, public entertainment, etc. 19c. First introduced by Byron (*Don Juan* III xcvii), who remarks that 'We've not so good a word, but have the thing'. Cf. TEMPS MORTS. [N,S]

loquat [Chin. *luh kwat* 'rush orange'] (the fruit of) the Japanese medlar, *Eriobotrya japonica*. 19c. [N,S]

loquitur [Lat.] . . . says, . . . speaks; always preceded by a name. 20c. The use of the term often implies the assumption by the speaker of an authority to which he is not entitled.

lorgnette/lorgnon [Fr.] (1) a pair of eyeglasses equipped with a long handle by means of which they may be held to the eyes; (2) an opera-glass. 19c. In current English usage *lorgnette* seems to be reserved for the first meaning, *lorgnon* for the second; but the current French distinction is nearly the opposite. In French *lorgnon* is equivalent to FACE-À-MAIN or PINCE-NEZ, and *lorgnette* means 'field-glass, opera-glass'. [N,S]

los von Rom [Ger.] 'away from Rome', the slogan of the early 20c. Austrian Nationalist party which resented the anti-German attitude of the clergy and worked for evangelical Christianity and union with Germany; *hence*, anti-Roman bias in religion, a break-away from Rome. 20c.

lotus/lotos [Lat. < Gk. λωτός] (1) *Myth.* a plant the fruit of which induces in the eater a state of dreamy forgetfulness; (2) the Egyptian water-lily, *esp.* as depicted in decorative art. 16c. [N,S]

louange perfide [Fr. 'treacherous praise'] praise designed to lead to unfortunate consequences for the person praised. 20c.

louche [Fr.] crooked, not straightforward, disingenuous. 19c. [N]

L.S.D./L.s.d./£.s.d.=LIBRÆ, SOLIDI, DENARII, pounds, shillings, and pence.

luce di sotto [It.] *Art* light coming from below, *esp.* in painting as a device for producing a dramatic effect. 20c.

lucri causa [Lat.] for pecuniary profit, in order to make money. 20c.

lucus a non (lucendo) [Lat.] 'a grove, so called because it is not light'; an absurd etymology; anything the qualities of which are the opposite of what its name suggests. 18c. Put forward as a serious etymology by Quintilian *De Institutione Oratoria* i 16. [S]

luge [Swiss] a sledge or sleigh. 20c. [N*]

lumachella [It. 'little snail'] a dark-coloured marble containing iridescent fossil shells. 18c. [N]

lumpen [Ger. *lumpen* 'rag, tattered clothing'] physically and mentally poverty-stricken. 20c.

Lumpenproletariat [Ger.] the ragged populace, the common people unredeemed by wealth or culture. 20c. The term was coined by Karl Marx.

lunette [Fr.] *Arch.* an arched aperture or window in a vaulted roof; a work of art fitted to a semicircular space in a ceiling or dome. 17c. [N,S]

lupanar [Lat.] a brothel. 19c. [N]

lupus in fabula [Lat.] 'the wolf in the story', a person who appears just as he is being spoken of. 16c. Cicero *Ad Atticum* XIII xxxiii 4. [S]

lusisti satis [Lat.] you have enjoyed yourself long enough, it is time for you to go. 20c. Horace *Epistles* II ii 214: *Lusisti satis, edisti satis atque bibisti: Tempus abire tibi est* 'you have played enough, you have eaten and drunk enough: it is time for you to go'.

lustrum, *pl.* **lustra** [Lat.] a period of five years. 16c. So called because of the ancient Roman ceremony of 'lustration' or purification, performed once every five years. Cf. QUINQUENNIUM. [N,S(*)]

lusus naturæ [Lat.] a 'sport', a freak of nature. 17c. The phrase, like its equivalent *sport*, implies that Nature has been playing a joke. [N,S]

luxe [Fr.] luxury, sumptuous elegance. 19c. Cf. DE LUXE; GRAND LUXE. [N]

lycée [Fr.] a (French) secondary school maintained by the state. 19c. The French equivalent of LYCEUM. [N,S]

lyceum [Lat. *Lyceum* < Gk. *Λύκειον*] an institute of higher education, *esp.* one situated on the continent of Europe. 18c. From the name of the garden in Athens, adjacent to the temple of Apollo, in which Aristotle taught his pupils. [N,S]

M

macabre [Fr.] gruesome, reminiscent of the DANSE MACABRE or Dance of Death. 19c. Fr. *macabre* is an error for earlier *macabré*, of unknown origin. [N,S]

macaroni *pl.* [Obs. It. *maccaroni*] *Cul.* a dried wheaten paste in the form of long tubes, used for a variety of savoury and sweet dishes. 16c. The current Italian form is *maccheroni*, with singular *maccherone*. Despite the plural form the word is normally construed in English as singular. Cf. CANNELLONI; PASTA; SPAGHETTI; VERMICELLI. [N,S]

macchia [It. 'stain'] *Art* a rough sketch giving a general impression of a scene; the underpainting of a finished painting. 20c.

macédoine [Fr. 'Macedonia'] (1) *Cul.* a dish consisting of a mixture of various kinds of vegetables or fruits; *hence* (2) a medley of unrelated things. 19c. [N*,S]

machair [Gael.] a strip of coastal plain, a sandy tract almost at sea-level. 20c. The Gaelic plural *machraichean* seems not to be in use in English.

machete [Sp.] a broad, heavy knife or cutlass. 19c. Current much earlier in such anglicized forms as *matchet*. [N,S]

macho [Sp.] (one who is) aggressively masculine, virile, 'tough'. 20c.

machree = MOCHREE, my darling.

Machtpolitik [Ger.] power politics, negotiations under the implied threat of violent action. 20c.

Machtübernahme [Ger.] a taking-over of power (*usu.* political power) by violent means. 20c. Used *esp.* of the coming to power of the German National Socialist party in 1933. Cf. COUP D'ÉTAT; PUTSCH.

macramé [Turk. *makrama* 'napkin' < Arab. *miqramah*] (the art of making) a fringe of knotted thread. 19c. [N,S]

macron [Gk. *μάκρον*] *Ling.* a short horizontal line ¯ placed over a vowel to indicate that it is long. 19c. [N,S]

macushla, *see* ACUSHLA, darling.

madame [Fr.] the proprietress of a brothel. 20c. In this sense the word is always preceded by the definite article; as a title of respect the word has been current since 13c. often anglicized to *madam*, *ma'am*.

madeleine [Fr.] *Cul.* a kind of small rich cake. 19c. [N*]

mademoiselle [Fr.] a French governess in an English family; the native

French mistress in a girls' school. 19c. The word has been current as a title of respect since 17c. Cf. FRÄULEIN. [N,S]

madonna [It. < *ma donna* 'my lady'] *Eccles.* a picture or statue of the Virgin Mary. 17c. [N,S]

maelstrom [Obs. Du.] a whirlpool, *esp.* a whirlpool in the Arctic Ocean west of Norway, supposed to engulf all shipping approaching it; *hence*, any influence drawing someone or something irresistibly to destruction. 17c. The current Dutch spelling is *maalstroom;* the Danish *malstrøm* and Swedish *malström* are probably from the Dutch. [N,S]

maestà [It. 'majesty'] *Art* a representation of the Virgin and Child seated on a throne surrounded by censing angels. 20c.

maestoso [It.] *Mus.* majestically. 18c. [N,S]

maestrale [It.] a strong cold north-west wind. 18c. The exact equivalent of the French MISTRAL. Cf. BISE; TRAMONTANA. [S]

maestro, *pl.* **maestri** [It.] one who has achieved mastery of some art, *esp.* that of music, either in composition or performance; *hence facet.* a form of address to a band-leader. 18c. Cf. MAÎTRE. [N,S(*)]

maestro di cappella [It.] *Mus.* the director of a church choir, *usu.* with its accompanying orchestra. The incorrect spelling *capella,* formerly common, seems now to be rare. Cf. KAPELLMEISTER. [S]

Magi, *see* MAGUS, wise man, astrologer.

magisterium [Lat.] *Eccles.* the authority of the Church in matters of doctrine; the authoritative teaching of the Church. 19c. [N]

magistras [Lat.] the collective body of those in authority. 20c.

Magna Charta [Lat.] (1) *Hist.* the Great Charter of liberties signed by King John in 1215; *hence* (2) any basic principle or document, *esp.* one conferring or implying liberty. 16c. The spelling *Magna Carta* is also common. [N,S(*)]

magna est veritas et prævalebit [Lat.] truth is great and shall prevail. 17c. Vulgate *I Esdras* iv 41: *magna est veritas et prævalet* 'truth is great and mighty above all things'. [S(*)]

magnanimitas [Lat.] nobility of intention, courage to do the right thing, fortitude. 20c. The Latin term is used to avoid confusion with English *magnanimity* 'generosity of feeling'.

Magnificat [Lat.] the hymn of the Virgin Mary 'my soul doth magnify the Lord', *esp.* when set to music; *hence*, any song of praise or exultation. 13c. Vulgate *St Luke* i 46: *magnificat anima mea Dominum.* [N,S(*)]

magnifico [It.] a nobleman of Venice; *hence*, any exalted personage. 16c. [N,S]

magno intervallo [Lat.] (divided) by a great interval (of space), (followed) after a great interval (of time). 19c. [S]

magnum [Lat.] a bottle containing two quarts of wine or spirits. 18c. [N,S]

magnum opus [Lat.] a great or important literary work; the most important production of an author. 18c. Often ironic in connotation. Formerly the phrase *opus magnum* was more common, but this seems now to be obsolete. [N,S]

Magus, *pl.* **Magi** [Lat. < Pers.] a member of the ancient Persian priesthood; *hence,* one skilled in astrology and magic; a wise man. 16c. Most commonly with reference to the 'wise men from the East' who brought offerings to the infant Christ. [N,S(*)]

maharajah [Hind. *mahā rājā* 'great king'] *A.-I.* an Indian prince. 17c. Cf. RAJAH. [N,S]

maharanee [Hind. *mahā rānī*] *A.-I.* the wife of a MAHARAJAH. 19c. *Occ.* written *maharani,* in closer conformity with the Hindustani. Cf. RANEE. [N]

mahatma [Sansk. *mahātman* < *mahā ātman* 'great soul'] an adept in esoteric Buddhism, supposed to possess supernatural powers. 19c. [N,S]

mahout [Hind. *mahāwat*] *A.-I.* an elephant-driver. 17c. [N,S]

maidan [Pers. *maidān*] *A.-I.* an open space near a town, used for sports and exercise. 17c. [N,S]

maillot jaune [Fr.] a yellow jersey worn each day by the current over-all leader in the *Tour de France,* the annual bicycle race held over a long and arduous circuit round France. 20c. The competitor who achieved the fastest time over the previous day's stage wears a *maillot vert,* a green jersey.

mairie [Fr.] the administrative office of a French municipality. 20c.

maison [Fr.] *Cul.* (a dish, etc.) which is a speciality of the restaurant in which it is served. 20c. Always placed after the name of the dish. Cf. SPÉCIALITÉ DE LA MAISON.

maison close [Fr.] a brothel. 20c.

maison de passe [Fr.] a disorderly house, a hotel or lodging-house which is in effect a brothel. 20c. Cf. STUNDENHOTEL.

maison de rendezvous [Fr.] a hotel or lodging-house offering accommodation to men and their mistresses. 20c. Cf. CABINET PARTICULIER.

maison de santé [Fr.] a nursing-home, a private hospital. 19c. [S]

maison de société [Fr.] a brothel. 20c.

maisonnette [Fr.] a dwelling-place forming only part of a building, but occupying more than one floor of it. 20c. Often miswritten *maisonette.* [N*]

maison tolérée [Fr.] a brothel licensed and inspected by the State. 20c. The normal French expression is *maison de tolérance,* but *maison tolérée* seems well established in English. Cf. QUARTIER TOLÉRÉ.

maître [Fr.] (a form of address to) one who has achieved mastery of some art or scholarly study; (a form of address or reference to) a French lawyer. 20c. Cf. MAESTRO.

maître de ballet, *f.* **maîtresse de ballet** [Fr.] *Ballet* the person responsible for the training of a company of dancers and for the conducting of rehearsals. 20c.

maître d'hôtel [Fr.] the manager of a hotel; a head-waiter. 19c. Formerly in use (from 16c.) in the sense 'steward, major-domo'. [N(*),S(*)]

maîtresse de ballet, *see* MAÎTRE DE BALLET, organizer of a company of dancers.

maîtresse en titre [Fr.] an acknowledged mistress, an 'official' mistress, *usu.* of a person of consequence. 20c. The 'official' mistress is thus distinguished from transitory concubines. Cf. AMANT ATTITRÉ.

maîtresse femme [Fr.] a competent, efficient woman; a masterful woman; a woman of the world. 20c.

majo, *f.* **maja** [Sp.] a gaily-dressed Spaniard of the lower classes. 19c. [N,S]

majolica [It. *maiolica*] a fine Italian pottery glazed with a tin enamel and highly decorated. 16c. Now often written *maiolica* to conform with Italian usage; but the traditional pronunciation requires the spelling *majolica.* The word may be derived from the name of the island of Majorca, where the finest pottery is said to have been made. Cf. FAÏENCE. [N,S]

makimono [Jap. 'roll-thing'] a Japanese painted scroll, so arranged as to unroll horizontally and reveal a series of pictures. 20c. Cf. KAKEMONO.

malade imaginaire [Fr.] a hypochondriac, one who imagines himself to be an invalid. 19c. From the title of Molière's last comedy (1673). [S]

maladresse [Fr.] clumsiness, awkwardness, lack of tact. 19c. [N,S]

mala fide [Lat.] *Law* in bad faith, with intent to deceive, fraudulently. 17c. Cf. BONA FIDE. [N,S]

mala fides [Lat.] *Law* bad faith, intent to deceive. 17c. Cf. BONA FIDES. [N,S]

malaise [Fr.] an ill-defined and inexplicable feeling of discomfort, either physical or mental. 18c. [N,S]

mal à propos [Fr.] inopportunely, unseasonably, inappropriately; inopportune, unseasonable, inappropriate. 17c. Cf. À PROPOS. [N,S]

mal d'amour [Fr.] the sickness of love, the pangs of love. 20c.

mal de mer [Fr.] sea-sickness. 18c. Now generally *facet.* [N,S]

mal du pays [Fr.] home-sickness. 19c. The earlier *maladie du pays* (18c.) seems now to be obsolete. [S]

mal du siècle [Fr.] distress at the condition of the world, pessimistic depression, weariness of life. 20c. Used by Sainte-Beuve in 1833 of the early Romantic poets. Also in the form *mal de siècle.* Cf. TÆDIUM VITÆ; WELTSCHMERZ.

maleficium [Lat.] the doing of evil by means of magic; sorcery; a malicious enchantment. 20c.

malentendu [Fr. < *mal entendu* 'misunderstood'] a misunderstanding, a misapprehension. 18c. [N,S]

malerisch [Ger. 'picturesque'] (a painter, a picture) expressing form by colour and tone, not by contour. 20c. The term was introduced by Heinrich Wölfflin in his *Kunstgeschichtliche Grundbegriffe* (1915).

malgré lui [Fr.] in spite of himself, against his will. 19c. [S]

malgré moi [Fr.] in spite of myself, against my own will. 20c.

malgré tout [Fr.] in spite of everything, all things considered. 20c.

mal mariée [Fr.] an unhappily married woman. 20c.

mal soigné, *f.* **mal soignée** [Fr.] unkempt, shabby, uncared for. 20c. Cf. SOIGNÉ.

mal vu [Fr.] viewed with disapproval, resented. 20c.

mana [Maori] supernatural or magical power or influence; *hence*, the spell-binding power of personality. 19c. The Maori word was taken over as an anthropological term, and has thence acquired a popular meaning. [N*]

Managerkrankheit [Ger.] physical and mental sickness and disturbance resulting from excessive executive responsibility. 20c. Cf. KRANKHEIT.

mañana [Sp.] tomorrow, *esp.* as a symbol of the tendency to procrastination supposed to be characteristic of the Mediterranean peoples. 20c.

mandamus [Lat. 'we command'] *Law* a writ issued by a superior authority, *esp.* one issued by the Court of Queen's Bench directing an inferior court or body to perform some specified act. 16c. [N,S]

mandorla [It. 'almond'] *Art* an almond-shaped panel or opening; an almond-shaped halo. 19c. [N,S]

manège [Fr.] (1) *Equ.* a riding-school; the art of training a horse; the performance of a trained horse. 17c. (2) *Ballet* an imaginary circle bounding the stage, the limit of the area in which the dancers perform; *hence*, a dance round the extreme limits of the stage. 20c. [N,S]

manes *pl.* [Lat.] the deified souls of departed ancestors; the shades of the dead, *esp.* considered as demanding vengeance. 14c. In the second sense the word is used also as a singular. [N,S]

maniéré, *f.* **maniérée** [Fr.] affected, characterized by artificial mannerisms. 18c. [S]

manierista, *pl.* **manieristi** [It.[a person addicted to artificial mannerisms and affectations. 20c. The word belongs rather with French MANIÉRÉ than with Italian MANIEROSO.

manieroso [It.] *Art* displaying the unmistakable touch of a master hand. 20c. Contrasted with DILIGENTE; wholly different in meaning from MANIÉRÉ.

manifesto [It.] a public declaration of policy. 17c. Cf. PRONUNCIAMENTO. [N,S]

mannequin [Fr. < Du. *manneken* 'little man'] (1) an artist's lay-figure; (2) a woman employed to display garments in a dressmaker's showroom. 19c. In the first sense there are earlier forms (from 17c.) derived directly from Du. *manneken.* [N(*),S]

manque [Fr.] *Roulette* any one of the numbers from 1 to 18 inclusive. 20c. Cf. PASSE.

manqué, *f.* **manquée** [Fr.] (1) unsuccessful, unsatisfactory, abortive; (2) (a person) who might have achieved great success in a profession or vocation other than the one he has chosen. 19c. In the second sense the word follows the name of the profession: 'an actor *manqué*', etc. Cf. RATÉ; VIE MANQUÉE. [S]

manque de goût [Fr.] absence of good taste. 20c.

mansuetæ naturæ [Lat.] (animals) of docile disposition; domesticated. 20c. Cf. FERÆ NATURÆ.

mantilla [Sp.] a head-scarf or veil, *usu.* of black lace. 18c. [N,S]

mantra [Sansk.] a sacred text, *usu.* from the Vedas, used as a prayer or incantation. 19c. [N]

manzanilla [Sp. 'camomile'] a dry, light, rather bitter sherry. 19c. [N,S]

maquereau [Fr. 'mackerel'] a pimp, a procurer. 20c.

maquette [Fr.] (1) *Art* a small model (of a piece of sculpture), a rough sketch (of a painting); (2) a full-size, non-working model (of a piece of machinery, etc.) 20c. In the second sense the French word is now often curiously anglicized as *mock-up*. Cf. BOZZETTO; MODELLO.

maquillage [Fr.] make-up, cosmetics; the art of make-up. 20c.

maquillé, *f.* **maquillée** [Fr.] wearing cosmetics, (heavily) made up. 20c.

maquis [Fr.] scrub-land, heath covered with undergrowth (in Corsica); *hence*, the organization of bandits which at one time infested this scrub-land; *hence*, the GUERRILLA organization in France during the Second World War, the RÉSISTANCE. 20c. The last sense is now much the most common.

maquisard, *f.* **maquisarde** [Fr.] a member of the MAQUIS, a GUERRILLA fighter in France during the Second World War. 20c.

marabout [Fr. < Arab. *murābit*] (1) a Moslem hermit or monk. 17c. (2) a tuft or plume of downy feathers, used to decorate a woman's dress or head-dress. 19c. These downy feathers are taken from beneath the wings and tail of a stork, said by the Arabs to be a 'holy' bird. In the second sense the spelling *marabou* is common in English though rare in French. [N(*),S]

marc [Fr.] the refuse which remains after the pressing of grapes. 17c. *Marc* is used for the manufacture of inferior wine and brandy. The *c* is not pronounced, even before a vowel.

Märchen, *pl.* **Märchen** [Ger.] a folk-tale, a fairy-story. 19c. [S]

marchesa [It.] a marchioness. 18c. [N,S]

Mardi Gras [Fr. 'fat Tuesday'] Shrove Tuesday, the last day of Carnival before Lent. 19c. [N*,S]

mare clausum [Lat.] a sea closed to international navigation by the unilateral action of a riparian nation. 19c. [S]

mare nostrum [Lat.] 'our sea', the Mediterranean, possession of which was claimed by Italy under the Fascist RÉGIME. 20c.

marginalia *pl.* [Lat.] marginal notes, *esp.* manuscript notes in a printed book or ancient manuscript. 19c. The singular *marginale* is not in use. [N,S]

mariage blanc [Fr.] an unconsummated marriage. 20c.

mariage de convenance [Fr.] a marriage of convenience, an arranged marriage, a marriage contracted with a view to material benefits, *usu.* financial. 19c. Contrasted with MARIAGE D'INCLINATION. [S]

mariage d'inclination [Fr.] a marriage for love, a marriage contracted without consideration for anything but passion or affection. 20c. Contrasted with MARIAGE DE CONVENANCE.

mari complaisant [Fr.] a complaisant husband, a husband who condones his wife's infidelities. 20c.

marijuana/marihuana [Sp.] a preparation of the flowers of a variety of hemp (*Cannabis sativa*), smoked as an intoxicant. 20c. The word is of native Mexican origin, but appears to have been influenced in form by the Spanish girls' names *Maria*, *Juana*.

marionnette [Fr.] a puppet manipulated by strings. 17c. The erroneous spelling *marionette* is common. [N,S]

marivaudage [Fr.] refinement of style and subtle analysis of sentiment, practised in an excessive degree. 18c. From the name of Pierre Carlet de Chamblain de Marivaux (1688–1763), whose prose comedies and romances were characterized by these features. [S]

marmite [Fr.] *Cul.* an earthenware stew-pot. 20c. [N*]

marocain [Fr. 'Moroccan'] a 'crinkly' fabric woven from specially twisted yarn. 20c. *Marocain* can be of cotton, silk, or wool, and the yarn used is normally specified—'silk *marocain*', etc. [N*]

marque [Fr.] (1) reprisal, *esp.* in the phrase 'letter of *marque*', a royal warrant authorizing a subject to carry out reprisals on the subjects of a hostile state. 15c. Cf. LETTRE DE MARQUE. (2) a make, *esp.* a highly-prized make (of motor-car, etc.) 20c. Cf. GRANDE MARQUE. [N]

marquise [Fr.] (1) a marchioness; (2) *Arch.* a glass roof projecting from the FAÇADE of a building, *usu.* over a flight of steps; (3) a style of cutting precious stones into a leaf-shape formed by the intersection of two arcs; a cluster of small jewels having the same outline. 19c. Cf. NAVETTE. [N(*),S]

marquisette [Fr.] a diaphanous open-mesh fabric resembling gauze. 20c. [N*]

marron glacé, *pl.* **marrons glacés** [Fr.] a kind of sweetmeat made of crystallized chestnut. 20c.

martellato [It. 'hammered'] *Mus.* (a note on a bowed instrument) played with a sharp decisive attack. 20c.

mascara [Sp.] a brown or black cosmetic for the eyelashes, applied with a small brush. 20c. The stress in Spanish is on the first syllable, in English on the second. The Spanish word, though it also has the meaning 'mask', is apparently not related to the English *mask*, but to the Romance verb represented by French *mâchurer* 'to blacken (the face)'.

mascherone [It.] *Arch., Art* a painted or carved mask, a grotesque human face, a gargoyle. 20c.

Maschinenstil [Ger.] *Art* industrial design suitable for manufacture by mass-production techniques. 20c.

massage [Fr.] *Med.* the pressing, rubbing and kneading of the human body for therapeutic purposes. 19c. [N,S]

massé [Fr.] *Billiards* (a stroke) made with the cue held vertical. 19c. [N]

masseur, *f.* **masseuse** [Fr.] a person who practises MASSAGE. 19c. [N,S]

massif [Fr.] a compact mountain range, a mountainous mass breaking up into individual peaks only at the summit; *hence*, a representative but pre-eminent figure. 19c. [N]

mastaba [Arab. *maçṭabah*] *Hist.* an ancient Egyptian tomb, rectangular in plan with a flat top and sloping sides. 19c. [N]

matador [Sp.] the bull-fighter whose task it is to kill the bull. 17c. [N,S]

maté [Sp. *mate* < Quechua *mati* 'gourd'] the South American shrub *Ilex paraguayensis*; the leaves of this shrub; an infusion or tea made from these leaves. So called because a gourd was *orig.* used for the preparation of the infusion. Cf. YERBA (MATÉ). [N,S(*)]

matelassé [Fr. 'mattressed'] (a silk fabric) with a raised pattern resembling quilting. 19c. [N]

matelot [Fr.] a (French) sailor. 20c. The word is also used in the Royal Navy as the standard colloquial term for 'sailor'.

Mater Dolorosa [Lat.] *Art* a representation of the Virgin Mary sorrowing. 19c. [S]

materfamilias [Lat.] the mother of a family. 19c. The plural *matres familiarum* is rare. Cf. PATERFAMILIAS. [N,S]

materia medica [Lat.] *Med.* the whole range of substances used in medical science and practice; the study of the use of drugs. 17c. [S]

matériel [Fr.] the total stock of material objects required for the conduct of some enterprise, *esp.* the arms, ammunition and commissariat of an army. 19c. Contrasted with PERSONNEL, the total force of persons required for the enterprise. [N,S]

matière [Fr.] *Art* the physical constituents (canvas, paint, etc.) of a picture. 20c.

matinée [Fr. 'morning'] a theatrical or film performance held in the afternoon; a special theatrical or film performance held at an unusual time. 19c. [N,S]

matinée musicale [Fr.] a concert held in the afternoon. 19c. Cf. MUSICALE; SOIRÉE MUSICALE; THÉ MUSICAL. [S]

matrimonio segreto [It.] a secret marriage. 20c.

matrix, *pl.* **matrices** [Lat.] (1) a mineral substance in which an object (*usu.* a precious stone) is found embedded. 17c. (2) the mould in which a piece of type is cast. 17c. A type-matrix is normally made by punching the symbol into copper with a steel punch. (3) *Math.* a rectangular arrangement of mathematical quantities. 19c. [N(*),S]

Matze [Ger. < Heb. *massōth*] the unleavened bread used by Jews at the Passover celebrations. 20c.

maudit [Fr.] (someone) who is beyond redemption, a lost soul; (someone) who is dogged by undeserved misfortune. 20c. Cf. POÈTE MAUDIT.

mausoleum, *pl.* **mausolea** [Lat. < Gk. *μαυσωλεῖον*] a building used as the burial place of a family, a stately sepulchral monument. 17c. Named from the tomb of Mausolos, king of Caria, at Halicarnassus, which was considered one of the seven wonders of the world. [N,S]

mauvais coucheur [Fr.] someone with whom it is very difficult to come to terms, a difficult person, a quarrelsome person. 20c.

mauvaise honte [Fr.] false shame, unreasonable diffidence; painful shyness. 18c. [N,S]

mauvais goût [Fr.] bad taste, lack of good taste. 20c.

mauvais moment [Fr.] an unpleasant or embarrassing moment, a passing embarrassment or discomfort. 20c. Cf. MAUVAIS QUART D'HEURE.

mauvais prêtre [Fr.] a renegade priest. 20c. A renegade priest is required for the proper celebration of a Black Mass.

mauvais quart d'heure [Fr.] an unpleasant quarter of an hour, an embarrassing scene. 19c. Cf. MAUVAIS MOMENT. [S]

mauvais sang [Fr.] bad blood, bad feeling, ill-will. 18c. [S]

mauvais sujet [Fr.] a 'bad lot', an irredeemable scoundrel. 19c. [N,S]

mavourneen [Ir. *mo mhurnín*] my darling. 19c. Irish idiom does not countenance the use of this expression as a form of address; the Irish vocative would be *a mhurnín* 'O darling'. For the spelling with *ma-* for *mo-* cf. MACHREE; MACUSHLA. [N,S]

maxima cum laude [Lat.] with the highest praise, with distinction. 20c. Used to distinguish those candidates who have achieved the greatest success in an examination in which Honours are not awarded. Cf. CUM LAUDE; SUMMA CUM LAUDE.

maxima debetur puero reverentia [Lat.] the greatest respect is due to a child, a child's susceptibilities must not be shocked by grossness or indecency. 19c. Juvenal *Satires* V xiv 47. [S]

mayonnaise [Fr.] *Cul.* a cold sauce made of yolk of egg, oil and vinegar with seasoning; a dish served with such a sauce. 19c. In the latter sense the word is *usu.* preceded by the main ingredient of the dish: 'lobster *mayonnaise*', etc. [N,S]

mazout [Russ. *mazut*] a thick oily substance which remains when crude oil is distilled. 19c. *Mazout* may be used either for lubrication or for fuel. [N*]

mazurka [Pol.] *Mus.* a lively Polish dance resembling a polka but in triple time; a piece of music composed in the rhythm of this dance. 19c. Pol. *mazurka* means 'a woman of Mazovia', the province in which the dance originated. [N,S]

mea culpa [Lat.] through my own fault. 14c. The phrase is from the Confession at the beginning of the Mass; now used to admit responsibility for some blunder. Cf. MEA MAXIMA CULPA; PECCAVI. [S]

mea maxima culpa [Lat.] through my own most grievous fault. 17c. Cf. MEA CULPA. [S]

méchanceté [Fr.] spitefulness, malicious ill-will. 18c. [S]

méchant, *f.* **méchante** [Fr.] spiteful, malicious, ill-natured. 19c. [N,S]

media, *pl.* **mediæ** [Lat. 'middle'] *Ling.* one of the voiced stops *b, d, g*. 19c. Priscian *Institutiones Grammaticæ* I xxvi: the voiced stops are considered as 'intermediate' between the voiceless stops (cf. TENUIS) and the aspirates. [N,S]

media aspirata, *pl.* **mediæ aspiratæ** [Lat.] *Ling.* one of the aspirated voiced stops *bh, dh, gh,* found in Sanskrit and the Dravidian languages, and postulated in the hypothetical Indo-European language. 20c.

medio tutissimus ibis [Lat.] you shall pass most safely in the middle, the moderate course of action is the safest. 17c. Ovid *Metamorphoses* ii 137. [S(*)]

medium, *pl.* **media** [Lat.] (1) *Art* any liquid with which pigments are mixed to render them suitable for painting with; *hence*, any of the types of painting distinguished according to the liquid used in the preparation of the paint; (2) a channel of communication, a system used for the dissemination of information; now *esp.* in the phrase 'mass *media*'. 19c. The word *medium* has other senses in English, but the others are fully anglicized and take the plural *mediums*. [N,S]

medulla oblongata [Lat.] *Med.* the back part of the brain which forms the continuation of the spinal cord. 17c. [N,S]

Meerschaum [Ger. 'sea-foam'] hydrous silicate of magnesium, a soft white clay used for the manufacture of pipes; a pipe made (mainly) of this clay. 18c. The German name is a literal translation of the Pers. *kef-i-daryā*. [N,S]

megalomania [Gk. μεγαλο- + μανία] an illusion of greatness, the mistaken belief that one is a most important person; a mania for surrounding oneself with magnificent objects and objects of large size. 19c. Cf. FOLIE DE GRANDEUR. [N]

megaron, *pl.* **megara** [Gk. μέγαρον] *Hist.* the oldest form of Greek house, consisting of a single rectangular room with an anteroom. 20c.

meiosis [Gk. μείωσις 'lessening'] *Ling.* a figure of speech in which emphasis is achieved by deliberate understatement. 16c. Often used as a synonym for LITOTES, which is properly only one form of *meiosis.* [N,S]

me judice [Lat.] in my opinion. 17c. [S]

melancholia [Lat. < Gk. μελαγχολία] *Med.* a morbid condition of the mind characterized by groundless fears and acute depression. 17c. The Greek word means 'having black bile', since black bile was believed to be the cause of the mental condition. [N]

mélange [Fr.] a medley, a conglomeration of heterogeneous constituents. 17c. [N,S]

mêlée [Fr.] a confused encounter between hostile parties, a 'free for all'; *hence*, a heated argument or debate. 17c. [N,S]

melisma, *pl.* **melismata** [Gk. μελίσμα] *Mus.* a melodic sequence of notes sung to a single syllable; an ornament in instrumental music. 19c. [N]

memento [Lat. 'remember!'] (1) *Eccles.* the commemoration of the living or the commemoration of the dead in the Canon of the Mass; *hence* (2) anything which serves to remind one of past events or absent persons, *esp.* some object kept specially for this purpose. 14c. [N,S(*)]

memento mori [Lat.] a reminder of death, *esp.* a skull displayed as a symbol of mortality. 16c. [N,S]

memoir [Fr. *mémoire* 'memory'] a record or report of things done, *esp.* a personal biographical sketch of a dead person; *hence* in *pl.*, a record of events within the personal knowledge of the writer, *esp.* an autobiographical narrative. 16c. Despite the change of spelling, the pronunciation remains quasi-French. [N,S]

memorabilia *pl.* [Lat.] memorable or noteworthy things. 19c. The singular *memorabile* is exceedingly rare. [N,S]

memorandum, *pl.* **memoranda** [Lat.] a note intended to refresh the memory, a record made for future reference; an informal letter from one official to another. 15c. [N,S(*)]

memoria technica [Lat.] a system of mnemonics, a device or system of devices to assist the memory. 18c. [N,S]

memsahib [*ma'am*+Hind. *çāḥib* 'friend' < Arab.] *A.-I.* a European married woman. 19c. This curious hybrid is the normal term by which Indian servants address or refer to their European mistress. Cf. SAHIB. [N]

ménage [Fr.] a household, *esp.* one consisting of a man and woman keeping house together; the management of a domestic establishment. 18c. Cf. EN MÉNAGE; FAUX MÉNAGE. [N,S]

ménage à trois [Fr.] a household consisting of a woman, her husband, and her lover, or of a man, his wife and his mistress. 20c.

ménager [Fr.] to treat gently and tactfully. 20c.

menhir [Breton *men hir* 'long stone'] *Hist.* a tall upright monumental stone of a type found throughout Europe but *esp.* in Brittany. 19c. [N,S]

meniscus, *pl.* **menisci** [Lat. < Gk. *μηνίσκος* 'crescent'] (1) a convexo-concave lens, a lens convex on one side and concave on the other so that its cross-section is crescent-shaped; (2) the convex or concave surface of a liquid in a tube, resulting from capillary attraction or surface tension. 17c. [N,S]

mensa [Lat. 'table'] *Arch.* the top stone slab of an altar. 19c. [N]

menses *pl.* [Lat. 'months'] *Med.* the monthly discharge from the womb of a fertile woman. 16c. [N,S]

menshevik [Russ. 'smaller'] a member of the more moderate section of the Russian Socialist Party. 20c. Often interpreted as the 'minority' party at the Second Congress of the Russian Social-Democratic Party, 1903; cf. BOLSHEVIK. [N*]

mens rea [Lat.] *Law* criminal intention, the state of mind necessary to make an act liable to the penalties of the law. 20c.

mens sana in corpore sano [Lat.] a healthy mind in a healthy body. 17c. Juvenal *Satires* IV x 356. [S(*)]

menstruum [Lat. 'monthly'] a solvent, a liquid in which a solid can be dissolved. 17c. *Orig.* (from 14c.) applied to the menstrual fluid or MENSES; the curious metaphorical meaning is due to a fancy of the mediæval alchemists. [N,S]

Mensur [Ger.] a fencing-match or duel between two German students. 20c.

menuisier [Fr.] a skilled joiner. 20c. Contrasted with ÉBÉNISTE, a skilled cabinet-maker.

menus plaisirs *pl.* [Fr.] the minor pleasures of life, *esp.* considered as involving the expenditure of money. 17c. [S]

meretrix, *pl.* **meretrices** [Lat.] a prostitute. 16c. [N]

méridional, *f.* **méridionale** [Fr.] a native of the south of France. 20c. Cf. (LE) MIDI.

meringue [Fr.] a confection made of icing-sugar and white of egg, made up into small cakes or spread over a pudding. 18c. The popular belief that the confection was invented by Napoleon's cook in honour of the victory of Marengo is discredited by the fact that the word appears in English as early as 1706, nearly a century before the date of the battle. [N,S]

mesa [Sp. 'table'] a high table-land, a high PLATEAU. 19c. [N,S(*)]

mésalliance [Fr.] an unsuitable marriage, *esp.* marriage with a person of inferior social condition. 18c. [N,S]

mesne [Obs. Fr.] (1) *Hist.* (a feudal lord) who holds an estate of a superior lord, not IN CAPITE; (2) *Law* occurring at a time intermediate between two dates. 16c. [N]

mesquin, *f.* **mesquine** [Fr.] sordid, shabby. 18c. [N,S]

mesquinerie [Fr.] shabbiness, little-mindedness. 19c. [S]

messa di voce [It. 'placing the voice'] *Mus.* the swelling and diminishing of a sustained note, *esp.* in singing. 20c.

mestizo, *f.* **mestiza** [Sp.] a Spanish or Portuguese half-caste, *esp.* the child of a Spaniard and an American Indian. 16c. Cf. MÉTIS. [N,S]

mesto [It.] *Mus.* sad, melancholy. 20c.

metamorphosis, *pl.* **metamorphoses** [Gk. *μεταμόρφωσις*] a transformation, a complete change of appearance, form, condition or nature. 16c. [N,S]

metathesis, *pl.* **metatheses** [Gk. *μετάθεσις*] *Ling.* the transposition of two sounds or letters in a word. 17c. [N,S]

metempsychosis, *pl.* **metempsychoses** [Lat. < Gk. *μετεμψύχωσις*] the transmigration of souls, the passage of a soul at death into a new body, either human or animal. 16c. [N,S]

métèque [Fr.] a person living in a country not his own, a resident alien. 20c. Always with a contemptuous connotation. From Gk. *μέτοικος* 'a foreigner living in Athens'.

métier [Fr.] a profession, vocation or calling; an occupation in which one has a special interest or skill, *esp.* *Art* the special subject-interest of a painter. 18c. [N,S]

métis, *f.* **métisse** [Fr.] the child of a European and an American Indian. 19c. Cf. MESTIZO. [N]

metri causa [Lat.] (an emendation in a text, made) for the sake of the metre, to correct a fault in the metre. 20c.

metteur au point [Fr.] one who makes a problem clear or throws new light upon it. 20c. Cf. MISE AU POINT.

metteur en scène [Fr.] the designer of the staging and production of a play; *hence*, the stage-manager of some dramatic event. 20c. Cf. MISE EN SCÈNE.

meum et tuum [Lat.] 'mine and yours', the principle of the rights of property. 17c. *Usu.* with reference to the neglect of the rights of property by thieves or small children. [N,S]

meurtrière [Fr. 'murderess'] *Arch.* a small loophole in a castle wall, so arranged that the defenders can fire on attackers from under cover. 19c. [N,S]

mezé [Turk. *meze*] a titbit served as an appetizer with a drink. 20c. The word has entered Modern Greek as *μεζές*, and the English usage may derive from this source.

mezza voce [It. 'half voice'] *Mus.* with a medium volume, neither very loud nor very soft. 18c. Properly *a mezza voce* 'at half voice'; but the full form is never now used. [N,S]

mezzo rilievo [It.] *Art* half relief; sculpture in which the figures project half their true proportion from the surface. 16c. Formerly often written *mezzo relievo*. Cf. ALTO RILIEVO; BASSO RILIEVO; CAVO RILIEVO; SCHIACCIATO RILIEVO. [N,S]

mezzo soprano [It.] *Mus.* (a woman having) a voice intermediate in compass between SOPRANO and CONTRALTO. 18c. [N,S]

miasma, *pl.* **miasmata** [Gk. μίασμα] noxious exhalations from putrescent matter; infectious emanations; atmospheric pollution. 17c. Since the singular has a plural meaning, singular and plural are used indiscriminately. [N,S]

mi-carême [Fr.] Mid-Lent. 20c.

(le) Midi [Fr. 'noon'] the south of France. 20c. An inhabitant of the *Midi* is called a MÉRIDIONAL.

midinette [Fr.] a girl apprenticed to a dressmaker, a milliner's assistant. 20c. Apparently a contraction of *midi* 'noon' and *dînette* 'snack'. [N*]

(le) mieux est l'ennemi du bien [Fr.] the best is the enemy of the good, in trying to achieve the best one often fails to achieve even the good. 20c. Voltaire *Dictionnaire Philosophique* s.v. *Art Dramatique*.

mignon, *f.* **mignonne** [Fr.] delicately small, dainty; a small delicate person. 16c. [N]

migraine [Fr.] a severe nervous headache, *esp.* one confined to one side of the head. 18c. Anglicized as *megrim;* ultimately from Gk. ἡμικρανία 'half skull'. [N,S]

Mikado [Jap. *mi kado* 'exalted door'] the title of the Emperor of Japan. 18c. The development of the meaning is exactly parallelled in *Sublime Porte* as a title of the Sultan of Turkey. Cf. SHOGUN. [N,S]

milieu [Fr.] (social) environment, (social) surroundings; (intellectual) atmosphere. 19c. [N,S]

mille feuilles [Fr. 'a thousand leaves'] *Cul.* a kind of 'puff' pastry consisting of multiple layers of thin flakes. 20c.

millefiori [It. 'a thousand flowers'] a kind of ornamental glass made by fusing together a number of threads of coloured glass and embedding a cross-section in transparent glass. 19c. Cf. LATTICINIO. [N,S]

millefleurs [Fr. 'a thousand flowers'] a perfume distilled from a large number of different kinds of flower. 19c. [N,S]

millegrain [Fr.] a setting for a precious stone in which the edge of the stone is gripped by a continuous band of minute beads of metal. 20c.

millennium [Lat.] a period of a thousand years, *esp.* the period of a thousand years during which Christ will reign on earth (*Revelation* xx 5); *hence*, a period of benevolent government and general happiness, envisaged as lying in the future. 18c. Cf. TAUSENDJÄHRIG. [N,S]

milord [Fr. < *my lord*] a wealthy Englishman travelling abroad. 19c. [N,S]

mimesis [Gk. *μίμησις*] imitation, mimicry, *esp.* the unconscious imitation by a living creature of some other animal or natural object. 18c. [N,S(*)]

minauderie [Fr.] affectation, coquettish manners. 18c. [N,S]

Minenwerfer, *pl.* **Minenwerfer** [Ger.] *Mil.* a trench-mortar. 20c.

minestrone [It.] *Cul.* a substantial soup made of rice, PASTA, and various kinds of vegetables; *hence*, a mixture of disparate things. 20c. The form *minestra*, of which *minestrone* is the augmentative, is commoner in Italy but seems to be unknown in England. Cf. LASAGNA.

minium [Lat.] *Art* vermilion, red crystalline mercuric sulphide; red lead, red oxide of lead. 14c. [N]

Minnesänger/Minnesinger, *pl.* **Minnesänger/Minnesinger** [Ger.] one of the German amatory lyric poets of the Middle Ages, a German TROUBADOUR. 19c. [N,S]

minuscule [Fr.] tiny, microscopic. 20c. Liable to confusion with the English *minuscule*, a term of palæography and typography. [N]

minuterie [Fr.] (1) small pieces of jeweller's work; (2) an automatic time-switch on the stairs of a block of flats, which extinguishes the lights at a fixed interval after they have been switched on. 20c.

minutia, *pl.* **minutiæ** [Lat.] a trivial detail, a minor particularity. 18c. The plural is much commoner than the singular, but each is sometimes used in error for the other. [N,S]

mir [Russ.] a Russian village community. 19c. [N*]

mirabile dictu [Lat.] wonderful to relate. 19c. Virgil *Georgics* ii 20. Cf. HORRIBILE DICTU. [S]

mirabile visu [Lat.] wonderful to behold. 20c. Formed after MIRABILE DICTU.

mirabilia *pl.* [Lat.] things to wonder at, astonishing things. 20c. The singular *mirabile* is not in use.

mirage [Fr.] an optical illusion observable in sandy deserts, which produces the appearance of sheets of water; the appearance of real objects which are beyond the horizon, resulting from unequal refraction in layers of hot air; *hence*, an illusion of something pleasant which has no real existence. 19c. [N,S]

miscellanea *pl.* [Lat.] a collection of writings on miscellaneous subjects. 16c. [N,S]

mise au point [Fr.] focussing, the clarifying and illuminating of an obscurity. 20c. Cf. METTEUR AU POINT.

mise en espace [Fr.] the staging of a play on an open stage in an amphitheatre. 20c. Formed after MISE EN SCÈNE.

mise en page [Fr.] the arrangement of printed matter on the page of a book, typographic design. 20c.

mise en scène [Fr.] the staging and production of a play; *hence*, the background against which some action takes place; the setting of a work of fiction. 19c. Cf. LOCALE. [S]

misère [Fr.] *Solo Whist* a declaration by which the caller undertakes not to win a single trick. 19c. [N]

misère ouverte [Fr.] *Solo Whist* a declaration by which the caller undertakes not to win a single trick although his hand is displayed after the first lead. 20c. Often in the erroneous form *misère ouvert*.

miserere [Lat.] (1) the fifty-first Psalm; a musical setting of this Psalm. 13c. (2) a misericord, a small bracket on the underside of a hinged seat arranged to give some support to a person standing in front of it. 18c. Vulgate *Psalm* l (li) 1: *Miserere mei, Deus, secundum magnam misericordiam tuam* 'Have mercy on me, O God, according to thy great mercy'. [N,S]

missa cantata [Lat.] *Eccles.* sung Mass, a low Mass accompanied by choral chants. 20c.

missa solemnis [Lat.] *Eccles.* High Mass, a Mass in which the celebrating priest is assisted by a deacon and subdeacon. 20c.

mission civilisatrice [Fr.] the duty of European nations to bring civilization to their colonial subject peoples. 20c.

mistral [Fr.] a strong cold north-west wind. 17c. The exact equivalent of It. MAESTRALE. Cf. BISE; TRAMONTANA. [N,S]

Mitteleuropa [Ger.] central Europe, *esp.* the Balkan states. 20c.

mittimus [Lat. 'we send'] *Law* the name of a writ from a justice of the peace to the keeper of a prison, ordering him to receive in custody the person named. 16c. [N,S]

moccasin [Powhatan *mockasin*] a shoe of soft leather, without a separate sole, worn by American Indians. 17c. The word occurs in numerous Indian dialects, but the Powhatan form is nearest to the English. [N,S]

mochree [Ir. *mo chroí* 'my heart'] my darling; a common and conventional form of endearment. 20c. A shortening of the full form *acushla mochree*, Ir. *a chuisle mo chroí* 'O pulse of my heart'; sometimes written *machree*, with *ma-* for *mo-* as in *macushla*, MAVOURNEEN. Cf. ACUSHLA; ALANNA; ASTHORE.

modello, *pl.* **modelli** [It.] *Art* a small version of a large picture, submitted for the approval of the patron who has commissioned it. 20c. Cf. MAQUETTE.

(der) moderne Bund [Ger.] 'the modern group', the title assumed by the group of Swiss artists led by the German painter Paul Klee. 20c.

modicum [Lat.] a small quantity, a moderate amount. 15c. [N,S]

modiste [Fr.] a fashionable dressmaker. 19c. This word, unlike COUTURIER, is applied only to women dressmakers. [N(*),S]

modulus, *pl.* **moduli** [Lat.] *Math.* a coefficient, *esp.* that by which Napierian logarithms must be multiplied to produce common logarithms; the absolute value of a complex quantity. 18c. [N,S]

modus operandi, *pl.* **modi operandi** [Lat.] the way in which a thing or person works; *hence*, a characteristic method of operation which may lead to the identification of a criminal. 17c. [N,S]

modus vivendi [Lat. 'way of living'] a working arrangement agreed between contending parties pending the final settlement of differences, or if the differences are felt to be irreconcilable. 19c. [N,S]

mœurs *pl.* [Fr.] the manners or customs of a place or period. 20c. Cf. MORES.

moiré [Fr.] (a fabric) having a watered or clouded appearance like watered silk. 19c. [N,S]

moire antique [Fr.] watered silk, *esp.* of a type with a large pattern. 19c. The word *moire* means 'mohair'; from 'watered mohair' the meaning was extended to include any watered fabric, *esp.* silk. In English usage *antique* adds little to the meaning. [N,S]

molleton [Fr.] swanskin, a heavy woollen fabric with a nap on both sides. 19c. [N]

moment critique [Fr.] the critical moment, a time of great importance in the development of something. 20c.

moment de défaillance [Fr.] a moment of weakness, a temporary lapse. 20c.

moment de vérité [Fr.] the 'moment of truth', the climax of a bull-fight in which the bullfighter and the bull are confronted and one or other will be killed; *hence*, an occasion on which one is brought face to face with stark reality. 20c. The current French version is *minute de vérité*.

moment psychologique [Fr.] the 'psychological moment', the most propitious point of time for embarking on a course of action involving another person. 20c. The phrase is translated from the German *das psychologische Moment* 'the psychological factor', much used by the German press at the time of the siege of Paris in 1870; in German *das Moment* means 'momentum' ('moment' is *der Moment*), but the misinterpretation is firmly established in both French and English.

momentum, *pl.* **momenta** [Lat.] the IMPETUS acquired through movement, the continuation of movement resulting from INERTIA. 17c. [N,S]

mondain, *f.* **mondaine** [Fr.] belonging to the world of fashion, fashionable. 20c. [N*]

monocoque [Fr. 'single shell'] (1) a type of aeroplane fuselage resembling an elongated egg; an aeroplane having such a fuselage; (2) (the hull of a boat or the body of a motor-car) manufactured in one piece, *esp.* from fibre-glass or plastic. 20c. [N*]

monologue intérieur [Fr.] an unspoken soliloquy, a passage in a work of fiction in which a character's thoughts are presented as they occur; the 'stream of consciousness' technique. 20c.

monsignore, *pl.* **monsignori** [It.] *Eccles.* a title given to domestic prelates of the Papal court. 17c. The shortened Italian form *monsignor* is very common in English. [N,S]

monsoon [Obs. Du. *monssoen* < Arab. *mausim*] a seasonal wind in southern Asia which blows from the south-west in summer and from the north-east in winter. 16c. The summer *monsoon* is accompanied by continuous rainfall. [N,S]

monstre sacré [Fr. 'sacred monster'] a notable figure (*usu.* a theatrical or cinema star) whose public appeal is enhanced by amiable or acceptable eccentricities in private life. 20c.

montage [Fr.] (1) *Art* a technique by which a picture is built up of fragments of photographs, drawings, etc. pasted to a surface; a picture produced in this way; (2) the cutting and editing of a cinema film. 20c. Cf. ASSEMBLAGE; COLLAGE; PAPIERS COLLÉS.

montant forfaitaire [Fr.] the 'agreed amount' of internal preference among members of the Common Market. 20c.

mont-de-piété, *pl.* **monts-de-piété** [Fr.] a pawnshop licensed by public authority. 19c. From It. MONTE DI PIETÀ; now more decorously named *crédit municipal.* [S]

monte [Sp. 'heap'] a Spanish gambling game played with a pack of forty-five cards. 19c. [N(*),S]

monte di pietà [It.] a pawnshop licensed by public authority. 17c. Cf. MONT-DE-PIÉTÉ. [S]

montre à tact, *pl.* **montres à tact** [Fr.] a watch without a glass, so designed that it is possible to tell the time in the dark by feeling the face. 20c.

montre grande sonnerie [Fr.] a clock or watch which strikes the quarter and the hour at every quarter. 20c. Cf. GRANDE SONNERIE.

monumentum ære perennius, *see* (EXEGI) MONUMENTUM ÆRE PERENNIUS (I have wrought) a monument more lasting than brass.

moquette [Fr.] a strong pile fabric of wool on a hempen base, a kind of Wilton carpeting. 19c. The word is probably connected in some way with *mohair*. [N]

mora, *pl.* **moræ** [Lat. 'delay'] *Ling.* a metrical unit equal to the duration of a single short syllable. 19c. [N(*)]

mora/morra [It.] an Italian game in which one player guesses the number of fingers simultaneously held up by another. 18c. [N,S]

moraine [Fr.] *Geog.* an accumulation of stones and earth carried down and deposited by a glacier; *hence*, a ridge of broken stones and earth in a rock-garden. 18c. [N(*),S]

morale [Fr. *moral*] the moral condition, loyalty, zeal, discipline, etc. (of a body of troops, citizens, etc.) 19c. The mis-spelling *morale* is securely established in English; attempts have been made since the later 19c. to introduce the more correct *moral*, but without success. Cf. LOCALE. [N,S]

moratorium [Lat.] *Law* a legal authorization to postpone payment of a debt for a specified period; *hence,* a temporary suspension of any kind of obligation. 19c. [N]

morbidezza [It.] *Art* lifelike smoothness and delicacy in the painting of flesh-tints; subtle gradation of tones and edges. 17c. [N,S]

morceau, *pl.* **morceaux** [Fr.] a short literary or musical composition. 18c. [N,S(*)]

morcellement [Fr.] (1) the parcelling out (of land, etc.) into small portions; (2) *Med.* the breaking up of a diseased organ into small pieces, as a curative measure. 19c. [N(*)]

more majorum [Lat.] according to the custom of our (their) ancestors. 17c. Cf. MOS MAJORUM. [S]

mores *pl.* [Lat.] the manners or customs of a place or period. 20c. Cf. MŒURS.

more Socratico [Lat.] in the manner of Socrates, (the imparting of information) by a process of question and answer. 20c.

more suo [Lat.] in his (her) own way, in his (her) characteristic fashion. 19c. [S]

morgue [Fr.] superciliousness, haughty behaviour, an attitude of superiority. 16c. The word is fully anglicized in the senses 'mortuary' and 'collection of obituary notices ready for future use'. [N,S(*)]

(la) morgue anglaise/(la) morgue britannique (Fr.] the haughty superciliousness supposed by foreigners to be characteristic of the English. 20c.

morituri te salutant [Lat.] 'those who are about to die salute you', the traditional greeting to the Roman Emperor from the gladiators in the arena. 20c. Suetonius *Claudius* xxi; often misquoted as *morituri te salutamus* 'we who are about to die salute you'.

morne [Fr.] dismal, dreary. 19c. The word is probably ultimately connected with the English verb *mourn.* [N]

morra=MORA, an Italian game.

mors janua vitæ (novæ) [Lat.] death, the gateway to (a new) life, death considered as the threshold of eternity. 20c.

morte lenta [It.] a slow death, a gradual decay or decadence. 20c. *Usu.* of a country or district suffering from adverse economic conditions.

mos majorum [Lat.] the custom of our (their) ancestors. 20c. Cf. MORE MAJORUM.

mot [Fr.] a witty remark, an epigram. 19c. Cf. BON MOT. [N,S]

mot à mot [Fr.] word for word, literally. 20c. Cf. VERBATIM.

mot de Cambronne [Fr.] the mildly indecent French expletive *merde.* 20c. This word is the traditional reply of General Pierre Cambronne (1770–1842) when called upon to surrender at Waterloo; the official version of his reply is *La garde meurt mais ne se rend pas* 'The Guards die but do not surrender'.

motif [Fr.] the theme of an artistic composition; a recurrent idea; the repeating feature of a regular design. 19c. This indispensable word is used in a variety of senses which blend imperceptibly one into another. Cf. LEITMOTIV. [N,S]

(le) mot juste [Fr.] the right word, the word which exactly serves the required purpose in a literary composition. 20c. The phrase is associated with the name of Gustave Flaubert (1821–1880), but seems not to be a quotation.

moto perpetuo [It.] *Mus.* continual movement, a passage of music in which the sequence of rapid notes continues without a break. 19c. Cf. PERPETUUM MOBILE. [S]

motoscafo, *pl.* **motoscafi** [It.] a motor-boat, a motor-launch. 20c.

motu proprio [Lat.] of one's own accord, of one's own free will; *hence Eccles.* a personal MEMORANDUM from the Pope to the clergy. 17c. [S]

moue [Fr.] a pout, an expression of petulance (often feigned). 19c. [N,S]

mouillé [Fr. 'moistened'] *Ling.* palatalized, *usu.* of the consonant *l.* 19c. Properly *l mouillé* is the sound heard in English *million;* the so-called *l mouillé* of modern French has the sound of English *y.*

moujik [Russ. *muzhik*] a Russian peasant; *hence,* a coat or cape similar to that worn by Russian peasants. 16c. [N,S(*)]

moulage [Fr.] (the making of) a plaster cast, *esp.* in police work for the preservation of footprints, etc. 20c.

moulinet [Fr.] the revolving wheel of a ROULETTE-table. 19c. Formerly in use in a number of other senses, all now obsolete. [S]

moussaka [Gk. *μουσακᾶς*] *Cul.* a Greek dish consisting of minced meat cooked with a variety of vegetables. 20c.

mousse [Fr.] *Cul.* a frothy confection made from fruit, etc. beaten up with cream and white of egg. 19c. [N(*)]

mousseux [Fr.] sparkling, frothy (wine). 19c. Distinct from PÉTILLANT 'semi-sparkling'. Cf. VIN MOUSSEUX. [S]

moutonnée [Fr.] *Geog.* (a rock in a glacial valley) ground smooth on the upper side but rough and rugged on the lower. 19c. Shortened from ROCHE MOUTONNÉE, and therefore always in the feminine form. [N]

mouvementé [Fr.] lively, animated, full of incident. 20c.

moyenâgeux [Fr.] mediæval, redolent of the Middle Ages. 20c. *Usu.* with the implication that the mediæval quality is spurious or exaggerated.

muezzin [Arab. *mu'aððin*] a public crier who calls the faithful of Moslem countries to prayer at the prescribed hours. 16c. The *muezzin* is not necessarily an IMAM. The Arabic word is pronounced in different ways in different dialects, and a wide variety of spellings have been current; in the later 19c. attempts were made to popularize the more correct *mueddin,* but without success. [N,S]

mufti [Arab. *muftī*] (1) a Moslem doctor of religion, *esp.* the official head of the Turkish Moslem clergy in Constantinople. 16c. (2) plain clothes worn by someone entitled to wear uniform. 19c. The relationship of the second meaning to the first is disputed, but there seems to be no doubt that the words are identical. [N,S]

mullah [Hind. *mullā* < Arab. *maulā*] a Moslem learned in theology or law. 17c. The Turkish form *molla* has given rise to English *mollah*, etc., but these forms seem to be obsolete. [N,S]

multum in parvo [Lat.] a great deal in a small compass. 18c. [N,S]

mu-mu=MUU-MUU, a straight simple dress.

musica ficta [Lat.] *Mus.* the alteration (sharpening or flattening) of certain notes in the ecclesiastical modes to secure more satisfactory harmonic progressions. 20c. *Musica ficta* was introduced to facilitate polyphonic composition without offending ecclesiastical susceptibilities.

musicale [Fr.] a musical party, *esp.* a musical evening. 19c. Shortened from MATINÉE MUSICALE or SOIRÉE MUSICALE. Cf. THÉ MUSICAL. [N]

musique concrète [Fr. 'concrete music'] *Mus.* a form of musical composition in which the sounds of conventional instruments are replaced by real or artificial sounds recorded on tape and edited so as to express the composer's intentions. 20c.

mutatis mutandis [Lat.] when the appropriate changes have been made. 17c. Used when applying a principle or rule which needs modification to fit a new set of facts. Cf. EXCEPTIS EXCIPIENDIS. [S(*)]

muu-muu/mu-mu [Haw.] a straight simple dress introduced into the Pacific islands by missionaries, a 'Mother Hubbard'. 20c.

mystique [Fr.] a quasi-religious reverence for certain pursuits and activities cultivated by those engaged in them; special skill in the management of some kind of enterprise, EXPERTISE; professional dexterity in performing some task; a trade secret. 20c. This word has recently undergone a very wide extension of its range of meanings.

mythopœia [Lat. < Gk. μυθοποιία] myth-making, the creation of myths. 20c. Applied either to the superstitions of primitive peoples or to contemporary credulity.

mythus, *pl.* **mythi** [Lat. < Gk. μῦθος] a myth; a cycle of mythological legends. 19c. Earlier (18c.), but now less commonly, in the Greek form *mythos*, with plural *mythoi*. [N,S]

N

nacelle [Fr. 'little boat'] the framework supporting the engine of an aeroplane; a bowl-like framework enclosing the front or rear lamps of a motor-car. 20c. [N*]

Nachtlokal [Ger.] a night-club. 20c. Cf. LOKAL.

Nacktkultur [Ger.] nudism, the expression of the belief that absence of clothing leads to emancipation of the spirit. 20c.

nadir [Arab. *naḍīr* 'opposite to'] the point in the celestial sphere opposite the zenith and therefore directly beneath the observer; *hence*, the lowest point, the place or time of greatest degradation. 15c. [N]

nævus, *pl.* **nævi** [Lat.] a birthmark, a mole. 17c. [N,S]

naïf, *f.* **naïve** [Fr.] natural, artless, unaffected; *hence*, simple, ingenuous. 16c. The feminine form *naïve* is now often used as the general form; it is sometimes written *naive* and pronounced as if English. Cf. FAUX NAÏF. [N,S]

naïveté [Fr.] artlessness, absence of affectation; ingenuousness. 17c. [N,S]

nappe [Fr. 'table-cloth'] *Geog.* (1) the sheet of water falling over a weir; (2) a type of geological fold or anticline. 20c. [N*]

narghile [Pers. *nārgileh* < *nārgīl* 'coconut'] an Oriental pipe in which the smoke bubbles through scented water before being inhaled through a long flexible tube. 19c. The tobacco-bowl was *orig.* made from a coconut. Cf. HOOKAH. [N,S]

narquois, *f.* **narquoise** [Fr.] bantering, mocking, sneering. 20c.

narthex [Gk. *νάρθηξ*] *Eccles.* the rear portion of the nave of an early Christian church, partitioned off for the use of women and catechumens. 17c. [N,S]

natura non facit saltum [Lat.] Nature does not make a jump, Nature works by gradual progression. 20c. Cf. SALTUS.

nature [Fr.] unadulterated, without the addition of any other substance. 20c. Always placed after the noun it qualifies.

naturel [Fr.] native character, temperament, or disposition. 19c. [N,S]

nature morte [Fr.] *Art* still life, a representation of cut flowers, vegetables, dead fish, etc. 20c.

navette [Fr. 'shuttle'] a style of cutting precious stones into a leaf-shape formed by the intersection of two arcs; a precious stone cut into this shape. 20c. Cf. MARQUISE.

N.B.=NOTA BENE, note well.

(le) néant [Fr.] nothingness, emptiness, vacuity. 20c. Used *esp.* with reference to existentialist philosophy.

nebula, *pl.* **nebulæ** [Lat. 'cloud'] a luminous patch of gaseous or stellar matter lying in space beyond the solar system. 18c. [N,S(*)]

necessarium [Lat.] a necessary house, a privy. 20c.

necrosis [Lat. < Gk. *νέκρωσις*] *Med.* the mortification or death of a piece of bone or tissue. 17c. [N,S]

nectar [Lat. < Gk. *νέκταρ*] *Myth.* the drink of the Gods (in Classical mythology); *hence*, any delicious drink; the sugary fluid produced by plants and collected by bees. 16c. Cf. AMBROSIA. [N,S]

née *f.* [Fr. 'born'] having the maiden name . . ., known before marriage as . . .; always followed by a surname. 19c. [N*,S]

nefas [Lat.] not right, not proper. 18c. The implication is *usu.* of social or conventional rather than of moral impropriety. Cf. FAS. [S]

négligé [Fr.] informal dress, *esp.* as worn by women; a 'wrap', a thin dressing-gown. 19c. In earlier use (18c.) in the anglicized form *negligee*. Cf. ROBE DE CHAMBRE. [N,S]

négritude [Fr.] the indigenous culture of negro peoples. 20c.

Nehrung [Ger.] *Geog.* a spit of land which nearly encloses the mouth of a river. 20c. Cf. HAFF.

nem. con.=NEMINE CONTRADICENTE, without opposition.

nemesis [Gk. *νέμεσις*] (1) *Myth.* the goddess of vengeance; *hence*, (2) retributive justice, *esp.* viewed as the inevitable consequence of misdoing. 16c. [N,S]

nem(ine) con(tradicente) [Lat.] without opposition, no one dissenting. 17c. The phrase does not imply that there were no abstentions, and is therefore not equivalent to 'unanimously'. [S(*)]

nemo dat quod non habet [Lat.] no one can give what he does not possess. 20c. Used to show that all the qualities of a thing must be present in its source.

nemo me impune lacessit [Lat.] no one can injure me with impunity. 17c. The motto of Scotland. [S]

nemo repente fuit turpissimus [Lat.] no one ever became a villain instantaneously. 19c. Modified from Juvenal *Satires* ii 83: *nemo repente venit turpissimus.*

ne plus ultra [Lat. 'no more beyond'] the uttermost limit, *usu.* of perfection. 17c. The words *ne plus ultra* were supposedly displayed on the Pillars of Hercules (the Straits of Gibraltar), the uttermost limit of navigation in the ancient world. [S]

netsuké [Jap. 'fasten-root'] a small piece of carved wood or ivory worn by the Japanese on a cord suspended from the belt. 19c. A *netsuké* can be distinguished by the presence of two holes through which the cord is passed. [N]

neue Folge [Ger.] new series. 20c. Used to distinguish the serial numbers of the volumes of a journal which has changed editorship or passed into different hands.

Neueinstudierung [Ger.] a fresh study of a work of art, a re-appraisal of an artist's intentions. 20c.

(die) neue Sachlichkeit [Ger.] the new Realism, the reaction against Impressionism which took place in Germany about 1920. 20c. Applied also to a type of poetry which rejects the traditional cult of beauty and seeks to be functional and utilitarian. Cf. SACHLICHKEIT.

Neuinszenierung [Ger.] a new production or staging of a dramatic or operatic work. 20c.

neurasthenia [Gk. *νευρο-* + *ἀσθένεια*] *Med.* functional nervous debility. 19c. [N]

neurosis, *pl.* **neuroses** [Pseudo-Gk. *νεύροσις*] *Med.* a functional nervous disorder. 18c. [N]

ne varietur [Lat. 'that it may not vary'] (a document, edition, etc.) intended to be definitive and authoritative. 20c.

névé [Fr.] *Geog.* the granulated snow on the upper part of a glacier, which has not yet been compressed into ice. 19c. Cf. FIRN. [N,S]

nexus [Lat.] a link or connection, *esp.* a causal connection or relation of interdependence; a cluster of connected ideas or images suggested by a single STIMULUS. 17c. [N,S]

niaiserie [Fr.] simplicity, foolishness; a simple or foolish action. 17c. [N,S]

niello, *pl.* **nielli** [It.] *Art* a black metallic composition used to fill in designs engraved on silver; the art of preparing engraved designs filled with this composition; a work of art produced in this way. 19c. [N,S]

nihil ad rem [Lat.] not at all to the point, quite irrelevant. 19c. Cf. AD REM. [S]

nihil obstat [Lat.] *Eccles.* 'there is no objection', a censor's statement that a religious book contains no unorthodox doctrine. 20c. The *nihil obstat* is followed by an IMPRIMATUR from the licensing authority.

nihil tetigit quod non ornavit [Lat.] he touched nothing that he did not adorn, he achieved notable success in everything he attempted. 20c. Based on Johnson's epitaph on Goldsmith (Boswell's *Life of Johnson* 22nd June 1776): *nullum quod tetigit non ornavit.*

nil admirari [Lat.] not to be surprised or excited at anything, (a state of) perfect equanimity. 18c. Horace *Epistles* I vi 1; such equanimity is the ideal of Stoicism. [S]

nil desperandum [Lat.] never despair! 17c. Horace *Odes* I vii 27. [S(*)]

nimbus, *pl.* **nimbi** [Lat. 'cloud'] a cloud of glory surrounding a person or thing; hence, a golden disk surrounding the head of a saint, a halo. 17c. [N,S]

nirvana [Sansk. *nirvāṇa*] *Rel.* the extinction of individual existence with its desires and passions, regarded by Buddhists as the ultimate reward of holiness. 19c. [N,S]

nisi [Lat. 'unless'] *Law* (a decree, order, etc.) which will come into force after a stated interval unless some implied contingency occurs. 19c. [N,S]

nisi prius [Lat. 'unless sooner'] *Law* the trial of a civil action before a judge and jury in a court of assize. 15c. ***Orig.*** the name of a writ commanding a sheriff to provide a jury at Westminster on a certain day, unless the justices of assize come to the county sooner. [N,S(*)]

Nō=NOH, a type of Japanese drama.

noblesse [Fr.] persons of noble rank, the aristocracy. 16c. [N,S(*)]

noblesse de robe [Fr.] those who have been ennobled for professional services to the State. 20c.

noblesse oblige [Fr.] noble birth has its obligations, the aristocracy must behave honourably. 19c. [S]

noche sombre [Sp.] *Rel.* the 'dark night of the soul', the conviction of utter desolation experienced by mystics as a stage in their spiritual development. 20c. The phrase is taken from the works of St John of the Cross.

nocturne [Fr.] (1) *Mus.* a composition of a dreamy, sleepy character; (2) *Art* a painting of a night-scene. 19c. The introduction of the term in music is due to the Irish composer John Field; in painting it was popularized by Whistler, but not introduced by him. [N]

Noh/Nō [Jap.] a type of Japanese drama performed on a curtainless stage by male actors in sumptuous costumes. 20c. The *Noh* drama had its origin in Buddhist temple dances, and reached its zenith in the fifteenth century: the subjects, historical and mythological, are treated melodramatically. Contrasted with KABUKI, the realistic popular drama.

noir [Fr.] *Roulette* any one of the black numbers. 20c. Cf. ROUGE.

noisette [Fr. 'nut'] *Cul.* a small piece of beef or mutton forming part of a savoury dish. 19c. The term *noisette* as the name of a kind of rose is from a proper name, and is unrelated to this. [N]

nolens volens [Lat. 'unwilling, willing'] willy-nilly, having no alternative. 16c. [N,S]

noli me tangere [Lat. 'do not touch me'] (1) *Art* a representation of Christ appearing to St Mary Magdalene at the Sepulchre; (2) a warning against meddling or interference. 16c. Vulgate *St John* xx 17. [N,S]

nolle prosequi [Lat.] *Law* an entry made on the record of a court when the prosecutor or plaintiff is unwilling to continue his suit against the defendant. 17c. *U.S.* usage has developed a verb 'to nolle-pross'. [N,S(*)]

nolo episcopari [Lat.] *Eccles.* 'I will not be a bishop', the formula by which the offer of a bishopric is refused; *hence*, the refusal of any great dignity or honour. 18c. [S]

nom de guerre [Fr. 'war-name'] a fictitious name, a pseudonym, *esp.* a literary pseudonym. 17c. Cf. SOBRIQUET. [S]

nom de plume [Pseudo-Fr. 'pen-name'] a literary pseudonym. 19c. The French equivalent is NOM DE GUERRE. Cf. SOBRIQUET. [S]

nom de théâtre [Fr. 'stage-name'] a pseudonym adopted in connection with the theatre; *hence*, any pseudonym. 19c. [S]

nonchalance [Fr.] indifference, unconcern, imperturbability, lack of enthusiasm. 17c. Cf. SANG FROID. [N,S]

nonchalant, *f.* **nonchalante** [Fr.] indifferent, unconcerned, imperturbable. 18c. Cf. POCO CURANTE. [N,S]

non compos (mentis) [Lat.] not of sound mind, incompetent to transact legal business. 17c. Used by Cicero *In Pisonem* xx 48; perhaps already a current phrase. Cf. COMPOS MENTIS. [N,S(*)]

non-ego [Lat. 'not I'] *Psych.* the not-self, everything that is not the conscious self; objective existence. 19c. Cf. EGO. [N,S]

non est (inventus) [Lat.] *Law* 'he has not been found', the answer returned by the sheriff when reporting to the issuer of a writ that the defendant cannot be located. 15c. Also in the form *non inventus.* [N,S]

non nobis (Domine) [Lat.] not unto us (O Lord). 19c. Vulgate *Psalm* cxiii 9 (cxv 1): *non nobis Domine, non nobis: sed nomini tuo da gloriam* 'not unto us, O Lord, not unto us, but unto thy name give glory'. [N,S]

non omnis moriar [Lat.] not all of me will die, something of me will survive death. 20c. Horace *Odes* II xxx 6.

non placet [Lat.] 'it does not please (me)', the formula used in giving a negative vote in university and ecclesiastical assemblies; *hence*, a negative vote. 16c. Cf. PLACET. [N,S(*)]

non possumus [Lat. 'we cannot'] (a plea of) inability to discuss or to act in a matter. 19c. [N,S]

non sequitur [Lat. 'it does not follow'] *Logic* a conclusion which does not follow from the premisses, an inconsequent statement. 16c. [N,S]

non sine gloria [Lat.] not ingloriously. 20c.

non sum qualis eram [Lat.] I am not such as I used to be. 19c. Horace *Odes* IV i 3: *Non sum qualis eram bonæ Sub regno Cinaræ* 'I am not such as I used to be in the reign of the good Cinara'.

nosce teipsum [Lat.] know yourself. 16c. A translation of the Greek *γνῶθι σεαυτόν*, GNOTHI SEAUTON. [S]

nostalgie de la boue [Fr. 'homesickness for mud'] the yearning of civilized man for physical degradation, *usu.* for sexual intimacy in sordid circumstances. 20c. Emile Augier (1820–89) *Le Mariage d'Olympe* I i.

nostrum [Lat. 'ours'] a secret medicine prepared by the person who recommends it, a patent medicine; *hence*, any remedy or specific cure recommended by its inventor. 17c. [N,S]

nota [Lat.] an abbreviation or shorthand sign, *esp.* one adopted by mediæval scribes from the ancient Roman system of 'Tironian notes'. 20c.

nota bene [Lat.] note well, take careful note. 17c. *Usu.* abbreviated to *N.B.* [N,S]

notabilia *pl.* [Lat.] noteworthy things, remarkable things. 19c. [S]

nougat [Fr.] a sweetmeat made of almonds and other nuts in a sugar paste. 19c. [N,S]

noumenon, *pl.* **noumena** [Gk. *νοούμενον*] *Psych.* an object of purely intellectual intuition. 18c. Introduced by Immanuel Kant (1724–1804); contrasted with PHENOMENON. [N,S]

nous [Gk. *νοῦς*] (1) mind, intellect; *hence* (2) commonsense, shrewdness. 17c. [N,S]

nous avons changé tout cela [Fr.] we have changed all that. 18c. Molière *Le Médecin Malgré Lui* (1666) II vi; spoken by the pretended doctor when it is pointed out that he has put the heart and liver on the wrong sides. [S]

nouveau riche, *f.* **nouvelle riche,** *pl.* **nouveaux riches** [Fr.] a person of humble origins who has recently acquired wealth. 19c. Always with the implication that the new wealth does not conceal the humble origins. Cf. NOVUS HOMO; PARVENU. [S]

nouveau roman [Fr.] the 'new novel', a 'novel' in which conventional plot and structure (and often grammar and punctuation) are discarded. 20c. The *nouveau roman* or *antiroman* 'anti-novel' was inaugurated by the French novelists Nathalie Sarraute and Claude Simon. Cf. ROMAN EXPÉRIMENTAL.

nouvelle [Fr.] a short novel, not so tightly knit in structure as a short story. 20c. Cf. NOVELLA; NOVELLE.

nouvelle vague [Fr. 'new wave'] a revolutionary technique of film-making combining a small budget, non-professional or little-known actors, and CINÉMA-VÉRITÉ camera-work. 20c. Now gradually being replaced by the English equivalent *new wave*. The *nouvelle vague* was initiated by Roger Vadim with his film *Et Dieu Créa la Femme*.

nova, *pl.* **novæ** [Lat.] a new star, *esp.* one that becomes visible because of a temporary increase in brightness. 19c. [N]

novella, *pl.* **novelle** [It.] a short story, *usu.* realistic, often satirical. 20c. This type of story was developed and cultivated by Giovanni Boccaccio (1313–1375). Cf. NOUVELLE; NOVELLE.

Novelle [Ger.] a long short story or short novel, *usu.* based on a strange episode from real life. 20c. A characteristic feature of the *Novelle* is the WENDEPUNKT, an unexpected turn of events. Cf. NOUVELLE; NOVELLA.

novena [Lat.] *Eccles.* a devotion consisting of special prayers recited on nine successive days. 19c. [N]

novio, *f.* **novia** [Sp.] a FIANCÉ(E); a bridegroom, a bride. 20c.

novus homo, *pl.* **novi homines** [Lat. 'new man'] an upstart, a person of humble origins who has recently come to rank and dignity. 17c. Cf. NOUVEAU RICHE; PARVENU. [S]

noyade [Fr.] execution by drowning. 19c. This method of execution was much used at Nantes in 1794 during the Reign of Terror. [N]

noyau [Fr. 'kernel'] a LIQUEUR made by steeping the kernels of certain fruits in brandy. 18c. [N,S]

nuance [Fr.] a shade of colour or tone; a delicate gradation; a fine shade of meaning. 18c. [N,S]

nuée ardente [Fr. 'glowing cloud'] *Geog.* a blast of hot, gas-charged fragments of lava emitted horizontally during the eruption of a volcano. 20c. The blast is not always incandescent.

nuit blanche [Fr. 'white night'] a sleepless night. 20c.

nulla bona [Lat.] *Law* the return made by the sheriff when a debtor has no goods to be distrained. 19c. [N,S(*)]

nullah [Hind. *nālā*] *A.-I.* a watercourse, *esp.* a dry watercourse, a gully. 18c. Cf. WADI. [N,S]

nulli secundus [Lat.] second to none. 20c.

numerus clausus [Lat.] a fixed or limited number (of vacancies, places in a school, etc.) 20c.

numnah [Hind. *namdā*] *Equ.* a saddle-cloth of thick felt, a felt pad placed under the saddle to prevent soreness. 19c. The more correct *numdah* is very rare. [N]

nunatak [Esk. *nunataq*] *Geog.* an isolated peak of rock protruding through an ice-field. 19c. [N]

nunc dimittis [Lat.] a declaration of willingness or joy at the prospect of departing from life or from some occupation. 17c. Vulgate *St Luke* ii 29: the first words of the Song of Simeon. [N,S]

nunc est bibendum [Lat.] now is the time to drink. 20c. Horace *Odes* I xxxvii 1.

nuncio/nuntio [Obs. It.] *Eccles.* a permanent diplomatic representative of the Pope. 16c. The current Italian form is *nunzio.* [N,S]

nux vomica [Lat. 'emetic nut'] the seed of an East Indian tree from which strychnine is obtained; a preparation of this seed used as an emetic. 16c. [N,S]

nymphæum, *pl.* **nymphæa** [Lat. < Gk. *νυμφαῖον*] *Hist.* a gallery in a Roman villa decorated to simulate the grotto of a nymph. 18c. [N,S]

O

O altitudo! [Lat.] a feeling or expression of religious exultation or elevated emotion. 17c. Vulgate *Romans* xi 33: *O altitudo divitiarum sapientiæ et scientiæ Dei*! 'O the depth of the riches both of the wisdom and knowledge of God!'

obbligato/obligato [It.] *Mus.* indispensable, not to be omitted; the opposite of AD LIB(ITUM). 18c. *Usu.* applied to an instrumental accompaniment to a vocal piece, where the instrumental part has an independent value. *Obbligato* is the current, *obligato* the older Italian spelling; both are common in English. [N,S]

obelus [Lat. < Gk. *ὀβελός* 'spit'] the typographical 'dagger' †, *esp.* when used to mark a spurious or suspect word or passage in an edited text. 14c. Also in the form *obelisk*, anglicized from the Greek diminutive. [N,S]

ob(iit) [Lat.] (he, she) died . . .; always followed by a date. 19c. [S]

obiit sine prole [Lat.] (he, she) died without issue. 20c. Frequent in genealogical works and in family trees; *usu.* abbreviated to *o.s.p.* Cf. DECESSIT SINE PROLE; SINE PROLE.

obiter [Lat. *ob iter* 'by the way'] (spoken) by the way, in passing, incidentally. 16c. [N,S]

obiter dictum, *pl.* **obiter dicta** [Lat.] an incidental remark, *esp. Law* a remark by a judge which does not form part of the judgment and is therefore not binding. 19c. Contrasted with RATIO DECIDENDI. [N,S]

objet d'art, *pl.* **objets d'art** [Fr.] a work of art in any medium, *usu.* of small size and suitable for display in a cabinet. 19c. [S]

objet de piété, *pl.* **objets de piété** [Fr.] a devotional object such as a crucifix or statuette. 20c. Cf. BONDIEUSERIE.

objet de vertu, *pl.* **objets de vertu** [Pseudo-Fr.] a work of art. 20c. The phrase purports to be a French version of English 'object of *vertu*', where *vertu* is a mis-spelling of VIRTÙ; but *vertu* has never had the required sense in French.

objet trouvé, *pl.* **objets trouvés** [Fr.] *Art* a natural object (a piece of stone or wood, etc.) or an artefact (not intended as a work of art) supposed to possess æsthetic significance. 20c. The æsthetic significance is not discernible until it is pointed out by the finder, who can therefore claim as much credit as if he had designed and made the object.

obligato=OBBLIGATO, indispensable; an instrumental accompaniment.

ob majorem cautelam [Lat.] *Law* by way of greater caution, to guard against every contingency. 20c. Cf. EX ABUNDANTI CAUTELA.

obscurum per obscurius [Lat.] an attempt to explain something obscure by reference to something even more obscure. 19c. Cf. IGNOTUM PER IGNOTIUS. [S]

octroi [Fr.] a tax levied on certain articles brought into towns in France and other European countries; the customs-station at which the tax is collected. 18c. Cf. DOUANE. [N,S]

odalisque [Fr. < Turk. *odalık* 'fit for the bedroom'] a female slave or concubine in an Oriental HAREM. 17c. [N,S]

oderint dum metuant [Lat.] let them hate, so long as they fear. 16c. Cicero *Philippic* i 14 and elsewhere; Suetonius *Caligula* xxx; the phrase is attributed to the poet Lucius Accius, only fragments of whose works are extant. [S]

odi et amo [Lat.] I love and I hate. 20c. The classic expression of the love-hatred syndrome. Catullus *Carmina* lxxxv: *Odi et amo. Quare id faciam, fortasse requiris. Nescio: sed fieri sentio, et excrucior.* 'I love and I hate. Perhaps you ask why I do it. I don't know, but I feel it happening, and I am in torment.'

odi profanum vulgus [Lat.] I hate the uninitiated crowd. 19c. Horace *Odes* III i 1. [S]

odium scholasticum [Lat.] the spitefulness of scholars. 20c. Modelled on ODIUM THEOLOGICUM.

odium theologicum [Lat.] the spitefulness of theologians, the acrimony of theological discussions. 18c. [N,S]

œdema, *pl.* **œdemata** [Lat. < Gk. *οἴδημα*] *Med.* a local dropsy, a swelling caused by the presence of a serous fluid in the tissues. 15c. [N,S]

œil-de-bœuf [Fr. 'ox-eye'] *Arch.* (1) a small round or oval window; (2) a circular or octagonal vestibule, so called from one at Versailles which was lighted by a small round window. 18c. [N,S(*)]

œillade [Fr.] a meaning look, an amatory glance or wink. 16c. [N,S]

œsophagus, *pl.* **œsophagi** [Lat. < Gk. *οἰσοφάγος*] *Med.* the gullet, the tube down which food passes from the throat to the stomach. 14c. [N,S]

œuvre [Fr.] the total output of an artist or man of letters. 20c. Cf. OPERA OMNIA.

ohne mich! [Ger.] count me out!, don't include me! 20c. The phrase became popular in Germany after the Second World War when the revival of the German armed forces was first suggested.

olla podrida [Sp. 'rotten pot'] (1) *Cul.* a Spanish dish consisting of many kinds of meat and vegetables stewed together; *hence* (2) a hotchpotch, a medley, a miscellaneous mixture. 16c. Cf. POT POURRI. [N,S]

oloroso [Sp.] a fragrant full-bodied dark sherry. 20c.

omadhaun [Ir. *amadán*] a fool, a madman. 19c. A common term of abuse in Ireland. [N,S]

ombré [Fr.] (a fabric) woven with variably dyed yarns so as to produce a shaded effect. 20c. Cf. ONDÉ.

ombres chinoises *pl.* [Fr. 'Chinese shadows'] a shadow pantomime, an entertainment in which the shadows of cut-out silhouettes are cast onto a translucent screen. 19c. [S]

ombudsman [Swed.] an official acting as an independent legal arbitrator between the State and the private citizen. 20c. The office has existed for 150 years in Sweden and has now been introduced in Denmark and New Zealand. The word is the modern form of Old Norse *umboðsmaðr* 'commissary'.

omne ignotum pro magnifico [Lat.] anything about which little is known is assumed to be wonderful. 19c. Tacitus *Agricola* xxx. [S]

omne scibile [Lat.] everything that can be known. 20c. Adapted from a phrase attributed to Pico della Mirandola: *de omni re scibile et quibusdam aliis* 'concerning everything that can be known and a few other things'.

(omnium consensu,) capax imperii nisi imperasset [Lat.] (everyone thought him) capable of exercising authority until he tried it. 20c. Tacitus *Histories* i 49; of the Emperor Galba.

omphalos [Gk. *ὀμφαλός*] (1) the boss on a shield; (2) a central point, a spiritual hub. 19c. *Orig.* applied to a stone in the temple of Apollo at Delphi which was reputed to mark the exact centre of the (flat) earth. [N,S]

ondé [Fr. 'wavy'] (a fabric) so treated as to produce an effect of shaded colour. 20c. Cf. OMBRÉ.

on dit [Fr. 'it is said'] a rumour, an item of gossip, something reported on hearsay. 19c. In English the phrase has a plural *on dits*. [N,S]

onomasticon [Gk. *ὀνομαστικόν*] an alphabetical list of proper names, *esp.* of names of persons. 18c. Formerly applied to any kind of vocabulary or glossary. Cf. INDEX NOMINUM. [N,S]

onomatopœia [Lat. < Gk. *ὀνοματοποιία*] *Ling.* (1) the formation of a word by vocal imitation of the sound associated with the thing or action in question; a word formed in this way; (2) the use of words the sounds of which help to reinforce the meaning intended. 16c. [N,S]

onus [Lat.] a burden; responsibility, duty. 17c. [N,S]

onus probandi [Lat.] the burden of proof, the duty of a person who makes a charge or allegation to prove it. 18c. [N,S]

oomiak=UMIAK, a large Eskimo boat.

op. cit.=OPERE CITATO, in the work quoted.

opéra bouffe [Fr.] comic opera, an operatic extravaganza. 19c. [N,S]

opera buffa [It.] comic opera, an operatic extravaganza. 19c. Cf. BUFFO. [N,S]

opéra comique [Fr.] opera which includes spoken dialogue, as distinct from grand opera in which all the dialogue is set to music. 18c. Cf. SINGSPIEL. [N,S]

opera minora *pl.* [Lat.] minor works, the less important works (of an author). 19c. [S]

opera omnia [Lat.] all the works, the whole output (of an author). 20c. Cf. ŒUVRE.

opera seria [It.] serious opera, as opposed to OPERA BUFFA. 20c. Cf. DRAMMA PER (LA) MUSICA.

operculum, *see* OPUSCULUM, a work on a small scale.

op(ere) cit(ato) [Lat.] in the work quoted. 19c. Used to avoid the repetition of a reference. Cf. IBID(EM); LOC(O) CIT(ATO). [S]

opérette [Fr.] an operetta, a short light opera. 20c.

operone [It.] an opera on a large scale, an opera produced with great magnificence. 20c.

opprobrium [Lat.] the disgrace consequent on shameful conduct; reproach, abuse. 17c. [N,S]

optimates *pl.* [Lat.] (1) *Hist.* the members of the patrician order in ancient Rome; *hence* (2) the aristocracy, the 'best people'. 16c. [N,S(*)]

optimum [Lat.] the best, the most favourable (conditions, circumstances, etc.) 19c. A recent formation based on *maximum* and *minimum.* [N]

opus, *pl.* **opera** [Lat.] a work, a composition; *esp.* one of a series of musical compositions numbered in order of publication. 19c. [N(*),S]

opus Alexandrinum [Lat.] *Art* a pavement made of circular slabs of marble with the interstices filled with geometrical patterns. 20c.

opus anglicanum [Lat.] English embroidery of the 13th century. 20c. Mediæval English embroidery was famous throughout Europe.

opusculum, *pl.* **opuscula** [Lat.] a literary or musical composition on a small scale. 17c. The word *operculum* 'lid' is *occ.* used by mistake for *opusculum*, presumably by confusion with *opera* the plural of OPUS. [N,S(*)]

opus Dei [Lat.] *Eccles.* the work of God, the performance of the liturgical offices considered as the most important part of monastic life. 20c.

opus operans [Lat.] *Theol.* an action (*esp.* a sacrament) the efficacy of which depends on the condition of the recipient or of the minister or of both; contrasted with OPUS OPERATUM. 16c. [S]

opus operatum [Lat.] *Theol.* an action (*esp.* a sacrament) the efficacy of which is independent of the merit of the minister; contrasted with OPUS OPERANS. 16c. Cf. EX OPERE OPERATO. [S(*)]

oraison funèbre [Fr.] a funeral oration, a funeral eulogy. 20c. Often with implied reference to the famous *Oraisons Funèbres* of Bossuet (1627–1704).

orangerie [Fr.] a building designed for the cultivation of orange-trees in climates in which they will not survive in the open. 20c. Also and better in the anglicized form *orangery*.

orang-outang [Mal. *ōrang ūtan* 'man of the woods'] an anthropoid ape (*Simia satyrus*) inhabiting the Malay archipelago. 17c. [N,S]

oratio obliqua [Lat.] *Ling.* indirect speech, reported speech. 19c. [N]

oratio recta [Lat.] *Ling.* direct speech, quoted speech. 19c. [N]

oratorio [It.] *Mus.* a choral work resembling an opera, but performed without action or scenery, and *usu.* based on a Scriptural story. 18c. The name is taken from the Oratory of St Philip in Rome, where musical dramas were performed in 16c. Cf. AZIONE (SACRA). [N,S]

ordonnance [Fr.] the systematic arrangement of the elements of a work of art or of literature. 17c. [N,S]

ordre du jour [Fr.] *Mil.* an order of the day, an announcement from the High Command on some special occasion. 19c. [S]

organum [Lat. < Gk. *ὄργανον*] *Mus.* a primitive mediæval form of polyphony in which a second part identical with the CANTO FERMO is added at an interval of a fourth or a fifth. 18c. Cf. ARS NOVA. [N]

oriflamme [Fr.] (1) *Hist.* the sacred orange-red banner of St Denis used by the early kings of France; *hence* (2) any banner or ensign which serves as a rallying point; (3) anything conspicuous, glorious, or golden. 15c. [N,S]

origami [Jap.] the Japanese art of cutting and folding paper into attractive forms and designs. 20c. Cf. PAPIERS DÉCHIRÉS.

O si sic omnes!/O si sic omnia! [Lat.] if only all (were, had been) thus! 19c. A form of praise, implying that if all things happened, or all people behaved, as in some specific instance, the world would be a better place; *omnes* refers to people, *omnia* to things. Perhaps based on Juvenal *Satires* IV x 123–4. [S]

o.s.p.=OBIIT SINE PROLE, died without issue.

osteria [It.] an inn, a tavern (in Italy). 17c. [N,S]

ostinato, *pl.* **ostinati** [It. 'obstinate'] *Mus.* (a theme or sequence of notes) which recurs again and again, *usu.* within a varied contrapuntal framework. 20c. Cf. BASSO OSTINATO.

ostrakon, *pl.* **ostraka** [Gk. *ὄστρακον*] a sherd of pottery engraved with an inscription. 19c. [N*]

O tempora, O mores! [Lat.] Oh, what times we live in, the way people behave! 16c. Cicero *In Catilinam* I i 2. [S(*)]

otium cum dignitate [Lat.] dignified leisure, graceful idleness; honourable retirement. 18c. Cicero *Pro Sestio* xlv 98 and elsewhere, in the form *cum dignitate otium.* [S]

ottava rima [It.] an Italian stanza of eight hendecasyllabic lines rhymed *a b a b a b c c;* an English stanza of eight five-stress lines rhymed in the same pattern. 19c. [N,S]

oubliette [Fr.] a secret dungeon reached only through a trap-door above. 19c. [N,S]

ouistiti [Fr. 'marmoset'] a pick-lock, a skeleton key. 20c. The development of the sense from 'marmoset' to 'pick-lock' is wholly obscure.

où sont les neiges d'antan? [Fr.] where are the snows of yesteryear? 20c. The refrain of Villon's *Ballade des Dames du Temps Jadis* (*Le Testament* 329–56).

outré [Fr.] exaggerated, eccentric, beyond the limits of convention. 18c. [N,S]

outremer [Fr.] overseas, *esp.* with reference to French colonial possessions. 20c.

outre-tombe [Fr.] from beyond the tomb; unearthly. 20c. *Usu.* with implicit reference to Chateaubriand's autobiographical *Mémoires d'Outre-tombe* (1849–50).

ouvreuse [Fr.] a woman employed to unlock the boxes in a French theatre and to show patrons to their seats; an 'usherette'. 20c.

ouzo [Gk. *οὖζον*] a Greek ardent spirit distilled from the lees of wine. 20c. The flavour is similar to that of ARAK.

ovum, *pl.* **ova** [Lat.] the reproductive cell of a female mammal. 18c. The erroneous plurals *ovas* and *ovæ* have sometimes been used. [N,S]

oyer [Obs. Fr. 'to hear'] *Law* in the phrase 'oyer and terminer', a commission to a judge empowering him to hold courts, *esp.* to try exceptional offences or in times of unusual civil disturbances. 15c. *Oyer* by itself is sometimes used as an abbreviation of the full phrase. [N,S]

oyez! [Obs. Fr. 'listen!'] a call for silence and attention made by a town-crier or court official. 15c. The traditional pronunciation is identical with that of English *Oh yes!* [N,S]

P

pabulum [Lat.] food, nutriment; *hence*, food for thought. 17c. [N,S]

pace [Lat.] by leave of . . .; always followed by the name of a person. 19c. Used in ironic apology for a contradiction. [N*,S]

padre [It. 'father'] a priest; a military or naval chaplain. 16c. Now often used to address an Anglican clergyman. [N,S]

padrone [It. 'patron'] an (Italian) employer of labour, *esp.* the proprietor of an inn or restaurant. 18c. [N,S]

paella [Sp. 'pan'] *Cul.* a dish consisting of chicken, bacon, pork and various shellfish cooked together with saffron rice. 20c.

pagoda [Port.] an Oriental temple, *esp.* a many-storied tower devoted to heathen worship. 16c. The normal Portuguese form is *pagode;* it may be derived from Pers. *but-kadah* 'idol temple'. [N,S]

paillette [Fr.] (1) *Art* a piece of coloured foil used to give brilliance to a painting in enamel; (2) a glittering ornament on a woman's dress, a spangle. 19c. In the first sense there is a variant form *paillon.* [N]

pair [Fr.] *Roulette* any one of the even numbers. 20c. Cf. IMPAIR.

palæstra [Lat. < Gk. *παλαίστρα*] (1) *Hist.* a place devoted to athletic exercises, *esp.* wrestling; *hence* (2) the practice of athletics, *esp.* wrestling. 15c. Cf. APODYTERIUM. [N,S]

palais (de danse) [Fr.] a dance-hall open to all on payment of an entrance-fee. 20c. [N*]

palazzo, *pl.* **palazzi** [It.] a fine mansion (in Italy). 19c. [S]

paletot [Fr.] a loose coat, a cloak with sleeves. 19c. [N,S]

palladium [Lat. < Gk. *Παλλάδιον*] (1) *Myth.* the image of Pallas at Troy, on which the safety of the city was supposed to depend; *hence* (2) anything on which the safety of a nation, institution, etc. depends; a safeguard. 16c. [N,S]

pallium, *pl.* **pallia** [Lat.] (1) *Hist.* the rectangular cloak worn as an outer garment (*esp.* by Greeks) in ancient Rome; (2) *Eccles.* the vestment conferred on an archbishop, *esp.* considered as a symbol of his office. 16c. [N,S]

palmam qui meruit ferat [Lat.] let him who has deserved the palm of victory wear it. 19c. Not, apparently, a quotation. [S]

palmette [Fr.] *Art* a fan-shaped ornament divided into branches like a palm-leaf. 19c. [N]

palomino [Sp.] a horse of a light colour ranging from cream to chestnut, with a light mane and tail. 20c.

pampas [Sp. 'steppes'] a giant ornamental grass. 19c. Properly *pampas-*grass, so called from the treeless plains south of the Amazon where the plant is found; it was introduced into Europe in 1843. [N,S]

panacea [Lat. < Gk. *πανάκεια*] a universal remedy for all diseases; *hence*, a cure for all troubles, a solution to all problems. 16c. Cf. CATHOLICON; ELIXIR. [N,S]

panache [Fr.] the plume of feathers on a helmet; *hence*, an air of gallantry, chivalrous pride, swagger. 16c. The figurative meaning, both in French and in English, dates from the famous use of the word in Edmond Rostand's *Cyrano de Bergerac* (1898). [N,S]

panada [Sp.] a ROUX or mixture of melted butter and flour heated with a quantity of liquid (*usu.* water or stock) and used to bind ingredients with no cohesive qualities into CROQUETTES, etc. 20c. In use from 16c. until recently in quite a different sense, 'a dish consisting of bread boiled to pulp and flavoured with sugar, spices, etc.' Cf. PANATELLA.

panatella [It.] *Cul.* an invalid dish made by boiling bread to pulp and flavouring it. 18c. [N]

pancratium/pancration [Lat. < Gk. *παγκράτιον*] an athletic contest combining boxing and wrestling; *hence*, a 'free-for-all'. 17c. [N,S]

panem et circenses [Lat.] 'bread and circuses', i.e. sustenance and entertainment considered as a means of pacifying the common populace. 19c. Juvenal *Satires* IV x 81; the phrase is in the accusative because it is the object of *optat* '(the populace) desires'; but in English usage the case is ignored. [S]

panneau décoratif [Fr.] *Art* a decorative panel, a drawing or print in which pictorial content is subordinated to decorative effect. 20c.

panta rhei [Gk. *πάντα ῥεῖ*] everything is in a state of flux. 20c. Attributed by Aristotle to Heraclitus.

Panzer [Ger.] armour-plating. 20c. Applied adjectivally to German armoured units during the Second World War.

papabile [It.] qualified for the office of Pope; *hence*, suitable for election or appointment to any high office. 20c.

paperasserie [Fr.] an accumulation of old papers; 'red tape'. 20c.

papier mâché [Fr. 'chewed paper'] paper reduced to pulp by boiling and macerating, mixed with whiting and size, and shaped by moulding. 18c. The phrase is of English formation; in French it has only its literal meaning, unless by recent borrowing from English. Cf. CARTON-PIERRE. [N,S(*)]

papier poudré, *pl.* **papiers poudrés** [Fr.] a sheet of paper lightly coated with face-powder, used *orig.* to improve the complexion without giving the appearance of 'painting', later for emergency repairs to make-up. 20c. Obsolescent or perhaps obsolete.

papiers collés *pl.* [Fr.] *Art* (a work of art consisting of) pieces of paper or cardboard glued to a canvas. 20c. Invented by Braque in 1909. Cf. COLLAGE; MONTAGE.

papiers déchirés *pl.* [Fr.] *Art* (a work of art consisting of) torn and twisted paper attached to a background. 20c. Developed by Picasso from the ancient Japanese art of ORIGAMI.

papiers découpés *pl.* [Fr.] *Art* (a work of art consisting of) paper cut into patterns and attached to a background. 20c.

paprika [Magyar] Hungarian red pepper, a condiment prepared from *Capsicum*. 19c. Cf. PIMENTO. [N*]

papyrus, *pl.* **papyri** [Lat. < Gk. *πάπυρος*] a writing-surface prepared from strips of the stem of the paper-rush; a document written on a surface prepared in this way. 18c. [N,S]

paramo [Sp. *páramo*] *Geog.* a high windy treeless PLATEAU in tropical South America. 18c. The Spanish word is from some South American Indian language. [N]

paranoia [Gk. *παράνοια*] *Med.* a chronic mental derangement characterized by delusions of grandeur or of persecution. 19c. [N]

paraphernalia *pl.* [Lat.] miscellaneous personal belongings, miscellaneous articles of equipment, 'bits and pieces' in general. 18c. The Latin word is from Gk. *παράφερνα* 'outside the dowry', and was *orig.* a technical legal term meaning 'the personal property of a married woman', over which the husband could exercise no rights without the wife's consent. [N,S]

par éminence [Fr.] pre-eminently, especially. 19c. [N]

parergon, *pl.* **parerga** [Gk. *πάρεργον*] (1) a subsidiary work, a by-product of a more important work; a hobby; (2) *Art* a subordinate detail in a pictorial composition, e.g. a glimpse of landscape in a portrait. 17c. Cf. BREVIORA. [N,S]

par excellence [Fr.] pre-eminently, in the highest possible degree. 17c. Cf. KAT' EXOCHEN. [N,S]

par exemple [Fr.] for instance. 19c. [N]

parfait [Fr. 'perfect'] *Cul.* a frozen pudding containing whipped cream and eggs. 20c.

parfum [Fr.] a scent, an odour, *esp.* a delicate or evanescent scent. 20c.

pariah [Tamil *paṛaiyar* 'drummers'] *A.-I.* a member of the lowest CASTE in India; a type of homeless mongrel dog which frequents Indian villages; *hence*, a social outcast, a reprobate. 17c. So called because the hereditary drummers at certain festivals belonged to the lowest *caste*. Numerous different spellings have been in use, notably *par(r)iar*. [N,S]

pari mutuel, *pl.* **paris mutuels** [Fr.] a totalisator system, a form of betting in which those who have backed the winning horse share the stakes placed on the losing horses. 19c. The only form of betting allowed in France since 1891. [N]

pari passu [Lat.] at an equal rate of progress, in step with one another; without preference on one side or another. 16c. [N,S]

Paris vaut bien une messe [Fr.] 'Paris is well worth a Mass', a material gain is well worth a sacrifice of principles. 20c. Attributed to the Huguenot Henri IV of France (1553–1610), who came to the throne at the price of religious conformity.

parka [Russ.] a light waterproof jacket with a hood, for use out of doors in bleak conditions. 19c. The word entered Russian from the Kamchadal language; the native *parka* was *orig.* made of skins. It is difficult to see why this word of long standing in the language has now been replaced by ANORAK. [N*]

parlando [It. 'speaking'] *Mus.* singing with a distinct articulation so that all the words are clearly audible. 20c.

parlante [It. 'speaking'] *Mus.* (a piano passage) played with crisp distinct articulation. 20c.

parole (d'honneur) [Fr. 'word (of honour)'] an undertaking by a prisoner that he will refrain from attempting to escape, or that he will return to custody after a stated period. 17c. [N,S(*)]

paronomasia [Gk. *παρονομασία*] a play upon words, a pun. 16c. [N,S]

parousia [Gk. *παρουσία*] *Theol.* the Second Coming of Christ. 19c. The word is used in this sense in the Greek text of *St Matthew* xxiv 27 and elsewhere. [N*]

parquet [Fr.] a flooring made of small pieces of wood arranged in patterns; the part of the floor of the auditorium of a theatre occupied by the stalls. 19c. [N,S]

parterre [Fr.] (1) a flower-garden consisting of a symmetrical arrangement of flower-beds; (2) (the occupants of) the 'pit' of a theatre. 17c. [N,S]

parthenogenesis [Gk. *παρθενο-* + *γένεσις*] reproduction without sexual intercourse, *esp.* parturition by a female without previous sexual congress. 19c. Cf. AUTOGENESIS. [N,S]

parti [Fr.] a marriageable person considered as a good or a bad match. 19c. [N,S]

partie carrée [Fr. 'square party'] a party of four persons, *usu.* two men and two women. 18c. [N,S]

parti pris [Fr. 'side taken'] a preconceived opinion; prejudice, bias. 19c. [N,S]

partir, c'est mourir un peu [Fr.] every parting is a step towards death. 20c. Edmond Harancourt 'Rondel de l'Adieu' in *Choix de Poésies* (1891).

parturiunt montes, nascetur ridiculus mus [Lat.] the mountains are in labour, and an absurd mouse will be born. 16c. Horace *Ars Poetica* 139; used when much fuss and labour produces an insignificant result. [S]

parure [Fr.] a set of matching pieces of jewellery designed to be worn together. 19c. [N,S]

parvenu, *f.* **parvenue** [Fr.] an upstart, a person of humble origins who has attained wealth and dignity. 19c. The implication is always that the wealth and dignity are undeserved. Cf. NOUVEAU RICHE; NOVUS HOMO. [N,S]

pas d'action [Fr.] *Ballet* a dance designed to tell a story or to illustrate a theme. 20c. Cf. BALLET D'ACTION.

pas de bourrée [Fr.] *Ballet* one of a large variety of dance steps in which the weight is transferred from one foot to the other three times. 20c. Cf. BOURRÉE.

pas de charge [Fr.] *Mil.* the double, the rapid pace used by infantry when going in to the attack. 19c. [S]

pas de chat [Fr.] *Ballet* a springing movement in which one foot jumps over the other. 20c.

pas de deux [Fr.] *Ballet* a dance or movement for two persons. 19c. [N,S]

pas de quatre [Fr.] *Ballet* a dance for four persons. 19c. [S]

pas de trois [Fr.] *Ballet* a dance for three persons. 18c. [S]

pas devant (les domestiques/les enfants) [Fr.] not in front of (the servants, the children). 20c. Used to warn other speakers that it would be indiscreet to continue the discussion in the presence of the servants or the children, who are presumed not to understand French.

paseo [Sp.] a leisurely walk, a constitutional; a broad street designed for leisurely walking. 19c. Cf. PASSEGGIATA; PROMENADE. [N*,S]

pasha [Turk. *paşa*] a Turkish title given to military commanders and governors of provinces; *hence*, a person characterized either by dictatorial manners or sexual promiscuity. 17c. [N,S]

paso doble [Sp.] the two-step; a musical composition suitable for this dance. 20c.

passacaglia [It. < Sp. *pasa calle* 'pace the street'] *Mus.* a slow Spanish dance in 3/4 time, rather slower than the CHACONNE, *usu.* on a ground-bass. 17c. [N,S]

passe [Fr.] *Roulette* any one of the numbers from 19 to 36 inclusive. 20c. Cf. MANQUE.

passé, *f.* **passée** [Fr.] past one's prime, *esp.* with reference to the beauty of a woman; out of date, out of fashion. 18c. [N,S]

passeggiata [It.] a leisurely walk, a constitutional. 20c. Cf. PASEO; PROMENADE.

passementerie [Fr.] a trimming of gold or silver lace, or of braid or bead-work. 19c. [N,S]

passe-partout [Fr.] (1) a master-key; *hence*, a solution to all difficulties; (2) an ornamental mount for a photograph or drawing; a simple frame for a photograph or drawing consisting of glass and cardboard held together by paper stuck over the edges; (3) (as a trade-name) coloured strips of paper gummed on one side, designed for the construction of such frames. 17c. [N,S]

passepied [Fr.] *Mus.* a French dance-tune resembling a minuet but quicker. 17c. [N,S]

pas seul [Fr.] *Ballet* a dance or movement for a single dancer. 19c. [N,S]

pas si bête! [Fr.] (I'm) not such a fool! what do you take me for? 19c. [S]

passim [Lat.] in various places, in many passages. 19c. Used after the title of a work to which reference is made to indicate the recurrence of relevant passages throughout the work. [N,S]

passionné, *f.* **passionnée** [Fr.] an enthusiastic devotee, a 'fan'. 20c. Cf. AFICIONADO.

pasta [It.] a food made of flour and water (and sometimes egg), cut or extruded into various shapes, dried, boiled, and served with a sauce. 20c. The generic name for CANNELLONI, LASAGNA, MACARONI, SPAGHETTI, VERMICELLI, etc.

pasticcio [It. 'pie'] a literary, musical, or graphic work consisting of fragments by various artists or from various sources ingeniously pieced together. 18c. *Occ.* used in the sense of PASTICHE. [N,S]

pastiche [Fr.] an avowed imitation of the style of another writer, composer or painter, *usu.* of an earlier period. 19c. *Occ.* used in the sense of PASTICCIO. [N]

pastille [Fr.] a cake of aromatic paste prepared to be burnt as a perfume or as a disinfectant; a flat round sweetmeat, *usu.* medicinal. 19c. Anglicized from 17c. as *pastil.* [N,S]

pastrami [Yidd. < Roumanian *pastramă*] smoked and highly seasoned meat, *esp.* beef. 20c. The Roumanian word has entered Turkish in the form *pastırma*, and has thence entered Modern Greek in the form παστουρμᾶς.

patchouli [Tamil *pach ilai* 'green leaf'] a penetrating perfume prepared from a plant native to the Malay peninsula. 19c. Known from 17c. in the partially translated form *patch-leaf.* [N,S]

pâté [Fr.] a pasty, a pie. 18c. [N,S]

pâté de foie gras [Fr.] a pie made of fatted goose liver, Strasburg pie. 19c. Now often used of the fatted goose liver itself. Cf. FOIE GRAS. [N,S]

pâte-de-verre [Fr.] a composition of powdered glass of various colours, moulded to shape and fired like ceramic. 20c. This technique, known to the ancient world, was revived in 1884 by the French sculptor Henri Cros.

pâte dure [Fr. 'hard paste'] natural kaolin clay used in the manufacture of porcelain; porcelain made from such clay. 19c. Contrasted with PÂTE TENDRE.

paterfamilias [Lat.] the father of a family, the head of a household. 15c. The plural *patres familiarum* is rare. Cf. MATERFAMILIAS; PÈRE DE FAMILLE. [N,S]

pater noster/paternoster [Lat. 'Our Father'] (1) the Lord's Prayer, *esp.* in the Latin version. 10c. (2) the larger type of bead in a rosary; *hence*, the rosary itself. 13c. (3) (a fishing-line) to which groups of hooks are attached at intervals. 19c. [N,S]

pater patriæ, *pl.* **patres patriæ** [Lat.] 'father of the country', a title given to Cicero after his suppression of Catiline's conspiracy in 63 B.C.; *hence*, applied to any person who has rendered signal service to his country. 16c. Cicero *Pro Sestio* lvii. [S]

pâte-sur-pâte [Fr.] a method of decorating with pottery 'slip', a dilute form of the clay from which the vessel is made. 20c. The 'slip' may be of a different colour from the ground, or it may be built up into a pattern in relief. Cf. BARBOTINE.

pâte tendre [Fr. 'soft paste'] an artificial clay used in the manufacture of porcelain, compounded of sand, nitre, salt and other substances; porcelain made from such clay. 19c. Contrasted with PÂTE DURE, natural kaolin clay. *Pâte tendre* was much used in early Sèvres porcelain, but was replaced by *pâte dure* about 1770 when natural kaolin deposits were discovered in France.

pathemata mathemata [Gk. *παθήματα μαθήματα*] painful experiences are instructive, one learns by suffering. 17c. Herodotus *Histories* i 207; *usu.* written in Greek characters. [S]

pathos [Gk. *πάθος* 'suffering'] the expression of a tender emotion, the power of evoking pity and compassion. 16c. [N,S]

patina [Lat. 'dish'] a greenish film produced by oxidation on bronze subjected to prolonged weathering; *hence*, any surface alteration produced by exposure to the elements or by prolonged use. 18c. [N,S]

patio [Sp.] an inner courtyard (open to the sky) in a Spanish house. 19c. [N,S]

pâtisserie [Fr.] any confection made of pastry; a place where such confections are sold, *usu.* for consumption on the premises. 18c. [N,S]

patois [Fr.] a dialect spoken in a particular district, differing substantially from the literary language of the country. 17c. A local dialect as distinct from an ARGOT or class dialect. [N,S]

patria potestas [Lat.] *Hist.* absolute power wielded by a father over his family, *esp.* the power wielded by the father in ancient Rome. 19c. [S]

patron, *f.* **patronne** [Fr.] the proprietor of a commercial establishment, *usu.* of an inn, café or restaurant. 20c. Always printed in italics to distinguish it from English *patron.*

pavane [Fr. < Sp. *pavana*] a slow and stately dance in which the dancers are magnificently dressed; the music appropriate to this dance. 16c. The Spanish word is probably derived from Sp. *pavo* 'peacock'. [N,S]

pavé [Fr.] (1) a cobbled street, *esp.* in France or Belgium; cobbled paving, *esp.* as conducive to discomfort in driving a motor-car; (2) a method of setting precious stones close together like the stones of a pavement so that no metal is visible between them. 18c. [N,S]

pavillon [Fr.] *Arch.* a small ornamental building set in a garden, a summerhouse. 20c.

pax [Lat.] 'peace', a call for truce used by children at play. 19c. [N]

pax Britannica [Lat.] the peace imposed by British rule within the British empire. 19c. Based on the better known PAX ROMANA; the phrase was invented by Joseph Chamberlain in 1893 to describe the results of British rule in India. [N]

pax Romana [Lat.] *Hist.* the peace imposed by Roman rule within the Roman Empire. 19c. [N]

paysage [Fr.] a rural scene, the countryside, the landscape; a representation of a rural scene, a landscape painting. 17c. [N,S]

(les) Pays Bas [Fr.] the Low Countries, Belgium and Holland. 19c. [S]

pays de mission [Fr.] *Rel.* a missionary country, a country in which proselytizing activity is planned or in progress. 20c.

pays sans frontière [Fr.] a country without frontiers, an international community; a country of the mind. 20c.

peau-de-soie [Fr. 'silk skin'] a thick silk fabric with a dull satin face on both sides. 19c. [N]

peccadillo [Sp. *pecadillo*] a trifling fault, a pardonable offence. 16c. [N,S]

peccavi, *pl.* **peccavimus** [Lat.] 'I have sinned', a confession of guilt or an admission of responsibility for an error. 16c. Now *usu.* jocular. Cf. MEA CULPA. [N,S]

péché mortel [Fr. 'mortal sin'] a CHAISE-LONGUE consisting of an upholstered arm-chair and a matching upholstered stool which can be removed. 18c. Cf. DUCHESSE. [S*]

peignoir [Fr.] a loose dressing-gown worn by women. 19c. From Fr. *peigne* 'comb'; the *peignoir* is worn while the hair is being combed. [N,S]

peine forte et dure [Fr. 'severe and cruel punishment'] *Law* pressing to death under heavy weights, the punishment formerly inflicted on those who refused to plead to a charge of felony. 16c. [N,S]

peintre de dimanche [Fr.] a 'Sunday painter', a painter who earns his living otherwise than by painting. 20c.

peinture [Fr.] *Art* the method of using paint adopted by an artist or school of artists. 20c.

peinture à la colle [Fr.] *Art* a method of painting with opaque powder-colour suspended in a solution of gum; poster-colour painting. 20c. Cf. GOUACHE.

pèlerine [Fr. 'pilgrim's cloak'] a woman's narrow cape with ends coming down to a point in front. 18c. The word has been fashionable at least six separate times, and the precise style denoted by it has probably been different each time. [N,S]

pelisse [Fr.] a woman's long loose cloak with holes for the arms. 18c. The *pelisse* was *orig.* lined with fur. [N,S]

pelota [Sp.] a game of Basque origin in which a ball is struck with a wicker racket attached to a leather glove. 19c. [N]

pelta [Lat. < Gk. πέλτη] (1) *Hist.* a small light shield used by the ancient Greeks and Romans; *hence* (2) *Art* a shield-like MOTIF in decorative art. 17c. [N]

penchant [Fr.] a strong or habitual inclination, a habitual liking. 17c. [N,S]

pendeloque [Fr.] a pendant, *esp.* a pear- or drop-shaped precious stone set as a pendant. 19c. [N,S]

pendente lite [Lat.] *Law* while the case is pending. 19c. [N,S]

penetralia *pl.* [Lat.] the innermost parts or recesses, *esp.* of a temple; the secret chambers (of the heart, etc.) 17c. The singular *penetrale* is very rare. [N,S]

pensée [Fr.] a thought or reflection put into literary form. 19c. *Usu.* by conscious analogy with Pascal's *Pensées* (1670). [N,S]

pension [Fr.] a boarding-house, a lodging-house with a fixed weekly or monthly rate, *usu.* in France or Italy. 18c. Cf. DEMI-PENSION; EN PENSION. [N,S]

pensionnaire [Fr.] one who is living as a boarder, paying a fixed weekly or monthly sum for board and lodging. 18c. [N,S]

pentathlon [Gk. πένταθλον] *Hist.* an athletic contest of the ancient world combining five different exercises—jumping, running, throwing the discus, throwing the spear, and wrestling. 18c. Revived in 1906 for the modern Olympic games; the men's *pentathlon* now includes 200 metre and 1500 metre races, discus, javelin, and long jump. [N,S]

pentimento, *pl.* **pentimenti** [It. 'repentance'] *Art* an alteration made in the process of executing a painting, *esp.* a detail effaced by the painter which becomes visible again in the course of time through the increasing translucence of the paint with age. 19c. [S]

peon [Sp.] a Mexican serf, a debtor held in servitude by his creditor until the debt is paid off. 19c. [N,S]

peplos [Gk. πέπλος] *Hist.* a rich robe or shawl worn by women in ancient Greece, hanging in folds and sometimes drawn over the head. 18c. [N]

peplum [Lat.] a woman's overskirt, supposed to resemble the ancient PEPLOS; *hence*, (a woman's jacket with) a flared skirt covering the upper part of the skirt beneath. 19c. The Latin word is irregularly derived from Gk. πέπλος; the more regular form *peplus* is very rare. [N,S]

per accidens [Lat.] by virtue of some non-essential circumstance, contingently. 16c. Opposed to PER SE. [N,S]

per annum [Lat.] (a sum of money paid) every year, yearly. 17c. [N,S]

percale [Fr. < Pers. *pargālah* 'rag'] a soft closely-woven cotton fabric. 19c. [N]

per capita [Lat. 'by heads'] (1) *Law* (a legacy) divided amongst a number of individuals in equal shares, not PER STIRPES; (2) (a payment made) in proportion to the number of persons who have benefited from some service. 17c. [N,S]

per cent(um) [Lat.] by the hundred, in each hundred. 16c. Commonly indicated by the arbitrary symbol %. [N,S]

perceptum, *pl.* **percepta** [Lat.] *Psych.* something perceived, a meaningful impression obtained through the senses. 20c.

percheron [Fr.] a breed of horse resembling a lightly-built cart-horse. 19c. *Orig.* bred in the district of *le Perche* in south Normandy, but now extensively bred in the United States. [N,S]

per contra [Lat.] on the other hand, on the other side of the argument. 16c. [N,S]

per diem [Lat.] (a sum of money paid) every day, daily, for a day's work. 16c. In use earlier than PER ANNUM. [N,S]

perdu. *f.* **perdue** [Fr. 'lost'] hidden away, out of sight; hidden but on the watch, in ambush. 17c. *Orig.* introduced in the phrase *sentinelle perdue* 'hidden sentry', and hence commonly written *perdue;* now distinguished according to the sex of the person referred to. [N,S]

père [Fr.] (the) father; always preceded by a name, and opposed to FILS '(the) son'. 19c. Cf. AÎNÉ; CADET. [S]

père de famille [Fr.] the father of a family. 19c. Cf. PATERFAMILIAS. [S]

peredyshka [Russ.] a breathing-space. 20c.

perfervidum ingenium [Lat.] extreme enthusiasm, ardent temperament. 19c. Sometimes completed by a Latin noun in the genitive case, e.g. *perfervidum ingenium Scotorum* 'the extreme enthusiasm of the Scots'. [S]

perfide Albion [Fr.] treacherous England. 19c. The traditional French view of England. The origin of the poetical name *Albion* is uncertain. [S]

pergola [It.] a covered walk formed of growing plants trained over trellis-work. 17c. Cf. BERCEAU. [N,S]

per impossible [Lat.] by an impossibility; supposing it were possible, which it is not. 20c. Used in argument when considering the hypothetical result of conditions which can never exist.

per incuriam [Lat.] *Law* through negligence, through carelessness. 20c.

per industriam hominis [Lat.] *Law* (the reclamation of land, etc.) through the industry of man. 19c. Such reclamation may provide grounds for a claim to ownership.

peripeteia [Gk. περιπέτεια] a sudden change of fortune or reverse of circumstances, *esp.* as providing the DÉNOUEMENT of a play or novel. 16c. Cf. WENDEPUNKT. [N,S]

periphrasis, *pl.* **periphrases** [Gk. περίφρασις] circumlocution, a roundabout way of speaking; a roundabout phrase or expression. 16c. [N,S]

periplus [Lat. < Gk. περίπλους] a circumnavigation, a circuit; *hence*, a primitive chart or sailing-guide. 18c. [N,S]

perito, *pl.* **periti** [It.] an expert. 20c. Used *esp.* of the experts called into consultation by the Second Vatican Council. The plural *periti* cannot be distinguished from that of the Latin equivalent *peritus.*

per mensem [Lat.] (a sum of money paid) every month, monthly. 17c. [N,S]

permis de séjour, *pl.* **permis de séjour** [Fr.] a licence to reside in a given place, issued by the police in certain foreign countries. 19c. [S]

perpetuum mobile [Lat.] *Mus.* continual movement, a passage of music in which the sequence of rapid notes continues without a break. 20c. Cf. MOTO PERPETUO.

per pro(curationem) [Lat.] by proxy, by the action of an official agent or deputy. 19c. Used to indicate that a letter or document has been signed by an agent on behalf of the principal: the correct sequence is '(principal) *per pro* (agent)', but the opposite sequence '(agent) *per pro* (principal)' is now almost universal; the abbreviation is often written *per/pro* and seems to be understood as 'for and on behalf of'. [N]

perron [Fr.] *Arch.* a platform in front of the main entrance of a building, *usu.* approached by a double flight of steps. 18c. [N,S]

perruque [Fr.] a wig, *esp.* a full-bottomed wig; *hence*, a pompous but vacuous person. 16c. [N,S]

per saltum [Lat.] by a jump, at a single step, without any intermediate stages. 17c. Cf. SALTUS. [N,S]

per se [Lat.] in itself, essentially, without reference to anything else. 16c. Opposed to PER ACCIDENS. [N,S]

persiennes *pl.* [Fr.] shutters constructed with movable slates like a Venetian blind. 19c. Cf. JALOUSIE. [N,S]

persiflage [Fr.] raillery, light-hearted banter; frivolous discussion of a subject. 18c. Cf. BADINAGE. [N,S]

persona, *pl.* **personæ** [Lat.] (1) a person's 'public image', the character in which one chooses to appear in public; (2) *Psych.* the part of the personality which is in touch with the outside world; the expression of the personality. 20c. In the second sense contrasted with ANIMA.

persona muta, *pl.* **personæ mutæ** [Lat.] a character in a play who has no speaking part. 17c. Cf. FIGURANT. [S]

persona non grata, *pl.* **personæ non gratæ** [Lat.] a person who is not wanted, *esp.* a diplomatic representative who is personally unacceptable to the authority to which he is accredited. 20c. The positive form *persona grata* is recorded from 19c; the negative form is recent, and seems to have displaced the other. [N,S]

personnel [Fr.] the total force of persons required for the conduct of some enterprise or for the continued functioning of some establishment or institution. 19c. Contrasted with MATÉRIEL, the stock of material objects required for the enterprise. [N,S]

per stirpes [Lat.] *Law* (a legacy) divided in equal shares between the branches of a family, the share of each branch being subdivided equally between the members of that branch. 17c. Cf. PER CAPITA. [N,S]

pétard [Fr. 'firework'] *Art* a work of art designed to startle. 20c.

pet de nonne [Fr. 'nun's fart'] *Cul.* a fritter. 20c.

pétillant [Fr.] sparkling (wit, etc.); semi-sparkling (wine). 20c. Distinct from MOUSSEUX 'sparkling, frothy (wine)'.

petit [Fr.] little, trivial, insignificant, *esp.* in phrases implying contempt or disparagement. 18c. Phrases of this type continue to be invented, e.g. *petit avantgardiste* 'an insignificant devotee of the AVANT-GARDE'. The pejorative connotation is not normally extended to the feminine *petite*.

petit beurre [Fr. 'little butter'] *Cul.* a plain sweet biscuit. 20c.

petit blanc, *pl.* **petits blancs** [Fr.] a 'poor white', a member of a mixed community whose only claim to distinction is European blood. 20c.

petit bourgeois, *f.* **petite bourgeoise** [Fr.] a member of the lower middle classes, a person of very limited mental horizons. 20c. Cf. PETITE BOURGEOISIE.

petite [Fr.] small and dainty (of a woman's figure). 18c. [N]

petite amie [Fr.] the female friend of a middle-aged man. 20c. Always with the implication that the friendship is not wholly Platonic. Cf. AMIE.

petite bourgeoisie [Fr.] the lower middle classes, supposedly very limited in their mental horizons. 20c. Cf. BOURGEOISIE; HAUTE BOURGEOISIE; PETIT BOURGEOIS.

petite entrée [Fr.] the privilege of admission (to Court, etc.) on a familiar footing, for informal private functions. 19c. Cf. ENTRÉE; GRANDE ENTRÉE. [S]

petite maison [Fr.] a 'love-nest', a flat or villa maintained for the residence of a mistress. 18c. Cf. APPARTEMENT MEUBLÉ. [S]

petite nature [Fr.] *Art* not quite life-size, between full-size and half-size. 20c.

petit four [Fr. 'little oven'] *Cul.* a small highly-decorated cake or biscuit. 19c. [N*]

petitio principii [Lat.] *Logic* begging the question, the logical fallacy of using a premiss which is either equivalent to or dependent on the conclusion. 16c. Cf. IGNORATIO ELENCHI. [N,S]

petit maître, *f.* **petite maîtresse** [Fr.] a dandy, a fop, a man full of affectation. 18c. [N,S]

petit mal [Fr.] *Med.* the less violent form of epilepsy in which the fits are abortive or incomplete. 19c. Cf. GRAND MAL. [N]

petit peuple [Fr.] people in a small way of business; the lower classes. 20c.

petit point [Fr.] (embroidery executed in) tent-stitch. 19c. Cf. GROS POINT. [N]

petit poulet [Fr.] a young fowl, a broiler fowl. 20c.

petits soins *pl.* [Fr.] little attentions, little services (*usu.* performed by a man for a woman). 19c. [S]

petit verre [Fr.] a glass of LIQUEUR. 19c. Not 'liqueur-glass'. [N,S]

peto [Sp.] a thick padded protective covering worn by horses participating in a bull-fight. 20c.

peuple [Fr.] characteristic of the working classes, plebeian. 20c.

phallus, *pl.* **phalli** [Lat. < Gk. *φαλλός*] a carved representation of the male generative organ, venerated in certain religions as the symbol of the generative power in nature. 17c. Cf. YONI. [N,S]

pharmacopœia [Lat. < Gk. *φαρμακοποιία* 'manufacture of drugs'] *Med.* a book containing authoritative formulæ for the preparation of drugs and medicines. 17c. [N,S]

pharos [Gk. *φάρος*] *Hist.* a (Greek or Roman) lighthouse. 16c. From *Pharos*, the name of an island off Alexandria, the site of a famous lighthouse built by Ptolemy Philadelphus. [N,S]

phenomenon, *pl.* **phenomena** [Lat. *phænomenon* < Gk. *φαινόμενον*] *Psych.* an appearance, an immediate object of perception (opposed to NOUMENON); *hence,* something extraordinary, a remarkable thing or person. 17c. The spellings *phainomenon* and *phænomenon* were formerly in use. [N,S]

philosophe [Fr.] a philosopher, *esp.* one tending towards freethinking or libertinism; a dabbler in philosophy, an amateur philosopher. 19c. [S]

phobia [Gk. *-φοβία*] a morbid fear or aversion. 19c. The form exists in Greek only as a suffix, not as an independent word. [N]

phrase toute faite [Fr.] a ready-made phrase, a commonplace, a CLICHÉ. 20c.

phylum, *pl.* **phyla** [Lat. < Gk. *φῦλον*] a group of organisms related by descent from a common ancestral form, *esp.* a primary division of the animal kingdom. 19c. [N,S]

physique [Fr.] physical constitution, bodily build, *esp.* the characteristic physical appearance of a person or race. 19c. [N,S]

piaffe [Fr. *piaffer*] *Equ.* to move with the same step as the trot, but more slowly. 18c. In the trot the two diagonally opposite legs are moved forwards simultaneously. [N]

pia fraus, *pl.* **piæ fraudes** [Lat.] a pious deceit, something dishonest done in the interest of religion or morality. 17c. Ovid *Metamorphoses* ix 710: *Impercepta pia mendacia fraude latebant* 'Unperceived lies lay hidden in a well-intentioned deceit'. Cf. FRAUDE PIEUSE. [S]

pianissimo [It.] *Mus.* very soft(ly); a very soft passage of music. 18c. The superlative of PIANO. [N,S]

piano [It.] (1) *Mus.* soft(ly); a soft passage of music. 17c. (2) a storey or floor in an Italian house. 19c. [N,S]

piano nobile [It.] the main floor of an Italian house on which the grand reception rooms are situated. 20c. Cf. APPARTEMENT DE PARADE; BEL ÉTAGE.

piastre [Fr.] the European name for various Oriental units of value, *esp.* the Turkish *kuruş*. 17c. The Turkish *kuruş*, one hundredth of a *lira*, has been much devalued, but the Egyptian *piastre* is still worth about a hundredth of a pound sterling. [N,S]

piazza, *pl.* **piazze** [It.] a public square, *esp.* in an Italian town; a colonnade, *esp.* round an internal courtyard in a building. 16c. [N(*),S]

pibroch [Gael. *piobaireachd*] a series of variations of martial character played on the bagpipe. 18c. [N,S]

picador, *pl.* **picadores** [Sp.] a horseman who opens a bull-fight by provoking the bull with a spear. 18c. [N,S]

picaresque [Fr.] (a type of fiction) dealing with the adventures of rogues and vagabonds. 19c. [N,S]

piccola morte [It. 'little death'] a temporary oblivion achieved by means of intoxicants, narcotics, etc.; the suspension of normal consciousness at the moment of orgasm in coition. 20c.

pice [Hind. *paisā*] *A.-I.* a coin worth one quarter of an ANNA. 17c. [N,S]

Pickelhaube, *pl.* **Pickelhauben** [Ger.] a German spiked helmet as worn during the First World War. 19c. [N*,S]

picot [Fr.] a small loop of twisted thread forming part of an edge to lace or ribbon. 19c. [N(*)]

pièce d'eau, *pl.* **pièces d'eau** [Fr.] an ornamental lake with a fountain. 20c.

pièce de résistance [Fr.] the most substantial dish in a meal; *hence*, the most important item in a collection, series, or programme. 19c. [N,S]

pièce de spectacle [Fr.] a work of art designed to gratify by its grandeur and splendour. 20c.

pièce d'occasion [Fr.] a literary or musical work composed for a special occasion. 19c. [S]

pièce justificative, *pl.* **pièces justificatives** [Fr.] a document serving as proof of an assertion, a document quoted as evidence. 18c. Now much more common in the plural than in the singular. [N,S]

pièce montée [Fr.] a 'set piece', something specially prepared or assembled, *usu.* from a number of constituent items. 20c.

pièce noire [Fr. 'black play'] a dramatic work with a tragic theme and a tone of unrelieved pessimism. 20c. *Pièces Noires* is the title given by Jean Anouilh to certain collections of his plays (1945 and later). Cf. COMÉDIE NOIRE.

pièce rose [Fr. 'pink play'] a dramatic work with an optimistic tone and a happy ending. 20c. *Pièces Roses* is the title given by Jean Anouilh to certain collections of his plays (1945 and later). Cf. COMÉDIE ROSE.

pied-à-terre [Fr. 'foot to ground'] a simple town residence, *esp.* considered as convenient when the owner is temporarily in town for business or pleasure. 19c. [S]

pied noir, *pl.* **pieds noirs** [Fr. 'black foot'] a European settler in Algeria. 20c. So called from the black shoes worn by Europeans but not by native Algerians.

pierrot, *f.* **pierrette** [Fr.] a clown with a whitened face and a long loose-sleeved costume, *esp.* one appearing in a travelling entertainment. 18c. [N,S]

pietà [It.] *Art* a representation of the Virgin Mary holding the dead body of Christ. 17c. [N,S]

pietas [Lat.] dutiful affection; devotion to the memory of a dead friend. 20c. Introduced to convey some of the earlier meanings of English *piety*, which has acquired a mainly religious connotation.

pietra commessa, *pl.* **pietre commesse** [It.] *Art* (a piece of) mosaic-work. 17c. Cf. INTARSIO; LAVORO DI COMMESSO; PIETRA DURA. [S]

pietra dura, *pl.* **pietre dure** [It.] *Art* mosaic-work in which hard semi-precious stones are set into a background, *usu.* of black marble. Cf. INTARSIO; LAVORO DI COMMESSO; PIETRA COMMESSA. [S]

pilav/pilaf [Turk. *pilâv* < Pers. *pilāw*] *Cul.* an Oriental dish consisting of rice boiled with pieces of meat, raisins and other ingredients. 17c. Earlier spellings in English (*pilaw*, etc.) represent the Persian form; *pilaf* represents the modern Turkish pronunciation. Cf. RISOTTO. [N,S]

pilotis *pl.* [Fr. 'stilts'] *Arch.* reinforced concrete columns used to support the weight of a building so as to leave the ground-space free. 20c.

pimento [Port. *pimenta*] *Cul.* allspice, a spice obtained from the aromatic berries of the tree *Pimenta officinalis*. 17c. Formerly, and now again increasingly, applied to *Capsicum*—'Red Pepper' or 'chilli'. Cf. PAPRIKA. [N,S]

pincé [Fr.] *Mus.* an ornament in which the main note is alternated with the note immediately below it. 20c.

pince-nez [Fr. 'pinch-nose'] a pair of spectacles held on the bridge of the nose by a spring clip. 19c. Formerly 'a *pince-nez*'; now generally construed as plural. [N,S]

pince-sans-rire [Fr. 'pinch-without-laughing'] a person of dry and mischievous humour. 20c. The word is unchanged in the plural.

pinna, *pl.* **pinnæ** [Lat.] a wing-like structure forming part of a living organism. 17c. Applied in the human being to the upper part of the external ear and to the lateral cartilage of the nose. [N]

pinto [Sp.] piebald; a piebald horse. 19c. [N]

pinx(it) [Lat.] (he) painted (it); always accompanied by a name and appended to a painting. 19c. Cf. CÆL(AVIT); DEL(INEAVIT); FEC(IT); SCULPS(IT). [S]

piquant, *f.* **piquante** [Fr.] pleasantly stimulating, exciting keen interest or curiosity. 17c. Partially anglicized in pronunciation, but still felt to be foreign, as the feminine form shows; often printed in italics. [N,S]

pique [Fr.] (1) a feeling of resentment, anger at some slight (real or fancied); (2) the winning of 30 points at PIQUET before the opponent has begun to score. 17c. [N,S]

piqué [Fr.] (1) a stiff cotton fabric woven with a raised pattern; (2) (ornamental work, *usu.* in tortoiseshell) inlaid with numerous minute points of gold. 19c. [N,S]

piquet [Fr.] a game for two players, played with 32 cards, in which points are scored for various combinations of cards. 17c. [N,S]

piqûre [Fr.] an injection (of some drug, etc.). 20c. The word refers rather to the operation of injecting the medicinal substance than to the nature of the substance injected.

pirogue [Fr.] a canoe hollowed out from the trunk of a tree; a native canoe, an open boat used by savage tribes. 17c. The French word is borrowed from some Carib dialect. [N(*),S]

pirouette [Fr.] (1) *Ballet* a full turn of the body on the point of the toe, with the toe of the free leg at the knee of the other; (2) *Equ.* a full turn made by a horse without changing his ground. 18c. Cf. TOUR. [N,S]

pis aller [Fr. 'go worst'] a last resource, that which must be accepted if no better can be had, a course of action to be adopted if the worst comes to the worst. 17c. Cf. FAUTE DE MIEUX. [N,S]

piscina, *pl.* **piscinæ** [Lat. 'fishpond'] *Eccles.* a stone basin with a drain serving for the priest's ablutions, *usu.* in a niche on the south side of the altar. 18c. [N,S]

pisé [Fr.] clay mixed with gravel and rammed between shutterings so as to form a wall; the building of a wall in this way. 18c. Cf. TERRE PISÉE. [N]

pistachio [Sp. *pistacho*, It. *pistacchio*] the green kernel of the tree *Pistacia vera*, used as a flavouring. 16c. The ultimate origin is Pers. *pistah.* Many spellings have been used in English; the current one seems to represent a compromise between the Spanish form (on which the pronunciation is based) and the Italian. [N(*),S]

piste [Fr.] the track or trail left by an animal; a race-track; a ski-run. 18c. [N,S]

piston [Fr.] 'influence' used in obtaining employment, etc. 20c. Cf. COUP DE PISTON.

pithos, *pl.* **pithoi** [Gk. πίθος] *Hist.* a large wide-mouthed rounded jar used by the ancient Greeks for storing wine or oil. 19c. [N]

piton [Fr.] an iron spike to which a rope can be attached when climbing a precipitous slope. 20c.

(le) pittoresque [Fr.] *Art* the quality in an arrangement of natural objects which makes it a fit subject for a picture. 20c. Cf. GENRE PITTORESQUE.

pizza [It.] *Cul.* a cake of dough covered with various vegetables and herbs and then baked. 20c.

pizzicato [It.] *Mus.* (a note or passage played on a bowed instrument) by plucking the string with the finger instead of using the bow. 19c. [N,S]

(une) place au soleil [Fr.] a place in the sun, an opportunity of enjoying the good things of life, circumstances of comfortable repose. 20c.

placebo [Lat. 'I shall be pleasing'] (1) *Eccles.* the Vespers in the Office for the Dead. 13c. (2) *Med.* a medicine prescribed to please rather than to cure the patient. 19c. Vulgate *Psalm* cxiv (cxvi) 9: *Placebo Domino in regione vivorum* 'I will walk before the Lord in the land of the living'. [N,S]

placet [Lat.] 'it pleases (me)', the formula used in giving a vote of assent in university and ecclesiastical conclaves; *hence*, a vote or expression of assent. 16c. Cf. NON PLACET. [N,S]

plage [Fr.] the beach, *esp.* at a Continental seaside resort; *hence*, a Continental seaside resort. 20c. [N]

planchette [Fr, 'little plank'] a heart-shaped board supported by two castors and a pencil-point, which traces out letters and words when one or more persons rest their fingers lightly upon it. 19c. The *planchette* was invented about 1855, and has been much used in the investigation of psychical phenomena. [N(*),S]

planetarium, *pl.* **planetaria** [Lat.] an orrery, a device for illustrating the positions or motions of the planets. 18c. [N,S]

plaque [Fr.] (1) a decorative plate or tablet of regular shape, designed to be hung as an ornament on the wall or to be inserted in a piece of furniture, etc.; a tablet bearing a commemorative inscription; (2) a circular token or counter used in gambling; (3) *Med.* a patch of eruption on the skin. 19c. [N,S]

plaquette [Fr.] *Art* an ornamental tablet cast in low relief in bronze or lead. 19c. [N]

plasma [Gk. πλάσμα] *Med.* the colourless liquid in which blood corpuscles float; protoplasm, the living matter of a cell. 19c. [N,S]

plasticage [Fr.] the committing of outrages with plastic bombs. 20c. Cf. PLASTIQUÉ; PLASTIQUEUR.

plastiqué [Fr.] attacked with or injured by a plastic bomb. 20c. A plastic bomb consists of an easily fragmented plastic container packed with explosive. Cf. PLASTICAGE; PLASTIQUEUR.

plastiqueur [Fr.] one who commits outrages with plastic bombs. 20c. Cf. PLASTICAGE; PLASTIQUÉ.

plastron [Fr.] the starched front of a dress-shirt; a 'dickey', a separate starched front worn to simulate a dress-shirt; a piece of material inserted to fill a large neck-opening in a woman's dress, a 'bib'-front. 19c. Cf. CHEMISETTE. [N,S]

plat du jour [Fr.] *Cul.* a dish specially recommended by the proprietor of a restaurant on a certain day. 20c.

plateau, *pl.* **plateaux** [Fr.] (1) *Geog.* a table-land, an elevated tract of level land; (2) a 'leaf' of an expanding dining-table. 18c. Cf. ALTIPLANO. [N,S]

plebs [Lat.] *Hist.* that part of the population of ancient Rome which belonged neither to the patrician families nor to the Knights; *hence*, the common people, the working-classes. 17c. [N,S]

plectrum, *pl.* **plectra** [Lat. < Gk. πλῆκτρον] *Mus.* a small pointed tool used for plucking the strings of a wire-strung instrument. 17c. [N,S]

plein air [Fr.] *Art* the 'open air' atmosphere achieved in certain landscape paintings. 20c.

plenum [Lat.] (1) a space completely filled with matter, the opposite of a *vacuum;* (2) the full meeting of a legislative assembly. 17c. [N,S]

plethora [Lat. < Gk. πλεθώρη] superabundance, excess; unhealthy repletion. 16c. [N,S]

plexus, *pl.* **plexus** [Lat.] a network, a tangled mass, a complicated interweaving. 17c. [N,S]

plié [Fr.] *Ballet* a movement in which the dancer slowly bends both knees with the feet turned out until the buttocks are as near the heels as possible. 20c.

pliqué à jour [Fr.] *Art* a kind of CLOISONNÉ-work in which the ground is removed when the application of transparent enamels is complete, so that the result resembles stained glass in miniature. 20c. This kind of work was popular in the 14th century. Both the origin and the correct form of the phrase seem doubtful; it is often printed *plique à jour*. Probably *pliqué* is an aphetic form of APPLIQUÉ. Cf. ÉMAILLERIE À JOUR.

plissé [Fr.] (a fabric) gathered in small pleats, or so woven as to have a shirred effect over parts of the surface. 20c. [N*]

plus ça change, plus c'est la même chose [Fr.] the more things change superficially the more they are fundamentally the same. 20c. Alphonse Karr (1808–1890) in *Les Guêpes* January 1849.

plus royaliste que le roi [Fr.] more royalist than the king; *hence*, more enthusiastic for some cause or project than the person most immediately concerned. 20c.

p.m.=POST MERIDIEM, after noon.

P.M.=POST MORTEM, (a dissection) after death.

pneuma [Gk. πνεῦμα] the spirit, the soul. 19c. Often distinguished from PSYCHE, the immaterial substance shared by mankind with the animal kingdom. Cf. ANIMUS. [N]

pochette [Fr.] a woman's handbag of cloth or leather. 20c. [N*]

poco curante, *pl.* **poco curanti** [It.] careless, indifferent, NONCHALANT; one who shows little interest or concern. 18c. [N,S]

podere [It.] a country estate, *esp.* in Italy. 20c.

podestà [It.] the chief magistrate of an Italian town. 16c. [N,S]

podium, *pl.* **podia** [Lat.] *Arch.* a projecting pedestal; a continuous raised platform running round the outside of a building or the inside of a room. 17c. [N,S]

podzol/podsol [Russ.] *Geog.* stratified soil in which substances are leached from the upper layers and deposited in a well-defined STRATUM. 20c. The upper surface is greyish-white. Such soil is found in sub-polar regions with high precipitation and low evaporation.

poeta nascitur non fit [Lat.] a poet is born, not made, i.e., you cannot become a poet by taking pains. 19c. [S]

poète maudit [Fr.] a poet insufficiently appreciated by his contemporaries. 20c. Verlaine's *Les Poètes Maudits* is a study of six such poets. Cf. MAUDIT.

pogrom [Russ. 'destruction'] an organized massacre aimed at the elimination of a class or type of people. 19c. Applied *esp.* to massacres of Jews. [N]

poilu [Fr. 'hairy'] a French private soldier. 20c. The nickname refers to the unkempt and unshaven appearance of the French soldier. [N*]

point d'Alençon [Fr.] a kind of lace made at Alençon. 19c. [N,S]

point d'appui [Fr.] a FULCRUM, a point of leverage. 19c. [N,S]

point de repère [Fr.] a point from which one takes one's bearings, a reference mark; *Mil.* a rallying-point. 19c. [N]

point de Venise [Fr.] a kind of lace made in Venice. 17c. [N,S]

point d'honneur [Fr.] a point of honour, something by which one feels one's honour to be impugned; a code of honour. 20c.

pointe [Fr.] *Ballet* the extreme point of the toe. 20c. Only DANSEUSES dance on the *pointes*, and they wear special shoes the toes of which are 'blocked' and darned to give extra support.

pointillisme [Fr.] *Art* the method developed by Impressionist painters of producing an effect of light by juxtaposing dots of pure colour which are blended by the eye. 20c. [N]

pointilliste [Fr.] *Art* a practitioner of POINTILLISME. 20c.

poitrine [Fr.] the chest; the bust. 19c. [S]

polder [Du.] a tract of land reclaimed from the sea and protected against inundation by dikes. 17c. [N,S]

polenta [It.] a kind of porridge made of maize, much eaten by the poorer classes in Italy. 19c. [S]

politesse [Fr.] good manners, the practice of etiquette. 18c. Often with the implication of excessive formality. [N,S]

politico [Sp.] a professional politician, an opportunist. 17c. Cf. POLITIQUE. [N,S]

politique [Fr.] a professional politician, an opportunist. 20c. Cf. POLITICO.

Poltergeist, *pl.* **Poltergeister** [Ger.] a spirit which makes its presence known by loud noises and by the displacement or removal of material objects. 19c. *Orig.* and properly applied to a 'noisy' spirit only; but the displacement of objects is now felt to be the most characteristic occupation of a *Poltergeist.* [N]

polypus, *pl.* **polypi** [Lat. < Gk. πολύπους 'cuttle-fish'] *Med.* a branching tumour growing from a mucous surface. 14c. Cf. SARCOMA. [N,S]

polysyndeton [Lat.] *Ling.* the use of a sequence of words or clauses linked together by (identical) copulative conjunctions. 16c. The (modern) Latin word is modelled on ASYNDETON. [N,S]

pommade [Fr.] *Cul.* a smooth creamy mixture, made of various ingredients, spread over slices of meat before cooking. 20c.

pompes funèbres [Fr.] obsequies, funeral rites. 20c. *Usu.* with an implication of morbid excess or ghoulish enjoyment in the external concomitants of death.

pompier [Fr.] (a style of writing characteristic of) a windy imitator of the style of others; derivative, banal, vulgar. 20c. The literal meaning is 'one who pumps', with reference to the idea of sucking in the wind of others and breathing it out again. Cf. STYLE POMPIER.

poncho [Sp.] a South American cloak consisting of a blanket or rectangular piece of cloth with a slit in the middle for the head; *hence*, any garment of similar design. 18c. The (South American) Spanish word is from a native Indian dialect. [N,S]

poncif [Fr.] *Art* (a work of art) commonplace and stereotyped in conception and execution. 20c.

pons asinorum [Lat.] 'the bridge of asses', the fifth proposition in the first book of Euclid; *hence*, any problem which the dull-witted find it difficult to solve. 18c. The proposition in question is the following: 'if two sides of a triangle are equal, then the angles opposite these sides are equal'. It is called 'the bridge of asses' because Euclid's diagram bears some resemblance to a bridge, and because the stupid cannot 'get over' it. [N,S]

pontifex maximus [Lat.] *Eccles.* the Supreme Pontiff, the Pope. 17c. *Orig.* the title of the Chief Priest in ancient Rome. Lat, *pontifex* has been understood to mean 'bridge-builder', and the title *pontifex maximus* interpreted in this sense; but the word is of Oscan-Umbrian origin, and has no connection with bridges. [N,S]

pontificalia *pl.* [Lat.] *Eccles.* the proper vestments of a pope, cardinal or bishop; the vestments of a priest. 16c. Cf. IN PONTIFICALIBUS. [N,S]

pont-levis [Fr.] *Arch.* a drawbridge. 15c. [N]

populus vult decipi (ergo decipiatur) [Lat.] the people want to be deceived (so let them be deceived). 17c. Attributed by Jacques de Thou (1553–1617) to Cardinal Giovanni Pietro Caraffa (1476–1559), later Pope Paul IV. Cf. QUI VULT DECIPI, DECIPIATUR. [S]

porcheria [It.] filthiness, disgusting behaviour. 20c. Cf. SCHWEINEREI.

porron [Sp.] a wine-flask with a long down-curving spout at the side. 20c.

portamento [It.] *Mus.* a continuous glide from one pitch to another in singing or in playing an instrument with variable pitch. 18c. Cf. GLISSANDO. [N,S]

port de bras [Fr.] *Ballet* the carriage of the arms; an exercise designed to improve the carriage of the arms. 20c.

porte-cochère [Fr.] a carriage entrance, a covered passage leading into an internal courtyard. 17c. [N,S]

portico [It.] *Arch.* a roofed arcade supported by pillars, *usu.* along the entrance-front of a building. 17c. Cf. STOA. [N,S]

portière [Fr.] a curtain hung over a door or doorway to eliminate draughts. 19c. [N,S]

portmanteau, *pl.* **portmanteaux** [Fr.] (1) a large suitcase or small trunk. 16c. (2) (something consisting of) a combination of two different things of the same kind. *esp.* (a factitious word) in which the sounds and meanings of two different words are blended. 19c. The second meaning was invented by Lewis Carroll, who devised a number of *portmanteau* words like *chortle* from *snort* and *chuckle;* a recent example is *smog* from *smoke* and *fog*. For an even more recent example cf. FRANGLAIS. [N,S]

posada [Sp.] an inn or tavern in Spain. 18c. [N,S]

posé [Fr.] *Ballet* a poising of the body by partially transferring the weight to the toe of an outstretched leg. 20c.

poseur, *f.* **poseuse** [Fr.] a person given to affectation, one who persists in an affected attitude in life. 19c. [N,S]

posse [Lat.] a force of constables or other persons with legal authority; a band of persons assuming quasi-legal authority. 17c. An abbreviation of *posse comitatus* 'the force of the county', the body of persons summoned by the sheriff of a county to maintain law and order. [N,S]

poste restante [Fr.] a department of the post office in which letters are kept until called for. 18c. [N,S]

post-facto [Lat.] after the event, retrospective. 20c. Irregularly formed from the phrase EX POST FACTO.

post hoc, ergo propter hoc [Lat.] 'later than that, therefore because of that'; the classic statement of the fallacy that succession in time implies a causal relationship. 19c. [S(*)]

postiche [Fr.] counterfeit; something superfluously and inappropriately added to a completed work; *hence*, a coil of false hair used to disguise the thinness of the natural hair. 19c. [N(*)]

post meridiem [Lat.] after noon, between noon and midnight. 17c. Normally abbreviated to *p.m.* Cf. ANTE MERIDIEM. [N,S]

post mortem [Lat.] after death; *hence Med.* the dissection of a corpse to determine the cause of death; *hence*, a discussion of some event recently concluded, *esp.* at the end of a hand of cards. 19c. Abbreviated to *P.M.* [N,S]

post obit(um) [Lat.] taking effect after someone's death; *esp.* a bond payable on the death of a named person from whom the borrower has expectations. 18c. [N]

post scriptum, *pl.* **post scripta** [Lat.] something added below the signature of a letter or document. 16c. Now always abbreviated to *P.S.*, which precedes the addition; a second addition is sometimes headed *P.P.S.* [N,S]

pot [Fr.] a woman's hat resembling an inverted flower-pot or similar vessel. 20c.

pot au feu [Fr.] *Cul.* boiled beef in broth. 18c. [S]

poteen [Ir. (*uisge*) *poitin* 'little pot (whisky)'] an ardent spirit brewed in Ireland in illicit stills. 19c. *Occ.* written *potheen*, *potsheen*, in imitation of the pronunciation of the word in different Irish dialects. [N,S]

pot pourri [Fr. 'rotten pot'] (1) a mixture of dried flower-petals and spices, kept in a jar to disseminate perfume; *hence* (2) a medley, a sequence of musical or literary extracts linked together to form a single composition. 18c. Cf. OLLA PODRIDA. [N,S]

pouf [Fr.] a low seat consisting of a case of leather or cloth completely filled with kapok or other stuffing. 19c. Often mis-spelt *pouffe*. [N(*)]

poule [Fr. 'hen'] a girl-friend; a woman of doubtful character. 20c.

poule de luxe [Fr.] a high-class girl-friend, a mistress maintained in luxury. 20c. Cf. GRANDE COCOTTE.

poulet [Fr. 'chicken'] a love-letter, a note of assignation. 19c. Cf. BILLET DOUX. [N]

poult-de-soie [Fr.] a fine corded silk. 19c. Anglicized from 17c. as *paduasoy*, by association with Padua, noted for its manufacture of silk. [N,S]

pourboire [Fr. 'for drinking'] a tip, a gratuity, a DOUCEUR. 19c. Cf. TRINKGELD. [N,S]

pour encourager les autres [Fr.] to encourage the others. 19c. Voltaire *Candide* xxiii: *il est bon de tuer de temps en temps un amiral pour encourager les autres* 'it's a good thing to kill an admiral from time to time to encourage the others'; with reference to the execution of Admiral Byng in 1757. [S]

pour épater les bourgeois [Fr.] to shock the middle classes, to startle the Philistines. 20c.

pour faire rire [Fr.] to cause amusement, as a joke. 20c.

pourparler [Fr.] an informal conference as a preliminary to diplomatic negotiation. 18c. [N,S(*)]

pour prendre congé [Fr.] (a visit or letter) to say goodbye on the eve of a prolonged absence. 19c. The abbreviation *p.p.c.* used to be written on a card left on the occasion of a farewell visit. Cf. CONGÉ. [S]

pour renfort de potage [Fr. 'to strengthen the soup'] to make matters worse. 20c.

pour rire [Fr.] light-hearted(ly); not to be taken seriously. 19c. Used adjectivally the phrase follows the noun it qualifies. [S]

pousse [Fr.] a dash (of bitters, etc., in a drink). 20c.

pousse-café [Fr.] a LIQUEUR taken after coffee, *esp.* a drink consisting of several different kinds of *liqueur* carefully poured into a glass in distinct layers. 19c. Cf. CHASSE. [N]

pou sto [Gk. *ποῦ στῶ*] a place to stand; a base from which to operate. 19c. [N,S]

P.P.S., *see* POST SCRIPTUM, an addition to a letter.

præmunire [Lat.] *Law* a writ summoning a person accused of prosecuting a suit in a foreign court, or *esp.* of maintaining the Papal jurisdiction in England. 15c. The *Statute of Præmunire* was promulgated by Richard II in 1392–3; the penalty was loss of liberty and property. [N(*),S]

præsente cadavere [Lat.] *Eccles.* (a REQUIEM Mass celebrated) in the presence of the corpse. 20c.

præsidium [Lat.] the executive committee of the Supreme Soviet of the U.S.S.R. 20c.

prahu/proa [Mal. *p(a)rā(h)ū*] a kind of boat used in the Malay Archipelago, propelled by sails or by oars and having an outrigger at one side. 16c. The form *proa* has been influenced by Port. *proa* 'prow (of a ship)'. [N,S]

praline [Fr.] a sweetmeat made by coating nuts or other small delicacies with boiling sugar. 19c. From the name of Marshal Duplessis-Praslin (1598–1675), by whose cook the sweetmeat was invented. Also found in anglicized forms *prawlin, prawling*. [N]

praliné [Fr.] *Cul.* (1) browned in boiling sugar; (2) (a confection) incorporating burnt almonds, *usu.* ground or chopped. 20c.

pratique [Fr.] permission allowing the crew of a ship to land in a port on the conclusion of quarantine, or on showing a clean bill of health. 17c. [N,S]

preces privatæ *pl.* [Lat.] *Eccles.* private prayers, as distinct from liturgical prayers recited in public. 20c.

précieux, *f.* **précieuse** [Fr.] absurdly affected, ridiculously over-refined; (a person) who cultivates absurd and affected refinement. 18c. Now often anglicized as *precious*. [N,S]

préciosité [Fr.] absurd affectation, ridiculous over-refinement. 20c.

précis [Fr.] an abridgement, a summary. 18c. Cf. RÉSUMÉ. [N(*),S]

predella [It.] *Art* a painted or carved panel at the back of an altar, which forms the base of the altar-piece above it; *hence*, a decorative panel at the foot of any picture. 19c. [N,S]

préfacier [Fr.] an author much given to contributing prefaces to the works of other writers, a professional writer of prefaces. 20c.

premier cru [Fr.] (a wine made from) the first (and best) growth of a vine. 20c. Cf. CRU; GRAND CRU.

premier danseur, *f.* **première danseuse** [Fr.] *Ballet* the leading dancer in a ballet company. 19c. Cf. DANSEUR; PRIMA BALLERINA. [S]

premier danseur étoile, *f.* **première danseuse étoile** [Fr.] *Ballet* the title of the highest rank in the ballet company of the Paris Opera. 20c.

première [Fr.] the 'first night' of a play or other entertainment. 19c. Now scarcely used except of the 'first night' of a film. Cf. URAUFFÜHRUNG. [N]

premier farceur [Fr.] the leading comedian in a dramatic company. 20c.

présalé [Fr.] *Cul.* a dish prepared from mutton from a sheep reared on a salt-marsh. 20c.

prestige [Fr.] reputation and influence resulting from past achievements. *hence*, social standing, STATUS. 19c. The earlier meaning was 'a conjuring trick', and current usage sometimes implies that present reputation is not wholly justified by past success. [N,S]

presto [It.] *Mus.* fast, in quick time (faster than ALLEGRO); a movement in quick time. 17c. [N,S]

prêt-à-porter [Fr.] ready to wear, 'off the peg'. 20c.

prétendant [Fr.] a claimant to the throne of France. 20c. The *prétendants* were banished from France by a law of June 1886, rescinded in June 1950.

Pretzel [Ger.] a salty biscuit baked in the form of a knot. 19c. *Usu.* eaten as a relish with beer. *Pretzel* is a South German dialect form of standard *Bretzel*, and this form has *occ.* been used in English. [N]

preux [Fr.] valiant, gallant. 19c. Felt to be the adjectival form of PREUX CHEVALIER. [N]

preux chevalier [Fr.] a valiant knight, a gallant knight; *hence*, a man who displays gallantry and protectiveness towards a woman. 18c. [N,S]

prie-dieu [Fr.] a piece of furniture designed for praying at, with a foot-piece to kneel on and a shelf to rest the arms on or to support a book. 18c. [N,S]

prima ballerina, *pl.* **prime ballerine** [It.] *Ballet* the DANSEUSE who performs the chief classical RÔLES in a ballet company. 20c.

prima ballerina assoluta [It.] *Ballet* a title of exceptional honour given to a DANSEUSE. 20c. The title was only given twice in the history of the Russian Imperial Ballet. Sometimes abbreviated to *assoluta*.

prima donna, *pl.* **prime donne** [It. 'first lady'] the principal female singer in an opera company. 19c. Cf. DIVA. [N,S]

prima facie [Lat.] at first sight, on the face of it; satisfactory enough to justify further investigation; (a prosecution case) strong enough to justify judicial proceedings. 15c. [N,S]

primeur [Fr.] anything new or early, *esp.* fruit or vegetables available before their normal season. 19c. More common in the plural than in the singular. [N]

primipara [Lat.] *Med.* (a woman or female animal) giving birth for the first time. 19c. [N]

primo [Lat.] firstly. 17c. Cf. SECUNDO. [S]

primum mobile [Lat. 'first mover'] a primary source of motion, an original cause of activity. 17c. *Orig.* applied to the outermost sphere in mediæval astronomy, which was supposed to be the cause of the motions of the stars and planets. [N,S]

primus inter pares [Lat.] first among equals, having precedence but no greater authority. 19c. [N,S(*)]

princesse [Fr.] a style of close-fitting woman's dress in which bodice and skirt are not divided by a seam but are formed by continuous strips of cloth. 20c.

princesse lointaine [Fr. 'far-off princess'] a woman humbly adored from afar, a remote and unattainable mistress. 20c. From the title of Rostand's verse play *La Princesse Lointaine* (1895).

principiis obsta [Lat.] make a stand against the first approaches (of a disease or other evil). 17c. Ovid *Remedium Amoris* 91. [S]

Privatdozent [Ger.] a lecturer recognized by a university but not a member of the salaried staff. 19c. Formerly often written *Privatdocent*. Cf. DOZENT. [N,S]

prix d'ami [Fr.] a special price for a friend, a price reduced for friendship's sake. 20c.

prix fixe [Fr.] (a meal, etc.) offered at an inclusive and fixed price. 20c. Cf. TABLE D'HÔTE.

pro [Lat.] for, in favour of (a proposition), *usu.* in the phrase '*pro* and CON(TRA)', for and against (or in the plural '*pros* and *cons*', arguments for and against). 15c. [N(*),S]

proa=PRAHU, a Malayan boat.

pro bono publico [Lat.] for the public good, for the benefit of the common people. 18c. [N,S]

proboscis, *pl.* **proboscides** [Lat. < Gk. *προβοσκίς*] a long flexible snout like an elephant's trunk; a tubular extension of the mouth of some insects. 17c. The plural is sometimes erroneously written *proboscces*. [N,S]

procès [Fr.] a lawsuit, a trial (in a French court). 19c. [S]

procès-verbal [Fr.] a written statement of evidence in support of a criminal charge (in a French court), a criminal information. 19c. [S]

procul este, profani! [Lat.] stay at a distance, you who are uninitiated! 20c. Virgil *Æneid* vi 258.

profil perdu [Fr. 'profile lost'] *Art* a portrait-pose in which the head of the sitter is turned nearly away from the viewer so that only the contour of the cheek is visible. 20c.

profit-à-prendre, *pl.* **profits-à-prendre** [Fr.] *Law* a right to the produce of soil belonging to another person. 17c. [N]

pro forma [Lat.] as a matter of form; as a gesture; as a formality in accordance with some legal requirement. 16c. Now often used as an abbreviation for '*pro forma* invoice', an invoice in accordance with legal requirements, or for any stereotyped form. [N(*),S(*)]

prognosis, *pl.* **prognoses** [Gk. *πρόγνωσις*] *Med.* a forecast of the probable course and duration of a disease. 17c. Cf. DIAGNOSIS. [N,S]

progressisme [Fr.] an optimistic belief that humanity is making and will make continuous progress towards greater prosperity and happiness. 20c.

pro hac vice [Lat.] for this occasion (only), as an exception. 17c. [N,S(*)]

prolegomenon, *pl.* **prolegomena** [Gk. *προλεγόμενον*] a preliminary treatise, a prefatory discourse. 17c. More common in the plural than in the singular, with the meaning 'introductory remarks'. Cf. EXORDIUM; PROŒMIUM. [N,S]

prolepsis, *pl.* **prolepses** [Gk. *πρόληψις*] anticipation; the assignment of an event to too early a date, an anachronism; the anticipation of objections by an opponent in an argument; *Ling.* the use of an adjective describing a condition which has not yet come into existence. 16c. [N,S]

promenade [Fr.] a leisurely walk, a constitutional; a public place designed for leisurely walking, *esp.* along the sea-front. 16c. Cf. PASEO; PASSEGGIATA. [N(*),S]

promenade en attitude, *pl.* **promenades en attitude** [Fr.] *Ballet* a slow turn on one foot with the other leg extended backwards, one arm raised and the other horizontal. 20c. Cf. ATTITUDE.

prononcé [Fr.] emphatic, conspicuous, strongly marked, exaggerated. 19c. [N,S]

pronto [Sp.] promptly, quickly. 20c. In colloquial use only. [N*]

pronunciamento [Sp.] a proclamation, *esp.* a MANIFESTO issued by the leaders of a revolution. 19c. [N(*),S]

proœmium [Lat. < Gk. *προοίμιον*] an introductory discourse, *esp.* the prefatory part of a speech. 15c. Also in the quasi-Greek form *proœmion.* Cf. EXORDIUM; PROLEGOMENON. [N,S]

propaganda [Lat.] (1) *Eccles.* the congregation DE PROPAGANDA FIDE, a committee of cardinals instituted in 1622 to superintend foreign missions; *hence* (2) any organized movement or systematic scheme for the propagation of a specific doctrine or theory. 18c. *Occ.* erroneously treated as a plural with a spurious singular *propagandum.* [N(*),S]

prophylaxis [Lat. < Gk. *πρό* + *φύλαξις*] *Med.* the prevention of disease by medical treatment. 19c. [N,S]

propylæum, *pl.* **propylæa** [Lat. < Gk. προπύλαιον] *Arch.* a gateway or entrance into a sacred enclosure, *esp.* when of architectural importance. 18c. [N,S]

pro rata [Lat.] in proportion, proportional(ly). 16c. [N,S(*)]

pro re nata [Lat. 'for a thing born'] for some unexpected contingency not previously provided for. 16c. [N,S]

prosciutto [It.] raw Parma ham. 20c.

prose rythmée [Fr.] rhythmical prose; free verse. 20c. Cf. VERS LIBRE.

prosit! [Lat. 'may it prosper!] 'your health!', a toast used in parts of Germany. 20c. Pronounced to rhyme with *toast*. Cf. GESUNDHEIT; SKÅL; SLÁINTE.

pro tanto [Lat.] so much, to such an extent. 18c. [N,S]

protégé, *f.* **protégée** [Fr.] one who is under the protection of another, one who receives benefits from a person of superior status. 18c. [N,S]

pro tem(pore) [Lat.] for the time being, temporarily. 15c. [N,S]

prothalamion [Pseudo-Gk.] a song or poem celebrating a coming marriage. 16c. Invented by Edmund Spenser: the title of a poem published in 1597. Cf. EPITHALAMIUM. [N,S]

protocolaire [Fr.] (a person) much addicted to insisting on the niceties of diplomatic etiquette. 20c.

proviso [Lat. 'provided'] a clause inserted into a formal document making some stipulation or limitation; a condition governing the execution of some undertaking. 15c. [N,S]

proxime accessit, *pl.* **proxime accesserunt** [Lat. 'he (she) came very near'] (a person who) obtained the next place to the actual winner of a prize, scholarship, etc. 19c. [N,S]

prox(imo) [Lat.] of the next month, in the next month. 19c. Cf. ULT(IMO). [N,S]

pruritus [Lat.] an itch, *esp. Med.* an itching of the skin without visible eruption. 17c. [N]

P.S.=POST SCRIPTUM, an addition to a letter or document.

pseudepigrapha *pl.* [Gk. ψευδεπίγραφα] spurious writings, books bearing false titles or ascribed to the wrong authors. 17c. [N]

pseudo [Gk. ψευδο-] spurious, counterfeit, bogus. 16c. The Greek form is used only as the first element of a compound. [N,S]

psyche [Lat. < Gk. φυχή] the spirit, the mind; the immaterial substance shared by mankind with the animal kingdom. 17c. Often distinguished from PNEUMA, the soul. Cf. ANIMA. [N,S]

psychosis, *pl.* **psychoses** [Lat. < Gk. φύχωσις] *Med.* any mental affliction or derangement which cannot be ascribed to an organic lesion. 19c. [N]

pudendum, *pl.* **pudenda** [Lat.] the privy parts, the external genital organs. 17c. Much more common in the plural than in the singular. Cf. GENITALIA. [N,S]

pudeur [Fr.] (excessive) sexual modesty. 20c.

pueblo [Sp.] a village in Spain or Spanish America. 19c. [N(*),S(*)]

puissance [Fr.] *Equ.* strength (in a horse); *hence*, (a competition) consisting of a small number of very high jumps. 20c.

pukka [Hind. *pakkā*] *A.-I.* substantial, permanent; certain, reliable; real, genuine. 18c. The spelling *pukka* is no older than 20c.; previously the normal spelling was *pucka.* [N,S]

punctum cæcum [Lat.] *Med.* the 'blind spot', the point on the RETINA from which the optic nerves radiate; *hence*, an obstinate refusal to see something obvious. 20c.

punctum delens [Lat.] a dot written under a letter in a mediæval manuscript to indicate deletion. 20c.

pundit [Hind. *paṇḍit*] a Hindu learned in Sanskrit, religion, and jurisprudence; *hence*, a person who claims to speak authoritatively on a wide variety of subjects. 17c. [N,S]

Punica fides [Lat.] 'the good faith of the Carthaginians', i.e. treachery. 19c. [S]

punkah [Hind. *pankhā*] *A.-I.* a large swinging fan worked by a cord; *hence*, any mechanical ventilating device or system. 19c. [N,S]

purana [Sansk. *purāṇá*] one of a group of Sanskrit religious poems containing the mythology of the Hindus. 17c. [N]

purdah [Hind. *pardah* 'curtain'] *A.-I.* the seclusion of Indian women of superior rank. 19c. [N(*),S]

purée [Fr.] *Cul.* anything reduced to the consistency of thick cream by passing it through a sieve; to cream something by passing it through a sieve. 19c. Formerly in the sense of 'broth'. [N,S]

purpureus pannus [Lat.] a 'purple patch', a passage in a work of literature consciously designed to display splendour of style. 20c. Horace *Ars Poetica* 15–16.

pur sang [Fr.] thoroughbred. 19c. [S]

Putsch [Swiss Ger.] a resolute revolutionary attack, a violent elimination of political opponents, *esp.* those in power. 20c. Popularized at the time of Hitler's abortive Munich *Putsch* in 1923. Cf. COUP D'ÉTAT; MACHTÜBERNAHME.

putto, *pl.* **putti** [It.] *Art* a naked infant (*usu.* very chubby) used as a decorative element in baroque art. 17c. [N]

puy [Fr.] *Geog.* a small volcanic cone, *esp.* one of those found in Auvergne. 19c. [N]

Q

Q.E.D.=QUOD ERAT DEMONSTRANDUM, which was to be proved.

Q.E.F.=QUOD ERAT FACIENDUM, which was to be done.

qq.v.=*quæ vide*, which see; *see* QUOD VIDE.

Q.S.=QUANTUM SUFFICIT, as much as suffices.

qua [Lat.] in so far as (it is), as being, in the capacity of. 17c. Cf. QUA SE. [N,S]

quadratista, *pl.* **quadratisti** [It.] *Art* an artist specializing in the transformation of interiors by TROMPE-L'ŒIL perspective paintings. 20c. Also in the form *quadraturista.*

quadratura [It.] *Art* the transformation of interiors by TROMPE-L'ŒIL perspective paintings. 20c.

quadriga, *pl.* **quadrigæ** [Lat.] *Hist.* a chariot drawn by four horses harnessed abreast. 18c. [N,S]

quadrille [Fr.] an obsolete square dance for four couples, containing five separate sets of figures. 18c. [N,S]

quadrivium [Lat.] *Hist.* the four-fold upper division of the seven liberal arts in the Middle Ages, comprising the mathematical sciences of arithmetic, geometry, astronomy, and music. 19c. Cf. TRIVIUM. [N,S]

quære [Lat.] 'inquire!', introducing a question or forming a memorandum that investigation is called for. 16c. [N,S]

quæsitum, *pl.* **quæsita** [Lat.] that which has to be decided or determined, the solution to a problem. 18c. [N,S]

quæ vide, *see* QUOD VIDE, which see.

quantum, *pl.* **quanta** [Lat. 'as much'] (1) *Law* the apportionment (of damages, an estate, etc.); the share due to a certain party. 17c. (2) a unit of energy emitted by an atom, proportional to the frequency of radiation. 20c. According to Planck's *quantum hypothesis* (1900) energy can only be emitted by atoms in *quanta.* [N(*),S]

quantum meruit [Lat. 'as much as he has deserved'] *Law* a fair recompense for services rendered where no rate of payment has been agreed. 17c. [S]

quantum mutatus ab illo [Lat.] how changed from him (I used to know)!, what a transformation I saw! 17c. Virgil *Æneid* ii 274, referring to Hector. [S]

quant(um) suff(icit) [Lat.] as much as suffices, a sufficient quantity. 17c. Common in medical prescriptions, but found in other contexts; often further abbreviated to *Q.S.* [N,S]

quartetto [It.] (1) *Mus.* a quartet; (2) a set of four nesting tables. 20c.

quartier [Fr.] a particular district in a (French) city or town. 19c. Often as an abbreviation for QUARTIER LATIN. [S]

quartier latin [Fr.] the 'Latin quarter' of Paris, the district on the left bank of the Seine inhabited by students, artists, and writers. 20c. Cf. RIVE GAUCHE.

quartier toléré [Fr.] the district in a city or town where the licensed brothels are located. 20c. Cf. MAISON TOLÉRÉE.

qua se [Lat.] in itself, by its own nature. 20c. Cf. QUA.

quasi [Lat.] apparently but not really; virtually; a kind of, a SIMULACRUM of. 17c. [N,S]

quattrocento [It. '400'] the fourteen hundreds, the fifteenth century, *esp.* the art and architecture of that century; characteristic of that century. 19c. Cf. CINQUECENTO; SEICENTO; SETTECENTO; TRECENTO. [N,S]

que diable allait-il faire dans cette galère? [Fr.] 'what the devil was he doing in the boat?', i.e. what business had he in that place (or company, occupation, etc.)? 20c. Cyrano de Bergerac *Le Pédant Joué* (1654) II iv; but Cyrano owed this scene to Molière, who later used the same phrase in *Les Fourberies de Scapin* (1671) II xi. Though the accurate quotation is recent, it has been used in garbled forms since 18c. [S]

Quellenforschung [Ger.] the investigation of sources (of literary works, etc.) 20c. *Usu.* cited as an unprofitable and stultifying type of research.

quem Deus vult perdere, prius dementat [Lat.] if God wishes to destroy a man, he drives him mad first. 19c. In the plural *quem* becomes *quos*. Based on Publilius Syrus *Aphorisms* 490: *stultum facit Fortuna quem vult perdere.* [S]

quenelle [Fr.] *Cul.* a ball made of meat or fish reduced to a paste, seasoned and fried. 19c. [N,S]

questionnaire [Fr.] a series of questions designed to elicit information from a number of people, *esp.* for statistical purposes. 20c. The current anglicization of the pronunciation is very recent. [N*]

quicunque vult [Lat. 'whoever wishes'] the Athanasian creed. 20c. So called from its first words.

quid pro quo [Lat.] one thing in exchange for another, something in return, a fair equivalent. 16c. [N,S]

quieta non movere [Lat.] let sleeping dogs lie. 18c. [S]

quietus [Lat.] a discharge from debt; a discharge from some office; *hence*, release from life, death. 16c. A shortened form of *quietus est* 'he is discharged'. [N,S]

qui facit per alium facit per se [Lat.] *Law* a man who does something by the agency of another does it himself, a man is responsible for whatever he authorizes. 19c. [S]

quinquennium, *pl.* **quinquennia** [Lat.] a period of five years. 17c. Cf. LUSTRUM. [N]

quis custodiet ipsos custodes? [Lat.] who is to guard the guardians themselves? i.e. who is to control those in authority? 18c. Juvenal *Satires* II vi 347. [S]

qui s'excuse s'accuse [Fr.] the man who makes excuses is admitting responsibility. 19c. [S]

qui vive [Fr.] the alert; only in the phrase 'on the *qui vive*', on the alert, keeping a sharp look out. 18c. *Orig.* a sentry's challenge; *qui vive?* '(long) live who?' The reply would be VIVE LE ROI '(long) live the King!' [N,S]

qui vult decipi, decipiatur [Lat.] if anyone wants to be deceived, let him be deceived. 20c. Cf. POPULUS VULT DECIPI (ERGO DECIPIATUR).

quod erat demonstrandum [Lat.] which was to be proved; added at the end of the proof of a theorem. 17c. Based on Euclid's ὅτι ἔδει δεῖξαι. Commonly abbreviated to *Q.E.D.* [S]

quod erat faciendum [Lat.] which was to be done or constructed; added at the end of the demonstration of a geometrical construction. 19c. Based on Euclid's ὅτι ἔδει ποιεῖν. Commonly abbreviated to *Q.E.F.* [S]

quod semper, quod ubique, quod ab omnibus (creditum est) [Lat.] what has been believed always, everywhere, and by everyone. 19c. St Vincent of Lérins *Commonitorium* ii. [S]

quod vide, *pl.* **quæ vide** [Lat.] which see. 19c. Used to indicate that further information can be found under the reference given. Commonly abbreviated to *q.v.*, *qq.v.* Cf. VIDE. [S]

quo jure? [Lat.] by what right?, by what authority? 17c. [S]

quondam [Lat.] former, that was formerly, that used to be. 16c. Cf. CI-DEVANT. [N,S]

quorum [Lat. 'of which'] the specified number of members of a body whose presence is necessary to validate the transactions of a meeting of that body. 17c. [N,S]

quorum pars magna fui [Lat.] of which I have been an important member, in which I have played a considerable part. 17c. Virgil *Æneid* ii 6. Occ. modified in modesty or mock-modesty to *quorum pars minima fui* 'in which I have played an insignificant part'. [S(*)]

quota [Lat. *quota* (*pars*) 'how great (a part)'] a proportional contribution or allocation of a specified part of a total amount. 17c. [N,S]

quot homines, tot sententiæ [Lat.] there are as many opinions as there are men, every man has his own opinion. 16c. Terence *Phormio* 454; quoted by Cicero *De Finibus* I v 15. Cf. DE GUSTIBUS (NON EST DISPUTANDUM). [S]

quo vadis? [Lat.] where are you going to? 20c. According to a legend told by St Ambrose (*Contra Auxentium*) St Peter fleeing from Rome encountered the figure of Christ, who addressed him in these words. St Peter had used the same words to Christ: Vulgate *St John* xiii 36.

quo warranto [Lat.] *Law* a writ calling upon a person to show by what warrant he holds some office or exercises some function. 16c. [N,S]

q.v.=QUOD VIDE, which see.

R

℞ = RECIPE, take!

raconteur, *f.* **raconteuse** [Fr.] someone skilled or gifted in the art of verbal story-telling. 19c. [N,S]

radix malorum [Lat.] the root of all evils, money. 20c. Vulgate *I Timothy* vi 10: *Radix enim omnium malorum est cupiditas* 'For the love of money is the root of all evil'.

ragoût [Fr.] *Cul.* a highly-seasoned stew of vegetables and small pieces of meat. 17c. [N,S]

raison d'état, *pl.* **raisons d'état** [Fr.] a reason connected with the safety of the state (as a justification for an apparently autocratic action). 20c.

raison d'être [Fr.] a reason for existing, a justification for the existence of something. 19c. [N,S]

raisonné [Fr.] rational, logical, systematically arranged. 18c. Cf. CATALOGUE RAISONNÉ.

raisonneur [Fr.] a character in a novel or play who draws conclusions from the behaviour of the other characters and moralizes upon the action. 20c. *Orig.* a term of dramatic criticism, now more commonly applied to the novel.

raj [Hind. *rāj*] *A.-I.* sovereignty, rule, authority. 19c. Most commonly in the phrase 'the British *raj*'. [N,S]

rajah [Hind. *rājā*] *A.-I.* an Indian prince or princeling, a Hindu chieftain. 16c. Cf. MAHARAJAH; RANEE. [N,S]

raki [Turk. *rakı*] an Oriental ardent spirit made from grain or grape-skins. 17c. Ultimately from Arab. *'araq*, 'juice'; cf. ARAK. [N,S]

râle [Fr.] *Med.* an abnormal noise accompanying breathing in morbid conditions of the lungs. 19c. Cf. SOUFFLE. [N]

rallentando [It.] *Mus.* becoming slower, slowing down. 19c. [N,S]

Ramadan [Arab. *ramaḍān*] *Rel.* the annual thirty days' fast in the ninth month of the Moslem year. 17c. *Ramadan* requires complete abstention from food and drink between sunrise and sunset; smoking is also forbidden. The form *Ramazan* from the Persian is also *occ.* used. [N,S]

ranchero [Sp.] a herdsman or overseer employed on a ranch; a small farmer. 19c. [N(*),S]

ranee [Hind. *rānī*] *A.-I.* the wife of a RAJAH. 17c. *Occ.* written *rani*, in closer conformity with the Hindustani. Cf. MAHARANEE. [N,S]

ranz-des-vaches [Swiss Fr.] a Swiss herdsman's melody played on an ALPENHORN. 19c. The meaning of *ranz* is unknown. [N,S(*)]

rappel [Fr.] a method of descending a cliff or rock-face on a double rope secured in such a way that the last man down can recover it. 20c. Cf. ABSEIL.

rappel à l'ordre [Fr.] a return to the question at issue, *esp.* a return to the application of basic principles (in criticism, etc.) 20c.

rapport [Fr.] a harmonious and intuitive understanding between two or more people. 19c. Cf. EN RAPPORT. [S]

rapporteur [Fr.] someone commissioned to make an investigation and report back (to a committee, etc.) 20c.

rapprochement [Fr.] a drawing together, a reconciliation; the establishment of harmonious relations. 19c. [N,S]

rara avis, *pl.* **raræ aves** [Lat.] a rare bird, a person or thing very rarely encountered, a remarkable person or thing. 18c. Horace *Satires* II ii 26; Juvenal *Satires* II vi 165. [N*,S]

rariora *pl.* [Lat.] the rarer items (in a collection, etc.) 20c.

raté, *f.* **ratée** [Fr.] (1) unsuccessful, unsatisfactory, abortive; (2) (a person) who might have achieved great success in a profession or vocation other than the one he has chosen. 20c. A more colloquial version of MANQUÉ.

Rathaus [Ger.] the town hall (of a German town). 20c. Cf. GEMEINDEHAUS.

ratio decidendi [Lat.] *Law* the essential part of a judgment, the reasons for deciding a case in a certain way. 20c. Contrasted with OBITER DICTUM.

rationale [Lat.] a reasoned explanation of principles; the fundamental rational basis (of anything). 17c. [N,S]

ratio scripta [Lat.] *Law* a judgment delivered in writing. 20c.

ratissage [Fr.] a police hunt for fugitives; the systematic combing out of territory by the military, etc. 20c.

ravioli *pl.* [It.] *Cul.* small portions of some savoury substance, *usu.* minced and seasoned meat, wrapped up in PASTA and boiled. 20c.

Realien *pl.* [Ger.] material objects forming the basis of scientific study; material objects used as teaching aids to stimulate the imagination. 20c.

Realpolitik [Ger.] a realistic policy which eschews idealism. 20c.

rebus sic stantibus [Lat.] *Law* things being as they are, in the given circumstances. 20c.

réchauffé [Fr. 'warmed-up dish'] a concoction of stale material, *esp.* a rehash of stale literary matter. 19c. Often mis-spelt *réchauffée*, *rechauffé*, *rechauffée*. [N,S]

recherché [Fr.] extremely choice, rare, or exquisite; exotic; far-fetched. 18c. *Occ.* mis-spelt *récherché*. [N,S]

recipe [Lat.] (1) *Med.* take (the following ingredients)!; *hence*, a medical prescription; (2) *Cul.* the instructions and list of ingredients for the preparation of a dish; (3) a means of attaining some end, *esp.* a method of curing some undesirable state of affairs. 15c. In the first meaning commonly abbreviated to ℞. [N,S]

recitativo, *pl.* **recitativi** [It.] *Mus.* a style of declamation between singing and speech, used in the narrative parts of operas; (a passage) intended to be declaimed in this style. 17c. The partially anglicized form *recitative* is from the Italian, not from French: the French form is *récitatif.* Cf. ARIOSO; SPRECHGESANG. [N,S]

recitativo secco [It.] *Mus.* the type of recitative in which the accompaniment is a mere framework which allows the singer to follow the natural rhythm of speech. 20c.

réclame [Fr.] the deliberate seeking of notoriety, the attainment of notoriety by self-advertisement. 19c. [N,S]

recto [Lat.] the right-hand page of an open book, the front of a leaf (as apposed to VERSO, the back of a leaf). 19c. For *recto folio* 'on a straight leaf' as opposed to a 'turned leaf'. [N,S]

rectum [Lat.] *Med.* the final section of the large intestine, leading directly to the ANUS. 16c. [N,S]

reculer pour mieux sauter [Fr.] to go back so as to jump better, to make a strategic retreat in order to make a more powerful attack. 20c.

rédacteur [Fr.] the editor (of a magazine or book). 19c. [N,S]

reddendum, *pl.* **reddenda** [Lat.] *Law* a stipulation or reserving clause in a deed. 17c. *Usu.* the clause of a lease stipulating the rental to be paid. [N,S]

redingote [Fr. < *riding-coat*] a woman's double-breasted coat with long plain skirts. 19c. [N,S]

reductio ad absurdum [Lat.] *Logic* the method of proving the falsity of a premiss by showing that the conclusion resulting from it is absurd; *hence*, pushing anything to an absurd extreme. 19c. [S]

referendum [Lat.] the submission of a question at issue to the arbitration of the whole body of voters, a plebiscite. 19c. The practice of the *referendum* was inaugurated in Switzerland. [N,S]

regalia *pl.* [Lat.] the emblems of royalty, *esp.* the crown, sceptre, and orb. 17c. Sometimes improperly used for the INSIGNIA of an order, etc. The singular *regale* is not now in use. [N,S]

regatta, *pl.* **regatte** [It.] a boat-race held on the Grand Canal at Venice; *hence*, a sporting event consisting of an organized series of aquatic contests. 17c. The word is peculiar to the Venetian dialect of Italian. [N,S]

Régence [Fr.] (the furniture and interior decoration characteristic of) the period (1715–23) of the regency of Philippe d'Orléans during the minority of Louis XV of France. 20c.

régime [Fr.] (1) a system of government, *esp.* considered as affecting social conditions; (2) a particular mode of living prescribed for reasons of health or punishment. 18c. Cf. ANCIEN RÉGIME. [N,S]

regimen [Lat.] a particular mode of living prescribed for reasons of health, *esp.* a course of diet adopted for medical reasons. 15c. [N,S]

regina [Lat.] the Queen, *esp.* as the theoretical prosecutor in a criminal prosecution. 19c. Cf. REX. [S]

régisseur [Fr.] *Ballet* the stage-manager who is also responsible for rehearsing the ballets in the RÉPERTOIRE of a company. 20c. Cf. RÉPÉTITEUR.

Regius [Lat.] appointed by the Crown; applied to certain professors in the older Universities. 17c. The Regius Chairs were founded by Henry VIII; the appointment is by the Crown after consultation with the University concerned. [S]

Reich [Ger.] a state, an empire. 20c. *Esp.* in the phrase 'the third *Reich*', referring to the German state from 1933 to 1945. This phrase is sometimes explained as if the third *Reich* had been so named to distinguish it from the 'first *Reich*', the Empire founded by Bismarck (1871–1918), and the 'second *Reich*', the Weimar Republic (1918–1933). In fact the phrase was used by Arthur Moeller van den Bruck (1876–1925) in a political interpretation of a development of the doctrine of the MILLENNIUM, in which a period of rule by the Holy Ghost was to follow periods of rule by the Father and by the Son; it is in this sense that the term was used by the propagandists of the National Socialist party. Cf. TAUSENDJÄHRIG.

relai (routier), *pl.* **relais (routiers)** [Fr.] one of a chain of roadside rest-houses in France, providing meals and sometimes beds at modest prices. 20c. *Orig.* set up for the use of long-distance lorry-drivers, now much used by the travelling public.

relatum, *pl.* **relata** [Lat.] one of a group of related things, *esp. Logic* one of the terms to which a logical relation proceeds. 20c.

relevé [Fr.] *Ballet* a step in which the body is raised on half or full POINTES. 20c.

religieuse [Fr.] a woman bound by religious vows, a nun. 18c. [N,S]

reliquiæ *pl.* [Lat.] remains, *esp.* the fossil remains of animals or plants. 17c. [N,S(*)]

rem acu tetigisti [Lat.] 'you have touched the thing with a needle', you have hit the nail on the head. 19c. Cf. Plautus *Rudens* V ii 19: *tetigisti acu.* [S]

remanet [Lat. 'it remains'] *Law* a suit the hearing of which is postponed. 18c. [N,S]

remanieur [Fr.] a writer who adapts or recasts the work of another. 20c.

renaissance [Fr. 'rebirth'] a regeneration or revival, a period of marked improvement following one of decay, *esp.* in literature or art. 19c. As a proper noun, *Renaissance* is used with special reference to the revival of art and letters from the fourteenth to the sixteenth century under the influence of Classical models. [N,S]

rencontre [Fr.] a casual or accidental meeting. 17c. [N,S]

rendezvous [Fr. 'betake yourselves!'] a place of meeting; a place and time appointed for a meeting; a place of common resort; to appoint a place of meeting, to meet at an appointed place. 16c. [N(*),S]

renouveau [Fr.] a period of renewal or refreshment, *esp.* in literature and art. 20c. The word lacks the implication of RENAISSANCE that the literature or art concerned was dead or moribund.

rentier [Fr.] one who lives without working, one who lives on profits derived from investments or property. 19c. Now *usu.* contemptuous. [N*,S]

renversement [Fr.] a reversal (of fortune), a complete transformation (of circumstances). 20c. *Usu.* with the implication of a change for the worse.

repêchage [Fr.] a supplementary heat in a rowing or sculling contest. 20c. The runners-up in the first heats compete together for a place in the final.

répertoire [Fr.] a stock of pieces which a company or performer is accustomed or able to perform; the extent of a person's proficiency in an art. 19c. [N,S]

repertorium [Lat.] a storehouse, a systematic collection. 19c. [N,S]

répétiteur [Fr.] a person responsible for conducting the rehearsals of a dramatic or musical performance. 20c. Cf. RÉGISSEUR.

répétition générale [Fr.] a full dress-rehearsal of a dramatic or musical performance, to which the press and members of the public are admitted. 20c. Sometimes abbreviated to *générale*.

replica [It.] *Art* a duplicate copy of a work of art, properly one made by the original artist; an exact copy of a work of art, a FACSIMILE. 19c. [N,S]

répondez, s'il vous plaît [Fr.] please reply. 19c. Normally abbreviated to *R.S.V.P.* and written or printed in the corner of an invitation card to indicate that a reply is expected. [N,S]

reportage [Fr.] a topical documentary, a running commentary on political occurrences, etc. 20c.

repoussé [Fr.] *Art* relief produced in ductile material by hammering the reverse side; raised in relief by this method. 19c. [N,S]

repoussoir [Fr.] *Art* a figure or object placed in the foreground to set off the rest of a picture; a foil to the beauty of something else. 20c.

reprise [Fr.] *Mus.* the resumption or repetition of a theme at the end of a development section. 19c. [N]

(la) république des lettres [Fr.] the commonwealth of literature, the whole body of men of letters all over the world. 20c. Molière *Le Mariage Forcé* (1664) vi.

requeté [Sp.] a recruit, *esp.* a recruit to the Carlist movement (1833–72) or a member of the Carlist regiments fighting with Generalissimo Franco during the Spanish Civil War (1936–9). 20c.

requiem [Lat.] *Eccles.* a Mass said or sung for the repose of the souls of the dead; a musical setting of the Mass for the Dead. 14c. From the opening words of the Introit of the Mass: *Requiem æternam dona eis, Domine* 'grant them eternal rest, O Lord'. [N,S]

requiescat in pace, *pl.* **requiescant in pace** [Lat.] may he (she) rest in peace! 16c. Commonly abbreviated to *R.I.P.* and often inscribed on sepulchral monuments. [S]

res adjudicata=*res judicata,* a matter already decided.

res gestæ *pl.* [Lat.] *Law* matters of fact, material facts, facts accepted by the court. 17c. [S]

residuum, *pl.* **residua** [Lat.] the remainder, what is left; *esp.* what remains after some process of combustion or evaporation. 17c. [N,S]

res integra [Lat.] *Law* a case raising a point of law which has not previously been decided. 18c. Contrasted with RES JUDICATA. [S]

res ipsa loquitur [Lat.] the matter speaks for itself, the matter is quite obvious. 20c.

(la) Résistance [Fr.] the resistance movement in France during the Second World War, the GUERRILLA activity conducted by those who refused to accept the armistice agreed upon by the Vichy government. 20c. Cf. MAQUIS; MAQUISARD.

res judicata [Lat.] *Law* a matter already decided, a point of law already determined. 19c. Also rarely in the form *res adjudicata;* contrasted with RES INTEGRA. Cf. CHOSE JUGÉE. [S]

res nihili/res nullius [Lat.] a thing of no importance, something wholly insignificant. 17c. [S]

respice finem [Lat.] look to the end, consider the result of what you are doing. 16c. Vulgate *Ecclesiasticus* vii 40. [S]

restaurant [Fr.] an eating-house, an establishment where refreshments and meals are served. 19c. [N,S]

restaurateur [Fr.] the proprietor or manager of a RESTAURANT. 18c. [N,S]

résumé [Fr.] a summary, an abstract, an EPITOME. 19c. Cf. PRÉCIS. [N,S]

resurgam [Lat.] I shall rise again. 17c. [S]

retenue [Fr.] self-possession, self-control, reserve. 19c. [N,S]

retina, *pl.* **retinæ** [Lat.] the reticulated light-sensitive coating on the back of the eyeball. 15c. [N,S]

retiré [Fr.] *Ballet* a step in which one foot is moved from the front to the back of the other foot by raising it as high as the knee of the other leg. 20c.

retro me, Satana [Lat.] behind me, Satan! 20c. Used in rejecting a tempting offer. Vulgate *St Mark* viii 33: *vade retro me, Satana!* 'get thee behind me, Satan!' Cf. VADE RETRO.

retroussage [Fr.] *Art* a process of smearing an etching in the course of printing so as to produce richer tones. 20c.

retroussé [Fr.] turned up. 19c. Applied only to noses. [N,S]

retsina/retzina [Gk. *ῥετσίνα*] a resinous wine drunk in Greece and the Levant. 20c. A more normal transliteration would be *rhetsina*.

revanche [Fr.] a return match, an opportunity for retaliation. 19c. Used *esp.* of the desire of the French to efface the defeat of 1870 by the recovery of Alsace-Lorraine. [S]

revanchisme [Fr.] a policy dictated by a desire for vengeance on an enemy. 20c.

réveillon [Fr.] a meal taken in the middle of the night, *esp.* a meal taken early on Christmas morning after Midnight Mass. 19c. [S]

revenant [Fr.] one who returns from the dead, a ghost. 19c. Used in preference to the vague *ghost* to distinguish one particular type of apparition. [N,S]

revenons à nos moutons [Fr.] 'let's get back to our sheep', let's get back to the point at issue. 19c. From the fifteenth-century French farce *Maistre Pierre Pathelin*, where the phrase (in the form *revenons à ces moutons*) is used by a judge to focus the attention of a witness who is confusing two different law-suits. The phrase became proverbial, and is used (in the form *retournons à nos moutons*) by Rabelais and others. [S]

rêverie [Fr.] a day-dream, a fit of abstracted musing; *hence Mus.* a musical composition suggesting a day-dream or fit of musing. 17c. Formerly also in the older French spelling *resverie;* now often written *reverie*. [N,S]

révolté [Fr.] an 'angry young man', one who rebels against contemporary conventions. 20c. Cf. JEUNE REFUSÉ.

revue d'esprit [Fr.] a revue in which the predominating element is wit rather than humour or farce. 20c.

revue intime [Fr.] an intimate revue, a revue designed for a small audience of initiates. 20c.

rex [Lat.] the King, *esp.* as the theoretical prosecutor in a criminal prosecution. 17c. Cf. REGINA. [N,S]

(la) Reyne le veult [Obs. Fr.] 'the Queen wishes it', the formula of royal assent to an Act of Parliament. 20c. Cf. (LE) ROY LE VEULT.

(la) Reyne s'avisera [Obs. Fr.] 'the Queen will think about it', the formula refusing royal assent to an Act of Parliament. 20c. The formula is now wholly obsolete, since the royal assent is never now refused. Cf. (LE) ROY S'AVISERA.

ria [Sp.] *Geog.* a long narrow inlet of the sea, *usu.* branching at the inner end. 19c. [N(*)]

riant [Fr.] smiling, gay, cheerful (landscape, etc.) 18c. Sometimes for no obvious reason in the feminine form *riante*. [N,S]

ricercare [It.] *Mus.* a FANTASIA or improvisation in which fugal imitation plays a leading part. 20c.

ricochet [Fr.] *Mil.* a glancing rebound made by a projectile before reaching its target; to make a glancing rebound. 18c. [N(*),S]

rictus [Lat.] a gaping of the mouth, a wide-open grin. 19c. [N]

ridotto [It.] a public assembly for music and dancing. 18c. Introduced into England in 1722, and exceedingly popular during 18c.; the word is now found only in historical contexts. [N,S]

rien ne va plus [Fr.] *Roulette* 'no more stakes accepted', the cry of the CROUPIER as the wheel begins to spin. 20c. Cf. FAITES VOS JEUX.

rifacimento [It.] a recasting of a literary work. 18c. Sometimes mis-spelt *rifacci(a)mento* as if it meant 'refacing'. [N,S]

rigor [Lat.] *Med.* a sudden chill accompanied by fits of violent shivering. 15c. Distinguished in pronunciation from English *rigour* by its long first vowel. [N,S]

rigor mortis [Lat.] *Med.* cadaveric rigidity, the stiffening of the body after death. 19c. [N,S]

rijsttafel [Du. 'rice-table'] *Cul.* a dish consisting of plain boiled rice accompanied by a variety of highly-seasoned foods. 20c.

riksmål [Norw.] the official language of Norway, thus distinguished from LANDSMÅL. 20c. The *riksmål* is not the historical descendent of ancient Norwegian but is a form of Danish influenced by Norwegian dialects.

rima chiusa [It. 'closed rhyme'] *Ling.* an arrangement of the rhymes in a quatrain such that the two outer and the two inner lines rhyme together. 20c.

rinceau [Fr.] *Art* an elaborately foliated scroll-pattern. 20c.

Rinderpest [Ger.] cattle-plague, a virulently infectious disease affecting ruminants. 19c. [N,S]

rinzaffato [It.] *Art* coarse plaster used for filling hollows and cracks in a wall before the application of the ARRICCIATO and the INTONACO. 20c. Cf. GESSO GROSSO.

R.I.P.=REQUIESCAT IN PACE, may he (she) rest in peace.

ripieno [It.] *Mus.* (an instrumental part) reinforcing the main orchestral parts by doubling them or filling in the harmony. 18c. [N,S]

riposte [Fr.] a quick counter-thrust, a prompt retaliation; to make a quick counter-thrust, to retaliate promptly. 18c. *Orig.* a fencing term; now in general use. [N,S]

risorgimento [It.] a resurgence of (nationalistic) feeling, *esp.* the movement for Italian unity and independence between 1815 and 1870. 20c.

risotto [It.] *Cul.* a dish made with boiled rice, meat or chicken broth, butter, etc. 19c. Cf. PILAV. [N]

risqué [Fr.] (a remark or anecdote) bordering on the indecent or suggestive of the obscene. 19c. [N*,S]

rissaldar [Hind. *risāladār*] *A.-I.* the native commander of an Indian cavalry regiment. 19c. Formerly more commonly *ressaldar*. [N,S]

risus sardonicus [Lat.] *Med.* an involuntary spasmodic grin induced by some morbid condition. 18c. [N]

rite de passage, *pl.* **rites de passage** [Fr.] a ritual or ceremony marking the passage from one period of life to another. 20c. *Orig.* an anthropological term, but now in more general use.

ritenuto [It. 'held back'] *Mus.* in slower time for a short period. 19c. [S]

ritornello, *pl.* **ritornelli** [It.] *Mus.* an instrumental prelude, interlude, or postlude in a vocal work. 17c. [N,S]

rive gauche [Fr.] the district of Paris on the left bank of the Seine inhabited by students, artists, and writers. 20c. Cf. QUARTIER LATIN.

riviera [It.] a coastal district, *esp.* a Mediterranean coastal district frequented by holiday-makers. 20c. The French *riviera* (properly the *Côte d'Azur*) extends from S.Raphael to Menton, the Italian *riviera* from Mentone to Spezia.

rivière [Fr. 'river'] a necklace of precious stones, *esp.* a necklace of more than one string. 19c. [N]

robe de chambre [Fr.] a dressing-gown, *esp.* a woman's dressing-gown suitable for an informal reception of friends. 18c. Cf. NÉGLIGÉ. [N,S]

robe de terrasse [Fr.] a woman's dress suitable for wearing on the terrace of a mansion in warm weather. 20c.

robusto [It.] *Mus.* a vigorous tenor suitable for virile operatic parts. 20c. Cf. HELDENTENOR.

rocaille [Fr.] *Art* a decorative design based on the forms of rocks and shells. 20c.

roche moutonnée, *pl.* **roches moutonnées** [Fr.] *Geog.* a rock in a glacial valley ground smooth on the upper side but rough and rugged on the lower. 19c. Cf. MOUTONNÉE. [N]

rococo [Fr.] *Art* (architecture, furniture, etc.) characterized by excessively florid and tasteless decoration. 19c. Applied *esp.* to a debased or frivolous development of BAROQUE. The French word is a fanciful extension of ROCAILLE. [N(*),S]

rodeo [Sp.] a rounding-up of cattle for inspection and marking; an enclosure into which cattle are rounded up; *hence*, an open-air entertainment at which cowboys exhibit their skill. 19c. [N(*)]

(le) roi est mort [Fr.] the king is dead. 20c. Cf. VIVE LE ROI.

roi fainéant, *pl.* **rois fainéants** [Fr.] a king who does nothing, a nominal king, *esp.* one of the later Merovingian kings of France whose power had been usurped by the Mayors of the Palace. 19c. Cf. FAINÉANT. [S]

(le) Roi Soleil [Fr. 'the Sun King'] Louis XIV of France. 20c.

rôle [Fr.] the part played by an actor in a dramatic performance; *hence*, the part played by a person in society, the function of some person or thing. 18c. [N,S]

Roma locuta est [Lat.] Rome has spoken, there is no more to be said. 20c. Often used derisively of a speech or message which arbitrarily puts an end to a discussion. St. Augustine *Sermon* cxxxi: *Roma locuta est, causa finita est* 'Rome has spoken, the dispute is finished'.

roman à clef [Fr.] a novel which portrays real events in recent history by concealing the identities of real persons under invented names. 20c. The 'key' referred to is an imaginary list identifying the invented with the real names of the characters.

roman à thèse [Fr.] a novel which sets out to prove some hypothesis or to express some specific point of view. 20c. Cf. DRAME À THÈSE.

romanesque [Fr.] resembling or having the characteristics of a novel. 20c. Distinguished from English *romanesque*, the architectural term, by italic type.

roman expérimental [Fr.] an experimental novel, a novel using untried techniques. 20c. Cf. NOUVEAU ROMAN.

roman-fleuve [Fr. 'river-novel'] a sequence of novels (each complete in itself) which follows the life and development of a character or group of characters. 20c.

roman poétique [Fr.] a poetic novel, a novel which achieves its effects by techniques normally associated with poetry. 20c.

roman policier [Fr.] a detective novel, a 'thriller'. 20c. More precise than any English term, since it expressly requires that the detective should be a policeman; but often used in a more general sense. Cf. KRIMINALROMAN.

rond-de-cuir [Fr. 'circle of leather'] a bureaucrat, a petty official. 20c. So called from the leather-topped stool formerly provided for the use of office workers. Cf. FONCTIONNAIRE.

rond de jambe [Fr.] *Ballet* a sweeping circular motion of the leg with the foot touching the ground. 20c.

rondeur [Fr.] a rounded outline, a rounded CONTOUR. 20c.

rond-point, *pl.* **ronds-points** [Fr.] a circus, a point where a number of streets meet. 20c. Cf. ÉTOILE.

rosé [Fr.] rose-coloured, pinkish (wine). 20c. Cf. VIN ROSÉ.

rosso antico [It.] a dark red marble used by the Ancients and now obtainable only by plundering ancient monuments. 19c. Cf. GIALLO ANTICO; VERDE ANTICO.

rostrum, *pl.* **rostra** [Lat.] (1) *Hist.* the platform for public speakers in the Forum of ancient Rome; *hence* (2) any platform designed for public speaking; any opportunity of addressing a wide public by speech or writing; (3) a platform erected for any public purpose, e.g. a conductor's platform at a concert. 16c. [N,S]

rota [Lat. 'wheel'] (1) a rotation of duties, a list of persons required to perform certain duties at specified times; (2) *Eccles.* the Roman supreme court for ecclesiastical and secular cases; (3) *Mus.* a 'round', a song in canon form. 17c. [N,S]

rôtisserie [Fr.] (1) an establishment where cooked food may be bought; (2) a device for roasting meat or fowl consisting of a spit continuously and automatically rotated inside an oven. 20c.

rotunda [Lat.] a circular building or hall, *usu.* with a dome. 17c. [N,S]

roturier, *f.* **roturière** [Fr. 'commoner'] plebeian; a person of low status in society. 16c. *Occ.* mis-spelt *rôturier*, as if connected with roasting. [N,S]

roué [Fr.] a profligate, a debauchee; one who leads a life wholly devoted to sensuality. 19c. The French word means 'broken on the wheel'; the implication is that the *roué* deserves this punishment. [N,S]

rouge [Fr.] (1) a red powder used to give artificial colour to the cheeks; a red powder used for polishing plate. 18c. (2) *Roulette* any one of the red numbers. 20c. Cf. NOIR. [N,S]

rouge-et-noir [Fr.] TRENTE-ET-QUARANTE, a gambling game played with cards, in which 30 is a winning and 40 a losing number. 18c. So called because the card-table is marked with two red and two black diamonds, on which the players place their stakes according to the colour they favour. [N,S]

rouge flambé [Fr.] a red colour found in porcelain, and produced by the reduction of copper. 20c. Cf. FLAMBÉ; SANG DE BŒUF.

roulade [Fr.] *Mus.* a rapid succession of notes joining one note of the melody to another, *esp.* in vocal music; any vocal or instrumental flourish. 18c. [N,S]

rouleau, *pl.* **rouleaux** [Fr.] (1) a cylindrical packet of identical coins; *hence*, a pile of counters ready for use in a game of hazard; (2) a decorative trimming to a woman's dress formed by a roll of cloth, lace, etc.; (3) *Art* a decorative moulding resembling a roll of paper, etc. 17c. [N,S]

roulette [Fr.] (1) a game of chance in which a ball is thrown so as to lodge in one of the numbered sections of a rotating wheel. 18c. (2) *Art* a small toothed wheel used as an engraving tool. 20c. Cf. BOULE. [N,S]

route nationale [Fr.] one of the main numbered arterial roads in France. 20c.

roux [Fr.] *Cul.* a mixture of melted butter and flour, *esp.* as used for thickening soups and gravies; hence, a greasy mixture. 19c. Cf. PANADA.

(le) Roy le veult [Obs. Fr.] 'the King wishes it', the formula of royal assent to an Act of Parliament. 20c. Cf. (LA) REYNE LE VEULT.

(le) Roy s'avisera [Obs. Fr.] 'the King will think about it', the formula refusing royal assent to an Act of Parliament. 20c. The formula is now wholly obsolete, since the royal assent is never now refused. Cf. (LA) REYNE S'AVISERA.

R.S.V.P.=RÉPONDEZ, S'IL VOUS PLAÎT, please reply.

ruat cœlum [Lat.] though the heavens fall, come what may. 17c. Cf. FIAT JUSTITIA, RUAT CŒLUM. [S]

rubato [It.] *Mus.* (a melody played or sung) with more regard to expression than to exact time-keeping. 19c. Abbreviated from TEMPO RUBATO 'stolen time', because any additional duration given to one note must be deducted from another. [N]

rubella [Lat.] *Med.* German measles. 19c. [N]

ruche [Fr. 'bee-hive'] a full frilling of gauze or other light fabric used as an ornament on a woman's dress. 19c. [N,S]

rupee [Hind. *rūpiyah*] *A.-I.* the monetary unit of India. 17c. There are about 15 rupees to the £ sterling. [N,S]

rusé, *f.* **rusée** [Fr.] cunning, wily, full of tricks. 19c. [S]

ruse de guerre [Fr.] a stratagem. 19c. [S]

rus in urbe [Lat.] the country in the city, an urban retreat so embowered as to seem rural. 18c. Martial *Epigrams* XII lvii 21. [S]

S

s.= SOLIDI, shillings.

s.a.=SUB ANNO, under the year . . .

sabot [Fr.] a shoe made of a single piece of wood hollowed out to fit the foot; a shoe with a thick wooden sole and uppers of leather. 17c. [N,S]

sabotage [Fr.] deliberate and systematic destruction, deliberate interference with the proper functioning of something; to destroy or interfere with the functioning of something. 20c. From the French verb *saboter* 'to make an ugly noise by walking in SABOTS', hence 'to perform badly, to mutilate'. [N*]

saboteur [Fr.] one who commits SABOTAGE. 20c. [N*]

sac-à-dos [Fr.] a rucksack, a bag designed to be hung on the back and supported by the shoulders. 20c.

saccadé [Fr.] jerky. 20c.

sachem [Narragansett] the supreme chief of an American Indian tribe. 17c. The word is used in varying forms by a large number of American Indian tribes. [N,S(*)]

sachet [Fr.] a small bag made of perfumed cloth; a small cloth packet containing dry perfume; a small sealed container (*usu.* made of plastic) for household liquids, e.g. shampoo. 19c. [N]

sachlich [Ger.] realist, objective (in art, etc.) 20c.

Sachlichkeit [Ger.] realism, objectivism (in art, etc.) 20c. Cf. (DIE) NEUE SACHLICHKEIT.

sæter [Norw.] a mountain pasture in Scandinavia where cattle remain during the summer months; a farmhouse on such a pasture. 19c. [N*]

sæva indignatio [Lat.] fierce indignation. 20c. From the epitaph of Jonathan Swift: *Ubi sæva indignatio ulterius cor lacerare nequit* 'Where fierce indignation can no more lacerate the heart'.

safari [Swahili] a journey on foot, *esp.* in search of big game; a party of travellers journeying together. 19c. Cf. SHIKAR. [N*]

saftig [Ger. 'full of sap'] juicy, succulent. 20c.

sage-femme [Fr. 'wise woman'] a midwife. 20c.

sahib [Hind. *çāḥib* 'friend' < Arab.] *A.-I.* a European gentleman. 17c. Used by native servants to address their masters; also added after a name as a title of respect equivalent to English *Mr.* Cf. BURRA SAHIB; MEMSAHIB. [N,S]

saison en enfer [Fr.] a period of intense misery and *usu.* of spiritual uncertainty. 20c. From the title of Rimbaud's volume of fragments *Une Saison en Enfer* (1873).

salaam [Hind. *salām* 'peace' < Arab.] an Oriental salutation, a low obeisance with the palm of the right hand on the forehead; to make such an obeisance. 17c. Properly Arab. *(as-)salām alaikum* 'peace be upon you'. The same root *s-l-m* appears in ISLAM. [N,S]

salami [It.] a kind of highly-seasoned Italian sausage. 19c. Properly the plural of It. *salame*, but in English always construed as singular. [N]

sal Atticus, *pl.* **sales Attici** [Lat. 'Attic salt'] (an example of) delicate wit. 19c. From the Greek province of Attica, the capital of which is Athens; Pliny *Natural History* xxxi 87. [S]

salina [Sp.] a salt-lake, a salt-marsh; a salt-pan, a salt-works. 17c. [N,S]

salle privée [Fr.] a private room (in a CASINO, etc.) for the use of gamblers who do not wish to play in public. 20c. Cf. CERCLE PRIVÉ.

salmi [Fr.] *Cul.* a RAGOÛT of minced game and spices. 18c. [N,S]

salon [Fr.] (1) a large reception room in a private house; a large public room; the main room of a hairdressing establishment, etc.; (2) the reception room of a lady of fashion in Paris; *hence*, a gathering or reunion of intellectuals in such a room or elsewhere. 18c. As a proper noun *Salon* denotes an exhibition of sculpture and painting by living artists, held annually in Paris (formerly in one of the *salons* of the Louvre). [N,S]

Salon des Refusés [Fr.] an exhibition organized in 1863 at the order of Napoleon III for the display of pictures rejected by the SALON; *hence*, any exhibition of works of art rejected by some official organization. 20c.

salpicon [Fr.] *Cul.* a stuffing for roast meat. 18c. [N,S]

saltarello [It.] a lively Italian or Spanish dance for one couple, which includes numerous jumps and skips; the music (in triple time) for such a dance. 18c. [N,S]

saltimbanque [Fr.] a mountebank, a quack doctor. 19c. The Italian form *saltimbanco* was formerly current but seems to be obsolete. [N]

salto mortale [It. 'deadly leap'] a somersault beginning with a standing jump; *hence*, a critical moment in life, a crucial undertaking. 20c.

saltus, *pl.* **saltus** [Lat.] a sudden transition, a breach of continuity, *esp. Math.* a 'step' in the graph of a function. 17c. Cf. NATURA NON FACIT SALTUM; PER SALTUM. [N]

salud y pesetas! [Sp.] health and money!; a Spanish phrase invoking good fortune for another person. 20c.

salus populi suprema (est) lex [Lat.] the well-being of the people is the highest law. 17c. Cicero *De Legibus* III iii 8. [S]

salvete [Lat.] greetings! 20c. Common in school magazines, *etc.* as a heading to a list of new members. Cf. AVETE; VALETE.

sal volatile [Lat.] an aromatic solution of ammonium carbonate used as a restorative in fainting-fits. 17c. [N,S(*)]

samadhi [Sansk. *samādhi*] *Rel.* the last stage of YOGA, in which profound meditation leads to a suspension of the link between soul and body. 19c. [N*]

samovar [Russ. 'self-boiler'] a Russian tea-urn heated by a central cylinder containing charcoal. 19c. [N,S]

sampan [Chin. *san-pan* 'three-board'] a small boat of Chinese type. 17c. [N,S]

samurai, *pl.* **samurai** [Jap.] a military retainer of a DAIMIO; a member of the Japanese military caste. 19c. Cf. BUSHIDO. [N,S]

sanatorium, *pl.* **sanatoria** [Lat.] a place, establishment, or quarter of a building designed or suitable for the care of invalids or convalescents. 19c. The *U.S.* equivalent is *sanitarium*, a spurious form based on English *sanitary*. [N(*),S]

sanbenito [Sp. *San Benito* 'St Benedict'] *Hist.* a long straight garment of yellow cloth with a red St Andrew's cross in front and behind, worn by penitent heretics under the Inquisition; a similar garment of black cloth ornamented with flames and devils, worn by impenitent heretics at an AUTO-DA-FÉ. 16c. So called because of the resemblance of the garment to the scapular introduced by St Benedict. [N,S]

sancta simplicitas [Lat.] holy simplicity, the NAÏVETÉ of the saintly. 20c. *O sancta simplicitas*! were the last words of John Huss at the stake in 1415. Cf. BEATA SIMPLICITAS.

sanctum (sanctorum) [Lat.] (1) *Hist.* the Holy of Holies of the Jewish Temple; *hence* (2) a private retreat secure from intrusion. 15c. The Latin phrase is a Hebraism, a literal translation of the Heb. *qōdesh haqqodāshīm*. Cf. ADYTUM. [N,S]

Sanctus [Lat.] *Eccles.* the conclusion of the Preface of the Mass, which begins *Sanctus*, *sanctus*, *sanctus* 'Holy, holy, holy'; a musical setting of this portion of the Preface. 14c. Vulgate *Isaias* vi 3. Cf. BENEDICTUS. [N,S(*)]

sang-de-bœuf [Fr. 'bullock's blood'] a deep red colour found in porcelain. 19c. Cf. ROUGE FLAMBÉ. [N,S]

sang froid [Fr. 'cold blood'] self-possession, coolness, absence of excitement. 18c. [N,S]

sans cérémonie [Fr.] unceremoniously, without formality. 17c. [N,S]

sansculotte [Fr. 'without breeches'] *Hist.* a republican of the poorest classes during the French Revolution; *hence*, a revolutionary, an anarchist. 18c. [N,S]

sans façon [Fr.] unceremoniously, without beating about the bush. 17c. [N,S]

sans-gêne [Fr.] lack of constraint, disregard of ordinary politeness or formality. 19c. Cf. DÉSINVOLTURE; GÊNE; LAISSEZ-ALLER. [N]

sans heures [Fr.] (a watch or clock) on the dial of which the numerals are replaced by thin rectangular marks known as BÂTONS. 20c.

sans peur et sans reproche [Fr.] fearless and blameless. 19c. Applied *orig.* to Pierre du Terrail, Seigneur de Bayard (1476–1524); the phrase occurs in the title of an anonymous biography published in 1527. [N,S]

sans phrase [Fr.] bluntly, without circumlocution, without qualification. 19c. From the formula *la mort sans phrase* used by the Abbé Siéyès (1748–1836) in voting for the death of Louis XVI. [N(*),S]

sans prétensions [Fr.] unpretentious, without affectation. 20c.

sarafan [Russ.] a long sleeveless cloak forming part of the national dress of a Russian peasant-woman. 18c. [N]

sarcoma, *pl.* **sarcomata** [Lat. < Gk. *σάρκωμα*] *Med.* a fleshy excrescence; a fibrous tumour. 17c. Cf. POLYPUS. [N]

sarcophagus, *pl.* **sarcophagi** [Lat. < Gk. *σαρκοφάγος* 'flesh-eating'] a stone coffin, *usu.* carved and inscribed. 18c. [N,S]

sari [Hind. *sāṛ(h)ī*] a long strip of silk worn by Hindu women. 18c. One end of the *sari* is passed several times round the waist to form a skirt, and the other covers the shoulders and head. Various different spellings have been current: until recently *saree* was the most common. [N,S]

sarong [Mal. *sārung*] the Malayan national costume of men and women, consisting of a strip of cloth wound round the waist like a skirt. 19c. [N,S]

sarsaparilla [Sp. *zarzaparrilla*] the dried roots of a kind of smilax, used in the preparation of an alterative and tonic medicine; a decoction of these roots. 16c. The Spanish word is perhaps derived from Basque. *Sarsaparilla* was formerly supposed to be a potent remedy for syphilis. [N,S]

sassafras [Sp.] the dried bark of a small North American tree, used in the preparation of an alterative medicine; a decoction of this bark. 16c. The Spanish word is probably from a native American name. [N,S]

Sassenach [Ir. *Sasanach*, Gael. *Sasunnach*] (the Irish or Scottish name for) an Englishman. 18c. The Welsh equivalent is *Saesneg*: all three Celtic words mean 'Saxon', taken as representative of Angles and Saxons. [N]

sastruga=ZASTRUGA, a furrow in snow.

Saturnalia *pl.* [Lat.] (1) *Hist.* the Roman festival of Saturn, celebrated as a time of universal merrymaking; *hence* (2) any period of unrestrained licence and noisy revelry. 16c. [N,S]

satyagraha [Sansk. *satya āgraha* 'faithful obstinacy'] passive resistance as a political policy. 20c. [N*]

Sauerkraut [Ger.] *Cul.* cabbage submitted to acid fermentation. 17c. A popular item of diet in Germany. [N,S]

sauna [Finn.] a Finnish steam-bath. 20c. The distinctive features of the *sauna* are (1) the production of steam by pouring water on heated stones, and (2) the fustigation with leafy birch-branches and the final cold plunge into a lake or snow-drift. A *sauna* is to be found in every Finnish village.

saut-de-lit, *pl.* **sauts-de-lit** [Fr. 'jump-out-of-bed'] a light dressing-gown, a morning wrap. 20c.

saut du même au même [Fr.] an error in copying caused by the omission of the passage between two occurrences of the same word or phrase. 20c. Cf. HOMŒOTELEUTON.

sauté [Fr. 'tossed'] *Cul.* fried in a pan with a little butter; a dish prepared in this way. 19c. [N,S]

sauve-qui-peut [Fr. 'save (himself) who can'] a general rout, a disorderly stampede. 19c. The phrase is sometimes said to have been first used by Napoleon at Waterloo, but it is recorded as early as 1802. [N,S]

savannah [Obs. Sp. *savana*] a treeless plain. 16c. The current Spanish form is *sabana;* the word is of Carib origin. [N,S]

savant [Fr.] a man professionally engaged in a learned occupation. 18c. Formerly often spelt *sçavant.* [N,S]

savoir faire [Fr.] instinctive knowledge of the right course of action in any circumstances. 19c. [N,S]

savoir vivre [Fr.] good breeding, experience of good society, knowing how to behave with propriety. 18c. [N,S]

sbirro, *pl.* **sbirri** [It.] an Italian police-officer. 17c. [N,S]

scagliola [It.] hard plaster painted to simulate stone or marble. 18c. [N,S]

scalpellino, *pl.* **scalpellini** [It.] *Art* an apprentice employed by a sculptor in the rough preparation of a block of stone; *hence,* an inferior sculptor, a mere chiseller. 20c.

scampi *pl.* [It.] Dublin Bay prawns. 20c. This variety of prawn, though named after Dublin Bay, is found also in parts of the Mediterranean and the Adriatic. The Italian singular *scampo* is not in use in English.

scarabæus, *pl.* **scarabæi** [Lat.] (1) a kind of beetle; (2) an ancient Egyptian jewel carved in the form of a beetle, with a design in INTAGLIO on the flat underside. 17c. [N,S]

scena [It.] *Mus.* a composition consisting mainly of dramatic recitative for one or more voices with instrumental accompaniment. 19c. [N]

scenario [It.] the outline of the plot of a play or film giving details of the sequences of scenes; *hence,* a plan of campaign prepared for adoption in the event of the outbreak of war. 19c. [N,S]

scène à faire [Fr.] a climactic scene (in a play or in real life) to which all the previous action is seen to lead up. 20c.

Schadenfreude [Ger.] malicious enjoyment of the discomfiture of others. 20c. [N*]

schema, *pl.* **schemata** [Lat. < Gk. σχῆμα] (1) a diagrammatic representation designed to simplify a complicated argument; (2) *Eccles.* an outline of a subject presented for discussion at the Second Vatican Council. 19c. [N,S]

schemozzle=SCHLEMOZZLE, a muddle, a quarrel.

scherzando [It.] *Mus.* played in a lively, sportive manner; a piece or movement played or designed to be played in such a manner. 19c. [N]

scherzo [It. 'joke'] *Mus.* a piece or movement of a lively, playful character. 19c. The second or third movement of the classical symphony or sonata is commonly a *scherzo*. Cf. BADINERIE. [N,S]

schiacciato rilievo [It. 'squashed relief'] *Art* a form of relief-carving in which the projection of the figures from the ground is reduced to the minimum consistent with adequate modelling. 20c. Cf. ALTO RILIEVO; BASSO RILIEVO; CAVO RILIEVO; MEZZO RILIEVO.

schizophrenia [Pseudo-Gk.] *Med.* split personality, a morbid condition of the mind in which two or more independent personalities occupy the consciousness in alternation or succession. 20c. Formerly known as DEMENTIA PRÆCOX. The word is sometimes misused in the sense 'divided loyalty'.

Schlachtruf [Ger.] a battle-cry, a signal for attack. 20c.

schlampig [Ger.] slovenly. 20c.

schlemiel/schlemihl [Yidd.] an uncomplaining man for whom everything goes wrong, one who is patient in undeserved adversity. 20c. The word became well-known in German as a result of the popularity of A. von Chamisso's *Peter Schlemihls wundersame Geschichte* (1814). Cf. SIMPLICISSIMUS.

schlemozzle/schemozzle/shemozzle [Yidd. < Ger. *schlimm* 'bad' + *Heb. mazzāl* 'luck'] a muddle, a mess; a quarrel, a row; to make off, to decamp. 19c. [N*]

Schloss [Ger.] a castle (in Germany). 19c. [N,S]

schmaltz [Yidd. < Ger. *Schmalz* 'grease'] anything repulsively sentimental; sugary sentimentality. 20c.

schmuck [Yidd. *shmok* < Slovene *šmok*] a fool, an innocent; one whose behaviour is *naïf* and unconventional. 20c.

Schnitzel [Ger.] *Cul.* a veal cutlet. 20c. Cf. WIENER SCHNITZEL. [N*]

Schnorchel [Ger.] an underwater breathing device, a tubular air-intake extending above the surface of the water. 20c. First used of a device fitted to submarines, now more commonly of a device facilitating underwater swimming; also extended to other breathing devices. Sometimes anglicized as *Snorkel*; the form *Schnörkel* is due to a confusion with an entirely different word meaning 'scroll'.

schnorrer [Yidd. < Ger. *Schnurrer*] a Jewish beggar. 19c. The word has re-entered German from Yiddish in the form *Schnorrer*. [N]

scholium, *pl.* **scholia** [Lat. < Gk. *σχόλιον*] a gloss, an explanatory note or comment, *esp.* an ancient comment on a Greek or Latin work. 16c. The Greek form *scholion* is also sometimes used. [N,S]

Schrecklichkeit [Ger.] 'frightfulness', a deliberate policy of committing atrocities to cow an enemy or a subject people. 20c.

Schuhplattler [Ger.] a folk-dance of Upper Bavaria in which the male dancers slap their thighs and knees and the soles of their shoes. 20c. The word is peculiar to the Bavarian dialect. Cf. ZAPATEADO.

Schuss [Ger. 'shot'] (to make) an unchecked descent on skis down a steep slope. 20c.

Schwärmerei [Ger.] extravagant enthusiasm, *esp.* the intense sentimental attachment of an adolescent to an adult of the same sex. 19c. [N*,S]

schwärmerisch [Ger.] addicted to intense sentimental attachments. 20c.

Schweinerei [Ger.] beastliness, an act which revolts decent feeling; a tendency to commit such acts. 20c. Cf. PORCHERIA.

Schwerpunkt [Ger. 'centre of gravity'] *Mil.* the point of main thrust, the point of main concentration of an attack. 20c.

scientia [Lat.] systematic knowledge. 20c. The word has been re-adopted in its Latin form because the anglicized *science* has come to be limited to the 'natural sciences'.

scientiæ causa [Lat.] (a painful experiment, etc., carried out) for the sake of science. 20c.

scil(icet) [Lat.] namely, that is to say. 14c. Commonly introducing a detailed list of things hitherto referred to only in general. Lat. *scilicet* is a contraction of *scire licet* 'it is permitted to know'. Cf. VIDELICET. [N,S]

scintilla [Lat. 'spark'] an atom, a minute particle (of doubt, truth, evidence, etc.) 17c. [N,S]

scire facias [Lat. 'cause (him) to know'] *Law* a writ issued as a warning of a pending execution of a judgment or revocation of a patent. 15c. [N,S]

scirocco=SIROCCO, a hot oppressive wind.

sclerosis [Lat. < Gk. *σκλήρωσις*] *Med.* a morbid hardening of any animal tissue. 14c. [N]

scoria, *pl.* **scoriæ** [Lat. < Gk. *σκορία*] dross remaining after the smelting of ore; volcanic clinker resulting from the cooling of a stream of lava. 14c. The singular *scoria* has sometimes been misconstrued as a plural, and a spurious singular *scorium* has been formed from it. [N,S]

scriptorium, *pl.* **scriptoria** [Lat.] a room (*usu.* in a religious house) set aside for the transcribing of manuscripts. 18c. [N,S]

scrutin de liste [Fr.] a system of proportional representation in which constituencies are grouped together and each voter may vote for as many candidates as there are constituencies in the group. 19c. [S]

scugnizzo, *pl.* **scugnizzi** [It.] a Neapolitan beggar-boy. 20c.

sculps(it) [Lat.] (he) carved (it); always accompanied by a name and inscribed on a piece of sculpture, etc. 19c. Cf. CÆL(AVIT); DEL(INEAVIT); FEC(IT); PINX(IT).

sculpture d'appartement [Fr.] *Art* a piece of sculpture on a small scale, designed for display in a dwelling-house. 20c.

séance [Fr.] a session; a meeting of a committee or society; a meeting held for the purpose of observing or evoking spiritualistic phenomena. 19c. [N,S]

séance d'essais [Fr.] the 'practice session' of a motor-race, the period set aside for a preliminary run-over of the course. 20c.

seau à bouteilles, *pl.* **seaux à bouteilles** [Fr.] a wine-cooler, a bucket containing iced water into which wine-bottles may be plunged. 20c.

sec [Fr.] dry (wine, champagne, etc.) 19c. [N*]

sécateur [Fr.] a pair of pruning shears resembling stout scissors. 19c. Now normally used in the plural *sécateurs.* [N]

secco [It.] *Art* painting on plaster which has been allowed to dry. 20c. The full phrase is FRESCO SECCO. Cf. A SECCO; IN SECCO.

secrétaire [Fr.] a writing-desk with small drawers and pigeon-holes, enclosed by a vertical front which can be let down to form a writing surface. 19c. Cf. BUREAU; ESCRITOIRE. [N,S]

secrétaire à abattant [Fr.] a fall-front writing-desk. 20c. There is no clear distinction between a *secrétaire* and a *secrétaire à abattant.*

secret de polichinelle [Fr.] an open secret, a supposed secret known to everybody. 20c.

secundo [Lat.] secondly. 17c. Cf. PRIMO. [S]

secundum quid [Lat.] in some particular respect only. 17c. Contrasted with SIMPLICITER. [N,S]

securus judicat orbis terrarum [Lat.] the judgment of the whole world is conclusive, the whole world cannot be wrong. 20c. St. Augustine *Contra Epistolam Parmenidis* iii 24.

sederunt [Lat. 'they sat'] a sitting of a court or similar body, *usu.* an ecclesiastical assembly; a meeting of a company of people for any purpose 17c. [N,S]

sede vacante [Lat.] *Eccles.* (during) the vacancy of an episcopal see, *esp.* the Papal see. 17c. [N,S]

sedia gestatoria [It.] *Eccles.* the chair carried on the shoulders of bearers, used by the Pope on certain ceremonial occasions. 20c.

sedilia *pl.* [Lat.] *Eccles.* a series of three seats (*usu.* recessed in the wall) on the south side of the chancel of a church for the use of the clergy. 18c. The singular *sedile* is exceedingly rare. [N,S]

séduisant, *f.* **séduisante** [Fr.] seductive, bewitching. 20c.

seguidilla [Sp.] a Spanish dance in triple time; the music for such a dance. 18c. [N,S]

Sehnsucht [Ger.] yearning, nostalgia. 19c. [S]

seicento [It. '600'] the sixteen hundreds, the seventeenth century, *esp.* the art and architecture of that century; characteristic of that century. 20c. Cf. CINQUECENTO; QUATTROCENTO; SETTECENTO; TRECENTO. [N]

seiche [Swiss Fr. < Ger. *Seiche* 'sinking'] *Geog.* a tide-like undulation of the surface of a lake; a wave resembling a tidal wave passing across the surface of a lake. 19c. The quasi-French pronunciation shows that the word does not come direct from German. [N]

seigneur [Fr.] a (French) feudal lord, a (French) noble taking his title from the name of his estate. 16c. Cf. GRAND SEIGNEUR. [N,S]

semper eadem [Lat.] always the same. 17c. The motto of Queen Elizabeth and of Queen Anne; since *eadem* is feminine the phrase is applicable only to women. [S]

semper fidelis, *pl.* **semper fideles** [Lat.] always faithful, always trustworthy. 20c.

se non è vero, è (molto) ben trovato [It.] if it is not true, it is a (very) happy invention. 19c. Used by Giordano Bruno in his *Degli Eroici Furori* (1585), but apparently already proverbial. Cf. BEN TROVATO; BIEN TROUVÉ.

senryu [Jap. *senryū*] a type of Japanese satirical verse. 20c. The name is derived from the pseudonym of a famous satirical poet.

sensibilia *pl.* [Lat.] *Psych.* the class of things capable of being perceived by the senses. 20c. Cf. SENSUM.

sensorium, *pl.* **sensoria** [Lat.] the centre in the brain to which sense-impressions are transmitted by the nerves; *hence facet.* the brain. 17c. [N,S]

sensum, *pl.* **sensa** [Lat.] *Psych.* something perceived by the senses, an object of sense-perception. 20c. Cf. SENSIBILIA.

sensu obscæno [Lat.] in an obscene sense, taking the obscene meaning of the word(s). 20c.

sensu stricto [Lat.] in the strict meaning of the word(s), strictly speaking. 20c.

sepoy [Hind. *sipāhī* < Pers.] *A.-I.* a native Indian soldier under British command. 18c. The original is much more exactly rendered by the Fr. SPAHI. The spelling *sipahi* (*occ.* found in English) is pedantic. [N,S]

septicæmia [Lat.] *Med.* septic blood-poisoning. 19c. The (modern) Latin word is based on Gk. σηπτικός 'septic' and αἷμα 'blood'. [N]

sequela, *pl.* **sequelæ** [Lat.] a consequence, a result, *esp.* a morbid condition resulting from a previous disease. 18c. Much more common in the plural than in the singular.

sérac [Fr.] *Geog.* a tower or pinnacle of ice on a glacier, formed by the intersection of CREVASSES. 19c. The word is Swiss French, and *orig.* meant a kind of white cheese. [N]

seraglio [It. *serraglio* 'lock-up'] the part of a Moslem house where the women live in seclusion, a HAREM; a polygamous household; a Turkish palace, *esp.* the palace of the Sultan in Constantinople. 16c. Despite the similarity of form the word is not etymologically related to Turk. *saray* < Pers. *serāī*, but it is regularly used as the English equivalent of the latter. Cf. ZENANA. [N,S]

serein [Fr.] a fine rain falling from a clear sky after sunset. 19c. [N]

serenata [It.] *Mus.* a CANTATA or orchestral piece suitable for performance in the open air. 18c. [N,S]

seriatim [Lat.] one by one in succession, one after another. 17c. [N,S]

sérieux, *f.* **sérieuse** [Fr.] serious-minded, earnest, not frivolous. 20c. Cf. FEMME SÉRIEUSE; HOMME SÉRIEUX; JEUNE FEMME SÉRIEUSE.

serinette [Fr.] *Mus.* a bird-organ, a small barrel-organ used for training song-birds. 19c. [N]

servante [Fr.] a concealed shelf beneath a table used for conjuring. 19c. [N]

servus servorum (Dei), *pl.* **servi servorum (Dei)** [Lat.] *Eccles.* 'the servant of the servants (of God)', one of the titles of the Pope. 16c. [S]

se tenant [Fr.] (different types of postage stamp) joined together in a single sheet 20c.

settecento [It. '700'] the seventeen hundreds, the eighteenth century, *esp.* the art and architecture of that century; characteristic of that century. 20c. Cf. CINQUECENTO; DIX-HUITIÈME; QUATTROCENTO; SEICENTO; TRECENTO.

sforzando [It.] *Mus.* (a note) to be specially emphasized, to be played markedly louder than its neighbours. 19c. [N,S]

sfumatezza [It.] *Art* the harmonizing and blending of two colours or shades one into another, SFUMATO. 20c.

sfumato [It. 'smoked'] (1) *Art* the softening of the transition between two colours or shades; (2) *Mus.* played in a vague indeterminate way. 19c. [N]

sgian dubh [Gael. 'black knife'] a small dagger worn thrust into the stocking by Scottish highlanders. 18c. More commonly written *skean dhu*, a spelling that has little to recommend it since it is neither Gaelic nor English. [N]

sgraffito, *pl.* **sgraffiti** [It.] *Art* (1) a method of architectural decoration produced by scratching through a thin layer of plaster to a layer of a different colour; GRAFFITO; (2) a method of decorating pottery by scratching through a thin layer of slip to reveal clay of a different colour. 18c. [N,S]

shadoof [Arab. *shādūf*] a primitive device used in Egypt to facilitate irrigation, consisting of a shaft loosely fastened in the middle to the top of a fixed pole, with a bucket at one end and a counter-weight at the other. 19c. [N,S]

shaman [Russ.] a priest or medicine-man amongst the tribes of northern Asia; *hence*, a medicine-man in any primitive tribe. 17c. The Russian word is borrowed from some Mongolian dialect. [N]

sharawaggi/sharawadgi [Unknown] *Art* the beauty of deliberate asymmetry or irregularity. 17c. First used in 1685 by Sir William Temple, who reports it as a Chinese word; but it cannot be Chinese, and no plausible alternative origin has yet been discovered. [N,S]

shashlik [Russ. *shashlyk*] *Cul.* a KEBAB, one of a variety of dishes consisting of meat cut into small pieces, seasoned, and roasted. 20c.

shebeen [Ir. *sibín*] an unlicensed house in which ardent spirits are sold; a low wayside public house. 18c. The word is probably not *orig*. Irish, and may be a diminutive of English *shop*. [N,S]

sheikh [Arab. *shaikh* 'old man'] the chief of an Arab family or tribe, the headman of an Arab village. 16c. Numerous different spellings have been used in English, but *sheikh* is now well established; to substitute *shaikh* is mere pedantry. [N,S]

shemozzle=SCHLEMOZZLE, a muddle, a quarrel.

sherpa [Tib. *shar pa* 'east-inhabitant'] a member of an eastern Tibetan tribe living south of the Himalayas. 20c. The *sherpas* are often used as bearers and guides by mountaineers in the Himalayas.

shibboleth [Heb. *shibbōleth* 'stream in flood'] a word used to detect foreigners by their mispronunciation; a peculiarity, *esp.* a peculiarity of pronunciation, distinguishing persons from a given district or of a given class; *hence*, a catchword or slogan adopted by members of a party or sect, by the use of which they may be distinguished from others. 17c. The Hebrew word was used by Jephthah at the crossing of the Jordan (*Judges* xii 4–6) to distinguish the fleeing Ephraimites, who could not pronounce *sh*, from his own followers the Gileadites. [N,S]

shikar [Hind. < Pers. *shikār*] *A.-I.* hunting big game as a sport. 17c. Cf. SAFARI. [N,S]

shikari [Hind. < Pers. *shikārī*] *A.-I.* a native huntsman who accompanies a European sportsman as a guide; a hunter of big game. 19c. Some recent writers have used *shikari* instead of SHIKAR in the sense 'hunting big game'. [N,S]

shiksa [Yidd. *shikse*] a non-Jewish girl; a non-practising Jewish girl, a girl Jewish by blood but not by religious conviction. 20c. The Yiddish word is ultimately from Heb. *sheqeṣ* 'blemish'. Cf. GOY.

shish kebab [Turk. *şiş kebab(ı)*] *Cul.* an Oriental dish consisting of small pieces of meat (often interspersed with pieces of vegetable) impaled on a skewer and roasted. 20c. Cf. KEBAB.

shogun [Jap. *shōgun* < Chin. *chiang chün* 'army leader'] the hereditary commander-in-chief of the Japanese army. 17c. Until 1867 the *shogun* was the virtual ruler of Japan. Cf. MIKADO; TYCOON. [N,S]

shufti/shufty [Arab. *shūf* 'look!'] have a look!; a look (at something). 20c. The origin of the English form is not clear. The earliest usage seems to be in the phrase *shufti* BINT 'an Egyptian woman willing to indulge in erotic exhibitionism'; the word may be a combination of the repeated *shūf!* used by such a woman, with the English ending *-ty* as in *shifty*, *flighty*, etc. Cf. DEKKO.

sic [Lat. 'thus'] 'thus in the original', a parenthetic insertion in a printed quotation or citation, indicating that an error or anomalous form is exactly reproduced from the original. 19c. Sometimes used as a discreet method of calling attention to the ignorance or carelessness of an earlier writer. [N]

siccum lumen [Lat. 'dry eye'] tearlessness, an absence of display of feeling on an occasion of grief. 20c. Tibullus *Elegies* I i 66; Lucan *Pharsalia* ix 1044; doubtless already a standard phrase.

sic itur ad astra [Lat.] this is the way to the stars, this is the way to achieve fame and immortality. 19c. Virgil *Æneid* ix 641. [S]

sic passim [Lat.] 'thus throughout in the original', a parenthetic insertion in a printed quotation or citation, indicating an error or anomalous form which occurs frequently or always in the original. 20c. Cf. SIC; PASSIM.

sic semper tyrannis [Lat.] such be the fate of tyrants! 20c. This phrase, the motto of the state of Virginia, was quoted by John Wilkes Booth as he assassinated Abraham Lincoln on 14th April 1865.

sic transit gloria mundi [Lat.] thus the glory of the world passes away. 16c. A reflection on the transitoriness of worldly success. Thomas à Kempis *The Imitation of Christ* I iii 6: *o quam cito transit gloria mundi!* 'Oh, how quickly the glory of the world passes away!' [S]

sierra [Sp. 'saw'] *Geog.* a range of mountains rising into peaks like the teeth of a saw. 17c. [N,S]

siesta [Sp.] an afternoon rest, *esp.* one taken during the hottest hours of the day in a tropical or sub-tropical climate. 17c. Ultimately from Lat. *sexta* 'sixth (hour)'. [N,S]

siffleur, *f.* **siffleuse** [Fr.] (1) a person skilled in the art of whistling; (2) someone hired to hiss and boo at a dramatic performance. 20c. [N*]

siglum, *pl.* **sigla** [Lat. < *sigillum* 'seal'] a letter or arbitrary mark used as an abbreviation for a word, *esp.* a letter or combination of letters used to denote a manuscript or printed text in the APPARATUS CRITICUS of a critical edition. 18c. [N,S]

si jeunesse savoit, si vieillesse pouvoit [Obs. Fr.] if youth had the knowledge, if old age had the strength. 20c. H. Estienne *Les Prémices* (1594) Epigram 191; often quoted with the modern French forms *savait, pouvait.*

silent leges inter armas [Lat.] laws are put to silence by armed force, the law is inoperative in time of war. 20c. Cicero *Pro Milone* iv 11.

si monumentum requiris, circumspice [Lat.] if you are seeking his monument, look about you. 19c. The epitaph of Sir Christopher Wren in St Paul's Cathedral. [S]

simoom [Arab. *semūm*] a hot dry sand-laden wind which periodically sweeps across the Arabian and Oriental deserts. 18c. [N,S]

simpatico, *f.* **simpatica** [It.] full of tender feeling, *hence* likable, congenial. 19c. Used (like Fr. SYMPATHIQUE) to avoid the connotation of commiseration implicit in English *sympathetic*. [N*,S]

simplesse [Fr.] artificial simplicity, cultivated artlessness. 20c.

simplex munditiis [Lat.] simple and neat, becomingly unadorned. 18c. Horace *Odes* I v 5. [S]

simplicissimus [Lat.] a simple-minded man who is constantly taken advantage of by others, but who accepts his misfortunes philosophically and survives them. 20c. From the title of H. J. C. von Grimmelshausen's romance *Der Abentheurliche Simplicissimus Teutsch* (1669). Cf. SCHLEMIEL.

simpliciter [Lat.] wholly, absolutely, unconditionally, not merely in one respect. 16c. Contrasted with SECUNDUM QUID. [N,S]

simpliste [Fr.] over-simple, too simple to be true. 20c.

simulacrum, *pl.* **simulacra** [Lat.] an exact image or representation; a counterfeit; an illusion, a phantasm. 19c. [N,S]

sine die [Lat.] (postponed) indefinitely, without any day being fixed for resumption or re-assembly. 17c. [N,S]

sine legitima prole [Lat.] without legitimate issue. 20c. Often abbreviated to *s.l.p.* Cf. SINE PROLE.

sine prole [Lat.] without issue. 20c. Often abbreviated to *s.p.* Cf. DECESSIT SINE PROLE; OBIIT SINE PROLE.

sine qua non [Lat. 'without which not'] some thing or person necessary and indispensable for the achieving of some purpose. 17c. The plural *sine quibus non* has been in use, but the singular is now used indiscriminately. Cf. CAUSA SINE QUA NON. [N,S]

sinfonia concertante [It.] *Mus.* a symphonic work with parts for a number of solo instruments. 20c. The *sinfonia concertante* normally displays the formal modifications of the symphony found in the CONCERTO. Cf. CONCERTANTE.

singerie [Fr.] *Art* a pictorial or plastic representation of monkeys in human situations or employed in human occupations. 20c. This kind of pictorial satire was fashionable in the eighteenth century.

Singspiel [Ger.] a quasi-operatic performance combining spoken dialogue with song; light opera. 19c. Cf. OPÉRA COMIQUE. [N*]

Sinn Fein [Ir. *sinn féin* 'we ourselves'] an Irish movement for self-government and cultural independence. 20c. The *Sinn Fein* movement was founded by Arthur Griffith in 1905; the term is now sometimes erroneously applied to the illegal Irish Republican Army. [N*]

sinopia [It.] *Art* a sketch made in red crayon on plaster as a preliminary to FRESCO painting. 20c.

sirdar [Hind. < Pers. *sardār*] a military leader, a general (in India and the East); *hence*, the British Commander-in-Chief of the Egyptian army. 17c. [N,S]

sirkar [Hind. < Pers. *sarkār*] *A.-I.* a house-steward. 18c. [N,S]

sirocco/scirocco [It. *scirocco* < Arab. *sharq* 'east'] a hot, humid, oppressive wind blowing from the south or south-east across the Mediterranean to southern Europe. 17c. The better form *scirocco* is less common in English than *sirocco*. Cf. KHAMSIN. [N,S]

sissonne [Fr.] *Ballet* a step in which the dancer leaps in the air and alights with one foot extended; the foot extended is then closed to the other. 18c. [N]

Sittlichkeit [Ger.] decorum, decency, morality. 20c.

si vis pacem, para bellum [Lat.] if you want peace, prepare for war. 20c. Based on Vegetius *De Re Militare* iii Prologue: *Qui desiderat pacem, præparet bellum* 'If anyone desires peace, let him prepare for war'.

sjambok [Afrik. < Mal *chamboq* < Hind. *chābuk*] a heavy whip made of rhinoceros or hippopotamus hide. 19c. [N]

skål! [Norw. 'bowl'] 'your health!', a toast used in Norway. 20c. Cf. GESUNDHEIT; PROSIT; SLÁINTE.

skean dhu=SGIAN DUBH, a Highland dagger.

skijöring [Norw. *skikjøring*] a method of skiing in which the skier is towed along behind a horse, reindeer, or motor vehicle. 20c. The form *skijöring*, apparently formed in English, has been adopted by a number of other languages.

sláinte! [Ir.] '(your) health!', a toast used in Ireland and Gaelic Scotland. 20c. Cf. GESUNDHEIT; PROSIT; SKÅL.

slalom [Norw. *slalåm*] a ski-race down a course marked out by artificial obstacles; *hence*, an obstacle-race in other sports, e.g. canoeing. 20c. [N*]

sloid/sloyd [Swed. *slöjd*] (instruction in) arts and crafts, handicrafts; (a school devoted to) the teaching of practical subjects. 20c. The English spelling *sloyd* is taken from the Swedish verb *sloyda*.

s.l.p.=SINE LEGITIMA PROLE, without legitimate issue.

smalto, *pl.* **smalti** [It.] *Art* (a fragment of) coloured glass or enamel used in mosaic work. 20c.

smörgåsbord [Swed. 'butter-goose-table'] *Cul.* a traditional Swedish dish consisting of a copious selection of various savouries (*usu.* cold) served on bread. 20c. It is possible that *smörgås* may refer to FOIE GRAS as an original element in the dish. The Norwegian spelling is *smørgåsbord*.

smørrebrød [Dan. 'butter-bread'] a sandwich. 20c. The meaning is sometimes influenced by the (mainly accidental) resemblance to the Swedish SMÖRGÅSBORD.

snobisme [Fr.] intellectual snobbery, an urge to follow the latest fashion in matters of intellect or culture. 20c. Much more precise than English *snobbery*. Cf. SUCCÈS DE SNOBISME.

sobriquet [Fr.] a nick-name; a pseudonym. 17c. Also erroneously written *soubriquet*. Cf. NOM DE GUERRE; NOM DE PLUME. [N,S]

sociétaire [Fr.] an actor of the Comédie Francaise who has a share in the profits made. 19c. [N*]

socle [Fr.] *Arch.* a plain pedestal or plinth supporting a statue, column or wall. 18c. [N]

soi-disant [Fr.] self-styled, would-be, pretended. 18c. Always with the implication of deliberate deceit. [N,S]

soigné, *f.* **soignée** [Fr.] well cared for, dressed or decorated with great care. 20c. Cf. MAL SOIGNÉ. [N*]

soirée [Fr.] an evening party, an evening assembly. 19c. [N,S]

soirée musicale [Fr.] a 'musical evening', an assembly in the evening for the purpose of making or hearing music. 19c. Cf. MATINÉE MUSICALE; MUSICALE; THÉ MUSICAL.

solarium [Lat.] a sunny terrace or balcony, *esp.* one designed to be exposed to the sun but protected from the wind. 19c. [N]

solatium [Lat.] a compensation, a sum of money given to make up for loss or inconvenience. 19c. [N,S]

solera [Sp.] (1) a blend of different vintages of sherry; (2) a large wine-cask. 19c. [N]

solfatara [It.] a volcanic area in which sulphurous vapours are emitted from vents in the ground. 18c. Formerly also written *solfaterra*, as if connected with *terra* 'earth'. Cf. FUMARUOLA. [N,S(*)]

solidus, *pl.* **solidi** [Lat.] (1) *Hist.* a Roman gold coin; (2) a shilling. 14c. *Usu.* abbreviated to *S.* or *s.* in the combination *L.S.D.*, *L.s.d.*, *£.s.d.* (LIBRÆ, *solidi*, DENARII). The singular *solidus* is used in typography to denote the oblique stroke /, which separates shillings from pence in such combinations as 10/6, and therefore in a sense denotes 'shillings'. [N(*),S]

soliste [Fr.] *Ballet* a solo dancer. 20c.

solitaire [Fr.] (1) a precious stone, *usu.* a diamond, set by itself; (2) a game which can be played by a single person, *esp.* a game played by moving marbles or pegs which fit into hollows or holes in a special board; (3) *U.S.* 'patience', a card-game for a single person. 18c. [N,S]

solo, *pl.* **soli** [It.] *Mus.* (a piece of vocal or instrumental music) performed or designed to be performed by a single singer or instrumentalist. 17c. The word remains foreign in this sense, but has been anglicized (with plural *solos*) and extended to a wide range of analagous meanings. [N(*),S]

solus [Lat. 'alone'] (an agreement) whereby a retailer undertakes to purchase supplies from one wholesaler only. 20c. Used *esp.* of the supply of petrol and lubricating oil.

solutis curis [Lat.] with all cares resolved, free from all anxiety. 20c.

solvitur ambulando [Lat. 'it is solved by walking'] the problem can only be solved by practical experiment. 19c. *Orig.* applied to the solution of the problem of the reality of motion, but now extended to the solution of any problem.

sol y sombra [Sp.] 'sun and shade', the name given to the medium-priced seats at a bullfight, which are exposed to the sun during part but not the whole of the afternoon. 20c.

soma [Sansk. *sōma*] an intoxicating drink much used in Vedic religious ceremonies. 19c. The plant from the juice of which *soma* was prepared has not been identified with certainty. [N,S]

sombrero [Sp.] a broad-brimmed felt hat of a type worn in Spain and Spanish America. 18c. [N,S]

sommelier [Fr.] a butler, a wine-waiter. 20c. [N*]

sonata [It.] *Mus.* a composition in several movements for the piano, or for piano and a solo instrument. 19c. In earlier usage (17c.) the sense was 'instrumental composition', contrasted with CANTATA. [N,S]

son et lumière [Fr. 'sound and light'] an entertainment performed in the precincts of an ancient building and illustrating its history by means of floodlighting, music, pageantry, and recorded commentary. 20c. First devised by the French architect Paul Robert-Houdin at Chambord in 1952; the first performance in England was at the Royal Naval College, Greenwich, in 1957.

soprano, *pl.* **soprani** [It.] *Mus.* the highest-pitched human singing voice; (a part) designed for or sung by such a voice; (a woman or boy) having such a voice. 18c. The normal compass of the *soprano* voice is from middle C to the note two octaves above it. [N,S]

sorites [Lat. < Gk. σωρείτης] *Logic* a series of syllogisms forming a consecutive argument, in which all the conclusions but the last are omitted. 16c. [N,S]

sortes Biblicæ *pl.* [Lat.] divination by the Bible: the volume is opened at random and the first phrase on which the eye falls is regarded as significant or prophetic. 20c. Based on SORTES VIRGILIANÆ. [N*]

sortes Homericæ *pl.* [Lat.] divination by the works of Homer: the volume is opened at random and the first phrase on which the eye falls is regarded as significant or prophetic. 17c. Based on SORTES VIRGILIANÆ. [N*,S]

sortes Virgilianæ *pl.* [Lat.] divination by the works of Virgil: the volume is opened at random and the first phrase on which the eye falls is regarded as significant or prophetic. 16c. [N*,S]

sortie [Fr.] *Mil.* a sally, a sudden attack made on the enemy by a besieged garrison. 18c. [N,S]

sostenuto [It.] *Mus.* (1) (a note) sustained or prolonged beyond its normal duration; (2) (a passage) played in a CANTABILE style. 18c. [N,S]

sottise [Fr.] a foolish action; a silly remark. 17c. [N,S]

sottisier [Fr.] a collection of silly remarks, an anthology of 'howlers'. 20c.

sotto in su [It.] *Art* the foreshortening of a figure painted on a cornice or ceiling so that it appears vertical to the viewer below. 20c. This foreshortening was a favourite device of Mantegna.

sotto voce [It.] (spoken or sung) in a low or subdued voice, in an undertone. 18c. [N,S]

sou [Fr.] a small French coin, a five-centime piece. 19c. Often used in a general sense as an example of a coin of very little value. [N,S]

soubresaut [Fr.] (1) the leaping motion characteristic of boiling liquids; (2) *Ballet* a leap in the air with both feet fully pointed one behind the other. 19c. [N]

soubrette [Fr.] the part of a maid-servant or lady's maid in a play; an actress accustomed to play such parts. 18c. [N,S]

soubriquet=SOBRIQUET, a nickname, a pseudonym.

souffle [Fr.] *Med.* a murmuring or whispering sound heard on auscultation. 19c. Cf. RÂLE. [N]

soufflé [Fr.] *Cul.* any dish made by mixing other ingredients with white of egg beaten into a froth and heating the whole in the oven until it puffs up. 19c. Sometimes mis-spelt *soufflée*. [N,S]

souffleur, *f.* **souffleuse** [Fr.] the prompter in a dramatic performance. 20c.

souk [Arab. *sūq*] an Oriental market-place, a BAZAAR. 19c. [N*]

soulagement [Fr.] relief, alleviation, *esp.* of mental distress. 18c. [S]

soupçon [Fr. 'suspicion'] a very small quantity, a slight trace. 18c. [N,S]

sourdine [Fr.] subdued, muffled. 19c. Cf. EN SOURDINE. [N]

sournois, *f.* **sournoise** [Fr.] sly, insincere, deceitful. 19c. [S]

sousentendu [Fr.] a hidden meaning, something left unexpressed but intended to be understood by the listener or reader. 20c. [N*]

sous l'angle du scandale [Fr.] from the point of view of scandal, taking into account the scandal that may be caused. 20c.

soutane [Fr.] a cassock, the long buttoned coat which forms the normal dress of ecclesiastics on the Continent. 19c. The wearing of the *soutane* has recently been made optional. [N]

souteneur [Fr.] a ponce, a man who lives on the immoral earnings of a prostitute. 20c. [N*]

souterrain [Fr.] a vault, an underground room, passage, or storehouse. 18c. [N,S]

souvenir [Fr. 'memory'] a keepsake, *esp.* something bought or received as a gift in remembrance of an occasion or a visit to a place. 18c. [N,S]

soviet [Russ.] a council elected by the inhabitants of a district in Russia to govern that district; a congress of delegates from these councils which governs the whole country. 20c. The word has now come to be used as an adjective meaning no more than 'Russian communist'. [N*]

sovkhoz [Russ.] a Russian state-owned farm. 20c. Contrasted with KOLKHOZ, a collective farm.

s.p.=SINE PROLE, without issue.

spaghetti *pl.* [It. 'cords'] *Cul.* a dried wheaten paste in the form of long thin sticks, intermediate in size between MACARONI (which are hollow) and VERMICELLI. 19c. Despite the plural form the word is normally construed in English as singular. Cf. CANNELLONI; PASTA. [N*]

spahi [Turk. *sipahi* < Pers. *sipāhi*] a cavalryman in the Turkish army; an Algerian horseman serving under the French government. 16c. Cf. SEPOY. [N,S]

spalliere, *pl.* **spallieri** [It.] *Art* a decorative painting on the back of a chair. 20c.

spalpeen [Ir. *spailpín*] a common labourer; a contemptible rascal; a young lad. 18c. [N,S]

spatula [Lat.] a flat blade of wood, ivory, or metal, used for various specialized purposes. 16c. The word is a diminutive of Lat. *spatha* 'sword' < Gk. σπάθη. [N,S]

spécialité de la maison [Fr.] a dish which is characteristic of or peculiar to a particular eating-house or restaurant; *hence facet.* anything characteristic of a person, writer, painter, etc. 20c. Cf. MAISON.

spectrum, *pl.* **spectra** [Lat.] the coloured band into which a beam of light is decomposed by a prism or diffraction grating; *hence*, a range of related but dissimilar things. 17c. [N,S]

speculum, *pl.* **specula** [Lat.] (1) *Med.* an instrument for the dilation of the various orifices of the body to facilitate examination; (2) the concave mirror of a reflecting telescope. 16c. [N]

spes ultima gentis [Lat.] the last hope of his race, the last hope of his family. 20c.

sphincter [Lat. < Gk. σφιγκτήρ] *Med.* a contractile muscular ring by which one of the openings of the body is normally kept closed. 16c. [N,S]

Spiegeleisen [Ger. 'mirror-iron'] a lustrous manganiferous cast-iron much used in the manufacture of steel by the Bessemer process. 19c. [N]

splendide mendax [Lat.] lying in an honourable cause. 19c. Horace *Odes* III xi 35. [S]

spolvero, *pl.* **spolveri** [It.] *Art* a cartoon or sketch pricked for reproduction by sprinkling it with coloured dust which will penetrate the holes. 20c.

sponte sua [Lat.] of his (her) own free will, voluntarily. 20c.

spotteur [Fr.] a police spy, a detective set to watch a suspected person. 20c.

Sprachgefühl [Ger.] a feeling for language, *esp.* a sensitiveness to the idiom, etc., of a foreign language. 20c.

Sprechgesang [Ger.] *Mus.* 'inflected speech', a kind of declamation which, while remaining speech rather than song, follows a preconcerted melodic pattern. 20c. Cf. ARIOSO; RECITATIVO.

Sprechstimme [Ger.] *Mus.* a vocal part written by a composer for performance according to the principles of SPRECHGESANG. 20c.

sprezzatura [It.] *Art* the NONCHALANCE and apparently effortless technique of the supreme artist. 20c. Applied by Baldassare Castiglione (1478–1529) to the ideal courtier, and now by extension to a great artist.

spurlos versunken [Ger.] sunk without trace, vanished without leaving any vestige behind. 20c.

sputnik [Russ. 'fellow-traveller'] an artificial satellite set in orbit round the earth. 20c. Used *esp.* of the first satellite, set in orbit in 1957, and of other (numbered) satellites of the same series.

sputum, *pl.* **sputa** [Lat.] *Med.* saliva, spittle, *esp.* as expectorated in morbid conditions of the lungs or throat. 17c. [N,S]

staccato [It. 'detached'] *Mus.* (a passage played) with the duration of each note reduced to a minimum so that successive notes are distinctly separated by rests; *hence*, jerky (manner of speech, etc.) 18c. Cf. DÉTACHÉ. [N,S]

Stahlhelm [Ger. 'steel helmet'] the name of a German ex-service association of nationalist and conservative tendencies, formed after the First World War. 20c. [N*]

stanza [It.] *Ling.* a group of lines of verse arranged according to a systematic and regularly recurring pattern. 16c. Cf. STROPHE. [N,S]

stasis [Gk. στάσις] *Med.* a stagnation or stoppage of the flow of any of the fluids in the body, *esp.* of the blood or of the contents of the bowels. 18c. [N]

status [Lat.] the state or condition of a thing or of things in general; the position or standing of a person in some profession or in society at large; (some visible object) denoting the possession of good standing in society. 18c. *Orig.* a legal term denoting some special class of rights or disabilities determined by law. Cf. PRESTIGE. [N,S]

status quo [Lat. 'the state in which'] the state of affairs existing (now or at some given date). 19c. Always with reference to a continuation or prolongation of some thing or condition already in existence. [N,S]

status quo ante [Lat.] the former state of affairs, the state of affairs existing before (the present or some given date). 19c. *Usu.* with reference to the restoration of some thing or condition not in existence. Cf. IN STATU QUO (ANTE). [S]

Stein [Ger. 'stone'] a large earthenware drinking-mug, the German equivalent of a tankard. 20c. [N]

stela, *pl.* **stelæ** [Lat. < Gk. στέλη] an upright slab carved with an inscription or decorative pattern. 18c. A *stela* may be a gravestone, a commemorative stone, or a milestone. [N,S]

stemma, *pl.* **stemmata** [Gk. στέμμα] a genealogical tree; *hence esp.* a diagram showing the genetic relationships of the manuscripts of a text. 19c. [N]

stengah [Mal. 'half'] a small whisky and soda. 20c. Sometimes corrupted into *stinger*. [N*]

steppe [Russ. *stepĭ*] *Geog.* a level treeless plain, *esp.* in southern Russia or Siberia. 17c. Cf. TUNDRA. [N,S]

stet [Lat.] 'let it stand', a direction that something which has been deleted or altered in a manuscript or proof is to remain uncorrected. 19c. [N,S]

stet processus [Lat. 'let the process stand'] *Law* an entry in the record of a court that by the consent of the parties concerned the proceedings are to be stayed. 19c. [N]

stichomythia [Lat. < Gk. στιχομυθία] dialogue in verse drama in which each speech occupies a single line. 17c. *Stichomythia* is characterized by antithesis and rhetorical repetition. The word is sometimes printed in Greek characters. [N,S]

stichos, *pl.* **stichoi** [Gk. στίχος] one of the units corresponding to a line of average length into which the contents of ancient manuscripts were sometimes divided to simplify the remuneration of the scribes. 19c. [N]

stigma [Gk. στίγμα] (1) a mark made by branding as a punishment; *hence*, a mark of infamy, a sign of condemnation; (2) *pl.* **stigmata,** marks resembling the wounds on the crucified body of Christ which sometimes appear on the bodies of devout persons. 16c. The first person to receive the *stigmata* was St Francis of Assisi. [N,S]

(De) Stijl [Du. '(the) Style'] *Art* a Dutch movement in architecture and abstract art which laid great emphasis on geometrical structure. 20c. The name is taken from that of a journal published from 1917 to 1928; one of the leaders of the movement was Piet Mondrian (1872–1944).

stiletto [It.] a short dagger with a thick narrow blade; *hence*, an instrument for making small circular holes; any round tapering sharp-pointed object. 17c. [N,S]

stilyaga, *pl.* **stilyagi** [Russ. 'stylish'] a (Russian) teddy-boy. 20c. Cf. BLOUSON NOIR; HALBSTARKE(R); JEUNE VOYOU; VITELLONE.

Stimmung [Ger.] the mood, tone, or atmosphere (of a work of literature, etc.) 20c.

stimulus, *pl.* **stimuli** [Lat. 'goad'] a spur, an incentive to activity; something that excites an organ or tissue in the body to specific activity. 17c. [N(*),S]

stoa, *pl.* **stoai** [Gk. στοά] *Arch.* a PORTICO, a roofed colonnade. 17c. The word *Stoic* comes from the *Stoa* in Athens where the philosopher Zeno lectured. [N,S]

Stock [Ger.] a ski-stick, a stick with an iron point and a metal ring attached near the point by leather thongs to prevent it from sinking into the snow. 20c. Cf. ALPENSTOCK.

stoep [Du.] a raised platform or VERANDAH along the front and sometimes also round the sides of a house. 19c. The *stoep* is characteristic of Dutch and Afrikander architecture, but has been adopted in parts of the United States, where the word is often anglicized as *stoop*. [N]

stratum, *pl.* **strata** [Lat.] a layer, *esp.* one of a number of layers superposed one on another; *Geog.* a bed of sedimentary rock. 16c. [N,S]

strega [It. 'witch'] an Italian LIQUEUR made at Benevento. 20c.

stretto [It.] *Mus.* (1) in quicker time; (2) a passage in a fugue in which the subject and the answer are made to overlap each other. 18c. [N]

stria, *pl.* **striæ** [Lat.] (1) *Arch.* the space between the adjacent flutings of a column; (2) a groove or ridge, *esp.* one of a series of grooves or ridges. 16c. [N,S]

strophe, *pl.* **strophæ** [Gk. στροφή 'turning'] *Ling.* the first group of lines in the metrical system of the Greek lyric, which is exactly repeated in the ANTISTROPHE; *hence*, any group of lines of verse arranged according to a systematic and recurring pattern, a STANZA. 17c. [N,S]

structures vivantes *pl.* [Fr.] *Art* works of plastic art which by mechanical means are maintained in constant motion, or which are so designed as to give the appearance of constant motion. 20c.

stucco [It.] *Arch.* a fine plaster, *esp.* a mixture of gypsum and pulverized marble, used for covering exterior walls in imitation of stone or marble, and for executing cornices, mouldings, etc., in the interior of buildings. 16c. [N,S]

stucco lustro [It.] *Arch.* STUCCO so treated as to give it a shiny surface. 20c.

Stundenhotel [Ger.] a disorderly house, a hotel or lodging-house which is in effect a brothel. 20c. Cf. MAISON DE PASSE.

stupa [Sansk. *stūpa*] a Buddhist sepulchral monument. 19c. [N]

stupor mundi [Lat.] the wonder of the world, a person who has achieved a world-wide reputation in which astonishment is mingled with awe. 20c.

Sturm und Drang [Ger.] 'storm and stress', the name given to a German romantic movement in the later eighteenth century characterized by extravagance in the representation of violent passion. 19c. The title of a play (1776) by F. M. Klinger, considered characteristic of the movement. [N,S]

(le) style, c'est l'homme [Fr.] the style is the man himself, the style of a writer is a reflection of his personality. 20c. Buffon *Discours sur le Style* (1753): *le style est l'homme même*. Cf. L'HOMME MÊME.

style champêtre [Fr.] *Art* the pastoral style in painting, the representation of idyllic rustic scenes. 20c.

style mécanique [Fr.] *Art* an angular and mechanistic style popular in the painting, sculpture and architecture of the 1920's and 1930's. 20c.

style périodique [Fr.] a literary style evolved in imitation of the long and complex periods of Ciceronian prose. 20c.

style pompier [Fr.] a windy derivative style drawing heavily on the work of others. 20c. Cf. POMPIER.

stylus, *pl.* **styli** [Lat.] a sharp-pointed instrument designed for inscribing letters on a wax tablet; *hence*, the sharp-pointed precious stone which follows out the grooves of a gramophone record. 19c. The Latin word is better written *stilus*, the spelling *stylus* being due to an erroneous association with Gk. στῦλος 'column'; but the spelling *stylus* is securely established in English. [N]

suave [Fr.] urbane, blandly polite, soothing in manner. 19c. [N,S]

suaviter in modo, fortiter in re [Lat.] urbanely in manner, resolutely in action. 18c. Applied to a person who with the utmost politeness refuses to budge from his intention. In the form *fortiter in re, suaviter in modo* the phrase occurs in a work entitled *Industriæ ad Curandos Animæ Morbos* (1606) by Rudolfo Acquaviva (1543–1615), fourth General of the Society of Jesus. [S]

subahdar [Hind. *çūbahdār* < Arab. *çūbah* 'province' + Pers. *dār* 'master'] *A.-I.* the governor of an Indian province; the native warrant-officer of a company of SEPOYS. 17c. [N,S]

sub anno [Lat.] under the year . . .; always followed by a date, with reference to an entry in a chronicle or series of annals. 20c. Abbreviated to *s.a.*

subbotnik [Russ.] an organized project of voluntary public service. 20c.

sub conditione [Lat.] *Eccles.* conditionally. 20c. *Usu.* with reference to a baptism, etc., administered conditionally in case a valid ceremony has already taken place.

sub judice [Lat. 'under a judge'] *Law* still being considered by a court of law, not yet decided, unsettled. 17c. [N,S]

subpœna [Lat. *sub pœna* 'under a penalty'] *Law* a writ commanding the presence in court of a defendant or witness under pain of fine or imprisonment; to serve such a writ upon (a person). 15c. When the word is used as a verb the past participle is *subpœnaed* or *subpœna'd.* [N,S]

subpœna duces tecum [Lat. *sub pœna, duces tecum* 'under a penalty, bring with you'] *Law* a writ commanding the production in court of the documents specified under pain of fine or imprisonment. 20c.

sub rosa [Lat. 'under the rose'] privately, secretly, in strict confidence. 17c. The origin of the expression is unknown, but the idiom is used in English, Dutch and German. [N,S]

sub sigillo [Lat.] under the seal (of confession), in inviolable confidence. 17c. [N,S]

sub silentio [Lat.] in silence, without making any remark; without paying any attention. 17c. [N,S]

sub specie æternitatis [Lat.] (considered) in relation to the one eternal Substance; without consideration of local or temporal conditions. 20c. Spinoza *Ethics* (1677) V xxxi: *sub æternitatis specie.*

substratum, *pl.* **substrata** [Lat.] a layer of one substance beneath another; a basis, a foundation; the substance in which qualities inhere. 17c. [N,S]

sub voce [Lat.] under the word . . .; used to indicate the head-word in a dictionary, etc., under which information may be found. 19c. Often abbreviated to *s.v.* [N]

succedaneum, *pl.* **succedanea** [Lat.] a makeshift, one thing substituted for another, *esp.* a drug of inferior quality substituted for another in a prescription. 17c. [N,S]

succès de ridicule [Fr.] success (of a work of art) resulting from its having been taken as a joke. 20c.

succès de scandale [Fr.] success (of a work of art) due wholly to the scandal created by it. 20c. [N*]

succès de snobisme [Fr.] success (of a work of art) due to its appeal to intellectual snobbery. 20c. Cf. SNOBISME.

succès d'estime [Fr.] success (of a work of art) which brings the approval of discerning critics but neither wide popularity nor financial reward. 19c. [N*,S]

succès fou [Fr.] success (of a work of art) marked by scenes of wild enthusiasm. 19c. [N*,S]

succubus, *pl.* **succubi** [Lat.] an evil spirit in female form which cohabits with a man during sleep. 14c. The apparently masculine form of the word is due to association with INCUBUS; the true feminine *succuba* is very rare. [N,S]

sudarium [Lat.] a face-cloth, *esp.* the cloth with which St Veronica wiped the face of Christ and on which His features were impressed. 17c. [N,S]

suède [Fr. 'Sweden'] undressed kid-skin. 19c. *Orig.* in the phrase *gants de Suède* 'Swedish gloves', and misunderstood as the name of the material. [N]

suggestio falsi [Lat.] the suggestion of what is false, the deliberate misrepresentation of something by speech or action without actually lying. 19c. *Usu.* in conjunction with SUPPRESSIO VERI. [N*,S]

sui generis [Lat.] belonging to a species all its own, unique. 18c. [N,S]

sui juris [Lat. 'of one's own right'] *Law* of full age and capacity, able to manage one's own affairs. 17c. [N,S]

suite [Fr.] (1) a retinue, a train of followers. 17c. (2) a number of rooms, *usu.* opening one into another, used by the same person or group of persons.

18c. Cf. EN SUITE. (3) a set of furniture, etc., of the same pattern. 19c. (4) *Mus*. a set of musical compositions designed to be played in sequence, *usu*. in the same key or in related keys. 19c. [N(*),S]

sul ponticello [It.] *Mus.* (the playing of a bowed instrument) with the bow very near the bridge, so as to produce a sound of characteristic quality. 20c. The use of the bow near the bridge elicits a higher proportion of upper partials than normal bowing does.

summa [Lat.] a summary treatise, a single work embracing the whole of a subject. 18c. Often with explicit or implied reference to the *Summa Theologica* of St Thomas Aquinas. [N,S]

summa cum laude [Lat.] with the highest praise, with distinction. 20c. Used to distinguish those candidates who have achieved the greatest success in an examination in which Honours are not awarded. Cf. CUM LAUDE; MAXIMA CUM LAUDE.

summum bonum [Lat.] the supreme Good, the ultimate object of all rational effort. 16c. Cicero *De Officiis* I ii 5. [N,S]

Sunna [Arab. *Sunnah*] the body of traditional sayings attributed to Mahomet and not contained in the Koran. 18c. Cf. HADITH. [N]

sunt lacrymæ rerum [Lat.] the way of the world is inevitably tragic. 20c. Virgil *Æneid* i 462 *Sunt lacrymæ rerum, et mentem mortalia tangunt* 'there are tears in life, and human sufferings distress the mind'. Virgil's well-known line is nearly untranslatable. Cf. LACRYMÆ RERUM.

suppressio veri [Lat.] the suppression of what is true, the misrepresentation of the truth by concealing something which ought to be made known. 18c. *Usu.* in conjunction with SUGGESTIO FALSI. [N*,S]

supra [Lat.] above, previously mentioned (referring to an earlier passage in a book, etc.) 16c. Cf. INFRA; UT SUPRA. [N,S]

supremo [Sp.] the commander-in-chief of a military force; an 'overlord', the overall supervisor of a number of government departments; the supreme authority on some question of taste. 20c. Cf. GENERALISSIMO.

surah [Arab. *sūrah*] a chapter of the Koran. 20c. In much earlier use (17c.) in the form *assora* from Arab. *as-sūrah* with the definite article. The same form is also used to denote a twilled silk fabric, but it is unlikely that there is any connection with the Arabic word.

Sûreté [Fr.] the criminal investigation department of a French police force. 20c. In full *Service de la Sûreté* 'Security Service'; but in English often used for *Sûreté Générale*, the French equivalent of Scotland Yard. [N*]

sur fond réservé [Fr.] *Art* EN PLEIN (enamel work), (enamel work) in which the ground (*usu.* of gold or silver) is carved in INTAGLIO, the hollows being filled with translucent enamel through which the modelling can still be seen. 20c. Cf. BASSE-TAILLE.

sur le cou du pied [Fr.] *Ballet* (with the heel of one foot) resting on the part of the other leg between the calf and the ankle. 20c.

sur le tapis [Fr. 'on the carpet'] under discussion, the subject of conversation. 18c. Cf. TAPIS. [S]

sur le vif [Fr.] *Art* (painted, etc.) from life. 20c. Cf. AD VIVUM; AU VIF.

sur place [Fr.] on the spot. 20c.

sursum corda [Lat.] 'lift up your hearts', the priest's exhortation immediately before the Preface of the Mass; *hence*, any comparable exhortation. 16c. [N,S]

surveillance [Fr.] watching over (a suspected person), spying (on a suspected person). 19c. Fully anglicized in the sense of 'supervision, control'. [N,S]

susurrus [Lat.] a low whispering, rustling or muttering. 19c. [N,S]

sutra [Sansk. *sūtra* 'string'] a short mnemonic rule, *esp.* as a summary of part of Buddhist sacred literature. 19c. [N,S]

suttee [Hind. *satī* 'good woman'] *A.-I.* a Hindu widow who burns herself on her husband's funeral pyre; *hence*, the burning of a Hindu widow on her husband's funeral pyre. 18c. The custom of *suttee* was abolished by law in 1829. The use of the spelling *sati* in English is pedantic. [N,S]

suzeraine [Fr.] a woman in authority over others, a woman having charge of an estate, etc. 19c. The masculine *suzerain* is fully anglicized. [N,S]

s.v.=SUB VOCE, under the word . . .

svelte [Fr. < It. *svelto*] slender, willowy; elegant. 19c. [N,S]

swami [Hind. *swāmī*] a Hindu religious teacher. 20c. Cf. GURU. [N]

swaraj [Sansk. *svarāj*] (the agitation in favour of) self-government for India. 20c. [N*]

swastika [Sansk. *svastika*] an ancient symbol of good fortune consisting of an equal-armed cross, each arm being continued by a limb at right-angles to it and pointing in a clockwise direction. 19c. Adopted under its German name *Hakenkreuz* as the symbol of the German National Socialist Party. [N]

syce [Hind. *sā'is* < Arab.] *A.-I.* a groom, a running footman. 17c. The use of the spelling *sais* in English is pedantic. [N,S]

syllepsis, *pl.* **syllepses** [Lat. < Gk. σύλληψις] *Ling.* a rhetorical device whereby a single word is to be construed with two other words in the same sentence, *usu.* in a slightly different sense. 16c. Cf. ZEUGMA. [N,S]

Sylvesterabend [Ger.] New Year's Eve. 20c.

symbiosis [Lat. < Gk. συμβίωσις] commensalism, the association of two organisms which contribute to each other's support by a kind of mutual parasitism. 19c. [N(*)]

sympathique [Fr.] likable, congenial. 20c. Cf. SIMPATICO.

symposium, *pl.* **symposia** [Lat. < Gk. συμπόσιον 'drinking together'] a collection of speeches delivered or articles written by a number of persons on the same topic. 18c. With implicit reference to the title of Plato's best-known dialogue. [N,S]

synæsthesia, *pl.* **synæsthesiæ** [Lat. < Gk. *συναίσθησις*] *Psych.* the production of a mental image of one kind from a sense-impression of a different kind, *esp.* the association of an image of colour with the hearing of certain sounds. 19c. The formation of the (modern) Latin word from the Greek is irregular in both form and meaning. [N]

syncope [Lat. < Gk. *συγκοπή*] (1) *Med*, suspension of the action of the heart, resulting in unconsciousness and *usu.* in death; (2) *Ling.* the contraction of a word by the omission of a medial vowel. 15c. [N,S]

synecdoche [Lat. < Gk. *συνεκδοχή*] *Ling.* a figure of speech in which the name of a part is used to designate the whole, or the name of the whole is used to designate a part. 14c. [N,S]

synopsis, *pl.* **synopses** [Lat. < Gk. *σύνοψις*] a condensed general survey or comprehensive view, a CONSPECTUS. 17c. [N,S]

synthesis, *pl.* **syntheses** [Lat. < Gk. *σύνθεσις*] the putting together of parts so as to make up a complex whole; a complex whole made up of parts put together. 18c. [N,S]

système D [Fr.] a policy of extracting oneself from difficult circumstances regardless of the interests of others. 20c. A contraction of *système* DÉBROUILLARD.

Systemzwang [Ger.] the influence exerted by a desire for systematic regularity. 20c.

T

tableau d'ensemble [Fr.] a general picture, a general survey (of a subject, etc.) 20c. Cf. ENSEMBLE; TOUT ENSEMBLE.

tableau (vivant), *pl.* **tableaux (vivants)** [Fr. 'living picture'] a representation of a scene or incident, or of a well-known painting or statue, by a group of silent and motionless persons; *hence*, an actual scene or incident which suggests the suspended animation of a painting or statue. 19c. [N,S]

table d'hôte [Fr. 'host's table'] a common table at an eating-house; *hence*, a fixed meal served at a standard price. 17c. Opposed to À LA CARTE. [N,S]

taboo [Tongan *tabu*] forbidden, prohibited to a certain class of persons, hedged round with arbitrary restrictions; the imposition of such prohibitions and restrictions; to impose such prohibitions and restrictions. 18c. The spelling *tabu* and the forms *tapu, tambu* found in other Polynesian and Melanesian languages are also in use, but savour of pedantry. The word was *orig*. an anthropological term, but has passed into general usage. [N,S]

tabouret [Fr. 'little drum'] a low stool without back or arms. 17c. [N]

tabula rasa [Lat. 'scraped tablet'] a blank surface ready to receive new impressions; *hence*, a mind wholly ignorant of a specified subject and ready to absorb information about it. 16c. The alternative forms *rasa tabula*, *abrasa tabula*, seem now to be wholly obsolete. [N,S(*)]

tacet [Lat. 'it is silent'] *Mus*. a direction that a voice or instrument is to remain silent for a time. 18c. [N]

tachisme [Fr.] *Art* 'action painting', the production of a work of art by spilling, pouring, and smearing the pigment on to the picture-surface. 20c. An example of the new movement in painting developed after the Second World War and known as ART AUTRE.

tædium vitæ [Lat.] weariness of life, a morbid disgust with life. 19c. Aulus Gellius *Noctes Atticæ* VII xviii 11. Cf. MAL DU SIÈCLE; WELTSCHMERZ. [N*,S]

tænia, *pl.* **tæniæ** [Lat. < Gk. ταινία] a tape-worm. 18c. [N]

(der) Tag [Ger.] 'the Day', i.e. the day of the outbreak of the First World War, looked forward to by enthusiastic German militarists as the beginning of German hegemony in Europe. 20c.

taiga [Russ.] *Geog*. a Siberian pine-forest. 19c. [N*]

taille d'épargne [Fr.] *Art* CHAMPLEVÉ enamel work, enamel work in which the metal ground is engraved or hollowed out, the hollows being filled with opaque enamel. 20c. Cf. CLOISONNÉ; EN TAILLE D'ÉPARGNE.

taille douce [Fr. 'soft cutting'] *Art* engraving on a metal plate, *esp.* copper-plate engraving; a work of art produced by this process. 17c. [N,S]

tailleur [Fr.] a woman's tailor-made costume. 20c. [N*]

talus [Fr.] (1) *Mil.* the sloping face of a wall or earthwork. 17c. (2) *Geog.* a sloping mound of fallen DÉBRIS at the foot of a cliff or precipice. Cf. GLACIS. [N,S]

tamasha [Hind. *tamāshā* < Arab.] *A.-I.* (1) an entertainment, a public function; *hence* (2) fuss and bother, a commotion. 19c. [N(*),S]

tambour [Fr. 'drum'] (1) an embroidery-frame consisting of one hoop fitting inside another; (2) *Tennis* the projection on the main wall of a tennis court near the GRILLE. 18c. [N]

tanist [Ir. *tánaiste*] the successor apparent to a Celtic chieftain. 16c. The title *Tánaiste* is now given to the deputy Prime Minister of the Republic of Ireland. [N,S]

tant bien que mal [Fr.] more or less well, moderately. 18c. [S]

tant mieux [Fr.] so much the better. 18c. [S]

tant pis [Fr.] so much the worse. 18c. *Usu.* with the implication 'it can't be helped'. [S]

tantra [Sansk. 'warp'] *Rel.* one of a class of Buddhist works of a magical or mystical nature. 18c. [N]

Tantum Ergo [Lat.] *Eccles.* the title of a hymn sung at Benediction; a musical setting of this hymn. 19c. The hymn consists of the last two stanzas of the hymn *Pange Lingua* by St Thomas Aquinas. The title is taken from the opening words: *Tantum ergo sacramentum Veneremur cernui* 'Bending low let us revere so great a sacrament'. [N*]

Taoiseach [Ir. 'chieftain'] the title given to the Prime Minister of the Republic of Ireland. 20c.

tapis [Fr. 'carpet'] in the phrase 'on the *tapis*', under discussion, the subject of conversation. 17c. Cf. SUR LE TAPIS. [N,S]

tapotement [Fr.] *Med.* percussion, striking with the edge of the hand (as part of the treatment in MASSAGE). 19c. [N]

tarantella [It.] a whirling dance popular in southern Italy since the fifteenth century; the music for such a dance. 18c. So called because the performance of the dance was believed to be a remedy for the bite of the TARANTULA spider. [N,S]

tarantula [Lat.] a kind of large spider found in Apulia and other Mediterranean regions, the bite of which is mildly poisonous. 16c. So called because it is commonly found near the city of Taranto. The spider's bite was believed to cause a hysterical malady characterized by involuntary dancing, which could be cured by dancing the TARANTELLA. [N,S]

tarboosh [Arab. *ṭarbūsh*] a Moslem cap of red felt with a tassel at the top, a fez. 18c. [N,S]

tarsia [It.] inlaid work in wood, bone, ivory and mother-of-pearl, INTARSIATURA. 17c. Cf. INTARSIO; LAVORO DI COMMESSO. [N,S]

tas-de-charge [Fr.] *Arch.* the lower courses of the ribs of a Gothic vaulted roof. 20c.

tausendjährig [Ger.] lasting a thousand years, millenary. 20c. A term derived from a development of the doctrine of the MILLENNIUM, in which a period of rule by the Holy Ghost is to follow the periods of rule by the Father and by the Son; applied by German National Socialist propagandists to the Third REICH.

tazza [It.] a shallow ornamental bowl supported on a foot. 19c. [N,S]

T.D.=TEACHTA DÁLA, a Member of the Irish Parliament.

Teachta Dála [Ir.] a Member of the Parliament of the Republic of Ireland. 20c. Usu. abbreviated to *T.D. Dála* is the genitive case of DÁIL.

Te Deum [Lat.] *Eccles.* an ancient Latin hymn of praise and thanksgiving, sung every day at Matins and on special occasions of victory or deliverance; a musical setting of this hymn. 14c. From the opening words of the hymn: *Te Deum laudamus* 'we praise Thee, God'. The hymn is doubtfully attributed to St Ambrose. [N,S]

Teil [Ger.] part (of a book, volume, etc.) 20c.

telæsthesia [Pseudo-Gk.] *Psych.* perception at a distance other than by means of the recognized channels of sense. 19c. The term was invented by F. W. H. Myers in 1882 to denote varieties of psychic perception not included in *telepathy*. [N]

telekinesis [Pseudo-Gk.] *Psych.* the movement of objects at a distance without contact with the motive agent. 19c. The term was invented by F. W. H. Myers in 1890. [N]

témoignage [Fr. 'testimony'] a factual account (of an important event, etc.) undistorted by prejudice. 20c.

tempera [It.] *Art* a method of painting in which the pigments are bound with yolk of egg. 19c. Formerly known as *distemper*, the connotations of which are now wholly concerned with interior decoration. [N,S]

tempo, *pl.* **tempi** [It.] (1) *Mus.* the relative speed of rhythmical movement, *esp.* the speed appropriate to some particular composition or type of composition. 18c. (2) *Bridge* the opportunity of leading a card as part of the strategy of playing a hand. 20c. Cf. A TEMPO. [N,S]

tempo giusto [It.] *Mus.* strict time. 20c. [N*]

temp(ore) [Lat.] in the time of . . ., always followed by a name, *usu.* that of a reigning monarch. 19c. Used to provide a rough dating when the exact date is uncertain.

tempo rubato [It. 'stolen time'] *Mus.* time slackened or hastened for the purposes of expression. 19c. Cf. RUBATO. [N]

temps levé [Fr.] *Ballet* a hop on one foot with the raised foot in any required position. 20c.

temps morts *pl.* [Fr.] dull moments, slack periods, LONGUEURS (in a work of literature or music). 20c.

temps perdu [Fr.] forgotten periods of the past. 20c. With reference to Marcel Proust's À LA RECHERCHE DU TEMPS PERDU.

tempus edax rerum [Lat.] time the devourer of all things. 16c. Ovid *Metamorphoses* XV 234. Cf. EDAX RERUM. [S]

tempus fugit [Lat.] time flies. 19c. Based on Virgil *Georgics* iii 284; *fugit irreparabile tempus* 'time flies, never to return'. [S]

tendre [Fr.] tender feeling, sentimental affection (towards someone). 17c. [N,S]

tendresse [Fr.] fondness, affection. 18c. [N,S]

tenebræ [Lat. 'darkness'] *Eccles.* the office of matins and lauds of the following day, formerly sung on the evenings of Wednesday, Thursday and Friday of Holy Week. 17c. Though the form of the Latin word is plural the meaning is singular, and it is construed as singular in English. [N]

tenet [Lat. 'he holds'] a doctrine, principle, or opinion held by a person, party, sect, etc. 16c. The plural *tenent* 'they hold' has been obsolete since 18c. [N,S]

tenue de ville [Fr.] town dress, city clothes. 20c.

tenuis, *pl.* **tenues** [Lat. 'thin'] *Ling.* one of the voiceless stops *p*, *t*, *k*. 17c. Cf. MEDIA; MEDIA ASPIRATA. [N,S]

tepidarium [Lat.] *Hist.* the warm room of a Roman bath. 16c. Cf. CALDARIUM; FRIGIDARIUM. [N,S]

tequila [Sp.] a fermented drink made in Mexico from the sap of the plant *Agave americana.* 19c. The name of a district in Mexico; the earlier name *pulque* (17c.), of uncertain origin, seems now to be obsolete. [N*]

terminer, *see* OYER.

terminus ad quem [Lat.] the point to which motion or action tends; *esp.* the end of a period of time in which some event, etc. must be dated. 16c. In the latter sense the form *terminus ante quem* is now sometimes used. [N,S]

terminus a quo [Lat.] the point from which motion or action starts; *esp.* the beginning of a period of time in which some event, etc. must be dated. 16c. In the latter sense the form *terminus post quem* is now sometimes used. [N,S]

terminus vitæ [Lat.] the end of life, death. 20c.

terra cotta [It. 'cooked earth'] a hard unglazed pottery of fine quality; a FIGURINE, etc., made of this substance; the characteristic brownish-red colour of this substance. 18c. [N,S]

terra firma [Lat.] the land as distinguished from the sea, dry land. 17c. [N,S]

terra incognita, *pl.* **terræ incognitæ** [Lat.] unknown territory, an unexplored region. 17c. [N,S]

terrazzo [It. 'terrace'] *Arch.* a surface made of chips of marble set in white or coloured cement. 20c. [N*]

terre à terre [Fr. 'earth to earth'] (1) *Ballet* (steps) in which the feet scarcely leave the ground, (dancing) without elevation of style; *hence* (2) down-to-earth, matter-of-fact, unimaginative. 18c. [N(*),S]

terre de pipe [Fr.] pipe-clay, a fine white clay; a kind of porcelain manufactured from this clay. 20c.

terre pisée [Fr.] clay mixed with gravel and rammed between shutterings so as to form a wall. 20c. Cf. PISÉ.

terre verte [Fr.] *Art* a natural green earth used as a pigment. 17c. [N]

terribilità [It.] *Art* qualities inspiring awe and dread in the mind. 20c. Also *occ.* in the form *terribiltà.*

tertium quid [Lat.] something related to two definite things but distinct from both of them; something which serves as a medium between two incompatible things. 18c. A translation of the Greek phrase *τρίτον τι*; the Latin form is found in Irenæus and Tertullian. [N,S]

terza rima [It. 'third rhyme'] *Ling.* a form of verse consisting of stanzas of three lines each, the first and third rhyming together and the second with the first and third of the following stanza. 19c. This is the form of verse used in Dante's *Divine Comedy.* [N,S]

tessera, *pl.* **tesseræ** [Lat. < Gk. *τέσσερα* 'four'] *Art* a small roughly cubical piece of marble or coloured stone for use in mosaic-work. 18c. *Τέσσερα* is Ionic Greek; the Attic form is *τέσσαρα.* [N,S]

tessitura [It. 'texture'] *Mus.* the part of the range of a vocal or instrumental part within which most of its notes lie. 19c. [N]

tête-à-tête [Fr. 'head to head'] a private conversation or interview between two persons; (two persons) in private together, without the presence of a third person. 17c. Cf. À DEUX; A QUATTR' OCCHI. [N,S]

tête-bêche [Fr.] (the printing of postage stamps) upside down or sideways in relation one to another; a set of stamps so printed. 19c. [N*]

tête folle [Fr.] a scatterbrain, an irresponsible person. 20c.

tetragrammaton, *pl.* **tetragrammata** [Gk. *τετραγράμματον* 'four-letter (word)'] the Hebrew word *YHWH* 'Jehovah', treated as a mysterious symbol of the name of God. 15c. [N,S]

texte intégral [Fr.] the complete text, a text not abridged or expurgated. 20c.

Textura [Ger.] a late mediæval form of handwriting closely resembling the 'Black Letter' of early printed books. 20c.

textus receptus [Lat.] the accepted text, the standard text (of an ancient work). 19c. *Orig.* applied to the second Elzevir edition of the Greek New Testament (1633), but now in general use. [N,S]

thalassa! thalassa! [Gk. θάλασσα] 'the sea! the sea!', an exclamation greeting the first glimpse of something long sought for. 20c. Xenophon *Anabasis* IV vii 24, describing the retreat of the Greeks from Asia to the Black Sea. Xenophon's own form of the word is the Attic θάλαττα; but the KOINE prefers the Ionic θάλασσα.

Thalweg [Obs. Ger.] *Geog.* the line joining the lowest points along a valley, the natural watercourse at the bottom of a valley. 19c. The current German spelling is *Talweg.* [N]

théâtre engagé [Fr.] (the composition of) dramatic works undertaken with a political or sociological purpose. 20c. Cf. ART ENGAGÉ; ENGAGÉ.

thé dansant [Fr.] an afternoon entertainment at which there is dancing and tea is served. 19c. [N*]

thé musical, *pl.* **thés musicaux** [Fr.] a musical tea-party, a social gathering at which music is performed and tea is served. 20c. Cf. MATINÉE MUSICALE; MUSICALE; SOIRÉE MUSICALE.

thesaurus, *pl.* **thesauri** [Lat. < Gk. θεσαυρός] a storehouse of knowledge, a dictionary, an encyclopædia. 19c. [N,S]

thesis, *pl.* **theses** [Gk. θέσις 'putting'] (1) *Ling,* an unstressed syllable in metre; (2) *Mus.* an unaccented note; (3) a proposition maintained in the course of an argument; (4) a dissertation written by a candidate for a University degree. 14c. In the first two senses always in contrast to ARSIS; but since by some writers the meanings of *arsis* and *thesis* are interchanged, both terms are better avoided. [N,S]

thyrsus, *pl.* **thyrsi** [Lat. < Gk. θύρσος] *Myth.* an emblematic staff tipped with a pine-cone and wreathed with ivy or vine-leaves, carried by Dionysus and his votaries. 16c. [N,S]

tiara [Lat. < Gk. τιάρα] (1) the triple crown worn by the Pope; (2) a richly jewelled coronet or frontal worn by ladies on formal occasions. 17c. [N,S]

tic (douloureux) [Fr.] *Med.* a severe form of neuralgia characterized by twitching of the facial muscles. 19c. [N,S]

tiers état [Fr.] the 'third estate', the commons in the French National Assembly before the Revolution. 18c. The first two 'estates' were the nobility and the clergy. [N,S]

tilde [Sp.] *Ling.* the diacritic mark ˜ used in Spanish to distinguish the palatalized from the normal *n* as in MAÑANA. 19c. The earlier Spanish usage was *nn*, preserved in English DUENNA: the *tilde* represents the second *n* written on top of the first. [N,S]

timbre [Fr.] the distinctive character or quality of a sound, *esp.* a musical or vocal sound; the quality of a sound which distinguishes it from other sounds of the same pitch and intensity. 19c. The *timbre* of a sound depends on the relative intensities of the overtones accompanying the fundamental. [N,S]

timeo Danaos et dona ferentes [Lat.] 'I fear the Greeks even when they bring gifts', i.e. apparent generosity on the part of the enemy is to be mistrusted. 17c. Virgil *Æneid* ii 49. [S]

timpani *pl.* [It.] *Mus.* kettle-drums. 20c. Cf. TYMPANUM.

tinnitus (aurium) [Lat.] *Med.* a persistent ringing in the ears. 19c. [N]

tirailleur [Fr.] *Mil.* a skirmisher, a sharpshooter, a soldier trained to take independent action. 18c. [N,S]

tisane [Fr. < Gk. πτισάνε 'barley'] barley-water; *hence,* any herbal decoction with mildly medicinal qualities. 19c. Early anglicized (from 14c.) in a variety of spellings, but re-adopted and felt to be a foreign word. Cf. INFUSION. [N,S]

tissu-éponge [Fr.] face-cloth, Terry towelling. 20c.

tmesis [Gk. τμῆσισ] *Ling.* the separation of the elements of a compound word by the insertion of another word or phrase. 16c. [N,S]

toccata [It.] *Mus.* a composition for a keyboard instrument designed to display the technique of the executant, and often having the character of an improvisation. 18c. [N,S]

toga [Lat.] *Hist.* the normal outer garment of a citizen of ancient Rome. 17c. In many Continental countries an academic gown is known as a *toga.* [N,S]

toga virilis [Lat.] *Hist.* the 'manly garment' adopted by an ancient Roman youth at puberty; *hence,* (any symbol of) intellectual maturity. 17c. [N,S]

tohu-bohu [Fr. < Heb. *thōhū wa-bōhū* 'emptiness and desolation'] chaos, utter confusion. 19c. In much earlier use (17c.) in the forms *Tohu vabohu* or '*Tohu* and *Bohu*'. The phrase is from *Genesis* i 2, and the standard rendering is 'without form and void'. [N,S]

toile [Fr.] a fabric used in dressmaking, *usu.* of linen, *esp.* a mixture of linen and silk. 19c. [N(*]]

toilette [Fr.] manner and style of dressing; the action or process of dressing. 18c. Also in anglicized form *toilet* in these and a number of other senses. [N,S]

tokonoma [Jap.] a shaded alcove in a Japanese house, used *esp.* for the display of arrangements of flowers.

tondo, *pl.* **tondi** [It.] *Art* a circular painting; a relief carving within a circular border. 19c. [N]

tonga [Hind *tāngā*] *A.-I.* a light two-wheeled Indian carriage. 19c. Cf. GHARRY. [N,S]

tonneau [Fr.] the rear part of a motor-car, the back seat of a motor-car. 20c.

topee [Hind. *ṭopī* 'hat'] a sun-helmet, an insulated hat designed to protect the wearer against sunstroke. 19c. The phrase *solā ṭopī* 'pith helmet' is often misunderstood as 'solar *topee*', as if referring to the rays of the sun. [N,S]

topos [Gk. τόπος 'place'] *Ling*. a figure of speech which has become stereotyped, a rhetorical CLICHÉ. 20c.

toque [Fr.] a woman's headdress resembling a low turban of twisted silk or other rich material. 19c. [N,S]

toqué. *f*. **toquée** [Fr.] 'cracked', dotty, irresponsible. 20c.

torchère [Fr.] a tall ornamental candlestick or lamp-stand. 20c. [N]

torchon [Fr. 'dish-cloth'] a coarse bobbin-lace of loose texture; a kind of rough paper used for water-colour painting. 19c. [N]

toreador [Sp.] a bull-fighter. 17c. *Orig*. applied to a bullfighter on horseback. The word is not now used in Spanish, having been replaced by TORERO. [N,S]

torero [Sp.] a bullfighter. 18c. *Orig*. applied to a bullfighter on foot, it is now used in Spanish to describe a bullfighter in general, and has displaced the earlier TOREADOR. [N]

torque [Fr.] *Hist*. a collar or bracelet made of a twisted strip of precious metal, *esp*. as worn by the Celtic peoples. 19c. The English word is perhaps not from the French, but an erroneous singular based on the Latin plural *torques* in the same sense. The scientific term *torque* 'rotatory force' is of different origin. [N]

torso, *pl*. **torsi** [It.] the trunk of the human body from neck to hip; the trunk of a nude statue; *hence*, (a work of literature, etc.) of which the main part but not the whole is extant. 18c. [N,S]

torticollis [Lat.] *Med*. a rheumatic affection of the muscles of the neck resulting in the permanent twisting of the head to one side. 19c. [N]

tortilla [Sp.] a thin round cake made of maize-flour. 17c. A staple article of diet in Mexico. [N,S]

tortillon [Fr.] *Art* a stump of paper rolled into the form of a pointed cylinder, used for shading chalk and pencil drawings. 19c. [N*]

totem [Algonquin *-t ote-m*] the hereditary emblem of a tribe or clan of American Indians or of other savage peoples. 18c. The *totem* is often an animal, and may be worshipped as the incarnation of a tutelary deity. [N,S]

Totentanz [Ger.] the Dance of Death, an allegorical representation of Death leading all conditions of men to the grave. 20c. Cf. DANSE MACABRE.

toties quoties [Lat.] as often as occasion demands, repeatedly. 16c. [N,S]

toto cælo [Lat. 'by the whole heaven'] by as much as the distance between the celestial poles, diametrically (opposed). 18c. [N,S]

Totschläger [Ger. 'dead-striker'] a heavy bludgeon. 20c.

touché [Fr.] well hit! you penetrated my defences there!; used to admit that a thrust in argument has gone home. 20c.

touche-à-tout [Fr.] a meddler, a busybody. 20c,

toujours de l'audace [Fr.] 'boldness all the time', audacity always pays. 20c. Danton to the Committee of Defence, 2nd September 1792: *De l'audace, et encore de l'audace, et toujours de l'audace!*

toujours la politesse [Fr.] politeness always pays. 20c.

toujours perdrix [Fr.] 'partridge all the time', too much of a good thing. 19c. [S]

toupet [Fr.] a patch of false hair to cover a bald place on the scalp. 18c. Also in the anglicized forms *toupée, toupee.* [N,S]

tour [Fr.] *Ballet* a full turn of the body on the point of the toe with the toe of the free leg at the knee of the other, a PIROUETTE. 20c. Cf. TOUR SUR PLACE.

tourbillon [Fr.] a whirlwind, a waterspout; a whirlpool, a VORTEX; an unceasing round (of gaiety, etc.) 18c. Also formerly in the anglicized form *tourbillion.* [N,S]

tour de chant [Fr.] an entertainment given by a singer, a performance of characteristic songs. 20c.

tour de force [Fr. 'feat of strength'] an instance of remarkable technical skill. 19c. Often with the implication that the display concerned has no other merit—'a mere *tour de force*'. [N,S]

tour d'horizon [Fr.] a general survey. 20c. Also erroneously in the form *tour de l'horizon.*

tour en l'air [Fr.] *Ballet* a leap in which the dancer rotates his body once or more before coming down. 20c.

tournedos [Fr.] *Cul.* fillet steak. 20c.

tourniquet [Fr.] *Med.* any device for stopping the flow of blood, *esp.* a bandage tightened by turning a stick passed through it. 17c. [N,S]

tournure [Fr.] manner or bearing, *esp.* a manner suited to polite society. 18c. [N,S]

tour sur place [Fr.] *Ballet* a full turn of the body on the point of the toe with the toe of the free leg at the knee of the other, a TOUR, a PIROUETTE. 20c.

tout comprendre, c'est tout pardonner [Fr.] to understand everything is to forgive everything. 20c. Based on Mme de Staël *Corinne* XVIII v: *tout comprendre rend très-indulgent* 'understanding everything makes you very forgiving'.

tout court [Fr.] without anything else added (to the word or phrase cited). 18c. *Usu.* with the implication that some additional phrase is required for accuracy or courtesy. [S]

tout de suite [Fr.] all at once, immediately. 18c. The original sense, still current in 18c. English, was 'consecutively'. [S]

tout ensemble [Fr.] the general effect (of a work of art, etc.), the whole of something considered without attention to details. 18c. Cf. ENSEMBLE. [N,S]

tout le bazar [Fr.] the whole lot. 20c.

tracasserie [Fr.] fuss and bother, a state of disturbance, a series of petty disagreements. 17c. [N,S]

trachea, *pl.* **tracheæ** [Lat. < Gk. (*ἀρτηρία*) *τραχεῖα* 'rough (artery)'] *Med.* the tube extending from the larynx to the BRONCHI, the windpipe. 16c. [N,S]

trachoma [Lat. < Gk. *τράχωμα*] *Med.* an infectious disease of the eyes characterized by roughness of the inner surface of the eyelids. 17c. [N]

tractatus, *pl.* **tractatus** [Lat.] a treatise. 20c.

traduttore traditore [It.] 'a translator is a traitor', it is impossible to translate without misrepresenting the original. 20c.

tragédienne [Fr.] an actress specializing in tragedy. 19c. Cf. COMÉDIENNE. [N,S]

Tragsitz [Ger.] a device for lowering injured persons in safety from mountain precipices. 20c.

(la) trahison des clercs [Fr.] the treason of the intellectuals, the entry of intellectuals (who should be guided by abstract principles) into the arena of nationalism and politics. 20c. The title of a work by Julien Benda (1927).

train de luxe, *pl.* **trains de luxe** [Fr.] a luxury train, a train in which no expense is spared in securing the comfort of the passengers. 20c. Cf. DE LUXE.

trait [Fr.] a distinguishing characteristic, *esp.* of the personality or cast of mind of a person. 18c. The accepted pronunciation is approximately French, though the final *s* in the plural *traits* is pronounced as *z*; but an anglicized pronunciation is becoming increasingly common. [N,S]

trait d'union [Fr. 'hyphen'] a bond or link which joins two disparate things. 20c.

tramontana [It.] a cold north wind blowing from a mountain-range, *esp.* from the Alps. 17c. Cf. BISE; MAESTRALE; MISTRAL. [N,S]

tranche [Fr.] the cut edge of a book (which may be gilded or painted), *esp.* the fore-edge. 20c.

tranche de vie [Fr.] a 'slice of life', an unadorned representation in a work of art or literature of scenes and events from real life. 20c.

transire [Lat.] a warrant issued by a custom-house permitting the passage of merchandise. 16c. [N]

trattoria, *pl.* **trattorie** [It.] an eating-house (in Italy). 19c. [N*,S]

trauma, *pl.* **traumata** [Gk. *τραῦμα* 'wound'] *Psych.* an unpleasant experience which induces hysteria or a morbid psychotic condition. 19c. [N(*)]

trecento [It. '300'] the thirteen hundreds, the fourteenth century, *esp.* the art and architecture of that century; characteristic of that century. 19c. Cf. CINQUECENTO; QUATTROCENTO; SEICENTO; SETTECENTO. [N,S]

tre corde [It. 'three strings'] *Mus.* (played on the piano) without the use of the 'soft' pedal, which shifts the hammers so as to strike only two strings or one. 20c. Contrasted with UNA CORDA.

trek [Afrik.] (one stage of) a journey by ox-wagon; to make a journey by ox-wagon; (to make) any kind of arduous journey across country. 19c. [N,S]

trembleuse [Fr.] (a cup) with a saucer provided with a socket into which the cup fits so that it will not be dislodged by a trembling hand. 19c. [N]

trente-et-quarante [Fr.] a gambling game played with cards, in which 30 is a winning and 40 a losing number. 17c. Cf. ROUGE-ET-NOIR. [N,S]

triclinium, *pl.* **triclinia** [Lat. < Gk. *τρικλίνιον*] *Hist.* a couch (used by the Romans for reclining on during meals) running round three sides of a dining-table; a dining-room equipped with such a couch. 17c. [N,S]

tricorne [Fr.] (a cocked hat) with the brim turned up on three sides. 19c. [N]

tricot [Fr.] a knitted fabric, *usu.* either a woollen fabric knitted by hand or a fabric machine-knitted from fine wool, cotton, silk or artificial fibre. 19c. [N]

tricoteuse [Fr.] one of the Frenchwomen who during the Revolution occupied themselves with knitting while watching the executions of the aristocrats; *hence,* any woman who watches scenes of violence unperturbed. 19c. [S]

tric-trac [Fr.] a form of backgammon popular in France. 17c. [N,S]

triennale [It.] (a fair, exhibition, etc.) held every three years. 20c. Cf. BIENNALE.

triforium, *pl.* **triforia** [Lat.] *Arch.* a gallery over the arches along the sides of the nave and choir of a Gothic church. 18c. The origin of the word is wholly obscure; it was first used by Gervase of Canterbury about 1185, and until 1800 it was applied only to Canterbury Cathedral. [N,S]

Trinkgeld [Ger. 'drink-money'] a tip, a gratuity, a DOUCEUR. 20c. Cf. POURBOIRE.

trio [It.] (1) *Mus.* a piece for three voices or instruments; (2) *Mus.* the middle section of a minuet or other dance movement (*orig.* always written in three parts); (3) a group or set of three persons or things. 18c. Cf. DUO. [N,S]

tripos [Lat. *tripus* 'tripod' < Gk. *τρίπους*] the final honours examination for the B.A. degree in the University of Cambridge. 19c. The name *tripos,* irregularly varied from the Latin on the basis of Greek nouns in *-os,* was *orig.* given to a bachelor of arts appointed to dispute with candidates for degrees, because he sat on a three-legged stool; it was then transferred to a set of humorous verses composed by this bachelor of arts; then to the list of successful candidates *orig.* printed on the back of the paper containing the verses; and finally to the examination itself. It was first used only of the examination in mathematics, and later extended to examinations in other subjects. [N]

triptyque [Fr. 'triptych'] a document issued by motoring associations to facilitate the movement of motor-cars across international frontiers. 20c. So called because it was *orig*. issued only in triplicate. [N]

triste [Fr.] sad, low-spirited, melancholy; dismal, depressing, dreary. 18c. [N,S]

tristesse [Fr.] melancholy, low spirits, depression. 18c. [N,S]

trivium [Lat.] (1) *Hist*. the three-fold lower division of the seven liberal arts in the Middle Ages, comprising grammar, rhetoric, and logic. 19c. (2) *pl*. **trivia,** trivialities, *esp*. the less serious works of a writer. 20c. The proper meaning of Lat. *trivium* is 'a place where three roads meet'; hence the meaning 'commonplace'. Cf. QUADRIVIUM. [N,S]

troika [Russ.] a carriage drawn by three horses abreast; *hence*, (an organization) jointly controlled by three different authorities. 19c. [N,S]

trois coups [Fr.] the three knocks which signal the start of a performance at the Comédie Française. 20c.

trois-temps [Fr. 'three-time'] the ordinary waltz as distinguished from the more rapid DEUX-TEMPS. 19c. [N]

trompe-l'œil [Fr.] *Art* so realistic as to deceive the eye, *esp*. (a perspective painting) which produces a vivid illusion of three-dimensional space. 20c. *Trompe-l'œil* perspective painting may be used in interior decoration to increase the apparent size of a room; cf. QUADRATURA.

tronc [Fr.] a 'pool' of money into which waiters in a hotel or restaurant place their tips and from which they receive payment in proportion to their seniority and exertion. 20c.

trotteur/trotteuse [Fr.] a short walking skirt; a walking shoe. 20c. The masculine and feminine forms are used indiscriminately. [N]

troubadour [Fr. < Prov. *trobador*] one of a group of Provençal lyric poets who flourished from the 11th to the 13th century. 18c. The *troubadours* produced mainly amatory lyrics. Cf. MINNESÄNGER; TROUVÈRE. [N,S]

troupe [Fr.] a company, *esp*. a company of actors or dancers. 19c. [N(*),S]

trousseau, *pl*. **trousseaux** [Fr.] a bride's outfit of clothes and household linen. 19c. [N,S]

trouvaille [Fr.] a lucky find, a windfall, something exceptionally good discovered by accident. 19c. [N,S]

trouvère [Fr.] one of a group of French epic poets who flourished from the 11th to the 14th century. 18c. The word is etymologically the equivalent of TROUBADOUR, but the connotation is different. [N,S]

trucage/truquage [Fr.] *Art* the faking of a work of art. 20c.

trumeau, *pl*. **trumeaux** [Fr.] *Arch*. a wall-space between windows; a pier-glass. 20c.

truquage=TRUCAGE, faking.

truqueur [Fr.] *Art* a faker of works of art. 20c.

tsar; tsarevitch; tsarina; tsaritsa, *see* CZAR; CZAREVITCH; CZARINA; CZARITZA.

tsuba [Jap.] the guard on the hilt of a (Japanese) sword. 20c. Cf. FUCHI-GASHIRA.

tuan [Mal.] 'master', a title of respect used by Malayans when addressing Europeans. 19c. [N*]

tufa [It.] any porous stone, *esp.* a stone formed by the consolidation of volcanic ash. 18c. [N,S]

tumulus, *pl.* **tumuli** [Lat.] a barrow, an ancient burial mound. 17c. [N,S]

tundra [Lapp] *Geog.* one of the arctic, level, treeless plains which make up the greater part of northern Russia. 19c. Cf. STEPPE. [N,S]

tu quoque [Lat. 'you too'] (a retort) implying that a charge made against the speaker can equally well be made against the accuser. 17c. [N,S]

turba [Lat. 'crowd'] *Mus.* a chorus representing the cries of the people in a setting of the Passion. 20c.

turquerie [Fr.] *Art* a picture with a pseudo-Turkish subject, of a kind popular in the 18th century. 20c.

tutti [It.] *Mus.* (a passage to be rendered) by all the performers together. 18c. [N,S]

tutti frutti [It.] *Cul.* (a confection) made with a number of different kinds of fruit or flavoured with a variety of fruit flavourings; *hence,* a conglomeration of different ideas or objects. 20c. [N*]

tutu [Fr.] *Ballet* the short classical ballet skirt; a longer skirt reaching halfway between knee and ankle, worn in certain ballets. 20c. The French word is the nursery corruption of *cul* 'bottom', and was *orig.* applied to the knickers which form the basis of the *tutu.*

tuyère [Fr.] the nozzle through which the blast is forced into a furnace; a nozzle which performs a similar function in a jet-engine. 18c. [N]

tycoon [Jap. *taikun* < Chin. *ta kiun* 'great prince'] the title by which the *shogun* of Japan was described to foreigners; hence, any person who has acquired great power, *esp.* in some branch of industry or commerce. 19c. [N,S]

tympanum, *pl.* **tympana** [Lat. < Gk. *τύμπανον*] (1) *Med.* the ear-drum; (2) *Arch.* the space between the cornices of a pediment; the space between the top of a square doorway and the head of a surrounding arch. 17c. [N,S]

typhoon [Chin. *tai fung=ta fêng* 'great wind'] a hurricane, a violent cyclonic storm frequent in the China seas between July and October. 18c. Three distinct words have coalesced: (1) dialectal (Cantonese) Chinese *tai fung;* (2) Arab. *tūfān* 'tornado'; (3) Gk. *Τυφῶν*, the name of the mythical monster who was father of the Winds. Before the current form was established in English earlier spellings (from 16c.) reflect the Arabic form rather than the Chinese or Greek. [N,S]

U

Übermensch [Ger.] a superman, a man who is superior to ordinary mortality and has no pity on those feebler than himself. 20c. The word and the idea are the invention of F. W. Nietzsche (1844–1900). Cf. BLONDE BESTIE.

uberrimæ fidei [Lat.] *Law* requiring the fullest confidence and good faith. 19c. Used of contracts in which one party is bound to communicate all relevant facts and circumstances to the other party.

uberrima fides [Lat.] *Law* full confidence and good faith (required for the validity of certain contracts). 19c.

ubi jus, ibi remedium [Lat.] *Law* where there is a right there is a (legal) remedy. 19c.

ubi sunt (qui ante nos fuerunt)? [Lat.] where are those who lived before us? 13c. The classic comment on the transitoriness of human life.

udarnik [Russ.] a 'shock'-worker, a member of a special labour-force dispatched to perform or help perform an urgent task. 20c.

Uhlan [Ger. < Turk. *oğlan* 'boy, servant'] a lancer, *esp.* a lancer in a quasi-Oriental uniform. 18c. Quasi-Oriental uniforms were popular *orig.* in Slavonic countries, latterly in the German empire. [N,S]

uhuru [Swahili] freedom. 20c.

uitlander [Du.] an alien settler in the South African Republic, *esp.* in the Transvaal. 19c. Cf. AUSLÄNDER. [N]

ukase [Russ. *ukaz*] a decree or edict issued by the Russian government; *hence*, any arbitrary or peremptory proclamation or decree. 18c. [N,S]

ukelele [Haw. *ukulele*] a four-stringed Hawaiian guitar. 20c. Numerous different spellings have been in use, but *ukelele* seems now to be the accepted form. [N*]

ultima ratio [Lat.] the final argument; *hence*, the use of force in preference to argument. 18c. The phrase *ultima ratio regum* 'the final argument of kings' was inscribed on cannon cast for Louis XIV after 1650; the variant *ultima ratio regis* appears on cannon cast for Frederick the Great after 1742. [S]

ultima Thule [Lat.] 'farthest Thule', the uttermost point accessible to exploration or discovery. 17c. Virgil *Georgics* i 30. Thule was supposed to be an island north of Britain beyond which there was no other land. [S]

ultimatum, *pl.* **ultimata** [Lat.] a final statement of terms, the rejection of which will lead to the severing of diplomatic relations and a state of hostility. 18c. [N,S]

ult(imo) [Lat.] of last month. 17c. Cf. PROX(IMO). [N,S]

ultra [Lat.] extreme; extremely, extravagantly. 19c. Also in very common use as the first element of a compound adjective. [S]

ultra vires [Lat.] beyond the legal power or authority (of a person, institution, etc.); opposed to INTRA VIRES. 18c. [N,S]

umiak [Esk. *umiaq*] a large Eskimo boat made of skins stretched over a wooden frame. 18c. *Occ.* written *oomiak*. The *umiak*, formerly a whaling-boat, is now used mainly by women for transporting their families, etc. Cf. CURRAGH; KAYAK. [N,S]

Umlaut [Ger.] *Ling.* mutation, a change in the quality of a vowel induced by the influence of a vowel or semivowel in the following syllable. 19c. Sometimes known as *metaphony*, as ABLAUT is known as *apophony*. The vowels of such pairs of English words as *man*, *men* are related by *Umlaut;* in this case the vowel inducing the change has disappeared. The word *Umlaut* is sometimes also used to denote the diacritic sign ¨ (properly called DIÆRESIS) because this sign is used in German to distinguish mutated vowels, as in *Mann*, *Männer*. [N,S]

Umschwung [Ger.] a sudden change (of opinion), a re-orientation. 20c. The connotation of 'reversal' implicit in VOLTE-FACE is absent from *Umschwung*.

una corda [It. 'one string'] *Mus.* (a passage played on the piano) with the use of the 'soft' pedal. 20c. In early pianos the pedal shifted the hammers so that they struck only one of the three strings allocated to each of the treble notes; in modern pianos the hammers never strike less than two of the three strings. Cf. TRE CORDE.

unappetitlich [Ger.] unappetizing, mildly repulsive. 20c.

unité d'habitation [Fr.] a 'dwelling unit', a building incorporating flats, shops, and all necessary services under a single roof. 20c. The term and the idea were originated by the French architect Le Corbusier. Cf. VILLE RADIEUSE.

unser . . . [Ger.] our . . .; always followed by a name. 20c. Used ironically of a claim to proprietary rights in a great man where no grounds for such a claim exist, e.g. the German use of *unser Shakespeare*.

(der) Untergang des Abendlandes [Ger.] the Decline of the West, the decay and proximal collapse of contemporary western civilization. 20c. The title of a work by Oswald Swengler (1880–1936).

uomo universale [It.] the universal man, the man who can claim competence in all the arts and sciences. 20c.

Upanishad [Sansk. *upa-nishád*] *Rel.* one of the treatises concerned with God and creation which form one of the divisions of Vedic literature. 19c. [N]

uræus [Lat. < Gk. *οὐραῖος*] *Hist.* a representation of the sacred asp worn on the head-dress of an ancient Egyptian monarch or deity as a symbol of supreme power. 19c. [N(*),S]

Uraufführung [Ger.] the first night (of a play), the PREMIÈRE (of a film). 20c.

urbanisme [Fr.] town-planning, the proper organization of urban life. 20c.

urbi et orbi [Lat.] 'to the city and to the world', (a formal proclamation) made by the Pope for general acceptance. 19c. [S]

Urfassung [Ger.] the original recension (of a text, etc.) 20c.

Urteilsbegründung [Ger.] a (judicial) summing-up. 20c.

Urtext [Ger.] the original text (of a work of literature, etc.) 20c.

usus [Lat.] *Law* the act of making use of something; the right to make use of something. 20c.

ut infra [Lat. 'as below'] see further below. 19c. Used to refer to a later passage in a book. Cf. INFRA. [S]

ut supra [Lat. 'as above'] see further above. 19c. Used to refer back to an earlier passage in a book. Cf. SUPRA. [S]

V

v.=VERSUS, against; VIDE, see.

vade mecum [Lat. 'go with me'] a handbook, a manual suitable for carrying about for ready reference. 17c. Cf. ENCHEIRIDION. [N,S]

vade retro [Lat.] get thee behind me! 19c. Used in rejecting a tempting offer. Vulgate *St Mark* viii 33: *vade retro me, Satana!* 'get thee behind me, Satan!' Cf. RETRO ME, SATANA. [S]

va-et-vient [Fr.] coming and going, fuss, commotion. 20c.

væ victis! [Lat.] woe to the conquered! 17c. Livy *Annals* V xlviii 9. [S]

vagantes *pl.* [Lat.] wandering ecclesiastics, mediæval clerics who wandered from place to place. 20c. A general term including both CLERICI VAGANTES and GYROVAGI.

valet [Fr.] a gentleman's personal attendant, a body-servant. 16c. Etymologically identical with *varlet.* [N,S]

valet de chambre [Fr.] a groom of the bed-chamber. 17c. Sometimes identical in meaning with *valet,* but often with reference to a position of honour in a royal or noble household. [N,S]

valete [Lat.] farewell! 20c. Common in school magazines, etc., as a heading to a list of departing members. Cf. AVETE; SALVETE.

vali [Turk. < Arab. *vali*] the civil governor of a Turkish province or VILAYET. 18c. [N]

valise [Fr.] a suitcase, a leather travelling-case; now *esp.* a soft travelling-case without a rigid framework. 17c. [N,S]

vallum [Lat.] *Hist.* a wall or rampart, *esp.* of earth or sods, erected by the Romans as part of a defensive fortification. 17c. [N,S]

vanitas vanitatum [Lat.] 'vanity of vanities', an exclamation at the transitorines of human happiness and worldly possessions. 16c. Vulgate *Ecclesiastes* i 2: *vanitas vanitatum, et omnia vanitas* 'vanity of vanities, and all is vanity'. [S]

vaporetto, *pl.* **vaporetti** [It.] a small passenger-steamer, *esp.* one plying in the Venetian lagoon. 20c.

vareuse [Fr.] a reefer-jacket; a loose sailor's jersey. 20c.

varia lectio, *pl.* **variæ lectiones** [Lat.] a variant reading (in the text of an ancient work, etc.) 17c. Abbreviated to *v.l.* with plural *vv.ll.* [S]

variatim [Lat.] in various ways. 20c.

variation [Fr.] *Ballet* a solo dance. 20c.

variorum [Lat.] (an edition of a text) in which are recorded the notes of previous commentators or the conjectures of previous editors. 18c. Cf. CUM NOTIS VARIORUM. [N,S]

vasculum [Lat.] an air-tight case used by botanists for carrying newly-collected specimens. 19c. [N,S]

vase de nuit [Fr.] a chamber-pot. 20c.

vaudeville [Fr.] a light dramatic entertainment consisting of songs, dances, and sketches. 19c. *Orig.* in the sense 'light popular song', and contracted from the phrase *chanson du Vau de Vire*, a name given to the songs composed by Olivier Basselin, who lived in the valley of Vire, in the fifteenth century. [N(*),S]

vécu [Fr. 'lived'] (a work of fiction) giving the impression that the writer has really experienced the events or emotions described. 20c.

vedette [Fr.] (1) a small passenger boat; (2) a 'star', a leading actor or actress on stage or screen. 20c. Earlier senses in English, now obsolete, were 'patrol boat' and 'mounted sentry'. Cf. GRANDE VEDETTE.

veduta, *pl.* **vedute** [It. 'view'] *Art* a painting of an identifiable place or scene. 20c.

veduta ideata, *pl.* **vedute ideate** [It.] *Art* a painting of an imaginary but realistic scene. 20c.

vedutista, *pl.* **vedutisti** [It.] *Art* a painter who specializes in depicting real places or scenes. 20c. The outstanding example of a *vedutista* is Canaletto.

V-Effekt=VERFREMDUNGSEFFEKT, an effect of strangeness and unfamiliarity.

veillée des armes [Fr.] *Hist.* the vigil spent by an aspirant knight alone in a chapel the night before he is to receive the accolade; *hence*, an ordeal preliminary to the bestowal of some privilege. 20c.

veilleuse [Fr.] a night-light; a sanctuary lamp; a chafing-dish heated by a small spirit-lamp. 19c. [N]

veldt [Obs. Du.] unenclosed country or open pastureland in South Africa. 19c. The current Dutch spelling *veld* is also in use, but *veldt* is the established English form. [N(*),S]

velours [Fr.] a fabric resembling velvet or plush used for dressmaking and for furnishings. 19c. [N]

velouté [Fr. 'velvety'] *Cul.* (1) smooth, creamy (in consistency); (2) a sauce made of white ROUX and veal or chicken stock. 20c.

vendetta [It.] a hereditary blood-feud, *esp.* in Corsica and southern Italy. 19c. [N,S]

vendeuse [Fr.] a shop-girl, a saleswoman. 20c.

veni, vidi, vici [Lat.] I came, I saw, I conquered. 16c. Julius Cæsar's laconic announcement of his defeat of Pharnaces at Zela in 47 B.C., the action which concluded his Pontic campaign: Suetonius *Divus Julius* xxxvii. Quoted by Seneca the Elder, *Suasoriæ* ii 22; perhaps a rendering of a Greek proverb preserved by the fifteenth-century rhetorician Apostolius. [S]

ventre à terre [Fr. 'belly to the ground'] at full gallop, at full speed. 19c. [S]

venue [Fr.] (1) *Law* the locality where a trial is to be held; (2) the scene of any real or imaginary event; (3) an appointed place of meeting, *esp.* for a match or athletic contest. 16c. [N]

vera causa [Lat.] the true cause which actually produces the effect in question. 19c. [N,S]

vera copula [Lat.] *Law* true sexual intercourse, e.g. that required for the legal consummation of a marriage. 20c.

veræ causæ [Lat.] *Law* relevant to the case at issue. 20c.

vera effigies [Lat.] the true likeness (of a person), an accurate portrait. 20c.

vera incessu patuit dea [Lat.] the goddess in person was revealed by her step. 20c. Virgil *Æneid* i 405.

verandah [Port. *varanda*] an open gallery with a roof supported by pillars, offering protection from sun and rain along the front and sometimes the sides of a house. 18c. The word is found in a number of Indian languages, but was adopted by these from Portuguese. Cf. STOEP. [N,S]

verbatim [Lat.] word for word, (a report, etc.) in the exact words as *orig.* spoken. 15c. Cf. MOT À MOT. [N,S]

verbum sap(ienti sat est) [Lat.] a word is enough for a wise man. 17c. Used to indicate that the foregoing remark is to be interpreted as a strong hint. Also abbreviated to *verb(um) sat.* The phrase is an adaptation of a Latin proverb *dictum sapienti sat est* quoted by both Plautus and Terence. [N,S]

verde antico [It. 'ancient green'] a greenish variety of ornamental marble, consisting mainly of serpentine. 18c. Cf. GIALLO ANTICO; ROSSO ANTICO. [N,S]

verdure [Fr.] *Art* a work of art, *esp.* a piece of tapestry, portraying mainly trees and foliage. 20c.

Verfremdungseffekt [Ger.] (a device designed to produce) an effect of strangeness and unfamiliarity in a theatrical production. 20c. The term was coined in 1935 by Bert Brecht to describe devices used by him for some years previously. Often abbreviated to *V-Effekt.*

verglas [Fr.] a thin coating of ice, *esp.* over rocks; a glass frost. 20c.

verismo [It.] realism, objectivity, *esp.* in expressionist painting. 20c.

vérité [Fr.] realism in film or television work, documentary technique. 20c. Also used in the plural *vérités*. Cf. CINÉMA-VÉRITÉ.

vermicelli *pl.* [It. 'little worms'] *Cul.* a dried wheaten paste in the form of long threads, the smallest variety of PASTA. 17c. In English often construed as a collective singular. Cf. CANNELLONI; MACARONI; SPAGHETTI. [N,S]

Vernichtungslager [Ger.] an extermination camp. 20c.

vernissage [Fr.] *Art* the application of a temporary coat of varnish to a painting; *hence*, varnishing-day at the Paris SALON; *hence*, the 'private view' at any exhibition of works of art. 20c.

verres églomisés *pl.* [Fr.] objects made of glass decorated by gilding the internal surface in patterns. 20c. Properly the process consists of affixing a pattern cut out of gold leaf and securing it by fusing over it a thin layer of powdered glass. From *Glomi*, the name of an eighteenth-century French picture-framer.

vers de société *pl.* [Fr.] light verse on topics of interest to polite society. 19c. [S]

vers libre [Fr.] 'free verse', verse consisting of unrhymed lines of irregular length arranged according to no regular pattern. 20c. Also used in the plural *vers libres*. Cf. PROSE RYTHMÉE. [N*]

verso [Lat.] the left-hand page of an open book, the back of a leaf (as opposed to RECTO, the front of a leaf). 19c. For *verso folio* 'on a turned leaf', as opposed to a 'straight leaf'. [N,S]

verst [Russ. *versta*] a Russian mile, equivalent to about two thirds of a standard mile. 16c. [N,S]

versus [Lat.] against, *esp.* of the two parties in an action at law, or of the two teams in a sporting event. 15c. Commonly abbreviated to *v*. [N,S]

vertigo [Lat.] giddiness, dizziness, a morbid condition producing a feeling of lack of EQUILIBRIUM; *esp.* the giddiness induced in some people by heights. 16c. [N, S]

verve [Fr.] energy, vigour, enthusiasm, *esp.* intellectual vigour displayed in works of art and literature. 19c. [N,S]

vestigium, *pl.* **vestigia** [Lat.] a trace, a mark left by something no longer in existence. 17c. [N,S]

veto [Lat. 'I forbid'] a prohibition designed to prevent legislation or political action; the right of imposing such a prohibition. 17c. [N,S]

vexata quæstio, *pl.* **vexatæ quæstiones** [Lat.] a disputed question, a point which has not yet been finally settled. 19c. [S]

via [Lat.] by way of . . ., by the route which passes through . . . 18c. [N,S]

Via Crucis [Lat.] *Eccles.* the Way of the Cross, the Stations of the Cross, a devotion performed in succession in front of each of fourteen representations of episodes in the Passion of Christ. 20c.

via dolorosa [Lat. 'sorrowful way'] the route followed by Christ on the way to Calvary; *hence*, a succession of painful experiences undergone for altruistic reasons. 20c.

via media [Lat.] a middle course, a course of action intermediate between two extremes. 19c. Cf. AUREA MEDIOCRITAS; JUSTE MILIEU. [S]

viaticum [Lat. 'journey-money'] *Rel.* the Eucharist administered to a person in danger of death. 16c. [N,S]

vibrato [It.] *Mus.* a tremulous quality of vocal or instrumental tone, involving fluctuation of both pitch and intensity. 19c. [N]

vice [Lat.] in place of; in succession to. 18c. In this prepositional usage the word is disyllabic; when compounded with another word (as in 'vice-president') it is monosyllabic. [N,S]

(le) vice anglais [Fr. 'the English vice'] homosexuality. 20c.

vice versa [Lat.] contrariwise, conversely, the relationship being transposed. 17c. [N,S]

vicisti, Galilæe! [Lat.] 'thou hast conquered, O Galilean!' 20c. The last words of Julian the Apostate.

victor ludorum, *f.* **victrix ludorum** [Lat.] the winner of the games, the person who has taken the first place in an athletic contest. 20c.

vicuña [Sp.] a kind of South American llama; the fine silky wool of this animal; fabric woven from this wool. 17c. The Spanish word is from the Quechuan language. Often written *vicuna* to avoid the use of the TILDE. [N,S]

(la) vida es sueño [Sp.] life is a dream. 20c. The title of a play by the Spanish dramatist Pedro Calderón de la Barca (1600–1681).

vide [Lat.] see, refer to (for further information). 16c. Often abbreviated to *v.* Cf. QUOD VIDE. [N,S]

videlicet [Lat.] namely, that is to say. 15c. Commonly introducing a more precise explanation of something already stated in general terms. Lat. *videlicet* is a contraction of *videre licet* 'it is permitted to see'; the word is often further abbreviated to *viz.*, in which *z* represents the mediæval mark of contraction ɜ. Cf. SCILICET. [N,S]

video meliora proboque, deteriora sequor [Lat.] I see and approve of the better things, but I follow the worse. 19c. Ovid *Metamorphoses* vii 20. [S]

vide-poche [Fr.] a small bedside table designed to accommodate the contents of one's pockets when retiring for the night. 20c.

vidimus [Lat. 'we have seen'] a copy of a document attested as authentic by some competent authority. 15c. Cf. INSPEXIMUS. [N,S]

vie amoureuse [Fr.] love-life, the history of a person's sexual encounters. 20c.

(la) vie de Bohème [Fr.] the unconventional and uninhibited life supposed to be led by artists and writers. 20c. From the title of Henry Murger's novel *Scènes de la Vie de Bohème* (1848).

vie de boudoir [Fr.] spending one's time dangling after women, regular attendance on ladies in their BOUDOIRS. 20c.

vie familiale [Fr.] family life, *esp.* considered as limiting or restricting the development of artistic or literary talent. 20c.

vie manquée [Fr.] a misdirected life, a life spent in a profession or vocation other than the one in which the greatest success might have been achieved. 20c. Cf. MANQUÉ.

vi et armis [Lat.] by force and armed power, by a display of menacing force. 17c. [S]

vieux jeu [Fr.] 'old hat', out of fashion, not up-to-date. 20c. Cf. DÉMODÉ.

vieux marcheur [Fr. 'old walker'] an old reprobate, a man who despite advanced age spends his time in pursuit of women. 20c. Current French, but taken from the title of a play by Henri Lavedan (1899).

vigilante [Sp.] *U.S.* a member of a self-appointed committee for the maintenance of law and order. 19c. [N]

vignette [Fr. 'little vine'] *Art* a drawing, engraving, or photograph not enclosed by a border, the edges of which are softened so as to blend imperceptibly into the background; *hence*, a representation in miniature, a brief sketch (of a scene or character) in a work of literature or on the stage. 19c. *Orig.* applied to a design of vine-leaves used as a decoration in a printed book, and transferred to other designs used for the same purpose. Cf. CAMEO. [N,S]

vilayet [Turk. < Arab. *welāyeh*] a Turkish province ruled by a VALI. 19c. [N,S]

villeggiatura [It.] living in a country house; a holiday spent in the country. 18c. Cf. EN VILLÉGIATURE. [N,S]

ville lumière [Fr.] the 'City of Light', Paris. 20c.

ville radieuse [Fr.] *Arch.* a town designed to consist of huge blocks of flats, so disposed as to trap the sun, and built on stilts so as to leave the ground free. 20c. The concept is due to the French architect Le Corbusier. Cf. UNITÉ D'HABITATION.

villino [It.] a small elegant house in the country or in a small park in a town. 20c.

vinaigrette [Fr.] (1) a smelling-bottle, a small bottle or box designed for holding aromatic or pungent salts. 19c. (2) *Cul.* a dressing of vinegar and oil. 20c. The second meaning is recorded once in 17c., but seems to have had no general currency until recently. [N,S]

vin blanc [Fr.] white wine. 20c.

vinculum, *pl.* **vincula** [Lat.] (1) a bond of union; (2) *Math.* a line drawn over two or more terms to indicate that they are subject to the same operation, as if they were enclosed in brackets. 17c. [N,S]

vin de table [Fr.] a table wine, a wine of inferior quality suitable for drinking with a meal. 20c. Cf. VIN ORDINAIRE.

vin d'honneur [Fr.] a reception in honour of a distinguished guest whose health is to be drunk, *esp.* on the occasion of the arrival or departure of the guest. 20c.

vin du pays [Fr.] local wine, wine produced in the neighbourhood. 19c. [S]

vingt-et-un [Fr. '21'] a card game in which the object is to score 21 or as near to this as possible without exceeding it by counting the pips on the cards, court cards being counted as 10. 19c. In earlier use (18c.) in the form *vingt-un*(*e*); now often corrupted to *pontoon*. Cf. BACCARA(T); CHEMIN DE FER. [N,S]

vin mousseux [Fr.] a sparkling, frothy wine. 20c. Cf. MOUSSEUX.

vin ordinaire [Fr.] non-vintage wine suitable for drinking with a meal. 19c. Cf. VIN DE TABLE. [S]

vin rosé [Fr.] wine of a pinkish colour intermediate between white and red. 20c. Cf. ROSÉ.

vin rouge [Fr.] red wine. 20c.

virago [Lat. 'heroic woman'] a violent woman, a termagant, a scold, a shrew. 14c. [N,S]

vir bonus dicendi peritus [Lat.] a reputable man skilled in speaking. 20c. Attributed by Quintilian to Cato the Censor; often quoted by Cicero as the classic description of the ideal orator.

virement [Fr.] transfer, clearing (in book-keeping and accountancy). 20c.

virginibus puerisque (canto) [Lat.] (I sing) for girls and boys. 19c. Used of literary works specially suitable for the young. Horace *Odes* III i 4.

virgo intacta [Lat.] an untouched virgin, a woman who is physically a virgin. 20c.

virtù [It.] *Art* supreme competence as an artist; artistic excellence; a love of fine art; a knowledge of fine art; a collection of works of art. 18c. Sometimes written *vertu* as if from French; but the French word has never had these meanings. Cf. OBJET DE VERTU. [N,S]

virtuoso, *pl.* **virtuosi** [It.] (1) a CONNOISSEUR of the fine arts; (2) *Mus.* a person who excels in technique in playing or singing; (a piece of music) designed to display technical skill. 17c. The feminine *virtuosa* seems no longer to be used in English. [N,S]

visagisme [Fr.] the care of the face, beauty treatment. 20c.

visagiste [Fr.] an expert in beauty treatment; a make-up expert. 20c. Cf. ESTHÉTICIEN.

vis a tergo [Lat.] pressure from behind. 20c.

vis-à-vis [Fr.] face to face (with), opposite (one another). 18c. [N,S]

viscera *pl.* [Lat.] *Med.* the internal organs, the bowels and other soft contents of the bodily cavities. 17c. The singular *viscus* is not now in use. [N,S]

vis inertiæ [Lat.] INERTIA, the tendency of matter to remain at rest (or to continue to move in a straight line) unless influenced by external forces. 18c. [S]

vis medicatrix naturæ [Lat.] the remedial power of nature, the tendency to recover from a disease without the help of medicine. 19c. [S]

vista [It.] a view or prospect, *esp.* a view down an avenue, a corridor, or a series of openings; a far-reaching mental vision. 17c. [N,S]

vita nuova [It.] a new life, turning over a new leaf. 20c. From the title of the first of Dante's principal works, which describes his encounters with Beatrice.

vitellone, *pl.* **vitelloni** [It. 'calf'] a young (Italian) hooligan, a teddy-boy. 20c. Cf. BLOUSON NOIR; HALBSTARKE(R); JEUNE VOYOU; STILYAGA.

viticulteur [Fr.] a (French) vine-grower. 20c.

vitrail, *pl.* **vitraux** [Fr.] a stained-glass window. 20c.

vitrine [Fr.] a glass show-case set in the wall of a room for the display of small works of art, etc. 19c. [N,S]

vivandière [Fr.] a female camp-follower. 19c. Properly 'a woman who sells provisions and liquor', but often implying 'prostitute'. [N,S]

vivarium, *pl.* **vivaria** [Lat.] a piece of ground or stretch of water specially adapted for the keeping or display of wild creatures under their natural conditions. 17c. Cf. AQUARIUM. [N,S]

vivat! [Lat. 'may he (she) live!'] long life and prosperity! 17c. [N,S]

viva voce [Lat. 'by the living voice'] (an examination) conducted by word of mouth instead of by writing. 19c. A *viva voce* examination is normally supplementary to a written examination; in colloquial usage contracted to *viva.* [N,S]

vive le roi! [Fr.] long live the king! 16c. In the collocation (LE) ROI EST MORT, *vive le roi*! used (often ironically) to acclaim the successor to a deceased or disgraced official. Cf. QUI VIVE. [S]

viveur [Fr.] a loose liver, a rake. 19c. Cf. BON VIVEUR. [S]

viz.=VIDELICET, namely.

v.l.=VARIA LECTIO, a variant reading.

vocalise [Fr.] a piece of vocal music without words, *esp.* one intended as an exercise in the technique of singing. 19c.

vodka [Russ.] a Russian ardent spirit *usu.* distilled from rye. 19c. [N,S]

vogue [Fr.] the prevailing fashion or tendency at a given place or time; success in popular esteem. 17c. [N,S]

vogue la galère [Fr. 'make the boat go!'] let's chance it, press on regardless. 18c. The phrase was used by Rabelais, but was doubtless already proverbial. [S]

voix célestes *pl.* [Fr. 'celestial voices'] *Mus.* an organ-stop consisting of two ranks of pipes tuned slightly out of unison so as to produce a tremulous effect. 19c. Cf. VOX ANGELICA.

volage [Fr.] fickle, inconstant, volatile. 18c. Early anglicized (16c.) but re-introduced from French. [N,S]

vol-au-vent [Fr. 'flight in the wind'] *Cul.* an individual pie made of very light puff pastry and containing meat, fish or fowl in a sauce. 19c. [N,S]

volenti non fit injuria [Lat.] *Law* no injury is done to someone who consents, no one can complain of damage resulting from an action to which he consented. 16c. Ulpian *Ad Edictum* lvi. [S]

(das) Volk dichtet [Ger.] 'the populace writes poetry', popular ballads and folk-songs are composed by the people at large. 20c. The doctrine expressed by the phrase is now accepted by few.

Völkerwanderung, *pl.* **Völkerwanderungen** [Ger.] tribal migration. 20c.

völkisch [Ger.] (aggressively) national, nationalistic. 20c. With particular reference to the nationalist policies of the German National Socialist Party; because of this connotation the word is now little used in German.

Volksbewegung, *pl.* **Volksbewegungen** [Ger.] a spontaneous instinctive upsurge of feeling experienced by a whole nation. 20c.

Volkslied, *pl.* **Volkslieder** [Ger.] a folksong. 19c. Cf. LIED. [S]

volkstümlich [Ger.] popular, unsophisticated. 20c.

volte-face [Fr.] a complete reversal of attitude or opinion. 19c. Cf. UMSCHWUNG. [N,S]

volupté [Fr.] sensual pleasure inclining towards sensuality. 20c.

vomitorium, *pl.* **vomitoria** [Lat.] *Hist.* a passage or opening in an ancient theatre or circus leading to or from the seats. 18c. There is no foundation for the belief that the Romans used this word to describe a room set aside for vomiting between the courses of a meal. [N,S]

vortex, *pl.* **vortices** [Lat.] a violent eddy or whirl (of water, flame, etc.); *hence*, a constant round of pleasure and entertainment. 17c. Cf. TOURBILLON. [N,S]

voulu [Fr.] intentional, deliberate. 20c.

vous l'avez voulu, (George Dandin, vous l'avez voulu)[Fr.] you wanted it, it's your own fault. 19c. Molière *George Dandin* (1661) I ix; the modern French spelling *Georges* is *occ.* substituted for the original *George.* [S]

voussoir [Fr.] *Arch.* one of the wedge-shaped stones of which an arch is constructed. 18c. [N,S]

vox angelica [Lat. 'angelic voice'] *Mus.* an organ-stop consisting of two ranks of pipes tuned slightly out of unison so as to produce a tremulous effect. 19c. Cf. VOIX CÉLESTES. [N]

vox et præterea nihil [Lat.] 'a voice and nothing more'; the voice of someone unseen; an ineffective utterance. 17c. *Orig.* used of the nightingale, the body of which is insignificant: Plutarch *Laconic Apophthegms* xiii 233a. [S]

vox humana [Lat.] *Mus.* an organ-stop supposed to simulate the sound of the human voice; *hence*, the exaggerated expression of emotion. 18c. [N,S]

vox nihili, *pl.* **voces nihili** [Lat. 'word of nothing'] a sequence of letters which do not form a word; a 'ghost-word', a word entered in a dictionary as a result of some misunderstanding. 19c. [S]

vox populi [Lat.] the voice of the people, an expression of popular or general opinion. 16c. [N]

vox populi, vox Dei [Lat.] the voice of the people is the voice of God. 16c. Alcuin *Epistola* cxxvii (Letter to Charlemagne); chosen by Walter Reynolds as the text of a sermon at the accession of Edward III in 1327. [N,S]

voyage à Cythère [Fr.] a journey to Cythera, the Greek island sacred to Aphrodite; *hence*, a quest for erotic experiences. 20c. Probably from the title of a poem by Baudelaire; but cf. also *L'Embarquement pour Cythère*, the name of a famous painting by Watteau.

voyage imaginaire [Fr.] (an account of) an imaginary journey. 20c.

voyant, *f.* **voyante** [Fr.] a seer, a person endowed with second sight. 20c. Cf. CLAIRVOYANT.

voyeur [Fr.] a peeping Tom, one who derives satisfaction from secretly watching the erotic activities of others. 20c.

vraisemblance [Fr.] verisimilitude, plausibility, the appearance of truth. 19c. [N,S]

vue d'ensemble [Fr.] a general view, an opinion taking everything into consideration. 20c.

vulgarisateur [Fr.] a popularizer, a person who writes popular books on academic or scientific subjects. 20c. Cf. ANIMATEUR; HAUTE VULGARISATION.

vulgo [Lat.] commonly, popularly; in the vernacular language. 17c. [N,S]

vv.ll. = VARIÆ LECTIONES, variant readings.

wadi [Arab. *wādi*] a dry water-course, a gulley. 19c. Cf. NULLAH. [N(*),S]

Wafd [Arab. 'deputation'] the Egyptian Nationalist party founded by Zaghlul Pasha in 1919. 20c. The name is derived from the deputation to the British High Commissioner led by Zaghlul Pasha at the foundation of the party.

wagon-lit [Fr.] a sleeping-coach on a Continental train. 19c. [N]

Wahlverwandtschaft, *pl.* **Wahlverwandtschaften** [Ger.] an 'elective affinity', a natural sympathy and intuitive understanding between two persons. 20c. From the title of Goethe's novel *Die Wahlverwandtschaften* (1809); Goethe's psychological ideas are based on pseudo-scientific premisses, and his title was borrowed from that of a treatise *De Attractionibus Electivis* (1775) by the Swedish chemist Torben Bergman.

wallah [Hind. *-wālā*] *A.-I.* a fellow; a minor official; often preceded by a noun suggesting the occupation of the person concerned. 18c. The Hindustani form is an adjectival suffix meaning 'connected with', so that the use of the word in conjunction with a noun indicating occupation is closest to the original usage; the sense 'minor official' comes from a contraction of the compound 'competition-*wallah*', meaning 'a civil servant appointed after a competitive examination'. [N(*),S(*)]

Walpurgisnacht [Ger.] the Eve of St Walburga, the night before 1st May when according to German belief witches and spirits are abroad to exercise their powers; *hence*, a witches' sabbath. 20c.

Wanderjahre *pl.* [Ger.] the years of wandering, the years spent by a journeyman travelling from one workshop to another to gain knowledge and experience. 20c.

Wanderlust [Ger.] fondness for travelling, *esp.* an urge to see the world. 20c. [N*]

Wandervogel, *pl.* **Wandervögel** [Ger.] a young person exploring the countryside or visiting foreign countries, *usu.* on foot and at little expense. 20c. The name *Wandervögel* was given to a mildly revolutionary German youth movement popular shortly before the First World War.

wedeln [Ger. 'to wag'] *Ski* to make a rapid descent following a wavy course by means of a regular oscillating movement of the skis. 20c. Cf. GODILLE.

Wehrwirtschaft [Ger.] war-time economy. 20c.

Weinstube, *pl.* **Weinstuben** [Ger.] an inn, a small drinking-house. 20c.

Weltanschauung, *pl.* **Weltanschauungen** [Ger.] an outlook on things in general, a philosophy of life. 20c.

Weltbürger, *pl.* **Weltbürger** [Ger.] a citizen of the world, a cosmopolitan. 20c.

Weltgeist [Ger.] the spirit of the world, the immanent spiritual quality of things. 19c. Cf. ZEITGEIST. [S]

Weltpolitik [Ger.] world politics, international politics. 20c.

Weltschmerz [Ger.] distress at the condition of the world, sentimental pessimism. 19c. Cf. MAL DU SIÈCLE; TÆDIUM VITÆ. [S]

Weltverbesserungswahn [Ger.] the illusion of progress, a mistaken belief that things get better and better. 20c.

Wendepunkt [Ger.] a turning-point, a dramatic turn of events in a NOVELLE. 20c. Cf. PERIPETEIA.

Wiegendruck, *pl.* **Wiegendrücke** [Ger. 'cradle-print'] a book printed before 1500, an incunable. 20c. Cf. INCUNABULA.

Wiegenlied, *pl.* **Wiegenlieder** [Ger.] a cradle-song, a lullaby. 20c. Cf. BERCEUSE.

Wiener Schnitzel [Ger. 'Vienna SCHNITZEL'] *Cul.* a veal cutlet coated with breadcrumbs in beaten egg before cooking, and garnished with lemon, capers, and sardines in the Viennese style. 20c. [N*]

(das) Wirtschaftswunder [Ger.] the economic miracle, the rapid economic recovery of West Germany after the Second World War. 20c.

wunderbar [Ger.] wonderful, marvellous. 20c. *Wunderbar!* is looked upon as the characteristic ejaculation of the unsophisticated German. Cf. KOLOSSAL.

Wunderkind, *pl.* **Wunderkinder** [Ger.] an infant prodigy. 20c.

Y

yamschik/yamstchik [Russ. *yamshchik*] the driver of a Russian coach. 18c. Cf. IZVOSCHIK. [N]

yashmak [Arab. *yashmaq*] the veil concealing the face below the eyes, worn by Moslem women in public. 19c. [N,S(*)]

yerba (maté) [Sp.] the South American shrub *Ilex paraguayensis*; the leaves of this shrub, used for making a kind of tea. 19c. The normal spelling of the first word in Spanish is *hierba;* but in this special combination the spelling *yerba* (an illiterate variant) has been established in Spanish as well as in English. Cf. MATÉ. [N,S]

yeti [Tib.] an 'abominable snowman', a creature as yet unidentified which leaves quasi-human tracks above the snowline in the Himalayas. 20c.

yoga [Hind.] *Rel.* 'union with the supreme spirit', a system of asceticism, meditation, and concentration practised by Hindu adepts. 19c. Cf. SAMADHI. [N,S]

yoghourt [Turk. *yoğurt*] fermented sour milk, consumed in Turkey and other countries in the Near East. 17c. Many different spellings are in use; such forms as *yaghourt* are etymologically unjustifiable. [N,S]

yogi [Hind. *yogi*] a Hindu ascetic, a devotee who practises YOGA. 17c. [N,S]

Yom Kippur [Heb. *Yom Kippūr*] the day of Atonement, the annual Jewish fast observed on the tenth day of the seventh month. 20c. The better Hebrew form is *Yom ha-Kippūrīm* 'day of Purgations' (*Leviticus* xxiii 27).

yoni [Sansk.] a representation of the female generative organ venerated by Hindus and others. 18c. Cf. PHALLUS. [N,S]

Z

zabaglione, *pl.* **zabaglioni** [It.] *Cul.* a confection of egg-yolks, sugar, and Marsala wine. 20c. The normal Italian spelling is *zabaione.*

zapateado [Sp.] slapping the ground with the shoes, as a feature of FLAMENCO dancing. 20c. Cf. COUP DE SAVATE; SCHUHPLATTLER.

zareba [Arab. *zarībah*] a breast-work made of thornbushes for defence against enemies or wild animals. 19c. [N,S]

zastruga, *pl.* **zastrugi** [Russ.] *Geog.* one of a series of parallel furrows made in loose snow by the action of the wind. 20c. Also in the form *sastruga.* [N*]

Zeilenstil [Ger.] *Ling.* a poetic style in which the natural breaks in the sense fall at the ends of the lines; opposed to HAKENSTIL. 20c.

Zeitgeist [Ger.] the spirit of the times, the 'climate of opinion' of a given period or age. 19c. Cf. WELTGEIST. [N(*),S]

Zeitnot [Ger.] (1) *Chess* shortage of time when playing by the clock; (2) slavery to the clock, the necessity in modern administrative work of adhering closely to a timetable. 20c.

zemstvo [Russ.] a provincial council in Russia elected for local government. 19c. [N,S]

zenana [Hind. *zenāna* < Pers. *zanāna*] the part of an Indian house where the women live in seclusion, a HAREM. 18c. Cf. SERAGLIO. [N,S]

zeugma [Gk. ζεῦγμα] *Ling.* a rhetorical device whereby a single word is to be construed with two other words in the same sentence, *usu.* in a slightly different sense. 19c. Cf. SYLLEPSIS. [N,S]

Zigeuner, *pl.* **Zigeuner** [Ger.] a gipsy. 20c.

ziggurat [Assyrian *ziqquratu*] an Assyrian sacred tower, so constructed that each storey is smaller than the one below and has a terrace all round it. 19c. [N]

zingaro, *pl.* **zingari** [It.] a gipsy. 17c. *I Zingari* 'The Gipsies' is the name of a famous cricket-club. [N,S]

Zollverein [Ger.] a customs union, a system whereby a number of states impose a common tariff against other countries and practise free trade amongst themselves. 19c. A *Zollverein* of all the German states was inaugurated in 1833. [N,S]

zombie [W. African *zumbi* 'image'] a corpse revivified and compelled to carry out certain actions by the magical power of Voodoo; *hence,* a person whose actions appear mechanical and involuntary, an AUTOMATON. 20c. *Orig*. the name given to the snake-deity of the Voodoo religion.

zouave [Fr.] a member of a body of French light infantry equipped in quasi-Oriental uniform. 19c. The name is derived from the Algerian tribe of *Zouaoua*, from amongst whom the *zouaves* were *orig*. recruited. [N,S]

zucchetto, *pl.* **zucchetti** [It.] *Eccles*. the skull-cap of an ecclesiastical dignitary, of the same colour as the costume appropriate to his rank. 19c. [N]

Zugzwang [Ger.] *Chess* (manœuvring one's opponent into) a blockade position where any move will lead to checkmate. 20c.

Zwieback [Ger.] a rusk. 20c.

APPENDIX

The appendix lists all the words and phrases which appear in the body of the dictionary, arranged according to their language of origin and the date of their introduction into English. The 'language of origin' is here interpreted as the language from which the word or phrase entered English; in many cases the ultimate origin is to be found in another language.

The appendix is divided into three main sections. The first section includes the six languages from which contributions to the English vocabulary have been the most numerous: French, Latin, Greek, Italian, German, and Spanish, listed in this order. The second section includes other European languages, listed in alphabetical order, with a final group of languages which have contributed only one word each. The third section includes non-European languages, listed in alphabetical order, with a final group of languages which have contributed only one word each.

Section I: French, Latin, Greek, Italian, German, and Spanish

1. French

Mediæval

adieu; avant-garde; avoirdupois; ballade; bedouin; béguine; bise; blancmange; bon voyage; congé; Dauphin; dragoman; faubourg; fleur de lis; marque; oriflamme; oyer; oyez!; pont-levis.

Sixteenth Century

armoire; auberge; bâton; bricole; cabochon; cache; caïque; canton; cap à pié; capriole; caravanserai; chamois; congé d'élire; devoir; éloge; enfant perdu; esprit; finesse; fricassée; greffier; honi soit qui mal y pense; jacquerie; kermesse; lèse majesté; memoir; mesne; mignon; morgue; naïf; œillade; panache; pavane; peine forte et dure; perruque; portmanteau; promenade; rendezvous; roturier; seigneur; valet; venue; vive le roi!

Seventeenth Century

aide de camp; aigrette; à la; à la mode; amende honorable; amour; ampoule; à propos; arabesque; aubade; au revoir; avant-courier; badinage; bagatelle; ballet; banquette; bas-relief; beau; bel esprit; belle; belles lettres; berceau; bienséance; bijou; billet doux; bisque; bizarre; blond; bocage; bouilli; bourgeois; bourgeoisie; boutade; brocatelle; brusque; bureau; canaille; caprice; caracole; cartel; cartouche; catafalque; chaconne; chagrin; chamade; chef d'œuvre; chevron; chicane; coiffure; commis; commune; compote; concierge; concordat; confidante; contour; coquette; cortège; couchée; coup d'état; courbette; critique; curé; dégagé; de haut en bas; démarche; démenti; dernier ressort; déshabillé; Dieu et mon droit; domino; douane; double entendre; doyen; éclaircissement; éclat; embonpoint; enceinte; en déshabillé; en passant; en prince; entremets; épopée; escritoire; étourdi; étui; exergue; façade; fainéant; fainéantise; fanfaronnade; fascine; faux pas; feme coverte; feme sole; fiacre; fiançailles; flambeau; foible; forte; gavotte; glacis; grand seigneur; grotesquerie; honnête homme;

je-ne-sais-quoi; jet d'eau; levée; lunette; mal à propos; manège; marabout; marc; mélange; mêlée; menus plaisirs; mistral; naïveté; niaiserie; noblesse; nom de guerre; nonchalance; odalisque; ordonnance; par excellence; parole (d'honneur); parterre; passe-partout; passepied; patois; paysage; penchant; perdu; piastre; piquant; pique; piquet; pirogue; pis aller; point de Venise; porte-cochère; pratique; profit-à-prendre; ragoût; rencontre; rêverie; rouleau; sabot; sans cérémonie; sans façon; sobriquet; sottise; suite; table d'hôte; tabouret; taille douce; talus; tapis; tendre; terre verte; tête-à-tête; tracasserie; tric-trac; valet de chambre; valise; vogue.

Eighteenth Century

abattu; abbé; accoucheur; acharnement; affiche; agréments; à la bonne heure; alambiqué; allée; amateur; à merveille; amie; ancien régime; à perte de vue; appliqué; à propos de bottes; artiste; aubergine; au contraire; au désespoir; au fait; au pied de la lettre; autrefois acquit; avalanche; ballet d'action; bal masqué; bandeau; barbette; barcarolle; bas bleu; batterie de cuisine; beau-pot; bêche-de-mer; bistre; bizarrerie; bon goût; bonhomie; bon mot; bonne bouche; bonnes fortunes; bon ton; bon vivant; boudoir; bougie; boulevard; bouleversement; bouquet; bourrée; bouts rimés; brochure; brouillon; brunette; brusquerie; buvette; cabriole; cabriolet; café au lait; carafe; carillon; carmagnole; carte blanche; casserole; catalogue raisonné; cestui que trust; chaise; chalet; chalumeau; chandelier; chapeau-bras; chaperon; charade; chargé d'affaires; charivari; château; chemise; chemisette; chenille; chère amie; chevalier d'industrie; chiffonnier; chignon; ci-devant; clique; colporteur; comme il faut; commissionnaire; commode; compagnon de voyage; confrère; connoisseur; contre-coup; contretemps; cordon bleu; corps; corps de bataille; corps diplomatique; corvée; coterie; couleur de rose; coup; coup de grâce; coup de main; coup de maître; coup d'essai; coup de théâtre; coup d'œil; coureur de bois; coûte que coûte; crampon; croquette; croupier; cuisine; cul-de-lampe; cul de sac; curette; dame de compagnie; débonnaire; débris; début; dedans; dénouement; déplacé; dépôt; désœuvré; détour; de trop; dévot; diablerie; distrait; douanier; douceur; douche; ébauche; échelon; élite; embarras de(s) richesse(s); embouchure; émigré; empressement; encore; en famille; en masse; ennui; en route; ensemble; en suite; en train; entrechat; entrée; entre nous; entrepôt; entresol; épergne; épuisé; esprit de corps; esprit fort; esquisse; étoile; étourderie; exigeant; farouche; faute de mieux; fauteuil; femme de chambre; fête; fête champêtre; feu de joie; figurant; fille de joie; fracas; fricandeau; gala; galantine; galère; gauche; gaucherie; girandole; gourmand; gouvernante; grille; grippe; grisette; guillotine; hauteur; homme d'esprit; hors de combat; hors d'œuvre; hôtel de ville; insouciance; jeu de mots; jeu d'esprit; jongleur; légèreté; lettre de cachet; liane; liqueur; lit de justice; locale; loge; malaise; mal de mer; malentendu; maniéré; marivaudage; mauvaise honte; mauvais sang; méchanceté; ménage; meringue; mésalliance; mesquin; métier; migraine; minauderie; moraine; morceau; nonchalant; nous avons changé tout cela; noyau; nuance; octroi; œil-de-bœuf; opéra comique; outré; papier mâché; partie carrée; pas de trois; passé; pâté; pâtisserie; pavé; péché mortel; pèlerine; pelisse; pension; pensionnaire; perron; persiflage; petit; petite; petite maison; petit maître; piaffe; pièce justificative; pierrot; pirouette; pisé; piste; plateau; politesse; poste restante; pot au feu; pot pourri; pourparler; précieux; précis; preux chevalier; prie-dieu; portégé; quadrille; qui vive; raisonné; recherché; régime; religieuse; restaurateur; riant; ricochet; riposte; robe de chambre; rôle; rouge; rouge-et-noir; roulade; roulette; salmi; salon; salpicon; sang froid; sansculotte; savant; savoir vivre; sissonne; soi-disant; solitaire; sortie; soubrette;

soulagement; soupçon; souvenir; sur le tapis; tambour; tant bien que mal; tant mieux; tant pis; tendresse; terre à terre; tiers état; tirailleur; toilette; toupet; tourbillon; tournure; tout court; tout de suite; tout ensemble; trait; triste; tristesse; troubadour; trouvère; tuyère; vis-à-vis; vogue la galère; volage; voussoir.

Nineteenth Century

abandon; à bas; abat-jour; abattoir; abat-voix; abbé de cour; abondance; abondance déclarée; à bras ouverts; absinthe; accablé; accouchement; à cheval; à contrecœur; à deux; affaire (de cœur); affaire d'honneur; à fleur d'eau; à fond (perdu); agent provocateur; à grands frais; à huis clos; aide-mémoire; aigre-doux; aigreur; aiguille; aiguillette; aîné; à la carte; à la lanterne; allonge; allure; à l'outrance; amazone; âme damnée; amourette; amour propre; aperçu; apéritif; aplomb; appartement; après coup; après nous le déluge; aquarelle; arête; argot; arrière-pensée; arrondissement; art nouveau; atelier; attaché; attentat; au courant; au fond; au grand sérieux; au gratin; au naturel; au sérieux; autrefois convict; avant-goût; baccara(t); baignoire; bain-marie; balle à la main; ballon d'essai; banal; barbotine; baroque; basque; batiste; battue; bayadère; bayou; beau idéal; beau monde; beaux yeux; béguinage; bel étage; bénéficiaire; béret; bergère; bête noire; bêtise; bévue; bibelot; bidet; bien entendu; bijouterie; bivouac; blague; blagueur; blanquette; blasé; bombe; bonbon; bonbonnière; bon enfant; bon marché; bonne; bon viveur; borné; bouchée; bouffant; bouillabaisse; boulevardier; bouleversé; Bourse; boutonnière; brassard; brasserie; bric-à-brac; brioche; briolette; broderie anglaise; brut; buffet; burnous; butte; cachet; cachou; cadet; cadre; café; café chantant; café noir; cahier; ça ira; calvaire; camaraderie; camouflet; canapé; canard; cancan; caporal; carte de visite; carton-pierre; caserne; cassette; cassolette; cause célèbre; causerie; causeuse; ça va sans dire; ce n'est pas une révolte, c'est une révolution; c'est-à-dire; c'est la guerre; chacun à son goût; chaise-longue; champlevé; chanson de geste; chantage; chapelle ardente; char-à-banc; charcuterie; chasse; chassé; chassé-croisé; château en Espagne; châtelaine; chatoyant; chaud-froid; chef; chef d'école; chef-lieu; chemise de nuit; chéri; cheval de bataille; chevaux de frise; chevet; chez nous; chic; chiffon; chinoiserie; chose jugée; chou(x); chronique scandaleuse; chypre; cire perdue; cirque; clairvoyance; clairvoyant; claque; claqueur; claveciniste; cliché; clientèle; cloche; cloisonné; clou; cocotte; cohue; coiffeur; col; colon; comble; (la) comédie humaine; comédienne; communard; communiqué; compère; compte rendu; concessionnaire; conférencier; confiseur; confrère; confrérie; conservatoire; console; consommé; conte; convenable; (les) convenances; cor anglais; cordon sanitaire; cornet à piston(s); corps de ballet; corps d'élite; corsetière; coryphée; costumier; coteau; cottage orné; coulisse; coup de temps; coupé; couturier; couvade; crèche; crème de la crème; crêpe; crêpe de Chine; crêpe lisse; crépon; crevasse; crève-cœur; criant; criard; crochet; croquet; croquis; croûton; cru; cuir bouilli; cuvée; cy-près; dame d'honneur; danse macabre; danseur; débâcle; déboutonné; débutante; déclassé; décolletage; décolletée; décousu; dégringolade; déjeuner à la fourchette; délassement; demimondaine; demi-monde; démodé; denier; dentelle; député; de règle; de rigueur; (le) dernier cri; désœuvrement; deux-temps; difficile; Directoire; diseuse; distingué; divertissement; divorcée; doctrinaire; dolmen; donnée; dossier; dot; doublure; douceur de vivre; dragée; duchesse; du tout; eau de Cologne; eau de Nil; eau de vie; eau forte; eau sucrée; écarté; éclair; écorché; écrin; écru; édition de luxe; élan; embarras de choix; émeute; emplacement; empressé; en avant; en bloc; en clair; enclave; en échelon; en évidence; enfant gâté; enfant terrible; en fête; en garçon; engobe; engouement; en grande tenue; enjambement; en l'air; en pension; en plein air; en prise; en rapport; en règle; en retraite; en revanche; entente; entente cordiale; entêté; entourage; en tout cas; entr'acte; entrain; entrecôte; entredeux; entrepreneur; en ventre sa mère; épée; épris; équestrienne; escargot; esclandre; espadrille; espiègle; espièglerie; estaminet; étagère; étrenne; étude; expertise; exposé; fabliau; façon de parler; faïence; fait accompli; famille jaune; famille noire; famille rose; famille verte; farandole; farceur; féerie; femme incomprise; femme savante; feuilleton; fiancé; fichu; figurine; filet; fils; fine (Champagne); flair; flambé; flèche; foie gras; folâtre; fondant; fond(s); fondue; force majeure; format; fougasse; foulard; fourchette; fourgon; foyer; franc tireur; frappé; fredaine; fronde; frondeur; frou-frou; galop; gamin; garçon; garde champêtre; garde mobile; garderobe; gastronome; gâteau; gendarme; gendarmerie; gêne; gêné; gens du monde; glacé; glissade; godet; gouache; gourmandise; gourmet; grand coup; (la) Grande Armée; grande dame; grande entrée; grande passion; grande tenue; grand mal; Grand Prix; grimoire; grisaille; gros de Naples; grosgrain; guerre à outrance; guichet; guilloche; guipure; habitué; haute bourgeoisie; haute école; haut ton; homme de lettres; hors concours; idée fixe; immortelles; impair; impasse; impayable; inconnu; ingénue; insouciant; intransigeant; jabot; j'adoube; jalousie; jardinière; jaspé; jeune premier; jeune première; jeunesse dorée; joue; juge d'instruction; juste milieu; képi; laissez-aller; laissez-faire; layette; levée en masse; lever de rideau; liaison; lingerie; lisse; littérateur; littoral; livraison; locataire; longueur; lorgnette; louche; luxe; lycée; macabre; macédoine; madeleine; mademoiselle; maison de santé; maître d'hôtel; malade imaginaire; mal du pays; malgré lui; mannequin; manqué; Mardi Gras; mariage de convenance; marionnette; marquise; massage; massé; masseur; massif; matelassé; matériel; matinée; matinée musicale; mauvais quart d'heure; mauvais sujet; mayonnaise; méchant; mesquinerie; métis; meurtrière; milieu; millefleurs; milord; mirage; mise en scène; misère; modiste; moiré; moire antique; molleton; mont-de-piété; moquette; morale; morcellement; morne; mot; motif; moue; mouillé; moulinet; mousse; mousseux; moutonnée; musicale; naturel; née; négligé; névé; noblesse oblige; nocturne; noisette; nom de plume; nom de théâtre; nougat; nouveau riche; noyade; objet d'art; ombres chinoises; on dit; opéra bouffe; ordre du jour; oubliette; paillette; paletot; palmette; par éminence; par exemple; pari mutuel; parquet; parti; parti pris; parure; parvenu; pas de charge; pas de deux; pas de quatre; passementerie; pas seul; pas si bête; pastiche; pastille; pâté de foie gras; pâte dure; pâte tendre; (les) Pays Bas; peau-de-soie; peignoir; pendeloque; pensée; percale; percheron; père; père de famille; perfide Albion; permis de séjour; persiennes; personnel; petite entrée; petit four; petit mal; petit point; petits soins; petit verre; philosophe; physique; picaresque; picot; pièce de résistance; pièce d'occasion; pied-à-terre; pince-nez; piqué; planchette; plaque; plaquette; plastron; point d'Alençon; point d'appui; point de repère; poitrine; portière; poseur; postiche; pouf; poulet; poult-de-soie; pourboire; pour encourager les autres; pour prendre congé; pousse-café; praline; premier danseur; première; prestige; preux; primeur; procès; procès-verbal; prononcé; purée; pur sang; puy; quartier; quenelle; qui s'excuse s'accuse; raconteur; raison d'être; râle; ranz-des-vaches; rapport; rapprochement; réchauffé; réclame; rédacteur; redingote; renaissance; rentier; répertoire; répondez s'il vous plaît; reprise; restaurant; résumé; retenue; retroussé; revanche; réveillon; revenant; revenons à nos moutons; risqué; rivière; roche moutonnée; rococo; (le) roi est mort; roi fainéant; roué; roux; ruche; rusé; ruse de guerre; sachet; saltimbanque; sang-de-bœuf; sans-gêne; sans peur et sans reproche; sans phrase; sauté; sauve-qui-peut; savoir faire; scrutin de liste; séance; sec; sécateur; secrétaire; seiche; sérac; serein; serinette; servante; sociétaire; soirée; soirée musicale; sou; soubresaut; souffle;

soufflé; sourdine; sournois; soutane; suave; succès d'estime; succès fou; suède; surveillance; suzeraine; svelte; tableau (vivant); tapotement; tête-bêche; thé dansant; tic (douloureux); timbre; tisane; tohu-bohu; toile; toque; torchon; torque; tortillon; toujours perdrix; tour de force; tragédienne; trembleuse; tricorne; tricot; tricoteuse; trois-temps; troupe; trousseau; vaudeville; veilleuse; velours; ventre à terre; vers de société; verve; vignette; vinaigrette; vin du pays; vingt-et-un; vin ordinaire; vitrine; vivandière; viveur; vocalise; voix célestes; vol-au-vent; volte-face; vous l'avez voulu, (George Dandin, vous l'avez voulu); vraisemblance; wagon-lit; zouave.

Twentieth Century

à bientôt; abonnement; académicien; accapareur de femmes; acharné; acte gratuit; actualité; affairé; affiché; à gogo; agrégé; à la guerre comme à la guerre; à la page; à la recherche du temps perdu; à la rigueur; à l'étroit; à l'impériale; à l'improviste; allumeuse; amant attitré; amant de cœur; ambiance; âme d'élite; âme incomprise; amitié amoureuse; amour courtois; amour de voyage; animateur; apache; appartement de parade; appartement meublé; après-ski; à propos de rien; à pur et à plein; à quoi bon?; arabesque fondue; arabesque penchée; à rebours; arriéré; arrière-goût; arrière-plan; arrivé; arriviste; art autre; art brut; art engagé; art moderne; assemblage; assemblé; à tâtons; à trois; attentat aux mœurs; attitude; attrapé; au grand galop; au pair; au poteau; au premier abord; au premier coup; autocritique; autres temps, autres mœurs; au vif; avec empressement; baccalauréat; bachot; badinerie; bafoué; bagarre; baguette; ballet blanc; ballet chanté; ballon; ballonné; ballotté; bal musette; banc; banco; banlieue; barbeau; baroquerie; barrage; barre; baryton-Martin; bascule; basse-taille; bateau-mouche; battement; battement dégagé; battement tendu; batterie de campagne; béarnaise; beau geste; beaux arts; béguin; (la) belle époque; belle indifférence; belle laide; belle peinture; berceuse; bergerie; bidonville; bien élevé; bien pensant; bien rangé; bien trouvé; bien vu; bistro; blanc de blancs; blanc-de-Chine; bleu-jaune; bloc; blouson; blouson doré; blouson noir; bois clair; bois de rose; boiserie; boîte; boîte de nuit; bombé; bombe surprise; bon copain; bondieuserie; bonheur-du-jour; bonne amie; bonne à tout faire; bonsens; bordereau; boucharde; bouché; bouche bée; bouche fermée; bouclé; bouillon; boule; bouquet garni; bouquiniste; boutique; boutonné; bras de lumière; brassière; brisé; brise-bise; brise-soleil; brisé volé; broché; brouhaha; bruit; brûlé; brûle-parfums; bruyant; bureau à cylindre; bureau de change; bureau plat; but du promenade; cabaret; cabinet particulier; cache-misère; cache-sexe; cache-torchons; cafard; café-concert; café filtre; café littéraire; cagnotte; cagoule; calque; camouflage; ça ne fait rien; capable de tout; caqueteuse; caractère; carnet; carnet vert; carrousel; carte d'identité; cartonnier; ça saute aux yeux; cas de conscience; cassant; casse-croûte; cassis; caste; cauchemar; cendré; cercle privé; c'est la vie; c'est magnifique, mais ce n'est pas la guerre; c'est pire qu'un crime, c'est une faute; c'est Vénus toute entière à sa proie attachée; chacun à son métier; chagrin d'amour; chahut; chambré; chanson de toile; chansonnier; charmeur; charmeuse; chasse-cousin(s); chasseur; chasseur alpin; chassis; chatoyance; chauffeur; chef d'orchestre; chemin de fer; chemise de bain; chenet; cherchez la femme; cher maître; chétif; chez; chichi; ci-gît; ciment fondu; cinéaste; cinéma-vérité; cinq-à-sept; ciré; ciselé; clair de lune; clef de voûte; clochard; cloqué; (le) cœur a ses raisons que la raison ne connaît point; coiffeur de dames; coiffure bouffante; collage; comblé; comédie larmoyante; comédie noire; comédie rose; comédie rosse; comme il se doit; (le) commencement de la fin; commerçant; commère; commis voyageur; concours; concours d'élégance; confiserie; confit; confort moderne; congé définitif; connaissance; conseil d'état; consommation; constatation; contenu; conte philosophique; contrarier; contrat de majorité; contrat social; contrepartie; coquillage; cordée; cordon militaire; cordon rouge; corniche; corsage; cotillon; couchette; coulant; coulé; couleur du temps; coup de foudre; coup de piston; coup-de-poing; coup de savate; coupe; coupé de ville; coup en passant; coureur; couture; couvert; craquelure; craquelure anglaise; crème brûlée; crépuscule; crève-cœur; cri de cœur; crime passionnel; crise d'adolescence; crise de cœur; crise de combat; crise de conscience; crise (de nerfs); croissant; croix de guerre; croûte; croyant; croyant et pratiquant; cruauté; crudités; cuirasse musclée; cuir ciselé; culotte; culte du moi; curettage; dada; dalle de verre; danse d'école; danse de vertige; danse du ventre; danseur noble; débrouillard; déchéance; décor; décor simultané; découpage; défaillance; (les) défauts de ses qualités; déformation professionnelle; déhanchement; déjà vu; de longue haleine; de luxe; déménagement; démeublé; demi-caractère; demi-castor; demi-pension; demi-pointe; demi-saison; demi-tasse; demi-toilette; demi-vierge; démon de midi; de nos jours; dentellière; dépaysé; déplacement; dépucellage; déraciné; déséquilibré; désinvolture; désordonné; désorienté; dessus de table; détaché; détente; détournement de jeunesse; détournement de mineurs; détraqué; deux-chevaux; Deuxième Bureau; dévalisé; développé; devoirs d'état; diagonale; dialogue des sourds; diamanté; diplomate de carrière; directeur de conscience; dirigisme; dirigiste; discothèque; dix-huitième; djellaba; dompteur; doyenné; drame à thèse; drame bourgeois; draperie mouillée; dressage; droit administratif; droit de cité; droit de seigneur; droit naturel; drôle; du dernier bateau; du meilleur rang; d'un certain âge; d'une longue haleine; duvet; ébéniste; ébénisterie; échange de vues; échappé; échoppe; école; écrasez l'infâme; écritoire; écriture artiste; écuelle; écurie; effleurage; égalité; égaré; élan vital; élévation; émaillerie à jour; embourgeoisement; embusqué; éminence grise; émotionné; empennage; en axe; en brochette; en brosse; en cabochon; en camaïeu; en casserole; enchaînement; encoignure; en dedans; en dehors; en détail; en diagonale; endimanché; en face; enfant chéri; enfant de miracle; enfant de son siècle; enfantillage; enfilade; en flèche; engagé; engagement; en garde; enjôleur; en ménage; ennuyeux; en pantoufles; en plein; en poste; en principe; en secondes noces; en sourdine; en taille d'épargne; entourloupette; en transi; en travesti; entre deux âges; entre deux guerres; en villégiature; en voyage; épanchement; épaule en dedans; épaulement; équipe; esprit de notaire; esprit d'escalier; esprit gaulois; esprit laïc; esprit libre; esthéticien; étalage; étape; étatisme; étrier; exalté; exclusivité; exécutant; exercice au milieu; exercice de style; expéditeur; explication de texte; façade d'honneur; face-à-main; facile; façonné; faible; faille; faire école; faisandé; faiseur de mots; faites vos jeux; faits divers; fantaisie; fantaisiste; (la) farce est jouée; farci; faunesque; fausse maigre; fauve; (Les) Fauves; fauvisme; faux amis; faux bonhomme; faux bourdon; faux dévot; faux ménage; faux naïf; fay ce que vouldras; féerique; femme de trente ans; femme du monde; femme du peuple; femme fatale; femme sérieuse; fête galante; fiche; fil d'Ariane; filet mignon; fille du régiment; filtre; fin de guerre; fin de non-recevoir; fin de race; fin de siècle; fine à l'eau; fine (de la) maison; fines herbes; fin gourmet; fin sourire; flâneur; flic; flou; folie; folie de doute; folie de grandeur; folklorique; fonctionnaire; fond de teint; force de frappe; formes libres; fouetté; fou rire; foutu; franchise; Franglais; fraude pieuse; fricatrice; frisson; froissé; frottage; fruit de mer; fugue; fumage; fumiste; fuselage; gaffe; galant; galanterie; galbe; gaminerie; garçon gratuit; garçonne; garçonnière; garni; gaufrette; gauloise; genre pittoresque; gens de bien; gens de couleur; gentilhommière; geste; gigolo; gigot; gilet; gloire; godille; grand amateur; grand atelier; grand cru; grande amoureuse; grand écart; grande cocotte; grande école; grande épreuve; grande marque; grandes machines; grande sonnerie; grande toilette; grande vedette; Grand Guignol; grand luxe; (le) Grand Monarque; (le) Grand Siècle; grasseyé; gratin; gros point; guéridon; guindé; habitué de la maison; haute couture; haute cuisine; haute époque; haute-lice; haute politique; haute vulgarisation; haut monde; historien de salon; homme de bien; homme de cœur; homme du monde; homme du peuple; homme moyen sensuel; homme-orchestre; homme sensible; homme sérieux; horizontale; hors catalogue; hors du jeu; hors série; hors texte; hôtelier; houille blanche; humour noir; idées reçues; il faut cultiver notre jardin; il faut souffrir pour être belle; il n'y a que le premier pas qui coûte; ils ne passeront pas; ils n'ont rien appris ni rien oublié; immobiliste; (les) Immortels; imprimé; inconséquence; inconvenable; infusion; insolite; instantané; intéressante; intime; intimiste; invité; j'accuse; je m'en fiche; je-m'en-foutisme; jeté; jeté battu; jeune amour; jeune femme sérieuse; jeune fille; jeune fille bien élevée; jeune fille fatale; jeune ingénue; jeune refusé; jeune voyou; (les) jeux sont faits; joie de vivre; jolie-laide; jour; jour de fête; journal intime; jubé; justification du tirage; j'y suis, j'y reste; la . . . ; laissez-passer; lambris d'appui; lambris de hauteur; lamé; langouste; langue de chat; larmes dans la voix; l'art pour l'art; Légion d'Honneur; Légion Étrangère; légionnaire; léproserie; les . . . ; l'état, c'est moi; lettre de marque; lettriste; levade; levée; l'homme même; libertin; lit-bateau; livre de chevet; l'œil du maître; louange perfide; madame; maillot jaune; mairie; maison; maison close; maison de passe; maison de rendezvous; maison de société; maisonnette; maison toléré; maître; maître de ballet; maîtresse en titre; maîtresse femme; maladresse; mal d'amour; mal du siècle; malgré moi; malgré tout; mal mariée; mal soigné; mal vu; manque; manque de goût; maquereau; maquette; maquillage; maquillé; maquis; maquisard; mariage blanc; mariage d'inclination; mari complaisant; marmite; marocain; marquisette; marron glacé; matelot; matière; maudit; mauvais coucheur; mauvais goût; mauvais moment; mauvais prêtre; ménage à trois; ménager; menuisier; méridional; métèque; metteur au point; metteur en scène; Mi-Carême; (le) Midi; midinette; (le) mieux est l'ennemi du bien; mille feuilles; millegrain; minuscule; minuterie; mise au point; mise en espace; mise en page; misère ouverte; mission civilisatrice; mœurs; moment critique; moment de défaillance; moment de vérité; moment psychologique; mondain; monocoque; monologue intérieur; monstre sacré; montage; montant forfaitaire; montre à tact; montre grande sonnerie; (la) morgue anglaise; mot à mot; mot de Cambronne; (le) mot juste; moulage; mouvementé; moyenâgeux; musique concrète; mystique; nacelle; nappe; narquois; nature; nature morte; navette; (le) néant; négritude; noblesse de robe; noir; nostalgie de la boue; nouveau roman; nouvelle; nouvelle vague; nuée ardente; nuit blanche; objet de piété; objet de vertu; objet trouvé; œuvre; ombré; ondé; opérette; oraison funèbre; orangerie; ouistiti; où sont les neiges d'antan?; outremer; outre-tombe; ouvreuse; pair; palais de danse; panneau décoratif; paperasserie; papier poudré; papiers collés; papiers déchirés; papiers découpés; parfait; parfum; Paris vaut bien une messe; partir, c'est mourir un peu; pas d'action; pas de bourrée; pas de chat; pas devant . . . ; passe; passionné; pastiche; pâte-de-verre; pâte-sur-pâte; patron; pavillon; pays de mission; pays sans frontière; peintre de dimanche; peinture; peinture à la colle; pétard; pet de nonne; pétillant; petit beurre; petit blanc; petit bourgeois; petite amie; petite bourgeoisie; petite nature; petit peuple; petit poulet; peuple; phrase toute faite; pièce d'eau; pièce de spectacle; pièce montée; pièce noire; pièce rose; pied noir; pilotis; pincé; pince-sans-rire; piqûre; piston; piton; (le) pittoresque; (une) place au soleil; plage; plasticage; plastiqué; plastiqueur; plat du jour; plein air; plié; pliqué à jour; plissé; plus ça change, plus c'est la même chose; plus royaliste que le roi; pochette; poète maudit; poilu;

point d'honneur; pointe; pointillisme; pointilliste; politique; pommade; pompes funèbres; pompier; poncif; port de bras; posé; pot; poule; poule de luxe; pour épater les bourgeois; pour faire rire; pour renfort de potage; pour rire; pousse; praliné; préciosité; préfacier; premier cru; premier danseur étoile; premier farceur; présalé; prêt-à-porter; prétendant; princesse; princesse lointaine; prix d'ami; prix fixe; profil perdu; progressisme; promenade en attitude; prose rythmée; protocolaire; pudeur; puissance; quartier latin; quartier toléré; que diable allait-il faire dans cette galère?; questionnaire; raison d'état; raisonneur; rappel; rappel à l'ordre; rapporteur; raté; ratissage; reculer pour mieux sauter; Régence; régisseur; relai (routier); relevé; remanieur; renouveau; renversement; repêchage; répétiteur; répétition générale; reportage; repoussé; repoussoir; (la) république des lettres; (la) Résistance; retiré; retroussage; revanchisme; révolté; revue d'esprit; revue intime; (la) Reyne le veult; (la) Reyne s'avisera; rien ne va plus; rinceau; rite de passage; rive gauche; robe de terrasse; rocaille; (le) Roi Soleil; roman à clef; roman à thèse; romanesque; roman expérimental; roman-fleuve; roman poétique; roman policier; rond de cuir; rond de jambe; rondeur; rond-point; rosé; rôtisserie; rouge flambé; route nationale; (le) Roy le veult; (le) Roy s'avisera; sabotage; saboteur; sac-à-dos; saccadé; sage-femme; saison en enfer; salle privée; Salon des Refusés; sans heures; sans prétensions; saut-de-lit; saut du même au même; scène à faire; sculpture d'appartement; séance d'essais; seau à bouteilles; secrétaire à abattant; secret de polichinelle; séduisant; sérieux; se tenant; siffleur; si jeunesse savoit, si vieillesse pouvoit; simplesse; simpliste; singerie; snobisme; socle; soigné; soliste; sommelier; son et lumière; sottisier; souffleur; sousentendu; sous l'angle du scandale; souteneur; souterrain; spécialité de la maison; spotteur; structures vivantes; (le) style, c'est l'homme; style champêtre; style mécanique; style périodique; style pompier; succès de ridicule; succès de scandale; succès de snobisme; Sûreté; sur fond réservé; sur le cou du pied; sur le vif; sur place; sympathique; système D; tableau d'ensemble; tachisme; taille d'épargne; tailleur; tas-de-charge; témoignage; temps levé; temps morts; temps perdu; tenue de ville; terre de pipe; terre pisée; tête folle; texte intégral; théâtre engagé; thé musical; tissu-éponge; tonneau; toqué; torchère; touché; touche-à tout; toujours de l'audace; toujours la politesse; tour; tour de chant; tour d'-horizon; tour en l'air; tournedos; tourniquet; tour sur place; tout comprendre, c'est tout pardonner; tout le bazar; (la) trahison des clercs; train de luxe; trait d'union; tranche; tranche de vie; trente-et-quarante; triptyque; trois coups; trompe-l'œil; tronc; trotteur; trouvaille; trucage; trumeau; truqueur; turquerie; tutu; unité d'habitation; urbanisme; va-et-vient; vareuse; variation; vase de nuit; vécu; vedette; veillée des armes; velouté; vendeuse; verdure; verglas; vérité; vernissage; verres églomisés; vers libre; (le) vice anglais; vide-poche; vie amoureuse; (la) vie de Bohème; vie de boudoir; vie familiale; vie manquée; vieux jeu; vieux marcheur; ville lumière; ville radieuse; vin blanc; vin de table; vin d'honneur; vin mousseux; vin rosé; vin rouge; virement; visagisme; visagiste; viticulteur; vitrail; volupté; voulu; voyage à Cythère; voyage imaginaire; voyant; voyeur; vue d'ensemble; vulgarisateur.

2. Latin

Mediæval

Agnus Dei; amphora; aqua vitæ; audi alteram partem; aurum potabile; ave Maria; benedicite; byssus; calx; capias; certiorari; cicada; colossus; confiteor; contra; cornea; Corpus Christi; de profundis; ecce signum; elixir; encænia; ergo; et alia; et cætera; ex; exeunt; explicit; fieri facias; gloria in excelsis (Deo);

gratis; habeas corpus; idem; imprimis; incubus; in pontificalibus; item; lapis lazuli; libra; limbo; Magnificat; manes; mea culpa; memento; memorandum; minium; miserere; modicum; nisi prius; non est (inventus); obelus; œdema; œsophagus; palæstra; paterfamilias; pater noster; placebo; polypus; præmunire; prima facie; pro; procœmium; pro tempore; proviso; recipe; regimen; requiem; retina; rigor; sanctum (sanctorum); Sanctus; scilicet; scire facias; sclerosis; scoria; solidus; subpœna; succubus; synecdoche; Te Deum; ubi sunt qui ante nos fuerunt?; verbatim; versus; videlicet; vidimus; virago.

Sixteenth Century

ab initio; ab origine; aborigines; ab ovo; absit omen!; acumen; ad clerum; ad hominem; adsum; affidavit; a fortiori; a latere; algæ; alias; aliquot; alter ego; anguis in herba; anno Domini; annulus; anonymus; ante meridiem; anus; aorta; apocrypha; a posteriori; aqua fortis; arbiter; arcanum; ars longa, vita brevis; asyndeton; atrium; aurum mosaicum; Bacchanalia; Bacchantes; ballista; basilica; bolus; bona fide; caduceus; cæsura; callus; catachresis; caveat; caveat emptor; cerebellum; cestus; chimæra; circus; colostrum; compendium; cornucopia; cranium; cum privilegio (ad imprimendum solum); dæmon; delirium; denarius; divide et impera; emporium; encomium; epicedium; epithalamium; erratum; et tu, Brute; etymon; exempli gratia; exeunt omnes; exit; ex nihilo nihil fit; ex officio; ex opere operato; exordium; experto crede; extempore; facia; factotum; ferula; fidus Achates; genius; genus; gradatim; gymnasium; hegira; helix; hendiadys; hinc illæ lacrymæ; hoc opus, hic labor (est); hydra; hyperbole; hysteron proteron; id est; ignis fatuus; ignoratio elenchi; ignotum per ignotius; in articulo mortis; in capite; in esse; in forma pauperis; in sæcula sæculorum; interim; interregnum; ipse dixit; ipso facto; jacta est alea; jure divino; jus gentium; latet anguis in herba; legatus a latere; lex talionis; littera scripta manet; locus communis; lotus; lupus in fabula; lustrum; Magna Charta; Magus; mandamus; memento mori; menses; meretrix; metempsychosis; miscellanea; mittimus; nectar; nolens volens; noli me tangere; non placet; non sequitur; nosce teipsum; nux vomica; obiter; oderint dum metuant; onomatopœia; optimates; opus operans; opus operatum; O tempora, O mores!; palladium; pallium; panacea; pari passu; parturiunt montes, nascetur ridiculus mus; pater patriæ; peccavi; per accidens; per centum; per contra; per diem; per se; petitio principii; placet; plethora; polysyndeton; pontificalia; post scriptum; pro forma; pro rata; pro re nata; quære; quid pro quo; quietus; quondam; quot homines, tot sententiæ; quo warranto; rectum; requiescat in pace; respice finem; rostrum; Saturnalia; scholium; sic transit gloria mundi; simpliciter; sorites; sortes Virgilianæ; spatula; speculum; sphincter; stratum; stria; summum bonum; supra; sursum corda; syllepsis; syncope; tabula rasa; tarantula; tempus edax rerum; tenet; tepidarium; terminus ad quem; terminus a quo; thyrsus; toties quoties; trachea; transire; vanitas vanitatum; veni, vidi, vici; vertigo; viaticum; vide; volenti non fit injuria; vox populi; vox populi, vox Dei.

Seventeenth Century

ab extra; abscissa; ab uno disce omnes; accidia; ad captandum (vulgus); addendum; ad finem; ad hoc; ad infinitum; ad inquirendum; ad libitum; ad majorem Dei gloriam; ad nauseam; ad rem; ad valorem; ad vivum; adytum; ætatis suæ; afflatus; agenda; album; alluvium; alumnus; amanuensis; ambo; a mensa et thoro; amicus curiæ; angelus; Anglice; animus revertendi; anno ætatis suæ; annus mirabilis; ante; antenna; apodyterium; apparatus; a priori; aqua regia;

arcanum imperii; ars est celare artem; auditorium; aurum fulminans; aut Cæsar aut nullus; bene esse; brutum fulmen; cæteris paribus; calculus; camera lucida; camera obscura; cannula; caput mortuum; caret; catena; causa sine qua non; cedant arma togæ; cento; ciborium; clepsydra; cogito, ergo sum; colloquium; compos mentis; congeries; copula; corona; corruptio optimi pessima; cortex; coryza; crisis; cucullus non facit monachum; cui bono; cum grano salis; datum; de bene esse; de die in diem; de facto; de fide; de gustibus (non est disputandum); Dei gratia; de jure; de minimis non curat lex; de novo; de propaganda fide; desideratum; desunt cætera; diæresis; dies non (juridicus); dulia; dum spiro, spero; ecce Homo; edax rerum; effluvium; ego et rex meus; ejusdem generis; elenchus; emphyteusis; ephebus; equilibrium; esse; ex animo; ex cathedra; ex debito justitiæ; ex dono; exegi monumentum ære perennius; ex hypothesi; exodus; ex parte; ex pede Herculem; ex post facto; exuviæ; faber fortunæ suæ; facetiæ; facilis descensus Averno; facsimile; fæces; farrago; fas est et ab hoste doceri; felo de se; feræ naturæ; festina lente; fiat; fiat lux; fibula; finis; finis coronat opus; flagrante delicto; florilegium; fœtus; forum; frustum; fulcrum; gravamen; halitus; hiatus; hic et ubique; hic jacet; homo unius libri; homunculus; honorarium; honoris causa; horresco referens; hortus siccus; hydrophobia; hypochondria; ibidem; ignoramus; impedimenta; imperium; impetus; imprimatur; impromptu; in bona parte; in commendam; index expurgatorius; index librorum prohibitorum; indicium; in mala parte; innuendo; in partibus (infidelium); in perpetuum; in posse; in propria persona; in puris naturalibus; insignia; inspeximus; instanter; in statu quo (ante); inter alia; in usum Delphini; in vacuo; juvenilia; labarum; lacuna; lamina; lapsus linguæ; lignum vitæ; linctus; lite pendente; litteratim; locum tenens; lusus naturæ; magna est veritas et prævalebit; mala fide; mala fides; materia medica; matrix; mausoleum; mea maxima culpa; medio tutissimus ibis; medulla oblongata; me judice; melancholia; meniscus; mens sana in corpore sano; menstruum; meum et tuum; modus operandi; momentum; more majorum; motu proprio; mutatis mutandis; nævus; necrosis; nemine contradicente; nemo me impune lacessit; ne plus ultra; nexus; nil desperandum; nimbus; nolle prosequi; non compos (mentis); nostrum; nota bene; novus homo; nunc dimittis; O altitudo!; onus; opprobrium; opusculum; pabulum; pancratium; pelta; penetralia; per annum; per capita; per mensem; per saltum; persona muta; per stirpes; phallus; pharmacopœia; phenomenon; pia fraus; pinna; plebs; plectrum; plenum; plexus; podium; pontifex maximus; populus vult decipi; posse; post meridiem; primo; primum mobile; principiis obsta; proboscis; prognosis; pro hac vice; pruritus; psyche; pudendum; qua; quantum; quantum meruit; quantum mutatis ab illo; quantum sufficit; quasi; quinquennium; quod erat demonstrandum; quo jure?; quorum; quorum pars magna fui; quota; rationale; reddendum; regalia; Regius; reliquiæ; res gestæ; residuum; res nihili; resurgam; rex; rota; rotunda; ruat cœlum; saltus; salus populi suprema (est) lex; sal volatile; sarcoma; scarabæus; scintilla; secundo; secundum quid; sederunt; sede vacante; semper eadem; sensorium; seriatim; servus servorum (Dei); sine die; sine qua non; sortes Homericæ; spectrum; sputum; stimulus; sub judice; sub rosa; sub sigillo; sub silentio; substratum; succedaneum; sudarium; sui juris; synopsis; tenebræ; tenuis; terra firma; terra incognita; tiara; timeo Danaos et dona ferentes; toga; toga virilis; trachoma; triclinium; tumulus; tu quoque; tympanum; ultima Thule; ultimo; vade mecum; væ victis!; vallum; varia lectio; verbum sap(ienti sat est); vestigium; veto; vice versa; vi et armis; vinculum; viscera; vivarium; vivat!; vortex; vox et præterea nihil; vulgo.

Eighteenth Century

ab urbe condita; acanthus; ad crumenam; ad eundem (gradum); ad interim; ad litem; ægis; ægrotat; alibi; alma mater; amor patriæ; anacoluthon; anæsthesia; angina pectoris; apparatus criticus; arbitrium; asphyxia; aurora australis; aurora borealis; bona fides; bronchi; cæstus; caldarium; campus; cantoris; caput lupinum; carcinoma; casus fœderis; casus omissus; censor morum; census; cilia; cippus; cognovit; coitus; collectanea; colophon; columbarium; condominium; consensus; contra bonos mores; contra mundum; corpus; credo quia impossibile est; curiosa felicitas; currente calamo; decani; dele; delineavit; de mortuis nil nisi bonum; Deo volente; desipere in loco; detritus; dictum; disjecta membra; dramatis personæ; dulce et decorum est pro patria mori; epiphenomenon; esto perpetua; exeat; experimentum crucis; ex voto; fas; fauna; flora; frigidarium; genius loci; gradus (ad Parnassum); habitat; hæc olim meminisse juvabit; herbarium; hoc genus omne; hypogeum; ictus; imperium in imperio; inertia; in flagrante delicto; in loco parentis; in medias res; insomnia; in toto; in utero; in vino veritas; lares et penates; larva; laudator temporis acti; limæ labor; litteræ humaniores; locus; locus pœnitentiæ; lucus a non (lucendo); lyceum; magnum; magnum opus; memoria technica; millennium; minutia; modulus; multum in parvo; nebula; nefas; nil admirari; nolo episcopari; nymphæum; odium theologicum; onus probandi; organum; otium cum dignitate; ovum; papyrus; paraphernalia; patina; pendente lite; periplus; piscina; planetarium; pons asinorum; post obitum; pro bono publico; propaganda; propylæum; pro tanto; quadriga; quæsitum; quieta non movere; quis custodiet ipsos custodes?; rara avis; remanet; res integra; risus sardonicus; rus in urbe; sarcophagus; scriptorium; sedilia; sequela; siglum; simplex munditiis; status; stela; suaviter in modo, fortiter in re; sui generis; summa; suppressio veri; symposium; synthesis; tacet; tænia; tertium quid; tessera; toto cælo; triforium; ultima ratio; ultimatum; ultra vires; variorum; via; vice; vis inertiæ; vomitorium; vox humana.

Nineteenth Century

abusus non tollit usum; ad misericordiam; adscriptus glebæ; ad usum filioli; ad vitam aut culpam; advocatus diaboli; æquam servare mentem; æquo animo; æs alienum; æs triplex; amœba; anacrusis; animus; animus furandi; animus revocandi; anno regni; aquarium; arbiter elegantiarum; arboretum; Arcades ambo; ars gratia artis; aurea mediocritas; ave atque vale; avizandum; bacillus; bacterium; beatæ memoriæ; beata simplicitas; bene decessit; Benedictus; bis dat qui cito dat; bona vacantia; cacoethes loquendi; cacoethes scribendi; cadit quæstio; cæcum; cætera desunt; canephorus; cantharus; carnivora; carpe diem; casus belli; causa causans; cave; chiasmus; circa; cloaca; codex; cognomen; confer; consortium; conspectus; coram populo; corpus delicti; corpus juris; corpus vile; corrigendum; cotta; credo; crematorium; crustacea; crux; cultus; cum; cum notis variorum; curia; curiosa; curriculum; cursus; damnosa hæreditas; damnum sine injuria; delirium tremens; dementia; desunt nonnulla; de te fabula (narratur); deus ex machina; dies iræ; differentia; difficilior lectio potior; Dominus illuminatio mea; ductus litterarum; dulce domum; dum vivimus, vivamus; editio princeps; ego; emeritus; enuresis; ergastulum; et hoc genus omne; et sequentes; ex abundanti cautela; exceptis excipiendis; excreta; excursus; ex delicto; ex libris; experientia docet; ex ungue leonem; facile princeps; fasciculus; fecit; fiat experimentum in corpore vili; fiat fustitia, ruat cœlum; filioque; floruit; fons et origo (mali); formicarium; gaudium certaminis; generalia; genitalia; hetæra; homœoteleuton; homo sapiens; homo trium literarum; horæ subsecivæ; hyperæsthesia; iconostasis;

idem sonans; Iesus Hominum Salvator; impluvium; in camera; incipit; in contumaciam; incunabula; index locorum; index nominum; index rerum; index verborum; in excelsis; in extenso; in extremis; infra; infra dignitatem; in limine; in memoriam; in re; in situ; in statu pupillari; intra vires; invenit; ipsissima verba; laborare est orare; lapsus calami; latifundia; laus Deo semper; lavabo; lex non scripta; loco citato; locus classicus; locus standi; lupanar; magisterium; magno intervallo; mare clausum; marginalia; Mater Dolorosa; materfamilias; maxima debetur puero reverentia; media; medium; memorabilia; mensa; mirabile dictu; modus vivendi; mora; moratorium; more suo; mythus; nemo repente fuit turpissimus; nihil ad rem; non-ego; non nobis, Domine; non possumus; notabilia; nova; novena; nulla bona; obiit; obiter dictum; obscurum per obscurius; odi profanum vulgus; omne ignotum pro magnifico; opera minora; opere citato; optimum; opus; oratio obliqua; oratio recta; O si sic omnes!; pace; palmam qui meruit ferat; panem et circenses; passim; patria potestas; pax; pax Britannica; pax Romana; peplum; perfervidum ingenium; per industriam hominis; per procurationem; phylum; pinxit; poeta nascitur non fit; post hoc ergo propter hoc; post mortem; primipara; primus inter pares; prophylaxis; proxime accessit; proximo; psychosis; Punica fides; quadrivium; quem Deus vult perdere prius dementat; qui facit per alium facit per se; quod erat faciendum; quod semper, quod ubique, quod ab omnibus (creditum est); quod vide; recto; reductio ad absurdum; referendum; regina; rem acu tetigisti; repertorium; res judicata; rictus; rigor mortis; rubella; sal Atticus; sanatorium; schema; sculpsit; septicæmia; sic; sic itur ad astra; si monumentum requiris, circumspice; simulacrum; solarium; solatium; solvitur ambulando; splendide mendax; status quo; status quo ante; stet; stet processus; stichomythia; stylus; sub voce; suggestio falsi; susurrus; symbiosis; synæsthesia; tædium vitæ; Tantum Ergo; tempore; tempus fugit; textus receptus; thesaurus; tinnitus (aurium); torticollis; tripos; trivium; uberrimæ fidei; uberrima fides; ubi jus, ibi remedium; ultra; uræus; urbi et orbi; ut infra; ut supra; vade retro; vasculum; vera causa; verso; vexata quæstio; via media; video meliora proboque, deteriora sequor; virginibus puerisque (canto); vis medicatrix naturæ; viva voce; vox angelica; vox nihili.

Twentieth Century

ad personam; allocutus; alternatim; angulus terrarum; anima; anima naturaliter Christiana; aquila; arcus senilis; argumentum a silentio; ars nova; auctoritate . . . ; auctoritate suo; avete; bifolium; bonæ memoriæ; boni et legales (homines); breviora; cælavit; cancellandum; cappa magna; caritas; catharsis; causa movens; certum est quia impossibile est; clausula; clerici vagantes; confessio fidei; consecutio temporum; continuum; coram episcopo; crux ansata; cujus regio, ejus religio; cum laude; curriculum vitæ; cursus honorum; cursus litterarum; da multos annos; decessit sine prole; dementia præcox; Deo Optimo Maximo; designatum; Deus absconditus; diabolus in musica; dis aliter visum; discordia concors; distinguo; dum sola (et casta); durum; ecclesiola; eheu fugaces; elegantiæ arbiter; entia non (sunt) multiplicanda præter necessitatem; episcopus vagans; esto; e tenebris lux; et in Arcadia ego; exceptio probat regulum; exemplum; ex gratia; ex necessitate; ex professo; ex silentio; extra metrum; favete linguis; filius nullius; floreat; fœderatus; fons vivus; functus officio; gaudeamus igitur; genius domus; gravitas; gyrovagi; homo ludens; horribile dictu; hortus conclusus; hortus inclusus; humanitas; hypotheses non fingo; id; ignorantia legis neminem excusat; ignotus; imago; imponderabilia; in absentia; in æternum; in consimile casu; in globo; in jure uxoris; in pari materia; in rebus; in rem; inter vivos; intra muros; in vivo; ipso jure; januis clausis; jure dignitatis; jus accrescendi; jus primæ noctis; lacrymæ rerum; lapsus memoriæ; lex domicili; lex fori; lex loci celebrationis; libido; limes; locus celebrationis; locus desperatus; loquitur; lucri causa; lusisti satis; magistras; magnanimitas; maleficium; mansuetæ naturæ; mare nostrum; maxima cum laude; media aspirata; mens rea; metri causa; mirabile visu; mirabilia; missa cantata; missa solemnis; mores; more Socratico; morituri te salutant; mors janua vitæ (novæ); mos majorum; musica ficta; mythopœia; natura non facit saltum; necessarium; nemo dat quod non habet; ne varietur; nihil obstat; nihil tetigit quod non ornavit; nisi; non omnis moriar; non sine gloria; non sum qualis eram; nota; nulli secundus; numerus clausus; nunc est bibendum; obiit sine prole; ob majorem cautelam; odi et amo; odium scholasticum; omne scibile; (omnium consensu,) capax imperii nisi imperasset; opera omnia; opus Alexandrinum; opus anglicanum; opus Dei; perceptum; per impossibile; per incuriam; perpetuum mobile; persona; persona non grata; pietas; postfacto; præsente cadavere; præsidium; preces privatæ; procul este, profani!; prosit; punctum cæcum; punctum delens; purpureus pannus; qua se; quicunque vult; qui vult decipi, decipiatur; quo vadis?; radix malorum; rariora; ratio decidendi; ratio scripta; rebus sic stantibus; relatum; res ipsa loquitur; retro me, Satana; Roma locuta est; sæva indignatio; salvete; sancta simplicitas; scientia; scientiæ causa; securus judicat orbis terrarum; semper fidelis; sensibilia; sensum; sensu obscæno; sensu stricto; siccum lumen; sic passim; sic semper tyrannis; silent leges inter armas; simplicissimus; sine legitima prole; sine prole; si vis pacem, para bellum; solus; solutis curis; sortes Biblicæ; spes ultima gentis; sponte sua; stupor mundi; sub anno; sub conditione; subpœna duces tecum; sub specie æternitatis; summa cum laude; sunt lacrymæ rerum; terminus vitæ; tractatus; turba; usus; vagantes; valete; variatim; vera copula; veræ causæ; vera effigies; vera incessu patuit dea; Via Crucis; via dolorosa; vicisti, Galilæe!; victor ludorum; vir bonus dicendi peritus; virgo intacta; vis a tergo.

3. GREEK

Mediæval

arsis; kyrie eleïson; tetragrammaton; thesis.

Sixteenth Century

acme; agape; agora; ambrosia; anathema; anathema sit; antipodes; antithesis; aposiopesis; apotheosis; cacodæmon; dilemma; encheiridion; ephemeris; epitome; eureka; gnome; gnomon; gnosis; kat' exochen; logos; meiosis; metamorphosis; nemesis; paronomasia; pathos; peripeteia; periphrásis; pharos; prolepsis; prothalamion; pseudo; stigma; tmesis.

Seventeenth Century

acroterion; agon; agonistes; amnesia; antistrophe; automaton; boustrophedon; catholicon; charisma; chlamys; cosmos; criterion; diagnosis; dogma; entasis; ephemeron; epidermis; euthanasia; exegesis; genesis; gnothi seauton; hapax legomenon; hoi polloi; lemma; litotes; metathesis; miasma; narthex; nous; parergon; pathemata mathemata; prolegomenon; pseudepigrapha; stoa; strophe.

Eighteenth Century

ankylosis; aroma; aura; bathos; ganglion; homoousion; mimesis; neurosis; noumenon; onomasticon; pentathlon; peplos; stasis.

Nineteenth Century

agapemone; agoraphobia; agraphon; anabasis; ananke; anonyma; aphasia; apologia; ascesis; autogenesis; catalysis; chiton; diaspora; eidolon; eirenicon; epos; erotica; ethos; homoiousion; hubris; ikon; katabasis; kerygma; koine; kudos; macron; megalomania; melisma; neurasthenia; omphalos; ostrakon; paranoia; parousia; parthenogenesis; phobia; pithos; plasma; pneuma; pou sto; stemma; stichos; telæsthesia; telekinesis; trauma; zeugma.

Twentieth Century

anti; deësis; enosis; euphoria; hamartia; kore; kouros; larnax; megaron; moussaka; ouzo; panta rhei; retsina; schizophrenia; thalassa! thalassa!; topos.

4. ITALIAN

Sixteenth Century

antipasto; bagnio; belvedere; biretta; bordello; cameo; canto; che sarà, sarà; cupola; duo; duomo; fresco; gondola; grottesca; inamorato; macaroni; magnifico; majolica; mezzo rilievo; nuncio; padre; piazza; podestà; seraglio; stanza; stucco.

Seventeenth Century

alto rilievo; amoretto; a rivederci; baldacchino; basso rilievo; campanile; capriccio; chiaroscuro; contadino; ditto; felucca; generalissimo; ghetto; gusto; incognito; intaglio; largo; lazaretto; lingua franca; literati; madonna; manifesto; monsignore; monte di pietà; morbidezza; niello; osteria; passacaglia; pergola; piano; pietà; pietra commessa; portico; presto; putto; recitativo; regatta; ritornello; sbirro; sirocco; solo; stiletto; tarsia; tramontana; vermicelli; virtuoso; vista; zingaro.

Eighteenth Century

adagio; al fresco; alla breve; allegretto; allegro; alto; andante; appoggiatura; aria; arietta; arioso; arpeggio; a tempo; ballerina; bambino; basso continuo; bravura; buffo; cadenza; cantabile; cantata; cantilena; canto fermo; casino; castrato; cavaliere servente; cicerone; cicisbeo; cinquecento; coda; cognoscenti; coloratura; con amore; concertante; concerto; concerto grosso; condottiere; contralto; conversazione; cortile; crescendo; czarina; da capo; del credere; dilettante; diminuendo; falsetto; fantasia; finale; giallo antico; impasto; impresario; in petto; larghetto; lava; lazzarone; libretto; loggia; lumachella; maestoso; maestrale; maestro; maestro di cappella; marchesa; mezza voce; mezzo soprano; mora; obbligato; oratorio; padrone; panatella; pasticcio; pianissimo; pietra dura; poco curante; portamento; ridotto; rifacimento; ripieno; saltarello; scagliola; serenata; sgraffito; solfatara; soprano; sostenuto; sotto voce; staccato; stretto; tarantella; tempo; terra cotta; toccata; torso; trio; tufa; tutti; verde antico; villeggiatura; virtù.

Nineteenth Century

accelerando; agitato; alla marcia; amorino; andantino; a quattr'occhi; basso profundo; beato; ben trovato; bersagliere; bottega; breccia; brio; calando; campo santo; cantatrice; capo d'opera; casa; cassone; cavatina; cavo rilievo; cipollino; con brio; confetti; con fuoco; con moto; con spirito; continuo; dal segno; diva; divertimento; dolce far niente; fata morgana; festa; fiasco; fioritura;

Seventeenth Century

cortes; desperado; duenna; embargo; guano; infanta; junta; matador; politico; salina; sierra; siesta; tortilla; vicuña.

Eighteenth Century

banderilla; banderillero; copaiba; estancia; fandango; mantilla; maté; paramo; picador; poncho; posada; seguidilla; sombrero; torero.

Nineteenth Century

adobe; aguardiente; amontillado; arroyo; bodega; bolas; bolero; bonanza; bronco; burro; camarilla; cañon; cascara (sagrada); chaparejos; chaparral; conquistador; corral; corrida (de toros); fiesta; flamenco; gaucho; gazpacho; gringo; guerrilla; guerrillero; hacienda; machete; majo; manzanilla; mesa; monte; pampas; paseo; patio; pelota; peon; pinto; pronunciamento; pueblo; ranchero; ria; rodeo; solera; tequila; tilde; vigilante; yerba (maté).

Twentieth Century

adios; afición; aficionado; altiplano; camino real; caudillo; copita; cuesta; fino; hasta la vista; hasta luego; incommunicado; macho; mañana; marijuana; mascara; noche sombre; novio; oloroso; paella; palomino; panada; paso doble; peto; porron; pronto; requeté; salud y pesetas!; sol y sombra; supremo; (la) vida es sueño; zapateado.

Section II: Other European Languages

1. Danish

Seventeenth Century: broch.
Twentieth Century: akvavit; smørrebrød.

2. Dutch

Sixteenth Century: monsoon.
Seventeenth Century: baas; maelstrom; polder.
Eighteenth Century: kraal.
Nineteenth Century: coleslaw; kopje; stoep; uitlander; veldt.
Twentieth Century: rijsttafel; (De) Stijl.

3. Gaelic

Mediæval: clachan; loch.
Eighteenth Century: gillie; pibroch; sgian dubh.
Twentieth Century: deoch-an-doruis; machair.

4. Irish

Mediæval: clairseach; curragh.
Sixteenth Century: coronach; tanist.
Eighteenth Century: banshee; Sassenach; shebeen; spalpeen.
Nineteenth Century: acushla; alanna; asthore; bohereen; cailleach; céad míle

fáilte; colleen; colleen bawn; crannog; feis; gombeen; gossoon; leprechaun; mavourneen; omadhaun; poteen.
Twentieth Century: céilidhe; Dáil; Erin go bragh; fáilte; mochree; Sinn Fein; sláinte; Taoiseach; Teachta Dála.

5. Magyar

Nineteenth Century: czardas; paprika.
Twentieth Century: goulash.

6. Norwegian

Seventeenth Century: fjord.
Eighteenth Century: kraken.
Nineteenth Century: landsmål; sæter.
Twentieth Century: riksmål; skål; skijöring; slalom.

7. Portuguese

Sixteenth Century: betel; pagoda.
Seventeenth Century: assegai; ipecacuanha; pimento.
Eighteenth Century: albino; auto-da-fé; ayah; verandah.
Nineteenth Century: amah; commando.
Twentieth Century: bossa nova.

8. Russian

Sixteenth Century: boyar; czar; kvas; moujik; verst.
Seventeenth Century: czaritza; shaman; steppe.
Eighteenth Century: balalaika; czarevitch; izba; kibitka; sarafan; ukase; yamschik.
Nineteenth Century: artel; ataman; bortsch; borzoi; doukhobors; feldsher; kulak; kurgan; mazout; mir; parka; pogrom; samovar; taiga; troika; vodka; zemstvo.
Twentieth Century: agrogorod; apparat; apparatchik; bolshevik; chernozem; commissar; dacha; duma; intelligentsia; izvoschik; kolkhoz; kulturny; menshevik; peredyshka; podzol; shashlik; soviet; sovkhoz; sputnik; stilyaga; subbotnik; udarnik; zastruga.

9. Swedish

Twentieth Century: ombudsman; sloid; smörgåsbord.

10. Welsh

Seventeenth Century: cromlech; englyn.
Eighteenth Century: gorsedd.
Nineteenth Century: eisteddfod; hwyl.
Twentieth Century: corgi; cwm; Cymru am byth; cynghanedd.

11. Other European Languages

Eighteenth Century: Edda (*Icelandic*).
Nineteenth Century: mazurka (*Polish*); menhir (*Breton*); tundra (*Lapp*).
Twentieth Century: luge (*Swiss*); sauna (*Finnish*).

Section III: Non-European Languages

1. Afrikaans

Nineteenth Century: biltong; Boer; Bond; kranz; laager; sjambok; trek.
Twentieth Century: apartheid.

2. Arabic

Mediæval: khan; nadir.
Sixteenth Century: hashish; muezzin; mufti; sheikh.
Seventeenth Century: arak; bulbul; couscous; djinnee; fakir; hajji; hakim; hammam; harem; imam; khamsin; Ramadan.
Eighteenth Century: fellah; hookah; simoom; sunna; tarboosh.
Nineteenth Century: dahabiyeh; djibbah; hadith; Islam; jehad; kif; mastaba; shadoof; souk; wadi; yashmak; zareba.
Twentieth Century: bint: imshi; kasbah; shufti; surah; wafd.

3. Australian

Eighteenth Century: boomerang; corroboree.
Nineteenth Century: billabong.

4. Chinese

Seventeenth Century: sampan.
Eighteenth Century: typhoon.
Nineteenth Century: kowtow; loquat.
Twentieth Century: cheong-sam; Kuomintang.

5. Eskimo

Eighteenth Century: kayak; umiak.
Nineteenth Century: igloo; nunatak.
Twentieth Century; anorak.

6. Hawaiian

Nineteenth Century: hula; kanaka.
Twentieth Century: aloha; lei; muu-muu; ukelele.

7. Hebrew

Seventeenth Century: shibboleth.
Nineteenth Century: kosher.
Twentieth Century: genizah; goy; kibbutz; Yom Kippur.

8. Hindustani

Sixteenth Century: bhang; rajah.
Seventeenth Century: dhoti; ghat; guru; havildar; lakh; maharajah; mahout; mullah; pice; pundit; ranee; rupee; sahib; salaam; shikar; sirdar; subahdar; syce; yogi.
Eighteenth Century: anna; babu; chi-chi; dak; khitmutgar; nullah; pukka; sari; sepoy; sirkar; suttee; wallah; zenana.
Nineteenth Century: burra; burra sahib; chapati; charpoy; chota; chota hazri;

dacoit; dacoity; dekko; dhobi; gharry; khaki; kukri; maharanee; memsahib; numnah; punkah; purdah; raj; rissaldar; shikari; tamasha; tonga; topee; yoga.
Twentieth Century: swami.

9. Japanese

Seventeenth Century: shogun.
Eighteenth Century: daimio; mikado.
Nineteenth Century: bushido; geisha; hara kiri; jinrickshaw; jiu jitsu; judo; kakemono; kimono; netsuké; samurai; tycoon.
Twentieth Century: banzai; bonsai; fuchigashira; haiku; kabuki; kamikaze; karate; kendo; kozuka; makimono; Noh; origami; senryu; tokonoma; tsuba.

10. Javanese

Nineteenth Century: atap; batik.
Twentieth Century: lahar.

11. Malay

Sixteenth Century: krees; prahu.
Seventeenth Century: orang-outang.
Nineteenth Century: agar-agar; gutta percha; sarong; tuan.
Twentieth Century: stengah.

12. Maori

Nineteenth Century: haka; mana.

13. Persian

Seventeenth Century: bakhsheesh; bazaar; cummerbund; durbar; firman; maidan.
Eighteenth Century: houri; howdah.
Nineteenth Century: narghile.

14. Sanskrit

Seventeenth Century: purana.
Eighteenth Century: avatar; tantra; yoni.
Nineteenth Century: karma; mahatma; mantra; nirvana; samadhi; soma; stupa; sutra; swastika; Upanishad.
Twentieth Century: ahimsa; satyagraha; swaraj.

15. Swahili

Nineteenth Century: bwana; safari.
Twentieth Century: uhuru.

16. Tamil

Seventeenth Century: catamaran; pariah.
Nineteenth Century: patchouli.

17. Tibetan

Seventeenth Century: lama.
Twentieth Century: sherpa; yeti.

18. Turkish

Sixteenth Century: bey; caftan; dervish; spahi.
Seventeenth Century: effendi; kaimakam; kebab; pasha; pilav; raki; yoghourt.
Eighteenth Century: vali.
Nineteenth Century: bimbashi; dolman; kismet; macramé; vilayet.
Twentieth Century: comitadji; kilim; mezé; shish kebab.

19. Yiddish

Nineteenth Century: schlemozzle.
Twentieth Century: pastrami; schlemiel; schmaltz; schmuck; schnorrer; shiksa.

20. Other Non-European Languages

Seventeenth Century: harmattan (*Fanti*); moccasin (*Powhatan*); sachem (*Narragansett*); sharawaggi (*Unknown*).
Eighteenth Century: karroo (*Hottentot*); taboo (*Tongan*); totem (*Algonquin*).
Nineteenth Century: atoll (*Maldive*); beri-beri (*Cingalese*); dhow (*Unknown*); get (*Aramaic*); indaba (*Zulu*); juju (*West African*); ziggurat (*Assyrian*).
Twentieth Century: basenji (*Basuto*); dghajsa (*Maltese*); zombie (*West African*).